WORKSHOPS IN COMPUTING
Series edited by C. J. van Rijsbergen

Also in this series

Women into Computing: Selected Papers 1988–1990
Gillian Lovegrove and Barbara Segal (Eds.)

3rd Refinement Workshop (organised by BCS-FACS, and sponsored by IBM UK Laboratories, Hursley Park and the Programming Research Group, University of Oxford), Hursley Park, 9–11 January 1990
Carroll Morgan and J. C. P. Woodcock (Eds.)

Designing Correct Circuits, Workshop jointly organised by the Universities of Oxford and Glasgow, Oxford, 26–28 September 1990
Geraint Jones and Mary Sheeran (Eds.)

Functional Programming, Glasgow 1990, Proceedings of the 1990 Glasgow Workshop on Functional Programming, Ullapool, Scotland, 13–15 August 1990
Simon L. Peyton Jones, Graham Hutton and Carsten Kehler Holst (Eds.)

4th Refinement Workshop, Proceedings of the 4th Refinement Workshop, organised by BCS-FACS, Cambridge, 9–11 January 1991
Joseph M. Morris and Roger C. Shaw (Eds.)

AI and Cognitive Science '90, University of Ulster at Jordanstown, 20–21 September 1990
Michael F. McTear and Norman Creaney (Eds.)

Software Re-use, Utrecht 1989, Proceedings of the Software Re-use Workshop, Utrecht, The Netherlands, 23–24 November 1989
Liesbeth Dusink and Patrick Hall (Eds.)

Z User Workshop, 1990, Proceedings of the Fifth Annual Z User Meeting, Oxford, 17–18 December 1990
J.E. Nicholls (Ed.)

IV Higher Order Workshop, Banff 1990
Proceedings of the IV Higher Order Workshop, Banff, Alberta, Canada, 10–14 September 1990
Graham Birtwistle (Ed.)

ALPUK91 Proceedings of the 3rd UK Annual Conference on Logic Programming, Edinburgh, 10–12 April 1991
Geraint A.Wiggins, Chris Mellish and Tim Duncan (Eds.)

Specifications of Database Systems,
1st International Workshop on Specifications of Database Systems, Glasgow, 3–5 July 1991
David J. Harper and Moira C. Norrie (Eds.)

7th UK Computer and Telecommunications Performance Engineering Workshop,
Edinburgh, 22–23 July 1991
J. Hillston, P.J.B. King and R.J. Pooley (Eds.)

Logic Program Synthesis and Transformation,
Proceedings of LOPSTR 91, International Workshop on Logic Program Synthesis and Transformation, University of Manchester, 4–5 July 1991
T.P. Clement and K.-K. Lau (Eds.)

Building Interactive Systems: Architectures and Tools,
Philip Gray and Roger Took (Eds.)

Declarative Programming, Sasbachwalden 1991,
PHOENIX Seminar and Workshop on Declarative Programming, Sasbachwalden, Black Forest, Germany, 18–22 November 1991
John Darlington and Roland Dietrich (Eds.)

continued on back page...

Rogardt Heldal, Carsten Kehler Holst and
Philip Wadler (Eds.)

Functional Programming, Glasgow 1991

Proceedings of the 1991 Glasgow Workshop on Functional Programming, Portree, Isle of Skye, 12–14 August 1991

Published in collaboration with the
British Computer Society

BCS

Springer-Verlag
London Berlin Heidelberg New York
Paris Tokyo Hong Kong
Barcelona Budapest

Rogardt Heldal, BSc
Carsten Kehler Holst, cand. Scient.
Philip Wadler, PhD
Department of Computing
The University
Glasgow G12 8QQ
Scotland

ISBN-13:978-3-540-19760-7 e-ISBN-13:978-1-4471-3196-0
DOI: 10.1007/978-1-4471-3196-0

British Library Cataloguing in Publication Data
Functional Programming, Glasgow 1991
Proceedings of the 1991 Glasgow Workshop on Functional Programming, Portree, Isle of Skye, 12-14 August 1991. – (Workshops in Computing Series)
I. Heldal, Rogardt II. Series
005.1'
ISBN-13:978-3-540-19760-7

Library of Congress Cataloging-in-Publication Data
Glasgow Workshop on Functional Programming (1991: Portree, Scotland)
Functional Programming, Glasgow 1991: Proceedings of the 1991 Glasgow Workshop on Functional Programming, Portree, Isle of Skye, 12-14 August 1991 / [edited by] Rogardt Heldal, Carsten Kehler Holst and Philip Wadler.
p. cm. – (Workshops in computing)
Includes index.
ISBN-13:978-3-540-19760-7
I. Functional programming (Computer science) –Congresses. I. Heldal, Rogardt, *1964–* . II. Holst, Carsten Kehler, *1962–* . III. Wadler, Philip, *1956–*
IV. Title. V. Series.
QA76.62.G58 1991 92-5442
005.1' 1–dc20 CIP

34/3830-543210 Printed on acid-free paper

Preface

The Glasgow functional programming group has held a workshop each summer since 1988. The entire group, accompanied by a selection of colleagues from other institutions, retreats to a pleasant Scottish location for a few days. Everyone speaks briefly, enhancing coherence, cross-fertilisation, and camaraderie in our work.

The proceedings of the first workshop were published as a technical report. Demand for this was large enough to encourage wider publication, and subsequent proceedings have been published in the Springer-Verlag *Workshops in Computing* series. These are the proceedings of the meeting held 12–14 August 1991, in Portree on the Isle of Skye.

A preliminary proceedings was prepared in advance of the meeting. Most presentations were limited to a brief fifteen minutes, outlining the essentials of their subject, and referring the audience to the pre-print proceedings for details. Papers were then refereed and rewritten, and you hold the final results in your hands.

A number of themes emerged at this year's workshop, including relational algebra and its application to hardware design, partial evaluation and program transformation, implementation techniques, and strictness analysis. We were especially pleased to see applications of functional programming emerge as a theme. One of the sessions was devoted to a lively discussion of applications, and was greatly enhanced by our industrial participants.

The workshop was organised by Kei Davis, Cordelia Hall, Rogardt Heldal, Carsten Kehler Holst, John Hughes, John O'Donnell, and Satnam Singh all from the University of Glasgow.

We would like to express our gratitude to our industrial sponsors: British Telecom, Hewlett Packard, and Software AG. Their financial support made the workshop possible.

Thanks also go to Nils Andersen, John Hannan, Fritz Henglein, Kristoffer H. Rose, Torben Mogensen, Mads Rosendahl, and Peter Sestoft, all from Copenhagen University, who refereed many of the papers in these proceedings.

University of Glasgow
January 1992

The Program Committee:

Rogardt Heldal
Carsten Kehler Holst
John Hughes
Nick Rothwell (Edinburgh)
Peter Sestoft (Copenhagen)
Philip Wadler (Chairman)

Contents

A Parallel Functional Database on GRIP

Gert Akerholt Kevin Hammond Simon Peyton Jones
Phil Trinder*

December 20, 1991

Abstract

GRIP is a shared-memory multiprocessor designed for efficient parallel evaluation of functional languages, using compiled graph reduction. This paper investigates the feasibility of processing persistent data on GRIP, and presents results obtained from a pilot implementation. A database implemented in a pure functional language must be modified *non-destructively*, i.e. the original database must be preserved and a new copy constructed. The naive implementation provides evidence for the feasibility of data processing in the form of modest real-time speed-ups, and acceptable real-time performance. The functional database is also used to investigate the GRIP architecture, compared with an idealised machine. The particular features investigated are the thread-creation costs and caching of GRIP's distributed memory.

1 Introduction

Multiprocessor machines potentially provide considerable computing power cheaply. Because they typically have large memories, multiprocessors are a particularly attractive choice for implementing data- or transaction-processing applications. It is believed that pure functional languages are easily made concurrent and hence particularly suitable for programming multiprocessors. Indeed, there are now several declarative multiprocessors, i.e. machines specifically designed to evaluate functional languages in parallel [3, 7, 8, 19].

There are many research issues which remain to be resolved for multiprocessor machines, for example locality, granularity, throttling and load balancing. Data processing poses an additional challenge for declarative systems because data structures must be modified *non-destructively*, that is, the original structure must be preserved and a new copy constructed. Because of the high cost of non-destructive update the designers of the Flagship declarative multiprocessor

---

* This work is supported by the SERC GRASP and Bulk Data Types Projects. Authors' address: Computing Science Dept, Glasgow University, Glasgow, Scotland. Email: {kh,simonpj,trinder}@uk.ac.glasgow.cs

provided side-effecting transactions as operating-system primitives. The Flagship machine has achieved some impressive transaction-processing results [23]. However, the side-effecting transactions made the semantics of programs complex, reasoning about programs difficult and evaluation-order significant.

An alternative purely-functional approach based on creating versions of trees was proposed in [1]. Essentially only a path from the root to the site of the update needs to be duplicated — the unchanged parts can be shared by the original tree and the new tree. Encouraging results were obtained for the simulated parallel evaluation of a prototype database using this approach [25, 26].

Preliminary results obtained from a prototype database implemented on the GRIP declarative multiprocessor are reported here. GRIP is intended to execute lazy functional languages efficiently in parallel. Two issues are investigated by the GRIP implementation. Since the implementation is the first pure functional database on a true multiprocessor, it provides insights into the feasibility of implementing a transaction manager in a pure, i.e. non-destructive manner. The second issue is whether the GRIP machine provides good real-time performance, in particular whether parallel evaluation of the database can produce real-time speed-ups.

From an architectural perspective, the database application is interesting in two respects:

- it bridges the gap between simple, well-understood parallel benchmarks such as *nfib*, and complex real functional programs such as the Veritas theorem prover. The parallel behaviour of the database is sufficiently understood for us to be able to draw useful conclusions about the performance of GRIP, yet it is complex enough to provide a satisfactorily realistic example program.
- it tests our policy of dynamic data distribution, and provides a benchmark we can exploit for measuring realistic local memory cache performance.

The results give some evidence that both lookup and update transactions can be handled efficiently in parallel, with real absolute speed-ups. The latter is particularly important - it is pointless to merely achieve good relative speed-ups. The costs of communication is also highlighted by this example, often approximating the reduction costs. This prompts us to suggest some architectural improvements.

Very little work has been done on changing persistent data in parallel functional languages other than the Flagship work already described. The AGNA system has demonstrated that parallel functional languages can be used to interrogate databases at speeds comparable with database machines [17]. However the problem of concurrent, consistent update is not addressed in AGNA.

It is not suggested that general-purpose declarative multiprocessors like GRIP are the best machines to implement transaction-processing databases on. Rather, the feasibility of processing data on declarative multiprocessors is being investigated. Specialised database machines, like Bubba and Gamma [6, 9], have a *shared-nothing* architecture that is designed to optimise database operations. Each node in the machine comprises a processor, some memory and a disk. The database is split (or *declustered*) over the nodes and a transaction is directed to the node containing the data it manipulates, hence minimising the communication. In contrast the GRIP architecture has a shared distributed memory and no disks. The database is randomly distributed over the shared memory. A transaction may be evaluated by several processors and the database-tree is communicated to the processor that requires it. These high communication costs are a feature of our results.

The remainder of the paper is structured as follows. Section 2 provides an overview of GRIP's architecture and that of the simulated machine. Section 3 describes the architecture of our database application, introducing the data manager and the mechanisms for generating parallelism. Section 4 presents comparative performance results for both GRIP and a simulated ideal machine. Section 5 concludes.

2 Machine Architectures

2.1 GRIP Architecture

2.1.1 Overview

GRIP consists of up to 20 printed circuit boards, each of which consists of up to four processing elements (PEs) and one Intelligent Memory Unit (IMU). The boards are interconnected using a fast packet-switched bus [19], and the whole machine is attached to a Unix host. A bus was chosen specifically to make the locality issue less pressing. GRIP still allows us to *study* locality, but does not require us to *solve* the locality problem before being able to produce a convincingly fast implementation. Communication between components on the same board is faster than between components on different boards, but otherwise no difference in communication protocol is perceived by either the sender or recipient.

Each unit which communicates with the bus therefore needs a fairly sophisticated bus interface processor (BIP) to store packets and forward them to their destination when the bus becomes available. A single BIP is shared between the IMU and the PEs.

Each PE consists of a M68020 CPU, a floating-point coprocessor, and 1Mbyte of private memory which is inaccessible to other PEs.

The IMUs collectively constitute the global address space, and hold the graph. They each contain 1M words of 40 bits, together with a microprogrammable data engine. The microcode interprets incoming requests from the bus, services them and dispatches a reply to the bus. In this way, the IMUs can support a variety of memory operations, rather than the simple READ and WRITE operations supported by conventional memories.

The following range of operations is supported by our current IMU microcode:

- Variable-sized heap nodes may be allocated and initialised.

- Garbage collection is performed autonomously by the IMUs in parallel with graph reduction, using a variant of Baker's real-time collector [4].

- Each IMU maintains a pool of executable threads. Idle PEs poll the IMUs in search of these threads.

- Synchronised access to graph nodes is supported. A lock bit is associated with each unevaluated node, which is set when the node is first fetched. Any subsequent attempt to fetch it is refused, and a descriptor for the fetching thread is automatically attached to the node.

When the node is overwritten with its evaluated form (using another IMU operation), any thread descriptors attached to the node are automatically put in the thread pool by the IMU.

The IMUs are the most innovative feature of the GRIP architecture, offering a fast implementation of low-level memory operations with great flexibility.

2.1.2 Graph reduction on GRIP

Our graph reduction model is based on the Spineless Tagless G-machine [22]. The expression to be evaluated is represented by a graph of *closures*, each of which is held in heap nodes. Each closure consists of a pointer to its *code*, together with zero or more *free-variable fields.* Some closures are in *normal form*, in which case their code is usually just a return instruction, while others represent unevaluated expressions, in which case their code will perform the evaluation.

A closure is evaluated by jumping to the code it points to, leaving a pointer to the closure in a register so that the code can access the free variables; this is called *entering* the closure. When evaluation is complete, the closure is *updated* with (an indirection to) a closure representing its normal form.

A *thread* is a sequential computation whose purpose is to reduce a particular sub-graph to weak head normal form. At any moment there may be many threads available for execution in a parallel graph reduction machine; this collection of threads is called the *thread pool.* A PE in search of work fetches a new thread from the thread pool and executes it. A particular physical PE may execute a single thread at a time, or may divide its time between a number of threads.

Initially there is only one thread, whose job is to evaluate the whole program. During its execution, this thread may encounter a closure whose value will be required in the future. In this case it has the option of placing a pointer to the closure in the thread pool, where it is available for execution by other PEs — we call this *sparking* a child thread.

If the parent thread requires the value of the sparked closure while the child thread is computing it, the parent becomes *blocked.* When the child thread completes the evaluation of the closure, the closure is updated with its normal form, and the parent thread is *resumed.*

We use the evaluate-and-die model of blocking/resumption, as described in [22, 13]. The advantage of this model is that blocking only occurs when the parent and child actually collide. In all other cases, the parent's execution continues unhindered.

Notice that in either case the blocking/resumption mechanism is the ***only*** form of inter-thread communication and synchronisation. Once an expression has been evaluated to normal form, then arbitrarily many threads can inspect it simultaneously without contention. This synchronisation provides the inter-transaction "locking" required by the functional database, as described in [25]. A transaction demanding the result of a previous transaction is blocked until the previous transaction has constructed the value it requires.

2.1.3 Mapping parallel graph reduction onto GRIP

We start from the belief that parallel graph reduction will only be competitive if it can take advantage of all the compiler technology that has been developed for sequential graph-reduction implementations [20]. Our intention is that, provided a thread does not refer to remote graph nodes, it should be executed exactly as on a sequential system, including memory allocation and garbage collection.

We implement this idea on GRIP in the following way. The IMUs together hold the *global heap*, a fixed part of the address space being supported by each IMU. Each PE uses its private memory as a *local heap*, in which it allocates new graph nodes and caches copies of global heap nodes. We ensure that there are no pointers into this local heap from outside the PE, so it can be garbage-collected completely independently of the rest of the system. When the IMUs run out of memory, the entire system is synchronised and global garbage collection is performed. Global garbage collection happens much less frequently than local garbage collections. In effect, local garbage collections recycle short-term "litter" without it ever becoming part of the global heap.

2.2 Metrics

We currently monitor two kinds of performance data: processor activity and spark usage. These are plotted as profiles against elapsed time. Although we also record total heap usage, we are not yet able to plot heap occupancy profiles.

Since garbage collection overheads are low, and the total available memory is high (128Mbyte for a fully-configured GRIP, or 42Mbyte in the system monitored here), space usage is not reported here. Obviously, the rate of heap consumption will affect the size of database which can reasonably be supported, but we believe that this is a secondary issue at present.

2.3 Processor activity

We break down the distribution of processor time into the following categories:

- Reduction: this corresponds almost exactly to what a sequential Spineless Tagless machine would do.
- Communication: this is almost entirely due to *flushing* out parts of the graph into global memory and *reading* other parts in.
- Idle: time spent looking for work.
- Garbage collection.
- Other overheads: time spent running other operating system tasks, or performing GRIP to host IO. This is always negligible.

The figures for communication time include the time taken to construct packets, in addition to the elapsed communication time. Measurements show that packet construction time generally exceeds the raw communication time, at least for a lightly loaded system.

As the program runs, each PE accumulates a profile of this breakdown against time, which is collected by the host when the program completes. Since the activities are interleaved quite finely, it is not adequate to refer to a real-time clock at the transition between activities. Instead, whenever there is a clock interrupt, we inspect a global variable which tells what the PE is currently doing, and increment an appropriate count. We maintain these counts in an array of 100 "buckets", each corresponding to a fixed time interval. When we run out of buckets, we combine the counts in adjacent buckets and double the time interval corresponding to a bucket. In this way we always have data with a time resolution of better than 2%, without having to decide any parameters in advance. Its precision within each bucket naturally depends on how many clock ticks correspond to a bucket. Each clock tick represents 1ms of elapsed time. The breakdown is plotted both on a processor-by-processor basis, and aggregated into a single plot.

2.4 Spark profiles

We accumulate a time profile of how sparks are generated and used, in three categories:

Sparks generated. This count is incremented whenever a processor sparks a new thread.

Sparks used. Incremented whenever a processor gets a new thread to execute. There will often be fewer of these than sparks generated, because of the ones discarded because they turn out to be in normal form or under evaluation by the time they are selected for execution.

Threads resumed. This is incremented whenever a processor resumes execution of an old thread, which had been blocked but which has now been freed for execution.

These profiles are accumulated in the same bucket array as the processor-activity profiles, and dynamically rescaled in the same way. We also plot IMU sparking profiles, and record the overall totals for sparking, the thread pool size etc.

2.5 The Simulated Machine Architecture

2.5.1 Overview

The hypothetical machine is implemented by a interpreter simulates parallel graph reduction. The hypothetical machine is intended to be an ideal declarative multiprocessor and it is interesting to compare GRIP's performance results with the results from such a machine. Fuller details of the architecture and instrumentation can be found in [25]. We simulate a MIMD shared-memory architecture.

The machine performs super-combinator graph reduction [20]. The evaluation strategy used in the machine is lazy except where eagerness is introduced by the primitives described in the following Section. In a machine cycle a processing element may either

- Perform a super-combinator reduction, or
- Perform a delta-reduction, i.e. evaluate a primitive such as 'plus', or
- Perform a house-keeping activity such as sparking a new thread.

The work to be performed by the program is broken into threads. Each thread reduces a subgraph of the program graph. Initially only one thread exists. New threads are sparked by the eager primitives described later. Thread synchronisation occurs as follows. A thread marks the nodes it is processing as busy. A thread encountering a busy node is marked as *blocked.* As soon as the required node is no longer busy the blocked thread resumes. A thread that is not blocked is termed *active.* The scheduling strategy used in the hypothetical machine is both simple and fair: every active thread is assigned to a processing agent and in a machine cycle the next redex in each active thread is reduced.

The machine is simplistic in not supporting throttling or granularity control, in having a uniform machine cycle and in reducing newly sparked threads immediately.

The hypothetical machine is instrumented to record the following statistics during the evaluation of a program: the number of super-combinator and delta-reductions, the number of graph nodes allocated, the number of machine cycles and the average number of active processes. In addition, every 20 machine cycles, the hypothetical records the average number of active threads. This information is used to plot graphs of the average number of active threads against time measured in machine cycles.

3 Database Architecture

3.1 Introduction

A *class* is a homogeneous set of data; it may represent a semantic object such as a relation or an entity set. For example a class might represent a collection of bank accounts. For simplicity the bulk data manager described in this paper supports operations on a single class of data. The same principles apply for operations on a database containing multiple classes of data. The design of a more realistic functional database that supports multiple classes, views, security, alternative data structures and two data models is given in [25].

In most existing languages only certain types of data may be permanently stored. Much of the effort in writing programs that manipulate permanent data is expended in unpacking the data into a form suitable for the computation and then repacking it for storage afterwards. The idea behind *persistent* programming languages is to allow entities of any type to be permanently stored. The length of time that an entity exists, or its persistence, is independent of its type. Several persistent functional languages have been constructed [15, 16, 17]

In a persistent environment a class can be represented as a data structure that persists for some time. Because of their size such structures are termed bulk data structures. Operations that do not modify a bulk data structures, for example looking up a value, can be implemented efficiently in a functional language. However, modifications to a data structure must be non-destructive in a pure functional language, i.e. a new version of the structure must be constructed. At first glance it appears to be prohibitively expensive to create a new version of a bulk data structure every time it is modified.

3.2 Trees

A new version of a tree can be cheaply constructed. For simplicity the prototype data manager uses a binary tree. In a more realistic database a B-tree would be used. The distinction between binary and B-trees does not affect the efficiency described in the next Section. A class can be viewed as a collection of entities and there may be a key function that, given an entity, will return its key value. If *et* and *kt* are the entity and key types then an abstract datatype *bdt*, for a tree can be written

$$bdt = Node\ bdt\ kt\ bdt \mid Entity\ et$$

That is, every element of the tree is either an internal node with a left sub-tree, a key and a right sub-tree, or a leaf containing an entity. Using this definition, a function to lookup an entity can be written as follows. If the lookup succeeds the result returned is the required entity tagged *Ok*. If the entity does not exist, an *Error* is reported.

$$\begin{aligned} lookup\ k'\ (Entity\ e) &= Ok\ e, \text{ if } key\ e = k' \\ &= Error, \text{ otherwise} \end{aligned}$$

$$\begin{aligned} lookup\ k'\ (Node\ lt\ k\ rt) &= lookup\ k'\ lt, \text{ if } k' \leq k \\ &= lookup\ k'\ rt, \text{ otherwise} \end{aligned}$$

A function to update an entity is similar except that, in addition to producing an output message, a new version of the tree is returned.

$$\begin{aligned} update\ e'\ (Entity\ e) &= (Ok\ e,\ Entity\ e'), \text{ if } key\ e = key\ e' \\ &= (Error,\ Entity\ e), \text{ otherwise} \end{aligned}$$

$$\begin{aligned} update\ e'\ (Node\ lt\ k\ rt) &= (m, Node\ lt'\ k\ rt), \text{ if } key\ e' \leq k \\ &= (m, Node\ lt\ k\ rt'), \text{ otherwise} \\ &\quad \text{where} \\ &\qquad (m, lt') = update\ e'\ lt \\ &\qquad (m, rt') = update\ e'\ rt \end{aligned}$$

The database-tree used to produce the results reported in the following Sections contains 2^{20} nodes. The database is lazily created by demanding the value of a database node. The entities at the leaves of the tree contain an account number, a balance a credit limit and a class. Because of GRIP has no fast access to permanent storage we assume that the entire database resides in primary memory for the present experiment. This is not as unreasonable as it might initially appear as a fully-configured GRIP has a 128Mb memory. Results already obtained using simulated disk accesses [26] are being verified in a further experiment on GRIP.

3.3 Efficiency

Let us assume that the tree contains n entities and is balanced. In this case its depth is $\log n$ and hence the update function only requires to construct $\log n$ new nodes to create a new version of such a tree. This is because any unchanged nodes are shared between the old and the new versions and thus a new *path* through the tree is all that need be constructed. This is best illustrated by the figure overleaf, that shows a tree which has been updated to associate a value of 3 with x.

A time complexity of $\log n$ is the same as an imperative tree update. The non-destructive update has a larger constant factor, however, as the new nodes must be created and some unchanged information copied into them. The functional update can be made more efficient using a reference count optimisation [25], but GRIP does not support this optimisation at present. However, when non-destructive update is used, a copy of the tree can be kept cheaply because the nodes common to the old and new versions are shared i.e. only a differential between the versions is required. This technique is similar to shadow paging [12] except that logical values, i.e. tree nodes, are being shadowed rather than fixed-sized pages.

As described in [1, 25], the cheap shadow versions have several uses. They make undoing an aborted transaction easy: the original database is simply reinstated. Section 5 demonstrates how the multiple versions permit an unusual degree of concurrency between transactions. It has also been noted, but not thoroughly investigated, that this versioning technique could provide an elegant checkpointing recovery mechanism if used in conjunction with a stable store [25].

3.4 Data Manager

The database-tree is controlled by a manager function that processes a stream of transactions to produce a stream of responses.

Original and New Trees

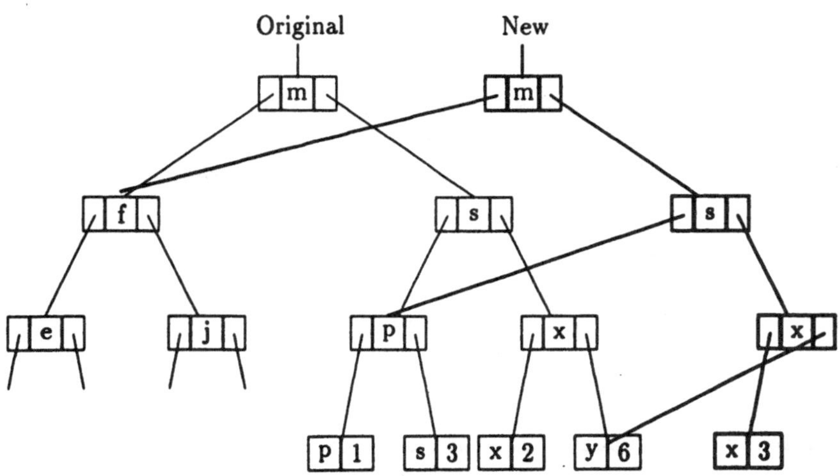

Transaction Functions

A transaction is a function that takes the database as an argument and returns some output and a new version of the database as a result. Let us call this type, $bdt \rightarrow (output \times bdt)$, txt. Transactions are built out of tree manipulating operations such as *lookup* and *update*. In the bank database, two functions that prove useful are *isok*, that determines whether an operation succeeded, and *dep* that increments the balance of an account.

$$\begin{aligned} &isok\ (Ok\ e) = True \\ &isok\ out = False \end{aligned}$$

$$dep\ (Ok\ Entity\ ano\ bal\ crl\ class)\ n \ = \ Entity\ ano\ (bal + n)\ crl\ class$$

Using *isok* and *dep*, a transaction to deposit a sum of money in a bank account can be written as follows.

$$\begin{aligned} deposit\ a\ n\ d &= update\ (dep\ m\ n)\ d, \text{ if } (isok\ m) \\ &= (Error, d), \text{ otherwise} \\ &\quad \textbf{where} \\ &\qquad m = lookup\ a\ d \end{aligned}$$

The arguments the *deposit* function takes are an account number a, a sum of money n and a database d. If the *lookup* fails to locate the account an error message and the original database are returned. If the *lookup* succeeds, the result of the function is the result of updating the account. The update replaces the existing account entity with an identical entity, except that the balance has been incremented by the specified sum. Note that *deposit* is of the correct type for a transaction-function when it is partially applied to an account number and a sum of money, i.e. *deposit a n* has type $bdt \rightarrow (output \times bdt)$.

The *deposit* transaction has a common transaction form: some operations are performed on the database and if they succeed the transaction commits, i.e. returns the updated database. If the operations fail, the transaction aborts and returns an unchanged database. Transactions that may commit or abort are termed *total*.

Manager

The database manager is a stream processing function. It consumes a lazy list, or stream, of transaction-functions and produces a stream of output. That is, the manager has type $bdt \rightarrow [txt] \rightarrow [output]$. A simple version can be written as follows.

$$\begin{aligned} manager\ d\ (f : fs) &= out : manager\ d'\ fs \\ &\quad \textbf{where} \\ &\qquad (out, d') = f\ d \end{aligned}$$

The first transaction f in the input stream is applied to the database and a pair is returned as the result. The output component of the pair is placed in the output stream. The updated database, d', is given as the first argument to the recursive call to the manager. Because the manager retains the modified database produced by each transaction it has an evolving state. The manager can be made available to many users simultaneously using techniques developed for functional operating systems [11]. Essentially streams of transactions from many users are non-deterministically merged into the single input stream consumed by the manager.

3.5 Concurrent Transactions

Total Transactions

Concurrency can be introduced between transactions by making the list constructor in the manager eager. A typical eager list constructor sparks a thread to evaluate the head of the list and continues to evaluate the tail of the list. The thread evaluating the head of the list, *out*, does so by applying the first transaction-function to the database, $f\ d$. The thread evaluating the tail of the list applies the manager to the updated database and the remaining transaction-functions, $manager\ d'\ fs$. The recursive call to the manager itself contains an eager list constructor that will spark a new thread to evaluate the second transaction and continue to apply the manager to the remaining transactions.

An eager manager provides ample concurrency between individual lookups and updates on the hypothetical machine [26]. However a total transaction, i.e. one that may commit or abort, can seriously restrict concurrency. This is because neither the original nor the updated database can be returned until the decision whether to abort or not has been taken. Therefore no other transaction may access any other part of the database until this decision has been made.

Friedman-and-Wise If

Essentially total transactions have the form,

$$if \text{ predicate db } then \text{ transform db } else \text{ db.}$$

In most cases the bulk of the database will be the same whether or not the transaction commits. This common, or unchanged, part of the database will be returned whatever the result of the commit decision. If there were some way of returning the common part early then concurrency would be greatly increased. Transactions that only depend on unchanged data can begin and possibly even complete without waiting for the preceding total transaction to commit or abort.

The common parts of the database can be returned early using *fwif*, a variant of the conditional statement proposed by Friedman and Wise [10]. A more complete description of *fwif* and its implementation in the hypothetical machine can be found in [25, 2]. To define the semantics of *fwif* let us view every data value as a constructor and a sequence of constructed values. Every member of an unstructured type is a zero-arity constructor — the sequence of constructed values is empty. Using C to denote a constructor, the semantics can be given by the following reduction rules.

$$fwif\ True\ x\ y \Rightarrow x$$
$$fwif\ False\ x\ y \Rightarrow y$$
$$fwif\ p\ (C\ x_0 \ldots x_n)\ (C\ y_0 \ldots y_n) \Rightarrow C\ (fwif\ p\ x_0\ y_0) \ldots (fwif\ p\ x_n\ y_n)$$

The third rule of *fwif* represents a family of rules, one for each constructor in the language. The third rule distributes *fwif* inside identical constructors, allowing the identical *then* and *else* constructor, C, to be returned before the predicate is evaluated. As an example, consider a conditional that selects between two lists that have 1 as the first element. Note how the first element of the list becomes available.

$$fwif\ p\ (cons\ 1\ xs)\ (cons\ 1\ ys)$$

$$= \{fwif\ 3\}$$

$$cons\ (fwif\ p\ 1\ 1)\ (fwif\ p\ xs\ ys)$$

$$= \{fwif\ 3\}$$

$$cons\ 1\ (fwif\ p\ xs\ ys)$$

To implement *fwif* the predicate and the two conditional branches are evaluated concurrently. The values of the conditional branches are compared and common parts are returned. When a part is found not to be common to both branches the evaluation of those branches ceases. Once the predicate is evaluated, the chosen branch is returned and the evaluation of the other is cancelled. This strategy amounts to speculative parallelism, the conditional branches being evaluated in the hope that parts of them will be identical.

4 Performance Measurements

In this section we present performance results gained from running small database transactions on both GRIP and the hypothetical machine. The GRIP results are discussed in some detail, including investigation of the architectural implications of our results. In contrast, the hypothetical machine results are merely summarised in order to provide a comparison with an ideal machine.

We present results for lookup and update transactions independently. Our results are for the 2^{20} node database described earlier. Only the update transactions use *fwif*.

4.1 Read-only Transactions

4.1.1 GRIP Results

Figure 1 shows the activity profiles for each of 6 PEs running 80 database lookups in 8 transactions. The reason for chosing around 10 operations per transaction is that the DebitCredit transaction-processing benchmark [24] uses a similar number (7). A typical lookup transaction is given in Appendix A.1. The GRIP database manager sparks a thread to evaluate each transaction in parallel.

In these results, a inverse relationship between reduction and communication time can be clearly observed. Generally the PEs are busy either computing or communicating. Reading and flushing (not separated in these plots) occur in roughly equal proportions throughout this run.

Figure 2 shows the activity and spark profiles for the same example aggregated over all PEs. The spark profile indicates that all sparks occurred early in the run. It also shows threads resuming after being blocked early in the run (the blocking is not shown). This blocking is a consequence of our distribution strategy, where a lookup transaction may not commence before the result of the previous transaction is known. Because the new, unchanged database is returned immediately from the lookups, the blocking period is always short.

The overall communication time is slightly higher than the overall reduction time (38% v. 37%). This indicates that few global nodes have been successfully cached. Given the random nature of the lookups and the fact that we are using a lazy caching algorithm, this is perhaps unsurprising. An eager caching scheme, where we prefetched graph nodes from global memory, might reduce PE communication overhead, as might a scheme which made better use of previously cached nodes.

The PEs are idle for 25% of the time. Idle time mainly occurs at the end of the run, when we are flushing the transaction pipeline. All PEs apart from PE 14.1 (which is running the transaction manager as the initial thread) are also partly idle at the start of the run. This presumably reflects the threads blocking on the root of the database, as noted earlier. The only significant idle time not mentioned so far occurs 75 ticks into PE 14.1's execution. This corresponds to the PE blocking, then resuming a transaction.

A rough estimate of absolute performance can made if the percentage reduction time is multiplied by the PEs in use. A single sequential processor performing no garbage collection or IO would have an absolute performance of 100%. For this example, our absolute performance is 222%. That is, we have definitely gained by using parallel evaluation in this case.

It is interesting to observe that threads are only created at the start of execution. That is, all transactions are sparked early in the run. Each PE obtains one thread and sparks one new thread (corresponding to the tail of the transactions). Because there are 8 transactions, but only 6 PEs, there are 3 "spare" threads (one of which is trivial). These threads are obtained by those PEs which block first, and are held "in reserve".

4.1.2 Results from the Hypothetical Machine

The hypothetical machine can support the GRIP strategy of sparking a single thread for each lookup transaction. The active thread graph for evaluation of the 8 read-only transactions is given in Figure 3. The idealised hypothetical machine achieves an absolute speed-up factor of 6.67 over the sequential execution. This is considerably better than GRIP achieves, reflecting the shared memory and low thread-sparking cost.

There is some similarity between the numbers of active threads in the two machines. The hypothetical machine reaches a stable state where it is utilising approximately 9 processors. These represent the manager and the 8 read-transactions. The GRIP machine usefully employs 6 processors. We believe that GRIP could utilise more processors to evaluate a larger number of read-only transactions.

Because threads are so cheap on the hypothetical machine, *fwif* can be used to spark a thread for each lookup within the transactions. So much parallelism is

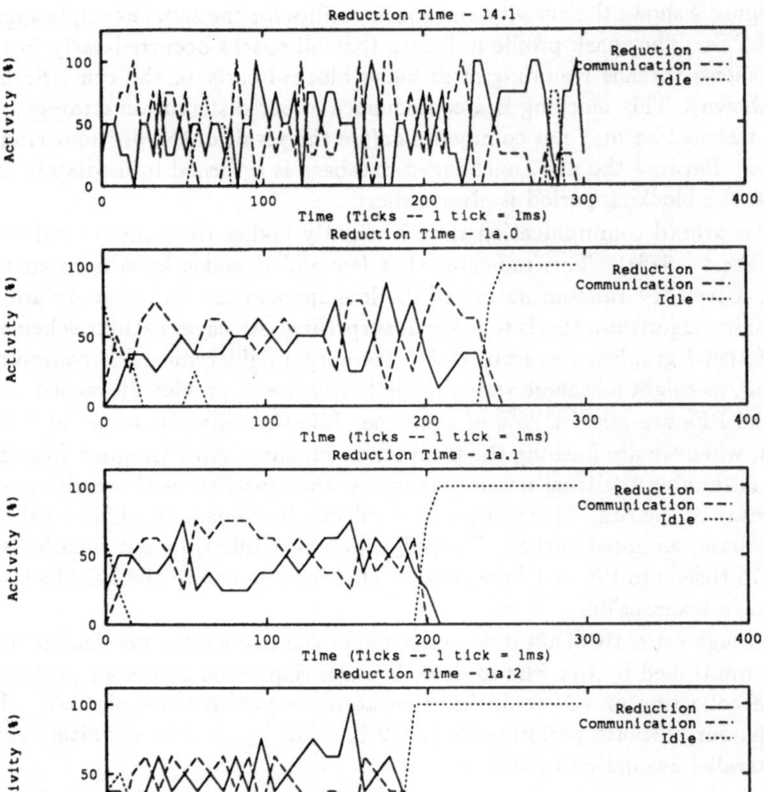

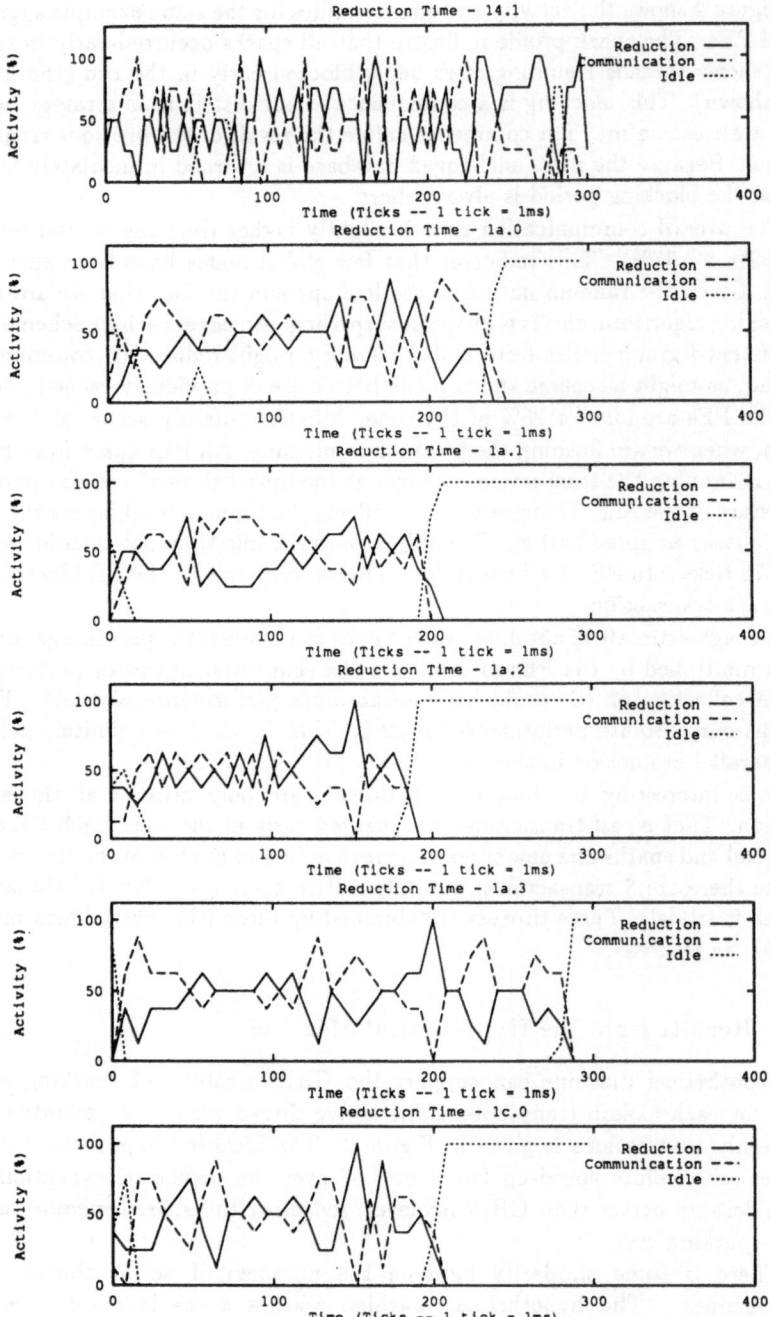

Figure 1: PE Activity Profiles: 80 lookups

generated by the program using *fwif* that 8 read-only transactions are not sufficient to reach a stable state. Hence Figure 4 plots the active thread graph for both a sequence of 8 read-only transactions (dotted line) and for a sequence of 32 read-only transactions (solid line). Assuming that thread sparking is so cheap is probably not reasonable if the hypothetical results are to be compared with GRIP results.

4.2 Update Transactions

4.2.1 GRIP Results

To test the performance of the parallel database under more realistic conditions, we have implemented two transaction mixes which include database updates, insertions and deletions as well as lookups. We use a variant of *fwif* to enhance inter-transaction parallelism, as described above. LML source code for a typical update transaction is given in Appendix A.3.

The first mix is a deliberately poor example, with poor locality. The second mix has better locality so that advantage can be taken of our cached copies of the database spine. For comparison, a typical update transaction in the first mix might update the records with keys 508440, 3420, 757150, 256330, 1001750, that is records in different parts of the database. Only the top two levels of the database are shared between the updates. A typical transaction in the second mix might update records with keys 8440, 3420, 7150, 6330, 1750. Now updates are occurring in the same part of the database, and the top 10 nodes of the cached tree may be reused for the second and subsequent updates. Data dependencies between transactions will also be reduced. The first mix contains 330 operations in 34 transactions; the second mix contains 480 operations in 48 transactions.

Figure 5 shows aggregate activity and spark profiles for the first mix of transactions running on 4 PEs. For clarity, we have separated the plots of reduction, communication and idle time. The startup and tail-off periods where the transaction pipeline is filling and being emptied, respectively, can be clearly seen.

In this example, communication time closely follows reduction time (overall, 30% of the total runtime each). Initially, similar times are spent flushing and reading graph. However, from tick 3, more time is spent reading than flushing and from tick 19, reading dominates flushing by a factor of 2. Clearly, the database is effectively distributed by tick 19, and most communication consists of creating cached copies of the database.

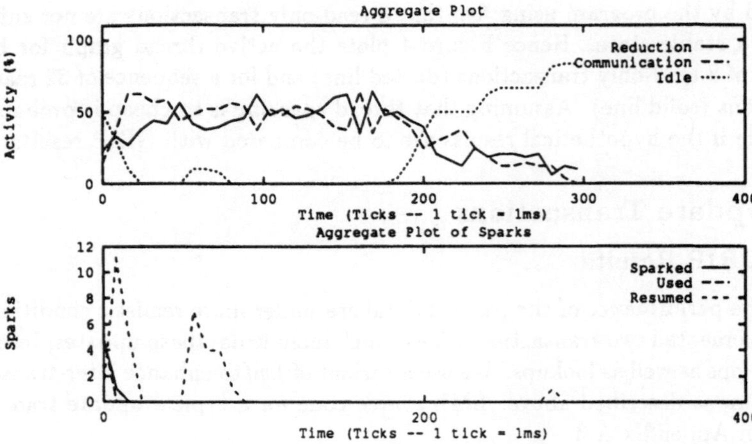

Figure 2: Aggregate Activity and Sparking Profiles: 80 lookups

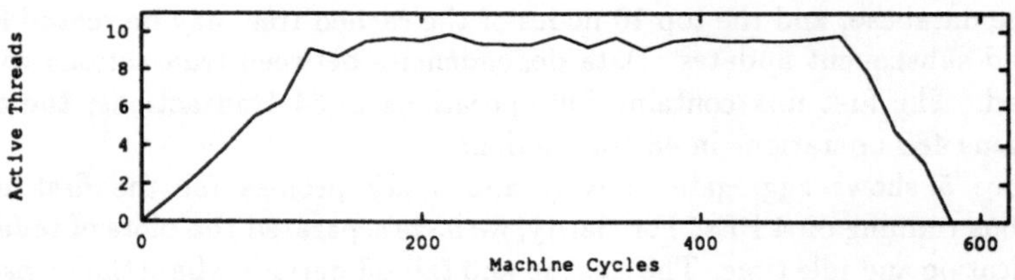

Figure 3: Simulator Results: 80 Lookups

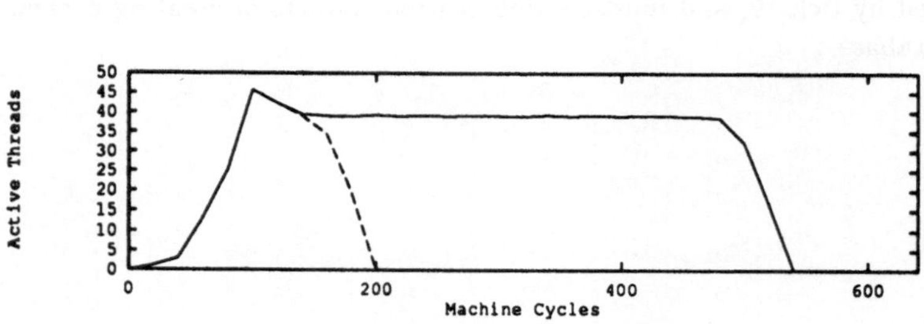

Figure 4: Simulator Results: Unrestricted Parallelism

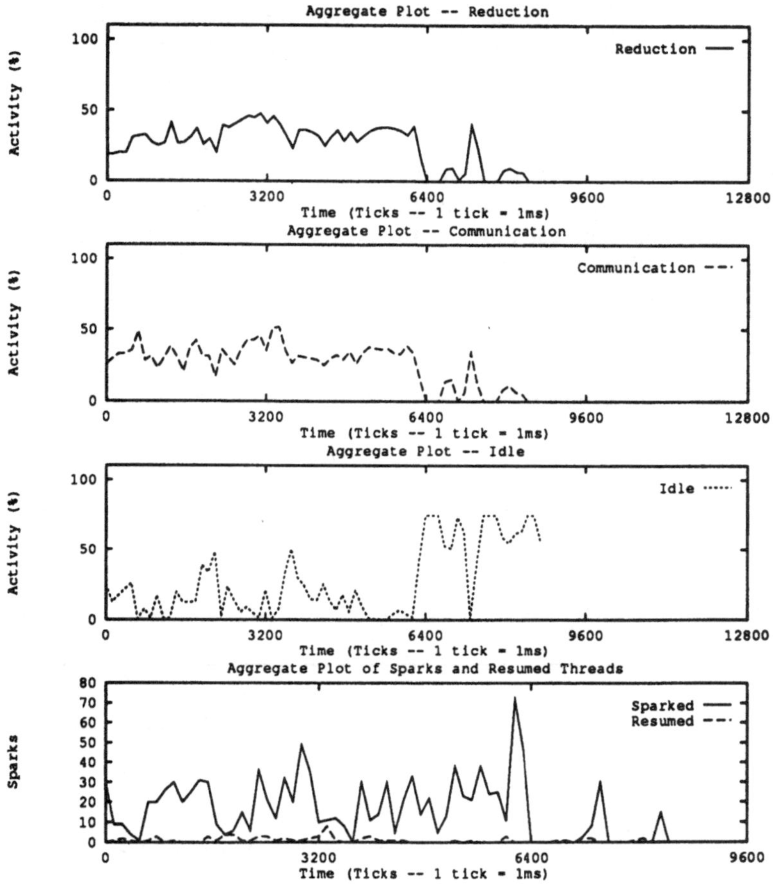

Figure 5: Aggregate Activity and Sparking Profiles: Mixed Transactions 1

Turning our attention to the sparking profiles, it is obvious that sparks are used to create threads almost immediately they are generated. The much higher sparking levels in this example reflect not only the additional transactions compared with the lookup example, but also the use of *fwif*, which in this version generates sparks to evaluate each level of the database in turn.

There is a small, but significant level of blocked thread resumption, corresponding to part of a database required by a later transaction being constructed by an earlier transaction. This will normally be the root of the database [25]. Thread resumption thus corresponds to the release of database locks, where the data dependencies have been detected dynamically.

Garbage collection accounts for 7% of the total runtime. This is the highest percentage rate we have yet observed on GRIP. The relatively high cost is presumably due to high heap occupancy, perhaps because we are retaining blocked threads locally as long as possible, in order to avoid the costs associated with flushing these to global memory.

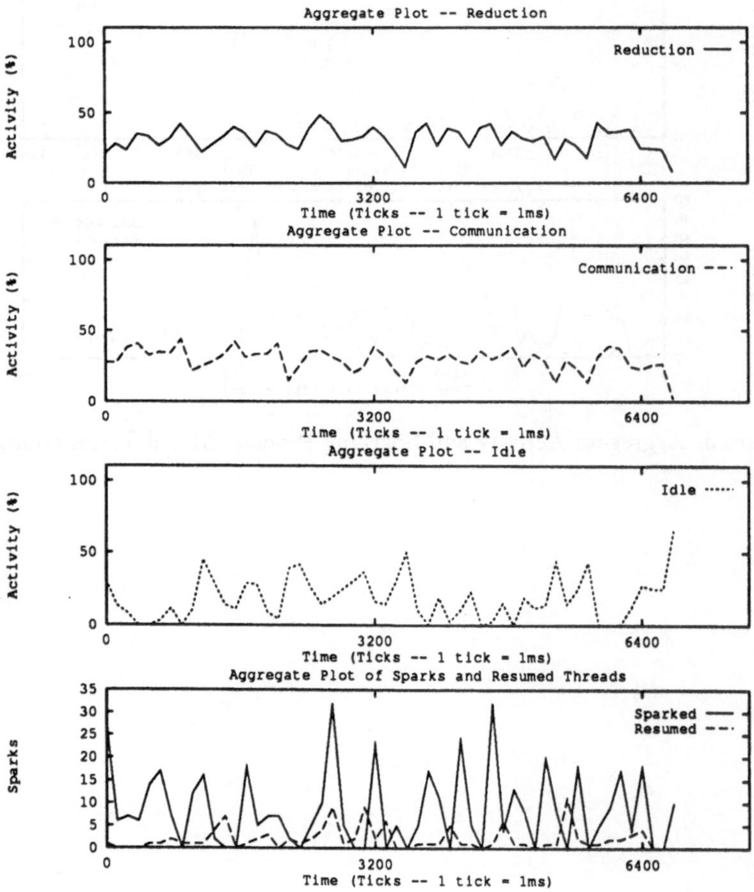

Figure 6: Aggregate Activity and Sparking Profiles: Mixed Transactions 2

Figure 6 shows the aggregate plots for the second (better) mix of transactions on 4 PEs. Once more, we have segregated the activity plots into communication, reduction and idle times. Compared with the fully random mix discussed above, the startup and tail-off times are reduced considerably. Communication costs are also slightly reduced relative to reduction time (38% reduction, 35% communication). Garbage collection costs are also reduced to < 5% of the total runtime.

The sparking profile shows that far fewer sparks are generated than before – 252 sparks for 188 threads, compared with 1093 for 948 threads.

Given that we are evaluating more transactions in this example, in less elapsed time, it is clear that implicitly caching part of the database has improved performance.

The following table shows the absolute timings for this example on varying numbers of PEs, from 1 to 18. Up to 4 PEs, there is an obvious improvement for each PE added. Beyond 4 PEs, it is clear that the advantage from adding more processors diminishes rapidly. For 8 PEs, we therefore achieve a maximum rate of 16 transactions processed per second. Significant performance improvements should result from tuning our system to reduce overheads and to take advantage of so far untapped processing resources.

PEs	Time(s)
1	13.248
2	7.456
3	3.885
4	3.570
5	3.424
6	3.398
8	3.005
10	3.338
12	3.141
18	3.325

4.2.2 Results from the Hypothetical Machine

The active thread graph for the hypothetical machine evaluation of the first update-transaction mix is given in Figure 7. For realism the thread-sparking strategy used is identical to that used in GRIP except where the *fwif* implementations and output drivers differ. The hypothetical machine achieves an absolute speed-up of a factor of 4.9 over the sequential evaluation. This ideal figure is considerably better than the GRIP absolute speed-up, though it is comparable with the relative speedup. The number of active threads in GRIP and in the hypothetical machine is similar. An average of 6.09 processors are active in the hypothetical machine while configuring GRIP to use more than 4 processors gains little improvement. The active thread graph for the second update-transaction mix is similar and is omitted.

5 Conclusion

We have implemented naive parallel data processing on the GRIP declarative multiprocessor. Our database relies on the multiple versions produced by

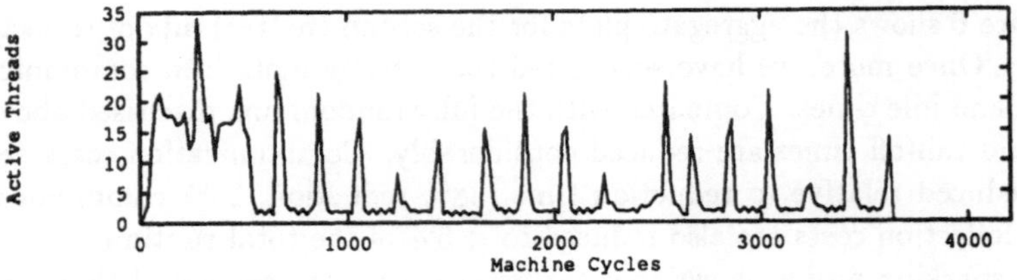

Figure 7: Simulator Results: Mixed Transactions 1

non-destructive updates to allow concurrent lookups and updates. Synchronisation between concurrent transactions is ensured by the normal thread synchronisation mechanism described above.

Our preliminary results show that we can achieve absolute speed-up over a sequential version of the database, even for small examples. Moreover, the real evaluation time for the sequences of transactions executed compares favourably with a more sophisticated database on existing machines. The results seem promising as early figures, especially if the communications overhead can be reduced and excessive data dependencies avoided. Tuning our system to take advantage of the unused processing capability should also improve our transaction throughput. These initial results have encouraged us and a more realistic transaction-processing example (part of the DebitCredit benchmark [24]) is now being implemented.

We have yet not attempted to tune our results, beyond experimenting with transactions with different locality, which improves the dynamic cache hit rate. This experiment demonstrated that absolute performance could be improved by 33%, with a 10% reduction in communication cost, and a 29% reduction in garbage collection costs.

Communication overhead might be reduced by:

- Implementing eager memory prefetch. By initiating memory accesses for the children of a node when the node is demanded we can reduce latency and also reduce packet construction costs (the major component of our communication overheads).

- Combining dynamic data distribution with a good initial static placement. This is an open research area.

The relatively high cost for garbage collection (5%-7%) is probably due to retaining large numbers of blocked threads in the PEs rather than flushing these to global memory. Since each thread currently uses a 50Kbyte stack drawn from the heap. By experimenting with smaller chunks, and by being more eager to flush blocked threads we should be able to reduce GC costs. The remainder of the increase in GC costs must be due to maintaining our database in primary memory. Further experiments will be needed to determine what proportion of the GC cost should be apportioned to using such a large data structure.

Bibliography

1. Argo G, Fairbairn J, Hughes RJM, Launchbury EJ, and Trinder PW,

"Implementing Functional Databases", *Proc Workshop on Database Programming Languages*, Roscoff, France (September 1987), pp. 87-103.

2. Akerholt G, "Extending A Parallel Functional Database", Senior Honours Project Report, Glasgow University Computer Science Dept., (1991), in preparation.

3. "Flagship Project — Alvey Proposal", Document Reference G0003 Issue 4, (May 1985).

4. Baker HG, "List processing in real time on a serial computer", *Comm. ACM* 21,4 (April 1978).

5. Bird RS and Wadler PL, *Introduction to Functional Programming*, Prentice Hall, (1988).

6. Boral H, Alexander W, and Clay L *et al.* Prototyping Bubba, A highly Parallel Database System. IEEE Trans. on Knowledge and Data Engineering 2,1 (March 1990).

7. Burton FW and Sleep MR, "Executing Functional Programs on a Virtual Tree of Processors", *Proc ACM Conference on Functional Programming Languages and Computer Architecture*, Portsmouth, New Hampshire, (1981).

8. Cox S, Glaser H, and Reeve M, "Compiling Functional Languages for the Transputer", *Proc Glasgow Workshop on Functional Programming*, Fraserburgh, Scotland, Springer Verlag, (August 1989).

9. De Witt DJ, Ghandeharizadeh S, Schneider DA *et al.* The Gamma Database Machine Project. IEEE Trans. on Knowledge and Data Engineering 2,1 (March 1990).

10. Friedman DP, and Wise DS, "A Note on Conditional Expressions", *Comm. ACM* 21(11), (November 1978).

11. Henderson P, "Purely Functional Operating Systems" in *Functional Programming and its Application*, Darlington J, Henderson P and Turner DA (Eds), Cambridge University Press, (1982).

12. Hecht MS, and Gabbe JD, "Shadowed Management of Free Disk Pages with a Linked List", *ACM Transactions on Database Systems* 8(4), (December 1983).

13. Hammond K, and Peyton Jones SL, "Some Early Experiments on the GRIP Parallel Reducer", *Proc 2nd International Workshop on Parallel Implementation of Functional Languages*, Plasmeijer MJ (Ed), University of Nijmegen, (1990).

14. Hammond K, and Peyton Jones SL, "Profiling Scheduling Strategies on the GRIP Parallel Reducer", submitted to *Journal of Parallel and Distributed Computing*, (1991).

15. McNally D, Joosten S, and Davie A Persistent Functional Programming. Proceedings of the 4th International Workshop on Persistent Object Systems, Martha's Vinyard, Mass., USA (September 1990).

16. Mathews DCJ A Persistent Storage System for Poly and ML. University of Cambridge Technical Report 102 (January 1987).

17. Nikhil RS Heytens ML List Comprehensions in AGNA, a Parallel Persistent Object System. Proceedings of the Conference on Functional Programming and Computer Architecture, Cambridge, Massachusetts (August 1991).

18. Peyton Jones SL, Clack, C, Salkild, J and Hardie, M "GRIP – a high-performance architecture for parallel graph reduction", *Proc FPCA 87*, Portland, Oregon, ed Kahn G, Springer-Verlag LNCS, (1987).

19. Peyton Jones SL, "Using Futurebus in a Fifth Generation Computer", *Microprocessors and Microsystems* 10(2), (March 1986), pp. 69-76.

20. Peyton Jones SL, *The Implementation of Functional Programming Languages*, Prentice Hall, (1987).

21. Peyton Jones SL, "FLIC - a Functional Language Intermediate Code", Department of Computer Science, University College, London, Internal Note 2048, (February 1987).

22. Peyton Jones SL, and Salkild J, "The Spineless Tagless G-machine", *Proc FPCA 89*, London, MacQueen (Ed), Addison Wesley, (1989).

23. Robertson IB, "Hope$^+$ on Flagship", *Proc 1989 Glasgow Workshop on Functional Programming*, Fraserburgh, Scotland, Springer Verlag, (August 1989).

24. Sawyer T. Serlin O. DebitCredit Benchmark - Minimum Requirements and Compliance List. Codd & Date Consulting Group, San Jose.

25. Trinder PW, *A Functional Database*, Oxford University D.Phil. Thesis, (December 1989).

26. Trinder PW, "Concurrent Data Manipulation in a Pure Functional Language", in *Proc 1990 Glasgow Workshop on Functional Programming*, Ullapool, Scotland, Springer Verlag, (August 1990).

Appendix A: LML Sources

A.1 GRIP fwif

The operational definition of the *fwif* we have implemented for GRIP is shown below, in pseudo-LML. To define this function precisely, we need to use a number of pseudo-functions:

boolval p determines whether the predicate *p* is *True*, *False* or not yet evaluated (*Unknown*).

eq p1 p2 determines whether *p1* and *p2* are identical local nodes or global pointers. Neither *p1* nor *p2* are evaluated.

seq x y evaluates *x* to weak head normal form, then evaluates and returns *y*.

par x y sparks *x* and continues execution of *y*.

C stands for an arbitrary n-ary constructor. All uses of *C* refer to the same constructor.

We assume that *fwif* is never applied to ⊥. For the database example described here, this is always the case.

```
rec fwif p x y =
  case boolval p in
       True : x
    || False : y
    || Unknown :
         if eq x y then x
         else seq x (seq y (
           if eq x y then x
           else case x in
             C x1 ... xn :
               case y in
                 C y1 ... yn :
                        let xy1 = fwif p x1 y1
                        ...
                        and xyn = fwif p xn yn in
                        par xy1 (... (par xyn (C xy1 ... xyn)) ... )

                 || _ : if p then x else y
               end
           end))
  end
```

For the database example, we know that only one branch of the constructor (node) will have changed between transactions. In fact, in general, it is likely that only some subnodes of an constructor will vary between *x* and *y*, and we need only spark *fwif* calls on non-identical children. Although the *fwif* threads would terminate immediately in the case where the children were identical, it is better to avoid the overhead of creating such fine-grained threads if possible. We therefore test for identity before creating the recursive calls.

```
let xy1 = fwif p x1 y1 and xy1' =
...
and xyn = fwif p xn yn in
if not (eq x1 y1) then
par xy1 xy2'
```

```
par xy1 (... (par xyn (C xy1 ... xyn)) ... )
```

Although we would prefer to return the constructor node immediately, and then nominate one spark as the successor of the *fwif*, this is not possible with the operations we have specified so far. Further work will investigate a version of *fwif* implemented in this way.

A.2 Read-only Transaction

This appendix gives a sample read-only transaction in LML. The transaction comprises 10 lookups on the same database (that is there is no interdependency between lookups). Since the database is unmodified by lookup operations, this result may be ignored. The new, unchanged database may be returned before any lookup is evaluated.

```
lookups d =
    let (o1,_) = lookup   1000     d in
    ...
    let (o10,_) = lookup  2010     d in
        ((if (isok o1) & (isok o2) & (isok o3) & (isok o4) & (isok o5) &
           (isok o6) & (isok o7) & (isok o8) & (isok o9) & (isok o10) then
         o10 else error "dep" 0),d)
```

A.3 Update Transaction

This appendix shows a sample update transaction written in LML. The transaction comprises 5 lookups, each of which is followed by an update of the same database node. The update is thus dependent on its associated lookup, and successive lookup/update pairs are dependent on their predecessors.

```
updates n d =
    let (o1,_) = lookup   508440     d in
    let (o2,d1) = update (deprec o1 n)     d in
    ...
    let (o9,_) = lookup   1001750     d in
    let (o10,d5) = update (deprec o9 n)     d4 in
    let test = (isok o2) & (isok o4) & (isok o6) &
               (isok o8) & (isok o10) in
    let d5 = fwifdb test d5 d in

    par d5 ((if test then o10 else error "ups1" 0),d5)
```

A New Sharing Mechanism for the TIM

Guy Argo[1]

Abstract

In this paper we introduce a new method of implementing lazy evaluation efficiently in the TIM. A major advantage of the TIM [4] over other abstract machines is that it can take advantage of the results of sharing analysis. In this paper, we demonstrate that despite this advantage the sharing mechanism of the original TIM suffers from two serious flaws: expensive shared partial applications (in both space and time); and redundant updates. We devise a more general notation for expressing sharing than that introduced in [4]. This allows us to demonstrate that the sole reason for the defects in the TIM sharing mechanism is its treatment of sharing as a local property of arguments. Consequently we propose a new scheme where sharing is treated as a global property of expressions. This eliminates the problem of redundant updates and opens the way for several improvements including: cheap shared partial applications (in both space and time); and better synergy between the caller and the callee.

Introduction

The paper is divided into three sections. The first section explains Fairbairn and Wray's Normal Order TIM, how they enhanced it to execute lazily, a general sharing notation to explain their enhancements and the problems with their lazy TIM. In the second section we investigate solutions to the original lazy TIM's problems within the framework of our sharing notation. In the fourth section we present our conclusions.

1. Closure reduction via the original TIM

The Three Instruction Machine [4], or TIM as it is more commonly known, has strongly influenced the design of recent lazy abstract machines. Its simple but radical design demonstrates that some of the decisions taken in the G-machine [1] [5] and the PAM [3] are open to question, thereby suggesting a whole spectrum of possible abstract machine architectures.

The TIM's key departure from its direct ancestor, the PAM, is to represent applications as closures instead of graphs. A closure is a pair whose first component is the code of a function and whose second component is a pointer to a frame in the heap containing the arguments (which are themselves closures).

[1]Mail to: Department of Computer Science, University of Glasgow, Glasgow, G12 8QQ, UK.
E-mail: guy@dcs.glasgow.ac.uk

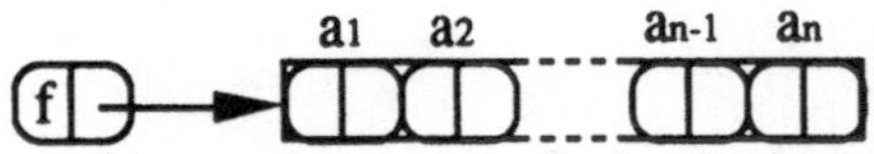

The advantage of this representation is that it is very simple to build - the arguments are passed via the stack and transferred into the frame by a block move at the start of the function. Accessing arguments is also straightforward - we do not have to go through the contortions of unwinding the spine of the graph onto the stack before executing the function body. The closure representation is also very compact. Consider an application of a function to n integers: the graph representation requires 3n words for the application nodes, 2n words for the integer arguments and 3 words for the function giving a total of 5n + 3 words; the closure representation requires 1 word for the frame header, 2n words for the integers in the frame and two words for the pair giving a total of 2n + 3, a saving of 3n words.

To be fair, partial applications as values are not handled so naturally by closures as by graphs but we shall return to this point later.

The TIM state consists of:

```
        (Code, Env)            Stack
```

representing the function `(Code, Env)` applied to the arguments on the `Stack`.

One of the innovations introduced by Fairbairn and Wray was to give constants an executable representation - a number is represented by the closure `(Int, 5)` where `Int` is a real code pointer not a data tag. But what should `Int` do ? If the closure part of the machine is a number it is because the expression under reduction has reached a normal form. In this situation the result is returned on top of the stack and the continuation on top of the stack is resumed. We can describe the behaviour of `Int` by the following rule:

```
        (Int, n)               cont:Stack
   ⇒    cont                   (Int, n):Stack
```

This provides the basis for an elegant normal order reducer. To implement laziness we must add a sharing mechanism.

1.1 A sharing mechanism for closure reduction

Fairbairn and Wray's original solution involves the introduction of a new object called a marker. During the evaluation of shared expressions a marker `≤U, i≥` is put on the stack:

```
        (C, E)                 a1:...:am:≤U,i≥:S
```

This indicates that the result of applying `(C, E)` to the arguments a_1:...:a_m is shared (whether that result is a base value or a partial application). When its computation terminates the result should be saved in a frame - in slot `i` of frame `U`.

But where do these markers come from? Sharing can only arise when an expression is bound to a name - that is, by parameter-passing and let-binding. Since let-bound variables are treated as formal parameters whose actual values are bound locally it suffices to consider shared parameters. Before evaluating any shared parameter, we place a marker on the stack using the instruction below.

```
      (PushMarker n; C, E)     S
⇒     (C, E)                   ≤E,n≥:S
```

So to evaluate the nth shared argument, the following sequence must be executed:

```
PushMarker n; Enter Arg n
```

instead of the usual

```
Enter Arg n
```

(The `Enter` instruction sets up the machine state to evaluate the closure described by its argument - in this case `Arg n`, the nth argument of the current environment.)

However, there is still a problem when a shared argument is passed to another function. We cannot simply copy it onto the stack, because this closure will not cause the original argument to be updated and so might lead to multiple evaluations. Instead we must pass an indirection to the argument, which when evaluated arranges for the slot to be updated properly. These indirections are themselves closures ! The code parts of the indirections can be shared between all functions - we need one piece of code for each slot index used in the program:

```
SI_1: PushMarker 1; Enter Arg 1
.........
SI_m: PushMarker m; Enter Arg m
```

Now instead of pushing a shared argument directly we push a "shared indirection" containing a reference to the frame to be updated. The actual updates are performed when the shared expression reduces to a weak head normal form. If, for example, it evaluates to an integer, then the update is performed by the `Int` reduction rule. We have to add an extra rule for `Int`:

```
      (Int, n)            ≤U,i≥:S
⇒     (Int, n)            S
      where U[i] := (Int, n)
```

So `Int` removes markers on the top of the stack, updates the locations they specify with the current value of the machine state and then resumes its continuation.

Having to augment `Int` with an extra rule is unfortunate. Now every computation that returns a basic value must test for the presence of markers, regardless of whether the result is shared. This in turn will reduce the efficacy of sharing/strictness analyses whose aim is to detect when markers are unnecessary because although omitting a marker enables an update to be avoided, the test for a marker will still have to be performed by every `Int` unless markers can be eliminated entirely. In the next section we present our solution to this problem.

So far we have only discussed first-order sharing (where the value shared is not a function). In the case of higher-order sharing, we eventually reach the following situation:

$$(f, E) \qquad a_1 : \ldots : a_m : \leq U, i \geq : a_{m+1} : \ldots : a_n : S$$

where f is a function of arity n. How should this situation be handled ? We must update the ith element of frame U with a representation of the shared partial application `(f a_1...a_m)`. The most logical place to do this is at the beginning of the code for the function f before it constructs its environment so that the markers are not mistaken for arguments. The instruction that performs this operation is called, `UpdateMarkers`. Its arguments are the function's code pointer, `f`, and its arity, `n`. It has the following execution rules:

```
      (UpdateMarkers f n;C, E)        a1:...:am:≤U,i≥:S
⇒     (UpdateMarkers f n;C, E)        I1:...:Im:S,          if m < n
      where U[i]   := (Partial f m, P)
            P^     = [a1,...,am]
            I1     = (SI_1, P)
            .........
            Im     = (SI_m, P)

      (UpdateMarkers f n;C, E)        a1:...:am:≤U,i≥:S
⇒     (C, E)                          a1:...:am:≤U,i≥:S,    if m ≥ n
```

`UpdateMarkers` loops until all shared partial applications have been stored in the location specified by their respective markers. Each shared argument a_i is pushed into a newly created frame, `P`. Its place on the stack is overwritten by an indirection I_i. This is necessary since otherwise the a_i copied into `P` will be evaluated separately from the a_i remaining on the stack, leading to a loss of sharing. Unfortunately this causes chains of indirections to build up - a problem we will return to later.

The `Partial` instruction takes two arguments: `f`, the code for the combinator which is being partially applied; and m, the number of arguments in the partial application. It pushes an indirection to each argument of the partial application onto the stack (to preserve sharing) and then executes `f`. This is specified by the following rule:

```
      (Partial f m, E)                S
⇒     (f, E)                          I1:...:Im:S
where        I1     = (SI_1, E)
             .........
             Im     = (SI_m, E)
```

The movement of the shared arguments into a new frame and their replacement by shared indirections ensure that laziness is preserved despite the fact that the same version of `f` is used for shared partial applications and ordinary full applications which may treat some of the arguments as unshared. Essentially this scheme treats the extra sharing of arguments caused by shared partial applications as exceptional and handles such cases dynamically at run-time in an interpretive fashion.

A problem with this scheme is that the representation of shared partial applications requires a new frame to be allocated to hold the arguments that are being partially applied. This seems wasteful as the function being partially applied will eventually build a frame containing these arguments anyway. We describe our first attempt to solve these two problems in the section 4.1.

1.2 Sharing via arguments in the original TIM

Having described how markers are employed in the original TIM to implement sharing, we introduce a notation which allows us to express alternative sharing strategies. In the following expression:

```
expr'n
```

the (') annotation indicates that result of evaluating `expr` should be written back to the variable `n`. (This is achieved by pushing a marker referring to `n` before `expr` is evaluated.) In the original TIM, every occurence of a shared parameter in the body of a function is annotated to update itself. For example:

```
let from n
      = n'n:(from (n'n + 1))
in from 1
```

This scheme requires no extra space to implement laziness: the annotated expressions are always arguments which already occupy a slot in a frame. However every time a shared argument is referenced a marker is pushed. This causes a phenomenon we call *identical updates* - an update is performed each time a shared argument is referenced, not just the first time. Of course if the shared value reduces to a base type, the effect of the marker is just to overwrite the reduced value with itself. However if the shared value reduces to a partially applied function then these *identical updates* are potentially quite expensive as they cause a new representation of the shared partial application to be created each time they are performed. This causes a new frame to be created for each identical update of a shared partial application!

Data structure elements are another major source of identical updates. To preserve laziness, every reference to an element of a data structure must be treated as the first. Thus all but the first reference to a data structure component causes an identical update. This is more serious than the identical updates associated with shared arguments as data structures could potentially be referenced very heavily e.g. lookup tables. Also data structures whose components are evaluated before the data structure is created or whose components are only used once are unfairly penalised by the adoption of this conservative attitude.

Another source of redundant updates is multi-level updates. Multi-level updates build up when an expression is passed down several levels of function call before being evaluated and is treated as shared at several of those levels. After the expression is evaluated, updates must occur at each level that treated the expression as shared. In our `from` example, the argument, `n`, is the source of multiple updates as it is shared both as an argument and as a component of a data structure - thus there are two updates where one would have sufficed.

The cost of updates should be paid only by those shared reductions necessary to preserve laziness. Later we will show how the TIM can be modified to achieve this.

2. Improved closure reduction

In the last section we described closure reduction as implemented by Fairbairn and Wray's TIM. In this section we discuss improvements which eliminate many of the shortcomings of the original TIM.

2.1 Eliminating identical updates with once-only indirections

The problem with the original TIM method of performing sharing via arguments is that it is difficult to avoid identical updates. This is because subsequent evaluations of an argument are treated in the same way as the first evaluation. To avoid this behaviour we declare a local variable for each shared argument which is used to store the value of the reduced argument after the first evaluation. We dub this a *once-only indirection* as its key property is that it will overwrite itself the first time it is followed. We demonstrate this technique by transforming our running example:

```
let from n =
        let new_n = n'new_n in
        new_n:(from (new_n + 1))
in from 1
```

Now the occurences of new_n do not themselves need a sharing annotation. The first time new_n is evaluated, it's overwritten by a closure that does not push a marker. Thus we replace an indirection which always causes an update, by a double indirection which only causes an update on its first use. Moreover, this first update short-circuits one level of indirection, since it is now the first indirection which is updated. This particularly benefits programs with shared partial applications because the updates associated with shared partial applications are relatively expensive operations.

To eliminate identical updates from data structures, constructors must be modified to build once-only indirections for every element. The selector functions must similarly be modified to access the original elements via the once-only indirections and not directly. This doubles the space required for data structures. Note that once an original component is evaluated the slot holding it becomes garbage but as frames cannot be compacted, the garbaged component becomes a "space gap". Space gaps have always been a problem in the TIM, this technique merely aggravates them.

The cost of building a data structure has doubled in both time and space, but the cost of selecting elements of a data structure has been reduced by eliminating identical updates. Assuming that the cost associated with an identical update is roughly twice that of creating a once-only indirection, an n-component data structure must be accessed at least n times before this technique becomes profitable. This is somewhat of a simplification as the internal fragmentation of frames may cause the garbage collector to thrash if the program has not been allocated sufficient memory.

This solution does not address the issue of multi-level updates. In the next section, we extend our solution to alleviate this problem.

2.2 Eliminating multi-level updates with global sharing

To avoid multi-level updates, we must always refer directly to the original expression without introducing an indirection chain. This is achieved by representing a shared expression as an unshared variable whose value is the expression annotated to update the variable's slot. As the variable itself is treated as unshared it can be freely copied and this guarantees that no chain of indirections will build up and no multi-level updates occur. This means it is actual parameters that are treated as shared and not formal parameters, i.e. sharing is administrated through globally shared expressions rather than locally shared arguments. For the `from` example, the annotations are as follows:

```
let from n =
      let new_n   = (n+1)'new_n in
      let new_tl = (from new_n)'new_tl in
      n:new_tl
in from 1
```

Global sharing may allocate as much space as local sharing but usually it allocates less. Consider the worst-case that every argument of every function is shared. Using local sharing causes every callee to double the size of its frame because each of its arguments requires an extra slot. Using global sharing causes every caller to allocate an extra slot for every argument of the functions it calls. Essentially global sharing hoists the sharing across the function call. This allows redundant sharing slots to be eliminated. We look at this idea more closely in the next section. In our example, the redundancy is caused by n being both a shared component of a data structure and a shared parameter.

This technique relieves data structures from the responsibility of administrating sharing. In fact the handling of data structures reverts to that used by the Normal Order TIM. With respect to data structures, our solution combines the strengths of the original TIM and our once-only indirections - construction is as cheap as the original TIM and interrogation is as cheap as a local sharing scheme using once-only indirections.

2.3 The caller-shares calling convention

In order to enforce our new design decision that sharing is a global property of expressions, we introduce a new function-call convention: *every argument passed must be copyable without loss of sharing*. This allows arguments to be manipulated with the same ease as in the normal order TIM, whilst still retaining laziness.

Although it is safe to regard every actual parameter as shared, this is too conservative to get good performance. The flexibility of our new function call convention allows us to create greater synergy between the caller and the callee by performing the minimum coercion on the actual parameters necessary to ensure laziness. This is summarised in the following table:

	Strict	Shared	Unshared
Constant or reduced	Copy	Copy	Copy
Unreduced variable	Force	Copy	Copy
Unreduced expression	Force	Share	Copy

The table contains three coercion operations: Copy pushes the actual parameter with no special treatment; Share pushes an unshared local variable which is bound to the shared expression as described in the last section; and Force forces the evaluation of the argument.

Each column denotes the calling convention of the formal parameter. Each row denotes the form of the actual parameter which must be one of the following: a reduced value, an unreduced variable or an unreduced expression. Note we distinguish between unreduced variables and expressions because arguments need no special treatment as variables must already have been shared if it was necessary. Unreduced expressions need special treatment because they are the base case; all sharing is performed through them.

So what is the cost of global sharing? Every globally shared expression requires the creation of a once-only indirection, i.e. allocating a closure in the current frame. If the shared expression is actually evaluated, a marker is created and subsequently an update is performed. Global sharing is faster than the original TIM's local sharing for shared expressions which are evaluated but for unevaluated shared expressions it bears the extra cost of creating a once-only indirection.

Of course the problem of space gaps in frames encountered in the last section is still with us - the frame of a function cannot be de-allocated until all the slots in the frame are unused. However, because fragmentation only now occurs in the frames of functions (and not data structures) it is a more tractable problem to solve.

Another cost involved in our new scheme is that the sharing information gleaned from the program must now be global information. The local information which sufficed for the original TIM is not suitable. This information is more expensive to compute but we feel this is a worthwhile trade-off.

2.4 Executable markers

To implement a sharing mechanism, Fairbairn and Wray added markers to the Normal Order TIM. Unfortunately this introduces an annoying irregularity in the TIM - markers are the only object in the TIM not represented by a closure ! The effect of this irregularity shows up most prominently in the rules for `Int`:

```
        (Int, n)            ≤U,i≥:S
⇒       (Int, n)            S
        where U[i] := (Int, n)
```

```
        (Int, n)            cont:Stack
⇒       cont                (Int, n):Stack
```

The Normal Order TIM requires only the second rule. If markers had a closure representation then the second rule would suffice for the lazy TIM too. The closure representing the marker would be the `Int`'s continuation resulting in the following state after `Int` has executed:

```
        (Marker_i, U)       (Int, n):Stack
```

Therefore `Marker_i` should update `U[i]` with the reduced value on top of the stack and then resume the continuation beneath the reduced value. This gives the following rule:

```
        (Marker_i, U)       value:cont:Stack
⇒       cont                value:Stack
        where U[i] := value
```

Now the rule for `Int` can revert to its Normal Order form. This small change has a marked effect on efficiency[2]. Only those reductions which are actually marked as shared bear the cost of the test and the update. In fact there is no test - it has been replaced by the extra jump caused by resuming the `Marker_i` continuation. Now the cost of the sharing mechanism is proportional to the number of reductions marked as shared. This results in a significant speedup in all programs, not just those which are intrinsically lazy.

2.5 Improved representation for shared partial application

In the original TIM, the `UpdateMarkers` instruction, which handles shared partial applications, is complicated by having to ensure that arguments which are part of a shared partial application are themselves treated as shared. This is achieved by moving every argument that is part of the shared partial application into a new frame and replacing them on the stack by shared indirections which point to their new location. In addition, the `Partial` instruction, used in the partial applications' representation, must ensure that sharing is still preserved when the arguments are reloaded onto the stack. Thus it pushes shared indirections to the arguments onto the stack not the arguments themselves.

This approach pays a high price for its conservative attitude towards sharing. If an argument is part of m shared partial applications a chain of m shared indirections will have built up by the time the body of the function is executed. If a function is successively applied to each of its arguments, one at a time, and each resulting partial application is shared, the space and time cost of building the partial applications' representations is quadratic in the number of arguments.

Essentially this poor behaviour is caused by the abstract machine trying to preserve sharing dynamically at run-time. However, in our new scheme where the caller handles sharing there is no need for this interpretive overhead. The rule for `UpdateMarkers` can be simplified thus:

[2]Executable markers were introduced independently in [Argo 1989] [Peyton Jones & Salkild 1989].

```
        (UpdateMarkers f n;C, E)        a1:...:am:≤U,i≥:S
   ⇒    (UpdateMarkers f n;C, E)        a1:...:am:S,          if m < n
        where U[i] := (Partial f m, P)
              P^ = [a1,...,am]

        (UpdateMarkers f n;C, E)        a1:...:am:≤U,i≥:S
   ⇒    (C, E)                          a1:...:am:≤U,i≥:S,    if m ≥ n
```

Clearly the environment `P` created on-the-fly for the shared partial application representation is a subset of the environment that will eventually be built by `f`. We can take advantage of this by arranging that the frame which will be used for f's environment is allocated before the `UpdateMarkers` instruction is executed. This allows `UpdateMarkers` to use that environment in shared partial application representations instead of creating one on-the-fly. Thus the rule for `UpdateMarkers` can be simplified further:

```
        (UpdateMarkers f n;C, E)        a1:...:am:≤U,i≥:S
   ⇒    (UpdateMarkers f n;C, E)        a1:...:am:S,          if m < n
        where U[i] := (Partial f m, E)

        (UpdateMarkers f n;C, E)        a1:...:am:≤U,i≥:S
   ⇒    (C, E)                          a1:...:am:≤U,i≥:S,    if m ≥ n
```

Similarly as sharing is guaranteed by the caller, the code for a shared partial application can reload the original arguments rather than introduce shared indirections:

```
        (Partial f m, E)            S
   ⇒    (f, E)                      E[1]:...:E[m]:S
```

The improvement in performance caused by these changes is quite dramatic. Previously if m shared applications were encountered by the `UpdateMarkers` instruction, m frames would be dynamically allocated and for each argument on the stack an indirection chain i long would be created, where i is the number of shared partial applications the argument is enclosed in. In our new scheme no new frames are dynamically allocated and no indirection chains are created. The only cost is what the caller paid to preserve sharing. As our scheme is global this is a cost that is paid only once.

It should be pointed out that this may lead arguments to be treated as shared more often if the identity of the function being applied is not known in advance. In practice this is a small price to pay for the removal of a large amount of interpretive overhead in the handling of shared partial applications.

3. Conclusion

Graph reduction provides a very natural method of implementing the sharing mechanism required to provide lazy evaluation. However in its original form, graph reduction cannot take advantage of information provided by sharing analysis and its handling of partial applications is clumsy. Burn, Peyton Jones and Robson's [2] Spineless G-machine avoided the former and Kieburtz and Agapiev [6] cured the latter. However subsequent efforts of Kieburtz and Agapiev to produce a hybrid which combined these strengths of the two approaches were not convincing.

Closure reduction via the TIM provides a simple and elegant normal order reducer. However although Fairbairn and Wray's lazy version of the TIM can take advantage of information provided by sharing analysis, we highlighted two major defects: expensive handling of shared partial application (in both space and time); and redundant updates in the sharing mechanism. Using a new notation to express sharing strategies, we showed that these defects were due to sharing being treated as a local property of arguments. We cured these defects by making sharing a global property of expressions. This also led to a compact and efficient representation of shared partial applications and better synergy between the caller and the callee. The resulting TIM combines the strengths of the Spineless G-machine, the S-machine and the original TIM whilst sharing none of their weaknesses.

Bibliography

1. Augustsson, L. 1987. Compiling Lazy Functional Languages, Part II. PhD thesis, Chalmers University of Technology.

2. Burn, G., Peyton Jones, S.L. and Robson, J.D. 1988. The Spineless G-machine. *ACM Symposium on Lisp and Functional Programming*.Salt Lake City.

3. Fairbairn, J. and Wray, S.C. 1986. Code generation techniques for functional languages. *Proceedings of the ACM Symposium on Lisp and Functional Programming*. Cambridge.

4. Fairbairn, J. and Wray, S.C. 1987. TIM: a simple abstract machine for executing super-combinators. *Proceedings of the Conference on Functional Languages and Computer Architecture*. Portland.

5. Johnsson, T. 1987. Compiling Lazy Functional Languages. PhD thesis. Chalmers University of Technology.

6. Kieburtz, R.B. and Agapiev, B. 1989. Optimizing the evaluation of suspensions. Unpublished draft.

BWM
a concrete machine for graph reduction

Lennart Augustsson
Department of Computer Science
Chalmers University of Technology
S-412 96 Göteborg, Sweden
Email: augustss@cs.chalmers.se

Abstract

This paper describes a machine for graph reduction. It is not another abstract machine, but instead a proposal for how actual hardware could be designed. The machine uses very large memory words. This makes it possible for a single instruction to do a lot (akin to VLIW machines), and also to construct and scrutinize large objects with few memory operations. Since construction of suspensions is a very common operation during graph reduction this is beneficial.

The machine is built around a stack and a multiplexor, not around an arithmetic unit as most stock processors. The reason for this is that this machine is not aimed at number crunching, but at manipulating data.

The paper also shows the results of some simulations of the machine.

1 Introduction

In the seventies and early eighties, before efficient compilers for functional languages existed, it was believed that special purpose hardware was needed to get efficient execution of functional languages. These were also the days when special purpose processors were considered a "good thing". With the advent of compilers for functional languages it was realized that relatively efficient execution was possible on stock hardware. Nowadays special purpose processors are no longer held in such high esteem; RISC, [3], is the buzz-word of today's computer design.

In this paper I will try to take a fresh look at designing a special purpose processor for lazy functional languages. Today's compilers with sophisticated analyses, strictness analysis in particular, can rival traditional languages for programs where most of the computation are with numbers and other flat domains.

On the other hand, when the data structures involved are trees or lists it is a different story. Here the strictness analyzers are no longer as powerful, and even if all strictness information could be deduced it is not clear how it can be used. One reason pure functional languages do worse then impure (i.e. those with updating) is that instead of updating they have to copy data structures. For lazy languages the problem is even worse since instead of computing a value a suspension of the computation often has to be created, to be scrutinized later on.

The main reason these things make programs run slower is that they increase the number of memory references. The machine presented in this paper has its origin in a single observation: the speed of functional programs (on traditional architectures) are then limited by the memory bandwidth. There are two ways of increasing memory bandwidth: reduce memory cycle time or increase the width of the memory. Since the first is decided by the available technology I will instead increase the second.

It has long been claimed that functional languages have inherent parallelism readily available which gives them great potential for multiprocessors. In an expression such as "`f` e_1 e_2", both "e_1" and "e_2" can be evaluated simultaneously. This is not the kind of parallelism we will use in this design.

We will also take advantage of parallelism, but on another level. It is on the same level as pipelining in ordinary processors, i.e. some kind of micro-parallelism. It is very much akin the VLIW [3] machines where Very Long Instruction Words are used to do several operations in parallel. The VLIW machines designed so far have been geared towards scientific computing, you could say that our design, the BWM (Big Word Machine) is a VLIW for lazy functional languages. If the expression "`f` e_1 e_2" is going to be evaluated in a lazy language both "e_1" and "e_2" have to be suspended and representations for them (e.g. closures) must be created in memory. Creating "e_1" and "e_2" takes time (possibly longer than evaluating them). The parallelism we are going to take advantage of is that there are no real data dependencies during the operations that create "e_1" and "e_2" so these operations can also in principle happen simultaneously.

To make it possible to construct a large object, like a closure, in a single operation requires that we know everything that has to be done without doing more than one instruction fetch - hence we must have wide instructions. But we must also be able to write the constructed object in a single operation - hence we need wide data words as well.

This paper will describe how the BWM works and the results of some preliminary simulations. The first section describes the basic design (without updating). The second section describes how data-types of different kinds can be added. The third section shows how the machine can be extended to handle updating. The fourth section contains some preliminary performance simulations and the last sections some thoughts on actual hardware.

I assume that the reader has some basic knowledge about the λ-calculus, the G-machine, the TIM, and hardware.

2 Basic machinery

The BWM is designed to execute the λ-calculus. In many ways it resembles the G-machine [4] and TIM [2], but in some ways it is even simpler. The basic machine can only run the pure λ-calculus by tree reduction. We will also assume that all applications will have few enough arguments to fit into a single big word. All these

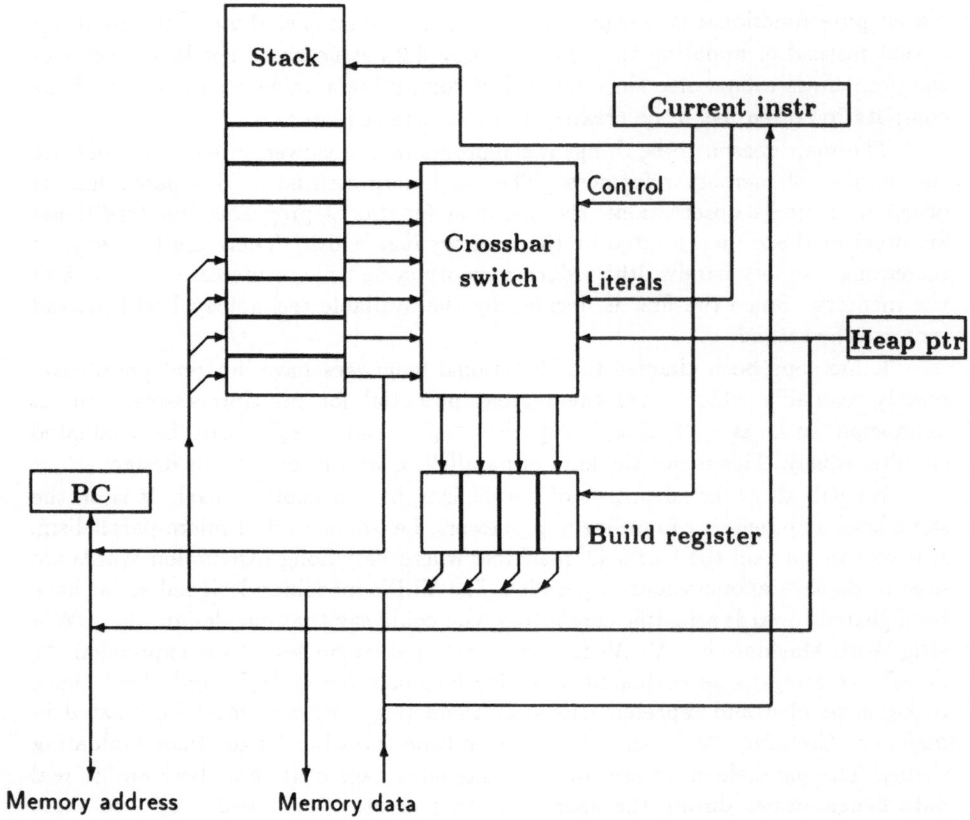

Figure 1: The basic BWM

restrictions will be lifted in later sections.

In figure 1 the basic machinery of the BWM is depicted. This machine is only able to perform string reduction, not graph reduction. Graph reduction and arithmetics will be explained in later sections. The machine has a single stack containing the arguments to the currently executing function. The arguments are represented by pointers to nodes. The first argument is on the top of the stack.

The machine has only got two instructions: **BUILD** and **UPDATE**. The **BUILD** instruction is used to construct new nodes in the heap, and the **UPDATE** is used to rearrange the stack and do a tail call (it also does updating in the graph reduction version). Both these instructions are very similar, they both construct a new object (node) in the **build register**, the **br**. The contents of the **br** comes from a cross-bar switch (or, to put it differently, a multiplexor for each slot in the **br**) that as its input has the top elements of the stack, some literal fields in the instruction and the heap pointer. The **br** can be regarded as the "accumulator" of the machine; this is where everything happens. The machine also contains a program counter (PC) which points to the next instruction to execute, and a heap pointer that points to the next free memory location.

An example: The code for the function

$f = \lambda n.\lambda z.\lambda s.s\ n$

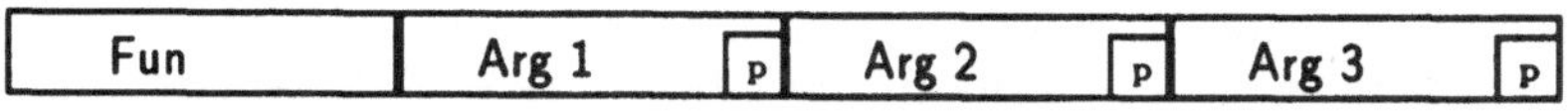

Figure 2: Node layout

should rearrange the stack removing n, z, and s and replacing them with s and n. All this is accomplished with a single instruction, namely an UPDATE. The instruction for this function would be:

```
UPDATE 3 2 0
```

The first 3 indicates that three elements are to be popped off the stack, the 2 and the 0 indicates what is going to be put onto the stack instead. The pushed elements are taken from the **br**. The first slot will get stack element two (counted from zero), i.e. s, and the second slot will get stack element zero, i.e. n. The last two slots are tagged as unused and are therefore not pushed.

When the stack has been rearranged the UPDATE instruction will enter what corresponds to the unwind mode in the G-machine. In this mode all arguments on the spine will be pushed until the function code is found (left most on the spine). This happens as follows: the top element of the stack is popped and examined, if it is a pointer to code it is put in the PC and execution of the function starts. If on the other hand it is a pointer to another node then the used parts of that node are pushed on the stack.[1]

The BUILD instruction will fill the **br** in the same way as the UPDATE instruction and then the **br** will be written to memory. It is written to the next free location (pointed to by the heap pointer, **hp**) and the heap pointer is incremented.

Another example: the function

$$g = \lambda x.\lambda y.\lambda z.x\ False\ (h\ y\ z)$$

will give the code

BUILD h 1 2
UPDATE 3 0 $False$ $hp - 1$

where $False$ and h designate that a literal field is used and $hp - 1$ designate that value, which is the address where the BUILD put the application. A literal is a (large) constant that usually represents a code pointer to a supercombinator. The BUILD instruction builds a node with h in the function position and stack entry 1 and 2 as arguments. The rest of the slots are tagged as unused.

The code for a function will always consist of a number (possibly zero) of BUILD instructions to build all function applications except the top one, followed by an UPDATE instruction for the top application (or variable).

2.1 Node layout

The node layout of the BWM is shown in figure 2. A node consist of a pointer to a function and a number of arguments (from zero to the word size less one) to that

[1] The actual hardware will, of course, not examine and pop the top like this, instead the value will be moved directly to the PC and used from there.

function. The arity of the function and the number of arguments need not coincide. In the unwind mode the node is pushed onto the internal stack. To know how much to push on the stack there is also a "present" bit on each argument to tell if this argument is used or not (these are the P fields in the figure). An example of an exact node layout is given in appendix B.

All nodes in the heap represent applications so there is no need to tag them in any way, all pointers to code represent abstractions (corresponding to the supercombinators). Since pointers to code and to heap have to be distinguished all pointers are tagged with this information. Furthermore a pointer to code also contains the arity of the function that it points to.

2.2 Instruction encoding

The BUILD and UPDATE instructions are very similar. They both contain information on how to assemble the br. The UPDATE also says how much the stack should be popped. The instruction layout is shown in figure 3 and in appendix A.

The fields are

- opc contains the opcode.
- cnt contains the number of arguments actually built.
- pop contains the number of elements to pop in UPDATE.
- arg$X$ contains a description of how to assemble the corresponding slot in br.
- lit$X$ contain literal values (large constants) that can be specified for a slot.

The description of a slot may contain

- a stack element number. The slot is filled with the stack element.
- a literal number (the literal is taken from the instruction). The slot is filled with the literal.
- a heap pointer offset. The slot is filled with the heap pointer plus the signed offset.
- a no-op. The slot is unaffected.
- a zero specifier. The slot is filled with 0.

If the node to be built contains more constants than the number of literals that are available in the instruction a special instruction BUILDN is used. It behaves as BUILD except that nothing is written to memory, the only thing that happens is that the br is changed. This is used to fill some slots in the br, and the next instruction(s) completes the job, leaving the initially filled slots unaffected.

opc	cnt	pop	Arg1	Arg2	Arg3	Arg4	Lit1	Lit2

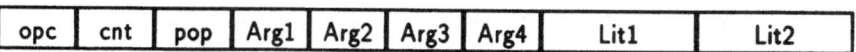

Figure 3: Instruction encoding

2.3 What word size?

The size of the words (i.e. how many pointers they can contain) is crucial for good performance. On one hand you want the word size to be as large as possible, because this will get more things done a once. On the other hand the word size should be as small as possible because of practical considerations: large words waste memory when they are not completely filled and large words require more hardware.

In this description I have used a word size of four pointers, but this is just an example. The actual value is not important for the description of the machine. The size should be determined by examining a large number of programs to figure out the "best" value. Measurement of number of arguments at function calls indicate that somewhere between four and eight is probably reasonable. Most closures created contain two arguments and a word size of four can contain up to three arguments, so very many of the closures can then be stored directly.

2.4 Host processor support

The BWM is intended to be a coprocessor. It is in no way designed to be a complete computer. Tasks such as loading the memory with the initial heap and printing are supposed to be handled by a host processor. The handling of stack overflow is another important task for the host. The BWM contains no hardware to handle stack over- and under-flows, instead it will generate an interrupt to the host which is responsible for dumping/filling the BWM stack. Obviously these interrupts must not be to frequent if a reasonable execution speed is to be expected. The actual size of the internal stack that is needed has yet to be determined (by simulations).

If the garbage collection is to be handled by the BWM additional instructions are probably necessary.

3 Argument overflow

If the number of arguments in an application is larger than the available number of pointers in a big word several big words have to be used. This is a simple transformation that can be done by the compiler or even the assembler. An application chain has to be built with all of the nodes except the top one containing as many arguments as possible.

The function

$$f = \lambda a.\lambda b.\lambda c.\lambda d.\lambda e.\lambda f.\lambda g.\ b\ c\ d\ e\ f\ g$$

would give the code

```
UPDATE 7 1 2 3 4 5 6
```

which can be transformed into the following (assuming four pointers per big word)

BUILD		1	2 3	4
UPDATE	7	$hp - 1$	4	5

This can be viewed as bracketing the function like this:

$$f = \lambda a.\lambda b.\lambda c.\lambda d.\lambda e.\lambda f.\lambda g.\ (b\ c\ d\ e)\ f\ g$$

BUILD instructions are transformed in a similar way.

4 Adding data types

4.1 Constructed data types

It is well known how data types corresponding to **data** declarations (those given by a number of constructors) can be encoded as λ-terms. One such encoding is used in [2]. We are using a variation on this which is more efficient with a large number of constructors. It is quite close to what is also proposed in [5].

Each constructor is encoded as a λ-expression taking first the arguments to the constructor and then a tuple with as many elements as the type has constructors. The n:th constructor function will pick out the n:th element of the tuple and apply it to its arguments, see figure 4 for a full explanation.

This can be made quite efficient by using a special encoding of the tuples and selector functions. Since the tuples are only used when translating a case expression and since the components are combinators, the tuples are constant expressions that can be built at compile time. This means that case analysis consists of pushing a single argument (the tuple) and then calling the scrutinized expression. The constructors functions themselves are very similar, they just select a component from the tuple and call it, the rest of the arguments can stay untouched on the stack (this is the reason for passing t around in the translation). To make constructors very efficient the tuples will be stored as vectors in memory and the constructor function itself will be encoded in a special way. It will not have any code, the code will instead be encoded into the code address itself. An extra bit will be used to tell if an address is a real address or a constructor. If it is a constructor the rest of the bits are used to encode the constructor number. Executing a constructor is very simple, the constructor number is simply used as an index into the vector to do an indexed jump.

An example: the program

```
data Tree a = Empty | Node (Tree a) a (Tree a)
mirror Empty = Empty
mirror (Node l x r) = Node (mirror r) x (mirror l)
```

is translated to

$$mirror = \lambda l.l\ \langle mirror0, mirror1\rangle$$
$$mirror1 = \lambda t.Empty$$
$$mirror2 = \lambda l.\lambda x.\lambda r.\lambda t.Node\ (mirror\ r)\ x\ (mirror\ l)$$

The data type declaration

$$\texttt{data}\ T = C_1\ t_1 \ldots t_k \mid \cdots \mid C_n\ s_1 \ldots s_m$$

will define the constructor functions in the following way

$$C_1 = \lambda x_1. \ldots \lambda x_k.\lambda t.sel_1^n\ t\ x_1 \ldots x_k\ t$$
$$\vdots$$
$$C_n = \lambda x_1. \ldots \lambda x_m.\lambda t.sel_n^n\ t\ x_1 \ldots x_m\ t$$

A scrutinizing expression

case e
  $C_1\ y_1 \ldots y_k$ => e_1
  $\vdots$
  $C_n\ y_1 \ldots y_m$ => e_n

is translated to

$$e\ \langle \lambda y_1. \ldots \lambda y_k.\lambda t.e_1, \cdots, \lambda y_1. \ldots \lambda y_m.\lambda t.e_n \rangle$$

where $\langle \cdots \rangle$ is an n-tuple constructor and sel_k^n the function to select the k-th component from the n-tuple.

Figure 4: Constructor coding

which will give the code

mirror :	UPDATE	1	0	*Jmirror*		
Jmirror :	JTAB	*mirror*0	*mirror*1			
*mirror*0 :	UPDATE	1	CON_1			
*mirror*1 :	BUILD		*mirror*	2		
	BUILD		*mirror*	0		
	UPDATE	4	CON_2	$hp-2$	1	$hp-1$

JTAB is simply a pseudoop to build a jump table in memory, CON_k is the encoding of constructor k.

4.2 Numbers

The λ-calculus encoding of numbers, and especially floating point numbers, is horrendously inefficient to compute with when compared to the special purpose hardware that is available. If numbers are to be used a lot the BWM should be extended with an arithmetic unit. This unit can be fed from two (or more) extra outputs from the cross-bar switch and the output of it fed back into the cross-bar. The time for an arithmetic operation need not be as small as the basic cycle time of the machine, the result could be available a number of cycles later. The compiler would then have to ensure that the result is picked up only when available.

The numbers can be encoded different ways, one way is to code a number as an application whith a special function, *self*, to the actual numeral. When a number is applied to a function *self* will call that function with the numeral as argument. A very similar encoding is used in [2].

5 Updating

The machine described so far can only do string reduction (the UPDATE instruction, as can be seen, does not really update). To do graph reduction we must unfortunately complicate the simple machinery.

To accomplish updating an extra stack is used. This stack contains pairs of a pointer to the node to be updated and an argument count. Every time a node is pushed a pointer to it together with the number of arguments in it is pushed.

When the code of a function is found the argument count on the top of the stack is compared with the arity of the function (which is encoded into the instruction pointer to allow overlap between this operation and the instruction fetch). If the top count is smaller than the function arity the top of the update stack is removed and the popped argument count is added to the next argument count. The comparison is then made again and the whole process is repeated until there are enough arguments.

Figure 5[2] shows the state of the machine when the application $((fx)y)zw$ has been unwound, but the update stack has not been adjusted yet. The update stack points to each node that has been pushed, and also contains the number of elements that was pushed from that node. Figure 6 shows the state after the update stack has

---

[2] I apologise for the ugly pictures. They look pretty nice in xfig, but LaTeXrefuses to spline the lines for me.

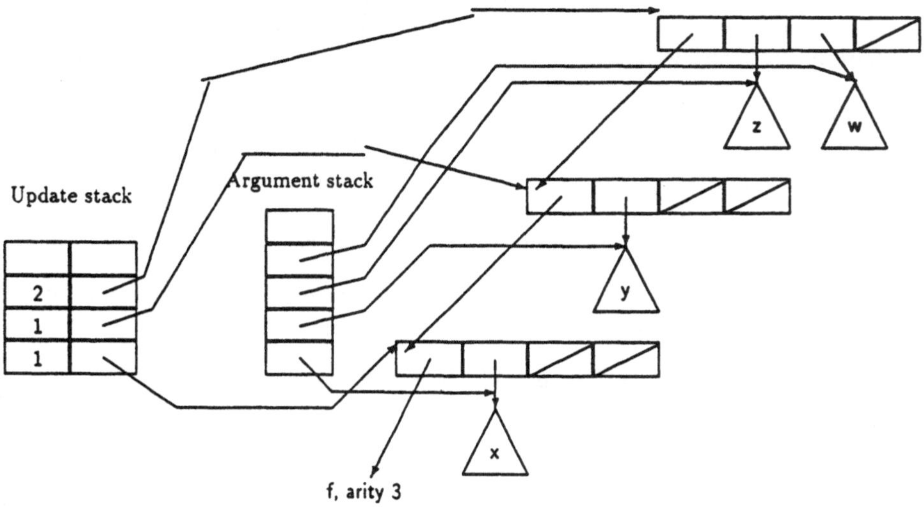

Figure 5: Machine state before update stack adjustment.

been adjusted. The update stack has been popped until the accumulated argument count (kept on top of the update stack) is not smaller than the function arity. The pointer at the top of the update stack now points to the node to update, and the count on the stack tells how many stack elements that "belong" to this node.

When an UPDATE instruction is executed the top of the update stack is used to determine which node is to be updated with the top of the stack and with how much. The UPDATE instruction changes the top argument count to reflect how much is now on the stack. This is the number of elements that should be written to the address on the top of the stack.

If the argument count exceeds the node size the updating becomes complicated. An easy solution to this problem is to generate an interrupt to the host processor and let it handle the difficult case. A faster, but more complicated, solution is to do it in the BWM itself. The updating consists of writing out the top elements to memory - basically executing a BUILD 0 1 2 3 - and replacing the top elements with a pointer to this node - almost an UPDATE 4 $hp - 1$ - and decrementing the argument count until the arguments fit in a single node.

The big disadvantage with the update mechanism is that it uses another stack, and also a comparator and adder to check the number of arguments. This whole popping loop also adds much control complexity to the machine. The extra time needed for the pushing and popping is probably negligible since it can be overlapped with memory operations. The update as such will of course take time, but that is unavoidable.

5.1 One bit reference counter

Updating should of course be avoided if possible since it involves a memory reference. A simple way to avoid some of them is to use the single bit reference counting trick

The simulated machine has an ALU and an update stack. The node and stack sizes are varied, some typical figures from the simulations are given in figures 7 and 8. Memory reads and writes are considered to take one cycle, except when they are done to consecutive locations when the take 0.5 cycles.[3] The ALU operations are considered to take two cycles, and comparisons one cycle. Stack overflow (underflow) is handled by swapping out (in) half the stack. This could be done by another processor, the time for this is set to 25 cycles per stack element plus 50 cycles in overhead. The argument and update stack had the same size.

Five simple benchmark programs were used (more elaborate tests are planned):

- mirror builds a binary tree with 32768 interior nodes and compares it to its mirror image. The program uses no arithmetic.
- nfib computes nfib 23. The program uses arithmetic heavily.
- 8q computes the number of solutions to the 8 queen problem. The program uses a lot of arithmetic, comparisons, and list handling.
- sem is a denotational semantics for LML, written in LML. The computation is of nfib 15. The program uses a little arithmetic, and a lot of tree manipulation.
- quad is a very higher order program, computing *quad quad inc* 0, where *quad* is *twice twice*.

Looking at the figures from the simulations here are some early observations (remember that this is for five silly benchmarks):

- The node size should be at least three words. Going above three does not give much improvement, four is probably a reasonable size.
- The stack size should be at least 50, but preferably higher. For some (abnormal?) programs, e.g. quad, the stack swapping did not get down to a reasonable level before the stack size was 1000, but in general a stack depth of a 100 seems adequate.
- The update stack was usually 50-70% of the size of the argument stack (indicating that the typical number of arguments per node is around two; which agrees well with the node size timings). The update stack could thus be made smaller than the argument stack.
- The number of updates where the number of stack elements exceeded the node size is 0-5% (for node size four). This figure is big enough that this condition has to be handled by hardware to get acceptable performance.
- The manipulation of the update stack takes about 10% of the exection time.

The absolute performance of the machine is hard to determine at this point, but some preliminary results are shown in figure 1. The BWM cycle time is 100 ns, and it does a read or write on one cycle (instruction fetch takes an extra cycle). The

[3] This is not an unreasonable assumption given that todays DRAM with nibble modes etc.

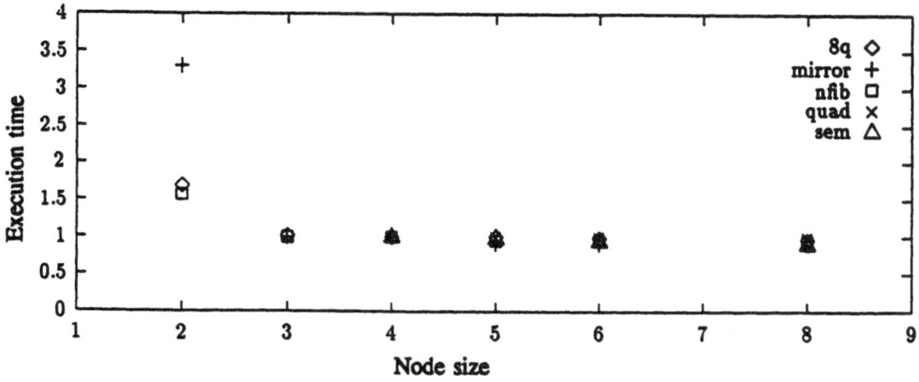

Figure 7: Relative execution time for different node sizes. Node size 4 is used as the reference. The stack size is 100.

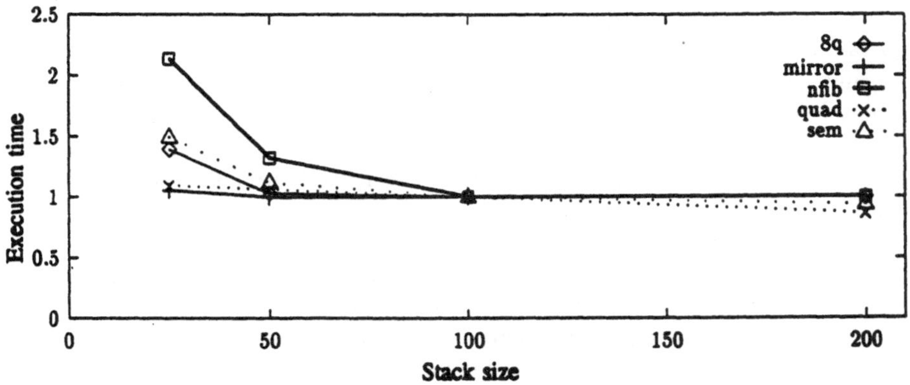

Figure 8: Relative execution time for different stack sizes. Stack size 100 is used as the reference. The node size is 4.

program	BWM	80386	M2000
8q	1.0	6.0	1.8
mirror	1.0	17.6	6.0
nfib	1.0	3.3	1.0
quad	1.0	1.8	0.51
sem	1.0	6.9	2.6

Table 1: Relative execution time for different processors. BWM with node size 4 and stack size 100 is used as the reference.

80386 has a 66 ns cycle time, it uses about three cycles to execute one instruction (including the instruction fetch). The MIPS M2000 has a 66 ns cycle time, it uses about 1.25 cycles to execute an instruction (including the instruction fetch). The absolute speedup is not great when compared to a modern RISC machine, so even if the BWM performance is improved it is an open question if it would be worthwhile to build.

7 Hardware

Alas, there is no hardware BWM yet. It only exists as a simulated machine. Quite a lot of consideration has been put into making the BWM as simple as possible in hardware terms, but as the actual hardware design has not begun yet it is hard to tell how complex it will be.

One problem that can be seen even now is how to connect a BWM chip to the outside world. A BWM with word size of for pointers would have a data path that is 128 bits wide, to this should be added address and control pins which bring the pin count up to around 200. This is a high, but possible pin count. An even more efficient BWM would have a Harvard architecture, i.e. separate buses for instructions and data, this would bring the pin count for the same word size up to 400! This is barely within todays packageing. Having bigger words would make things even worse.

Because of the simple internal structure of the BWM I expect a short cycle time to be easily attainable. Something in the order of 50 or 100 ns should be no problem at all. The big problem is having a memory that can keep up with this speed. Memory speed can probably be improved by interleaving the memory, this helps both for instruction fetches (assuming some fancy prefetching) and the many consecutive writes from BUILD instructions (again assuming they have been prefetched).

References

1. L. Augustsson and T. Johnsson. The Chalmers Lazy-ML Compiler. *The Computer Journal*, 32(2):127 - 141, 1989.

2. J. Fairbairn and S. C. Wray. TIM: A simple, lazy abstract machine to execute supercombinators. In *Proceedings of the 1987 Conference on*

Functional Programming Languages and Computer Architecture, Portland, Oregon, September 1987.

3. J. L. Hennessy and D. A. Patterson. *Computer architecture: a quantitative approach.* Morgan Kaufmann Publishers, Palo Alto, 1990.

4. T. Johnsson. *Compiling Lazy Functional Languages.* PhD thesis, Dept. of Computer Science, Chalmers University of Technology, Göteborg, Sweden, February 1987.

5. S. L. Peyton Jones and Jon Salkild. The Spineless Tagless G-machine. In *Proceedings of the 1989 Conference on Functional Programming Languages and Computer Architecture*, London, Great Britain, 1989.

6. W. Stoye. *The Implementation of Functional Languages using Custom Hardware.* PhD thesis, University of Cambridge, Computer Laboratory, 1985.

Appendix

A Instruction encoding

The description is given in pseudo-C, where we assume that bit fields are packed in a suitable way. All addresses are assumed to be big word aligned thus having four lsb zeroes that need not be stored.

```
typedef enum { stack, literal, heapptr, noop, unused }  argtype;

typedef struct {
    argtype type:3;             /* argument type */
    int value:5;                /* stack pos, heap offset, or literal no */
} argspec;

typedef enum { BUILD, BUILDN, UPDATE, ALU, CMP } opcode;

typedef int literal;

typedef struct {
    opcode opc:8;               /* operation code */
    int pop:8;                  /* pop count */
    int cnt:2;                  /* argument count */
    int :14;                    /* filler */
    argspec args:8[4];          /* argument descriptors */
    literal lits:32[2];         /* literals */
} instr;
```

B Node layout

```
/* Address encodings */
typedef int memaddr;                  /* Generic address */

typedef struct {
    int arity:5;                      /* arity of function */
    bool constr:1;                    /* constr/addr flag */
    union {
        memaddr address:23;           /* address of function */
        int constrno:23;              /* constructor function number */
    } ucode;
} codepointer;                        /* pointer to code */

typedef struct {
    bool share:1;                     /* is node possibly shared? */
    memaddr address:28;               /* address of node */
} nodepointer;                        /* pointer to node */

typedef struct {
    bool code:1;                      /* code/node flag */
    union {
        codepointer cptr:29;          /* code or */
        nodepointer nptr:29;          /* node pointer */
    } uptr;
} pointer;                            /* pointer in heap and stack */

/* Node layout */
typedef struct {
    bool used:1;                      /* Word used/unused flag */
    bool ptr:1;                       /* Pointer/data flag */
    union {
        pointer ptr:30;               /* Pointer or */
        int data:30;                  /* data */
    } uword;
} word;                               /* Word in the heap */

typedef struct {
    word ptrs[4];                     /* Four pointers (or whatever) */
} node;
```

ACTRESS: an Action Semantics Directed Compiler Generator (Summary)

Deryck F. Brown*
Hermano Moura†
David A. Watt

Abstract

We report progress on the development of a compiler generator based on action semantics. A number of components have been implemented in Standard ML. These can be fitted together to construct either an action notation compiler or a simple compiler generator. We also outline continuing research which is aimed at improving the quality of the compiler generator. A full version of this paper can be found in Brown et al. [2].

1 Introduction

A *compiler generator* is a system that constructs a compiler automatically, given syntactic and semantic descriptions of the source language. Ideally, these are the same formal descriptions that are written by the language designer and consulted by users of the language. Processing of syntactic descriptions has long been practised, but processing of semantic descriptions remains an open research problem.

The key efforts have been attempts to generate compilers from denotational semantic descriptions [4, 7, 9]. The generated compiler translates the source program to a λ-expression, then reduces the λ-expression as much as it can. The residual λ-expression is the generated compiler's "object program". There are many fundamental problems with this approach, which are analysed in detail in Lee [3]. Reduction of λ-expressions is very slow. Environments and stores are passed around like ordinary values. Consequently, the generated compilers are enormously inefficient. (The performance penalty relative to a hand-crafted compiler is typically 100–1000, both at compile-time and at run-time.) The only hope of generating efficient compilers from denotational descriptions is for the compiler generator to

* Supported by SERC, UK.

† Supported by CNPq, Brazil. On leave from Caixa Econômica Federal, Brazil.
Authors' address: Department of Computing Science, The University, Glasgow, G12 8QQ, UK.
E-mail {deryck, moura, daw}@dcs.glasgow.ac.uk.

"understand" the special properties of environments, stores, and continuations, rather than to treat them as ordinary values.

Action semantics [5] promises to be a better basis for compiler generation. An action-semantic description in effect specifies a translation from the source language to *action notation.* Although designed for producing readable and modular semantic descriptions, action notation has several other properties that are useful for our purposes. The primitive actions and action combinators correspond quite closely to simple operational concepts. The store is by definition single-threaded, and bindings are by definition scoped. And action notation has numerous algebraic and other laws that will provide a basis for code-improving transformations. This paper outlines an action-semantics directed compiler generator, ACTRESS, that we are currently developing. Our ultimate goal is to generate compilers that are conventionally-structured and efficient. (We aim for a performance penalty relative to hand-crafted compilers of much less than 10.)

2 Overview

ACTRESS supports a well-defined subset of action notation, which is rich enough to write semantic descriptions of interesting programming languages. This subset includes the functional, declarative, and imperative facets; the main primitive actions and combinators associated with these facets; recursive actions; and abstractions. ACTRESS consists of a number of modules, which may be composed in various ways. Some of these modules are shown in Figure 1, and are explained below.

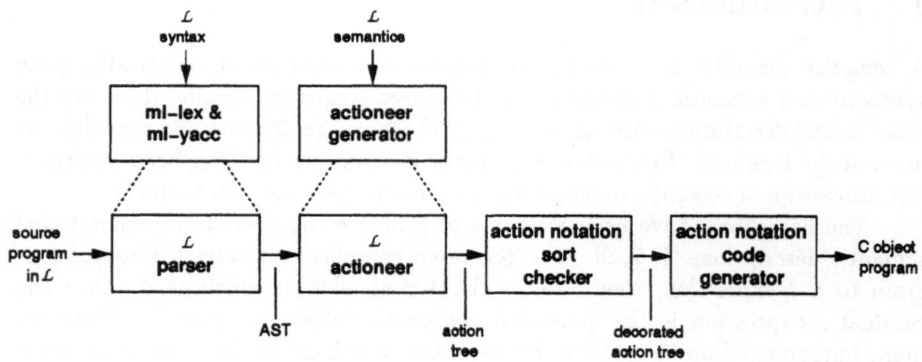

Figure 1: The structure of an automatically generated compiler.

The *action notation parser* parses a textual action term, and translates it to the corresponding action notation abstract syntax tree (*action tree*).

The *action notation sort checker* has a role similar to that of the contextual analyser in a conventional compiler. It traverses the action tree, inferring the sorts of the data flowing into and out of each action, in the functional and declarative facets. Ill-sorted actions are detected, and the action tree is decorated with sort information for use by the code generator.

The *action notation code generator* translates the decorated action tree to C object code. Sort information is used to guide register allocation, to generate code for any run-time sort checks, and especially to guide the translation of recursive actions and abstractions. The object program operates on a global store, passes transients in registers, and explicitly manipulates bindings.

The action notation parser, sort checker, and code generator, when composed, form the *action notation compiler*. This translates a textual action to a C object program, which can then be compiled and executed in the usual way. Alternatively, the action tree can be fed into the *action notation interpreter* [6].

The *actioneer generator* accepts the dynamic action semantics of a source language $\mathcal{L}$, and generates an $\mathcal{L}$ actioneer. The latter is a module that translates the abstract syntax tree (AST) of an $\mathcal{L}$ program to its denotation, an action tree.

Composing an $\mathcal{L}$ parser with the generated $\mathcal{L}$ actioneer and the action notation sort checker and code generator gives us a generated $\mathcal{L}$ compiler. (See Figure 1.)

3 Sort Checking

The action notation sort checker is similar in principle to an ordinary type checker, but is in fact significantly more complicated. It traverses the action tree, and decorates each action with the tagged sorts of information flowing into and out of that action. This is done for both the functional facet (transients) and the declarative facet (bindings). The sort information is represented by record types, similar to those used by Even and Schmidt [8]. Each action is decorated by four records, representing the sorts of input and output transients, and input and output bindings. For example, a record for transients (data tagged by numbers) might be $\{0 \mapsto \textsf{integer}, 1 \mapsto \textsf{truth-value}\}$, and a record for bindings (data tagged by tokens) might be $\{\mathbf{x} \mapsto 5, \mathbf{y} \mapsto \textsf{integer}, \mathbf{z} \mapsto \textsf{cell}\}$. In each case the record fields are action notation sorts. Individual values, such as 5, are treated as singleton sorts. In the latter example, the sort checker has inferred that **x** is bound to the known integer 5, but **y** is bound to some unknown integer, and **z** is bound to some unknown cell.

The sorts inferred by the sort checker have been specified using a set of inference rules, somewhat analogous to the type inference rules of a programming language. The sort inference algorithm is based on the one developed by Even and Schmidt [8]. However, it has been enhanced in several ways. In particular, our action notation subset is significantly richer, including as it does recursive actions and abstractions. For more information on sort checking and a full description of the sort rules, see Brown [1].

4 Code Generation

The actual translation of an action tree into C object code is done by the action notation code generator. In the object code, transients and bindings are stored in registers (C variables). The flow of information between actions guides the allocation and deallocation of registers. The object program consists of four parts: the C main program, generated from the given action; a set of C functions, generated from the abstractions present in the given action; declarations for the used registers; and the run-time environment.

Transient data are contained in what we call *d-registers*; each d-register contains a single datum. For example, the object code of action "**give** D **label** $\#N$" assigns the value of D to a d-register, allocated at translation-time. The association between N and that d-register is noted, and the object code of "**the** $S\#N$" just accesses the d-register associated with N.

A second kind of register called a *b-register* is used to contain a set of bindings. The object code of action "**bind** T **to** D" just assigns a single binding to a b-register, allocated at translation-time. The object code of "**the** S **bound to** T" just searches for token T in the appropriate set of bindings. Sets of bindings are constructed and searched by run-time functions.

Storage is represented by an array. The object code of action "**store** D **in** C" just assigns the value of D to the array element indexed by the value of C. The object code of "**the** S **stored in** C" just indexes the array by the value of C.

Some of these operations, such as "**the** $S\#N$", require that the result is of sort S. If this cannot be guaranteed by the sort checker, the code generator is warned and generates a run-time sort check.

An abstraction is represented at run-time by a C structure with three fields: a pointer to a C function, whose body is the object code of the encapsulated action; a transient datum (the one given to the abstraction, if any); and a set of bindings (the ones received by the abstraction, if any). The enactment of an abstraction is just a call to the function representing it, with the transient datum and the set of bindings as arguments.

Action combinators, such as "**and**", "**and then**", "**then**", "**or**", and "**unfolding**", are translated into efficient object code. Control structures such as if- and while-commands are described in terms of these combinators, and we find that our generated compilers translate these control structures into good object code.

5 Further Work and Conclusion

Our experience with ACTRESS shows that the generated compilers are already far better, in terms of object code quality, than those generated by the classical denotational semantics directed compiler generators. Nevertheless, we are working on further major improvements.

Action notation aims for maximum generality, so bindings, storage allocation, and sort (type) checking are all dynamic. If the source language $\mathcal{L}$ really does require dynamic storage allocation and is dynamically typed and scoped, we suspect that our generated $\mathcal{L}$ compiler would be competitive with a hand-crafted compiler, in terms of object code quality. But if $\mathcal{L}$ is statically typed and scoped, the generated $\mathcal{L}$ compiler would generate object code that still contains dynamic type checks and bindings. Our current work is aimed at discovering and exploiting important special properties of the source language from its semantic description, such as whether it is statically typed and/or scoped.

We intend to apply a simple and general binding-elimination technique in a future version of the action notation code generator. The object code of "**the** S **bound to** T" will be simply the value bound to token T, if that value is known at compile-time; otherwise the object code will fetch the unknown value bound to T from a known address where it was previously stored. Thus all bindings can be eliminated from the object program, provided that the source language is statically scoped. We aim to formalise this property in a manner that permits it to be tested on the source language's semantic description.

Rather than dynamic storage allocation, the generated compiler should use static or stack allocation wherever possible. Not only is this more efficient, but also our binding-elimination technique will work better, since the affected variables will have known (at compile-time) addressing functions. By analysing the flow of control, we aim to classify each **allocate** action as static allocation, stack allocation, or dynamic allocation.

To conclude, action semantics has opened up a rich field of ideas to be explored. Action semantics imposes useful structure on the description of the source language, unlike classical denotational semantics. We have been able to exploit this structure to build a working and tolerably efficient compiler generator, in a comparatively short time. We intend to exploit this structure further to analyse source languages in ways not yet achieved by any compiler generator.

Bibliography

1. D. F. Brown. Sort inference in action semantics. Research report, Department of Computing Science, The University, Glasgow, Scotland, 1991. In preparation.

2. D. F. Brown, H. Moura, and D. A. Watt. ACTRESS: an action semantics directed compiler generator. Research report, Department of Computing Science, The University, Glasgow, Scotland, 1992. In preparation.

3. P. Lee. *Realistic Compiler Generation.* MIT Press, Cambridge, Massachusetts, 1989.

4. P. D. Mosses. SIS – semantics implementation system, reference manual and user guide. Departmental Report DAIMI MD–30, Computer Science Department, Aarhus University, Denmark, 1979.

5. P. D. Mosses and D. A. Watt. The use of action semantics. In M. Wirsing, editor, *Formal Description of Programming Concepts.* North Holland, Amsterdam, Netherlands, 1987.

6. H. Moura. An implementation of action semantics. Research report, Department of Computing Science, The University, Glasgow, Scotland, 1991. In preparation.

7. L. Paulson. *A compiler generator for semantic grammars.* PhD thesis, Stanford University, California, 1981.

8. D. A. Schmidt and S. Even. Type inference for action semantics. In N. Jones, editor, *ESOP '90, 3rd European Symposium on Programming*, pages 118–133. Springer-Verlag, Berlin, 1990. Lecture Notes in Computer Science, Volume 432.

9. M. Wand. A semantic prototyping system. *SIGPLAN Notices (SIGPLAN '84 Symp. On Compiler Construction)*, 19(6):213–221, June 1984.

The Abstract Interpretation of Higher-Order Functional Languages: From Properties to Abstract Domains[1] (Technical Summary)

G L Burn

Department of Computing, Imperial College of Science, Technology and Medicine, 180 Queen's Gate, London SW7 2BZ, United Kingdom

Abstract

Over recent years a number of analysis techniques have been developed for higher-order lazy functional languages, and although a few studies have been made comparing the techniques, no fundamental basis for their comparison has yet been found. We suggest that studying the *properties* an analysis technique can represent, and the ways it has for combining and decomposing them, provides such a basis. Using this notion, we are able to give a rational reconstruction of the use of the *tensor product* in abstract interpretation. Furthermore, it enables us to see what the appropriate notion of a *relational method* for the abstract interpretation of a higher-order functional language is, and to show that using the tensor product is *not* sufficient for defining such an analysis. The paper concludes with observations about several open problems.

1 Introduction

An almost bewildering array of semantics-based program analysis techniques have been developed for functional languages: *abstract interpretation* — see [21, 3, 27, 23, 16, 11, 13] for example; *projection analysis* — see [26, 8] for example; and *'type' inference* — see [17, 28, 15] for example. Moreover, some of these analyses can be performed in either a *forwards* or a *backwards* way — see [12] for example.

In trying to understand the relationships between these analyses, we have come to the conclusion that the main question we have to ask about an analysis technique is: What *properties* does the technique allow us to reason about? For example, analyses based on [5, 4] can reason about the Scott-closed set behaviour of functions, whilst those based on projections naturally capture (total) relations between values [26, 6][2].

There are two subsidiary questions that we must ask about the properties of constructed data types:

---

[1] This research was partially funded by the Semantique Project — ESPRIT BRA 3124.

[2] The natural way of combining two total relations to give a relation over a function space does not give a total relation. This is why projections cannot be used to capture properties of higher-order functions in a natural way [6].

- Can we build representations of all of the properties of a constructed data type from the representations of the properties of its constituent parts?; and
- Can the representation of a property of a constructed data type be decomposed into representations of the properties of its constituent parts?

The work reported in [22, 23, 10] can be seen as attempts to answer the first question, whilst the second seems to be particularly important in studying the relationship between forwards and backwards analyses [12].

In this paper we deal exclusively with a BHA-style abstract interpretation, and we will address the first question. Furthermore, we make the following *Property Assumption*:

> *Given a* finite *set of properties on the base types, we consider only those properties of a constructed type which can be expressed using a construction of the properties on its constituent types.*

This is consistent with the philosophy that abstract domains need only be provided to capture properties of the base types, with the rest of the abstract domains being defined by appropriate constructions over those for simpler types (see [23, 4] for examples of this).

The question then reduces to trying to define abstract domains and constructions over them which accurately model properties and the ways they can be combined.

This work has a number of results: it gives a rational reconstruction of the need for using the ***tensor product*** for the abstract interpretation of products; it shows that using the tensor product can be smoothly integrated into an abstract interpretation framework for higher-order functions; it gives insights into what should be meant by the terms ***independent attribute*** and ***relational*** methods for giving abstract interpretations for languages with higher-order functions; it shows that solely using the tensor product does not give the most informative relational analysis for such languages; and gives insights into a number of open problems.

The paper is organised as follows. We formally define what we mean by a property and combination of a number of properties in the next section. In Section 3, we show how the tensor product arises naturally when we consider trying to represent properties of pairs, and demonstrate an abstract interpretation which uses it. In Section 4 we show that this abstract interpretation allows the expression of ***conjunctions*** of properties of functions, but not ***disjunctions***, implying that using the tensor product does not give the most relational analysis. This work has given further insights into both the BHA-style of abstract interpretation and a number of open problems. These are summarised in Section 5.

2 Properties, Their Combination and Their Representation

In the classical BHA-style analysis, an abstract domain point represents a ***non-empty Scott-closed set***[3]. For the purposes of this paper, a ***property is a Scott-closed set***. A

[3] Hunt has developed an abstract interpretation in the BHA-style where abstract domain points represent partial equivalence relations [13]. We will only consider this in Section 5.

subset S of a domain D is *Scott-closed* if:

1. $x \sqsubseteq s \in S$ then $x \in S$, and

2. $X \subseteq S$ and X is directed, then $\bigsqcup X \in S$.

Given a ***finite*** set of properties for some type, there are three operations we might want to perform on them: intersection; union; and negation. Finite unions and intersections of Scott-closed sets are Scott-closed, which says that combinations of properties using finite ***conjunctions*** and ***disjunctions*** are also properties. The complement of a Scott-closed set is not necessarily Scott-closed, so we cannot express the negation of a property.

We will say that a set of properties satisfies the *Closure Property* if it is closed under *all* finite unions and intersections. A set of properties of a domain D can only have the closure property if it contains both D, the empty intersection, and $\{\bot_D\}$, the empty union.

Finite lattices of abstract values are often used to represent properties in abstract interpretation. For a given type, we have to make sure that the meets and joins of these finite lattices accurately represent the intersection and union operations on the sets of properties. This can be formalised in the following way. If σ is a type, γ_σ is a function from the abstract values for the type σ to the set of properties over that type, and p and q are points in the abstract domain, then we will say that our abstract domain has the *Representation Property* if the following two conditions hold:

- $\gamma_\sigma\ (p \sqcap q) = (\gamma_\sigma\ p) \bigcap (\gamma_\sigma\ q)$; and

- $\gamma_\sigma\ (p \sqcup q) = (\gamma_\sigma\ p) \bigcup (\gamma_\sigma\ q)$.

If these hold, then finite combinations of properties using intersections and unions can be modelled accurately by combinations of abstract domain points using meets and joins. We can paraphrase these equations in words:

- the abstract domain point $p \sqcap q$ represents the intersection (conjunction) of the properties represented by p and q; and

- the abstract domain point $p \sqcup q$ represents the union (disjunction) of the properties represented by p and q.

The question "Can we build representations of all of the properties of a constructed data type from the representations of the properties of its constituent parts?" can be rephrased as "For each way of constructing new types, can we define a construction on abstract domains which have the Representation Property such that the resulting domain has the Representation Property for the constructed type?".

We will see that this can be done for products using the tensor product construction, but the problem is still open for function types.

3 Properties of Pairs and Tensor Products

3.1 Representing Properties of Pairs

In this subsection we will show that if we have *finite* sets of properties $\mathcal{P}$ and $\mathcal{Q}$ over domains D and E with the Closure Property, and abstract domains $\bar{\mathcal{P}}$ and $\bar{\mathcal{Q}}$ with the Representation Property, then a tensor product of $\bar{\mathcal{P}}$ and $\bar{\mathcal{Q}}$ gives an abstract domain with the Representation Property for $D \times E$.

Suppose we have finite sets of properties $\mathcal{P} = \{P_i | i \in I\}$ and $\mathcal{Q} = \{Q_j | j \in J\}$ over D and E respectively, each with the Closure Property, and that we want to express properties of pairs of values from $D \times E$ such that the P_i express properties of the first element of a pair and the Q_j express properties of the second element. What properties can we express over the product?

First of all we note that the properties D and E essentially contain no information. So to express the property that the first element of a pair has property P_i (and we do not know anything about the second element of the pair), we can use the pair of properties (P_i, E). Similarly, (D, Q_j) represents the property that second element of a pair has property Q_j (and we know nothing about the first element). Let us see what happens when we introduce intersections and then unions of properties.

Suppose that we have two properties (P_{i_1}, Q_{j_1}) and (P_{i_2}, Q_{j_2}), then by a simple calculation,

$$(P_{i_1}, Q_{j_1}) \bigcap (P_{i_2}, Q_{j_2}) = (P_{i_1} \bigcap P_{i_2}, Q_{j_1} \bigcap Q_{j_2}),$$

and since $\mathcal{P}$ and $\mathcal{Q}$ are closed under intersections, $\exists i \in I, \exists j \in J$ such that $P_{i_1} \bigcap P_{i_2} = P_i$ and $Q_{j_1} \bigcap Q_{j_2} = Q_j$. In words this says that *the conjunction of properties of pairs is a pair of properties.*

> *If* $\bar{\mathcal{P}} = \{p_i | i \in I\}$ *and* $\bar{\mathcal{Q}} = \{q_j | j \in J\}$ *are the abstract lattices with the Representation Property for* $\mathcal{P}$ *and* $\mathcal{Q}$ *respectively, such that* $\forall i \in I, P_i = \gamma\ p_i$ *and* $\forall j \in J, Q_j = \gamma\ q_j$*, then the calculation*
>
> $$\begin{aligned} (p_{i_1}, q_{j_1}) \sqcap (p_{i_2}, q_{j_2}) &= (p_{i_1} \sqcap p_{i_2}, q_{j_1} \sqcap q_{j_2}) \\ &= (p_i, q_i) \text{ by the Representation Property} \end{aligned}$$
>
> *shows that pairs of abstract values are sufficient to represent all conjunctions of properties.*

Adding disjunctions of properties is more problematic, for

$$(P_{i_1}, Q_{j_1}) \bigcup (P_{i_2}, Q_{j_2}) = (P_{i_1} \bigcup P_{i_2}, Q_{j_1} \bigcup Q_{j_2})$$

does not hold in general. How are we to proceed? First of all we note that intersection distributes over union (and vice versa, but that is of no use to us here), so that

$$[(P_{i_1}, Q_{j_1}) \bigcup (P_{i_2}, Q_{j_2})] \bigcap (P_{i_3}, Q_{j_3}) = [(P_{i_1}, Q_{j_1}) \bigcap (P_{i_3}, Q_{j_3})] \bigcup [(P_{i_2}, Q_{j_2}) \bigcap (P_{i_3}, Q_{j_3})].$$

This means that all properties can be expressed as a union of intersections of properties. From our discussion of intersections of properties, we know that any finite intersection of properties of pairs is equivalent to a pair of properties. Putting these two pieces of information together, the only properties we can express on pairs can be reduced to finite unions of pairs of properties, that is $\bigcup\{(P_i, Q_j) | i \in I' \subseteq I \wedge j \in J' \subseteq J\}$.

We have seen that the intersection of properties can be represented by values from $\bar{\mathcal{P}} \times \bar{\mathcal{Q}}$. How can we represent unions? A natural way is to represent

$$\bigcup\{(P_i, Q_j) | i \in I' \subseteq I \wedge j \in J' \subseteq J\}$$

by

$$\{(p_i, q_j) | i \in I' \subseteq I \wedge j \in J' \subseteq J\}.$$

However, this representation is not quite what we want because it fails to capture two important properties of union.

The first property it fails to capture is that

$$P_{i_1} \subseteq P_{i_2} \wedge Q_{j_1} \subseteq Q_{j_2} \Rightarrow (P_{i_1}, Q_{j_1}) \bigcup (P_{i_2}, Q_{j_2}) = (P_{i_2}, Q_{j_2}).$$

This means that we must 'equate' the sets $\{(p_{i_1}, q_{j_1}), (p_{i_2}, q_{j_2})\}$ and $\{(p_{i_2}, q_{j_2})\}$. The standard way of doing this is to define the *left-closure*, of a set S, $\mathbf{LC}(S)$, by

$$\mathbf{LC}(S) = \{s | \exists s' \in S \wedge s \sqsubseteq s'\},$$

and then we can say that the property

$$\bigcup\{(P_i, Q_j) | i \in I' \subseteq I \wedge j \in J' \subseteq J\}$$

is represented by

$$\mathbf{LC}\{(p_i, q_j) | i \in I' \subseteq I \wedge j \in J' \subseteq J\}.$$

The second property of union that it fails to capture is that if Q_j is some property, then

$$(P_{i_1}, Q_j) \bigcup (P_{i_2}, Q_j) = (P_{i_1} \bigcup P_{i_2}, Q_j).$$

This means that the set containing (p_{i_1}, q_j) and (p_{i_2}, q_j) must also contain $(p_{i_1} \sqcup p_{i_2}, q_j)$, for this represents the property $(P_{i_1} \bigcup P_{i_2}, Q_j)$ as $\bar{\mathcal{P}}$ has the Representation Property. Clearly the same argument holds for the second elements of pairs.

This motivates the following definition.

Definition 3.1

If $\bar{\mathcal{P}}$ and $\bar{\mathcal{Q}}$ are abstract domains for the domains D and E respectively, then define the abstract domain for $D \times E$ by

$$\begin{aligned} &\{Y \subseteq D \times E | Y = \mathbf{LC}(Y) = \mathbf{CC}_1(Y) = \mathbf{CC}_2(Y)\} \\ \textit{where}\ &\mathbf{CC}_1(Y) = \{(d_1 \sqcup d_2, e) | (d_1, e), (d_2, e) \in Y\} \\ &\mathbf{CC}_2(Y) = \{(d, e_1 \sqcup e_2) | (d, e_1), (d, e_2) \in Y\} \end{aligned}$$

□

> *The abstract lattice construction we have motivated and defined above is the definition of the* tensor product *of two finite lattices D and E with respect to* linear *(or* additive*)* functions *[24]*[4]. *The discussion of this section has shown that if the abstract domains for the constituent types of a product type have the Representation Property, and their related sets of properties have the Closure Property, then using the tensor product (with respect to linear maps) gives an abstract domain with the Representation Property for the product.*

We return to this in Section 5.

In passing, we note that Nielson's discussion of tensor products in [22] is restricted to *atomically generated* lattices. An atom l of a lattice L is a value such that $l \neq \perp_L$ and $\forall l' \in L, l' \sqsubseteq l \Rightarrow l' = l$. In words, the atoms of a lattice are all the elements immediately above the bottom of the lattice. If the set of atomic elements of the lattice L is denoted by A_L, then we say that L is atomically generated if $\forall l' \in L,\ l' = \bigsqcup\{l \in A_L | l \sqsubseteq l'\}$. This restriction is not required by our work.

Fact 3.2

If we repeat the process with the *smash* product, then we derive the construction

$$\begin{array}{l} \{Y \subseteq D \star E | Y = \mathrm{LC}(Y) = \mathrm{CC}_1(Y) = \mathrm{CC}_2(Y)\} \bigcup \{\perp_{D\star E}\} \\ \textit{where}\ \ \mathrm{CC}_1(Y) = \{(d_1 \sqcup d_2, e) | (d_1, e), (d_2, e) \in Y\} \bigcup \{\perp_{D\star E}\} \\ \qquad\qquad \mathrm{CC}_2(Y) = \{(d, e_1 \sqcup e_2) | (d, e_1), (d, e_2) \in Y\} \bigcup \{\perp_{D\star E}\} \end{array}$$

where $D \star E$ is the smash product of D and E. This is the lattice which results from taking the tensor product with respect to *strict* linear functions between D and E [2].

3.2 A Language and Its Abstract Interpretation Using the Tensor Product

We will use the language Λ_T defined in Figure 1 to demonstrate the use of the tensor product in an abstract interpretation framework, and apply it to giving a strictness analysis. The type system of Λ_T is defined inductively by

$$\sigma ::= B | \sigma \rightarrow \sigma | \sigma \times \sigma$$

---

[4] A function f is *linear* if for all x, y, $f\ (x \sqcup y) = (f\ x) \sqcup (f\ y)$. A tensor product construction for finite lattices actually has more structure than just giving a lattice of values. It consists of a pair $(\otimes_L, \mathit{cross})$, where $\otimes_L$ with respect to linear maps is the construction we have derived in this section, and *cross* is a separately linear function from $D \times E$ to $D \otimes_L E$ (i.e. linear in each element of the pair separately), such that if f is any separately linear function, then there exists a unique linear function $f^{\otimes_L}$ such that $f = f^{\otimes_L} \circ \mathit{cross}$. In our case, we can define *cross* by $\mathit{cross}\ (d, e) = \mathrm{LC}\{(d, e)\}$. Note that we have persisted in referring to the tensor product *with respect to* maps with a particular property. This is because considering different functions gives us different tensor products. In general, a tensor product is used to convert a function which has some property separately in each element of its argument pair into one which has it in its argument pair considered as one argument — consult an advanced textbook on algebra, [19] for example, to get the details.

$$(1)\quad x^\sigma : \sigma \qquad\qquad (2)\quad c_\sigma : \sigma$$

$$(3)\quad \frac{e_1 : \sigma \to \tau,\ e_2 : \sigma}{(e_1\ e_2) : \tau} \qquad\qquad (4)\quad \frac{e : \tau}{(\lambda x^\sigma . e) : \sigma \to \tau}$$

$$(5)\quad \frac{e : \sigma \to \sigma}{\mathbf{fix}_{(\sigma\to\sigma)\to\sigma}\ e : \sigma} \qquad\qquad (6)\quad \frac{e_1 : \sigma_1, e_2 : \sigma_2}{\mathbf{tuple}_{\sigma_1\times\sigma_2}(e_1, e_2) : \sigma_1 \times \sigma_2}$$

Abstract Syntax of Λ_T

$\mathbf{true}_{bool}$	$\mathbf{false}_{bool}$	$\mathbf{if}_{bool\to\sigma\to\sigma\to\sigma}$
$\{\mathbf{0}_{int}, \mathbf{1}_{int}, \mathbf{2}_{int}, \ldots\}$	$\mathbf{plus}_{(int\times int)\to int}$	
$\mathbf{fst}_{\sigma_1\times\sigma_2\to\sigma_1}$	$\mathbf{snd}_{\sigma_1\times\sigma_2\to\sigma_2}$	

The Constants of Λ_T

Figure 1: Definition of the Language Λ_T

where B is an arbitrary base type. 'Base types' may include recursively defined data types such as lists, but our example strictness abstract interpretation will only distinguish between the properties of being definitely bottom and being any possible value for these types.

Note that we have given **plus** the type ($int \times int \to int$). It will act as our prototypical function which is bottom if either the elements of its argument pair is bottom.

The standard interpretation of Λ_T is obtained from the parameterised abstract interpretation in Figure 2 by setting $\mathbf{I}(\times)$ to be product and $\mathbf{I}(\mathbf{tuple})(d, e)$ to be (d, e), and giving the usual interpretations to the base types and constants. We denote the standard interpretation of the type σ by $\mathbf{S}_\sigma$, and the standard interpretation of the expression e in the environment $\rho^{\mathbf{S}}$ by $\mathbf{S}\ [\![e]\!]\ \rho^{\mathbf{S}}$.

To use the tensor product in an abstract interpretation, we set $\mathbf{I}(\times)(D, E)$ to be $D\otimes_L E$, the tensor product with respect to linear maps of D and E[5], and $\mathbf{I}(\mathbf{tuple})(d, e)$ to be $cross(d, e)$ where $cross$ is an injection of $D \times E$ into $D\otimes_L E$, defined by

$$cross\ (d, e) = \mathbf{LC}\ \{(d, e)\}.$$

A specific abstract interpretation can be defined by giving particular interpretations for the base domains and each of the constants. For the purposes of this paper we will assume that the abstract interpretation of each base domain is a finite lattice. We denote the abstract interpretation of the type σ by $\mathbf{A}_\sigma$, and the abstract interpretation of the expression e in the environment $\rho^{\mathbf{A}}$ by $\mathbf{A}\ [\![e]\!]\ \rho^{\mathbf{A}}$.

---

[5] The symbol $\otimes_L$ should not be confused with the smash product. It is standard in mathematics to use the symbol $\otimes$ for the tensor product, and it is unfortunate that it has also been adopted for the smash product. The subscript L is to remind us that it is defined with respect to linear maps.

$$
\begin{aligned}
\mathbf{I}_B &= \text{some domain for the base type } B\\
\mathbf{I}_{\sigma_1\to\sigma_2} &= \mathbf{I}_{\sigma_1} \to \mathbf{I}_{\sigma_2}\\
\mathbf{I}_{\sigma_1\times\sigma_2} &= \mathbf{I}(\times)(\mathbf{I}_{\sigma_1},\mathbf{I}_{\sigma_2})
\end{aligned}
$$

Interpretation of the Types

$$
\begin{aligned}
&\mathbf{I}\ [\![x^\sigma]\!]\ \rho^{\mathbf{I}} = \rho^{\mathbf{I}}\ x^\sigma\\
&\mathbf{I}\ [\![c_\sigma]\!]\ \rho^{\mathbf{I}} = \mathbf{K}^{\mathbf{I}}\ [\![c_\sigma]\!]\\
&\mathbf{I}\ [\![e_1\ e_2]\!]\ \rho^{\mathbf{I}} = (\mathbf{I}\ [\![e_1]\!]\ \rho^{\mathbf{I}})\ (\mathbf{I}\ [\![e_2]\!]\ \rho^{\mathbf{I}})\\
&\mathbf{I}\ [\![\lambda x^\sigma.e]\!]\ \rho^{\mathbf{I}} = \lambda d \epsilon \mathbf{I}_\sigma.\mathbf{I}\ [\![e]\!]\ \rho^{\mathbf{I}}[d/x^\sigma]\\
&\mathbf{I}\ [\![\mathbf{fix}_{(\sigma\to\sigma)\to\sigma}\ e]\!]\ \rho^{\mathbf{I}} = \bigsqcup_{i\geq 0}\ (\mathbf{I}\ [\![e]\!]\ \rho^{\mathbf{I}})^i\ \bot_{\mathbf{I}_\sigma}\\
&\mathbf{I}\ [\![\mathbf{tuple}_{\sigma_1\times\sigma_2}(e_1,e_2)]\!]\ \rho^{\mathbf{I}} = \mathbf{I}(\mathbf{tuple})(\mathbf{I}\ [\![e_1]\!]\ \rho^{\mathbf{I}},\mathbf{I}\ [\![e_2]\!]\ \rho^{\mathbf{I}})
\end{aligned}
$$

Interpretation of Language Terms

Figure 2: A Parameterised Interpretation of Λ_T

3.3 The Correctness of the Abstract Interpretation

It is routine to prove the correctness of this abstract interpretation by adding cases for product types in the relevant theorems in [1]. The paper uses a *logical relation* framework for its proof of correctness. Given a relation $\mathbf{R}_B$ on each base type B, the relation on $\sigma \to \tau$ is defined inductively by

$$f\ \mathbf{R}_{\sigma\to\tau}\ g \iff [\forall s \in \mathbf{S}_\sigma, \forall a \in \mathbf{A}_\sigma . s\ \mathbf{R}_\sigma\ a \Rightarrow (f\ s)\ \mathbf{R}_\tau\ (g\ a)],$$

and it is this definition which makes the relation *logical* in the sense of [25]. By doing trivial manipulation of the definition, the following property can be obtained:

$$
\begin{aligned}
f\ \mathbf{R}_{\sigma_1\to\ldots\to\sigma_n\to\tau}\ g \iff & \forall s_1,\ldots,s_n.\forall a_1,\ldots,a_n.\\
& \textstyle\bigwedge_{i=1}^n s_i\ \mathbf{R}_{\sigma_i}\ a_i \Rightarrow (f\ s_1\ \ldots\ s_n)\ \mathbf{R}_\tau\ (g\ a_1\ \ldots\ a_n)
\end{aligned}
$$

[1, p.15]. Extending the proof to include products involves using the relation on product types defined by:

$$(s_1,s_2)\ \mathbf{R}_{\sigma_1\times\sigma_2}\ \{(a_{i1},a_{i2})|i \in I\} \iff [\exists j \in I.(s_1\ \mathbf{R}_{\sigma_1}\ a_{j1}) \wedge (s_2\ \mathbf{R}_{\sigma_2}\ a_{j2})].$$

From the logical relation we can define a concretisation map:

$$\forall \sigma, \forall a \in \mathbf{A}_\sigma, \gamma_\sigma\ a = \{s|s\ \mathbf{R}_\sigma\ a\}.$$

It is easy to prove that this is equivalent to the concretisation map which is defined when this abstract interpretation is presented using abstraction and concretisation maps as in [4].

The following theorem states what we mean for the abstract interpretation to be correct.

$$\mathbf{K^A}\ [\![\mathbf{true}]\!] = 1 = \mathbf{K^A}\ [\![\mathbf{false}]\!] = \mathbf{K^A}\ [\![0]\!] = \mathbf{K^A}\ [\![1]\!] = \ldots$$

$$\mathbf{K^A}\ [\![\mathbf{plus}_{int \times int \to int}]\!]\ v = \begin{cases} 1 & \text{if } v = \mathbf{LC}\{(1,1)\} \\ 0 & \text{otherwise} \end{cases}$$

$$\mathbf{K^A}\ [\![\mathbf{if}_{bool \to \sigma \to \sigma \to \sigma}]\!]\ x\ y\ z = \begin{cases} \bot_{\mathbf{A}_\sigma} & \text{if } x = 0 \\ y \sqcup z & \text{if } x = 1 \end{cases}$$

$$\mathbf{K^A}\ [\![\mathbf{fst}_{\sigma_1 \times \sigma_2 \to \sigma_1}]\!]\ Y = \bigsqcup\{s_1 | (s_1, s_2) \in Y\}$$

$$\mathbf{K^A}\ [\![\mathbf{snd}_{\sigma_1 \times \sigma_2 \to \sigma_1}]\!]\ Y = \bigsqcup\{s_2 | (s_1, s_2) \in Y\}$$

Figure 3: Abstract Interpretation of the Constants in Λ_T

Theorem 3.3 (Correctness Theorem)

Let $\mathbf{R} = \{\mathbf{R}_\sigma\}$ *be a logical relation. Suppose that* $\mathbf{K^S}\ [\![c_\sigma]\!]\ \mathbf{R}_\sigma\ \mathbf{K^A}\ [\![c_\sigma]\!]$ *for all constants* c_σ. *Then* $\forall e : \sigma, \forall \rho^{\mathbf{S}}, \rho^{\mathbf{A}}$,

$$\rho^{\mathbf{S}}\ \mathbf{R}\ \rho^{\mathbf{A}} \Rightarrow (\mathbf{S}\ [\![e]\!]\ \rho^{\mathbf{S}})\ \mathbf{R}_\sigma\ (\mathbf{A}\ [\![e]\!]\ \rho^{\mathbf{A}}).$$

(Here $\rho^{\mathbf{S}}\ \mathbf{R}\ \rho^{\mathbf{A}}$ *means* $\forall x^\sigma.(\rho^{\mathbf{S}}\ x^\sigma)\ \mathbf{R}_\sigma\ (\rho^{\mathbf{A}}\ x^\sigma)$.*)*

3.4 A Strictness Abstract Interpretation for Λ_T

As in [21, 5], let 0 represent the property $\{\bot_{\mathbf{S}_B}\}$ and 1 the property $\mathbf{S}_B$ for every base type B. If we are to have the Representation Property at the base types, then we must define the following relation for all base types B:

$$\bot_{\mathbf{S}_B}\ \mathbf{R}_B\ 0$$
$$s\ \mathbf{R}_B\ 1 \text{ for all } s \in \mathbf{S}_B$$

This interpretation of the base types induces the abstract interpretations for the constants given in Figure 3. For example, the abstract interpretation of **plus** says that if it is possible that both elements of its argument pair are defined, then it is possible that the result will be defined, otherwise it is definitely undefined. It is routine to prove that $(\mathbf{K^S}\ [\![c_\sigma]\!])\ \mathbf{R}_\sigma\ (\mathbf{K^A}\ [\![c_\sigma]\!])$ for all constants c_σ in Λ_T. As a corollary of the Correctness Theorem, we then have the following Strictness Theorem.

Theorem 3.4 (Strictness Theorem)

Suppose that $\rho^{\mathbf{S}}\ \mathbf{R}\ \rho^{\mathbf{A}}$, *that* $e : \sigma_1 \to \ldots \to \sigma_n \to \tau$, *and that*

$$\mathbf{A}\ [\![e]\!]\ \rho^{\mathbf{A}}\ \top_{\mathbf{A}_{\sigma_1}}\ \ldots\ \top_{\mathbf{A}_{\sigma_{i-1}}}\ \bot_{\mathbf{A}_{\sigma_i}}\ \top_{\mathbf{A}_{\sigma_{i+1}}}\ \ldots\ \top_{\mathbf{A}_{\sigma_n}} = \bot_{\mathbf{A}_\tau}.$$

Then $\forall j \in \{1, \ldots, n\}, \forall s_j \in \mathbf{S}_{\sigma_j}$, $\mathbf{S}\ [\![e]\!]\ \rho^{\mathbf{S}}\ s_1\ \ldots\ s_{i-1}\ \bot_{\mathbf{S}_{\sigma_i}}\ s_{i+1}\ \ldots\ s_n = \bot_{\mathbf{S}_\tau}$.

Hunt defined the following two functions in order to show that one needed to be able to represent both conjunctions and disjunctions of properties in an abstract interpretation:

```
f c u =  g c u u
         where
         g c v w = if c then v else w
h c x = plus (if c then (x,3) else (2,x))
```

[14]. We need to be able to represent conjunctions to show that the first function is strict in its second argument: if its second argument is bottom, then *both* the second and third arguments of the conditional in the body of g are bottom, so the application must return bottom. We need to be able to represent disjunctions to show the strictness of the second function in its second argument: if its second argument is bottom, then the conditional will return a pair, where *either* its first element is bottom *or* its second element is, and in either case the application of plus will return bottom. Combining the functions by

```
p c x = h c (f c x)
```

gives a function which requires us to reason about both conjunctive and disjunctive properties in order to show its strictness in its second argument. It is a simple exercise to translate this into Λ_T and to determine that:

$$\mathbf{A}\ [\![f]\!]\ \{\} = \lambda c_\epsilon \mathbf{2}.\lambda u_\epsilon \mathbf{A}_\sigma.\begin{cases} \bot_{\mathbf{A}_\sigma} & \text{if } c = 0 \\ u & \text{otherwise} \end{cases}$$

$$\mathbf{A}\ [\![h]\!]\ \{\} = \lambda c_\epsilon \mathbf{2}.\lambda x_\epsilon \mathbf{2}.\begin{cases} 0 & \text{if } c = 0 \\ \mathbf{K^A}\ [\![\mathbf{plus}]\!]\ (cross(x,1) \sqcup cross(1,x)) & \text{otherwise} \end{cases}$$

$$\mathbf{A}\ [\![p]\!]\ \{\} = \lambda c_\epsilon \mathbf{2}.\lambda x_\epsilon \mathbf{2}.\begin{cases} 0 & \text{if } c = 0 \\ \mathbf{K^A}\ [\![\mathbf{plus}]\!]\ (cross(x,1) \sqcup cross(1,x)) & \text{otherwise} \end{cases}$$

The Strictness Theorem can then be used to determine that the standard interpretation of p is strict in its second argument.

4 Properties of Functions

The abstract interpretation in Section 3.2 uses the monotonic function space to construct abstract domains for function types. It is not difficult to show that that this construction gives an abstract domain which satisfies the first condition of the Representation Property if it is satisfied by the base types. This is stated by the following proposition.

Proposition 4.1

> *If for all base types B,* $\gamma_B\ (a_1 \sqcap a_2) = (\gamma_B\ a_1) \bigcap (\gamma_B\ a_2)$*, then for all types* σ*,* $\gamma_\sigma\ (s_1 \sqcap s_2) = (\gamma_\sigma\ s_1) \bigcap (\gamma_\sigma\ s_2)$.

Unfortunately, the same is not true of unions. It is a simple exercise to show that the standard interpretation of the definition

$$f = \lambda c^{bool}.\mathbf{if}\ c\ (\lambda x^{bool}.\lambda y^{bool}.x)\ (\lambda x^{bool}.\lambda y^{bool}.y)$$

is in the concretisation of $\lambda c_\epsilon \mathbf{2}.\lambda x_\epsilon \mathbf{2}.\lambda y_\epsilon \mathbf{2}.x \sqcup \lambda c_\epsilon \mathbf{2}.\lambda x_\epsilon \mathbf{2}.\lambda y_\epsilon \mathbf{2}.y$ $(= \lambda c_\epsilon \mathbf{2}.\lambda x_\epsilon \mathbf{2}.\lambda y_\epsilon \mathbf{2}.x \sqcup y)$, but not in the concretisation of either $\lambda c_\epsilon \mathbf{2}.\lambda x_\epsilon \mathbf{2}.\lambda y_\epsilon \mathbf{2}.x$, or $\lambda c_\epsilon \mathbf{2}.\lambda x_\epsilon \mathbf{2}.\lambda y_\epsilon \mathbf{2}.y$, and so is not in the union of their concretisations.

This means that the monotonic function space construction does not give us abstract domains with the Representation Property. It remains an open question if there is such a construction. This issue is discussed further in the subsection headed "Linear Functions" in the next section.

5 Observations and Open Problems

Independent Attribute and Relational Methods

In their 1981 paper, Muchnick and Jones distinguished between two different sorts of program analyses. The first, *independent attribute* methods, treated each element of a pair separately. This corresponded to representing properties of pairs as pairs of abstract properties. The second, *relational* methods, allowed the expression of relationships between the elements of a pair. This corresponded to representing properties of pairs as sets of pairs of properties. Nielson claimed that using the tensor product in an abstract interpretation is the appropriate generalisation of the relational method [22, 23].

The discussion in Sections 3 and 4 gives a number of further insights into the distinction for higher-order functional languages, where properties are Scott-closed sets (rather than arbitrary sets as in [20], or relations as in [26], or pers as in [13]). Given some sets of properties,

- independent attribute methods correspond to allowing finite intersections of properties. When the properties of the elements of a pair are closed under finite intersections, we saw that taking pairs of properties gave us all the properties we could get by taking finite intersections of the properties of the elements of the pairs;
- the notion of a relational method for a language with higher-order functions is unclear. For a first-order language, our discussion has shown that a relational method corresponds to being able to accurately model unions of properties by joins in an abstract domain. For higher-order functions, there are several degrees of accuracy that could be achieved by different abstract interpretations, so some terminology to describe these has to be agreed upon. Perhaps we should say that an analysis is relational for a particular set of type constructors, where the most accurate analysis would be relational for all type constructors. The analysis in Section 3.2 would then be relational on the base types and on products, but not on function types. This hones the claim made by Nielson that the tensor product generalises the relational method [22, 23].
- although the original BHA-framework [5] did not include products explicitly, because of the isomorphism

$$\mathbf{A}_\sigma \rightarrow \mathbf{A}_\tau \rightarrow \mathbf{A}_\upsilon \cong \mathbf{A}_\sigma \times \mathbf{A}_\tau \rightarrow \mathbf{A}_\upsilon,$$

  and because we have seen that taking pairs of abstract values to represent properties of pairs gives an independent attribute method, the original BHA-framework is an independent attribute method. Intuitively, this should come as no surprise, because the interpretation of a curried function is a curried function, and so there is no obvious way that any record can be kept of any relationships between the arguments, as they are provided one at a time.

An unfortunate side-effect of the last point is that, even if we use the tensor product in an abstract interpretation, suboptimal information will be determined about a program where functions are presented in a curried form rather than in an uncurried form. If this is not obvious, then consider the following example. Let $\mathbf{plus'}_{int \to int \to int}$ be the curried version of $\mathbf{plus}_{int \times int \to int}$. It has abstract interpretation

$$\mathbf{K^A}\ [\![\mathbf{plus'}_{int \to int \to int}]\!]\ x\ y = \begin{cases} 1 & \text{if } x = 1 = y \\ 0 & \text{otherwise} \end{cases}$$

The following two definitions have the same standard interpretation (that is, they denote the same function):

$$\begin{aligned} \mathbf{f} &= \lambda \mathbf{x}^{int \times int}.\mathbf{plus}_{int \times int \to int}\ x \\ \mathbf{f'} &= \lambda \mathbf{x}^{int \times int}.\mathbf{plus'}_{int \to int \to int}\ (\mathbf{fst}\ x)\ (\mathbf{snd}\ x) \end{aligned}$$

However, if we apply the abstract interpretation of each function definition to $(cross\ (0,1)) \sqcup (cross\ (1,0))$, then we find that the first one returns 0, whilst the second returns 1.

Linear Functions

The fact that

$$\mathbf{A}_\sigma \to \mathbf{A}_\tau \to \mathbf{A}_\upsilon \cong \mathbf{A}_\sigma \times \mathbf{A}_\tau \to \mathbf{A}_\upsilon.$$

arises from the fact that domains with continuous functions forms a *cartesian closed category*. More generally, this property is expressed as

$$Hom(A \times B, C) \cong Hom(A, B \to C).$$

A similar isomorphism holds for the tensor product with respect to linear maps:

$$Hom(A \otimes_L B, C) \cong Hom(A, B \to_L C),$$

where $B \to_L C$ is the set of linear maps from B to C. We conjecture that if a linear function space was used in an abstract interpretation, then the abstract domain for function types would have the Representation Property. Unfortunately it is possible to write non-linear functions in the typed lambda-calculus, and so using the linear function space in an abstract interpretation in a naïve way, by defining

$$\mathbf{A}_{\sigma \to \tau} = \mathbf{A}_\sigma \to_L \mathbf{A}_\tau$$

will not work. This is simply a result of the more fundamental fact that any model of a typed lambda calculus must be a cartesian closed category [18], and a category satisfying the final isomorphism above is not necessarily cartesian closed. It is possible to embed a non-linear function space in a linear function space, but the problem is doing it in such a way that the resultant abstract domains have the Representation Property, and so that a computable abstract interpretation using the relational properties of these domains can be defined. This is currently being investigated by Jensen as an extension of his work reported in [15].

Tensor Product and Pers

Hunt has defined an abstract interpretation where the abstract domain points represent partial equivalence relations (pers), and has shown that it can capture both the Scott-closed set behaviour of functions (strictness, for example) and their relational behaviour (head-strictness, for example) [13]. We are investigating the use of the tensor product in this analysis framework.

The Tensor Product and Abstract Domains for Recursively Defined Algebraic Data Types

In 1987 Wadler introduced an abstract domain for lists which seems to enable us to capture the sort of information we want to know about list structures [27]. It has been noted by a number of authors that the construction can be defined by:

$$\mathbf{A}_{list\ \sigma} = ((\mathbf{A}_\sigma)_\bot)_\bot,$$

that is, the abstract domain for a list type can be obtained by doubly lifting the abstract domain for the type of the elements in the list. The Nielsons have recently argued that a better abstract domain is given by

$$\mathbf{A}_{list\ \sigma} = ((\mathcal{O}(\mathbf{A}_\sigma))_\bot)_\bot,$$

where $\mathcal{O}(\mathbf{A}_\sigma)$ is the set of Scott-open sets of $\mathbf{A}_\sigma$ [24]. Whilst this may be the case, we have yet to see at any deep level where these constructions come from. Perhaps using the (symmetric) tensor product in solving an appropriate recursive domain equation, and applying sensible filters to the result (c.f. [9]) will enable us to give a rational reconstruction of the above domains.

A Relational Analysis for Sums

If the argument of Section 3.1 was repeated for sums, then we would find that all intersections of properties could be represented by sums of abstract domains, but unions require products of abstract domains. This is a further argument for equating independent attribute methods with representing intersections of properties, and relational methods with unions.

Forwards versus Backwards Analysis

We have found it helpful in understanding analyses to think of the properties that can be represented in our analyses. In fact, we believe that the key questions one has to ask of an analysis technique are how properties are combined to give properties of structured data types, and how properties of a structured data type can be factored into properties over its constituent parts[6]. In fact, this is what was done in part in [12]. Focusing on these issues should give further insights into the forwards versus backwards question. Perhaps if we used constructions/factorings which were inverses of each other in some way, then we would find that forwards and backwards analyses are equally powerful.

[6] Note that function application is the destructor corresponding to the constructor lambda-abstraction.

What is a Property?

In this paper a property has been a Scott-closed set. We could have been more general, and talked about logics of properties, and given interpretations of the logics in different mathematical structures (e.g. Scott-closed sets or pers). This should give further insight, and is being studied by Thomas Jensen.

Combining Analyses

In this paper we have only considered combinations of representations of properties for constructed types. Another way we might combine analyses is to take two different sets of properties and abstract domains representing those properties *for one type*, and define combinations on the two abstract domains which reflected all the properties one could obtain by combining the properties from the two different sets. It should be clear that this is a different problem to the one we have been tackling in this paper. The first work in this area was reported in [7], and has been further developed in [10]. Unfortunately the latter work tackles both this issue and the issues being addressed in this paper (but only for a first-order framework), and so is quite complex.

Relationship to Other Work

After completing the initial draft of this work, I became aware that the Nielsons had been working with the tensor product at the same time, reported in [24]. They too have shown that the tensor product can be used in an abstract interpretation in the sense given by the Correctness Theorem (Theorem 3.3), although, as they do not give a complete definition of their language, it is not clear whether they have a higher-order language or not. They make the further interesting observation that doing this means that functions over lists need no longer be expressed in terms of a case construct, for using tensor product allows us to express the property "the first element of the list is undefined and all the rest of the elements are defined, *or*, the first element of the list is defined and at least one of the elements in the tail must be undefined".

6 Conclusion

We have shown that focusing on the properties a program analysis technique can express, and how they can be combined and factored is an important step in understanding the technique.

As an example of this, we demonstrated that the tensor product of abstract domains arises naturally if we consider representing a combination of properties of a product type as a combination of the representations of properties of its constituent types.

Focusing on properties has also allowed us to clarify the notions of independent attribute and relational methods for a higher-order language. As a result of this, we have seen that just using the tensor product does not give the most accurate relational method for a higher-order language, bringing into question the sense in which the tensor product generalises the relational method.

We have found that this work has given us some insights into a number of open problems, discussed in the previous section, which we believe will be fruitful lines of further research.

Acknowledgements

This work was originally inspired by Sebastian Hunt pointing out to me that to determine the strictness of some functions we needed to be able to represent disjunctive properties. Recalling the title of Flemming Nielson's paper "Tensor Products Generalise the Relational Data Flow Analysis Method" I set out to see if the tensor product could be smoothly integrated into a higher-order framework, and whether it gave the required information. I have benefited greatly from extensive discussions with Samson Abramsky, Eric Goubault, Sebastian Hunt, Thomas Jensen, and Dave Sands, and the atmosphere provided by the Semantique Project. In particular I am grateful to Samson for putting on the course on higher-order categorical logic, which has given me the grounding in some of the areas I needed to undertake this work. I cannot recall whether or not I had the idea of trying to get a rational reconstruction of Phil Wadler's domain for lists. Certainly it was suggested to me by at least Dave Sands and Samson Abramsky. Eric Goubault suggested that the symmetric tensor product (rather than the ordinary tensor product) might be useful in trying to do this. Finally, I would like to thank Flemming and Hanne Nielson who have given of their time to help me understand their work, including paying for me to visit them for a few days in December 1990.

Bibliography

1. S. Abramsky. Abstract interpretation, logical relations and Kan extensions. *Journal of Logic and Computation*, 1(1):5–39, 1990.

2. H.-J. Bandelt. The tensor product of continuous lattices. *Mathematische Zeitschrift*, 172:89–96, 1980.

3. G.L. Burn. *Abstract Interpretation and the Parallel Evaluation of Functional Languages.* PhD thesis, Imperial College, University of London, March 1987.

4. G.L. Burn. *Lazy Functional Languages: Abstract Interpretation and Compilation.* Research Monographs in Parallel and Distributed Computing. Pitman in association with MIT Press, 1991. 238pp.

5. G.L. Burn, C.L. Hankin, and S. Abramsky. Strictness analysis of higher-order functions. *Science of Computer Programming*, 7:249–278, November 1986.

6. G.L. Burn and L.S. Hunt. Relating projection- and abstract interpretation-based analyses. *Draft Manuscript*, Department of Computing, Imperial College, 180 Queen's Gate, London, SW7 2BZ, UK, July 1991.

7. P. Cousot and R. Cousot. Systematic design of program analysis frameworks. In *Proceedings of the Sixth Annual Symposium on Principles of Programming Languages*, pages 269–282. ACM, January 1979.

8. K. Davis and P. Wadler. Strictness analysis: Proved and improved. In *Proceedings of the Second Annual Glasgow Workshop on Functional Programming, 21–23 August, 1989, Fraserburgh Scotland*, Springer Workshops in Computing. Springer-Verlag, 1990.

9. C. Ernoult and A. Mycroft. Uniform ideals and strictness analysis. In *Proceedings of ICALP'91*. Springer-Verlag Lecture Notes in Computer Science, 1991.

10. P. Granger. Combinations of semantic analyses. In INRIA, editor, *Proceedings of Informatika 88 (French-Soviet Workshop)*, pages 71–88, Nice, February 1988.

11. P. Hudak and J. Young. Higher order strictness analysis in untyped lambda calculus. In *Proceedings of 12th ACM Symposium on Principles of Programming Languages*, pages 97–109, January 1986.

12. R.J.M. Hughes and J. Launchbury. Towards relating forwards and backwards analyses. In *Proceedings of the Third Annual Glasgow Workshop on Functional Programming*, pages 145–155, Ullapool, Scotland, 13–15 August 1990.

13. L.S. Hunt. PERs generalise projections for strictness analysis. In *Proceedings of the Third Annual Glasgow Workshop on Functional Programming*, pages 156–168, Ullapool, Scotland, 13–15 August 1990.

14. L.S. Hunt. Forwards and backwards strictness analysis: Continuing the comparison. Unpublished manuscript, Department of Computing, Imperial College, 180 Queen's Gate, London SW7 2BZ, UK, 3rd May 1991.

15. T.P. Jensen. Strictness analysis in logical form. In *Proceedings of the Conference on Functional Programming and Computer Architecture*, Cambridge, Massachussets, USA, 26–28 August 1991.

16. N.D. Jones and F. Nielson. Abstract interpretation: a semantics-based tool for program analysis. In S. Abramsky, D.M. Gabbai, and T.S.E. Maibaum, editors, *Handbook of Logic in Computer Science*, volume 3. Oxford University Press, 1992. To appear.

17. Tsung-Min Kuo and P. Mishra. Strictness analysis: a new perspective based on type inference. In *Proceedings of the Conference on Functional Programming Languages and Computer Architecture*, pages 260–272, London, 11–13 September 1989. ACM.

18. J. Lambek and P.J. Scott. *Introduction to Higher Order Categorical Logic*. Number 7 in Cambridge Studies in Advanced Mathematics. Cambridge University Press, 1986.

19. S. Lang. *Algebra*. Addison-Wesley, second edition, 1984.

20. S.S. Muchnick and N.D. Jones, editors. *Program Flow Analysis: Theory and Applications*. Prentice-Hall Software Series. Prentice-Hall, 1981. ISBN 0-13-729681-9.

21. A. Mycroft. *Abstract Interpretation and Optimising Transformations for Applicative Programs.* PhD thesis, University of Edinburgh, Department of Computer Science, December 1981. *Also* published as CST-15-81.

22. F. Nielson. Tensor products generalize the relational data flow analysis method. In *Proceedings of the 4th Hungarian Computer Science Conference*, pages 211–225, 1985.

23. F. Nielson. Two-level semantics and abstract interpretation. *Theoretical Computer Science*, 69:117–242, 1989.

24. F. Nielson and H. Riis Nielson. The tensor product in Wadler's analysis of lists. Preliminary version of Chapter 8 of Two-level Functional Languages, CUP, 1992.

25. G.D. Plotkin. Lambda definability and logical relations. Technical report, Department of AI, University of Edinburgh, 1973.

26. P. Wadler and R. J. M. Hughes. Projections for strictness analysis. In G. Kahn, editor, *Proceedings of the Functional Programming Languages and Computer Architecture Conference*, pages 385–407. Springer-Verlag LNCS 274, September 1987.

27. P.L. Wadler. Strictness analysis on non-flat domains (by abstract interpretation over finite domains). In S. Abramsky and C.L. Hankin, editors, *Abstract Interpretation of Declarative Languages*, chapter 12, pages 266–275. Ellis Horwood Ltd., Chichester, West Sussex, England, 1987.

28. D.A. Wright. A new technique for strictness analysis. In *Proceedings of TAPSOFT91*, Brighton, UK, 8–12 April 1991.

A Note on the Choice of Domains for Projection-Based Program Analysis

Kei Davis

Department of Computing Science
University of Glasgow
Glasgow G12 8QQ, UK
email: davismk@dcs.glasgow.ac.uk

Abstract

Various nonstandard interpretations of functional programs have been proposed in which the basic nonstandard values are *projections*. We show that every *stable* function is completely determined by an appropriate abstract value in the backward analysis, and that every *continuous* function is completely determined by an appropriate value in the forward analysis.

1 Introduction

Strictness analysis by abstract (or non-standard) interpretation is an important part of several compilers for lazy functional languages (e.g. [1], [2]), and a wide variety of strictness analysis techniques have been proposed. The term *forward* is used to describe abstract interpretations in which the goal is to discover information about an entire expression given information at its leaves, while *backward* describes interpretations in which information flows in the other direction: the goal is to determine information at the leaves of an expression, given information about the entire expression.

The development of backward strictness analysis was motivated in part by the need for a method that could detect certain forms of *data structure strictness* such as *head strictness*, since a forward technique was not forthcoming, and suspected to be impossible by any forward analysis BHA framework ([3]).

A *projection* may be used to specify upper and lower bounds of the definedness of values (a semantic interpretation), or upper and lower bounds on evaluation (an operational interpretation); see e.g. [4]. In particular, projections can usefully encode head strictness as well as ordinary strictness ([5]). Program analysis techniques based on the use of projections include backward strictness analysis techniques ([5], [6], [7], [8]), and a forward analysis technique for use in partial evaluation ([9]).

A domain projection is a continuous, idempotent function that approximates the identity. The set of projections on a given domain forms a complete lattice under the usual domain ordering, with the identity ID as the greatest element, and the function BOT that maps every element to $\bot$ as the least element. For example, let projections F and S be defined on pairs as follows. For all values u and v,

$$F\ (u,v) = (u,\bot),$$
$$S\ (u,v) = (\bot,v).$$

Let $\mathit{fst}\ (u,v) = u$, then $\mathit{fst} = \mathit{fst} \circ F$, indicating that the second component of any argument of *fst* need never be evaluated, and we say that *fst* is F strict. Let $\mathit{swap}\ (u,v) = (v,u)$. If only the first component of the result of *swap* is required, for example if it were the argument of *fst*, then S may be safely applied to its argument, that is, $F \circ \mathit{swap} = F \circ \mathit{swap} \circ S$, and we say that *swap* is S strict in an F-strict context. Here F and S specify upper bounds on evaluation, by mapping those components of their arguments that will never be evaluated to bottom, and leaving those that might be evaluated unchanged.

In backward analysis, the central problem is, given γ and f, to find δ such that $\gamma \circ f = \gamma \circ f \circ \delta$, or equivalently, $\gamma \circ f \sqsubseteq f \circ \delta$. Taking δ to be ID always satisfies this inequality, but tells nothing about f; smaller δ is more informative. More generally, given f we seek to determine the least *projection transformer* τ, a function from projections to projections, such that for all γ, $\gamma \circ f \sqsubseteq f \circ (\tau\ \gamma)$. This inequality is the *safety condition* for τ and any τ satisfying the safety condition will be called a *backward abstraction* of f. For forward analysis we wish to determine the greatest *forward abstraction* τ such that for all δ, $\tau\ \delta \circ f \sqsubseteq f \circ \delta$.

Two questions will be addressed. Firstly, given f, does there always exist a least backward (or greatest forward) abstraction? Secondly, how much information about a function can be determined by a backward (or forward) abstraction? This paper proceeds as follows. Starting with backward analysis, a simple example—the *parallel-or* function—demonstrates that a continuous function may not have a least backward abstraction. However, there is a useful set of functions for which least backward abstractions do exist: the *stable* functions. Hunt states but does not prove this fact ([10]); we provide the proof here. Roughly speaking, the stable functions include the *sequential* functions; another example shows that the converse is not true. Next we show that even simple strictness (i.e. that $f\ \bot = \bot$) is not determined by the least backward abstraction of a stable function. We give a remedy first described in [5]: stable function f is transformed to a function $f_\bot$ such that the least backward abstraction of $f_\bot$ determines simple strictness in f. Our main result shows that this determines not just simple strictness of f, but completely determines f, so that in some sense this transformation is the 'right' one. Intuitively, this transformation makes straightforward the specification with projections of lower bounds on evaluation. For forward analysis, the results are similar: every *continuous* function f has a greatest forward abstraction; this abstraction does not determine even simple strictness; and, the greatest forward abstraction of the transformed function $f_\bot$ determines f.

2 Backward Analysis

For continuous f, there does not necessarily exist a least backward abstraction. For example, there is no least backward abstraction of parallel-or, defined by

$$\begin{aligned} &POR\ (\perp, v) = v, \\ &POR\ (u, \perp) = u, \qquad u \neq \perp, \\ &POR\ (u, v) = u \vee v,\ u \neq \perp,\ v \neq \perp. \end{aligned}$$

To see this, let δ_1 be the greatest projection such that $\delta_1\ (true, true) = (true, \perp)$, and δ_2 be the greatest projection such that $\delta_2\ (true, true) = (\perp, true)$. Then $ID \circ POR \sqsubseteq POR \circ \delta_1$ and $ID \circ POR \sqsubseteq POR \circ \delta_2$, but since $(\delta_1 \sqcap \delta_2)\ (true, true) = (\perp, \perp)$, it is not true that $ID \circ POR \sqsubseteq POR \circ (\delta_1 \sqcap \delta_2)$.

However, least backward abstractions do exist for the *stable* functions. The theory of stability was developed by Berry ([11]) in an attempt to extend the characterisation of *sequential* functions to include higher order functions. At first order the stable functions are a superset of the sequential functions, and this is hypothesised to be the case at higher order.

Definition. A continuous function f is *stable* if for all x and y such that $y \sqsubseteq f\ x$, there exists a least value $M(f, x, y) \sqsubseteq x$ such that $y \sqsubseteq f\ (M(f, x, y))$. □

Parallel-or plays an important role in the development of the theory of stability, and is in a sense the archetypical non-stable function (though it is not the simplest.) An example (due to Berry) of a function that is stable but not sequential is the least monotonic function h such that $h\ (true, false, \perp) = h\ (\perp, true, false) = h\ (false, \perp, true) = true$. Note that h is not the three-argument analog of parallel-or (which is not stable), since $h\ (false, true, \perp) = \perp$.

A well-known and useful consequence of the definition of stability is the following.

Lemma. Given stable f, for all x_1, x_2 such that there exists y such that x_1, $x_2 \sqsubseteq y$, we have $f\ (x_1 \sqcap x_2) = (f\ x_1) \sqcap (f\ x_2)$.

Proof. We have $f\ x_1 \sqcap f\ x_2 \sqsubseteq f\ y$ (monotonicity of f), so there is a least $x' \sqsubseteq y$ such that $f\ x_1 \sqcap f\ x_2 \sqsubseteq f\ x'$. Since x_1, $x_2 \sqsubseteq y$ it must be that $x' \sqsubseteq x_1$, x_2 and hence $x' \sqsubseteq x_1 \sqcap x_2$, so $f\ (x_1 \sqcap x_2) \sqsupseteq (f\ x_1) \sqcap (f\ x_2)$. However, $f\ (x_1 \sqcap x_2) \sqsubseteq f\ x_1$, $f\ x_2$, so $f\ (x_1 \sqcap x_2) \sqsubseteq (f\ x_1) \sqcap (f\ x_2)$. We conclude that $f\ (x_1 \sqcap x_2) = (f\ x_1) \sqcap (f\ x_2)$. □

Hunt states, but does not prove, the following theorem.

Theorem 1. For stable f there exists a least function τ such that for all γ, $\gamma \circ f \sqsubseteq f \circ \tau\ \gamma$. Further, τ is continuous.

Proof. That stable function f has a least backward abstraction means that for each α there is a least projection β such that $\alpha \circ f \sqsubseteq f \circ \beta$. Let $f : V \rightarrow W$ and α be fixed and let β be the least function satisfying this inequality. Then β is clearly weaker than the identity; to show that it is a projection we show that it is monotonic, continuous, and idempotent, in that order.

Let $a,\ b \in V$, with $a \sqsubseteq b$. Now

$$\begin{array}{ll} \alpha\ (f\ a) & \\ \sqsubseteq \alpha\ (f\ b) & \text{monotonicity } f \text{ and } \alpha, \\ \sqsubseteq f\ (\beta\ b) & \text{definition } \beta. \end{array}$$

Since $\beta\ a$ is the least value below a such that $\alpha\ (f\ a) \sqsubseteq f\ (\beta\ a)$, $\beta\ a$ cannot be larger than $\beta\ b$. If $\beta\ a$ were incomparable to $\beta\ b$, then $\beta\ a \sqcap \beta\ b$ would be strictly smaller than $\beta\ a$ or $\beta\ b$, and

$$\begin{array}{ll} f\ (\beta\ a \sqcap \beta\ b) & \\ = f\ (\beta\ a) \sqcap f\ (\beta\ b) & \beta\ a \sqsubseteq a,\ \beta\ b \sqsubseteq b,\ f \text{ stable}, \\ \sqsupseteq \alpha\ (f\ a) \sqcap \alpha\ (f\ b) & \text{definition } \beta, \text{ property } \sqcap, \\ = \alpha\ (f\ a) & \text{monotonicity of } f, \end{array}$$

contrary to $\beta\ a$ being least. Hence $\beta\ a \sqsubseteq \beta\ b$ and we conclude that β is monotonic.

In the following write $f\ X$ to mean $\{f\ x \mid x \in X\}$ and $X \circ f$ to mean $\{x \circ f \mid x \in X\}$.

Let $X \subseteq V$ be a directed set. The image of a directed set under a monotonic function is directed, so $\beta\ X$ is directed. Then $\beta\ (\sqcup X) \sqsupseteq \sqcup(\beta\ X)$ again since β is monotonic. Now

$$\begin{array}{ll} \alpha\ (f\ (\sqcup X)) & \\ = \sqcup(\alpha\ (f\ X)) & \text{continuity } f, \alpha, \\ \sqsubseteq \sqcup(f\ (\beta\ X)) & f,\ \beta \text{ monotonic}, \alpha \circ f \sqsubseteq f \circ \beta, \\ = f\ (\sqcup(\beta\ X)) & f \text{ continuous}, \\ \sqsubseteq f\ (\beta\ (\sqcup X)) & \beta \text{ monotonic}. \end{array}$$

Since $\beta\ (\sqcup X)$ is by definition the least value weaker than $\sqcup X$ such that $\alpha\ (f\ (\sqcup X)) \sqsubseteq f\ (\beta\ (\sqcup X))$, and $\sqcup(\beta\ X) \sqsubseteq \sqcup X$ (since β is weaker then the identity), it must be that $\sqcup(\beta\ X) = \sqcup X$. We conclude that β is continuous.

Let $x \in V$, then $\alpha\ (f\ x) \sqsubseteq f\ (\beta\ x)$. Now $\beta\ (\beta\ x)$ is by definition the least value bounded above by $\beta\ x$ such that $\alpha\ (f\ (\beta\ x)) \sqsubseteq f\ (\beta\ (\beta\ x))$. Since $\alpha \circ f \circ \beta = \alpha \circ f$, it must be that $\beta\ (\beta\ x)$ is the least value bounded above by $\beta\ x$ such that $\alpha\ (f\ x) \sqsubseteq f\ (\beta\ (\beta\ x))$. However, $\beta\ x$ is the least value bounded above by x such that $\alpha\ (f\ x) \sqsubseteq f\ (\beta\ x)$; hence it must be that $\beta\ x = \beta\ (\beta\ x)$, and we conclude that β is idempotent.

Finally, we show that the least backward abstraction τ of f is continuous. It is clear that τ is monotonic. Let X be a directed subset of the projections on V. Since τ is monotonic $\tau\ X$ is directed and $\sqcup(\tau\ X) \sqsubseteq \tau\ (\sqcup X)$, and since f is monotonic, $X \circ f$ and $f \circ (\tau\ X)$ are directed, so

$$\begin{array}{ll} (\sqcup X) \circ f & \\ = \sqcup(X \circ f) & \text{continuity of } f, \\ \sqsubseteq \sqcup(f \circ (\tau\ X)) & \text{safety condition for } \tau, \text{ property } \sqcup, \\ = f\ (\sqcup(\tau\ X)) & \text{continuity of } f, \end{array}$$

so $\sqcup(\tau\ X) \sqsupseteq \tau\ (\sqcup X)$, since by definition $\tau\ (\sqcup X)$ is the least value satisfying the safety condition. We conclude that $\sqcup(\tau\ X) = \tau\ (\sqcup X)$, and hence that τ is continuous. □

The least backward abstraction of a stable function f determines head strictness in f. Define projection H by

$$\begin{aligned} H\ \bot &= \bot, \\ H\ nil &= nil, \\ H\ (cons\ \bot\ xs) &= \bot, \\ H\ (cons\ x\ xs) &= cons\ x\ (H\ xs),\ \text{if } x \neq \bot. \end{aligned}$$

Then f is head strict if $f = f \circ H$. If τ is the least backward abstraction of f then f is head strict iff $\tau\ ID \sqsubseteq H$. However, the least backward abstraction of f may not contain all of the information in f, that is, f may not be determined by its least backward abstraction. In particular, it may not determine simple strictness when f is strict. Consider all of the monotonic functions from **2** to **2**, where **2** is the two-point domain $\{\bot, \top\}$, $\bot \sqsubset \top$, defined by

$$\begin{aligned} &bot\ \bot = \bot, \qquad && id\ \bot = \bot, \qquad && top\ \bot = \top, \\ &bot\ \top = \bot, && id\ \top = \top, && top\ \top = \top. \end{aligned}$$

There are only two projections on **2**, ID and BOT. The least backward abstractions of *bot* and *top* are the same, the function that maps both ID and BOT to BOT, though *bot* is strict and *top* is not. The least backward abstraction of *id* is the identity.

As shown in [5], by mapping a function $f : V \to W$ to $f_\bot : V_\bot \to W_\bot$, such that $f_\bot\ \bot = \bot$ and $f_\bot\ (lift\ x) = lift\ (f\ x)$, and defining the projection STR by

$$\begin{aligned} STR\ \bot &= \bot, \\ STR\ (lift\ \bot) &= \bot, \\ STR\ (lift\ v) &= lift\ v,\ \text{if } v \neq \bot, \end{aligned}$$

then f is strict if and only if $STR \circ f_\bot \sqsubseteq f_\bot \circ STR$. Put another way, if τ is the least backward abstraction of $f_\bot$, then f is strict if and only if $\tau\ STR \sqsubseteq STR$. In fact, we can make a stronger statement. Note that for any f the function $f_\bot$ is strict and bottom reflecting, that is, $f_\bot\ x = \bot$ if and only $x = \bot$, function f is stable if and only if $f_\bot$ is stable, and $f_\bot$ determines f and vice versa. We have

Theorem 2. Every stable, strict, bottom-reflecting function is determined by its least backward abstraction.

Proof. We will write $|V|$ to denote the lattice of projections on domain V, and $|f|$ to denote the least backward abstraction of f. Let $f \in A \to B$ be strict, stable, and bottom reflecting, then $|f| \in |B| \to |A|$. Given domain T, For all $c \in T$ let $\gamma_c \in |T|$ be defined by

$$\begin{aligned} &\gamma_c\ x = x,\ x \sqsupseteq c, \\ &\gamma_c\ x = \bot,\ x \not\sqsupseteq c. \end{aligned}$$

Let $b \in B$, $b \neq \bot$, $\beta = \gamma_b \in |B|$, $\alpha = |f|\ \beta$. We show that for all $a \in A$, $a \neq \bot$,

$$\begin{aligned} &f\ a = b \\ \Leftrightarrow\ &(\alpha\ a \neq \bot)\ \wedge\ (\forall b' \sqsupset b. |f|\ \gamma_{b'}\ a = \bot), \end{aligned}$$

so, together with the fact that f is strict and bottom reflecting, f may be reconstructed from $|f|$. First, for all $a \in A$,

$$\begin{array}{ll} \alpha\ a \neq \bot & \\ \Leftrightarrow (f \circ \alpha)\ a \neq \bot & \Leftarrow f \text{ strict}, \Rightarrow f \text{ bottom reflecting}, \\ \Leftrightarrow (\beta \circ f)\ a \neq \bot & \Leftarrow \text{safety condition}, \Rightarrow \text{leastness of } \alpha, \\ \Leftrightarrow \beta\ (f\ a) \neq \bot & \text{definition } \circ, \\ \Leftrightarrow f\ a \sqsupseteq b & \Leftarrow \text{defn } \beta; \Rightarrow f\ a \neq \bot, \text{defn } \beta, b \neq \bot. \end{array}$$

Second, let $b' \sqsupset b$, $\beta' = \gamma_{b'} \in |B|$, $\alpha' = |f|\ \beta'$. The chain of equivalences above has been cast so that we may substitute b' for b, β' for β, α' for α, and negate the first and last proposition to yield, for all $a \in A$, $a \neq \bot$,

$$\begin{array}{l} \alpha'\ a = \bot \\ \Leftrightarrow f\ a \not\sqsupseteq b' \end{array}$$

Since this holds for every $b' \sqsupset b$, we have that $f\ a \not\sqsupset b$, hence $f\ a = b$. □

This theorem tells us nothing about how a backward abstraction might be exploited in practice. We have seen how it may be used to detect simple strictness head strictness; it may be used similarly to determine other forms of strictness, such as tail strictness and head strictness in a head-strict context. Since every stable function f is determined by the least backward abstraction of $f_\bot$, determining this least backward abstraction is not computable. So, as is usual in abstract interpretation, the goal is to find as good an abstraction as possible. Importantly, such approximations to abstractions of $|f_\bot|$ defined on finite abstract domains of projections can still reveal head strictness and ordinary strictness. These practical issues are addressed in [5].

The mapping from stable functions to their least backward abstractions is not monotonic. For example, for *bot*, *id*, and *top* be as previously defined we have $bot \sqsubset id \sqsubset top$ in the usual domain ordering, but $|bot| = |top|$ and $|bot| \sqsubset |id|$. However, as Hunt states ([10]) the mapping is monotonic when the ordering on the argument domain is the *stable ordering* $\sqsubseteq_s$, where for stable f and g we have $f \sqsubseteq_s g$ if $f \sqsubseteq g$ and for all x, y, if $y \sqsubseteq f\ x$ then $M(f,x,y) = M(g,x,y)$. The proof is as follows.

Theorem 3. For all stable functions f and g, $f \sqsubseteq_s g$ implies $|f| \sqsubseteq |g|$.

Proof. Let f, $g : V \to W$ be stable functions with $f \sqsubseteq_s g$, and let $\alpha : |W|$. Then by the definition of $\sqsubseteq_s$ we have $f \sqsubseteq g$ and for all x we have $M(f,x,\alpha\ (f\ x)) = M(g,x,\alpha\ (f\ x))$. Now since $f \sqsubseteq g$ we have $\alpha\ (f\ x) \sqsubseteq \alpha\ (gx)$, so that $M(f,x,\alpha\ (f\ x)) \sqsubseteq M(g,x,\alpha\ (g\ x))$, since M is monotonic in its third argument. Since $M(f,x,\alpha\ (f\ x)) = |f|\ \alpha\ x$, and similarly for g, we have that $f \sqsubseteq_s g$ implies $|f| \sqsubseteq |g|$ □

For example, for *bot*, *id*, and *top* as defined before we have $bot \sqsubset_s id$, $bot \sqsubset_s top$, but $id \not\sqsubset_s top$ and $top \not\sqsubset_s id$.

3 Forward Analysis

The forward analysis does not fall within the BHA framework, so we might ask whether it is potentially able to detect head strictness, or even ordinary strictness. We start with:

Theorem 4. Every continuous f has a greatest forward abstraction, and it is continuous.

Proof. Let f and δ be fixed. Let X be the set of projections γ such that $\gamma \circ f \sqsubseteq f \circ \delta$. Since the lattice of projections is continuous and X is not empty (it always contains BOT), $\sqcup X$ always exists. So

$$
\begin{aligned}
& (\sqcup X) \circ f \\
= & \sqcup (X \circ f) && \text{continuity } \circ \\
\sqsubseteq & f \circ \delta && \text{safety condition}
\end{aligned}
$$

Since $\sqcup$ in the lattice of projections and $\sqcup$ for projections in the domain of continuous functions is the same, $\sqcup X$ is the greatest projection satisfying the safety condition. The proof that the greatest forward abstraction is continuous is analogous to the corresponding proof for the least backward abstraction. □

Head strictness of any continuous function f is determined by its greatest forward abstraction τ: we have that f is head strict iff $\tau\ H = ID$. In general, however, a continuous function is not determined by its greatest forward abstraction; even simple strictness is not determined. To see this, take ***bot***, ***id*** and ***top*** defined as before. The greatest forward abstractions of ***bot*** and ***top*** are the same, namely the function that maps *ID* and *BOT* to *ID*. The greatest forward abstraction of ***id*** is the identity. Similarly to the backward case, we have that f is strict iff $\tau\ STR = STR$, where τ is the greatest forward abstraction of $f_\perp$. Further:

Theorem 5. Every continuous, strict, bottom-reflecting function is determined by its greatest forward abstraction.

Proof. We will write $|f|$ to denote the greatest forward abstraction of f. Let $f \in A \to B$ be continuous, strict, and bottom reflecting, then $|f| \in |A| \to |B|$. Given domain T, For all $c \in T$ let $\gamma_c \in |T|$ be defined by

$$
\begin{aligned}
& \gamma_c\ x = \perp,\ x \sqsubseteq c, \\
& \gamma_c\ x = x,\ \ x \not\sqsubseteq c.
\end{aligned}
$$

It is not hard to see that for $x \in A$, it must be that $|f|\ \gamma_x = \gamma_{(f\ x)}$. Since $\gamma_c = \gamma_d$ iff $c = d$, it is straightforward to reconstruct f from $|f|$. □

The mapping from continuous functions to their greatest forward abstractions is not monotonic. For example, ***bot*** $\sqsubseteq$ ***id*** $\sqsubseteq$ ***top***, but $|$***bot***$| = |$***top***$|$ and $|$***id***$| \sqsubset |$***bot***$|$. This mapping is not monotonic even when the ordering on ***bot***, ***id***, and ***top*** is the stable ordering.

4 Conclusion

As mentioned, the purpose of the transformation of function f to $f_\perp$ in [5] is to enable determination of simple strictness with a backward abstraction. We have shown that this transformation is also sufficient for the same purpose for forward abstraction, and in both cases determines not just simple strictness in the function, but completely determines the function.

Head strictness is determined by both least backward and greatest forward abstractions. An argument presented in [12] suggests that any projection-based forward *program analysis* will not be able to detect head strictness, unlike the backward analysis of [5].

We conjecture that every continuous (as opposed to stable) function is determined by the set of all of its (continuous) backward abstractions, and that every continuous function from a finite domains to a finite domain is determined by its minimal (monotonic) backward abstractions.

We suspect that there is an ordering of continuous functions closely related to the stable ordering, such that the mapping of these functions to their greatest forward abstractions is monotonic.

References

1. Wray, S. "A new strictness detection algorithm." In *Proceedings of the Workshop in Implementation of Functional Languages* (Aspenäs, Sweden). L. Augustsson et. al., eds. Report 17, Programming Methodology Group, Department of Computer Sciences, Chalmers University of Technology and University of Göteborg, Göteborg, Sweden.

2. Augustsson, L. and Johnson, T. "The Chalmers Lazy ML Compiler." Department of Computer Science, Chalmers University of Technology, Göteborg, Sweden, 1988.

3. Abramsky, S. and Hankin, C. "An introduction to abstract interpretation." Ch. 1 of *Abstract Interpretation of Declarative Languages.* Abramsky, S. and Hankin, C. (eds.). Ellis-Horwood, 1987.

4. Burn, G.L. "Using projection analysis in compiling lazy functional programs." In *Proceedings of the ACM Conference on Lisp and Functional Programming* (Nice, June 1990).

5. Wadler, P., and Hughes, J. *Projections for Strictness Analysis.* Report 35, Programming Methodology Group, Department of Computer Sciences, Chalmers University of Technology and University of Göteborg, Göteborg, Sweden, 1987.

6. Davis, K. and Wadler, P. "Strictness analysis: Proved and improved." In *Functional Programming, Glasgow 1989: Proceedings of the 1989 Glasgow Workshop on Functional Programming, 21-23 August 1989, Fraserburgh, Scotland.* K. Davis and J. Hughes, eds. Springer Workshops in Computing. Springer-Verlag, 1990.

7. Hughes, R.J.M. and Launchbury, J. *Projections for polymorphic strictness analysis.* CS Report Series CSC 90/R33, Department of Computing Science, University of Glasgow, 1990.

8. Davis, K. and Wadler, P. "Strictness analysis in 4D." In *Functional Programming, Glasgow 1990: Proceedings of the 1990 Glasgow Workshop on Functional Programming, 13-15 August 1990, Ullapool, Scotland.* Simon L. Peyton Jones *et al.*, eds. Springer Workshops in Computing. Springer-Verlag, 1991.

9. Launchbury, J. *Projection Factorisation in Partial Evaluation.* Ph.D. thesis, Department of Computing Science, University of Glasgow, 1990.

10. Hunt, S. *Projection analysis and stable functions.* Unfinished manuscript.

11. Berry, G. "Stable models of typed lambda-calculi." In *Proceedings of the 5th ICALP* pp 375-387, LNCS 62. Springer-Verlag, Berlin, 1978.

12. Hughes, R.J.M. and Launchbury, J. "Towards relating forwards and backwards analysis." In *Functional Programming, Glasgow 1990: Proceedings of the 1990 Glasgow Workshop on Functional Programming, 13-15 August 1990, Ullapool, Scotland.* Simon L. Peyton Jones *et al.*, eds. Springer Workshops in Computing. Springer-Verlag, 1991.

Extended abstract

An Operational Model of Strictness Properties and its Abstractions

ALAIN DEUTSCH*
Laboratoire d'Informatique de l'Ecole Polytechnique (LIX)
F-91128 Palaiseau Cedex - France.
deutsch@lix.polytechnique.fr

Abstract

We study the problem of strictness analysis. We start from a new semantic model of strictness properties, and then derive an efficient and *on-line* algorithm for statically determining strictness properties of first order languages with structured data. This algorithm is based on a new algebraic structure which we first developed for alias analysis: the *lattice of unitary-prefix monomial relations on a rational language.* This algorithm discovers accurate strictness properties not found by existing algorithms and is formalised in the framework of operational abstract interpretation.
Keywords: automata and theory of formal languages, abstract interpretation based data flow analysis, logics and semantics of programming languages, rational transductions, strictness analysis, modal logic.

1 Introduction

Global and On-Line Analysis Algorithms We introduce a new terminology for classifying program analysis methods into *global* and *on-line* analysis algorithms. Although both kinds of algorithms exist since the mid seventies, we are not aware of an existing terminology for distinguishing them. An interprocedural program analysis algorithm is called *on-line* if:

1. procedures are analysed independently of their invocation context;

2. an infinite number of abstract contexts can be distinguished.

---

* Also at INRIA. This work was partly funded by the CNRS (URA 1439), by the French Department of Research and Technology and by the EEC ESPRIT project Sémantique #3124.

Historically, on-line program analyses have appeared independently in several areas of program analysis:

1. *interprocedural semantic analyses based on relational lattices* [13]: the lattice of collections [13] and the lattice of linear restraints [19] have been the first relational lattices used for analysing procedures. Procedures are analysed once for all (modulo the local fixpoint iteration) by representing relations between their input and output values with an element of a relational lattice;

2. *effect analyses for procedural languages*, for instance [2, 4];

3. *Milner-style polymorphic type inference* [30]: ML `let` polymorphism is in essence on-line: consider the ML expression ⟦`let x = N in M`⟧. Then the subexpression `N` is analysed once for all, producing a type scheme σ which is then instanciated as an unquantified (open) type for each particular occurrence of the variable `x` in `M`.

On-line analysis algorithms [1] have the property of analysing each procedure only once and are usable with modern module-based languages such as ADA or Standard ML. On the opposite, *global* interprocedural analysis algorithms process procedures by partitioning finitely their abstract invocation contexts and reanalyse each procedure for every such context. This is in essence the second analysis framework presented in [13] and its successors [38] (also called Minimal Function Graphs (MFG) in [25]) which is used in a very large number of program analyses from constant propagation to strictness analysis. On-line algorithms can be much more precise than global algorithms because of their ability to distinguish an infinite number of abstract invocation contexts, which is important for analysing recursive procedures.

A given data flow problem can be solved by both global and on-line algorithms. Take for instance the DFA[2] problem Constant Propagation for a procedural language and as a particular example the following Pascal program:

```
program ConstantPropagation;
 var n: integer;

 procedure Add(x,y: integer; var z: integer);
 begin
 if x > 0 then Add(x-1, y+1, z) else z := y
 end

begin
 Add(3, 4, n);
 writeln(n)
end.
```

[1] Algorithms for inferring polymorphically invariant program properties [1] can also be on-line algorithms. Another example of on-line data flow analysis is the constant propagation of [8].

[2] Data Flow Analysis

and a global algorithm using the well-known lattice of singletons C =

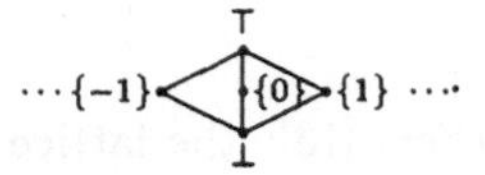

The DFA solution associates each program point and each variable with an element of C. The result for the example above is that $\mathbf{n} \in \mathbf{Z}$ before **writeln** : the algorithm fails to discover that $\mathbf{n} \in \{7\}$. The on-line algorithm uses a relational numerical lattice such as the lattice of affine subspaces of $\mathbf{R}^n$ [27]. The DFA solution is computed in two phases:

1. The first one associates each procedure with an element of the relational lattice that relates values of the parameters at entry to their values upon exit. This phase is properly on-line.
2. The second phase (called the propagation phase) resembles the global algorithm except that procedure calls are processed by using the relations computed by the previous phase rather than reanalysing the called procedure.

In the above example, phase 1 determines for the procedure **Add** the relation $z = x + y$ and phase 2 determines in particular that $\mathtt{n} = 7$ before **writeln**. In general algorithms that analyse each procedure once by *enumerating* the abstract domain (or part of it) are not on-line, even though procedures are analysed independently of their invocation context.

Access Paths In order to express program properties that involve data structures, we introduce *access paths*. An access path π is a sequence $\sigma_1.\dots.\sigma_n$ of *data selectors*. A data selector $\sigma \in \Sigma$ can be either a variable name, a constructor name (for sums and variants) or a record field selector. The alphabet Σ is determined by the type declarations of the program. Consider the Standard ML type declaration:

```
datatype 'a BinaryTree =
    Leaf
  | Node of 'a * ('a BinaryTree) * ('a BinaryTree);
```

then if the program variable `t` is of type **'a BinaryTree** the access path π = `t.Node.1`, refers to the key attached to the root node of tree `t`. This can be explained as follows: the one element path `t` refers to the root node itself, the path `t.Node` select the `Node` variant of the root and finally `t.Node.1` selects the first element of the triple found as the `Node` variant of `t`. Similarly the access path `t.Node.2.Node.1` selects the key of the left subtree of the root node `t`.

First-order and Second-Order Strictness Properties We distinguish two classes of strictness properties according to the signature of the program predicates implicitly computed. *First-order strictness determination algorithms* compute program predicates of the form $strict_G \in Lab \rightarrow \mathsf{P}(\Sigma^*)$ such that $strict_G(L)$ is a subset [3] of the data access paths that can be safely evaluated each time program point L is reached. *Second-order strictness predicates* are of the form

[3] Determining the exact set of paths that can safely be evaluated is undecidable.

$strict_L \in ProcId \rightarrow \mathsf{P}(\Sigma^*) \rightarrow \mathsf{P}(\Sigma^*)$ such that $strict_L(f)(\Pi)$ is the set of access paths that can safely be evaluated upon entry to function f when f is in a context [4] where all the paths in Π can be safely evaluated on exit of f. Most existing strictness determination algorithms produce second-order predicates.

Relational Strictness Properties Another useful concept for classifying strictness analyses is the distinction between *relational* and *independent attribute* program analyses [31]. Relational strictness properties are able to express relations between the strictness of two different objects. For instance the function $f(x, y, z) =$ **if** x **then** y **else** z is strict in x but strict in either y or z even though f is not strict in y (resp. z). Head strictness [39] is also an example of relational strictness property. On the other hand, independent strictness properties cannot express relations between the strictness of different objects.

Uniform Strictness Properties In order to compare algorithms for strictness determination we introduce the concept of *inductively-closed* or *uniform* strictness predicates. Informally, a strictness predicate is uniform if all elements of an inductive data type (such as a list) are described as having the same strictness. Of course, analysers that produce non-uniform strictness properties are likely to be more precise than others.

Related Work Most existing strictness analysers (see for instance [32, 6, 23, 7, 16, 24, 20, 34, 37, 26, 36]) produce second-order strictness predicates. However these algorithms are not on-line, because they are of an enumerative nature. The only on-line algorithm we are aware of is presented in [40].

Contributions of the paper The contributions of the paper are:

1. *An operational semantic model of strictness properties for a fragment of ML with call-by-name.*
   We present an exact, dynamic operational semantics of a polymorphic first order subset of ML with normal order semantics. An important aspect of our model is that it is *operational* although it describes a normal order language. Classical semantic models of strictness are based on denotational semantics [32, 33] and domain theory. In contrast, our model is operational, based on set theory and *trace semantics.*

2. *Algorithms for statically estimating strictness properties of programs.*
   The second contribution is to our knowledge the first *on-line* algorithm that infers *non-uniform* strictness properties. It is an abstract interpretation based data flow analysis algorithm for statically estimating strictness properties of polymorphically typed programs based on the class UPR($\mathcal{L}, \alpha_*$) of *unitary-prefix monomial relations on a rational language* $\mathcal{L}$ [15]. It is both more accurate that existing algorithms and compatible with *type inference* systems and module based languages, because it is on-line. We give two versions of

---

[4] The notion of context will be given an exact, semantic definition bellow.

v ∈ *Var*	L ∈ *Lab*	n ∈ *Num*	t ∈ *TyCon*
f ∈ *Field*	ϕ ∈ *ProcId*	c ∈ *Constructor*	τ ∈ *TyVar*

pgm	::=	tdecl pdecl
tdecl	::=	**datatype** $(\vec{\tau}_1)t_1$ = c_1^1 **of** ty_1^1 | ... | $c_1^{m_1}$ **of** $ty_1^{m_1}$
		and $\cdots$ **and** $(\vec{\tau}_n)t_n$ = c_n^1 **of** ty_n^1 | ... | $c_n^{m_n}$ **of** $ty_n^{m_n}$
ty	::=	τ | **int** | $(\vec{ty})t$ | $\{f_1: ty_1, \ldots, f_n: ty_n\}$
pdecl	::=	**fun** $\phi_1(v_1)$ = e_1 **and** $\cdots$ **and** $\phi_n(v_n)$ = e_n
e	::=	v | n | $\{f_1=e_1, \ldots, f_n=e_n\}$ | op e | ϕ e
		| **case** e **of** c_1 v_1 => e_1 | $\cdots$ | c_n v_n => e_n
op	::=	c | #f | ...

Figure 1: Syntax of a pure Standard ML subset

this algorithm: (1) a global and first order version, (2) an on-line, second order version. The on-line algorithm is based on finite representations of the effects of functions, or more precisely on representations of *sets of trace segments.* This algorithm is very different from existing algorithms as it relies on our new results in semantics and formal language theory mentioned above.

2 An Operational Semantic Model of Strictness Properties

In this section we present an exact, dynamic, non-compositional, partitionable [5], transition-based and operational semantics of a first order polymorphic fragment of Standard ML with call-by-name semantics. The exact semantics of programs is defined by a *transition system* $[State, \rightarrow_\tau]$, where *State* is a non-necessarily finite set of states (or configurations), and $\rightarrow_\tau \subseteq State \times State$ is the transition relation. The set of *finite and infinite execution traces* [11] $\Sigma[State, \rightarrow_\tau, \Phi] \subset State^\infty = State^* \cup State^\omega$ generated by this transition system is the set of sequences of states such that $\gamma_0 \in \Phi$ and that consecutive states are related by $\rightarrow_\tau$: $\gamma_0 \rightarrow_\tau \gamma_1 \rightarrow_\tau \cdots \rightarrow_\tau \gamma_n \rightarrow_\tau \ldots$ We syntactically associate a pair of *labels* $(\mathrm{L}, \mathrm{L}') \in Lab^2$ with each expression. By convention, a labelled expression will be written as: $[\![(e)^{\mathrm{L}}_{\mathrm{L}'}]\!]$. Label L (resp. L′) can be understood as the program point just before initiating (resp. after completing) execution of the expression $[\![e]\!]$. We say that state $\gamma = (\mathrm{L}', \ldots) \in State$ is at point L iff L = L′ and we write $at_{\mathrm{L}}(\gamma)$.

Definition 1 (Semantic Objects)

[5] Partitionable semantics, or more precisely transition-based semantics with a partitionable set of states are useful for constructing abstract interpretations [10].

(L, t, κ)	$\in$	*State*	=	$Lab \times Tree \times Dump$	configurations
σ	$\in$	Σ	=	$Var \cup Constructor \cup Field \cup \{\zeta\}$	selectors
t	$\in$	*Tree*	=	$\Sigma^* \rightarrow Ev$	finite value trees
κ	$\in$	*Dump*	=	Lab^*	control dumps
ev	$\in$	*Ev*	=	$\mathbf{Z} \cup \{\Omega\}$	tree node labels

A *selector* $\sigma \in \Sigma$ can be a record field name, a summand name or a variable name [6]. We use *finite trees* ($t \in Tree$), with edges labelled by selectors and nodes labelled with elements of Ev that can be either a natural number for representing integer values, or Ω for representing structured values (such as records, delay thunks, sum objects or activation records). Finite trees represent in an uniform manner values such as records or sums and internal components of states such as delay thunks or activation records. These rational trees are encoded as partial maps from words over Σ (i.e: access paths) to Ev.

DEFINITION 2 (OPERATIONS ON *Tree*) *Operations on value trees are defined for all* $t \in Tree$ *as:*

$t_\pi = \{\pi' \mapsto ev \mid t(\pi.\pi') = ev\}$	*subtree extraction*
$t\text{-}_\pi = \{\pi' \mapsto ev \mid t(\pi') = ev \ \wedge \ \pi \not\leq \pi'\}$	*subtree elimination*
$t\text{-}_S = \{\pi' \mapsto ev \mid t(\pi') = ev \ \wedge \ \forall \pi \in S.\ \pi \not\leq \pi'\}$	*subtrees elimination*
$t[\pi \mapsto t'] = t\text{-}_\pi \cup \{\pi.\pi' \mapsto ev \mid t'(\pi') = ev\}$	*subtree substitution*

The transition relation $\rightarrow_\tau \subseteq State \times State$ is defined relative to a program $P \in Pgm$. As noted above, this semantics differs from Structured Operational Semantics [21] or Natural Semantics [9] in that it does not use induction at all but is nevertheless defined at the source level, without translation to an intermediate language. For lack of space, the transition relation $\rightarrow_\tau$ will not be shown in this summary. A noteworthy property of this semantics is that all values are named by an access path $\pi \in \Sigma^*$. We have seen that each instance of formal parameters and local variables was given a unique name. But even expression values are named. Suppose that the program $[\![P]\!]$ contains a subexpression of the form $[\![(\mathrm{e})_\mathrm{L}]\!]$, and that a state $\gamma = (\mathrm{L}, t, \kappa)$ is reached. Then the value of the expression $[\![\mathrm{e}]\!]$ is stored in the value tree t at the position designated by the access path L.

2.1 First-order strictness predicates

We now define an exact, first order strictness predicate:

DEFINITION 3 (EXACT FIRST-ORDER STRICTNESS PREDICATE) *Given a program* $[\![P]\!]$ *and a set of initial states* $\Phi \in \mathbf{P}(State)$, *the set* $strict_G(\mathrm{L})$ *of globally*

---

[6] Selectors also include in particular ζ that refers to the last activation record. For instance during the execution of a recursive function `f(x)`, the current value of the parameter `x` is denoted by the access path `x` and the value of `x` in the previous (stacked) invocation of `f` is denoted by the access path ζ.`x`. In the general case, variable values are denoted by access paths of the form ζ^n.`v` where $n \in \mathbf{N}$ and `v` is a variable name.

strict access paths at program point L *is defined as:*

$$strict_G(\mathrm{L}) = \bigcap\{strictat(L,\theta) \mid \theta \in \Sigma[State, \rightarrow_\tau, \Phi]\}$$

$$strictat(L,\theta) = \bigcap\{\overline{defined(\theta_i)} \cup readafter(i,\theta) \mid \|\theta\| < \omega \ \wedge \ i < \|\theta\| \ \wedge \ at_L(\theta_i)\}$$

$$readafter(i,\theta) = \{\pi \in \Sigma^* \mid i < j < \|\theta\| \ \wedge \ (\forall k \in [i,j].\ defined(\theta_k)(\pi)) \ \wedge \ locallyread(\theta_j)(\pi)\}$$

$$locallyread(\mathrm{L},t,\kappa) = \{\pi \in \Sigma^* \mid ((\mathrm{L},t,\kappa) \rightarrow_\tau) \Rightarrow ((\mathrm{L},t',\kappa) \not\rightarrow_\tau) \ \wedge \ t' = t\text{-}_\pi\}$$

where $defined(\mathrm{L},t,\kappa)(\pi) \Leftrightarrow \pi \in Dom(t)$

We say that path π is locally read in state γ (noted $locallyread(\gamma)(\pi)$ [7]) whenever making π undefined in γ prevents further *local* transitions to take place. This is a semantic operational definition of locally read data, contrary to the syntactic definition given in [22]. In contrast the denotational characterisation $f(\perp) = \perp$ is not local: whereas $\pi \in locallyread(\gamma)$ means that π is needed for the next reduction step, $f(\perp) = \perp$ means that the parameter of f is needed at some step of the reduction sequence starting with $f(\perp)$. An alternate, more concise formulation of the $strict_G$ predicate can be given using *temporal logic* [28]:

DEFINITION 4 (TEMPORAL SPECIFICATION) *Equivalent definition of strictness based on temporal logic:*

$$strict_G(\mathrm{L}) = \{\pi \in \Sigma^* \mid \Box(at_\mathrm{L} \Rightarrow [\ \ \neg defined(\pi) \ \vee \ (\forall \circ)(defined(\pi) \rhd locallyread(\pi))])\}$$

where $\Box$ *ranges only over finite traces.*

The set $readafter(i,\theta)$ contains all data access paths π that are valid from time i (i.e: trace position i) to time j and ultimately read at time j. Given a trace θ, $strictat(L,\theta)$ is the set of all data access paths that are read (or undefined) each time program point L is reached along the finite execution trace θ. Note that if θ is an infinite trace then $strictat(L,\theta)$ contains all possible data paths: this accounts for the fact that if a computation loops (i.e: θ is infinite) then it is safe to pre-evaluate every data path π, as we do not want to distinguish between two non-terminating computation sequences.

EXAMPLE 1 *Consider the program* ⟦`hd(append(1::2::nil,loop()))`⟧ [8] *where* **append**(x,y) *is the usual list concatenation function and* **loop** *is some non terminating function. If* **append**$_{in}$ *is the program label at entry of* **append**, *then the set of globally strict paths at* **append**$_{in}$ *is:* $strict_G(\textbf{append}_{in}) = \{x, x.cons, x.cons.hd\}$ [9].

---

[7] In the remainder we use interchangeably sets and their characteristic functions.

[8] We use the ML abbreviations `x::y` ≡ `cons{hd=x, tl=y}` and `(x,y)` ≡ `{1=x, 2=y}`.

[9] We assume that lists are defined as:

```
datatype 'a list = nil | cons of {hd: 'a, tl: 'a list};
```

2.2 Second-order strictness predicates

DEFINITION 5 (EXACT SECOND-ORDER STRICTNESS PREDICATE) *Given a program* $[\![P]\!]$ *and a set of paths* $\Pi \subseteq \Sigma^*$ *then the set* $strict_L(f)(\Pi)$ *of strict access paths at the entry of function* f *when* f *is in a* Π*-strict context is defined as:*

$$strict_L(f)(\Pi) = \bigcap\{strictat(f_{in}, \theta) \mid \theta \in \Sigma[State, \rightarrow_\tau, State] \wedge \Pi \subseteq strictat(f_{out}, \theta)\}$$

Intuitively, $strict_L(f)(\Pi)$ is the set of paths that are read after the entering f on each trace θ that is Π-strict. We say that the execution trace θ is Π-strict at program point L if every data access path $\pi \in \Pi$ is read each time L is reached. Second order strictness predicates are not arbitrary functions from sets of paths to sets of paths. Indeed, sets of paths are *downward closed sets* (or "semi-ideals"[10]) w.r.t to the prefix ordering on access paths, and strictness predicates are monotonic. This is because if f cannot be strict in access path π without also being strict in each prefix of π.

PROPOSITION 1 *For any ML function* f *the corresponding second order strictness predicate* $strict_L(f)$ *satisfies :* $strict_L(f) \in mon(\mathbf{P}_\downarrow(\mathcal{L}) \rightarrow \mathbf{P}_\downarrow(\mathcal{L}))$.

EXAMPLE 2 *Consider the function* `length(l)` *and the strictness context* $\Pi = \$$, *where* $\$$ *is the implicit variable containing the result of* `length`. *Then the set of strict access paths at entry of* `length` *when this function is in any* Π*-strict execution context (i.e: any context in which the result of* `length` *is ultimately used) is:* $strict_L(\texttt{length})(\Pi) = \downarrow(x.(cons.tl)^*)$.

EXAMPLE 3 *Consider the function:* `f(x,y)= if x then f(x,y) else y;`, *our model correctly captures that* `f` *is strict in* y *as on each* finite *trace* y *is ultimately used :* $strict_L(f)\{\$\} = \{\mathtt{x}, \mathtt{y}\}$.

3 Global Strictness Analysis using Unitary-prefix Monomial Sets

As the strictness predicate $strict_G$ is generally not computable, we may first think about looking for an underestimate of the set of strict paths $strict_G(\mathrm{L})$. Of course we want an underestimate because of the particular program transformation that exploit strictness properties in order to replace call by need by call by value. However the framework of semantic analysis is particularly well suited for finding upper approximations of sets rather than lower approximations. Therefore we consider the dual of the sets $strict_G(L)$: these sets contain all the access paths that are not strict. We now look for an upper approximation of $\overline{strict_G(\mathrm{L})}$, where $\overline{X}$ is the complement of X relative to $\mathcal{L}$. We are thus left with the problem of finding an upper approximation to a set of words (access paths). The crucial observation for finding such an approximation is the following: the sets of strict paths $strict_G(\mathrm{L})$ corresponding to any polymorphically typed ML program are subsets of a rational

[10] Given a poset P the set $\mathbf{P}_\downarrow(P)$ of semi-ideals of P defined as $\mathbf{P}_\downarrow(P) = \{S \subseteq P \mid S = \downarrow S\}$ where $\downarrow S = \{\pi' \mid \pi \in S \wedge \pi' \leq \pi\}$ and $\leq$ is the prefix ordering is a complete lattice ordered by inclusion.

language $\mathcal{L} \subseteq \Sigma^*$ determined by the program types. Because of this rationality property, we can use the lattice of *unitary-prefix monomial relations* of $\mathcal{L}$, written $\mathrm{UPR}^n(\mathcal{L}, \alpha_*)$ [15]. This original construction relies in part on the *unitary-prefix monomial* decomposition of the rational subset $\mathcal{L}$ due to Samuel Eilenberg [17]. We initially developed this lattice for the purpose of alias and interference analysis, and specifically for representing alias relations. It is an upper approximation of $\mathsf{P}(\mathcal{L}^n)$:

THEOREM 1 ($\mathrm{UPR}^n(\mathcal{L}, \alpha_*)$ ABSTRACTS $\mathsf{P}(\mathcal{L}^n)$, SEE [15]) *Given a rational subset $\mathcal{L} \in Rat(\Sigma^*)$ and an abstraction function α_*, $UPR^n(\mathcal{L}, \alpha_*)$ is a complete lattice with widening ∇, and there exists a semi-dual Galois connection (α_2, γ_2) between $\mathsf{P}(\mathcal{L}^n)$ and $UPR^n(\mathcal{L}, \alpha_*)$.*

Here the abstraction function α_* is defined on $\mathsf{P}(\mathsf{N}^{kn})$, where n is the degree of the relations we consider ($n = 1$ for the global analysis) and k is a positive integer that depends on the rational language $\mathcal{L}$. Suitable choices of the abstraction α_* are relational numerical lattices (see appendix B). The lattice $\mathrm{UPR}^1(\mathcal{L}, \alpha_*)$ has neither finite width nor finite height and can represent exactly rational and even algebraic subsets of $\mathcal{L} \in Rat(\Sigma^*)$. Based on this lattice, our algorithm performs *global strictness analysis using upper approximations of sets of non-strict paths.* If at some program point this semantic analysis determines a unitary-prefix monomial relation R that denotes a set of access paths $S = \gamma_2(R)$, then this means that the program is strict in every access path $\pi \notin S$, as $S \supseteq strict_G(L)$ implies $\overline{S} \subseteq \overline{strict_G(L)}$. We now give examples of sets of non-strict access paths that are concretisations of elements of $\mathrm{UPR}^1(\mathcal{L}, \alpha_*)$ and the corresponding duals sets of strict access paths:

- $\bot$: $\gamma_2(\bot) = \emptyset$ is the hyper-strict context (strict $= \Sigma^*$)
- $\top$: $\gamma_2(\top) = \Sigma^*$ is the fully lazy context (strict $= \emptyset$)
- $\{(cons.tl)^{k_1}.cons.hd \mid k_1 \in 2\mathsf{N}\}$: the odds strict context (strict $= \{(cons.tl)^{k_1}.cons.hd.\Sigma^* \mid k_1 \in 2\mathsf{N} + 1\}$)

The global algorithm itself is not described in this summary and consists in (1) deriving a system of approximate semantic equations, (2) solving this system in the lattice $\mathrm{UPR}^1(\mathcal{L}, \alpha_*)$. Because this lattice has infinite antichains, the algorithm cannot analyse separately functions for each abstract value. The proof of correctness is easily structured and not inductive because we use a small step operational semantics and relies on a semi-dual Galois connection between the set of traces $\Sigma[State, \rightarrow_\tau, State]$ and the subsets of non-strict paths $\mathsf{P}(\mathcal{L})$, which then are abstracted by $\mathrm{UPR}^1(\mathcal{L}, \alpha_*)$.

4 On-Line Strictness Analysis based on Unitary-prefix Monomial Relations

The global method presented above provides a usable analysis algorithm, but: (1) functions can be reanalysed many times, (2) it is not very suitable for languages with modules. In this section we present an on-line strictness analysis.

In the previous section we abstracted a set of traces by a (super-)set $strict_G(f)$ of corresponding non-strict paths. As to on-line strictness analysis, we have to abstract the function $strict_L(f)$ (see definition 5) on and to sets of strict access paths. This is more complicated than abstracting sets of paths. Indeed rather that abstracting sets of complete traces, we now abstract *sets of execution trace segments*. More precisely we abstract sets of trace segments that begin at the entry of a function f and end up at its exit.

4.1 Monomorphic Analysis using Strictness Triples

Using the same duality argument as in the previous section, we turn the problem of representing $strict_L(f) \in mon(\mathbf{P}_\downarrow(\mathcal{L}) \to \mathbf{P}_\downarrow(\mathcal{L}))$ into the problem of representing:

$$\overline{strict_L(f)}(\Pi) = \overline{strict_L(f)(\overline{\Pi})}$$

From proposition 1 it follows that $\overline{strict_L(f)}$ is a monotonic function on *upward closed sets* of access paths. Sets $\Pi \subseteq \mathbf{P}(\Sigma^*)$ of non-strict access paths are upward closed sets (or "dual semi-ideals"): if $\pi \in \Pi$, which means that the access path π may be unused, then each subcomponent π' of π (i.e: $\pi' > \pi$) may also be unused. Hence $\Pi = \uparrow\Pi$ [11]. The dual semi-ideals of a poset $[L, \sqsubseteq, \perp]$ form a complete lattice $[\mathbf{P}_\uparrow(L), \subseteq, \emptyset, L]$ [12] isomorphic to the complete lattice of *sets of minimal elements* (or "crowns") $[\mathbf{P}_{\min}(L), \sqsubseteq, \emptyset, \{\perp_L\}]$, where the set of incomparable elements of L is $\mathbf{P}_{\min}(L) = \{S \in \mathbf{P}(L) \mid \forall x, y \in S.\ x \not\sqsubseteq_L y\}$ and the order relation is defined as: $S \sqsubseteq S' \Leftrightarrow \forall x \in S.\ \exists x' \in S'.\ x \sqsupseteq_L x'$ (see [5, ch. VIII.2]). The lattice isomorphism $\phi_\uparrow \in \mathbf{P}_\uparrow(L) \to \mathbf{P}_{\min}(L)$ is defined as: $\phi_\uparrow(S) = \min(S)$ [13]. Another useful isomorphism: the complete boolean algebra (CBA) of monotone functions from a poset P to a CBA L is isomorphic to the set of antimonotonic functions [14] from P to L through the morphism $\phi_{\text{mon}}(f) = \lambda x. f(x) \setminus \bigsqcup\{f(x') \mid x' \sqsubset x\}$.

Consider a second order strictness predicate $\overline{strict_L(f)} \in mon(\mathbf{P}_\uparrow(\mathcal{L}) \to \mathbf{P}_\uparrow(\mathcal{L}))$. We can show that: $mon(\mathbf{P}_\uparrow(\mathcal{L}) \to \mathbf{P}_\uparrow(\mathcal{L})) \cong mon(\mathcal{L} \to \mathbf{P}_\uparrow(\mathbf{P}_\uparrow(\mathcal{L})))$ through the morphism $\phi_{\text{inv}}(f) = \lambda\pi.\ \{\Pi \mid \pi \in f(\Pi)\}$, and thus we can find a function $f_0 = \phi_{\text{inv}}(\overline{strict_L(f)})$ such that: $f_0 \in mon(\mathcal{L} \to \mathbf{P}_\uparrow(\mathbf{P}_\uparrow(\mathcal{L})))$. Using the isomorphism ϕ_{mon} (as $\mathbf{P}_\uparrow(\mathbf{P}_\uparrow(\mathcal{L}))$ is a CBA) we obtain the function $f_1 = \phi_{\text{mon}}(f_0)$ such that: $f_1 \in \overline{mon}(\mathcal{L} \to \mathbf{P}_\uparrow(\mathbf{P}_\uparrow(\mathcal{L})))$. Now as $\mathbf{P}_\uparrow(L) \cong \mathbf{P}_{\min}(L)$ we can find a function $f_2 = \mathbf{P}(\phi_\uparrow) \circ \phi_\uparrow(f_1)$ such that: $f_2 \in \overline{mon}(\mathcal{L} \to \mathbf{P}_{\min}(\mathbf{P}_{\min}(\mathcal{L})))$. Consider an access path π. It is a subpath of some parameter of the ML function **f**, and $f_0(\pi)$ is the set of sets of possibly unused (non-strict) subpaths of the result of **f** such that π may be unused [15]. The set of sets of access paths $f_2(\pi)$ is just a representation of $f_0(\pi)$ based on the structure of the function f_0. What is the structure of $f_2(\pi)$? Either $\emptyset \in f_2(\pi)$, which means that π may be unused even when the function **f** is in the totally strict context $\emptyset$, or $f_2(\pi)$ can contain singletons $\{\pi'\} \in f_2(\pi)$, which means that the subcomponent π of the parameter of **f** may be unused when **f** is in a context which is nonstrict in π', or $f_2(\pi)$ can contain sets $\{\pi_1, \ldots, \pi_n\} \in f_2(\pi)$

[11] The upward closure of S is : $\uparrow S = \{\pi' \mid \pi \in \Pi \wedge \pi' \in \pi.\Sigma^*\}$

[12] $\mathbf{P}_\uparrow(L) = \{S \in \mathbf{P}(L) \mid S = \uparrow S\}$

[13] The set of minimal elements of S is : $\min(S) = \{x \in S \mid y \in S \Rightarrow y \not\sqsubset_L x\}$

[14] The set $\overline{mon}(P \to L)$ of anti-monotone functions from the poset P to the lattice L is defined as: $\overline{mon}(P \to L) = \{f \in P \to L \mid x \sqsubset_P x' \Rightarrow f(x) \not\sqsubseteq_L f(x')\}$.

[15] $f_0(\pi)$ is the set of contexts in which **f** possibly does not use the access path π.

(with $n \geq 2$) which means that `f` is not strict in π when each of the subcomponents $\pi_1, \ldots, \pi_n$ of the result of `f` may be unused. This represents *conjunctive strictness properties.*

EXAMPLE 4 *Consider for instance the ML function:*

```
fun f(x,y) = (x.1, x.2);
```

where `x.1` *and* `x.2` *represent respectively the first and second components of the pair* `x`*. Then its exact second order strictness predicate is:*

$$\begin{aligned}
\overline{strict_L(f)}(\emptyset) &= \{\mathtt{y}\}\\
\overline{strict_L(f)}(\{\$.1\}) &= \{\mathtt{x.1}, \mathtt{y}\}\\
\overline{strict_L(f)}(\{\$.2\}) &= \{\mathtt{x.2}, \mathtt{y}\}\\
\overline{strict_L(f)}(\{\$.1, \$.2\}) &= \{\mathtt{x}, \mathtt{x.1}, \mathtt{x.2}, \mathtt{y}\}\\
\overline{strict_L(f)}(\{\$, \$.1, \$.2\}) &= \{\mathtt{x}, \mathtt{x.1}, \mathtt{x.2}, \mathtt{y}\}
\end{aligned}$$

We see that $\overline{strict_L(f)}$ *is monotonic, but not additive as* $\overline{strict_L(f)}\{\$.1, \$.2\} \supset \overline{strict_L(f)}\{\$.1\} \cup \overline{strict_L(f)}\{\$.2\}$. *The corresponding function* f_0 *and* f_2 *are defined as:*

π	$f_0(\pi)$	$f_2(\pi)$
`x.1`	$\{\{\$.1\}, \{\$.1, \$.2\}, \{\$, \$.1, \$.2\}\}$	$\{\{\$.1\}\}$
`x.2`	$\{\{\$.2\}, \{\$.1, \$.2\}, \{\$, \$.1, \$.2\}\}$	$\{\{\$.2\}\}$
`x`	$\{\{\$.1, \$.2\}, \{\$, \$.1, \$.2\}\}$	$\{\{\$.1, \$.2\}\}$
`y`	$\{\emptyset, \{\$.1\}, \{\$.2\}, \{\$.1, \$.2\}, \{\$, \$.1, \$.2\}\}$	$\{\emptyset\}$

The non-additivity of $\overline{strict_L(f)}$ *has as counterpart conjunctive strictness property* $f_2(\mathtt{x}) = \{\{\$.1, \$.2\}\}$, *which means that the parameter* `x` *may be unused when* both *$.1 and $.2 may be unused.*

We now have to find finite representations for arbitrary functions f_2. Consider a set of variables X, then $\mathsf{P}(\mathsf{P}(X))$ is isomorphic to the set of *propositional logic formulas* over X in Disjunctive Normal Form (DNF). In our case, we have $X = \mathcal{L}$, which means that we are considering propositional formulas built over an infinity of variables, and hence infinite formulas can arise. We illustrate the correspondence between encoded second order strictness predicates and propositional formulas (PFs) for the the function f_0 derived from $\overline{strict_L(f)}$: we associate to each access path π subcomponent of the input of `f`, a PF whose variables are access paths subcomponents of the output of `f`:

input path	`x.1`	`x.2`	`x`	`y`
associated PF	$.1	$.2	($.1 ∧ $.2) ∨ $	*true*

The first approximation consists in replacing arbitrary conjunctions (of $n > 2$ terms) by sets of *binary conjunctions.* We will therefore decompose the range of f_2 into empty sets, singletons and sets of two elements. Therefore we can approximate f_2 with an element of the lattice $\mathsf{P}(\mathcal{L}) \times (\mathcal{L} \rightarrow \mathsf{P}(\mathcal{L}) \times \mathsf{P}(\mathcal{L} \times \mathcal{L}))$ which itself can be represented by an element:

$$f_3 \in \mathsf{P}(\mathcal{L}) \times \mathsf{P}(\mathcal{L} \times \mathcal{L}) \times \mathsf{P}(\mathcal{L} \times \mathcal{L} \times \mathcal{L})$$

which we call a *concrete strictness triple* (CST). For the particular ML function **f** discussed above, we have:

$$f_3 = (\{y\},\ \{(x.1,\$.1),(x.2,\$.2)\},\ \{(x,\$.1,\$.2)\})$$

which means that: (a) **f** is never strict in **y**, (b) **f** may ignore **x.1** only when used in a context not strict in $.1 (similarly for **x.2**), (c) **f** is not strict in **x** only when in a context neither strict in **x.1** nor strict in **x.2**. Now using theorem 1, we approximate and represent finitely the CST f_3 by an *abstract strictness triple* (AST):

$$f^{\#} \in \mathrm{UPR}^1(\mathcal{L},\alpha_*) \times \mathrm{UPR}^2(\mathcal{L},\alpha_*) \times \mathrm{UPR}^3(\mathcal{L},\alpha_*)$$

Therefore :

PROPOSITION 2 *Given a monomorphic ML function f its on-line strictness predicate $strict_L(f) \in mon(\mathsf{P}_\downarrow(\mathcal{L}) \to \mathsf{P}_\downarrow(\mathcal{L}))$ can be finitely represented by an abstract strictness triple : there exists a semi-dual Galois connection (α,γ) between the lattices $mon(\mathsf{P}_\uparrow(\mathcal{L}) \to \mathsf{P}_\uparrow(\mathcal{L}))$ and $UPR^1(\mathcal{L},\alpha_*) \times UPR^2(\mathcal{L},\alpha_*) \times UPR^3(\mathcal{L},\alpha_*)$.*

EXAMPLE 5 *Consider the addition function* `+: int * int -> int`, *then if its formals parameters are denoted by* **x** *and* **y**, *we obtain the CST:* $(\emptyset,\{(x,\$),(y,\$)\},\emptyset)$.

EXAMPLE 6 *Consider the function* `fun g(x: int list) = cons(hd(x), tl(x))`, *its CST is* (Δ,R_2,R_3) *where :*

$$\begin{aligned}
&\Delta = \emptyset,\\
&R_2 = \{(x.(cons.tl)^m.cons.hd,\ \$.(cons.tl)^n.cons.hd) \mid m = n\} \cup\\
&\qquad \{(x.(cons.tl)^m,\ \$.(cons.tl)^n) \mid m = n\},\\
&R_3 = \{(x,\ \$.cons.hd,\ \$.cons.tl)\}
\end{aligned}$$

EXAMPLE 7 *Consider the monomorphic instance of the function* `append: int list * int list -> int list` *with formal parameters* **x** *and* **y**, *its CST is* (Δ,R_2,R_3) *where :*

$$\begin{aligned}
&\Delta = \emptyset\\
&R_2 = \{(x.(cons.tl)^m,\ \$.(cons.tl)^n) \mid m = n\} \cup\\
&\qquad \{(x.(cons.tl)^m.cons.hd,\ \$.(cons.tl)^n.cons.hd) \mid m = n\} \cup\\
&\qquad \{(y.(cons.tl)^m,\ \$.(cons.tl)^n) \mid m \leq n\}\\
&R_3 = \emptyset
\end{aligned}$$

This strictness triple can be interpreted as follows:

1. *if* **append** *is in a totally strict context, then both* **x** *and* **y** *are totally needed (as* $\Delta = \emptyset$*) ;*

2. *if* **append** *is in a context* T_n *non-strict in the nth tail of the result list, then* **f** *is not strict in the nth tail of* **x** *and in* **y** *(this is because the length of* **x** *may be greater than n, in which case* **y** *is not used at all);*

3. *if* **append** *is in a context* H_n *not strict in the nth head of the result list, then the only data paths that can be ignored are: (1) the nth head of* x, *(2) the n first heads of* y.

This CST can be represented exactly as an AST using the lattice of unitary-prefix monomial functions parametrised by the numerical lattice of convex polyedra [14].

4.2 Polymorphic analysis using a correspondence between polymorphic invariance and right-regular relations

The representation of strictness predicates by strictness triples is not very satisfactory. For example the strictness triple (Δ, R_2, R_3) corresponding to a monomorphic instance of the polymorphic identity function `id: 't -> 't` can be quite involved: the relation R_2 associates with each well typed path $\$.\pi$ the path $\mathtt{x}.\pi$ (where \$ is the name of the result, and `x` is the name of the formal parameter). Although there are only a finite number of monomorphic instances of `id` effectively used, we cannot predict at what types the polymorphic identity will be used by solely looking at its definition : doing so would require the whole program, which is incompatible with an on-line analysis. We cannot enumerate the monomorphic (ground) instances, but nevertheless we need a way of generating the CST of the function for any of its instances.

Given a CST $(\Delta, R_2, R_3) \in \mathbf{P}(\mathcal{L}) \times \mathbf{P}(\mathcal{L} \times \mathcal{L}) \times \mathbf{P}(\mathcal{L} \times \mathcal{L} \times \mathcal{L})$ we can partition R_2 into two relations R_2^m and R_2^p such that $R_2 = R_2^m \cup R_2^p$ and R_2^p is a *right-regular relation* [16]. Similarly, R_3 can be decomposed into R_3^m and R_3^p. In fact right regularity has the same purpose as polymorphic invariance and type schemes: there is no need to describe the abstraction of a function at each monotype. Therefore R_2^p can be abstracted (and finitely represented) by first computing the least relation R_2^{rp} whose right-regular closure yields R_2^p. Following a similar development for R_3^p, we obtain a *polymorphic concrete strictness triple* (PCST) :

$$(\Delta, (R_2^m, R_2^{rp}), (R_3^m, R_3^{rp})) \in \mathbf{P}(\mathcal{L}) \times \mathbf{P}(\mathcal{L}^2)^2 \times \mathbf{P}(\mathcal{L}^3)^2$$

which is abstracted by a *polymorphic abstract strictness triple* (PAST) :

$$f_4 \in \mathrm{UPR}^1(\mathcal{L}, \alpha_\bullet) \times \mathrm{UPR}^2(\mathcal{L}, \alpha_\bullet)^2 \times \mathrm{UPR}^3(\mathcal{L}, \alpha_\bullet)^2$$

where R_2^m and R_3^m represent monomorphic information and R_2^{rp} and R_3^{rp} are their (reduced) polymorphic counterparts. Therefore :

PROPOSITION 3 *Given a polymorphic ML function f its on-line strictness predicate $strict_L(f) \in mon(\mathbf{P}_\downarrow(\mathcal{L}) \rightarrow \mathbf{P}_\downarrow(\mathcal{L}))$ can be finitely represented by a polymorphic abstract strictness triple : there exists a semi-dual Galois connection (α, γ) between $mon(\mathbf{P}_\uparrow(\mathcal{L}) \rightarrow \mathbf{P}_\downarrow(\mathcal{L}))$ and $UPR^1(\mathcal{L}, \alpha_\bullet) \times UPR^2(\mathcal{L}, \alpha_\bullet)^2 \times UPR^3(\mathcal{L}, \alpha_\bullet)^2$.*

EXAMPLE 8 *Consider the polymorphic function:*
`append: 'a list * 'a list -> 'a list` *with formal parameters* `x` *and* `y`, *its PCST is* $(\Delta, (R_2^m, R_2^{rp}), (R_3^m, R_3^{rp}))$ *where :*

$$\begin{aligned}
\Delta &= \emptyset \\
R_2^m &= \{(x.(cons.tl)^m, \$.(cons.tl)^n) \mid m = n\} \\
R_2^{rp} &= \{(x.(cons.tl)^m.cons.hd, \$.(cons.tl)^n.cons.hd) \mid m = n\} \cup \\
&\quad\ \{(y.(cons.tl)^m, \$.(cons.tl)^n) \mid m \leq n\} \\
R_3^m &= \emptyset \\
R_3^{rp} &= \emptyset
\end{aligned}$$

---

[16] A relation $R \subseteq A \times A$ on a monoid $[A, .]$ is right-regular iff $xRy \Rightarrow \forall a \in A.\ x.aRy.a$. The right-regular closure $\rho_c(R)$ of an arbitrary relation $R \subseteq A \times A$ is the least right-regular relation $R' \supseteq R$, and $R' = \{(x.a, y.a) \mid xRy \wedge a \in A\}$. Ternary right-regular relations are defined similarly.

And finally an example that exhibits polymorphic conjunctive strictness properties :

EXAMPLE 9 *Given the function* `fun h(x) = (x,x)`, *its PCST is* $(\Delta, (R_2^m, R_2^{rp}), (R_3^m, R_3^{rp}))$ *where :*

$$\Delta = \emptyset$$
$$R_2^m = R_2^{rp} = \emptyset$$
$$R_3^m = \emptyset$$
$$R_3^{rp} = \{(x, \$.1, \$.2)\}$$

As R_3^{rp} *represents a right-regular (hence polymorphic) relation,* `h` *may be non strict in* $\mathtt{x}.\pi$ *only when both* $\$.1.\pi$ *and* $\$.2.\pi$ *may be unused.*

5 Significance of the results

As evidenced by many publications, strictness analysis methods are very often based on denotational models of strictness properties. We have presented an operational, set based semantics of first order functional programs with inductive data types and a formal definition of strictness properties based on this model.

The strictness analysis methods we have presented are based on this new model of strictness properties and on the lattice of unitary-prefix monomial relations. Although we have designed this lattice in order to solve the specific problem of aliasing determination, we have then tried to reformulate its formalisation as independently as possible from that particular problem. We now believe it is a general tool for the semantic analysis of languages with structured data and we are studying potential applications to other problems.

Our algorithm is likely to be efficient and accurate in practice because it is on-line and produces non-uniform strictness information. Potential extensions of our work include: (1) relational strictness properties such as head strictness, (2) higher-order functions, (3) relations between our semantic model of strictness properties, classical (denotational) models and projection based models, (4) our method captures conjunctive strictness properties but only binary conjunctions, it would be interesting find an abstract representation of arbitrary conjunctions.

Finally we think this work provides a significantly new theoretical and practical basis for solving strictness problems.

6 Acknowledgments

Thanks are due to David Sands for pointing out an error in a preliminary version of this work, to Patrick Cousot for suggesting the idea that strictness analysis can be formalised using operational semantics and to Alan Mycroft for discussions and comments.

A Notations and Definitions

If $w \in \Sigma^\infty = \Sigma^* \cup \Sigma^\omega$ then $\|w\|$ is the (ordinal) length of the (infinite) word w. Given an alphabet Σ, $Rat(\Sigma^*)$ is the set of *rational* (i.e: recognizable, or regular) subsets of the free monoid Σ^*. Given two posets $[A, \sqsubseteq_A]$ and $[B, \sqsubseteq_B]$, a pair (α, γ) of mappings $\alpha \in A \rightarrow B$, $\gamma \in B \rightarrow A$ is a *semi-dual Galois connection* between A and B [35] if: $\forall x \in A.\ \forall y \in B.\ \alpha(\gamma(y)) \sqsubseteq_B y \ \wedge\ x \sqsubseteq_A \gamma(\alpha(x))$. In the context of abstract interpretation based data flow analysis, (α, γ) is called a ***pair of adjoined functions***, α is called a ***abstraction function*** and γ is the associated ***concretisation function*** [12]. A ***widening operator*** ∇ on a complete lattice $[L, \sqsubseteq]$ [12] is defined as: (a) $x \sqcup y \sqsubseteq x \nabla y$, (b) for any sequence $x_1, \ldots, x_i, \ldots \in L$ the sequence defined by $y_0 = \perp$ and $y_{n+1} = y_n \nabla x_{n+1}$ is not strictly increasing.

B Relational Lattices

Given a semi-dual Galois connection (α, γ) between $\mathbf{P}(U^n)$ and a lattice L, then L is called a *relational lattice* iff there exists at least one $y \in L$ such that the concretisation of y cannot be described as a cartesian product of subsets of U. An example is the lattice of *affine subspaces* [27]: it is an abstraction of $\mathbf{P}(\mathbf{R}^n)$ and consists of the empty set and all subsets of $\mathbf{R}^n$ of the form $\vec{o} + (\vec{v_1}, \ldots, \vec{v_m})\mathbf{R}^n$ where $(\vec{v_1}, \ldots, \vec{v_m})$ forms the basis of a m-dimensional linear subspace of $\mathbf{R}^n$ and the origin $\vec{o}$ is some point of $\mathbf{R}^n$. This lattice has height $n + 1$ and infinite width. Other numerical relational lattices include: *convex polyedra* [14], *simple sections* [3], *linear congruence equalities* [18] and *congruential trapezoids* [29].

References

1. S. Abramsky. Strictness analysis and polymorphic invariance. In *Proc. Programs as Data Objects*, volume 217 of *Lecture Notes on Computer Science*. Springer Verlag, 1986.

2. F.E. Allen. Interprocedural data flow analysis. In *Information Processing 74*, pages 398–402. North-Holland Pub. Co., 1974.

3. V. Balasundaram and K. Kennedy. A technique for summarizing data access and its use in parallelism enhancing transformations. In *SIGPLAN'89 Conference on Programming Language Design and Implementation*, volume 24(7) of *Sigplan Notices*, pages 41–53, June 1989.

4. J.P. Banning. *A Method for Determining the Side Effects of Procedure Calls*. PhD thesis, Stanford University, Stanford Linear Accelerator Center, August 1978.

5. G. Birkhoff. *Lattice Theory*, volume XXV. AMS Colloquium Publications, 1979.

6. A. Bloss and P. Hudak. Variations on strictness analysis. In *Proc. of the 1986 ACM Conf. on Lisp and Functional Programming*, pages 132–142, Cambridge, MA, August 1986.

7. G. Burn, C. Hankin, and S. Abramsky. The theory of strictness analysis for higher-order functions. In *Proc. Programs as Data Objects*, volume 217 of *Lecture Notes on Computer Science*. Springer Verlag, 1986.

8. D. Callahan, K.D. Cooper, K. Kennedy, and L. Torczon. Interprocedural constant propagation. In *Proc. SIGPLAN Symp. on Compiler Construction*, volume 21(6) of *Sigplan Notices*, pages 152–161, 1986.

9. D. Clement, J. Despeyroux, T. Despeyroux, and G. Kahn. A simple applicative language: Mini-ML. In *Conference Record of the 1986 ACM symposium on LISP and Functional Programming*, pages 13–27, Boston, August 1986.

10. P. Cousot. Semantic foundations of program analysis. In *Program Flow Analysis: Theory and Applications*, pages 303–342. Prentice-Hall, 1981.

11. P. Cousot. Methods and logics for proving programs. In *Handbook of Theoretical Computer Science*, volume B. Elsevier Science Publisher, 1990.

12. P. Cousot and R. Cousot. Abstract interpretation : a unified lattice model for static analysis of programs by construction of approximation of fixpoints. In *Fourth Annual ACM Symposium on Principles of Programming Languages*, pages 238–252, Los Angeles, January 1977.

13. P. Cousot and R. Cousot. Static determination of dynamic properties of recursive procedures. In *Working Conf. on Formal Description of Programming Concepts*, St-Andrews,Canada, August 1977. IFIP WG 2.2, North-Holland.

14. P. Cousot and N. Halbwachs. Automatic discovery of linear restraints among variables of a program. In *Fifth Annual ACM Symposium on Principles of Programming Languages*, pages 84–97, Tucson, Ariz., January 1978.

15. A. Deutsch. A storeless model of aliasing and its abstractions using finite representations of right-regular equivalence relations. In *Proceedings of the IEEE 1992 International Conference on Computer Languages*, San Francisco, April 1992.

16. P. Dybjer. Inverse image analysis. In *Proc. 14th International Colloquium on Automata, Languages and Programming*, volume 267 of *Lecture Notes on Computer Science*, pages 21–30. Springer Verlag, July 1987.

17. S. Eilenberg. *Automata, Languages and Machines*, volume A. Academic Press, 1974.

18. P. Granger. Static analysis on linear congruence equalities among variables of a program. In *TAPSOFT'91*, volume 493 of *Lecture Notes on Computer Science*, pages 169–192. Springer Verlag, 1991.

19. N. Halbwachs. *Détermination automatique de relations linéaires vérifiées par les variables d'un programme.* PhD thesis, Université Scientifique et Médicale de Grenoble & Institut National Polytechnique de Grenoble, Grenoble, France, March 1979.

20. C.V. Hall and D.S. Wise. Compiling strictness into streams. Technical Report 209, Indiana University, Computer Science Dept., Bloomington, December 1986.

21. M.C.B. Henessy and G.D. Plotkin. Full abstraction for a simple programming language. In *Proc. Mathematical Foundations of Computer Science*, volume 74 of *Lecture Notes on Computer Science*, pages 108–120, 1979.

22. S. Horwitz, P. Pfeiffer, and T. Reps. Dependence analysis for pointer variables. In *Conference on Programming Language Design and Implementation*, volume 24(7) of *SIGPLAN Notices*, pages 28–40, June 1989.

23. P. Hudak and J. Young. Higher-order strictness analysis in untyped lambda calculus. In *Thirteenth Annual ACM Symposium on Principles of Programming Languages*, pages 97–109, St Petersburg, Florida, January 1986.

24. R.J.M. Hughes. Backwards analysis of functional programs. In D. Bjorner, A.P. Ershov, and N.D Jones, editors, *Proc. Workshop on Partial Evaluation and Mixed Computation*, pages 155–169. North-Holland, October 1987.

25. N.D. Jones and A. Mycroft. Data flow analysis of applicative programs using minimal function graphs. In *Thirteenth Annual ACM Symposium on Principles of Programming Languages*, pages 296–306, Florida, January 1986.

26. S.B. Jones and D. Le Métayer. A new method for strictness analysis on non-flat domains. In *Functional Programming, Proc. of the 1989 Glasgow Workshop*, pages 1–11, Fraserburgh, Scotland, August 1989. Springer Verlag.

27. M. Karr. Affine relationships among variables of a program. *Acta Informatica*, 6:133–151, 1976.

28. Z. Manna. Logics of programs. In S.H. Lavington, editor, *Information Processing 80*, pages 41–51. IFIP, North Holland Pub. Co., 1980.

29. F. Masdupuy. Using abstract interpretation to detect array data dependencies. In Kyushu University Press, editor, *Proceedings of the International Symposium on Supercomputing*, pages 19–27, Fukuoka, nov 1991. ISBN 4-87378-284-8.

30. R. Milner. A theory of type polymorphism in programming. *Journal of Computer and System Sciences*, 17(3):348–375, December 1978.

31. S. Muchnick and N.D. Jones. Complexity of flow analysis inductive assertion synthesis and a language due to dijkstra. In *Program Flow Analysis: Theory and Applications*, pages 380–393, New Jersey, 1981. Prentice-Hall.

32. A. Mycroft. The theory and practice of transforming call-by-need into call-by-value. In *Proc. International Symposium on Programming*, volume 83 of *Lecture Notes on Computer Science*, pages 269–281, 1980.

33. A. Mycroft and F. Nielson. Strong abstract interpretation using power domains. In *Programs as Data Objects*, volume 217 of *Lecture Notes on Computer Science*, pages 536–547. Springer Verlag, October 1985.

34. S. Ono. Relationships among strictness-related analyses for applicative languages. In K. Fuchi and L. Kott, editors, *Programming of Future Generation Computers*, pages 257–283. Elsevier Science Publishers B.V., 1988.

35. O. Ore. Galois connections. *Transactions Amer. Math. Soc.*, 55:493–515, 1944.

36. R.C. Sekar, S. Pawagi, and I.V. Ramakrishnan. Small domains spell fast strictness analysis. In *Seventeenth Annual ACM Symposium on Principles of Programming Languages*, pages 169–183, San Francisco, January 1991.

37. P. Sestoft and G. Argo. Detecting unshared expressions in the improved three instruction machine. unpublished note, November 1989.

38. M. Sharir and A. Pnueli. Two approaches to interprocedural data flow analysis. In S. Muchnick and N.D. Jones, editors, *Program Flow Analysis: Theory and Applications*, pages 189–234. Prentice-Hall, 1981.

39. P. Wadler and R.J.M. Hughes. Projections for strictness analysis. In *Functional Programming Languages and Computer Architecture*, volume 274 of *Lecture Notes on Computer Science*, pages 385–407, Portland, September 1987. Springer Verlag.

40. D.A. Wright. A new technique for strictness analysis. In S. Abramsky and T.S.E Maibaum, editors, *Proc. TAPSOFT'91*, volume 494 of *Lecture Notes on Computer Science*, pages 235–258, Brighton, April 1991. Springer Verlag.

A Novel Approach Towards Peephole Optimisations

Andrew Gill
Department of Computing Science
University of Glasgow
andy@dcs.glasgow.ac.uk

Abstract

In this paper we examine alternative approaches towards the traditional optimisation technique of peepholing. Three simple methods of generating quality code are given. The first method improves poor juxtapositions while generating code, the second is an alternative usage of a solution to the knapsack problem. A third hybrid algorithm combines the strong points of both these solutions, and is presented as an alternative to conventional peepholing.

Introduction

Conventional optimising code generators can be considered as a pipeline consisting of two parts, the code generator and the target code optimiser. For example the code generator might take some type of intermediate representation, and emit assembly language. The second stage of this pipeline then performs cost cutting transformations on the assembly language.

Intermediate Code ⇒ [Code Generator] ⇒ Assembly Language ⇒ [Optimiser] ⇒ Optimised Assembly Language

To give clarity to this process, a concrete example of both an intermediate form and an assembly language are given. The intermediate form used here is a small subset of Cardelli's Functional Abstract Machine (FAM) [3]. The target language is a simple assembly language, which is a subset of the 68000 assembly language. The 68000 like structure was chosen because of its non-regular register set. For example, in the assembly language arithmetical operations act on the **D** register, and indirection can only be done from an address register (ie. **A** or **S**). The syntax for both of these (overly simplistic) languages are given in Figure 1. The informal semantics of the intermediate code is included in the Appendix (Figure 5). There is also an explanation of how the simple assembly language maps onto 68000 syntax (Figure 6).

When combining code generators with peephole optimisers, the method of code generation is often macro expansion. This is where every construct of the

IntermediateCode	=	GetLocal < *int* >
	|	MakeInt < *int* >
	|	Add
	|	Mul
	|	Head
Addressing	=	D | #< *int* > | A | (A) | < *int* >(S) | (S)+ | -(S)
AssemblyLanguage	=	**move** < *Addressing* > , < *Addressing* >
	|	**add** < *Addressing* >
	|	**mul** < *Addressing* >

Figure 1: Syntax of the Intermediate Code and Assembly Language

$\mathcal{M}$ ⟦ Getlocal *n* ⟧	= **move** *n***(S),-(S)**
$\mathcal{M}$ ⟦ Head ⟧	= **move (S)+,A ; move (A),-(S)**
$\mathcal{M}$ ⟦ Mul ⟧	= **move (S)+,D ; mul (S)+ ; move D,-(S)**
$\mathcal{M}$ ⟦ Add ⟧	= **move (S)+,D ; add (S)+ ; move D,-(S)**
$\mathcal{M}$ ⟦ MakeInt *n* ⟧	= **move #***n***,-(S)**

Figure 2: Simple Code Generation

intermediate code is replaced with short sequences of equivalent assembly language instructions. Figure 2 uses this macro strategy for translating from our intermediate code into our assembly language.

As an example, take the code generated for the expression "**(hd x)*y+4**", where **hd** is a function that, when applied to a list, returns its head. By walking the syntax tree, it is straightforward to generate intermediate code for this expression. Presuming the stack has the values of **x** and **y** in its top and second places respectively, the walk would produce the sequence:

GetLocal 0, Head, GetLocal 2, Mul, MakeInt 4, Add

Using the macro expansion code generation technique on this sequence gives the following assembly language:

⟦ GetLocal 0 ⟧ ⇒	**move 0(S),-(S)**
⟦ Head ⟧ ⇒	**move (S)+,A** **move (A),-(S)**
⟦ GetLocal 2 ⟧ ⇒	**move 2(S),-(S)**
⟦ Mul ⟧ ⇒	**move (S)+,D** **mul (S)+** **move D,-(S)**
⟦ MakeInt 4 ⟧ ⇒	**move #4,-(S)**
⟦ Add ⟧ ⇒	**move (S)+,D** **add (S)+** **move D,-(S)**

This is inefficient code, basically because of poor register usage. Objects are always pushed back onto the stack after use, and each code macro has no notion of state, but is a complete block in its on right. It is this code that peephole optimisers take, and transform into a more efficient form. They work by viewing the generated code through a *peephole* window, recognising streams of instructions, and replacing them with shorter, equivalent sequences. It should be observed that peephole optimisations can be independent from other general optimisation techniques, like the sophisticated register allocation schemes given in [1], or the simulated stack technique given in [7]. In almost every case, further optimisations can be achieved by using peepholing after assembly language generation.

Peepholers generally perform two distinct types of optimisation:

- Improving poor juxtapositions of pairs of instructions. An example of the type of inefficiency that is to be removed is when items are pushed onto then immediately recovered from a stack.
- Replacing known inefficient sequences with more efficient ones. This could typically be where a boolean intermediate value is created then immediately consumed. More efficient code would make use of the internal flags of the target machine.

Unfortunately large numbers of patterns are required to provide sufficient mappings to generate consistently clean code. Although initially straightforward peepholing gives very good results, patterns become increasingly complex to cover specialised cases.

It is in the context of the functionality of peepholers that the novel approaches to this optimisation paradigm can be explained. All are extensions to the code generation algorithm given above, removing the need for the post code generation peepholing stage totally. The first technique explained is called "simple dominoing". It addresses optimisations achieved by the first type of peepholing, improving poor juxtapositions. The second technique, called "dynamic code building", addresses the second type of optimisation made by a peepholer, rewriting inefficient sequences. The final technique, called "dynamic dominoing", is a hybrid of these two algorithms, and together this addresses both possible types of optimisation.

Simple Domino Optimisations

Dominos is a simple game where rectangular blocks are placed in a chain. Each block has two halves, and each half has a small number of dots. The blocks can be added to the end of a chain if the two connecting halves have the same number of dots. This concept is applied to the stack usage problem in code generation, as this is a typical example of where poor juxtapositions of instructions happens.

Corresponding to the dots on the sides of dominos, we invent a small set of stack *states*. We also define all possible transformations between these states, to allow code that provides movement from state to state to be easily generated. The purpose of these states is to allow different interpretations of the orientation of the stack to be used at different times. For example, efficiency considerations dictate that the top of the stack will sometimes be required to be kept in a register, and there are two types of registers. So in this example of dominoing, we will have three states.

The first state is the "normal" state, where the virtual stack of the intermediate language is held in the memory locations of the target machine stack. This state is called **SK** (it should be noticed that if we only had this one state, then the code would be identical to the code produced by the naïve macro expansion technique).

The second state is called **DR**, where the top of the stack has been popped into the "**D**" register. To transform from **SK** into **DR**, the instruction "**move (S)+,D**" is executed. The instruction "**move D,-(S)**" is used to transform back.

The final state is where the top of the stack has been popped into the "**A**" register, and is called **AR**. The transformation to and from **SK** can use "**move (S)+,A**" and "**move A,-(S)**" respectively. Also the transformation between **AR** and **DR** can be performed, using "**move A,D**" and "**move D,A**" respectively.

Where two consecutive instructions share the same stack state their assembly language equivalents can be concatenated. So where there is:

$$[\![\text{GetLocal } n]\!] \Rightarrow (SK \text{ , } \mathbf{move}\ n\mathbf{(S),D} \text{ , } DR)$$

$$[\![\text{Mul}]\!] \Rightarrow (DR \text{ , } \mathbf{mul\ (S)+} \text{ , } DR)$$

the following transformation during code generation can take place:

$$[\![\text{GetLocal } n \text{ ; Mul}]\!] \Rightarrow (SK \text{ , } \mathbf{move}\ n\mathbf{(S),D\ ;\ mul\ (S)+} \text{ , } DR)$$

The macro for "GetLocal *n*" leaves its answer in "D", (its top of stack), and "**mul**" can immediately use this registered value, because it presumes that its top of stack is the same register. This simple technique goes some way towards needless pushing and popping of values.

When the two touching sides of consecutive macros have different values, an intermediate stage, like a bridging domino, must be inserted that converts from the output state of the first macro to the input state of the second. These are simply small definitions that contain the state transformation code sequences given earlier. So for the definitions:

$$[\![\text{Add}]\!] \Rightarrow (DR \text{ , } \mathbf{add\ (S)+} \text{ , } DR)$$

$$[\![\text{Head}]\!] \Rightarrow (AR \text{ , } \mathbf{move\ (A),D} \text{ , } DR)$$

the following translation happens:

$$[\![\text{Add ; Head}]\!]$$

$$\Downarrow$$

$$(DR \text{ , } \mathbf{add\ (S)+} \text{ , } DR)$$
$$\qquad\qquad (AR \text{ , } \mathbf{move\ (A),D} \text{ , } DR)$$

$$\Downarrow$$

$$(DR \text{ , } \mathbf{add\ (S)+} \text{ , } DR)$$
$$\qquad\qquad (DR \text{ , } \mathbf{move\ D,A} \text{ , } AR)$$
$$\qquad\qquad\qquad\qquad (AR \text{ , } \mathbf{move\ (A),D} \text{ , } DR)$$

$$\Downarrow$$

$$(DR \text{ , } \mathbf{add\ (S)+\ ;\ move\ D,A\ ;\ move\ (A),D} \text{ , } DR)$$

State	= SK | DR | AR
$\mathcal{B}$ SK SK	= ϵ
$\mathcal{B}$ SK DR	= **move (S)+,D**
$\mathcal{B}$ SK AR	= **move (S)+,A**
$\mathcal{B}$ DR SK	= **move D,-(S)**
$\mathcal{B}$ DR DR	= ϵ
$\mathcal{B}$ DR AR	= **move D,A**
$\mathcal{B}$ AR SK	= **move A,-(S)**
$\mathcal{B}$ AR DR	= **move A,D**
$\mathcal{B}$ AR AR	= ϵ
$\mathcal{D}$ ⟦ Getlocal *n* ⟧	= (SK , **move *n*(S),D** , DR)
$\mathcal{D}$ ⟦ Head ⟧	= (AR , **move (A),D** , DR)
$\mathcal{D}$ ⟦ Mul ⟧	= (DR , **mul (S)+** , DR)
$\mathcal{D}$ ⟦ Add ⟧	= (DR , **add (S)+** , DR)
$\mathcal{D}$ ⟦ MakeInt *n* ⟧	= (SK , **move #*n*,D** , DR)

Figure 3: Simple Domino Code Generation

An example of the simple domino compilation scheme for our small language is given in Figure 3. Taking the example used earlier, the same sequence of intermediate code is translated using dominoing.

⟦ GetLocal 0 ⟧	⇒	**move 0(S),D**
		move D,A
⟦ Head ⟧	⇒	**move (A),D**
		move D,-(S)
⟦ GetLocal 2 ⟧	⇒	**move 2(S),D**
⟦ Mul ⟧	⇒	**mul (S)+**
		move D,-(S)
⟦ MakeInt 4 ⟧	⇒	**move #4,D**
⟦ Add ⟧	⇒	**add (S)+**
		move D,-(S)

This code is better that the original code, especially if the realistic overhead of external memory access (ie. stack access) is taken into account. There remains however, fundamental inefficiencies in the code generated by this simple scheme.

A Straightforward Improvement to Dominoing

Though the code produced by dominoing is better than naïve macro expansion, there are still examples of poor juxtapositioning. The first instruction in the example produced earlier should have been "**move 0(S),A**" rather than the observed "**move 0(S),D ; move D,A**". Problems like this stem from the fundamental flaw that dominoing is a locally greedy algorithm, doing what is locally the lowest cost, in hope of global efficiency.

$$State = \mathrm{SK} \mid \mathrm{DR} \mid \mathrm{AR} \mid \mathrm{ANY}\ (State \rightarrow AssemblyLanguage^*)$$

$\mathcal{B}$ SK SK	$= \epsilon$
$\mathcal{B}$ SK DR	= **move (S)+,D**
$\mathcal{B}$ SK AR	= **move (S)+,A**
$\mathcal{B}$ DR SK	= **move D,-(S)**
$\mathcal{B}$ DR DR	$= \epsilon$
$\mathcal{B}$ DR AR	= **move D,A**
$\mathcal{B}$ AR SK	= **move -(S),A**
$\mathcal{B}$ AR DR	= **move A,D**
$\mathcal{B}$ AR AR	$= \epsilon$
$\mathcal{B}$ (ANY f) a	= f a

$\mathcal{D}$ ⟦ Getlocal n ⟧	= (SK , ϵ , ANY (λ SK → **move** n**(S),-(S)**
	| DR → **move** n**(S),D**
	| AR → **move** n**(S),A**))
$\mathcal{D}$ ⟦ Head ⟧	= (AR , ϵ , ANY (λ SK → **move (A),-(S)**
	| DR → **move (A),D**
	| AR → **move (A),A**))
$\mathcal{D}$ ⟦ Mul ⟧	= (DR , **mul (S)+** , DR)
$\mathcal{D}$ ⟦ Add ⟧	= (DR , **add (S)+** , DR)
$\mathcal{D}$ ⟦ MakeInt n ⟧	= (AR , ϵ , ANY (λ SK → **move #**n**,-(S)**
	| DR → **move #**n**,D**
	| AR → **move #**n**,A**))

Figure 4: Improved $\mathcal{B}$ and $\mathcal{D}$

One possible way to improve the algorithm is to delay the code production until the preferred next state is known, and *then* use this information in a greedy fashion. Improved definitions of $\mathcal{B}$ and $\mathcal{D}$ using this extension are given in Figure 4.

Again taking the example used earlier, the intermediate sequence is translated using the improved domino algorithm.

⟦ GetLocal 0 ⟧	⇒	**move 0(S),A**
⟦ Head ⟧	⇒	**move (A),-(S)**
⟦ GetLocal 2 ⟧	⇒	**move 2(S),D**
⟦ Mul ⟧	⇒	**mul (S)+**
		move D,-(S)
⟦ MakeInt 4 ⟧	⇒	**move #4,D**
⟦ Add ⟧	⇒	**add (S)+**
		move D,-(S)

This again is better code. However, it would have been nice if the algorithm could recognise that the final two intermediate instructions could use "**add #4**", rather than creating the constant "4" as a conventional stack citizen. A method for allowing this functionality to be included in the final algorithm is introduced by the technique presented in the next section.

Dynamic Code Building

This section considers the problems with replacing longer sequences with shorter, equivalent sequences. For example, for the four arbitrary intermediate constructs "$A; B; C; D$", macro expansion gives:

$$[\![A \; ; \; B \; ; \; C \; ; \; D]\!] \Rightarrow a \; ; \; b \; ; \; c \; ; \; d$$

Upper case letter represent opcodes, and lower case letters represent assembly language. Now include a mapping:

$$[\![B \; ; \; C]\!] \Rightarrow x$$

Where the execution of "x" is preferable (eg. faster) than "b ; c". A good code generation algorithm should perform the mapping:

$$[\![A \; ; \; B \; ; \; C \; ; \; D]\!] \Rightarrow a \; ; \; x \; ; \; d$$

This can be compared to conventional peepholing. However, the pattern matching is being done on the intermediate code, via extra mappings, rather than on the assembly language itself. Something similar to this was done in an early version of LML [5].

The simple idea of linear usage of these mappings could easily be used; however it has an important defect, due to the order in which replacements are considered. To give a concrete example, there are five mappings, and each mapping has a weight (which is, typically, the time to execute the assembly language sequence):

$$[\![A]\!] \Rightarrow (a \; , \; 5) \qquad [\![B]\!] \Rightarrow (b \; , \; 10) \qquad [\![C]\!] \Rightarrow (c \; , \; 15)$$

$$[\![A \; ; \; B]\!] \Rightarrow (x \; , \; 10) \qquad [\![B \; ; \; C]\!] \Rightarrow (y \; , \; 10)$$

When translating the following sequence with a simple replacement algorithm, the code generated is sub-optimal to what is possible from the given definitions.

$$[\![A \; ; \; B \; ; \; C]\!] \quad \Rightarrow \quad (x \; , \; 10); [\![C]\!] \quad \Rightarrow \quad (x \; ; \; c \; , \; 25)$$

This is better than the macro expansion technique, that would give a cost of 30. Yet abandoning the left to right ordering, the following code can be generated:

$$[\![A \; ; \; B \; ; \; C]\!] \quad \Rightarrow \quad [\![A]\!]; (y \; , \; 5) \quad \Rightarrow \quad (a \; ; \; y \; , \; 15)$$

It can be clearly seen that a systematic method of choosing the best possible mappings should be found in order to achieve the ultimate objective of reasonable code generation. Simply scanning the stream for the longest matches will not necessarily result in the best code. Even some multi-pass conventional peepholers fall prey to this subtlety.

To accomplish the aim of picking the best sequence a dynamic programming algorithm can be used. The algorithm given here is a variation of a solution to the knapsack problem [8]. The principle difference here is that the ideal solution has the least rather than the greatest cost. The mappings from the simple example above are used to explain it.

The algorithm uses a (opcode * cost * code list) list. At the start the stack is empty:

Opcode	Cost	Code List	Comments
—	0	—	Empty stack.

Then the first opcode considered is A. The only mapping for this goes to $(a, 5)$. So the stack look like:

Opcode	Cost	Code List	Comments
A	5	a	Only one possibility.
—	0	—	Empty Stack.

Concerning the second mapping; there are two possibilities, mapping $[\![B]\!] \Rightarrow (b, 10)$, and mapping $[\![A ; B]\!] \Rightarrow (x, 10)$. The first possibility would give a cost of $5 + 10 = 15$. For the second possibility, the top opcode is retrieved from the stack, allowing A to be appended to B, and thus allowing $[\![A ; B]\!]$ to be applied to find $(x, 10)$ This second possibility gives a cost of $0 + 10 = 10$ (ie. cost one deep down the stack, plus the cost of $[\![A ; B]\!]$). This is the cheapest total, which mean the new stack becomes:

Opcode	Cost	Code List	Comments
B	10	x	Both possibilities have been considered.
A	5	a	Only one possibility.
—	0	—	Empty stack.

When considering the final opcode, there are two possible mappings for code generator: $[\![C]\!] \Rightarrow (c, 15)$ and $[\![B ; C]\!] \Rightarrow (y, 10)$. The first of these would give a cost of $10 + 15 = 25$. The second, by digging one deep down the stack (to find the extra needed opcode and cost) would give a cost of $5 + 10 = 15$. The second choice is used, and the stack therefore becomes:

Opcode	Cost	Code List	Comments
C	15	$a ; y$	Optimal sequence.
B	10	x	Both possibilities have been considered.
A	5	a	Only one possibility.
—	0	—	Empty stack.

This is how the optimal sequence is dynamically found, since the code list at the top is the optimal one. The algorithm would simply continue as explained for longer sequences, and would dig deeper down the stack to match longer patterns.

This algorithm is more expensive computationally than dominoing, but should be cheaper than applying a similar technique to map assembly language to assembly language. The time complexity of the algorithm is $O(kcn)$, where k is the maximum number of places mappings can look back, c is the maximum possible mappings from one intermediate construct, and n is the length of the sequence being translated. Since both k and c are small (in the implementation described later, both were always less that three), this runtime is reasonable.

It should be clear that the strength of the code generated using this method depends on the size of and number of multiple mapping supplied, therefore an example is not given. What is useful is that this algorithm gives the possibility of replacing recognised inefficient streams of (automatically generated) assembly language with shorter, more efficient ones.

Dynamic Domino Optimisations

The final algorithm captures the properties of both the improved domino scheme and the possibility of choosing from multiple definitions. The basic solution is to produce a cross product of the possible states and the dynamic streams. The dynamic output is treated like a thread of code, which has input and output states for each touching macro. There can only be one thread per stack state at each stage.

The algorithm looks into the state list as before to find viable assembly language sequences. For each of the possible mappings the algorithm again digs down into the stack if necessary, to find previous costs. The difference now is that dominoing has to be included. For each opcode, the algorithm stores:

- The opcode
- A list of (code list * cost * domino stack state)

The code for each item in the list is "optimal" for its particular stack state. So rather that there being one "optimal" code list for the code sequence for each opcode, there are now several. The considerations at each macro are now multiplied by the number of possible stack states available. The algorithm considers each viable code sequence by inserting a bridging domino if necessary, as previously done during normal domino code generation. The bridging dominos now have a cost and this cost must be included in the calculations. The improvement to simple dominoing can be included by simply building the code in reverse, because the inputs contain no wild card.

This algorithm gives a complexity value of $O(kcsn)$, where the new variable s is the number of possible stack states in domino optimisations, the other variables stand for the same as the simple dynamic case. Since all of k, c, s are small values, this again is a reasonable runtime value.

Observations and Conclusion

The complete algorithm has been successfully used to improve the quality of code created by a native code producing version of Edinburgh ML [4]. The code generator took a version of Cardelli's FAM, and produced 68000. The same number of stack states were used as in the early examples (ie. three stack state, plus an exit wild card). These states optimise operations that relied on using the argument stack. Only a minimal amount of multiple mappings from several intermediate instructions were used, concentrating on improving commonly used operations (like sequences containing **GetLocal** n) rather than exotic instruction sequences. Even though no attempt was made at register allocation (other than the allocation via the domino effect) performance was still found to be reasonable.

Comparisons between macro expansion and dynamic dominoing over a wide range of examples saw the execution time of the produced code drop by about 50%. The code size also dropped significantly. A further increase in quality would be possible with more complete mappings, possibly based on extensive profiling of the relative frequency of intermediate instruction usage.

The code produced by the augmented Edinburgh ML showed comparable execution speed with the production ML compilers PolyML [6] and Standard ML of New Jersey [2]. Edinburgh ML generally gave slightly favourable observed performance, however there are too many mitigating factors (for example different intermediate code generation strategies, the usage of different heap allocation and garbage collecting methods, possibly of arbitrary precision arithmetic, etc.) to draw any firm conclusions from this.

One advantage of the algorithm given here is the way it handles abstract objects. As no comparisons are done at the assembly language level, the code generator could pre-assemble commonly used intermediate mappings, and manipulate raw bit patterns rather than assembly language. The domino bridging function should also have this optimisation added. The assembler would still be needed to compute jumps etc. but this pass could be trivialised, resulting in a reduction in total execution time of the code generator.

The principle advantage of work presented in this paper is that because dynamic dominoing takes as its specification a derived form of macro expansion, prototype optimising code generators that produce reasonable code can be written quickly.

Acknowledgements

This paper is a version of part of my Honours thesis [4], completed while studying at Edinburgh University. I would like to thank my undergraduate supervisor Russell Green for all his help and encouragement. I would also like to thank both my girlfriend and my parents for proof reading this paper, and Kevin Mitchell (one of the original implementors of Edinburgh ML) and Dave Matthews (the implementor of PolyML) for several enlightening conversations on the topic of code generation.

Appendix

$$
\begin{array}{ll}
\langle \overbrace{s_1 \ldots s_n}^{n \text{ items}} \bullet s' \bullet S, M, \text{GetLocal } n \bullet C \rangle & \Rightarrow \langle s' \bullet \overbrace{s_1 \ldots s_n}^{n \text{ items}} \bullet s' \bullet S, M, C \rangle \\
\langle S, M, \text{MakeInt } n \bullet C \rangle & \Rightarrow \langle n \bullet S, M, C \rangle \\
\langle s \bullet s' \bullet S, M, \text{Add} \bullet C \rangle & \Rightarrow \langle s + s' \bullet S, M, C \rangle \\
\langle s \bullet s' \bullet S, M, \text{Mul} \bullet C \rangle & \Rightarrow \langle s * s' \bullet S, M, C \rangle \\
\langle s \bullet S, M, \text{Head} \bullet C \rangle & \Rightarrow \langle M(s) \bullet S, M, C \rangle
\end{array}
$$

Figure 5: Semantics of the Intermediate Language

$$
\begin{array}{ll}
\mathcal{A} [\![\text{ D }]\!] & = \text{d0} \\
\mathcal{A} [\![\ \#n \ ]\!] & = \#n \\
\mathcal{A} [\![\text{ A }]\!] & = \text{a0} \\
\mathcal{A} [\![\text{ (A) }]\!] & = \text{(a0)} \\
\mathcal{A} [\![\ n\text{(S)} \ ]\!] & = \langle n * 4 \rangle\text{(a5)} \\
\mathcal{A} [\![\text{ (S)+ }]\!] & = \text{(a5)+} \\
\mathcal{A} [\![\text{ -(S) }]\!] & = \text{-(a5)} \\
\\
\mathcal{T} [\![\textbf{ move a,b }]\!] & = \text{move.l } \mathcal{A} [\![\textbf{ a }]\!] \text{ , } \mathcal{A} [\![\textbf{ b }]\!] \\
\mathcal{T} [\![\textbf{ add a }]\!] & = \text{add.l } \mathcal{A} [\![\textbf{ a }]\!] \text{,d0} \\
\mathcal{T} [\![\textbf{ mul a }]\!] & = \text{muls } \mathcal{A} [\![\textbf{ a }]\!] \text{,d0}
\end{array}
$$

Figure 6: Translation of the Assembly Language to 68000

Bibliography

1. Alfred V. Aho, Ravi Sethi and Jeffrey D. Ullman. *Compilers: Principles, Techniques and Tools.* Addison-Westley, 1986.

2. Andrew W. Appel and David B. MacQueen. A Standard ML compiler. In *Functional Programming Languages and Computer Architecture*, pages 301–324. Springer-Verlag, 1987.

3. Luca Cardelli. The Functional Abstract Machine. *Polymorphism*, 1(1), 1983.

4. Andrew J. Gill. A Sun 3 Native Code Generator for Edinburgh ML. Honours thesis, Edinburgh University, May 1991.

5. T. Johnsson. Target Code Generation from G–Machine code. In *Workshop on Graph Reduction*, pages 119–159. Springer-Verlag, 1986.

6. David Matthews. Papers on PolyML. Technical report, Computer Laboratory, University of Cambridge, February 1989.

7. Simon Peyton-Jones. *The Implementation of Functional Programming Languages.* Prentice-Hall, 1987.

8. Robert Sedgewick. *Algorithms.* Addison Wesley, 2nd edition, 1988.

Evaluation Order Analysis for Lazy Data Structures

Carsten K. Gomard and Peter Sestoft
DIKU, Department of Computer Science, University of Copenhagen
Universitetsparken 1, DK-2100 Copenhagen Ø, Denmark
E-mail: gomard@diku.dk, sestoft@diku.dk

Abstract

We describe a method to statically infer evaluation order information for data structures in a typed lazy first order functional language. The evaluation order of subexpressions of an expression is described by two relations, depicted as arrows. One says "expression e_1 must be evaluated before e_2" (strongly precedes), the other says "if expression e_1 is evaluated at all, then it must be before e_2" or in other words "e_1 is not evaluated after e_2" (weakly precedes). Strongly precedes implies weakly precedes.

Evaluation order for a data structure is described by a *context*, or *evaluation order type*, which is the type of the data structure together with relations describing the order of evaluation of its components. For recursively defined types such as `natlist ::= Nil | Cons nat natlist`, only uniform descriptions are allowed: the recursive components (those of type `natlist`) must all have the same description.

The analyses work *backwards*: from the context of an expression we find the contexts of the free variables and the order in which the free variables are evaluated.

This work extends the work of Bloss and Hudak's "path analysis"[2] because the backwards approach allows analysis of data structures. The information obtained can for example be used to optimize the implementation of suspensions (or "thunks") in lazy languages as in [3].

1 Introduction

Previous work covers evaluation order analysis of lazy languages without data structures. For example, Bloss and Hudak analyse the expression

```
letrec f(x,y,z) = if x=0 then y else z
in     f(v+5,w,u+w)
```

and find that the variables `v` and `w` may be evaluated in the following orders: First `v`, then `w`; or first `v`, then `u`, then `w`, assuming that "+" evaluates its arguments from left to right [2]. This finding would be expressed by a set of paths, where a *path* is a finite sequence of variable names. The path set for the above example is {<v,w>, <v,u,w>}.

Bloss and Hudak's path analysis is a forwards analysis in which one concatenates the paths for argument expressions in the order in which the corresponding variables are used. Variables can occur at most once in a path: in a lazy language the argument expression bound to a variable is evaluated at most once.

Forwards analysis does not work in the presence of lazy data structures. The order of evaluation of `x` and `y` in `e` ≡ `(Pair x y)` depends on the context of expression `e`. Assume again that "+" evaluates its arguments from left to right. Now if the expression `e` ≡ `(Pair x y)` occurs in `(f e)` where `f z = (fst z) + (snd z)`, then `x` is evaluated before `y`. On the other hand, if `e` occurs in `(g e)` where `g z = (snd z) + (fst z)`, `y` would be evaluated before `x`.

We therefore suggest an analysis in which one works *backwards*: from the demand order on the result of an expression to its subexpressions, and from these to the variables occurring in the expression.

1.1 Evaluation order

The origin of evaluation order in a lazy functional program is the printer's demand on the result of the entire program. The printer's demand is *preorder* and *left to right.* The printer first obtains the weak head normal form to know which constructor to print, then recursively evaluates and prints the arguments to that constructor from left to right.

Example 1 Consider the data type `natlist` and the function `take` which computes a prefix of a given list:

```
natlist ::= Nil | Cons nat natlist
take : natlist × nat → natlist
take xs n = case xs of
              Nil       => Nil
              Cons y ys => case n=0 of
                             True  => Nil
                             False => Cons y (take ys (n-1))
```

where `take` has type `natlist × nat → natlist`. Assume that a call to `take` is to be evaluated and printed. In the `natlist` type, constructor `Cons` has arguments of types `nat` and `natlist`, of which the printer demands the `nat`-component before the `natlist` component. We shall denote this evaluation order type by $\mathtt{natlist}_{\mathtt{Cons}:1\rightarrow 2}$.

When the demand on `(take xs n)` is $\mathtt{natlist}_{\mathtt{Cons}:1\rightarrow 2}$, then this is also the demand on each of the `case` branches. This means that the value of variable `y` will be demanded before that of subexpression `(take ys (n-1))`; in particular, `y` will be demanded before `ys`. Moreover, the demand on `(take ys (n-1))` is also $\mathtt{natlist}_{\mathtt{Cons}:1\rightarrow 2}$, so `ys` is in the same context as `xs`.

From the evaluation order on `y` and `ys` we conclude that the demand on `xs`, which is being matched with `Cons y ys`, is $\mathtt{natlist}_{\mathtt{Cons}:1\rightarrow 2}$. □

Section 2 introduces a first order example language with lazy data structures. Section 3 introduces tools for describing evaluation order of subexpressions and data structures, so-called evaluation order types. Section 4 defines evaluation order in the example language and gives an evaluation order analysis. Section 5 presents several examples of evaluation order analysis. Section 6 discusses related work and Section 7 outlines topics for further study.

2 A first order example language

We shall use a simple example language to illustrate the evaluation order analysis. It is a lazy, simply typed, first order functional language with (directly or indirectly) recursive data types. Standard examples of (possibly) recursive data types are tuples, lists of naturals, lists of lists of naturals *etc.*

2.1 Syntax

A program consists of data type definitions, a set of recursive function definitions, and a program body.

program	::=	*typedef*$_1$ ... *typedef*$_n$ *letrec*
typedef	::=	*t* `::=` *summand*$_1$ "`|`" ... "`|`" *summand*$_n$
summand	::=	*C texp*$_1$ ... *texp*$_m$
texp	::=	`nat` | *t*
letrec	::=	`letrec` *def*$_1$ ... *def*$_n$ `in e`
def	::=	`f x`$_1$ ... `x`$_n$ `= e`
`e`	::=	`x` | `A e`$_1$ ... `e`$_n$ | *C* `e`$_1$ ... `e`$_n$ | `f e`$_1$ ... `e`$_n$ | `case e`$_0$ `of` *branch*$_1$ ... *branch*$_n$
branch	::=	*C* `x`$_1$ ... `x`$_m$ `=> e`

A type expression is either a *base type* or the name of a *data type*. A data type is a set of *summands*, each of which consists of a *constructor* and a list of type expressions. Note that data types may be recursive. All names of types, constructors, functions and variables must be distinct. The language is simply (monomorphically) typed and all expressions are assumed to be type correct, but we shall not give a formal type system here.

2.2 Informal semantics

Expressions are assumed to be evaluated or reduced towards weak head normal form (whnf) according to these rules:

A variable `x` is reduced to whnf by reducing the closure bound to the variable (if it is not already reduced to whnf), or by returning the whnf (if already reduced).

A base function application `A e`$_1$ ... `e`$_n$ is reduced to whnf by reducing the (base type) arguments `e`$_1$ ... `e`$_n$ to whnf from left to right, then applying the (base type) function denoted by `A`. The whnf of a base type expression is its value.

A constructor application *C* `e`$_1$ ... `e`$_n$ is reduced to whnf by making suspensions (*i.e.*, closures) for the arguments `e`$_1$ ... `e`$_n$, and returning a package consisting of the constructor and these closures.

An application `f e`$_1$ ... `e`$_n$ of a function defined by `f x`$_1$ ... `x`$_n$ = `e` is reduced to whnf as follows. First suspensions are made for the arguments `e`$_1$ ... `e`$_n$. Then these are bound to the formal parameters $\mathtt{x}_1 \ldots \mathtt{x}_n$, and the body $\mathtt{e}$ of $\mathtt{f}$ is reduced to whnf.

A **case** expression **case** $\mathtt{e}_0$ **of** *branch*$_1$ ... *branch*$_n$ is reduced to whnf as follows. First $\mathtt{e}_0$ is reduced to a whnf of form $(C_i\ \mathtt{u}_1 \ldots \mathtt{u}_{c(i)})$, selecting the i'th case branch $C_i\ \mathtt{x}_{i1} \ldots \mathtt{x}_{ic(i)}$ `=>` $\mathtt{e}_i$. Then the suspensions $\mathtt{u}_1 \ldots \mathtt{u}_{c(i)}$ are bound to the formal parameters $\mathtt{x}_{i1} \ldots \mathtt{x}_{ic(i)}$, and the right hand side $\mathtt{e}_i$ is reduced to whnf.

Thus we assume a very pure lazy evaluation or reduction strategy. Namely, we assume the language is evaluated non-speculatively, and sequentially "on a single processor".

3 Describing evaluation order

In any particular evaluation of a lazy program, the subexpressions of the program will be evaluated to *weak head normal form* (abbreviated *whnf*) in some order, ultimately determined by the printer's demand for a result to print. The precise order cannot be inferred unless one has the program's input data available, so that the program can be run. Our goal is to describe *approximately* the order of evaluation of subexpressions for all possible evaluations of the program, independently of its concrete input data. We will give this approximate description as a relation on the *subexpression occurrences* in the program.

This section introduces tools for describing the evaluation order of subexpressions as well as of substructures of data structures.

3.1 Occurrences

An *occurrence* in an expression $\mathtt{e}$ is a finite sequence of indexes, which are natural numbers. An occurrence p is used to point out a subexpression of $\mathtt{e}$ which we will denote by $\mathtt{e}[p]$. The empty sequence $p = \varepsilon$ labels the entire expression $\mathtt{e}$, the occurrence $p = [1]$ labels the first subexpression *etc.* More formally, we have $\mathtt{e}[\varepsilon] \equiv \mathtt{e}$, and for $\mathtt{e} \equiv (\mathtt{op}\ \mathtt{e}_1 \ldots \mathtt{e}_i \ldots \mathtt{e}_n)$, we have $\mathtt{e}[i.p] \equiv \mathtt{e}_i[p]$. Here $\equiv$ denotes syntactical identity. In examples we shall be less formal and use integers for labels instead of sequences of integers. We will sometimes use an integer i when we mean a sequence $[i]$ of length one. We shall also talk about "an expression" when we really mean "the subexpression at occurrence p".

3.2 Evaluation order relations

An *evaluation order relation (eor)* on the finite set D is a pair $r = (r_s, r_w)$ of reflexive relations on D for which $r_s \subseteq r_w$. Thus the set $Eor(D)$ of evaluation order relations on D is

$$Eor(D) = \{ (r_s, r_w) \mid I_D \subseteq r_s \subseteq r_w \subseteq D^2 \}$$

where $I_D = \{ (p,p) \mid p \in D \}$ is the identity relation on D. We order the set $Eor(D)$ of eor's on D by componentwise reverse set inclusion, so

$$r_1 \leq r_2 \text{ if and only if } r_{1s} \supseteq r_{2s} \text{ and } r_{1w} \supseteq r_{2w}$$

With this ordering $Eor(D)$ is a lattice. The join operation or least upper bound $\sqcup$ is componentwise set intersection. Since the lattice has finite height it is trivially complete. The least element of the lattice is the complete relation $\bot_{Eor(D)} = (r_s, r_w) = (D^2, D^2)$ in which all occurrences are related by r_s (and hence by r_w).

For $r = (r_s, r_w)$ we shall write the relation r_s as $\xrightarrow{r}$ and the relation r_w as $\overset{r}{\dashrightarrow}$. The relation r_s (or $\xrightarrow{r}$) is called *strongly precedes* and r_w (or $\overset{r}{\dashrightarrow}$) is called *weakly precedes*. The inverse relations r_s^{-1} and r_w^{-1} are written as reversed arrows.

When clear from the context we will leave out the superscript r on arrows. The lattice $Eor\{1, 2\}$ of evaluation order relations on the two-element set $\{1, 2\}$ is shown in Figure 1 using the arrow notation.

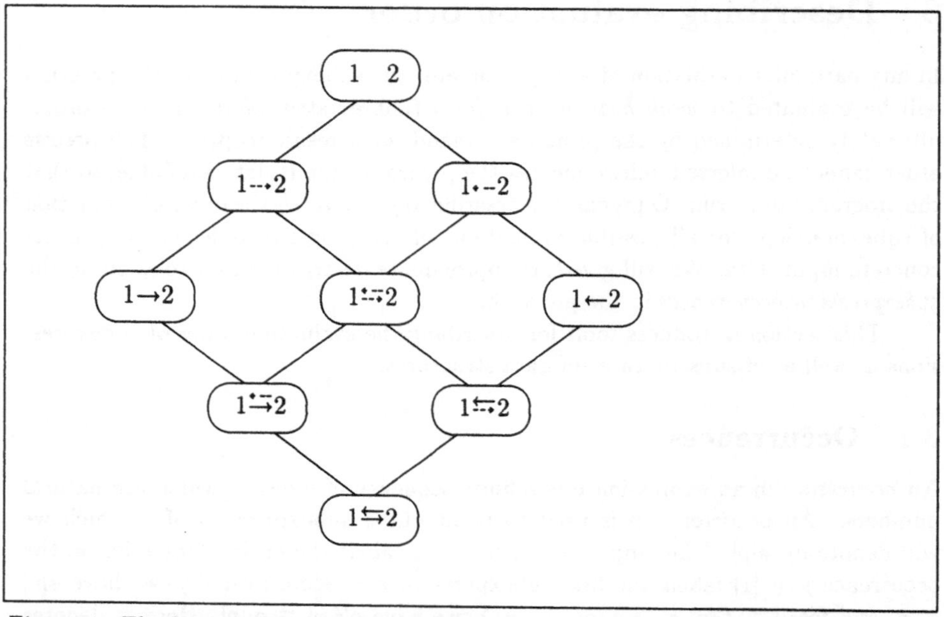

Figure 1: The lattice of two-point evaluation order relations

3.2.1 Evaluation order

We study the order in which expressions reach their whnf's (as opposed to the order in which they are demanded, or their evaluation initiated). Evaluation order relations are interpreted as follows. Let e_1 and e_2 be two subexpression occurrences.

The assertion $e_1 \rightarrow e_2$ means: if e_2 is evaluated at all, then e_1 has been evaluated *before* e_2. Here and elsewhere, "before" means "no later than". Correspondingly, "after" means "strictly later than".

The assertion $e_1 \dashrightarrow e_2$ means: either e_1 is not evaluated at all, or it is evaluated before e_2. In other words: e_1 is *not* evaluated after e_2.

The following special cases are particularly interesting. If we have $e_1 \dashrightarrow e_2$ as well as the converse $e_2 \dashrightarrow e_1$, then at most one of the subexpressions can be evaluated. If in addition $e_1 \rightarrow e_2$, then at most e_1 can be evaluated. If $e_1 \rightarrow e_2$ and $e_2 \rightarrow e_1$ and e_1 and e_2 are *distinct*, then none of them can be evaluated.

Example 2 Consider the program copy where we have superscripted expressions with labels.

```
copy xs = (case xs⁶ of
             Nil       => Nil⁵
             Cons y ys => (Cons y¹ (copy ys²)³)⁴
          )⁷
```

To express that the root expression (labelled 6) is evaluated before each of the branches, we write $6 \rightarrow 5$ and $6 \rightarrow 4$. To express that it must reach a whnf before the entire **case** expression does, we write $6 \rightarrow 7$. That the branches are mutually exclusive is expressed by $4 \mathrel{\substack{\dashleftarrow \\ \dashrightarrow}} 5$. Note that without knowing the context for an application (copy **xs**) of copy we are unable to relate, say, 1 and 3. □

3.2.2 Properties of evaluation order relations

Here we shall state some properties of evaluation order relations. Some properties follow from the intuitive interpretations given above and hold true for all evaluation order relations.

- Subrelation: If $e_1 \rightarrow e_2$, then $e_1 \dashrightarrow e_2$.
- Transitivity of $\rightarrow$: If $e_1 \rightarrow e_2$ and $e_2 \rightarrow e_3$, then $e_1 \rightarrow e_3$.
- Weak transitivity: If $e_1 \dashrightarrow e_2$ and $e_2 \rightarrow e_3$, then $e_1 \dashrightarrow e_3$. It is possible to have $e_1 \rightarrow e_2$ and $e_2 \dashrightarrow e_3$, and yet not $e_1 \dashrightarrow e_3$ (consider the case where e_3 is evaluated before e_1, and e_2 is never evaluated). Thus $\dashrightarrow$ is not transitive.

Other properties hold only because of our assumptions about the implementation of the lazy example language made in Section 2.2. Namely, we assumed it is evaluated non-speculatively, and sequentially "on a single processor".

It follows from non-speculative evaluation that the evaluation of subexpression e' of e will not be initiated (and not reach whnf) before evaluation of e is initiated. In particular, if evaluation of e is never initiated, then evaluation of e' is not initiated either.

It follows from sequential evaluation that for disjoint expressions e_1 and e_2, expression e_1 cannot reach its whnf after evaluation of e_2 is initiated but before it reaches whnf.

- Context: Assume e_1 and e_2 are disjoint expressions. If $e_1 \rightarrow e_2$, then it holds also that $e_1 \rightarrow e_2'$ for all subexpressions e_2' of e_2. Similarly, if $e_1 \dashrightarrow e_2$, then it holds also that $e_1 \dashrightarrow e_2'$.

  To prove the $\rightarrow$ case, assume that e_1 reaches its whnf before e_2 does. From disjointness and sequentiality it follows that e_1 reaches its whnf before evaluation of e_2 is initiated, but by non-speculative evaluation this is also before evaluation of e_2' (is initiated and) reaches its whnf.

  To prove the $\dashrightarrow$ case, we prove the contrapositive and assume that e_1 reaches its whnf only after e_2' reaches its whnf. By non-speculative evaluation this is after evaluation of e_2 is initiated, and by disjointness and sequentiality therefore also after e_2 reaches its whnf.

- Alternatives: Assume $\mathbf{e}_1$ and $\mathbf{e}_2$ are disjoint expressions and alternatives, that is, if evaluation of one is ever initiated, then evaluation of the other will never be initiated. Then $\mathbf{e}_1' \overset{\bullet -}{\dashrightarrow} \mathbf{e}_2'$ for all subexpressions $\mathbf{e}_1'$ of $\mathbf{e}_1$ and $\mathbf{e}_2'$ of $\mathbf{e}_2$.

  Assume without loss of generality that evaluation of $\mathbf{e}_1$ is never initiated, and let $\mathbf{e}_1'$ be a subexpression of $\mathbf{e}_1$. Then by non-speculative evaluation, evaluation of $\mathbf{e}_1'$ is never initiated and therefore never reaches whnf, so $\mathbf{e}_1' \overset{\bullet -}{\dashrightarrow} \mathbf{e}'$ for all expressions $\mathbf{e}'$, in particular for all subexpressions $\mathbf{e}_2'$.

3.2.3 Argument evaluation order

The order in which a function `f` evaluates its arguments is described by an ***argument evaluation order relation (argument eor)***, and is an evaluation order relation on the set $D = \{ \varepsilon, 1, \ldots, n \}$ of occurrences. Here ε labels the entire function application (`f` $\mathbf{e}_1$ ... $\mathbf{e}_n$), and i labels the i'th argument position. To relate evaluations of the arguments $\mathbf{e}_i$, it relates *first* uses of the corresponding variables $\mathbf{x}_i$. Thus the argument eor $1 \rightarrow 2$ does not mean that variable $\mathbf{x}_1$ is not used after variable $\mathbf{x}_2$ in the body of `f`; it means that the first use of $\mathbf{x}_1$ precedes the first use of $\mathbf{x}_2$. In a lazy language this means that argument $\mathbf{e}_1$ is evaluated (once) before argument $\mathbf{e}_2$. The argument eor $1 \rightarrow \varepsilon$ would mean that the first argument will evaluate to a whnf before the function application does: the function is *strict* in the first argument.

In summary, to describe argument evaluation order and strictness of an n-argument function `f` $\mathbf{x}_1$ ... $\mathbf{x}_n$ `=` $\mathbf{e}$ we use an element of $Aeor_\varepsilon(n)$ where

$$Aeor_\varepsilon(n) = Eor\{ \varepsilon, 1, \ldots, n \}.$$

When we are not interested in strictness information, we exclude ε from the set of possible occurrences:

$$Aeor(n) = Eor\{ 1, \ldots, n \}.$$

The ε-free relations are used when analysing constructor contexts as explained in Section 3.3 below. Section 4.1 below describes how to compute the argument eor for a function from an evaluation order relation on the function body.

3.2.4 Application contexts

An argument evaluation order relation provides only a "top level" description of the evaluation order in a function application (`f` $\mathbf{e}_1$ ... $\mathbf{e}_n$): the evaluation order to whnf of the n argument expressions. We would also like to know how the function consumes the value of each individual argument expression $\mathbf{e}_i$. This is expressed by the context or evaluation order type of $\mathbf{e}_i$.

We define an *application context* to be a pair $(a,(\tau_1,\ldots,\tau_m))$ of a (top level) argument eor a and a tuple $(\tau_1,\ldots,\tau_m)$ of argument contexts. The argument contexts τ_i are evaluation order types.

We have yet to define evaluation order types, but for now let $Eot(t)$ denote the set of evaluation order types over type t. Let function `f` have type $t_1 \times \ldots \times t_n \rightarrow t$. The set $Actx(t_1 \ldots t_m)$ of possible application contexts is defined as follows:

$$Actx(t_1 \ldots t_m) = Aeor_\varepsilon(m) \times \prod_{j=1}^{m} Eot(t_j)$$

Assuming that $Eot(t_j)$ is a lattice of finite height for each j, also $Actx(t_1 \ldots t_m)$ can be organized as a lattice of finite height.

3.3 Evaluation order types

An evaluation order type (eot) describes the evaluation order of the components of a value. Evaluation order types over base types such as **nat** are trivial, because **nat** values are atomic. There is only one evaluation order relation $\tau_b = \varepsilon{\rightarrow}\varepsilon \in \{ \varepsilon{\rightarrow}\varepsilon \} = Eor\{\varepsilon\} = Aeor_\varepsilon(0) = Actx()$.

Evaluation order types over composite values, that is, values of a data type t, are more interesting. We shall first discuss evaluation order types for non-recursive data types, then consider one example of a recursive data type, `natlist`. To avoid excessive technicalities we do not consider the general case of recursive types in this paper.

3.3.1 Constructor contexts

Data types involve constructors, so to introduce evaluation order types, one must understand how to represent the evaluation order of constructors' arguments. The evaluation order of arguments to a constructor application such as $(C\ \mathbf{e}_1 \ldots \mathbf{e}_m)$ is determined by the context of the application, *not* by the constructor C itself.

For a constructor C of type $t_1 \times \ldots \times t_m \rightarrow t$ and arity m, a consumer function will have type $t_1 \times \ldots \times t_m \rightarrow t'$ and arity m. As seen in the preceding section, such functions can be described as application contexts in the lattice $Actx(t_1 \ldots t_m)$.

However, for constructors we do not consider strictness, so constructor contexts are elements of $Cctx(t_1 \ldots t_m)$ where

$$Cctx(t_1 \ldots t_m) = Aeor(m) \times \prod_{j=1}^{m} Eot(t_j)$$

3.3.2 Non-recursive data types

For a given (non-recursive) data type t, we can finally define an *evaluation order type (eot)* to be a tuple of constructor contexts, one for each constructor. Thus the set $Eot(t)$ of evaluation order types is:

$$\begin{aligned} Eot(\mathbf{nat}) &= \{ \tau_b \} \\ Eot(t) &= \prod_{i=1}^{n} Cctx(t_{i1} \ldots t_{ic(i)}) \\ &\quad \text{where } t ::= C_1\ t_{11} \ldots t_{1c(1)} \mid \ldots \mid C_n\ t_{n1} \ldots t_{nc(n)} \end{aligned}$$

Unfolding this definition for a given non-recursive data type t yields a finite product of *Aeor*'s, which in turn are just *Eor*'s. Thus the ordering inherited from the component lattices $Eor(D)$ makes the set $Eot(t)$ into a complete lattice of finite height. Its least element is denoted by $\bot_{Eot(t)}$.

3.3.3 Recursive data types

For a recursive data type such as `natlist ::= Nil | Cons nat natlist`, we require *uniformity* in the recursive components. Thus evaluation order information for all the elements of a list are identified. As a consequence, the analysis can collect only information which is valid for all elements of a list.

Space does not permit inclusion of the details on how to define and manipulate uniform evaluation order types (two different solutions can be found in the authors' theses [5] [7]). The general idea is to follow the scheme for non-recursive types, but ignore the recursive structure:

$$\begin{aligned} Eot(\texttt{natlist}) &= Cctx() \times Cctx(\texttt{nat natlist}) \\ &= Aeor(0) \times Aeor(2) \end{aligned}$$

Since $Aeor(0)$ has only one element, the product $Aeor(0) \times Aeor(2)$ is isomorphic to $Aeor(2)$, which is $Eor\{1,2\}$. Thus evaluation order types over **natlist** correspond to evaluation order relations r on $\{ 1, 2 \}$. As in the introduction we shall write $\texttt{natlist}_{\texttt{Cons}:r}$ for these evaluation order types.

For example, $\texttt{natlist}_{\texttt{Cons}:1\rightarrow 2}$ is the context induced by the printer, which evaluates the head before the tail. Similarly, $\texttt{natlist}_{\texttt{Cons}:1 \overset{\leftarrow}{\dashrightarrow} 2}$ is a context which will ignore all heads (*i.e.*, elements) of the list. Section 5 gives more examples.

3.4 Combining evaluation order relations

The evaluation order relation r on a composite expression $\mathbf{e} \equiv (\mathtt{op}\ \mathbf{e}_1\ \ldots\ \mathbf{e}_n)$ is expressible as a combination of the evaluation order relations $r_1 \ldots r_n$ on each of its components $\mathbf{e}_1 \ldots \mathbf{e}_n$. The way $r_1 \ldots r_n$ are combined depends on the operator **op**, and on the evaluation order of the arguments given by $a \in Aeor_\varepsilon(n)$ or $a \in Aeor(n)$.

Let $a \in Aeor_\varepsilon(n)$ (or $Aeor(n)$) be an argument evaluation order relation, and $r_i \in Eor(D_i)$ be evaluation order relations, $i = 1, \ldots, n$. Then $r = a(r_1, \ldots, r_n)$ is an evaluation order relation in $Eor(\{\varepsilon\} \cup \{\ i : p | p \in D_i, 1 \le i \le n\})$, called the *a-combination* of $r_1, \ldots, r_n$. It is generated from the following definitions and from the general eor properties transitivity, context rule, *etc.* listed in Section 3.2.2.

$$\begin{array}{ll} i{:}p \overset{r}{\longrightarrow} i{:}q & \text{if } p \overset{r_i}{\longrightarrow} q \\ i{:}p \overset{r}{\dashrightarrow} i{:}q & \text{if } p \overset{r_i}{\dashrightarrow} q \\ i \overset{r}{\longrightarrow} j & \text{if } i \overset{a}{\longrightarrow} j \\ i \overset{r}{\dashrightarrow} j & \text{if } i \overset{a}{\dashrightarrow} j \end{array}$$

In Section 4.2 below we list the argument eor's appropriate for describing evaluation order of composite expressions in our example language.

4 Evaluation order analysis

The purpose of evaluation order analysis is to find evaluation order information about a given program `letrec ... in` $\mathbf{e}_0$. We represent this information as an *evaluation order description* ζ such that for every function **f** of type $t_1 \times \ldots \times t_n \rightarrow t$ in the program, $\zeta\mathtt{f}$ has type $Eot(t) \rightarrow Actx(t_1\ \ldots\ t_n)$, and function $\zeta\mathtt{f}$ maps the context τ of an application (`f` e_1 ... e_n) to an application context $(a, (\tau_1, \ldots, \tau_n))$ for `f`.

Below we define two analysis functions to compute this application context. Function $\mathcal{T}$ computes the τ_i, and $\mathcal{R}$ is used when computing the a. Actually, $\mathcal{R}$ computes an eor r on the body of `f`, and another analysis function $\mathcal{A}_\varepsilon$ extracts the argument eor a from r.

4.1 Computing argument evaluation order

The function $\mathcal{A}_\varepsilon$ constructs an argument eor a for function `f` $x_1 \ldots x_n$ `=` `e` from an eor r on the body `e` by analysing all occurrences of the variables $x_1 \ldots x_n$ (and ε) in `e`, so that $a = \mathcal{A}_\varepsilon(e,(x_1 \ldots x_n),r) \in Eor\{\varepsilon, 1, \ldots, n\}$. Note that this may include strictness information such as $x_1 \rightarrow \varepsilon$.

To define $\mathcal{A}_\varepsilon$, we let the symbol x^j range over occurrences of `x`, and let ε^j denote just ε. We define the argument eor $a = \mathcal{A}_\varepsilon(e,(x_1 \ldots x_n),r)$ as follows:

$$p \xrightarrow{a} q \text{ if } \forall q^i.\exists p^j.p^j \xrightarrow{r} q^i$$

$$p \overset{a}{\dashrightarrow} q \text{ if } \forall q^i.((\forall p^j.p^j \overset{r}{\dashrightarrow} q^i) \vee (\exists p^j.p^j \xrightarrow{r} q^i))$$

A similar analysis function $\mathcal{A}$ finds the argument eor a on pattern variables $x_1 \ldots x_n$ occurring in the right hand side `e` of a case branch C $x_1 \ldots x_n$ `=>` `e`. This is just $\mathcal{A}$ restricted to non-ε occurrences.

Example 3 Consider the program fragment

```
f x y z = (... x¹ ... y² ... x³ ...)⁴
```

Assume the eor on the function body is $1 \rightarrow 2$, $2 \rightarrow 3$, and $2 \rightarrow 4$. Then the argument eor a computed by function $\mathcal{A}_\varepsilon$ is $x \xrightarrow{a} y$, $x \xrightarrow{a} z$, $y \xrightarrow{a} z$, $z \overset{a}{\dashrightarrow} x$, $z \overset{a}{\dashrightarrow} y$, $x \xrightarrow{a} \varepsilon$, $y \xrightarrow{a} \varepsilon$, $\varepsilon \xrightarrow{a} z$, $z \overset{a}{\dashrightarrow} \varepsilon$. □

4.2 Evaluation order in the example language

The evaluation order of a syntactic construct is characterized by an argument eor a which shows how to combine the eor's of subexpressions into an eor for the entire construct. These combiners reflect the informal evaluation rules listed in Section 2.2. Let r_i be an evaluation order relation on subexpression e_i.

The combined eor for $e \equiv$ (`A` $e_1 \ldots e_n$) is $R_{An}(r_1, \ldots, r_n)$, where R_{An} contains $i \rightarrow \varepsilon$ for $i = 1, \ldots, n$, and $i \rightarrow j$ for $1 \leq i < j \leq n$.

The combined eor for $e \equiv (C_i\ e_1 \ldots e_m)$ is $a_i(r_1, \ldots, r_m)$ where a_i is the argument eor associated with constructor C_i in the context τ of the constructor application.

The combined eor for $e \equiv$ (`f` $e_1 \ldots e_n$) is $a_f(r_1, \ldots, r_n)$ where a_f is the argument eor for `f` (in the given context τ), found using $\zeta f \tau$.

The combined eor for $e \equiv$ `case` e_0 `of Nil =>` e_1 `Cons x xs =>` e_2 is $R_{case}(r_0, r_1, r_2)$, where $R_{case} = \{ 0 \rightarrow \varepsilon, 0 \rightarrow 1, 0 \rightarrow 2, 1 \dashrightarrow \varepsilon, 2 \dashrightarrow \varepsilon, 1 \overset{\cdot}{\dashrightarrow} 2\}$. If the entire `case` expression or any of the branches are evaluated then the root expression e_1 has indeed been evaluated first. None of the branches is evaluated *after* the full expression has been evaluated. Furthermore, the two branches are *alternatives*. None is evaluated after the other.

Note the need for the ζ map in the analysis of function application.

4.3 Computing variable contexts

The *context analysis function* $\mathcal{T}$ finds the context for a variable y (of type t_v) in an expression e (of type t) in context τ, assuming a function description ζ. Letting $\mathrm{Var}(t_v)$ denote the set of variables of type t_v, we have $\mathcal{T}[\![\,\mathtt{e}\,]\!]\zeta$: $Eot(t) \to \mathrm{Var}(t_v) \to Eot(t_v)$. The analysis function is defined by

$$
\begin{array}{lll}
\mathcal{T}[\![\,\mathtt{x}\,]\!]\zeta\tau\mathtt{y} & = \tau & \text{if } \mathtt{x} = \mathtt{y} \\
 & = \bot_{Eot(t)} & \text{otherwise} \\
\mathcal{T}[\![\,\mathtt{A}\ \mathtt{e}_1\ \ldots\ \mathtt{e}_n\,]\!]\zeta\tau\mathtt{y} & = \bigsqcup_{i=1}^{n} \mathcal{T}[\![\,\mathtt{e}_i\,]\!]\zeta\tau\mathtt{y} & \\
\mathcal{T}[\![\,\mathtt{Nil}\,]\!]\zeta\tau\mathtt{y} & = \bot_{Eot(t)} & \\
\mathcal{T}[\![\,\mathtt{Cons}\ \mathtt{e}_1\ \mathtt{e}_2\,]\!]\zeta\tau\mathtt{y} & = \mathcal{T}[\![\,\mathtt{e}_1\,]\!]\zeta\tau_b\mathtt{y} \sqcup \mathcal{T}[\![\,\mathtt{e}_2\,]\!]\zeta\tau\mathtt{y} & \\
\mathcal{T}[\![\,\mathtt{f}\ \mathtt{e}_1\ \ldots\ \mathtt{e}_n\,]\!]\zeta\tau\mathtt{y} & = \bigsqcup_{i=1}^{n} \mathcal{T}[\![\,\mathtt{e}_i\,]\!]\zeta\tau_i\mathtt{y} & \\
 & \text{where } (a_{\mathtt{f}}, (\tau_1,\ldots,\tau_n)) = \zeta\mathtt{f}\tau &
\end{array}
$$

$$
\mathcal{T}\left[\!\!\left[\begin{array}{l}\mathtt{case}\ \mathtt{e}_0\ \mathtt{of} \\ \quad \mathtt{Nil} \qquad\quad \mathtt{=>e}_1 \\ \quad \mathtt{Cons}\ \mathtt{x}_1\ \mathtt{x}_2\mathtt{=>e}_2\end{array}\right]\!\!\right]\zeta\tau\mathtt{y} = \mathcal{T}[\![\,\mathtt{e}_0\,]\!]\zeta\tau_0\mathtt{y} \sqcup \mathcal{T}[\![\,\mathtt{e}_1\,]\!]\zeta\tau\mathtt{y} \sqcup \mathcal{T}[\![\,\mathtt{e}_2\,]\!]\zeta\tau\mathtt{y}
$$

$$
\begin{array}{lll}
\text{where } \tau_0 & = & \tau_2 \sqcup \tau_{22} \\
\tau_2 & = & \mathcal{A}(\mathtt{e}_2,(\mathtt{x}_1,\mathtt{x}_2),r_2) \\
\tau_{22} & = & \mathcal{T}[\![\,\mathtt{e}_2\,]\!]\zeta\tau\mathtt{x}_2 \\
r_2 & = & \mathcal{R}[\![\,\mathtt{e}_2\,]\!]\zeta\tau
\end{array}
$$

Explanation: If x and y are the same variable, then an occurrence of x contributes to the context of y, otherwise it does not.

The first argument of a `Cons` must be of type `nat` and so is in context τ_b; the second argument has the same context τ as the entire `Cons` expression (by uniformity).

For a function application, the argument contexts must first be found using ζ, then the argument expressions are analysed in these contexts.

To find the context of y in a **case** expression we must analyse $\mathtt{e}_0$ in the context τ_0 found from the branches (computed using $\mathcal{R}$, defined below). The two branches are analysed in the same context as the entire **case** expression. The context τ_0 of $\mathtt{e}_0$ is found as the least upper bound of the argument eor τ_2 for the pattern variables $\mathtt{x}_1$ and $\mathtt{x}_2$, and the context τ_{22} of $\mathtt{x}_2$ in $\mathtt{e}_2$. (We take the least upper bound to get a uniform context τ_0. The argument eor τ_2 doubles as evaluation order type because we work with the restricted case of `natlist`, see Section 3.3.3). To find τ_2 we need the evaluation order relation r_2 on the second case branch.

4.4 Computing evaluation order relations

The *evaluation order analysis* function $\mathcal{R}$ finds an eor $r = \mathcal{R}[\![\,\mathtt{e}\,]\!]\zeta\tau$ on expression e in context τ, assuming a function description ζ. For an expression e of type t whose set of occurrences is D, $\mathcal{R}[\![\,\mathtt{e}\,]\!]\zeta$: $Eot(t) \to Eor(D)$. The analysis functions is defined by

$$
\begin{aligned}
&\mathcal{R}[\![\mathtt{x}]\!]\zeta\tau && = \varepsilon \rightarrow \varepsilon \\
&\mathcal{R}[\![\mathtt{A}\ \mathtt{e}_1\ \ldots\ \mathtt{e}_n]\!]\zeta\tau && = R_{A_n}(\mathcal{R}[\![\mathtt{e}_1]\!]\zeta\tau, \ldots, \mathcal{R}[\![\mathtt{e}_n]\!]\zeta\tau) \\
&\mathcal{R}[\![\mathtt{Nil}]\!]\zeta\tau && = \varepsilon \rightarrow \varepsilon \\
&\mathcal{R}[\![\mathtt{Cons}\ \mathtt{e}_1\ \mathtt{e}_2]\!]\zeta\tau && = \tau(\mathcal{R}[\![\mathtt{e}_1]\!]\zeta\tau_b, \mathcal{R}[\![\mathtt{e}_2]\!]\zeta\tau) \\
&\mathcal{R}[\![\mathtt{f}\ \mathtt{e}_1\ \ldots\ \mathtt{e}_n]\!]\zeta\tau && = a_{\mathtt{f}}(\mathcal{R}[\![\mathtt{e}_1]\!]\zeta\tau_1, \ldots, \mathcal{R}[\![\mathtt{e}_n]\!]\zeta\tau_n) \\
& && \quad \text{where } (a_{\mathtt{f}}, (\tau_1, \ldots, \tau_n)) = \zeta\mathtt{f}\tau
\end{aligned}
$$

$$
\mathcal{R}\left[\!\!\left[\begin{array}{l}\mathtt{case}\ \mathtt{e}_0\ \mathtt{of} \\ \quad \mathtt{Nil} \qquad\quad \mathtt{=>e}_1 \\ \quad \mathtt{Cons}\ \mathtt{x}_1\ \mathtt{x}_2\mathtt{=>e}_2\end{array}\right]\!\!\right]\zeta\tau = R_{\mathtt{case}}(r_0, r_1, r_2)
$$

$$
\begin{aligned}
\text{where } r_0 &= \mathcal{R}[\![\mathtt{e}_0]\!]\zeta\tau_0 \\
\tau_0 &= \tau_2 \sqcup \tau_{22} \\
\tau_2 &= \mathcal{A}(\mathtt{e}_2, (\mathtt{x}_1, \mathtt{x}_2), r_2) \\
\tau_{22} &= \mathcal{T}[\![\mathtt{e}_2]\!]\zeta\tau\mathtt{x}_2 \\
r_i &= \mathcal{R}[\![\mathtt{e}_i]\!]\zeta\tau \qquad \text{for } i = 1, 2
\end{aligned}
$$

An expression which is a variable occurrence has only one label, ε, and therefore the only possible eor is $\varepsilon \rightarrow \varepsilon$.

The rest of the equations should be self-explanatory after Section 4.2. The **case** equation is very similar to that in function $\mathcal{T}$ above.

Example 4 For an example, consider again the copy function from Example 2.

```
copy xs = (case xs⁶ of
              Nil        => Nil⁵
              Cons y ys => (Cons y¹ (copy ys²)³)⁴
          )⁷
```

First we note that in the argument eor, $\mathtt{xs} \xrightarrow{a} \varepsilon$ because $6 \rightarrow 7$ in the function body.

Next assume there is a call (copy xs) in the (uniform) context $\tau = \mathtt{natlist}_{\mathtt{Cons}:1\rightarrow 2}$. This context induces $1 \rightarrow 3$, and by the context rule $1 \rightarrow 2$. Thus $\mathtt{y} \xrightarrow{a} \mathtt{ys}$ in the Cons branch. By uniformity, also $(\mathtt{copy}\ \mathtt{ys}^2)^3$ is in context $\mathtt{natlist}_{\mathtt{Cons}:1\rightarrow 2}$, so the context of ys is the same as that of xs. Hence the description (ζ copy) should map the context $\mathtt{natlist}_{\mathtt{Cons}:1\rightarrow 2}$ for the application to the context $\mathtt{natlist}_{\mathtt{Cons}:1\rightarrow 2}$ for xs. The notation

$$\mathtt{copy} : \{\ \mathtt{xs} \xrightarrow{a} \varepsilon\ \},\ \mathtt{natlist}_{\mathtt{Cons}:1\rightarrow 2} \rightarrow \mathtt{natlist}_{\mathtt{Cons}:1\rightarrow 2}$$

is used to summarize these findings about copy. □

4.5 Doing evaluation order analysis

In the analysis we seek the least solution ζ to the simultaneous equations

$$
\begin{aligned}
\zeta\mathtt{f}\tau = (a, (\tau_1, \ldots, \tau_n)) \\
\text{where } a &= \mathcal{A}_{\varepsilon}(\mathtt{e}, (\mathtt{x}_1, \ldots, \mathtt{x}_n), r) \\
\tau_i &= \mathcal{T}[\![\mathtt{e}]\!]\zeta\tau\mathtt{x}_i \qquad \text{for } i = 1, \ldots, n \\
r &= \mathcal{R}[\![\mathtt{e}]\!]\zeta\tau \\
\text{and } & \ \mathtt{f}\ \mathtt{x}_1 \ldots \mathtt{x}_n = \mathtt{e} \text{ in the program has type } \mathtt{f} : t_1 \times \ldots \times t_n \rightarrow t
\end{aligned}
$$

To analyse a given program `letrec ...` in e_0 where the goal expression e_0 has type t_0, we start by finding the evaluation order type τ_0 expressing the printer's order of demand on values of type t_0. If t_0 is a base type, then this evaluation order type is the trivial τ_b. If t_0 is **natlist**, then τ_0 is represented as the argument evaluation order relation $1 \rightarrow 2$ as mentioned in Section 3.3.3. For other data types, τ_0 can be expressed similarly, reflecting that the printer evaluates and prints all data structures in preorder and from left to right.

5 Examples of evaluation order analysis

In this section we will show the results of applying our analysis to some small programs.

```
length : natlist → nat
length xs = case xs of
                 Nil        => 0
                 Cons y ys  => 1 + (length ys)
```

$$\texttt{length} : \texttt{xs} \xrightarrow{a} \varepsilon,\ \texttt{natlist}_{\texttt{Cons}:1 \leftrightarrows 2} \rightarrow \texttt{nat}$$

The evaluation order relation $1 \leftrightarrows 2$ on the components of **Cons** means that the first component **y** is never evaluated. This was one of the special cases mentioned in Section 3.3.3. It is also found that `length xs` is strict in `xs`.

```
sum : natlist → nat
sum xs = case xs of
              Nil        => 0
              Cons y ys  => y + (sum ys)
```

$$\texttt{sum} : \texttt{xs} \xrightarrow{a} \varepsilon,\ \texttt{natlist}_{\texttt{Cons}:1 \rightarrow 2} \rightarrow \texttt{nat}$$

The **sum** function evaluates its argument from left to right.

```
take : natlist × nat → natlist
take xs n = case xs of
                 Nil        => Nil
                 Cons y ys  => case n=0 of
                                    True  => Nil
                                    False => Cons y (take ys (n-1))
```

$$\texttt{take} : \{\texttt{xs} \xrightarrow{a} \varepsilon, \texttt{xs} \xrightarrow{a} \texttt{n}\},\ \texttt{natlist}_{\texttt{Cons}:1 \rightarrow 2} \times \texttt{nat} \rightarrow \texttt{natlist}_{\texttt{Cons}:1 \rightarrow 2}$$
$$\texttt{take} : \{\texttt{xs} \xrightarrow{a} \varepsilon, \texttt{xs} \xrightarrow{a} \texttt{n}\},\ \texttt{natlist}_{\texttt{Cons}:2 \rightarrow 1} \times \texttt{nat} \rightarrow \texttt{natlist}_{\texttt{Cons}:2 \rightarrow 1}$$

That **take** is strict in **xs** and evaluates **xs** before **n** is independent of the context. In a $\texttt{natlist}_{\texttt{Cons}:1 \rightarrow 2}$ context, **xs** is in context $\texttt{natlist}_{\texttt{Cons}:1 \rightarrow 2}$, and in a $\texttt{natlist}_{\texttt{Cons}:2 \rightarrow 1}$ context, **xs** is in context $\texttt{natlist}_{\texttt{Cons}:2 \rightarrow 1}$.

```
reverse : natlist × natlist → natlist
reverse xs zs = case xs of
                  Nil       => zs
                  Cons y ys => reverse ys (Cons y zs)
```

$$\texttt{reverse} : \{\texttt{xs}\stackrel{a}{\rightarrow}\varepsilon, \texttt{xs}\stackrel{a}{\rightarrow}\texttt{zs}\},$$
$$\texttt{natlist}_{\texttt{Cons}:1\leftarrow 2} \times \texttt{natlist}_{\texttt{Cons}:1\rightarrow 2} \rightarrow \texttt{natlist}_{\texttt{Cons}:1\rightarrow 2}$$
$$\texttt{reverse} : \{\texttt{xs}\stackrel{a}{\rightarrow}\varepsilon, \texttt{xs}\stackrel{a}{\rightarrow}\texttt{zs}\},$$
$$\texttt{natlist}_{\texttt{Cons}:1\leftarrow 2} \times \texttt{natlist}_{\texttt{Cons}:1\leftarrow 2} \rightarrow \texttt{natlist}_{\texttt{Cons}:1\leftarrow 2}$$

Reverse is strict in **xs**, evaluates **xs** before **zs**, and evaluates tail before head in **xs** regardless of context.

```
append : natlist × natlist → natlist
append xs zs = case xs of
                 Nil       => zs
                 Cons y ys => Cons y (append ys zs)
```

$$\texttt{append} : \{\texttt{xs}\stackrel{a}{\rightarrow}\varepsilon,\ \texttt{xs}\stackrel{a}{\rightarrow}\texttt{zs}\},$$
$$\texttt{natlist}_{\texttt{Cons}:1\rightarrow 2} \times \texttt{natlist}_{\texttt{Cons}:1\rightarrow 2} \rightarrow \texttt{natlist}_{\texttt{Cons}:1\rightarrow 2}$$
$$\texttt{append} : \{\texttt{xs}\stackrel{a}{\rightarrow}\varepsilon,\ \texttt{xs}\stackrel{a}{\rightarrow}\texttt{zs}\},$$
$$\texttt{natlist}_{\texttt{Cons}:2\rightarrow 1} \times \texttt{natlist}_{\texttt{Cons}:2\rightarrow 1} \rightarrow \texttt{natlist}_{\texttt{Cons}:2\rightarrow 1}$$

The first type above does not say that all elements of the first sublist have been evaluated when the evaluation of the first element of the second sublist begins. This illustrates that some information about evaluation order between substructures of different data structures is lost by our concept of evaluation order type.

```
natlist     ::= Nil | Cons nat natlist
natlistlist ::= ListNil | ListCons natlist natlistlist
concat : natlistlist -> natlist
concat xss = case xss of
                 ListNil           => Nil
                 ListCons ys yss => append ys (concat yss)
```

$$\texttt{concat} : \{\texttt{xss}\stackrel{a}{\rightarrow}\varepsilon\},\ \texttt{natlistlist}_{\texttt{Cons}:1\rightarrow 2,\ \texttt{ListCons}:1\rightarrow 2} \rightarrow \texttt{natlist}_{\texttt{Cons}:1\rightarrow 2}$$
$$\texttt{concat} : \{\texttt{xss}\stackrel{a}{\rightarrow}\varepsilon\},\ \texttt{natlistlist}_{\texttt{Cons}:2\rightarrow 1,\ \texttt{ListCons}:2\rightarrow 1} \rightarrow \texttt{natlist}_{\texttt{Cons}:2\rightarrow 1}$$

6 Related work

The forwards path analysis by Bloss and Hudak [3] [1] is more precise but also considerably more expensive than our backwards analysis. Path sets are more expressive than evaluation order relations: an evaluation order relation corresponds to a prefix-closed set of paths. For example, a path set can give information such as "whenever variable **x** is evaluated, variable **y** will definitely also be evaluated", whereas our evaluation order relations cannot. However, Bloss and Hudak's forwards path analysis cannot handle lazy data structures, unlike our analysis.

Could we not simply encode data structures as higher order functions and apply Bloss and Hudak's higher order path analysis, thus obviating the need for a whole new theory? One answer is that the complexity of higher order path analysis is (at least) exponential in the complexity of types in the expressions being analysed, and the encoding of data structures as functions give very complex types. Furthermore, higher order path analysis cannot be expected always to terminate when applied to recursively defined data structures encoded as functions [6, pp. 103–104].

Draghicescu and Purushothaman present another forwards evaluation order analysis, restricted to first order languages without data structures [4]. That analysis can accommodate also evaluation strategies which make use of strictness information to move evaluation of arguments earlier.

7 Topics for further study

7.1 Improving the framework

In two respects this version of our theory is unsatisfactory. First, the analysis of **case** expressions cannot discover neededness of a variable (even) when it is needed in all branches. Second, the function definitions `g y = g y` and `f x = x` both have argument eor $\varepsilon \leftrightarrows$**x**, which makes the interpretation of this argument eor uselessly weak. A consequence is that we can describe a two-argument function as a "black hole", using the argument eor $1 \leftrightarrows 2 \rightarrow \varepsilon$, but we cannot so describe a one-argument function.

In a generalization of the present framework, one may use path sets instead of evaluation order relations to describe subexpression evaluation order. Path sets offer the advantage of being more intuitive and previously used in the literature. The definition of evaluation order type is unchanged (but based on path sets instead of eors). Also, the analysis functions $\mathcal{T}$ and $\mathcal{R}$ are virtually unmodified.

The resulting backwards path set analysis is more precise (but more expensive) than the analysis presented in this paper, which can be seen as a "cheap" abstraction. More details on this may be found in the authors' Ph.D. theses [5] [7].

7.2 Possible extensions

The framework could be extended in two directions: application to higher order languages, and polymorphism in the evaluation order component of the type of a function. (Recall that our example language is first order and simply typed). A higher order extension is suggested in Gomard's thesis [5].

We conjecture that functions which are (Damas-Milner) polymorphic in some component of their types are also "evaluation order polymorphic" in those components. Consider the polymorphic type of the function **append**: `(List` α`)` $\times$ `(List` α`)` $\rightarrow$ `(List` α`)`. Since **append** does not inspect the list elements, these may be of any type α. Moreover, for the same reason **append** cannot change the order of evaluation of subcomponents of type α; hence any evaluation order relation on these will be preserved by **append**.

8 Conclusion

We have presented a method and supporting concepts for inferring the order of evaluation of subexpressions in a functional language with lazy data structures. The method presented here is restricted to simply typed first order languages. The main contribution of this paper is the handling of lazy data structures. We specified the analysis in detail, but we have not implemented it.

The evaluation order information obtained can be used for optimizing the suspensions which hold unevaluated argument expressions, as demonstrated by Bloss, Hudak, and Young [3] [1, Sec. 4.3]. The optimization of suspensions requires detecting whether at a given occurrence of a variable, the expression is always not previously evaluated, always already evaluated, always not later used, *etc.*

Acknowledgements

The second author was supported by the Danish Natural Science Research Council. Thanks to Lisa Wiese for LaTeX'ing Figure 1, and to Neil D. Jones and the referees Alain Deutsch, John Hughes, and Patrick Sansom, for providing useful comments and suggestions.

Bibliography

1. A. Bloss. *Path Analysis and the Optimization of Non-Strict Functional Languages.* PhD thesis, Computer Science Department, Yale University, New Haven, Connecticut, USA, May 1989. Also: Research Report YALEU/DCS/RR-704. 129 pages.

2. A. Bloss and P. Hudak. Path semantics. In M. Main et al., editors, *Mathematical Foundations of Programming Language Semantics, 3rd Workshop, New Orleans, Louisiana. (Lecture Notes in Computer Science, vol. 298)*, pages 476–489. Springer-Verlag, 1988.

3. A. Bloss, P. Hudak, and J. Young. Code optimizations for lazy evaluation. *Lisp and Symbolic Computation*, 1(2):147–164, September 1988.

4. M. Draghicescu and S. Purushothaman. A compositional analysis of evaluation-order and its application. In *1990 ACM Conference on Lisp and Functional Programming, Nice, France*, pages 242–250. ACM Press, 1990.

5. C.K. Gomard. *Program Analysis Matters.* PhD thesis, DIKU, University of Copenhagen, Denmark, November 1991. Also DIKU Report 91/17.

6. P. Hudak and J. Young. Higher-order strictness analysis in untyped lambda calculus. In *Thirteenth ACM Symp. Principles of Programming Languages, St. Petersburg, Florida, 1986*, pages 97–109, 1986.

7. P. Sestoft. *Analysis and Efficient Implementation of Functional Programs.* PhD thesis, DIKU, University of Copenhagen, Denmark, October 1991.

Strictness Analysis Using Hindley-Milner Type Inference

Cordelia Hall

December 22, 1991

Department of Computing Science
University of Glasgow
Glasgow, Scotland
cvh@dcs.glasgow.ac.uk

1 Introduction

For many years, abstract interpretation has been thought of as the best way to formalize the analysis of semantic properties of functions, such as strictness. Recent publications suggest this may be changing. A number of new papers [1, 5] use sophisticated type systems to learn more about properties of functions. The goal of this work is to encapsulate a function's properties in its type. However, there is no uniform framework in which to prove these analyses safe, whereas one of the advantages of abstract interpretation is that it provides a well understood framework for such proofs. In addition, the compiler which uses them must contain a new type-checker for each analysis. These typecheckers may be large, complex pieces of code if they are to perform analyses which can also be done using abstract interpretation, as Jensen has shown [4] that abstract interpretation cannot be modeled by a type system which does not handle subtypes. Finally, how do we know that there isn't a much simpler and cheaper solution to the problem? For example, what happens if a garden variety Hindley Milner typechecker is given code that has been slightly modified - can it do a 'poor man's' strictness analysis which is worth having?

The goal of this paper is to investigate how far we can get using Hindley-Milner type inference, which will be used to construct a fast first order strictness analysis over flat domains. A function f will be transformed into a new function f' with a type which summarises the propagation of bottom through the definition's body, much as abstract values are propagated during abstract interpretation[6]. The first section discusses the translation, and the second proves it safe.

2 The Transformation

The syntax of programs is defined as

program ::= **bind**$_1$ ... **bind**$_n$ **expr**
bind ::= **fun var**$_1$ ... **var**$_k$ = **expr**

```
expr ::= const
       | var | prim expr₁ expr₂
       | if expr₁ expr₂ expr₃ | fun expr₁ ... exprₘ
```

The transformation is defined as

$$
\begin{aligned}
&T[[\mathtt{bind}_1 \ldots \mathtt{bind}_n\ \mathtt{expr}]] = T[[\mathtt{bind}_1]] \ldots T[[\mathtt{bind}_n]]\ T[[\mathtt{expr}]] \\
&T[[\mathtt{fun\ var}_1 \ldots \mathtt{var}_k = \mathtt{expr}]] = \mathtt{fun\ var}_1 \ldots \mathtt{var}_k = T[[\mathtt{expr}]] \\
&T[[\mathtt{const}]] = \mathtt{one} \\
&T[[\mathtt{var}]] = \mathtt{var} \\
&T[[\mathtt{prim\ expr}_1\ \mathtt{expr}_2]] = \mathtt{and}\ T[[\mathtt{expr}_1]]\ T[[\mathtt{expr}_2]] \\
&T[[\mathtt{if\ expr}_1\ \mathtt{expr}_2\ \mathtt{expr}_3]] = T[[\mathtt{expr}_1]] \\
&T[[\mathtt{fun\ expr}_1 \ldots \mathtt{expr}_i]] = \mathtt{fun}\ T[[\mathtt{expr}_1]] \ldots T[[\mathtt{expr}_i]]
\end{aligned}
$$

The transformation uses primitives functions **one** and **and**, defined as

```
one :: a
one = one

and :: a -> a -> a
and x y = head [x,y]
```

We write f' when referring to the transformed version of function f. Given the definition

$$f'\ v_1 \ldots v_n = e$$

if the type inferred for e is the type of some v_i, then f' is *typestrict* in v_i, which means that the original function f is strict in v_i. For example,

```
g a b c = if (a+1) then b else c
g' :: x -> y -> z -> x
g' a b c = and a one
```

The transformation T is extremely simple; all constants are replaced by **one** and primitive function names excluding conditionals are replaced by the name **and**. Transformed conditional applications contain only the code for the predicate.

Types propagate through the function body of a transformed function in much the same way as abstract values do during abstract interpretation. It's easy to see that this is the case for constants, variables and arithmetic primitives. The constant 1 does not propagate the value of any variable bound in the function definition. In the same way, the polymorphic type of **one** unifies with everything, but does not affect the type environment. If two variable values were needed by a primitive operation, then the result would be bottom if either of those values were bottom. In the same way, if the types of arguments to **and** depend on the types of two variables, then they and the result type of the application are all given the same type. The function **one** is analogous to the constant value 1 in Mycroft's domain, and **and** is analogous to his & function.

2.1 Transforming Conditionals

It is apparently not possible to represent both the least upper bound and greatest lower bound functions used in abstract interpretation within a type inference system as weak as Hindley-Milner [4]. If we represent the greatest lower bound operation with **and**, then the conditional, which has an abstract interpretation using both functions [6], must be given a transformation which produces less information than would be available during abstract interpretation. We choose a transformation which propagates the type of the predicate. This is weaker than Mycroft's abstract conditional at only one possible combination of arguments, 1, 0 and 0, which is a common case.

2.1.1 Analysing the Code for Conditional Branches

Suppose we choose to analyse the code for the conditional branches, even though their types are not propagated through the conditional. Then it is essential that variables occurrences are separated, otherwise an unsafe analysis could take place. For example, we could have the function g

```
g a b c = if (a <= 0) (a + b) c.
```

with the translation

```
g' a b c = if (and a one) (and a b) c.
```

The translation g' would be typestrict in b but g would not be strict in b. This problem could be avoided if each variable was given a tuple type in which each occurrence received a field of the type. We would then have the translation

```
g' a b c = if (and (fst a) one) (and (snd a) b) c.
```

The translation g' would no longer be typestrict in b.

Unfortunately, it is prohibitively expensive to separate variable occurrences, because the tuple types that result create a significant overhead during unification. This problem becomes serious when recursive function definitions are transformed. When abstract interpretation is used to perform strictness analysis, fixpoints are found by iterating the application of the recursive function to successive, better and better defined argument values. The iteration can be terminated when the fixpoint is found, and it is guaranteed to be found in a finite number of steps that depends directly upon the height of the abstract domain and the number of function arguments, in this case 2^n where n is the number of function arguments. The transformation must do the same, but it produces code without knowing anything about the code's type, so must provide the maximum number of applications. Even though this number is significantly reduced because the conditional is weak enough to justify treating this analysis as a form of backwards analysis[3], it is still proportional to the number of function arguments. This means that as each application is typed, the argument tuple types grow more and more complex, causing the final type of the function to be big.

For example, here is the factorial function

```
fac n a = if (0 = a) 1 (fac (n - 1) (n * a))
```

We'll assume that the transformation introduces the following projections on tuples:

```
s31 (a,b,c) = a
s32 (a,b,c) = b
s33 (a,b,c) = c
```

First, the transformation creates a polymorphic function which is the higher order definition of `fac`. It must pass in a separate version of the higher order function for each application of `fac` in the function body, otherwise the type propagated would be unsafe. The iteration takes place during type checking of the body of `fac`, after the bottom type (`bottom` is `and`) provides the initial value.

```
fac_rec fac0 n a
  = if (and (s31 n) one)
       (fst a)
       (fac0 (and (s33 n) one) (and (s32 n) (snd a))))


fac' n a
  = (fac_rec fac_rec3 n a)
    where
    fac_rec3 n a  = (fac_rec fac_rec2 n a)
    fac_rec2 n a  = (fac_rec fac_rec1 n a)
    fac_rec1 n a  = (fac_rec fac_rec0 n a)
    fac_rec0 n a  = (bottom [n,a])
```

The final type correctly shows that `fac` is strict in its first argument, but is too large to be practical.

```
fac' :: (a, (b, (c, (d, e))), (f, (c, (d, e)), (g, (d, e), (h, e, e))))
                  -> (i, (b, (c, (d, e)))) -> a

fac_rec :: (a -> b -> c) -> (d, b, a) -> (e, b) -> d
```

2.1.2 Removing the Code for Conditional Branches

Actually, we have learned nothing new from `fac'` that would not have been learned if the transformed `fac` had been

```
fac' n a = and n one
```

The reason is that this abstract conditional is simply too weak to take advantage of the new information learned through calculating fixpoints. Thus, there is no point in including code for the branches of the conditional, and some harm is done if it is included.

What about recursions in predicates? If the recursion is of the form

```
f a b = if (g (f e1 e2)) e3 e4
```

and `g` is strict in its argument, then `f` will not terminate. If `g` is not strict in its argument, then the function will terminate but may not use the result of the recursion. We'll assume that the transformer recognises functions with recursions in predicates and either approximates immediately or treats them as if they were ill-formed.

3 Typestrictness Analysis is Safe for Non-recursive Functions

We'll prove that when f' is *typestrict* in a given argument, then first order strictness analysis will show that the original function f is strict in that argument.

First, we define what it means for f' to be *typestrict* in one or more of its arguments.

Definition 1 *Let $f'\ y_1 \ldots y_n\ =\ e'$. We say that f' is* typestrict *in y_i iff f' is non-recursive and for some i, y_i has the same type as e'. We say that e' is typestrict in y_i iff y_i is free in e' and f' is typestrict in y_i.*

For example, let $f'\ y_1\ y_2\ =\ e'$ such that $f'\ ::\ \alpha \rightarrow \beta \rightarrow \beta$. Then f' is typestrict in y_2 but not in y_1.

We define what it means for the abstract interpretation of f, written as f^{abs}, to be strict in an argument.

Definition 2 *Let $f^{abs}\ y_1 \ldots y_n\ =\ e^{abs}$. We say that f^{abs} is* strict *in y_i iff*

$$f^{abs}\ 1_1\ \ldots\ 1_{i-1}\ 0\ 1_{i+1} \ldots\ 1_n\ =\ 0$$

We say that e^{abs} is strict in y_i iff y_i is free in e^{abs} and f^{abs} is strict in y_i.

Other research has proven that if f^{abs} is strict in y_i then f is strict in its corresponding argument, x_i [6], so we'll concentrate on relating f' to f^{abs}.

We'll need the following lemma:

Lemma 1 *Let the expression $g'\ e'_1\ \ldots\ e'_m$ have free variables $v_1 \ldots v_n$. Then it is typestrict in v_i iff the following hold:*

1. *for some j such that $1 \leq j \leq m$, g' is typestrict in its jth argument*
2. *the expression e'_j is typestrict in v_i.*

For example, let $g'\ x_1\ x_2\ x_3\ =$ and x_1 (and x_2 one). The function g' is typestrict in x_1 and x_2. The expression g' (and $v_1\ v_2$) $v_3\ v_4$ is typestrict in v_1, v_2, and v_3.

Theorem 1 *Let $x_1 \ldots x_n$ be free in e, let $y_1 \ldots y_n$ be free in e' and let $z_1 \ldots z_n$ be free in e^{abs}. If e' is typestrict in y_i then e^{abs} is strict in z_i.*

Proof: By structural induction. The non-trivial case, for function application, is as follows:

Assume $g'\ e'_1\ \ldots\ e'_m$ is typestrict in y_i. We must show that $g^{abs}\ e^{abs}_1\ \ldots\ e^{abs}_m$ is strict in z_i. By Lemma 1, g' is typestrict in its jth argument for some j, and e'_j is typestrict in y_i.

There are m cases, of which we will do just the first.

We know that if $g^{abs}\ e^{abs}_1\ \ldots\ e^{abs}_m$ is strict in z_i then g^{abs} is strict in at least one of its arguments, and the corresponding expression e^{abs}_k is strict in z_i. We'll assume that g' is typestrict in its first argument and that e'_1 is typestrict in y_i. By induction, g^{abs} is strict in its first argument and e^{abs}_1 is strict in z_i, so the implication holds. The rest of the cases are similar.

4 Conclusion

The transformation can be performed during dependency analysis, which needs to be done before typechecking in any case. We have seen that the weakness of the conditional allows us to avoid calculating fixpoints, which slows many compile-time analyses down. This may also mean that the analysis is simply too weak to be useful in significant pieces of software. Empirical tests will determine whether this analysis is useful in practice. However, it is interesting that a recent implementation of LML contains a strictness analyser which approximates instead of fully calculating fixpoints. There is an additional advantage of making a typechecker do the analysis in a language with modules like Haskell[2], which sums up static information about a function by giving that function's type in a module interface. The translation of that function can also be given a type in the interface, making separate compilation easy.

Bibliography

1. Henglein, F. *Efficient Type Inference for Higher-Order Binding-Time Analysis*, in J. Hughes (ed.) *Proceedings of 5th ACM Conference on Functional Programming Languages and Computer Architecture*, pp. 448-472.

2. Hudak, P., Wadler, P.L., Peyton Jones, S.L. et al., "Report on the Programming Language Haskell", Dept. of Computing Science, University of Glasgow, August (1991).

3. Hughes, R. J. M. *Backwards Analysis of Functional Programs.* Departmental Research Report CSC/87/R3, Department of Computing Science, University of Glasgow, 1987.

4. Jensen, T. *Strictness Analysis in Logical Form*, in J. Hughes (ed.) *Proceedings of 5th ACM Conference on Functional Programming Languages and Computer Architecture*, pp. 352-366.

5. Leung, A. and P. Mishra, *Reasoning about Simple and Exhaustive Demand in Higher-Order Lazy Languages*, in J. Hughes (ed.) *Proceedings of 5th ACM Conference on Functional Programming Languages and Computer Architecture*, pp. 328-351.

6. Mycroft, A., *Abstract interpretation and optimising transformations for applicative programs*, Phd. thesis, University of Edinburgh , 1981.

Extending Deforestation for First Order Functional Programs

G.W. Hamilton
S.B. Jones

Department of Computing Science and Mathematics,
University of Stirling,
Stirling FK9 4LA

September 1991

Abstract

Intermediate data structures are widely used in functional programs. Programs which use these intermediate structures are usually a lot easier to understand, but they result in loss of efficiency at run time. In order to reduce these run-time costs, a transformation algorithm called *deforestation* was proposed by Wadler which could eliminate intermediate structures. However, this algorithm is only applicable to a subset of all first-order functional terms. In this paper, it is shown how deforestation can be extended to be made applicable to all first-order functional terms. This is achieved by performing static analysis to determine which intermediate data structures can be eliminated. Using this extended form of deforestation, the majority of garbage which can be detected at compile-time will not be generated at run-time.

1 Introduction

One advantage which functional languages offer over their imperative counterparts is that they include no explicit storage management operations. The programmer can thus concentrate upon writing programs which resemble the structure of the original problem without worrying about the underlying storage requirements. As a result of this lack of explicit storage management operations, a substantial proportion of the execution time of functional programs is spent on storage management.

A wide variety of schemes for performing this garbage collection as efficiently as possible have been suggested. These schemes only serve to 'shut the stable door after the horse has bolted'. This is because, in the majority of cases, the inefficiency lies in the actual program definition itself.

Another advantage of functional languages is that they allow greatly improved modularisation (as described in [8]). Functions can be defined in terms of smaller and simpler functions which are 'glued' together to give their result. These smaller functions are easier to construct and reuse. A lot of these smaller functions either form a structure as their result, or decompose a structured argument into its constituent elements. Whenever these functions are put together to form compound terms, a lot of structures are formed only to be decomposed again. These intermediate structures are the glue which hold the functions together. The use of these intermediate structures aids clarity, but it results in inefficiency at run-time. Each intermediate structure must be allocated, traversed, and subsequently deallocated. These compound terms can be transformed instead to avoid the building of intermediate structures. For example, consider the following function definition:

$$\mathit{factorial}\ n \;=\; \mathit{product}\ (\mathit{upto}\ 1\ n)$$

The function call *upto* 1 n creates a list of the numbers from 1 to n, and *product* decomposes this list again into its constituent elements and multiplies them together. Transforming this definition to eliminate this intermediate list gives the following:

$$\begin{array}{lll} \mathit{factorial}\ n & = & f\ 1\ 1\ n \\ & & \textbf{where} \\ & & f\ a\ m\ n \;=\; \textbf{if}\ m > n \\ & & \qquad\qquad\quad \textbf{then}\ a \\ & & \qquad\qquad\quad \textbf{else}\ f\ (a * m)\ (m+1)\ n \end{array}$$

This definition is more efficient because all operations on lists have been eliminated. In [13], a transformation algorithm called deforestation was proposed which can eliminate these intermediate structures. However, this algorithm is only applicable to a subset of all first-order functional terms. It is shown in [7] how deforestation can be made applicable to a larger subset of functional terms. This work is further extended in this paper so that deforestation can be applied to all first-order functional terms. These extensions are achieved by performing static analysis to determine which data structures can be eliminated. A brief description is given of the static analysis which is required. The extended deforestation algorithm is illustrated with examples, and an outline proof of its termination is given.

2 Deforestation

2.1 Language

Deforestation (as proposed in [13]) is now described for a simple first order language with the grammar as shown in Figure 1. This language is similar to that described in [4]. The basic functions are the built-in functions of the language (such as $+, -, =, <$, etc.) which cannot be unfolded in any way. Function arguments are used for pattern matching, rather than the case terms used in [13]. This is because the size of sub-terms to be transformed can become rather large when case expressions are used. This is because terms containing case expressions are unfolded before anything profitable may be done

fn	::=	$f\ v_1 \ldots v_n$	$=$	t	function definition
	|	$g\ p_1\ v_1 \ldots v_n$	$=$	t_1	
			$\vdots$		function definition with pattern match
		$g\ p_m\ v_1 \ldots v_n$	$=$	t_m	
p	::=	$c\ v_1 \ldots v_k$			pattern
t	::=	v			variable
	|	$b\ t_1 \ldots t_n$			basic function application
	|	$c\ t_1 \ldots t_n$			constructor application
	|	$f\ t_1 \ldots t_n$			user-defined function application
	|	$g\ t_0 \ldots t_n$			

Figure 1: Language grammar

with them. The patterns used in the definitions of pattern matching functions may not be nested. Methods to transform pattern matching functions with nested patterns into ones without nested patterns are described in [1] and [14].

The intended operational semantics of the language is normal order reduction of the lambda calculus. However, pattern matching is strict, and when a pattern matching function is applied, the pattern matching argument is evaluated to head normal form before the body is entered. Some example definitions are shown in Figure 2.

list α	::=	*Nil* | *Cons* α (*list* α)
append	:	*list* $\alpha \rightarrow$ *list* $\alpha \rightarrow$ *list* α
append Nil ys	=	*ys*
append (*Cons x xs*) *ys*	=	*Cons x* (*append xs ys*)
reverse	:	*list* $\alpha \rightarrow$ *list* $\alpha \rightarrow$ *list* α
reverse Nil ys	=	*ys*
reverse (*Cons x xs*) *ys*	=	*reverse xs* (*Cons x ys*)

Figure 2: Some example definitions

2.2 Treeless Form

In [13], a treeless form of definition is characterised which uses no intermediate trees. The grammar of treeless form for the given language is shown in Figure 3. The restriction that every argument of a function must be a variable guarantees that no intermediate trees are created. In addition, treeless terms must be linear in all variables. A term is said to be linear if no variable appears in it more than once. This restriction guarantees that

$$
\begin{array}{rcll}
tfn & ::= & tf\ v_1 \ldots v_n = tt & \\
 & | & tg\ p_1\ v_1 \ldots v_n = tt_1 & \text{treeless function definitions} \\
 & & \vdots & \\
 & & tg\ p_m\ v_1 \ldots v_n = tt_m & \\
 & & & \\
tt & ::= & v & \\
 & | & b\ v_1 \ldots v_n & \\
 & | & c\ tt_1 \ldots tt_n & \text{treeless terms} \\
 & | & tf\ v_1 \ldots v_n & \\
 & | & tg\ v_0 \ldots v_n &
\end{array}
$$

Figure 3: Treeless Form Grammar

unfolding a function application will not introduce repeated computations. The definition of *append* given in Figure 2 is in treeless form, whereas the definition of *reverse* is not, because the function argument (*Cons x ys*) is not a variable. The *deforestation theorem* (as given in [13]) states that every linear term, containing only occurrences of functions with treeless definitions, can be effectively transformed to an equivalent treeless term, without loss of efficiency. The algorithm which carries out this transformation is called the *deforestation algorithm.*

$$
\begin{array}{lll}
(1) & \mathcal{T}[\![v]\!] & = v \\
(2) & \mathcal{T}[\![b\ t_1 \ldots t_k]\!] & = b\ \mathcal{T}[\![t_1]\!] \ldots \mathcal{T}[\![t_k]\!] \\
(3) & \mathcal{T}[\![c\ t_1 \ldots t_k]\!] & = c\ \mathcal{T}[\![t_1]\!] \ldots \mathcal{T}[\![t_k]\!] \\
(4) & \mathcal{T}[\![\cdots f\ t_1 \ldots t_k \cdots]\!] & = \mathcal{T}[\![\cdots t[t_1/v_1, \ldots, t_k/v_k] \cdots]\!] \\
 & \text{where } f \text{ is defined by } f\ v_1 \ldots v_k = t & \\
(5) & \mathcal{T}[\![\cdots g\ (c\ t'_1 \ldots t'_n)\ t_1 \ldots t_k \cdots]\!] & \\
 & & = \mathcal{T}[\![\cdots t[t'_1/v'_1, \ldots, t'_n/v'_n, t_1/v_1, \ldots, t_k/v_k] \cdots]\!] \\
 & \text{where } g \text{ has a defining equation } g\ (c\ v'_1 \ldots v'_n)\ v_1 \ldots v_k = t & \\
(6) & \mathcal{T}[\![\cdots g\ v_0\ t_1 \ldots t_k \cdots]\!] & = g'\ v_0\ v'_1 \ldots v'_n \\
 & \text{where } g' \text{ is a new function defined by:} & \\
 & g'\ p_1\ v'_1 \ldots v'_n \ = \ \mathcal{T}[\![\cdots g\ p_1\ t_1 \ldots t_k \cdots]\!] & \\
 & \qquad \vdots & \\
 & g'\ p_m\ v'_1 \ldots v'_n \ = \ \mathcal{T}[\![\cdots g\ p_m\ t_1 \ldots t_k \cdots]\!] & \\
 & \text{and } g \text{ is defined by:} & \\
 & g\ p_1\ v_1 \ldots v_k \ = \ t'_1 & \\
 & \qquad \vdots & \\
 & g\ p_m\ v_1 \ldots v_k \ = \ t'_m & \\
 & \text{and } v'_1 \ldots v'_n \text{ are the variables in the original term (except } v_0) &
\end{array}
$$

Figure 4: Transformation Rules

2.3 The Deforestation Algorithm

The deforestation algorithm is a set of transformation rules which will convert a term satisfying the preconditions of the deforestation theorem into a treeless equivalent. The transformations rules for the given language are shown in Figure 4. The notation $\cdots t \cdots$ denotes a context of nested pattern matching parameters in function calls. It is defined as follows:

$$\cdots t \cdots ::= t \mid g\ (\cdots t \cdots)\ t_1 \ldots t_n$$

This notation is used to identify an innermost function call which is about to be unfolded.

As they stand, these transformation rules will not necessarily terminate. For example, consider the deforestation of *append* (*append xs ys*) *zs* shown in Figure 5.

$$
\begin{array}{lcll}
\multicolumn{3}{l}{\mathcal{T}[\![append\ (append\ xs\ ys)\ zs]\!] =} & \\
\multicolumn{3}{l}{g\ xs\ ys\ zs} & \text{(By 6)} \\
\multicolumn{3}{l}{\text{where}} & \\
g\ Nil\ ys\ zs & = & \mathcal{T}[\![append\ (append\ Nil\ ys)\ zs]\!] & \text{(By 6)} \\
 & = & \mathcal{T}[\![append\ ys\ zs]\!] & \text{(By 5)} \\
 & = & append\ ys\ zs & \text{(By 6,5,1,3)} \\
g\ (Cons\ x\ xs)\ ys\ zs & = & \mathcal{T}[\![append\ (append\ (Cons\ x\ xs)\ ys)\ zs]\!] & \text{(By 6)} \\
 & = & \mathcal{T}[\![append\ (Cons\ x\ (append\ xs\ ys))\ zs]\!] & \text{(By 5)} \\
 & = & \mathcal{T}[\![Cons\ x\ (append\ (append\ xs\ ys)\ zs)]\!] & \text{(By 5)} \\
 & = & Cons\ x\ (\mathcal{T}[\![append\ (append\ xs\ ys)\ zs]\!]) & \text{(By 3,1)}
\end{array}
$$

append (*append xs ys*) *zs* therefore transforms to:

$$
\begin{array}{lcl}
\multicolumn{3}{l}{g\ xs\ ys\ zs} \\
\multicolumn{3}{l}{\text{where}} \\
g\ Nil\ ys\ zs & = & append\ ys\ zs \\
g\ (Cons\ x\ xs)\ ys\ zs & = & Cons\ x\ (g\ xs\ ys\ zs)
\end{array}
$$

Figure 5: Deforestation of *append* (*append xs ys*) *zs*

The transformation rules are applied until we obtain a sub-term which is a renaming of the original. This non-termination can be avoided if we keep a list of all terms which have already been transformed. Whenever we encounter (a renaming of) any term for the second time, we introduce an appropriate function definition, and replace each instance of the term by a corresponding call of the function. For the given example, we introduce a new function definition:

$$g\ xs\ ys\ zs = \mathcal{T}[\![append\ (append\ xs\ ys)\ zs]\!].$$

Any sub-terms which match the right hand side of this equation (modulo renaming) are replaced by an appropriate call of this function, resulting in the term shown in Figure 5.

2.4 Blazing

The definition of treeless form shown in Figure 3 is quite restrictive. For example, consider the definition of *upto* shown in Figure 6.

$$
\begin{array}{lcl}
\mathit{upto} & : & \mathit{int} \rightarrow \mathit{int} \rightarrow \mathit{list\ int} \\
\mathit{upto}\ m\ n & = & \mathit{upto}'\ (m > n)\ m\ n \\
\\
\mathit{upto}' & : & \mathit{bool} \rightarrow \mathit{int} \rightarrow \mathit{int} \rightarrow \mathit{list\ int} \\
\mathit{upto}'\ \mathit{True}\ m\ n & = & \mathit{Nil} \\
\mathit{upto}'\ \mathit{False}\ m\ n & = & \mathit{Cons}\ m\ (\mathit{upto}\ (m+1)\ n) \\
\\
\mathit{product} & : & \mathit{list\ int} \rightarrow \mathit{int} \\
\mathit{product}\ xs & = & \mathit{product}'\ xs\ 1 \\
\\
\mathit{product}' & : & \mathit{list\ int} \rightarrow \mathit{int} \rightarrow \mathit{int} \\
\mathit{product}'\ \mathit{Nil}\ a & = & a \\
\mathit{product}'\ (\mathit{Cons}\ x\ xs)\ a & = & \mathit{product}'\ xs\ (a * x)
\end{array}
$$

Figure 6: More example definitions

Some function arguments are not variables ($m > n$ and $m + 1$), and the definition is not linear in the variable m. However, these intermediate values are only integers.

This situation is resolved in [13] by introducing *blazing* of terms (blazing is a term used in forestry for the marking of a tree by making a cut in its bark). This blazing is

$$
\begin{array}{lclcll}
\mathit{btfn} & ::= & \mathit{btf}\ v_1 \ldots v_n & = & \mathit{btt} & \\
 & | & \mathit{btg}\ p_1\ v_1 \ldots v_n & = & \mathit{btt}_1 & \text{blazed treeless function definitions} \\
 & & & \vdots & & \\
 & & \mathit{btg}\ p_m\ v_1 \ldots v_n & = & \mathit{btt}_m & \\
\\
\mathit{btt} & ::= & \mathit{ett} & & & \\
 & | & (c\ \mathit{btt}_1 \ldots \mathit{btt}_n)^{\oplus} & & & \text{blazed treeless terms} \\
 & | & (\mathit{btf}\ \mathit{ett}_1 \ldots \mathit{ett}_n)^{\oplus} & & & \\
 & | & (\mathit{btg}\ \mathit{ett}_0 \ldots \mathit{ett}_n)^{\oplus} & & & \\
\\
\mathit{ett} & ::= & v & & & \\
 & | & (b\ \mathit{ett}_1 \ldots \mathit{ett}_n)^{\ominus} & & & \\
 & | & (c\ \mathit{ett}_1 \ldots \mathit{ett}_n)^{\ominus} & & & \text{extractable treeless terms} \\
 & | & (\mathit{btf}\ \mathit{ett}_1 \ldots \mathit{ett}_n)^{\ominus} & & & \\
 & | & (\mathit{btg}\ \mathit{ett}_0 \ldots \mathit{ett}_n)^{\ominus} & & &
\end{array}
$$

Figure 7: Blazed Treeless Form Grammar

performed according to the type of each term. All terms of a structured type (*list* α or *tree* α) are blazed $\oplus$, and all terms of an atomic type (*int* or *bool*) are blazed $\ominus$. We only want to eliminate ('fell') all intermediate terms ('trees') which are blazed $\oplus$.

Treeless form is now generalised to ***blazed treeless form*** which has the grammar as shown in Figure 7. Function arguments are restricted to be either variables or terms blazed $\ominus$, and terms are only required to be linear in variables blazed $\oplus$. The definitions of *upto* and *product* shown in Figure 6 are in blazed treeless form.

The ***blazed deforestation theorem*** given in [13] states that every term linear in variables blazed $\oplus$, containing only occurrences of functions with blazed treeless definitions, can be effectively transformed to an equivalent blazed treeless term, without loss of efficiency.

The deforestation algorithm is extended to accommodate blazing in the following way. Any sub-terms blazed $\ominus$ which arise during transformation are extracted by introducing **let** terms. For example, applying extraction to the inefficient definition of *factorial* given in Section 1:

$$product'\ (upto\ 1\ n)\ 1$$

we obtain the term:

$$\begin{array}{l} \mathbf{let}\ v_0 = 1 \\ \mathbf{in}\quad \mathbf{let}\ v_1 = 1 \\ \qquad \mathbf{in}\ \ product'\ (upto\ v_0\ n)\ v_1 \end{array}$$

Later in the same transformation, applying extraction to the term:

$$product'\ (upto\ (v_0 + 1)\ n)\ (v_0 * v_1)$$

we obtain the term:

$$\begin{array}{l} \mathbf{let}\ v_2 = v_0 + 1 \\ \mathbf{in}\quad \mathbf{let}\ v_3 = v_0 * v_1 \\ \qquad \mathbf{in}\ \ product'\ (upto\ v_2\ n)\ v_3 \end{array}$$

The inner term of this expression is a renaming of the inner term of the previous expression. The following new function is therefore defined:

$$f\ v_0\ v_1\ n = \mathcal{T}[\![product'\ (upto\ v_0\ n)\ v_1]\!]$$

The inner terms are replaced with calls to f, giving a term similar to the efficient definition of *factorial* given in Section 1.

Extraction forces all function arguments blazed $\ominus$ to be variables, so it is not necessary for terms to be linear in variables blazed $\ominus$, because unfolding will only replace these variables with other variables, and no duplication of a term can occur. The following extra transformation rule is required to handle extracted terms:

$$(7)\quad \mathcal{T}[\![\mathbf{let}\ v^{\ominus} = t_0^{\ominus}\ \mathbf{in}\ t_1]\!] \;=\; \mathbf{let}\ v^{\ominus} = \mathcal{T}[\![t_0^{\ominus}]\!]\ \mathbf{in}\ \mathcal{T}[\![t_1]\!]$$

3 Extending Deforestation

We now show how deforestation can be extended to all first-order functions. This extension can be made if *inheritance analysis* and *creation analysis* are performed on all sub-terms of the term being transformed. A brief description of these analyses is given below. For a more detailed study, the interested reader is referred to [5].

3.1 Inheritance Analysis

Blazed treeless form (as shown in Figure 7) is still not the most general form of term which contains no intermediate structures. Not all function arguments which are of a structured type will be intermediate structures. For example, consider the term:

$$append\ xs\ (append\ ys\ zs)$$

This term contains no intermediate structures because the structure *append ys zs* will appear directly in the result of the term. No transformation is therefore required on this term to eliminate intermediate structures. However, this term is transformed using the deforestation algorithm into the same term resulting from the deforestation of *append* (*append xs ys*) *zs* shown in Figure 5.

Transformation of terms which contain no intermediate structures can be avoided if we can determine which sub-terms are not intermediate structures, and extract them in the same manner as terms blazed $\ominus$ are extracted in blazed deforestation. In order to be able to determine which sub-terms are not intermediate structures, we perform *inheritance analysis*. Inheritance analysis is a backward analysis similar to the transmission analysis described in [11] and [6]. It is used to determine if a sub-term of structured type will definitely appear in the result of the overall term of which it is a part (is inherited by it). A sub-term of structured type is defined to be an *intermediate structure* if it is not inherited by the overall term of which it is a part.

3.2 Creation Analysis

Not all intermediate structures can be eliminated by the deforestation algorithm. For example, consider the term:

$$append\ (reverse\ xs\ ys)\ zs$$

If we apply the transformation rules to this term, we obtain sub-problems of ever increasing size, and the transformation does not terminate. The reason for this non-termination is that the intermediate term *reverse xs ys* will never construct a structure as its result (because the value of *xs* is not known). If an intermediate term does not construct a structure as its result, then it will not be possible to decompose it again into its component parts. In order to be able to determine which terms may be created, we perform *creation analysis*. Creation analysis is a forward analysis which is used to determine whether a term may construct a structure as its result during transformation. Any such terms which are intermediate structures (as determined by inheritance analysis) are called *constructed intermediate structures*.

3.3 Extending the Deforestation Algorithm

The deforestation algorithm can now be extended to all first-order functions in the following way. First of all, inheritance analysis and creation analysis are performed upon all sub-terms of the term to be transformed. Then, any of these sub-terms which have been found to be constructed intermediate structures are blazed $\oplus$, and can be eliminated using the extended deforestation algorithm. Any sub-terms which have been found *not* to be constructed intermediate structures are blazed $\ominus$, and are extracted as in blazed deforestation. The overall term is then transformed using the blazed deforestation algorithm as described earlier. In addition to the given transformation rules, after any function calls have been unfolded (transformation rules 4 and 5), all sub-terms of the unfolded body must be blazed in the manner described before any further transformation.

If all sub-terms are blazed in this way, *extended treeless form* can be defined in exactly the same way as blazed treeless form as shown in Figure 7. The definition of *reverse* shown in Figure 2 is in extended treeless form. Any term can be transformed by the extended deforestation algorithm into extended treeless form. There is no requirement for the functions in the term to have extended treeless definitions. This transformation may, however, produce a less efficient term as its result if functions are not linear in all their arguments. This situation can be avoided if all non-linear function arguments are also blazed $\ominus$, and are extracted before unfolding.

The *extended deforestation theorem* now states that every term can be effectively transformed to an equivalent extended treeless form, without loss of efficiency. In fact,

$\mathcal{T}[\![\textit{reverse}\ (\textit{append}\ xs\ ys)\ zs]\!] =$			
$g\ xs\ ys\ zs$			(By 6)
where			
$g\ \textit{Nil}\ ys\ zs$	$=$	$\mathcal{T}[\![\textit{reverse}\ (\textit{append}\ \textit{Nil}\ ys)\ zs]\!]$	(By 6)
	$=$	$\mathcal{T}[\![\textit{reverse}\ ys\ zs]\!]$	(By 5)
	$=$	$\textit{reverse}\ ys\ zs$	(By 6,5,1,3)
$g\ (\textit{Cons}\ x\ xs)\ ys\ zs$	$=$	$\mathcal{T}[\![\textit{reverse}\ (\textit{append}\ (\textit{Cons}\ x\ xs)\ ys)\ zs]\!]$	(By 6)
	$=$	$\mathcal{T}[\![\textit{reverse}\ (\textit{Cons}\ x\ (\textit{append}\ xs\ ys))\ zs]\!]$	(By 5)
	$=$	$\mathcal{T}[\![\textit{reverse}\ (\textit{append}\ xs\ ys)\ (\textit{Cons}\ x\ zs)]\!]$	(By 5)
	$=$	$\mathcal{T}[\![$ **let** $v = \textit{Cons}\ x\ zs$ **in** $\textit{reverse}\ (\textit{append}\ xs\ ys)\ v]\!]$	
	$=$	**let** $v = \textit{Cons}\ x\ zs$ **in** $\mathcal{T}[\![\textit{reverse}\ (\textit{append}\ xs\ ys)\ v]\!]$	(By 7,3,1)

reverse (*append xs ys*) *zs* therefore transforms to:

$g\ xs\ ys\ zs$		
where		
$g\ \textit{Nil}\ ys\ zs$	$=$	$\textit{reverse}\ ys\ zs$
$g\ (\textit{Cons}\ x\ xs)\ ys\ zs$	$=$	$g\ xs\ ys\ (\textit{Cons}\ x\ zs)$

Figure 8: Extended deforestation of *reverse* (*append xs ys*) *zs*

there will be a gain in efficiency if the original term contained any sub-terms blazed ⊖. The deforestation of *reverse* (*append xs ys*) *zs* by the extended deforestation algorithm is shown in Figure 8. Note that non-termination will result if this term is transformed by the original unextended deforestation algorithm.

3.4 Outline of Termination Proof

In this section, we outline a proof of termination of the extended deforestation algorithm. A more detailed proof is contained in [5] for the interested reader.

In order to be able to prove that the extended deforestation algorithm terminates, it is sufficient to show that there is a bound on the size of the terms encountered during transformation. If there is such a bound, then there will be a finite number of terms encountered (modulo renaming of variables), and a renaming of a previous term must eventually be encountered. The algorithm will therefore be guaranteed to terminate.

After applying transformation rules (1-3), the size of the subsequent terms to be transformed are smaller than the original term. Whenever unfolding of a function call is performed in transformation rules (4-5), the only compound terms (non-variables) which will be passed into the function body will be constructed intermediate structures. These terms may construct a structure which is subsequently decomposed in the function body. If they do not, they will be extracted before further transformation. Thus the size of a term can not be increased by the unfolding of a function call. In transformation rule (6), a variable pattern matching argument of a function is replaced by a pattern. This pattern will subsequently be decomposed when pattern matching occurs, so the size of the term will not be increased. There is therefore a bound on the size of the terms encountered during transformation, so the extended deforestation algorithm must terminate.

4 Related Work

Deforestation grew out of earlier work by Wadler on *listlessness* (described in [16] and [15]). This work involved transformations that eliminate intermediate lists. These transformations are not source-to-source and give a non-functional result. Also, the definition of treeless form is simpler than the definition of listless form. However, listlessness does allow transformations on non-linear functions, unlike deforestation.

It is shown in [7] how the deforestation algorithm described in [13] can be made applicable to a larger subset of functional terms. This is achieved by making use of information obtained from inheritance analysis. This work is further extended in this paper to show how the deforestation algorithm can be made applicable to all first order functional terms. This is achieved by also making use of information obtained by creation analysis.

Other work has already been done on trying to extend deforestation for all first order functional programs in [2] and [3]. This work is explained using a *producer-consumer* model of functions. A function is a good consumer if its arguments are linear and non-accumulating. Any arguments not satisfying these criteria are blazed ⊖, and are extracted before transforming function calls. A function argument is a good producer if it satisfies an extended treeless form. Function arguments are forced to be good producers by extracting those terms which are preventing the argument from being treeless. Thus only good producers will be fused with good consumers during transformation.

The work presented here could also be described in terms of a producer-consumer model. A term is a good producer if it constructs a structure as its result, as determined by creation analysis. A term is a good consumer of its sub-terms if they do not appear in the result of the term, as determined by inheritance analysis. This is perhaps more intuitive than the criteria described in [2] and [3].

Preliminary studies have shown that although both these methods are applicable to all first-order functional programs, more intermediate structures can be eliminated using the method described here. More work needs to be done to compare the two methods. In the work described in [2] and [3], functions appearing in a term must have their definitions transformed to treeless form before transforming the overall term, and special consideration must be given to recursive functions. In the work described here, any term can be immediately transformed into treeless form.

Only first order functions have been considered in this paper. It is shown in [13] how deforestation can be applied to a restricted class of higher order functions. This is achieved by defining these functions as higher order macros. A method is described in [2] for extending deforestation for all higher order porgrams. This method involves removing some of the higher order features from a program before performing deforestation.

Analyses similar to the inheritance analysis and creation analysis described in this paper can also be used to determine what garbage can be collected at compile time. Similar analyses are described in [12], [10] and [9] which are used for performing compile-time garbage collection.

5 Conclusion

We have extended deforestation (as described in [13]) such that all first order functional programs can be transformed safely into an extended treeless form. It is no longer necessary to transform function definitions into treeless form before transforming terms composed of calls of these functions. This has been achieved through the use of inheritance analysis and creation analysis to determine which data structures can be eliminated. An implementation of the ideas presented here is required in order to be able to assess their worth.

This extended form of deforestation can be viewed as compile-time garbage avoidance. Variations of inheritance analysis and creation analysis can also be used to determine what garbage can be collected at compile-time. It can be shown that the majority of the garbage which can be detected at compile time can be avoided by the transformations described here. Research is continuing in this area.

Bibliography

1. L. Augustsson. Compiling pattern matching. *Lecture Notes in Computer Science*, 201:368–381, 1985.

2. Wei-Ngan Chin. *Automatic Methods for Program Transformation.* PhD thesis, Imperial College, University of London, July 1990.

3. Wei-Ngan Chin. Generalising deforestation for all first-order functional programs. In *Journées de Travail sur L'Analyse Statique en Programmation Equationnelle, Functionnelle et Logique*, pages 173–181, October 1991.

4. A.B. Ferguson and P.L. Wadler. When will deforestation stop? In *1988 Glasgow Workshop on Functional Programming*, pages 39–56, August 1988.

5. G.W. Hamilton. *Compile-Time Garbage Avoidance.* Technical Report TR 74, Dept. of Computing Science and Mathematics, University of Stirling, 1991.

6. G.W. Hamilton and S.B. Jones. *Compile-Time Garbage Collection by Necessity Analysis.* Technical Report TR 67, Dept. of Computing Science and Mathematics, University of Stirling, 1990.

7. G.W. Hamilton and S.B. Jones. Transforming programs to eliminate intermediate structures. In *Journées de Travail sur L'Analyse Statique en Programmation Equationnelle Fonctionnelle et Logique*, pages 182–188, October 1991.

8. R.J.M. Hughes. Why functional programming matters. *The Computer Journal*, 32(2):98–107, April 1989.

9. S. Hughes. *Static Analysis of Store Use in Functional Programs.* PhD thesis, Imperial College, University of London, 1991. In preparation.

10. K. Inoue, H. Seki, and H. Yagi. Analysis of functional programs to detect runtime garbage cells. *ACM Transactions on Programming Languages and Systems*, 10(4):555–578, October 1988.

11. S.B. Jones and D. Le Metayer. Compile-time garbage collection by sharing analysis. In *Proceedings of the Fourth International Conference on Functional Programming Languages and Computer Architecture*, pages 54–74, 1989.

12. A. Mycroft. *Abstract Interpretation and Optimising Transformations for Applicative Programs.* PhD thesis, University of Edinburgh, 1981.

13. P. Wadler. Deforestation: transforming programs to eliminate trees. *Lecture Notes in Computer Science*, 300:344–358, 1988.

14. P. Wadler. Efficient compilation of pattern matching. In *The Implementation of Functional Programming Languages*, pages 78–103, Prentice Hall, 1987. S.L. Peyton Jones.

15. P. Wadler. Listlessness is better than laziness II: Composing listless functions. *Lecture Notes in Computer Science*, 217:282–305, 1985.

16. P. Wadler. Listlessness is better than laziness: Lazy evaluation and garbage collection at compile-time. In *Proceedings of the ACM Conference on LISP and Functional Programming*, pages 45–52, 1984.

Efficient Type Inference Using Monads (Summary)

Kevin Hammond, Glasgow University*.

Abstract

Efficient type inference algorithms are based on graph-rewriting techniques. Consequently, at first sight they seem unsuitable for functional language implementation. In fact, most compilers written in functional languages use substitution-based algorithms, at a considerable cost in performance. In this paper, we show how monads may be used to transform a substitution-based inference algorithm into one using a graph representation. The resulting algorithm is faster than the corresponding substitution-based algorithm.

1 Introduction

Type inference accounts for much of the cost of compiling a functional program. Typically around half of the total space and time requirements of a compilation in the Glasgow prototype Haskell compiler, or the Chalmers LML compiler, can be attributed directly to the costs of type inference. To some extent this reflects the nature of type inference — in general type-inference has time requirements which are exponential in the size of its input [7,8]. To some extent also, it reflects the state of functional compiler technology. Even so, it seems clear that the cost of type inference can be significantly reduced if the substitution-based algorithms used by many compilers writtem in functional languages can be replaced by the graph-rewriting techniques employed in the more efficient type-inference algorithms used by imperative compilers such as Standard ML of New Jersey.

Because this paper is a summary of a full paper, some details such as instantiation of non-generic type variables are necessarily omitted here. These details are entirely standard, however.

1.1 Type Inference

We define type inference with respect to a simple expression language, with variables, function applications, lambda abstractions and local definitions, as shown in Figure 1. The syntax of types and the associated type inference rules in Figures 2 & 3 respectively are entirely conventional, and are derived directly from those in e.g. [2,10].

1.2 Monads

A monad comprises a triple of a type constructor **M**, which is parameterised on a single type variable, plus two operations: `unitM`: $\forall\alpha.\ \alpha \rightarrow M\ \alpha$ and `thenM`: $\forall\alpha,\beta.\ M\ \alpha \rightarrow (\alpha \rightarrow M\ \beta) \rightarrow M\ \beta$. These operations must be related by the following laws [15]:

* Author's address: Department of Computing Science, 17 Lilybank Gardens, Glasgow, UK.
Electronic mail: kh@dcs.glasgow.ac.uk.

Identifiers	x	
Expressions	e ::=	x | $e_0\, e_1$ | $\lambda x.e$ | let x = e_0 in e_1

Figure 1: Formal syntax of expressions.

Type Variables	α	
Type Constructors	χ	
Types	τ ::=	$(\tau \rightarrow \tau')$ | α | $\chi(\tau_1 \ldots \tau_n)$
Type-schemes	σ ::=	$\forall \alpha.\sigma$ | τ

Figure 2: Formal syntax of types.

$$(unitM\ t)\ \text{`}thenM\text{`}\ (\lambda x.\ v) = v\,[t/x] \quad (1)$$

$$u\ \text{`}thenM\text{`}\ (\lambda x.\ unitM\ x) = u \quad (2)$$

$$u\ \text{`}thenM\text{`}\ (\lambda x.\ v\ \text{`}thenM\text{`}\ (\lambda y.\ w)) = (u\ \text{`}thenM\text{`}\ (\lambda x.\ v))\ \text{`}thenM\text{`}\ (\lambda y.\ w) \quad (3)$$

(we use the syntactic convention that `f `g` h = g f h`). The operation `thenM` is simply a reformulation of the Kliesli operator: `k* u = u `thenM` k`.

The structure-preserving properties of monads suggest their application to programming language semantics and also to issues of state, such as that presented here.

For example, for the monad of Lists:

$$unitList\ x = [x]$$

$$[]\ \text{`}thenList\text{`}\ k = []$$

$$(x : u)\ \text{`}thenList\text{`}\ k = (k\ x) +\!\!+ (u\ \text{`}thenList\text{`}\ k)$$

The papers by Moggi and Wadler [11,12,14,15] contain many more examples of monads, including the state-transformer and error-handling monads exploited in this paper.

2 Substitution-Based Type Inference

In this section we present a conventional type inference algorithm based on substitutions. Our algorithm is written in a "literate" dialect of Haskell [6], extended with macro-expanding "packages". A package is defined by **package** `P { f1, ..., fn }`, and used by **use** `P { a1, ..., an }`. When used, the body of the package is inserted in-line but with the formal parameters f_i replaced by the corresponding actual parameters a_i.

First we define the monad T which will be used for substitution-based type inference. This is a simple error-handling state-transformer monad, which is defined over substitutions and a type variable supply. The type variable supply provides new unique type variables where required by the algorithm.

In addition to the obvious **thenT** and **unitT** we also provide the primitive function **failT** to create new failure nodes. It is easy to verify that T does in fact constitute a monad.

Maybe a is used to encapsulate failures. For simplicity, we define only one kind of failure, **Fail**.

```
> package Monad { Repr, getReprT, putReprT } where

> data Maybe a =   Succ a                              {- Successes}
>                | Fail                                {- Failures-}

> type T a =       Repr -> Tyvars -> Maybe (Repr, Tyvars, a)

> thenT :: T a -> (a -> T b) -> T b
> k `thenT` cont =   \ r vs ->
>                    case k r vs of
>                        Succ (r', vs', res) ->  cont res r' vs'
>                        Fail ->                 Fail

> unitT :: a -> T a
> unitT a =          \ r vs -> Succ (r,vs,a)

> failT :: T a
> failT =            \ r vs -> Fail
```

Functions **getReprT**, **putReprT**, **getVsT** and **putVsT** may be used to acces monads components.

```
> getReprT :: T a -> Repr
> getReprT a =      \ r vs -> r

> putReprT :: Repr -> T ()
> putReprT r' =     \ r vs -> Succ (r', vs, () )

> getVsT :: T a -> Tyvars
> getVsT a =         \ r vs -> vs

> putVsT :: Tyvars -> T ()
> putVsT vs' =      \ r vs -> Succ (r, vs', () )
```

Now we define some basic types which will be used throughout this paper.

```
> package Types { Type } where
> data TypeR =      TyVar  Tyvars         {- Type Variables        -}
>                 | TyCon  Name [Type]    {- Type Constructors     -}
```

TAUT	$A, x:\sigma \vdash x:\sigma$
SPEC	$\dfrac{A \vdash e : \forall\alpha.\sigma}{A \vdash e : \sigma[\tau/\alpha]}$
GEN	$\dfrac{A \vdash e : \sigma}{A \vdash e : \forall\alpha.\sigma}$ α not free in A
COMB	$\dfrac{A \vdash e : (\tau' \to \tau),\quad A \vdash e' : \tau'}{A \vdash (e\ e') : \tau}$
ABS	$\dfrac{A_x, x : \tau' \vdash e : \tau}{A \vdash (\lambda x.e) : (\tau' \to \tau)}$
LET	$\dfrac{A \vdash e : \sigma,\quad A_x, x : \sigma \vdash e' : \tau}{A \vdash (\text{let } x = e \text{ in } e') : \tau}$

Figure 3: Hindley/Milner Type Inference Rules.

```
> data Expr =     Var    Name              {- Variables                -}
>               | Lambda Name Expr         {- λ name . expr            -}
>               | Let    Name Expr Expr    {- let name = expr in expr' -}
>               | Apply  Expr Expr         {- expr1 expr2              -}

> type Tyvars =   Int                      {- Type Variables are nos.  -}
> type Name =     String                   {- Identifiers              -}

> type Subst =    [(Tyvars,Type)]          {- Substitutions            -}

> type NgEnv =    [Tyvars]                 {- NonGeneric Type Var Env. -}
> type NTEnv =    [(Name,Type)]            {- Name/Type Environment    -}
> type Env =      (NgEnv,NTEnv)            {- Combined Environment     -}
```

2.1 The Basic Algorithm

The most commonly presented type inference algorithms are based on algorithm *W* [2,10]. This uses the notion of *substitutions* — environments mapping type variables to types — to implement type unification. The corresponding monadic algorithm, in Haskell, is presented below. The syntax `\ i1 ... ik -> e` is a Haskell lambda-expression equivalent to $\lambda i_1. \ldots \lambda i_n. e$ and `v@p` is a so-called named- (or as-) pattern. Guards appear on the lhs of a definition following a vertical bar ("|").

The most interesting case is function application (that is the implementation of the **COMB** rule of Figure 3). This uses the unification algorithm `unify` to unify two types: the type of the function part `t1`; and a function from the type of the argument part `t2` to a new type `tr`. The unification algorithm returns a substitution which can be used to replace type variables in the original expressions with their unified types. After substitution, `tr` is returned as the type of the application.

The environment `env` contains a name-to-type mapping, updated by *let* expressions. It also contains an environment of nongeneric type variables, updated by λ-expressions. This environment is used during the instantiation of types as a result of `lookup`. Any *generic* type variable will be replaced (consistently) by a new type variable in the type returned by `lookup`. Nongeneric type variables, however, are not replaced by new type variables but are used directly in the type returned by `lookup`. This implements the SPEC rule of Figure 3. The GEN rule is implemented implicitly by the scoping of the nongeneric type variable environment.

Any of the recursive calls to `infer`, or the unification in the **COMB** rule may fail. Propagation of failures is handled implicitly by `thenT`. This is one advantage of the monadic approach.

```
> package Infer ( Type, substT, newType, newTyvar ) where

> infer :: Env -> Expr -> T Type
> infer env (Var x) =
>         lookup env x                             `thenT` ( \ t    ->
>         substT t                                         )

> infer env (Apply e1 e2) =
>         infer env e1                             `thenT` ( \ t1   ->
>         infer env e2                             `thenT` ( \ t2   ->
>         newTyvar                                 `thenT` ( \ tr   ->
>         applyT t2 tr                             `thenT` ( \ at   ->
>         unify t1 at                              `thenT` ( \ ()   ->
>         substT tr                                        )))))

> infer env (Lambda i e) =
>         newTyvar                                 `thenT` ( \ ti   ->
>         makeNonGeneric ti (bindEnv env i ti)     `thenT` ( \ env' ->
>         infer env' e                             `thenT` ( \ te   ->
>         substT ti                                `thenT` ( \ ti'  ->
>         applyT ti' te                                    ))))

> infer env (Let i e1 e2) =
>         infer env e1                             `thenT` ( \ ti   ->
>         infer (bindEnv env i ti) e2                      )

> applyT t1 t2 =  newType (TyCon  "->" [t1, t2])    {- t1 → t2 -}
```

The implementation of the unification algorithm is similarly straightforward. A most general substitution is created if the algorithm succeeds.

```
> package Unify { Type, unify, unifyV, substT } where

> unifyR :: TypeR -> TypeR -> T ()
> unifyR  (TyVar v1)         (TyVar v2) | v1 == v2 =   unitT ()
> unifyR  t1@(TyVar v)       t2 =                      unifyV v t2
> unifyR  t1                 t2@(TyVar v) =            unifyR t2 t1
> unifyR  (TyCon tc1 ts1)   (TyCon tc2 ts2)
>         | tc1 == tc2 =                               unifyList ts1 ts2
> unifyR t1 t2 =                                       failT
```

unifyList unifies two lists of types.

```
> unifyList :: [Type] -> [Type] -> T ()
> unifyList [] [] =                                    unitT ()

> unifyList (t1:t1s) (t2:t2s) =
>     substT t1                                        `thenT` ( \ t1' ->
>     substT t2                                        `thenT` ( \ t2' ->
>     unify t1' t2'                                    `thenT` ( \ ()  ->
>     unifyList t1s t2s                                        )))
```

We can now complete the substitution algorithm by defining the primitive substitution operations. The function substT applies a substitution to a type; newSubst creates a new substitution and newTyvar operates on the type variable supply to generate a new type variable. **unifyV** unifies a type variable with a type, creating a new substitution. It fails if the type variable to be substituted already occurs in the type, i.e. if a cyclic substitution would be ceated.

```
> module Subst where

> use Types { Type }
> use Monad { Subst, getSubstT, putSubstT }
> use Unify { Type, unify, unifyV, substT }
> use Infer { Type, substT, unitT, newTyvar }

> type Type = TypeR

> unifyV :: Tyvars -> TypeR -> T ()
> unifyV t1 t2 =  substT t1 `thenT` unifyvs
>     where  unifyvs t1'@(TyVar v') | occurs v' t2 = failT
>                                   | otherwise =    newSubst v' t2
>            unifyvs t1' =                           unify t1' t2
```

```
> substT ::    Type -> T Type
> substT t =
>       getSubstT                                    `thenT`  ( \ s  ->
>       unitT (applyS s t)                                    )

> newSubst :: Tyvars -> Type -> T ()
> newSubst v t =
>       getSubstT                                    `thenT`  ( \ s  ->
>       putSubstT (extendSubst s v t)                         )

> newTyvar :: T Type
> newTyvar =
>       getVsT                                       `thenT`  ( \ vs ->
>       putVsT (vs+1)                                `thenT`  ( \ () ->
>       unitT (TyVar vs)                                      ))
```

In the definitions of `infer` and `unify`, we have assumed that substitutions are idempotent (that is, that $s \,.\, s = s$). A proof may be found in Milner's paper [10].

3 The Graph-Rewriting Algorithm

This algorithm is based on Henglein's unification algorithm *A* [4], which is in turn derived from the unification algorithms of Paterson and Wegman [13], and Martelli and Montanari [9]. A similar algorithm is described by Aho, Sethi and Ullman [1]. The basic data structure required is a heap of type nodes, which we represent by a pure functional array. An index associated with each heap node defines the equivalence class of that node. This will be used for efficient comparison of nodes which have already been unified. We also change the basic representation of types so that the arguments to type constructors are now indexes into the heap. This creates an acyclic graph whose nodes are type constructors and virgin type variables and whose arcs are children of type constructors and type variables which have been unified with other types.

The monad T becomes an error-handling state-transformer monad over the heap and an index. The index is overloaded both as a heap "high-water mark" and as a type variable supply. This implies that each new type variable created will use a new heap location. The heap may be garbage-collected to free short-lived types by traversing the graphs of all live types. This would either require a compacting collector, or the use of a free list in place of the simple type variable supply used here.

```
> module Heap where

> use Types { Type }
> use Monad { Heap, getHeapT, putHeapT }
> use Unify { Type, unifyH, unifyV, unitT }
> use Infer { Type, unitT, newType, newTyvar }
```

```
> type Index =    Tyvars
> type Type =     Index
> type Heap =     Array Index (TypeR,Index)
```

`newTyvar` now returns a new heap location, which is initialised to a type variable. `newType` is similar, but returns a new heap location initialised with the specified type.

```
> newTyvar :: T Type
> newTyvar =
>       getHeapT                                       `thenT` ( \ h  ->
>       getVsT                                         `thenT` ( \ vs ->
>       putHeapT (h // (vs := (TyVar vs,vs)))          `thenT` ( \ () ->
>       putVsT   (vs+1)                                        )))

> newType :: TypeR -> T Type
> newType t =
>       newTyvar                                       `thenT` ( \ v  ->
>       updateT v t                                    `thenT` ( \ () ->
>       unitT v                                                ))
```

Conceptually, the graph-based algorithm is quite simple. A two-level unification algorithm is used in place of the one-level algorithm used earlier. The outer level unifies references, short-circuiting unification when two nodes are identical or in the same equivalence class. The inner level unifies types, and is identical to the substitution algorithm except that rather than creating a new substitution, the heap node corresponding to a type variable is updated.

At the outer level (unifying heap nodes), two nodes which are in the same equivalence class must have been unified already, therefore any attempt to unify these nodes will terminate successfully. Two nodes which are to be unified are joined into the same equivalence class before unification. Identical nodes (those with the same reference) also unify trivially.

Because the algorithm will unify cyclic structures without failing [13] the *occurs* check may be omitted here. Since the equivalence classes of the nodes are updated before type unification, any two nodes which have already been unified will belong to the same equivalence class. It follows that unification will always succeed immediately the second time two nodes are encountered, and therefore the algorithm will terminate. However, because types are required to be acyclic, it is still necessary to check for acyclicity at the outermost level of unification. This can be done using a simple linear graph-traversal algorithm, recording nodes as they are visited. This trades one traversal at each substitution of a type variable for one traversal at each call to `unify` in the type inference algorithm.

Figure 5 shows the unification of two types represented as graphs. Double lines represent unification of equivalence classes. Dashed lines represent unification of type variables with types. Unification proceeds top-down.

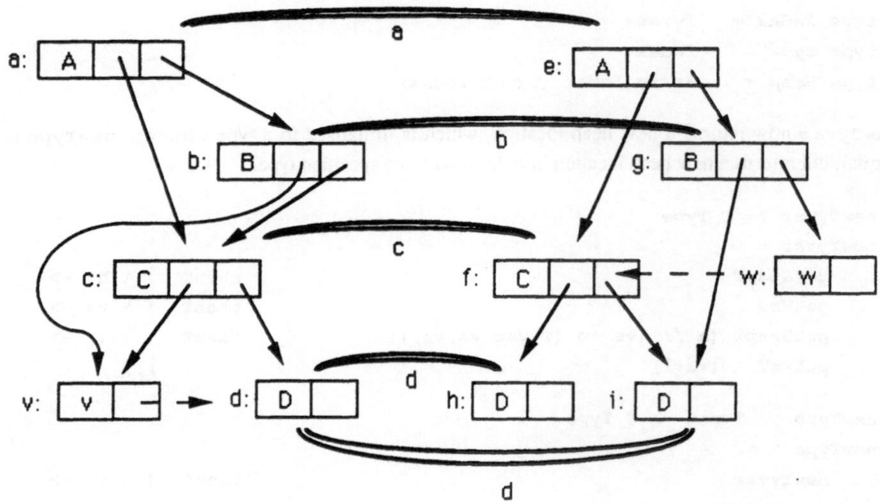

Figure 5: Unifying two types using the graph-rewriting algorithm.

This algorithm updates the base equivalence classes (determined by **followEqs**). This is important, since the effects of the unification will then be shared by other nodes in the same equivalence class. A minor optimisation to our algorithm is to update also the equivalences on the nodes themselves. This avoids the necessity to follow a chain of equivalences during subsequent unifications involving the same nodes.

unifyV is identical to the substitution version, but uses (**updateT v t2**) instead of (**newSubst v t2**) and has no *occurs* check.

```
> unify :: Type -> Type -> T ()
> unify r1 r2 | r1 == r2 =                        unitT ()
>             | otherwise =
>     derefH r1                                   `thenT` ( \ (_,eq1)   ->
>     derefH r2                                   `thenT` ( \ (_,eq2)   ->
>     followEqs eq1 r1                            `thenT` ( \ (t1,eq1') ->
>     followEqs eq2 r2                            `thenT` ( \ (t2,eq2') ->

>     if eq1' == eq2' then unitT ()
>     else
>        ( updateH eq1' eq2'                      `thenT` ( \ () ->
>          unifyR t1 t2                                   ) ) ))))

> unifyV :: Tyvars -> TypeR -> T ()
> unifyV v t2 =                                   updateT v t2
```

The basic heap operations which we have used in the unification algorithm are defined below. `h!r` returns the value referenced by element `r` of `h`. `h // (r := (t,eq))` is a Haskell expression which updates element `r` of `h` with the value `(t,eq)`.

```
> derefH :: Index -> T (TypeR,Index)
> derefH r =
>     getHeapT                                    `thenT` ( \ h  ->
>     unitT (h!r)                                         )

> updateEq :: Index -> Index -> T ()
> updateEq r eq =
>     getHeapT                                    `thenT` ( \ h  ->
>     putHeapT (h // (r := (t,eq)))
>     where (t,_) = h ! r                                 )

> updateT :: Index -> TypeR -> T ()
> updateT r t =
>     getHeapT                                    `thenT` ( \ h  ->
>     putHeapT (h // (r := (t,eq)))
>     where (_,eq) = h ! r                                )

> followEqs :: Index -> T Index
> followEqs r =
>     derefH r                                    `thenT` ( \ (t,eq) ->
>     if r == eq then  unitT eq  else followEqs eq        )
```

Since all operations on the heap are encapsulated within the monad, it is easy to verify that the heap is never duplicated or erased by any function call [14]. It follows that the array representing the heap may be updated destructively, since all references following an update to the heap will use the updated value rather than the original value [5]. In fact, a similar argument also applies to the sequential substitution algorithms presented above: substitutions may also be represented by a destructively updatable aggregate data structure, such as an imperative array.

The new definition of `infer` is identical to that used for substitutions, but with `substT` replaced by `unitT`, and `newType` used to create the new apply types in function application and lambda abstraction. Type instantiation in `lookup` must also create new heap types explicitly rather than simply returning the instantiated types as values.

The graph-based algorithm is a significant improvement over the substitution-based algorithms presented earlier. Type variables will be substituted for types exactly once, rather than many times; two terms will be unified at most once (zero times if they are identical, or they have identical equivalence classes from other unifications). Identical terms need not be traversed. However, the algorithm may still traverse a sub-graph many times if there are multiple roots to that sub-graph. It is possible to avoid this behaviour by performing any necessary unification for the parents of each node before performing unification for that node. All equivalences for a single node may then be unified simultaneously [13]. This results in a linear unification algorithm, where each node is examined exactly once during the unification of two graphs. However, the associated overheads are high: each node must record its parents; it is necessary to use a set of equivalences rather than the single equivalence used here; and it is also necessary to delete unified nodes during unification. The latter constraint implies that two graphs to be unified must each be traversed twice before unification to unset their deleted markers (the second traversal is to reset the traversal marker for each node).

4 Efficiency of Substitutions versus Graphs

Given the theoretical result that ML type inference is DTIME($2^{n^{O(1)}}$) complete, even with a linear unification algorithm [7,8], it is clear that we can only improve on the constant associated with the complexity of type inference, rather than the order of the complexity. However, even this constant factor reduction may be significant in practice. For space reasons, a detailed comparison is omitted here, but may be found in the full paper. Results show that this constant factor should be at least 2, perhaps higher.

5 Summary and Conclusions

Using monads, we have developed a fast, efficient type inference algorithm from a simple substitution-based algorithm. The algorithm which has been developed is based on graph rewriting, but has been specified in a pure functional language. Since this algorithm is single-threaded [5], the principal data structures used here may be updated destructively. Although our unification algorithm is not linear in the size of its inputs, as is claimed for at least one algorithm [13], it is likely to be more efficient in practice than these algorithms since it has less overhead for small terms. In the full paper, we have also shown how a "pruning" substitution algorithm and a parallel substitution algorithm may be developed from the same basis. Even though we have been unable to reformulate inference as a purely monadic operation, clearly monads are a powerful structuring technique. Using simple unfolding transformations, the overheads of using monads may be considerably reduced.

We had hoped that by using monads we could derive a parallel graph-rewriting type inference algorithm similar to that of [3] by combining the parallel substitution algorithm with the sequential graph-rewriting algorithm. However, this does not seem to be possible without splitting and recombining the heap in the **COMB** rule: an unacceptable overhead for distributed parallel machines. A locking mechanism is also necessary to prevent multiple writes to the same heap node, but without serialising access to the heap. These are particularly hard problems for a pure functional language.

Acknowledgements

I would like to thank Rysard Kubiak and Cordy Hall for reading and commenting on an earlier draft of this paper. The referees also provided much useful feedback, which I have attempted to use. This work was supported by the SERC GRASP project.

References

1. Aho A, Sethi R, Ullman J. *Compilers: Principles, Techniques, and Tools*, Addison Wesley, 1986.

2. Damas L, Milner R. "Principal type schemes for functional programs", *Proc. 9th ACM POPL*, Albuquerque, NM, 1982, pp 207-212.

3. Hammond K, *Parallel SML: A Functional Language and its Implementation in Dactl*, Pitman Research Monographs in Parallel and Distributed Computing, Pitman Press, 1991.

4. Henglein F. "Type Inference with Polymorphic Recursion", *To appear in ACM TOPLAS*, 1992.

5. Hudak P, Bloss A. "The Aggregate Update Problem in Functional Programming Systems", *Proc. 12th. ACM POPL*, 1985, pp 300-314.

6. Hudak P, Wadler PL (Eds.). "Report on the Programming Language Haskell, Version 1.0", *Technical Report of the Universities of Glasgow and Yale*, 1990.

7. Kfoury AJ, Tiuryn J, Urzyczyn P. "ML Typability is DEXPTIME-Complete", *Proc. CAAP 90*, Springer Verlag LN, 1990, pp 206-220.

8. Mairson HG. "Deciding ML Typability is Complete for Deterministic Exponential Time", *Proc. 17th. ACM POPL*, 1990, pp 382-401.

9. Martelli A, Montanari U. "An Efficient Unification Algorithm", *TOPLAS*, 4(2):258-282, April 1982.

10. Milner RJ. "A Theory of Type Polymorphism in Programming", *J Comp Sys Sci*, 17:348-75, 1978.

11. Moggi E. "Computational Lambda-Calculus and Monads". In *Symp. Logic in Comp. Sci.*, 1989.

12. Moggi E. "The Mathematical Structure of Programming Languages", *unpublished report*, University di Genova, May 1991.

13. Paterson M. Wegman M. "Linear Unification", *J. Comp. Sys. Sci.*, 16:158-167, 1978.

14. Wadler PL. "Comprehending Monads", In *Proc. Lisp & FP 90*, Nice, 1990.

15. Wadler PL, "The Essence of Functional Programming", Proc. 18th. ACM POPL, 1992.

Generating More Practical Compilers by Partial Evaluation

Rogardt Heldal*

Abstract

Given an abstract machine code specified denotationally as a set of combinators, and given a semantics for a programming language in terms of these combinators, this paper shows how to automatically generate native-code compilers.

1 Introduction

In this paper we discuss the generation of compilers by partial evaluation. Recall that a partial evaluator *Mix* is a program transformer which given a program p and some of its inputs s, generates a specialised program p_s such that for all remaining input d,

$$p_s\ d = p\ s\ d$$

In general, the specialised program is more efficient than the original. Given an interpreter *int* for some programming language L, together with an L-program *prog* we may use partial evaluation to "compile" the L-program by specialising *int* [4, 8] such that for all suitable input data *data*,

$$int_{prog}\ data = int\ prog\ data$$

So int_{prog} can be thought of as a compiled version of *prog*. Of course, int_{prog} is expressed in the language in which this *int* is written, not in a machine-like language as one might expect. Moreover, if *sint* is a self interpreter (written in the same language it interprets) then it is a stated goal of partial evaluation that for any program p,

$$sint_p = p$$

This is usually interpreted to mean that the partial evaluator has "removed an entire layer of interpretation". But we can also interpret it as saying that no compilation has taken place. Our goal is to perform realistic compilation by partial evaluation: to generate "code" of a low-level nature, in which structures such as stacks and heaps are explicitly manipulated. Our specialised program can be regarded as abstract

* Department of Computing Science, University of Glasgow, 17 Lilybank Gdns, Glasgow G12 8QQ, United Kingdom. Supported by the Norwegian Government, Email: heldalr@dcs.glasgow.ac.uk

machine code and translated straightforwardly to a C program. To achieve this we specialise non-standard interpreters in which low-level operations are made explicit. Of course, partial evaluation can also be used to generate stand-alone compilers for the language interpreted by *int*. We have built tools for generating stand-alone compilers: the generated code is a C program. In the remainder of this paper we take a simple first-order strict functional language as an example, and show how we can generate a compiler to C via abstract machine code for a stack machine. Knowledge about partial evaluation and functional languages is assumed. In the following we use a subset of LML [1].

2 Stack interpreter for the example language

Using LML, we define stack operations corresponding to abstract machine instructions, e.g. `loadnum`, `loadarg`, `add`, `discard`, `testzero` etc. The `loadnum` operation pushes an element onto a stack, the `loadarg` finds an argument in the environment and pushes it onto a stack, `add` pops two arguments from a stack and adds them together and pushes the result onto the stack, `discard` removes the actual arguments pushed onto the stack before a function call, and leaves the result of the function call on the top of the stack, and `testzero` test if the top element of a stack is zero.

We define an interpreter in terms of these operations. To see how this is done, look at the following extract from the interpreter.

```
eval prog f_args a_args (Num n) s = loadnum n s
eval prog f_args a_args (Add e1 e2) s = add (eval prog f_args a_args e2
                                              (eval prog f_args a_args e1 s))
...

eval prog f_args a_args (Parm x) s = loadargs (position f_args x) a_args s
eval prog f_args a_args (Call f_name a_args') s =
              discard (number a_args')
                      (eval_function prog (prog_lookup prog f_name)
                         (map_eval prog f_args a_args a_args' s))
eval prog f_args a_args (If e1 e2 e3) s =
              jump prog f_args a_args e2 e3 (eval prog f_args a_args e1 s)

jump prog f_args a_args e1 e2 s =
              if testzero s then eval prog f_args a_args e1 (pop s)
              else eval prog f_args a_args e2 (pop s)

eval_function prog (f_name, f_args, body) a_args =
              eval prog f_args a_args body a_args

loadnum n s = n.s
add s       = (hd (tl s) + hd s).tl (tl s)
```

The function **eval** takes a stack **stack**, and an expression **exp**, and gives as result the stack with the evaluation of **exp** on the top of **stack**. The function **eval** also has as arguments a variable environment and a function environment **prog**. The variable environment is split up into a list of actual arguments **actual** and a list of formal arguments **formal**.

3 Specialising the stack interpreter

In this section we consider specialising the above interpreter to particular programs: that is, compiling by partial evaluation. The specialiser we have distinguishes between two kinds of function calls: *eliminable* calls, which are unfolded, and *residual* calls which are replaced by calls to versions of the functions specialised to their static (known) parameters. Therefore only the dynamic parameters need be passed to specialised functions. The programmer chooses which calls will be residual and which parameters will be static by annotating the program that is to be specialised: the details of how this is done will not concern us here.

The arguments **prog**, **formal** and **exp** will disappear because they will be annotated as static. We choose to make calls of **eval_function** and **jump** residual, but we do not want the functions corresponding to abstract machine instructions to be specialised: it would be silly for example to create a specialised "instruction" for loading argument three. The way of solving this problem is to introduce a new type of annotation. We annotate all machine instructions as *machine* calls. The specialiser will evaluate the static arguments in functions annotated as machine calls, but will not remove the static arguments as in a residual call. The definitions of machine calls will be ignored. Some care has to be taken when the interpreter is annotated because of problems such as code duplication, call duplication, infinite unfolding, etc. [6]. If we specialise the interpreter to the program **power** defined by:

```
power n x = if n then 1 else x * power (n - 1) x
```

we obtain the following generated code:

```
run a_args = eval_function a_args

eval_function a_args = jump a_args (loadargs 0 a_args a_args )

jump a_args s =
     if testzero s then loadnum 1 (pop s)
     else mul (discard 2
             (eval_function (sub (loadnum 1 (loadargs 0 a_args
             (loadargs 1 a_args (loadargs 1 a_args (pop s))))))))
```

If we look at the generated code we can see that the function **eval_function** corresponds to the function **power** and the function **jump** corresponds to the **if-expr**. We can think of this as machine code, having only machine instructions, conditions and function calls.

4 Implementing the abstract machine code in C

By construction, all functions in the specialised code are strict, and there are no data structures other than the stack. If we ignore the definition of the abstract machine calls, we have residual code which contains only conditions, function calls, and abstract machine calls. We can therefore give a straightforward translation into C of the previously generated **power** function.

```
#include <stdio.h>
#include "genlib.h"

int *run_0();
int *eval_function_1();
int *jump_2();

int *run_0(a_args)
int *a_args;
    {
    return eval_function_1(a_args);
    }

int *eval_function_1(a_args)
int *a_args;
    {
    return jump_2(a_args,loadargs(0,a_args,a_args));
    }

int *jump_2(a_args,s)
int *a_args;
int *s;
    {
    return (testzero(s))
    ? loadnum(1,pop(s))
    : mul(discard(2,eval_function_1(sub
                (loadnum(1, loadargs(0,a_args, loadargs(1,a_args,
                 loadargs(1,a_args,pop(s)))))))));
}
```

We supply a library with the abstract machine code instructions implemented in C. When we wrote the interpreter we ensured that the stack was single-threaded by only passing one copy around. The C definition can take advantage of the stack being single-threaded and implement it as an updatable array. The C definitions can therefore be made much more efficient than the LML definitions.

5 Related work

There have been some efforts to produce compilers from denotational semantics, one of the earliest being SIS [5]. The problem with this system is that the compilers produced are extremely slow compared with hand-written ones. Also, the denotational description can be very complex and for that reason hard to write and change.

Wand has worked on transforming interpreters to compilers [7]. His idea is to take an interpreter and replace the functions with code representations. By doing this he produces a compiler. This is similar to what we are trying to do, except that we are trying to do this automatically by partial evaluation.

Holst wrote a partial evaluator which generates machine code [3]. The approach Holst used is related to the one here. Instead of his partial evaluator producing residual programs in *Scheme*, they produced SECD style machine code. This meant that machine code could be produced for any residual program, but at the cost of a more general evaluation strategy.

At Glasgow there is a group investigating the use of *action semantics* to define the syntax and semantics of programming languages and from the definition produce compilers automatically. This project is still in an initial phase; but they have a prototype compiler generator, ACTRESS [2].

6 Conclusion

By specialising a stack interpreter with explicit machine call instructions we have managed to produce code for an abstract machine. For *nfib*, compilation produces a speed up factor of 28 over interpretation. The code runs 5 times slower than the code produced for nfib by the LML compiler. We are still working on improving the time efficiency, for example, by using macros instead of functions.

Our next goal is to find out whether this technique of writing and annotating interpreters can be applied to other programming languages, e.g. imperative languages and logical languages.

We will also make an annotation which globalises arguments such as the stack and store, for example; we do not want the C functions to pass around the store.

We will also write interpreters in a continuation-passing style and see if they can be easily transformed into compilers producing abstract machine code.

We hope to find an automatic binding-time analysis which includes our new annotations.

7 Acknowledgements

Thanks are due to my supervisor John Hughes, for direction and encouragement, and to Carsten Kehler Holst and John Launchbury for comments.

Bibliography

1. Lennart Augustsson and Thomas Johnsson. *Lazy ML user's manual.* Dept. of Computer Science, Chalmers University of Technology, Gøteborg, Sweden, 1990.

2. Deryck F. Brown, Hermano Moura, and David A. Watt. Towards a realistic semantics-directed compiler generator. *Glasgow Workshops in Functional Programming, Draft Proceedings*, pages 59–74, 1991.

3. Carsten Kehler Holst. Program specialization for compiler generation. Master's thesis, DIKU, University of Copenhagen, 1989.

4. N.D. Jones, P.Sestoft, and H. Søndergaard. Mix: A self-applicable partial evaluator for experiments in compiler generation. *Lisp and Symbolic Computation*, pages 9–50, 1989.

5. P. D. Mosses. Sis – Semantics Implementation System, Reference Manual and User Guide. DAIMI MD - 30, Computer Scince Department, Århus University, Denmark, 1979.

6. Peter Sestoft. Automatic call unfolding in a partial evaluator. *IFIP TC2 Workshop on Partial Evaluation and Mixed Computation*, pages 485–506, 1988.

7. Mitchell Wand. From inerpreter to compilers: A representational derivation. *Springer Lecture Notes in Computer Science*, pages 306–324, 1985.

8. Y.Futamura. Partial evaluation of computation process – an approach to a compiler-compiler. *System, Computers, Controls*, pages 45–50, 1971.

A Loop-Detecting Interpreter for Lazy Programs

Carsten Kehler Holst and John Hughes*

Abstract

This paper develops a loop detecting interpreter for a lazy language. The loop detection scheme is a further development of what takes place in memoising interpreters and in pending analysis. It is our hope that the work described in this paper, in the end, will help to improve both of these, and be a stepping stone towards a non-trivial partial evaluator for a lazy language.

Keywords: Termination, interpreter, partial evaluation, pending analysis, laziness.

1 Introduction

Imagine that a compiler writer wishes to evaluate constant expressions at compile-time. There is an immediate problem: evaluation of any particular expression may fail to terminate, but we expect compilers to terminate for all inputs. The compiler must therefore avoid evaluating any expression that loops infinitely. Since it is impossible to identify such expressions precisely, the compiler must be conservative and leave unevaluated some expressions that would, in fact, terminate.

How is the compiler to select expressions for evaluation? One possibility is to try to evaluate all constant expressions, but place an ad-hoc bound on the depth of recursion permitted. If the bound is exceeded, the expression is classified as potentially non-terminating and left in its original form. While this strategy works it is unattractive: if the bound is set low, only trivial expressions can be evaluated by the compiler, while if it is set high much time may be wasted trying to evaluate truly non-terminating expressions. Much more appealing is for the compiler to *prove* that certain expressions terminate, for example by syntactic detection of primitive recursion, and then evaluate those expressions however long they take.

But now suppose that the compiler uses a non-standard interpreter to evaluate constant expressions—a *loop detecting* interpreter that terminates more often than the standard interpreter, sometimes producing the special value 'LOOP'. We call expressions on which this interpreter terminates *quasi-terminating*. Now it's sufficient for the compiler to prove an expression quasi-terminating before evaluating it, and in general this is easier. (Of course, even if an expression can only be

---

* Both at: Department of Computing Science, University of Glasgow, Glasgow G12 8QQ, Email: {kehler, rjmh}@dcs.glasgow.ac.uk

proved quasi-terminating its evaluation may well terminate). Thus the use of a loop-detecting interpreter allows the compiler to adopt a more aggressive strategy when choosing expressions to evaluate.

Other applications are partial evaluation and abstract interpretation. In partial evaluation the evaluation of static expressions corresponds closely to the evaluation of constant expression described above. Probably more important: function specialisation might loop, giving either infinite unfolding or infinite specialisation. In abstract interpretation we can use normal evaluation instead of calculation of the minimal fixpoint by iteration if we can prove that the abstract function terminates. If the abstract function only is quasi-terminating the loop-detecting evaluation corresponds to pending analysis; the 'LOOP' is approximated by $\perp$ and one iterates until a minimal fixpoint is found.

A very simple loop-detecting interpreter just compares the arguments of recursive function calls with those of dynamically enclosing calls of the same function. If the arguments match those of an earlier call an infinite loop has been detected. An analysis that can prove expressions quasi-terminating with respect to this interpreter is presented in Holst [1].

However, this approach fails for a lazy language, because it requires function arguments to be evaluated at the point of call for comparison with the arguments of enclosing calls. The loop-detecting interpreter might go into an undetected loop while evaluating a parameter that would never actually be used, and therefore fail to terminate in a case when the ordinary lazy evaluator would! This is unacceptable.

A more subtle problem is that this interpreter fails to detect some quite obvious loops. Consider the function

```
f x y = if x=0 then 1 else f x (y+1)
```

If `x` is non-zero this function loops infinitely, yet no two recursive calls have the same arguments. However, the second parameter is irrelevant since it isn't tested in the condition, and an interpreter which ignored it and just compared first parameters could detect the loop. This is also related to laziness: a lazy interpreter would never evaluate `y` and so should be able to detect this loop.

In the remainder of the paper we'll take the very simple loop-detecting interpreter as a starting point, and show how to modify it first to detect loops such as the one above in strict programs. Having done so, it is fairly easy to modify it further to work for lazy programs.

2 Language

The language is a simple first-order language with flat domains and no structures. The syntax of the language can be found in figure 1. We shall consider both strict and non-strict semantics.

2.1 Standard Semantics

The standard semantics is given in figure 2. It is for a strict version of the language as can be seen by the test on $\perp$ in the semantic function $\mathcal{F}$. By removing this test we get the non-strict semantics. The semantic function $\mathcal{P}$ is going to be

$$x, x_i, \ldots \in \text{Var},\ e, e_i, \ldots \in \text{Exp},\ f, f_i, \ldots \in \text{Fnames},\ o \in \text{Operators}$$

$$\text{Prog} ::= f_1(x_1, \ldots, x_{n_{f_1}}) = e_1,\ \ldots,\ f_m(x_1, \ldots, x_{n_{f_m}}) = e_m$$

$$\text{Exp} ::= x_i \mid o(e_1, \ldots, e_{n_o}) \mid e_1 \rightarrow e_2 [\!] e_3 \mid f(e_1, \ldots, e_{n_f})$$

Figure 1: Syntax

$$\begin{array}{lcl} \text{Val} & = & D \\ \text{Venv} & = & \text{Vnames} \rightarrow \text{Val} \\ \text{Fenv} & = & \text{Fnames} \rightarrow \text{Val} \rightarrow \ldots \rightarrow \text{Val} \\ \mathcal{O} & = & \text{Operators} \rightarrow \text{Val} \end{array}$$

$$\mathcal{P} :: \text{Prog} \rightarrow \text{Fenv}$$

$$\mathcal{P}[\![\ f_1(x_1, \ldots, x_n) = e_1,\ \ldots, f_m(x_1, \ldots, x_n) = e_m\ ]\!] = fix\ \lambda\phi.[\ldots\ f_i \mapsto \mathcal{F}[\![\ f_i(x_1, \ldots, x_n) = e_i\ ]\!]\phi, \ldots]$$

$$\mathcal{F} :: \text{Def} \rightarrow \text{Fenv} \rightarrow \text{Fenv}$$

$$\mathcal{F}[\![\ f(x_1, \ldots, x_n) = e\ ]\!] = \lambda v_1 \ldots v_n.\ \text{if any } v_i = \bot \text{ then } \bot \text{ else } \mathcal{E}[\![\ e\ ]\!][\ldots, x_i \mapsto v_i, \ldots]\phi$$

$$\mathcal{E} :: \text{Exp} \rightarrow \text{Venv} \rightarrow \text{Fenv} \rightarrow \text{Val}$$

$$\begin{array}{lcl} \mathcal{E}[\![\ x\ ]\!]\rho\phi & = & \rho\ x \\ \mathcal{E}[\![\ o(e_1, \ldots, e_n)\ ]\!]\rho\ \phi & = & \mathcal{O}[\![\ o\ ]\!]\ (\mathcal{E}[\![\ e_1\ ]\!]\rho\ \phi) \ldots (\mathcal{E}[\![\ e_n\ ]\!]\rho\ \phi) \\ \mathcal{E}[\![\ e_1 \rightarrow e_2 [\!] e_3\ ]\!]\rho\phi & = & \mathcal{E}[\![\ e_1\ ]\!]\rho\ \phi \rightarrow \mathcal{E}[\![\ e_2\ ]\!]\rho\ \phi [\!] \mathcal{E}[\![\ e_3\ ]\!]\rho\ \phi \\ \mathcal{E}[\![\ f(e_1, \ldots, e_n)\ ]\!]\rho\ \phi & = & \phi\ f\ (\mathcal{E}[\![\ e_1\ ]\!]\rho\ \phi) \ldots (\mathcal{E}[\![\ e_n\ ]\!]\rho\ \phi) \end{array}$$

Figure 2: Standard Semantics

the same in all our interpreters so we shall omit it in the future. $\mathcal{O}$ is the semantic function giving meaning to the primitive operations. The primitive operations are strict.

3 A Simple Loop-Detecting Interpreter

The simplest loop detection scheme compares every call with all the *dynamically* surrounding calls. If a call turns out to be a repetition of one of the surrounding calls we have encountered a loop and return 'LOOP'.

Perhaps the most obvious scheme would be to keep a list of all the surrounding calls made so far, and pass the list inwards at every call. Our approach is different. Our interpreter returns the value of each expression paired with a *history* recording which function calls were made. The value domain is lifted with the new bottom value 'LOOP', V_{LOOP}. The interpretation of a function call looks down the history of the evaluation of its body checking if a repeated call is made, and if so returns

'LOOP'. Otherwise it returns the value together with the history augmented with information about itself. A history is a sequence of events. The empty sequence is denoted by ϵ, and concatenation of sequences is denoted by juxtapositioning. The events are descriptions of function calls of the form (Call $f\ v_1 \ldots v_n$), meaning that function f was called with argument values $v_1 \ldots v_n$. $\mathcal{O}$ is strict in both $\bot$, and LOOP.

$$
\begin{array}{lcl}
\text{Val} & = & (V_{\text{LOOP}}, \text{Hist}) \\
\text{Event} & = & \text{Call}(\text{Fname}, \text{V}^*) \\
\text{Hist} & = & \text{Event}^* \\
\text{Venv} & = & \text{Vnames} \rightarrow \text{Val} \\
\text{Fenv} & = & \text{Fnames} \rightarrow \text{Val} \rightarrow \ldots \rightarrow \text{Val} \\
\mathcal{O} & = & \text{Operators} \rightarrow V \rightarrow \ldots \rightarrow V
\end{array}
$$

$$\mathcal{F} :: \text{Def} \rightarrow \text{Fenv} \rightarrow \text{Val} \rightarrow \ldots \rightarrow \text{Val}$$

$$
\begin{array}{lcl}
\mathcal{F}[\![\, f(x_1, \ldots, x_n) = e \,]\!]\phi & = & \lambda(v_1, h_1) \ldots (v_n, h_n). \\
 & & \text{if any } v_i = \bot \text{ then } (\bot, \epsilon) \\
 & & \text{elsf any } v_i = \text{LOOP then } (\text{LOOP}, \epsilon) \\
 & & \text{elsf } (\text{Call } f\ v_1 \ldots v_n) \in h \text{ then } (\text{LOOP}, \epsilon) \\
 & & \text{else } (r, h_1 \ldots h_n\ (\text{Call } f\ v_1\ \ldots\ v_n))\ h) \\
 & & \text{where } (r, h) = \mathcal{E}[\![\, e \,]\!][\ldots, x_i \mapsto (v_i, \epsilon), \ldots]\phi
\end{array}
$$

$$\mathcal{E} :: \text{Exp} \rightarrow \text{Venv} \rightarrow \text{Fenv} \rightarrow \text{Val}$$

$$
\begin{array}{lcl}
\mathcal{E}[\![\, x \,]\!]\rho\ \phi & = & \rho\ x \\
\mathcal{E}[\![\, o(e_1, \ldots, e_n) \,]\!]\rho\ \phi & = & (\mathcal{O}[\![\, o \,]\!]v_1 \ldots v_n, h_1 \ldots h_n) \\
 & & \text{where } (v_i, h_i) = \mathcal{E}[\![\, e_i \,]\!]\ \rho\ \phi \\
\mathcal{E}[\![\, e_1 \rightarrow e_2 \square e_3 \,]\!]\rho\ \phi & = & (v_1 = \text{LOOP}) \rightarrow (\text{LOOP}, h) \square (v, h) \\
 & & \text{where } \ (v_i, h_i) = \mathcal{E}[\![\, e_i \,]\!]\rho\ \phi \\
 & & \qquad\qquad (v, h) = (v_1 \rightarrow v_2 \square v_3, h_1(v_1 \rightarrow h_2 \square h_3)) \\
\mathcal{E}[\![\, f(e_1, \ldots, e_n) \,]\!]\rho\ \phi & = & \phi\ f\ (\mathcal{E}[\![\, e_1 \,]\!]\rho\ \phi) \ldots (\mathcal{E}[\![\, e_n \,]\!]\rho\ \phi)
\end{array}
$$

Figure 3: Strict Loop Detecting Interpreter

3.1 Complexity

The interpreter outlined in this section has complexity $O(n^2)$ where n is the runtime of the program being interpreted. We do not expect this to be a problem in practice, for the applications we have in mind.

4 A Loop-Detecting Interpreter Using Dependencies

The interpreter developed in the last section does not terminate on the example in the introduction. The reason, of course, is that the example program never makes a repeated call. The second argument of the function increases at every call, but on the other hand the second argument has no influence on whether the program terminates or not since the value is never tested.

If a function calls itself unconditionally, either directly or indirectly, there is an infinite loop. A "typical" example of this is the following function:

```
f x = f (x+1)
```

This function calls itself regardless of the value of its argument. Even if the call is not unconditional it still might only depend on some of its arguments. In the following example the second argument grows while the first argument remains the same, and the condition only depends on the first argument. So we have an infinite loop if the first argument is 0.

```
f x y = if x=0 then f x (y+1) else y
```

Considering only the arguments which the tests depend on is too naive, as the following example shows.

```
f x y = if x=0 then f y (y+1) else y
```

Consider the call `f 0 0`: only the first argument is tested and `f` is called with the same first argument value again (`f 0 1`). But this does not mean that we have an infinite loop. The value of the first argument depends on the second argument, and it is a coincidence that it turns out to be 0. The fact that the first argument depends on the second and that the second argument changes makes it impossible to conclude that the function loops. As a matter of fact the function terminates with result 2. When, in the following, we say that a function call depends on some arguments, we mean the ones that are tested, and disregard the fact that the value of these arguments in the inner call might depend on something else.

Conjecture 1. Suppose that a call of f gives rise to yet a call to f, such that the first call dynamically surrounds the second call.

$$f\ x_1 \ldots x_n \ \rightarrow \ldots \rightarrow \ f\ e_1 \ldots e_n$$

If the flow of control between the two calls only depends on the variables in D_0 and the value of e_i only depends on the variables in D_i and we define D as the smallest set satisfying $D = D_0 \cup \bigcup_{\{i|x_i \in D\}} D_i$. Then the second call constitutes an infinite loop if the value of the arguments in D are the same. □

Realise that the two extremes are the cases where D is the complete set of variables, in which case the calls has to match exactly, and the case where D_0 is empty, in which case the values of the arguments does not matter.

We improve our interpreter by adding dependency information to the history, and use the dependency information as suggested by conjecture 1.

The dependency information is the set of variables the value depends on. This representation is relative to a certain scope. When changing scope we have to change the representation too, so when interpreting a function call we have to change the representation. Suppose the actual function call had arguments with dependencies $D_1 \ldots D_n$, each D_i being a set of variable names. Let D be a dependency relative to the function called, then $(\bigcup_{\{i|x_i \in D\}} D_i)$ is the dependency in the outer scope (x_i is the variable at position i). *I.e.*, if it depends on the first argument inside the function it depends on what the first argument depends on outside the function.

$$
\begin{array}{lll}
\text{Val} & = & (V_{\text{LOOP}}, \text{Hist}, \text{Depn}) \\
\text{Event} & = & \text{Call}(\text{Fname}, \text{Depn}, (D, \text{Depn})^*) \\
\text{Hist} & = & \text{Event}^* \\
\text{Depn} & = & \wp(\text{Vnames}) \\
\text{Venv} & = & \text{Vnames} \to \text{Val} \\
\text{Fenv} & = & \text{Fnames} \to \text{Val} \to \ldots \to \text{Val} \\
\mathcal{O} & = & \text{Operators} \to V \to \ldots \to V
\end{array}
$$

$\mathcal{F}$ :: Defn $\to$ Fenv $\to$ Val $\to \ldots \to$ Val

$$
\begin{array}{l}
\mathcal{F}[\![f(x_1,\ldots,x_n) = e]\!]\phi = \\
\qquad \lambda(v_1,h_1,d_1)\ldots(v_n,h_n,d_n). \\
\qquad \text{if any } v_i = \bot \text{ then } (\bot,\epsilon,\emptyset) \\
\qquad \text{elsf any } v_i = \text{LOOP then } (\text{LOOP},\epsilon,\emptyset) \\
\qquad \text{elsf } (\text{Call } f\ \emptyset\ (v_1,\emptyset)\ldots(v_n,\emptyset)) \text{ matched-in } h \text{ then LOOP} \\
\qquad \text{else } (r,h',\delta\ d) \\
\qquad \text{where} \\
\qquad h' = h_1\ldots h_n(\text{Call } f\ d\ (v_1,d_1)\ldots(v_n,d_n))(\text{update } \delta\ h) \\
\qquad (r,h,d) = \mathcal{E}[\![e]\!][\ldots,x_i \mapsto (v_i,\epsilon,\{x_i\}),\ldots]\phi \\
\qquad \delta d = \bigcup_{\{i \mid x_i \in d\}} d_i
\end{array}
$$

$\mathcal{E}$ :: Exp $\to$ Venv $\to$ Fenv $\to$ Val

$$
\begin{array}{lll}
\mathcal{E}[\![x]\!]\ \rho\ \phi & = & \rho\ x \\
\mathcal{E}[\![o(e_1,\ldots,e_n)]\!]\ \rho\ \phi & = & (\mathcal{O}[\![o]\!]v_1\ldots v_n,\ h_1\ldots h_n, d_1 \cup \ldots \cup d_n) \\
 & & \text{where} \\
 & & (v_i,h_i,d_i) = \mathcal{E}[\![e_i]\!]\rho\ \phi \\
\mathcal{E}[\![e_1 \to e_2 [\!] e_3]\!]\ \rho\ \phi & = & (v,h,d) \\
 & & \text{where} \\
 & & (v_i,h_i,d_i) = \mathcal{E}[\![e_i]\!]\rho\ \phi \\
 & & v = (v_1 = \text{LOOP}) \to \text{LOOP} [\!] (v_1 \to v_2 [\!] v_3) \\
 & & h = h_1(v_1 \to \text{mark } d_1\ h_2 [\!] \text{mark } d_1\ h_3) \\
 & & d = d_1 \cup (v_1 \to d_2 [\!] d_3) \\
\mathcal{E}[\![f(e_1,\ldots,e_n)]\!]\ \rho\ \phi & = & \phi\ f\ (\mathcal{E}[\![e_1]\!]\rho\ \phi)\ldots(\mathcal{E}[\![e_n]\!]\rho\ \phi)
\end{array}
$$

mark :: Depn $\to$ Hist $\to$ Hist

mark $d\ (\ldots(\text{Call } f\ d_f\ v_1\ldots v_n)\ldots) = \ldots(\text{Call } f\ (d_f \cup d)v_1\ldots v_n)\ldots$

matched-in :: Event $\times$ Hist $\to$ Bool

$(\text{Call } f\ \emptyset\ (v_1',\emptyset)\ldots(v_n',\emptyset)$ matched-in $(\ldots(\text{Call } f\ d_f\ (v_1,d_1)\ldots(v_n,d_n))\ldots)$
iff $\forall x_i \in D : v_i = v_i'$ where $D = d_f \cup \bigcup_{\{i \mid x_i \in D\}} d_i$

update :: (Depn $\to$ Depn) $\to$ Hist $\to$ Hist

update $\delta\ (\ldots(\text{Call } f\ d_f\ (v_1,d_1)\ldots(v_n,d_n))\ldots)$
$= \ldots(\text{Call } f\ (\delta d_f)\ (v_1,\delta d_1)\ldots(v_n,\delta d_n))\ldots$

Figure 4: Strict Loop Detecting Interpreter Using Dependencies

The call descriptions are augmented to record which arguments the occurrence of the call depended on, (the arguments determining the control flow), and the argument values in the call description are augmented with information about which arguments their value depend on.

The interpreter outlined in figure 4 makes use of three auxiliary functions: mark, matched-in, and update. A few comments about these functions: "mark" marks *all* the events in the history. "matched-in" return true if *any* of the call descriptions in the history match. D is the least set of dependencies satisfying the equation. "update" updates *all* the events in the history.

Example 2. To give some intuition about how this works we shall examine the history of an example. Consider the following program:

```
f x y = if x=0 then f y (y+1) else y
```

The initial call is `f 0 0` and successive calls become `f 0 1` and `f 1 2`. The history collected by the semantics in figure 4 becomes:

(Call `f` {x} $(0, \{y\})$ $(1, \{y\})$)
(Call `f` {x,y} $(1, \{y\})$ $(2, \{y\})$)

Starting with the inner most call `f 1 2` we get the empty history since this call does not give rise to any calls. The penultimate call `f 0 1` gives rise to the call `f 1 2` and so we collect the event (Call `f` $\emptyset$ $(1, \{y\})$ $(2, \{y\})$) since the control flow depends on the variable `x` this event is then marked with `x` giving the event (Call `f` {x} $(1, \{y\})$ $(2, \{y\})$). Like wise the outermost call `f 0 0` gives rise to the event (Call `f` {x} $(0, \{y\})$ $(1, \{y\})$) as can be seen in the history above. The second call in the history is the updated version of the history of the call `f 0 1`. The update makes the dependencies relative to the call place instead of the the formal arguments of the function, in this case it changes dependencies on the variable `x` to be dependencies on the variable `y`. This is why the control flow depends on `y`. It depends on `x` for the same reason that the first call event depends on `x`. □

5 A Lazy Loop-Detecting Interpreter

In this section we consider a lazy language. The ideas are the same as for the previous loop detecting interpreters. The language is lazy, but still first-order with flat domains.

The first change we must make is the order in which the history is generated. It is no longer correct to put the history of the arguments before the history of the body of the function as in the strict case. Instead we must insert the history of the arguments at the points in the history of the body where the arguments are referred to. To be able to do so we invent a new type of events that record the reference to a variable. We shall record which variable that was referred and what that reference depended on just as for the function calls. For example the event (Arg x_i d) means that variable x_i was referenced and that the control flow was determined by the variables in d. When a function returns "update" will substitute the "Arg" events in the history of the body with the appropiate argument histories.

Another problem is that the argument values are not present when the function is called so we cannot add a "Call" event with the values of the arguments at the

$$
\begin{array}{lcl}
\text{Val} & = & (V_{\text{LOOP}}, \text{Hist}, \text{Depn}) \\
\text{Event} & = & \text{Arg}(\text{Vname}, \text{Depn}) + \text{Call}(\text{Fname}, \text{Depn}, (\text{Depn},(V + \bullet)^*)) \\
\text{Hist} & = & \text{Event}^* \\
\text{Depn} & = & \wp(\text{Vnames}) \\
\text{Venv} & = & \text{Vnames} \to \text{Val} \\
\text{Fenv} & = & \text{Fnames} \to \text{Val} \to \ldots \to \text{Val} \\
\mathcal{O} & = & \text{Operators} \to V \to \ldots \to V
\end{array}
$$

$$\mathcal{P} :: \text{Defn} \to \text{Fenv} \to \text{Val} \to \ldots \to \text{Val}$$

$$
\begin{array}{l}
\mathcal{F}[\![\, f(x_1, \ldots, x_n) = e \,]\!]\phi = \\
\quad \lambda(v_1, h_1, d_1) \ldots (v_n, h_n, d_n). \\
\quad \text{if (Call } f\ \emptyset\ (v_1, \emptyset) \ldots (v_n, \emptyset)) \text{ matched-in } h \\
\quad \text{then LOOP} \\
\quad \text{else } (r,\ (\text{Call } f\ \emptyset\ \bullet \ldots \bullet)\ h',\ \delta\ d) \\
\quad \text{where} \\
\quad (r, h, d) = \mathcal{E}[\![\, e \,]\!]\ [\ldots x_i \mapsto (v_i,\ \text{Arg } x_i\ \emptyset, \{x_i\}) \ldots]\ \phi \\
\quad \delta\ d = \bigcup_{\{i \mid x_i \in d\}} d_i \\
\quad h' = \text{update } \delta\ f\ ((v_1, h_1, d_1), \ldots, (v_n, h_n, d_n))\ h
\end{array}
$$

$$\mathcal{E} :: \text{Exp} \to \text{Venv} \to \text{Fenv} \to \text{Val}$$

$$
\begin{array}{lcl}
\mathcal{E}[\![\, x \,]\!]\ \rho\ \phi & = & \rho\ x \\
\mathcal{E}[\![\, o(e_1, \ldots, e_n) \,]\!]\ \rho\ \phi & = & (\mathcal{O}[\![\, o \,]\!]\ v_1 \ldots v_n,\ h_1 \ldots h_n,\ d_1 \cup \ldots \cup d_n) \\
& & \text{where} \\
& & (v_i, h_i, d_i) = \mathcal{E}[\![\, e_i \,]\!]\rho\ \phi \\
\mathcal{E}[\![\, e_1 \to e_2 [\!] e_3 \,]\!]\ \rho\ \phi & = & (v, h, d) \\
& & \text{where} \\
& & (v_i, h_i, d_i) = \mathcal{E}[\![\, e_i \,]\!]\rho\ \phi \\
& & v = (v_1 = \text{LOOP}) \to \text{LOOP} [\!] (v_1 \to v_2 [\!] v_3) \\
& & h = h_1 (v_1 \to \text{mark } d_1\ h_2 [\!] \text{mark } d_1\ h_3) \\
& & d = d_1 \cup (v_1 \to d_2 [\!] d_3) \\
\mathcal{E}[\![\, f(e_1, \ldots, e_n) \,]\!]\ \rho\ \phi & = & \phi\ f\ (\mathcal{E}[\![\, e_1 \,]\!]\rho\ \phi) \ldots (\mathcal{E}[\![\, e_n \,]\!]\rho\ \phi)
\end{array}
$$

Figure 5: Lazy Loop Detecting Interpreter Using Dependencies

time of the call. Instead we will add "Call" events with partial information about the arguments. We will use a new special value '$\bullet$' meaning this value not yet know. (This is quite different from 'LOOP', meaning known to be $\perp$.) so the call event (Call f d_f $(3, d)$ $(\bullet, \emptyset)$) means that f has been called and that the value of the first argument was 3 and that we still do not know the value of the second argument.

Where, in the strict interpreter, each function call gave rise to *one* call event, a function call in the lazy interpreter gives give rise to a sequence of call events, with improving information about the argument values. The first call event comes immediately when the function is called. At that time we can only record that a function call has taken place since we have no knowledge about the argument values. Such a call event looks like: (Call f d_f $(\bullet, \emptyset) \ldots (\bullet, \emptyset)$) where d_f are the set of arguments that determine the control flow. The improved versions of this call event has to be added to the history at the points where one of the arguments are evaluated. So when the history of the body is "updated" we add an improved version of the call event at the point each argument event.

$$\text{mark} :: \text{Depn} \rightarrow \text{Hist} \rightarrow \text{Hist}$$

$$\text{mark}\ d\ (\ldots(\text{Call}\ f\ d_f\ v_1 \ldots v_n)\ldots) = \ldots(\text{Call}\ f\ (d_f \cup d)\ v_1 \ldots v_n)\ldots$$
$$\text{mark}\ d\ (\ldots(\text{Arg}\ x_i\ d_i)\ldots) = \ldots(\text{Arg}\ x_i\ (d_i \cup d))\ldots$$

$$\text{matched-in} :: \text{Event} \times \text{Hist} \rightarrow \text{Bool}$$

$$(\text{Call}\ f\ \emptyset\ (v_1', \emptyset)\ldots(v_n', \emptyset)\ \text{matched-in}\ (\ldots(\text{Call}\ f\ d_f\ (v_1, d_1)\ldots(v_n, d_n))\ldots)$$
$$\text{iff}\ \ \forall x_i \in D : v_i = v_i'\ \text{where}\ D = d_f \cup \bigcup_{\{i|x_i \in D\}} d_i$$

$$\text{update} :: (\text{Depn} \rightarrow \text{Depn}) \rightarrow \text{Fname} \rightarrow \text{Val}^n \rightarrow \text{Hist} \rightarrow \text{Hist}$$

$$\text{update}\ \delta\ f\ ((v_1, h_1, d_1)\ldots(v_n, h_n, d_n))\ (\ldots(\text{Call}\ f\ d_f\ (v_1, d_1)\ldots(v_n, d_n))\ldots)$$
$$= \ldots(\text{Call}\ f\ (\delta\ d_f)\ (v_1, \delta\ d_1)\ldots(v_n, \delta\ d_n))\ldots$$
$$\text{update}\ \delta\ f\ ((v_1, h_1, d_1), \ldots, (v_n, h_n, d_n))\ (\ldots(\text{Arg}\ x_i\ d')\ldots)$$
$$= \ldots(\text{mark}\ (\delta\ d')\ h_i)(\text{Call}\ f\ (\delta\ d')\ w_1 \ldots w_n)\ldots$$
$$\text{where}\ w_i = (x_i \in d') \rightarrow (v_i, d_i) \,[\!]\, (\bullet, \emptyset)$$

Figure 6: Auxiliary functions for the lazy interpreter

Very little is changed, in the interpreter, apart from the order in which the history is created. The "mark" function, shown in figure 6, now also marks the Arg events. "matched-in" is exactly as in the strict case with the difference that some of the values in the call events might have the value '•'. Of course '•' does not match anything. "update" works as before for call events. An argument event gives rise to the insertion of an improved call event and to the insertion of the history of the argument. The history of the argument is already relative to the outer scope so we need not change the dependencies, but the reference to the variable, which in the end was what caused the computation described in the argument history, depended on d'. So the inserted argument history has to be marked with this dependency changed such that it is relative to the outer scope.

5.1 Optimisations

The outlined interpreter collects a call-by-name history and not a lazy history. It would be easy enough to change this by only keeping the first Arg event for each argument in the history and throw the succeeding ones away. But this way we might detect fewer loops than with this interpreter because the dependencies of the later argument events might be different. For example one of the late argument events could be unconditional and an infinite loop might therefore be detected which would otherwise not be detected.

The following example illustrates this behavior. If we use an interpreter with call-by-name behavior the second unconditional reference to **x** in **f** which turns out to be a unconditional recursive call of **g** is a detectable infinite loop. On the other hand if we disregard the second reference to **x** because we try to model lazy evaluation we cannot detect the infinite loop because the reference to x in f is dependent on y. In the body of g f's second argument is x so the recursive call to g is dependent on g's first argument which grows so we cannot conclude that there is an infinite loop.

```
g x = f (g (x+1)) x
f x y = (if y = 0 then x else x) + x
```

A safe optimisation would be to throw all the Arg events away where the dependencies were a super set of the dependencies in a previous Arg event.

Example 3. Consider the following program:

```
f x y = if x=0 then f (f x y) y else 0
```

The initial call is `f 0 0` and the history becomes:

(Arg x $\emptyset$)
(Call f {x} $(\bullet, \emptyset)$ $(\bullet, \emptyset)$)
(Call f {x} $(\bullet, \emptyset)$ $(\bullet, \emptyset)$)
(Call f {x} $(0, \{x\})$ $(\bullet, \emptyset)$)

First there is an argument event recording the evaluation of x in the test. If this call had been a call in the program and not the initial call the argument event would have been substituted for the history of that argument and an improved call event. The next event is the first approximation to the function call in the then branch. Then comes the history of the body of the call `f (f x y) x`, first x is evaluated in the test. That gives rise to an argument event that is then substituted with the history of the argument, in this case `f x y` with x, and y bound to 0. First event in the argument history is (Call f {x} $(\bullet, \emptyset)$ $(\bullet, \emptyset)$) next event is an argument event evaluating x (here x is bound to 0 so the evaluation history of this argument is empty and we add an improved version of the call `f x y` which was first argument to the call `f (f x y) x`. At this point (Call f {x} $(0, \{x\})$ $(\bullet, \emptyset)$) the infinite loop is detected. The call depends on the first argument and the value of the first argument in the inner call only depends on the first argument of the outer call, and the two first arguments are equal. □

6 Applications

Why this sudden interest in loop detecting interpreters? Because of its application in partial evaluation. In this section we shall argue that some kind of loop-detection is needed to make a non-trivial partial evaluator. Furthermore, we conjecture a connection between the loop detecting strategies revealed in this paper and memoisation.

6.1 Partial Evaluation

A partial evaluator, in essence, is an interpreter capable of handling unbound variables. Expressions containing these unbound variables are left as residual code, partial evaluation of a program resulting in a residual program which computes the final result when the unbound variables become bound. Consider the following standard example:

```
ack m n = if m=0 then m+1 else
          if n=0 then ack (m-1) 1 else
             ack (m-1) (ack m (n-1))
```

If partial evaluators employed a standard depth first evaluation strategy they would loop on calls like: `ack 3 n`, because of the recursive call `(ack m (n-1))`. But, partial evaluators, like Mix [4], use a memoising call strategy, so instead of looping they generate specialised versions of the function `ack` for `m` bound to 3, 2, 1, and 0.

The problem is that partial evaluation is over-eager, it evaluates both branches in conditionals, and therefore it has a tendency to fall into loops. Even in the "simple" strict case a partial evaluator needs some kind of loop detecting evaluation strategy. In the lazy case the difference in "eagerness" between partial evaluation and lazy evaluation makes it even more likely, than in the strict case, that the partial evaluator falls into loops. That is why we need a loop detecting interpreter (partial evaluator).

It is our hope that by using a loop detecting interpreter as the heart of a partial evaluator for lazy languages, an interesting class of lazy programs can be partially evaluated with success.

6.2 Quasi-Termination

A program is terminating if it terminates on all input; it is quasi-terminating if the program terminates on all inputs when evaluated by the loop-detecting interpreter in question. I.e., quasi-termination is defined relative to some loop-detecting interpreter. So, it makes sense to have a quasi-termination analysis that establish if a program is terminating relative to a particular evaluation strategy. The finiteness analysis described in Holst [1] is an example of such a quasi-termination analysis. The analysis match the simple loop-detecting interpreter described in section 3.

In Holst [1] a quasi-termination analysis was used to find out how to restrict the partial input, such that partial evaluation of the program, with respect to the restricted partial input, was guaranteed to terminate.

It is our hope that a quasi-termination analysis, matching the loop-detecting interpreter for a lazy language, can be used, in a similar fashion, to change the program, and restrict the partial input so partial evaluation is guaranteed to terminate.

The combination of a quasi-termination analysis and a loop-detecting interpreter is well suited for off-line partial evaluation. In on-line partial evaluators, like Fuse [5], a terminating interpreter is used. By necessity such a scheme has to be more conservative than a loop-detecting interpreter. So a combination of the two schemes would be beneficial. First do the quasi-termination analysis, and then use the terminating interpreter on the parts of the program that could not be found to be quasi-terminating.

6.3 Memoisation

A memoising interpreter for a functional language record function calls, as variable binding, return value pairs. When reaching a function call with a set of previously encountered variable bindings it is immediately returns the previously computed return value.

This scheme is capable of detecting the same loops as the strict loop detecting interpreter described in section 3. We conjecture that the more advanced loop-detecting strategies can show the way to more advanced memoising strategies. In particular it might be possible to have a memo-function that is not hyper-strict, as for example the memo-function described in Holst and Gomard [2], or relying on the underlying representation as the lazy-memo-functions described by Hughes [3].

7 Further Work

The future work falls into three categories: Improving the interpreter by making it more fine grained. Extending the language with tuples recursive data types, and higher-order functions. Constructing a quasi-termination analysis, that tells if a program is terminating relative to the evaluation strategy. Finally the correctness of the interpreter ought to be formally proven, and a quasi-termination analysis has to be designed.

7.1 Non-Flat Domains

It would be interesting to handle tuples, lists, and higher-order functions. The following two examples should make clear why this is not as obvious as one might expect.

```
f x = (x, fst(f x))
g x = (x, snd(g x))
```

First, we cannot conclude that a function, like `f`, is looping just because a call of `f` gives rise to a call of `f` with the same arguments. Only `g` is looping (`f x = (x, x)` while `g x = (x,⊥)`). Some kind of context information is needed to tell that the second part of `g`'s value is needed while computing the second part of `g`'s value. When considering recursively defined data types like lists, another problem is that part of a data structure might be equal to the whole, like in:

```
ones = 1:ones
many = length ones
```

The problem here is that `length ones` should be recognized as a loop.

7.2 Formal Correctness and Quasi-Termination

A formal proof of correctness might give some insight. It has turned out to be difficult to understand precisely what non-termination means in the non-flat case. It is our hope that a more formal approach might help here. A formal understanding of the interpreter will probably also be the starting point for the quasi-termination analysis.

8 Conclusion

In this paper we have developed a loop-detecting interpreter for a lazy first-order language with flat domains.

It is not possible to conclude anything yet. We believe that some kind of loop-detecting interpreter is crucial if one wants to make a non-trivial partial evaluator for a lazy language. The loop-detecting interpreter in this paper is quite advanced, compared to the kind of loop-detection used in partial evaluator for strict languages, but it still does not handle non-flat domains or higher-order functions, two rather important aspects of lazy languages. Furthermore we have not made a partial evaluator for a lazy language.

Nevertheless, we believe that this is a important stepping stone in our attempt to make a partial evaluator for a lazy language, and that the relationship between loop-detection and pending analysis is worth looking into.

Acknowledgments

The referees Geoffrey Burn and Peter Sestoft both offered valuable comments on an earlier draft.

References

1. Carsten Kehler Holst. Finiteness analysis. In John Hughes, editor, *Functional Programming Languages and Computer Architectures*, volume 523 of *Lecture Notes in Computer Science*, pages 473–495, Cambridge, Massachusetts, USA, August 1991. ACM, Springer-Verlag.

2. Carsten Kehler Holst and Carsten Krogh Gomard. Partial evaluation is fuller laziness. In Paul Hudak and Neil D. Jones, editors, *Partial Evaluation and Semantic Based Program Manipulation*, volume 26,9 of *SIGPLAN NOTICES*, pages 223–233, New Haven, Connecticut, USA, June 1991. ACM, ACM Press.

3. John Hughes. Lazy memo-functions. In Jean-Pierre Jouannaud, editor, *Functional Programming Languages and Computer Architectures*, volume 201 of *Lecture Notes in Computer Science*, pages 129–146, Nancy, France, September 1985. Springer-Verlag.

4. Neil D. Jones, Peter Sestoft, and Harald Søndergaard. Mix: A self-applicable partial evaluator for experiments in compiler generation. *Lisp and Symbolic Computation*, 2(1):9–50, 1989.

5. Daniel Weise, Roland Conybeare, Erik Ruf, and Scott Seligman. Automatic online partial evaluation. In John Hughes, editor, *Functional Programming Languages and Computer Architectures*, volume 523 of *Lecture Notes in Computer Science*, pages 165–191, Cambridge, Massachusetts, USA, August 1991. ACM, Springer-Verlag.

Making functionality more general

Graham Hutton, University of Glasgow
Ed Voermans, Eindhoven University of Technology*

January 6, 1992

Abstract

The notion of functionality is not cast in stone, but depends upon what we have as types in our language. With *partial equivalence relations* (pers) as types we show that the functional relations are precisely those satisfying the simple equation $f = f \circ f^{\cup} \circ f$, where "$\cup$" is the relation converse operator. This article forms part of "A calculational theory of pers as types" [1].

1 Introduction

In calculational programming, programs are derived from specifications by a process of algebraic manipulation. Perhaps the best known calculational paradigm is the Bird–Meertens formalism, or to use its more colloquial name, Squiggol [2]. Programs in the Squiggol style work upon trees, lists, bags and sets, the so–called Boom hierarchy. The framework was uniformly extended to cover arbitrary recursive types by Malcolm in [3], by means of the F–algebra paradigm of type definition, and resulting catamorphic programming style. More recently, Backhouse et al [4] have made a further generalisation by choosing to work within the relational calculus.

Of fundamental importance to Backhouse's relational approach is the treatment of types not as separate entities from programs, but as special kinds of programs. Specifically, partial identity relations, called monotypes in [4], are adopted as types. Working in this style allows programs and type information to be manipulated withing the single framework of the relational calculus, and is fundamental to the use of type information to "inform and structure" program calculation. We in this paper take a more general approach than Backhouse, adopting partial equivalence relations as types. The extra generality allows us to handle types whose constructors are required to satisfy equations, so–called "types with laws". The present article forms part of [1], to which the reader is referred for omitted proofs.

In the relational style, both specifications and implementations are viewed as binary relations. Thinking of which binary relations should be accepted as implementations, functional (or deterministic) relations naturally come to mind. With

*Authors e–mail addresses: `graham@dcs.glasgow.ac.uk`, `wsinedv@win.tue.nl`.

pers as types however, we have a more general notion than normal of what constitutes an element of a type. It is natural then to expect a more general notion of what constitutes a function. We find that functional relations in the "pers as types" world are precisely those satisfying the simple equation $f = f \circ f^{\cup} \circ f$, where "$^{\cup}$" is the relation converse operator. Such relations f are known as *difunctionals*.

1.1 Notation

Our per–based paradigm is developed within the axiomatic theory of relations as presented in [4]. The axiom system comprises three layers, respectively dealing with the ***powerset lattice*** structure of relations, the ***composition*** operator, and the ***converse*** operator. Collectively, the three axiomatic layers are known as the ***spec calculus***. Since most readers will already have some knowledge of relational calculus, and there are only a few calculations in this article, we don't mention anything further about the axiom system. (See [4, 1] for more details.)

Rather than working with the normal "$\subseteq$", "$\cup$", and "$\cap$" operators from set–theory, Backhouse adopts in his axiomatic framework the more anonymous lattice–theoretic symbols "$\sqsubseteq$", "$\sqcup$" and "$\sqcap$". The term *spec* (abbreviating specification) is used by Backhouse in preference to *relation*, keeping a clear distinction between the axiomatic theory and the meta–language (predicate calculus.) Throughout this article capital letters $R, S, T, \ldots$ are used to denote arbitrary specs.

To avoid confusion with the use of the capital letter "T" to denote an arbitrary spec, the supreme spec (with respect to the implicit universe) is denoted by "$\top\!\!\top$" rather than the more usual lattice theoretic symbol "$\top$". The empty–spec is written as "$\bot\!\!\bot$". The composition operator for specs is denoted by "$\circ$", and the identity spec with respect to this operator by "I". For relation converse (an operator which swaps the components of each pair in a binary relation) the anonymous notation $R^{\cup}$ is used rather than the more usual R^{-1}; writing R^{-1} might have led us to suspect that R^{-1} is the inverse of R with respect to the composition operator "$\circ$", which is not true in general. For reference we give below pointwise definitions for the operators as used in this article. For R a binary relation, $x\ R\ y$ may be read as "x is related by R to y." Formally then, $x\ R\ y$ is just an abbreviation for $(x, y) \in R$.

$$\begin{array}{lcl}
x \perp\!\!\perp y & \hat{=} & \mathit{false} \\
x \top\!\!\top y & \hat{=} & \mathit{true} \\
R \sqsupseteq S & \hat{=} & \forall (x, y :: x\ R\ y \Leftarrow x\ S\ y) \\
x\ (R \sqcup S)\ y & \hat{=} & x\ R\ y \ \vee\ x\ S\ y \\
x\ (R \sqcap S)\ y & \hat{=} & x\ R\ y \ \wedge\ x\ S\ y \\
x\ (\neg R)\ y & \hat{=} & \sim\!(x\ R\ y) \\
x\ (R \circ S)\ z & \hat{=} & \exists (y :: x\ R\ y \ \wedge\ y\ S\ z) \\
x\ I\ y & \hat{=} & x = y \\
x\ (R^{\cup})\ y & \hat{=} & y\ R\ x
\end{array}$$

1.2 Quantification

For quantified expressions, we adopt the *Eindhoven notation* [5]. The general pattern is $Q\ (x : p.x : t.x)$, where Q is some quantifier (e.g. "$\forall$" or "$\bigsqcup$"), x is a sequence of free variables (sometimes called *dummies*), $p.x$ is a predicate which must be satisfied by the dummies, and $t.x$ is an expression defined in terms of the dummies. For the special cases of "$\forall$" and "$\exists$", we have the following links with standard notation:

$$\forall\ (x : p.x : q.x) \quad \equiv \quad \forall x.\ (p.x \Rightarrow q.x)$$

$$\exists\ (x : p.x : q.x) \quad \equiv \quad \exists x.\ (p.x \wedge q.x)$$

1.3 Monotypes and domain operators

In the next section, we introduce our notion of types: "partial equivalence relations". Backhouse in [4] works with less general types: "partial identity relations". Following Backhouse, we refer to partial identity relations as *monotypes*.

Definition 1: spec A is a *monotype* $\triangleq$ $I \sqsupseteq A$

To aid reading of formulae, monotypes are always denoted by letters A, B, C, etc. Set–theoretically, a monotype is just the identity relation on some set. For example, $\{(\mathsf{false}, \mathsf{false}), (\mathsf{true}, \mathsf{true})\}$ is a monotype representing a type of booleans.

We often need to refer to the domain and range of a spec. In order to avoid confusion with decision to have the input part of functional relations on their right–side (explained later on in this article), we use the terms *left domain* and *right domain*. In the case of functional relations then, the right domain is the input part. In the spec calculus, a left domain of a spec R is represented by a monotype A satisfying $A \circ R = R$; similarly a right domain of R is represented by a monotype B satisfying $R \circ B = R$. Specs in general have many domains; the smallest left and right domains are given by operators "$<$" and "$>$", defined as follows:

Definition 2:

$$R< \ \triangleq \ I \sqcap (R \circ R^{\cup})$$

$$R> \ \triangleq \ I \sqcap (R^{\cup} \circ R)$$

Using "$<$" and "$>$" we can define what it means for two specs to be disjoint:

Definition 3: $disj.R.S \ \triangleq \ R< \sqcap S< \ = \ R> \sqcap S> \ = \ \perp\!\!\!\perp$

2 Partial equivalence relations

A *partial equivalence relation* (per) on a set $\mathcal{S}$ is a symmetric and transitive relation on $\mathcal{S}$. To aid reading of formulae, we always use letters A, B and C for pers. In the spec–calculus, we have three equivalent definitions for the *per* notion.

Definition 4: $per.A \;\hat{=}$

(a) $A = A^{\cup} \;\wedge\; A \sqsupseteq A \circ A$

(b) $A = A^{\cup} \;\wedge\; A = A \circ A$

(c) $A = A \circ A^{\cup}$

Consider for example definition 4a. The calculation below shows that the $A \sqsupseteq A \circ A$ part corresponds to the set–theoretic notion of transitivity; a similar calculation would show that the $A = A^{\cup}$ part corresponds to the symmetry condition.

$$
\begin{array}{ll}
 & A \sqsupseteq A \circ A \\
\equiv & \quad \{ \text{ def } \sqsupseteq \ \} \\
 & \forall (x, z :: x\ A\ z \Leftarrow x\ A{\circ}A\ z) \\
\equiv & \quad \{ \text{ def } \circ \ \} \\
 & \forall (x, z :: x\ A\ z \Leftarrow \exists (y :: x\ A\ y \wedge y\ A\ z)) \\
\equiv & \quad \{ \ \exists \text{ elimination } \} \\
 & \forall (x, y, z :: x\ A\ z \Leftarrow x\ A\ y \wedge y\ A\ z)
\end{array}
$$

A per on a set $\mathcal{S}$ that is reflexive on $\mathcal{S}$ is called an *equivalence relation* on $\mathcal{S}$. We use the notation $\mathcal{S}^2$ for the *full relation* $\mathcal{S} \times \mathcal{S}$ on $\mathcal{S}$. Formally then we have $x\ \mathcal{S}^2\ y \;\hat{=}\; x, y \in \mathcal{S}$. For example, $\{a, b\}^2 = \{(a, a), (a, b), (b, a), (b, b)\}$. It is clear that $\mathcal{S}^2$ is an equivalence relation on $\mathcal{S}$, indeed it is the largest such. The set–theoretic notion of a full relation can be cast in the spec calculus as follows:

Definition 5: spec X is a *full relation* $\;\hat{=}\; X = X \circ \top\!\!\top \circ X^{\cup}$.

We always use letters X, Y and Z for full relations. A well known result is:

Lemma 6: every per can be written in a unique way as the union of disjoint full relations, each such relation representing an *equivalence class* of the per.

With "pers as types", it is these disjoint full relations that we refer to as *elements* of types. Aiming towards defining an "$\in$" operator for pers, we see that two properties of a set $\mathcal{S}$ are required such that $\mathcal{S}^2$ may be called an element of a per A:

(1) $\forall (x, y \;:\; x, y \in \mathcal{S} \;:\; x\ A\ y)$

(2) $\forall (x, y : \; x \in \mathcal{S} \;\wedge\; x\ A\ y \;:\; y \in \mathcal{S})$

The first clause says that $\mathcal{S}$ is an equivalence class of A, being just the set-theoretic expansion of $\mathcal{S}^2 \sqsubseteq A$. The second clause ensures that $\mathcal{S}$ is as big as possible. The following calculation shows that (2) is equivalent to $\mathcal{S}^2 \circ A \sqsubseteq \mathcal{S}^2$.

$$
\begin{array}{ll}
 & \mathcal{S}^2 \circ A \sqsubseteq \mathcal{S}^2 \\
\equiv & \qquad \{ \text{ def} \sqsubseteq \ \} \\
 & \forall (x,z:\ z\ \mathcal{S}^2{\circ}A\ x:\ z\ \mathcal{S}^2\ x) \\
\equiv & \qquad \{ \text{ def} \circ \ \} \\
 & \forall (x,y,z:\ z\ \mathcal{S}^2\ y \wedge y\ A\ x:\ z\ \mathcal{S}^2\ x) \\
\equiv & \qquad \{ \text{ def } \mathcal{S}^2 \ \} \\
 & \forall (x,y,z:\ y,z \in \mathcal{S} \wedge y\ A\ x:\ x,z \in \mathcal{S}) \\
\equiv & \qquad \{ \text{ calculus } \} \\
 & \forall (x,y,z:\ y,z \in \mathcal{S} \wedge y\ A\ x:\ x \in \mathcal{S}) \\
\equiv & \qquad \{ \ \forall (x,y:\ y \in \mathcal{S} \wedge y\ A\ x:\ \exists (z\ ::\ z \in \mathcal{S}))\ \} \\
 & \forall (x,y:\ y \in \mathcal{S} \wedge y\ A\ x:\ x \in \mathcal{S})
\end{array}
$$

Given $\mathcal{S}^2 \sqsubseteq A$ we find that $\mathcal{S}^2 \circ A \sqsubseteq \mathcal{S}^2$ is equivalent to the equality $\mathcal{S}^2 \circ A = \mathcal{S}^2$. Since the equality implies the containment, the following proof is sufficient:

$$
\begin{array}{ll}
 & \mathcal{S}^2 \circ A \\
\sqsupseteq & \qquad \{ \text{ assumption: } A \sqsupseteq \mathcal{S}^2 \ \} \\
 & \mathcal{S}^2 \circ \mathcal{S}^2 \\
= & \qquad \{ \text{ full relations } \} \\
 & \mathcal{S}^2
\end{array}
$$

We give now a spec–calculi definition for an "$\in$" operator:

Definition 7: For X a full relation and A a per,

$$X \in A \ \hat{=}\ X \sqsubseteq A \ \wedge\ X \circ A = X$$

To clarify our interpretation of pers as types, let us consider an example. A *rational number* may be represented as a pair of integers (a,b), with $b \neq 0$. The interpretation is that (a,b) represents the rational a/b. This representation is not unique: pairs (a,b) and (c,d) represent the same rational iff $ad = bc$. We see then that rational numbers induce a per, RAT say, on the set $\mathbb{Z}\times\mathbb{Z}$:

$$(a,b)\ RAT\ (c,d) \ \hat{=}\ ad = bc \ \wedge\ bd \neq 0$$

Partiality arises in the denominator of a rational being restricted to non-zero integers; equivalence classes arise in the representation as pairs of integers being non-unique. Viewing the per RAT as a type, it is important to understand that elements of type RAT are not simply pairs of integers, but full relations on equivalence classes of pairs of integers.

3 Partial orderings on types

Consider the types of (non–empty) *trees*, *lists* and *uplists*. (We use the term *uplist* for a list whose elements are ascending with respect to some partial ordering.) Elements of all three types can be built from constructors [–] (making singleton elements) and "++" (joining two elements together). The three types are different however in the properties required of the constructors. We introduce in this section three orderings on types; these orderings allow us to make precise such relationships.

When used as a constructor for trees, "++" is not subject to any laws. When used with lists however, we require that "++" be associative. For example, we require that $[1] + \!\!+ ([2] + \!\!+ [3]) = ([1] + \!\!+ [2]) + \!\!+ [3]$. More formally, while the two expressions form distinct (singleton) equivalence classes in the type of trees, they are the members of the same equivalence class in the type of lists. In standard list notation, this equivalence class is denoted by $[1, 2, 3]$. With uplists the "++" constructor becomes partial, in that certain constructions are forbidden. In particular, $X + \!\!+ Y$ is only defined if the last element of X is at most the first element of Y. For example, although $[1, 3]$ and $[2, 4]$ are both uplists, their combination, $[1, 3, 2, 4]$ is not. More formally, $[1, 3, 2, 4]$ does not represent an equivalence class in the type of uplists.

We introduce now three orderings on types: "$\subseteq$", "$\lhd\!|$", and "$\lhd$". Writing *uplist* $\subseteq$ *list* would express that uplists are a special kind of list: every uplist is a list, but the reverse in general does not hold. Writing *list* $\lhd\!|$ *tree* would say that every list is an equivalence class of trees. Writing *uplist* $\lhd$ *tree* would combine the previous two statements: uplists are made from trees by coalescing and discarding equivalence classes. Each of the three operators is first defined using the "$\in$" operator, after which an equivalent but simpler formulation is given.

Definition 8: Given pers A and B,

$$A \subseteq B \;\; \hat{=} \;\; \forall (X : X \in A : X \in B)$$

We read $A \subseteq B$ as "A is a subtype of B", i.e. the type A is formed by discarding elements of type B. We observe now that "$\subseteq$" is a partial ordering on pers, with $\perp\!\!\!\perp$ as a least element. (Pers in fact form a "$\sqcap$" semi–lattice under "$\subseteq$".)

Lemma 9: $A \subseteq B \;\; \equiv \;\; A \circ B = A \;\wedge\; A \sqsubseteq B$

Given a full relation X and a per A, we say that X *coalesces* A if all the elements of A are combined to form the single element of X. For example, $\{a, b, c\}^2$ coalesces $\{a, b\}^2 \cup \{c\}^2$. In the spec calculus, coalescence can be defined as follows:

Definition 10: For X a full relation and A a per,

$$X \; coalesces \; A \;\; \hat{=} \;\; X = A \circ \top\!\!\top \circ A$$

This notion is used in the definition of the "$\lhd$" ordering:

Definition 11: Given pers A and B,

$$A \lhd B \;\hat{=}\; \forall(X : X \in A : \exists(C : C \subseteq B : X \textit{ coalesces } C))$$

We read $A \lhd B$ as "A is a per on B" — the type A is formed by discarding and coalescing elements of type B. We note that "$\lhd$" is a partial ordering on pers, with "$\perp\!\!\perp$" as least element, and "I" as greatest element. (Pers in fact form a lattice under "$\lhd$".) We work in practice with a simpler formulation:

Lemma 12: $A \lhd B \;\equiv\; A \circ B = A$

From the symmetry of A and B (i.e. $A = A^{\cup}$ and $B = B^{\cup}$), it follows that $A \lhd B \;\equiv\; B \circ A = A$. We note also that "$\subseteq$" can be expressed in terms of "$\lhd$":

Lemma 13: $A \subseteq B \;\equiv\; A \lhd B \;\wedge\; A \sqsubseteq B$

Writing $A \lhd B$ expresses that A is a partial equivalence relation on B. If A is an equivalence relation on B (i.e. no elements have been discarded in moving to A from B) we write $A \lhd\!| B$. It can be shown that "$\lhd\!|$" is a partial ordering on types, with $\top\!\!\top$ as greatest element. (Pers in fact form a "$\sqcup$" semi-lattice under "$\lhd\!|$".)

Definition 14: Given pers A and B,

$$A \lhd\!| B \;\hat{=}\; A \lhd B \;\wedge\; \forall(X : X \in B : \exists(Y : Y \in A : Y \sqsupseteq X))$$

Lemma 15: $A \lhd\!| B \;\equiv\; A \lhd B \wedge A \sqsupseteq B$

4 Typing judgements for specs

In set-theoretic approaches to relational calculus, it is common to write $R \subseteq A \times B$ (where A and B are sets) in the form of a *typing judgement* $R \in A \sim B$. In this section we seek to define the set $A \sim B$ in our approach to relational calculus, with A and B being pers. In writing $R \in A \sim B$, we require that R on its left-side respects the elements of A, and on its right-side respects the elements of B. Let us consider the A part in more detail. Recall that elements of pers are full relations. By a relation R "respecting on its left-side" a full relation $\mathcal{S}^2$, we mean that the image through R of each member of $\mathcal{S}$ is the same set; that is, we require that

$$\forall(a, b, c : a, b \in \mathcal{S} : a\,R\,c \;\equiv\; b\,R\,c)$$

(That such an image set may be empty means that R is not required to be total on A.) We call such a full relation $\mathcal{S}^2$ a *left equivalence class* of R. We find that the predicate above can be written in relational calculus as $R \sqsupseteq \mathcal{S}^2 \circ R$:

$$
\begin{array}{ll}
 & \mathcal{S}^2 \circ R \sqsubseteq R \\
\equiv & \quad \{ \text{ def } \sqsubseteq \ \} \\
 & \forall (a,b : a\ \mathcal{S}^2 \circ R\ b : a\ R\ b) \\
\equiv & \quad \{ \text{ def } \circ \ \} \\
 & \forall (a,b : \exists (c :: a\ \mathcal{S}^2\ c \wedge c\ R\ b) : a\ R\ b) \\
\equiv & \quad \{ \ \exists \text{ elimination } \} \\
 & \forall (a,b,c : a\ \mathcal{S}^2\ c \wedge c\ R\ b : a\ R\ b) \\
\equiv & \quad \{ \text{ def } \mathcal{S}^2 \ \} \\
 & \forall (a,b,c : a,c \in S \wedge c\ R\ b : a\ R\ b) \\
\equiv & \quad \{ \text{ shunting } \} \\
 & \forall (a,b,c : a,c \in S : c\ R\ b \Rightarrow a\ R\ b) \\
\equiv & \quad \{ \text{ predicate calculus } \} \\
 & \forall (a,b,c : a,c \in S : a\ R\ b \equiv c\ R\ b)
\end{array}
$$

Similarly we can define a *right equivalence class* of a relation R as a full relation $\mathcal{S}^2$ for which $R \sqsupseteq R \circ \mathcal{S}^2$. We make now two definitions in the spec calculus:

Definition 16:

A *left equivalence class* of a spec R is a full relation X for which $R \sqsupseteq X \circ R$;

A *right equivalence class* of R is such an X for which $R \sqsupseteq R \circ X$.

Using these notions we can define the "~" operator:

Definition 17: For A and B pers, $R \in A\text{\textasciitilde}B \ \hat{=}$

$$
\begin{array}{l}
\forall (X : X \in A : R \sqsupseteq X \circ R) \wedge A \circ R \sqsupseteq R \wedge \\
\forall (X : X \in B : R \sqsupseteq R \circ X) \wedge R \circ B \sqsupseteq R
\end{array}
$$

We call such a per A a *left domain* of R, and B a *right domain*. The clauses $A \circ R \sqsupseteq R$ and $R \circ B \sqsupseteq R$ above, equivalent respectively to $A \sqsupseteq R<$ and $B \sqsupseteq R>$, are needed to ensure that pers A and B are big enough to serve as domains of R. In practice we work with a simpler but equivalent formulation of "~":

Lemma 18: $R \in A\sim B \ \equiv \ A \circ R = R = R \circ B$

The right–side of Lemma 18 can be written in fact as a single equality:

Lemma 19: $R \in A\sim B \ \equiv \ A \circ R \circ B = R$

5 Typing judgements difunctionals

We view relational programming as a generalisation of functional programming: relations for us are the primitive notion, functions are regarded as special kinds of relation. In the last section we introduced a typing notation $R \in A{\sim}B$ for specs. In this section we introduce a typing notation $f \in A \leftarrow B$ for functional specs, and show that the functional specs are precisely those f satisfying $f = f \circ f{\cup} \circ f$.

Normally the "input part" of a functional relation is on its left-side. Following [4] however, we view the right-side of a functional relation as its input part, writing $A \leftarrow B$ for the set of all functions to A from B. This choice avoids confusion between written and diagrammatic order for composition of functions, and is consistent with placing the argument to the right of the function symbol during application.

Definition 20: Give a spec R and a full relation X, the *image* of X back through R is given by the full relation $R.X \;\widehat{=}\; R \circ X \circ R{\cup}$

In writing $f \in A \leftarrow B$, we require two properties: f has a valid typing $A{\sim}B$ as a spec (i.e. typed functions are a special case of typed specs); applying f to an element of per B gives an element of per A (i.e. f is functional to A from B.)

Definition 21:

$$f \in A \leftarrow B \;\;\widehat{=}\;\; f \in A{\sim}B \;\;\wedge\;\; \forall(X \;:\; X \in B \;:\; f.X \in A)$$

In practice as usual we work with a simpler but equivalent formulation:

Lemma 22: $f \in A \leftarrow B \;\;\equiv\;\; f \in A{\sim}B \;\;\wedge\;\; A \sqsupseteq f \circ f{\cup}$

In the monotypes world [4], functional specs are characterised as those f satisfying $I \sqsupseteq f \circ f{\cup}$. It is shown below how this definition corresponds to the normal set-theoretic definition of a relation being functional:

$$\begin{array}{ll} & I \sqsupseteq f \circ f{\cup} \\ \equiv & \quad \{\ \text{def} \sqsupseteq\ \} \\ & \forall(x,y :: \; x\, I\, y \Leftarrow x\, f \circ f{\cup}\, y) \\ \equiv & \quad \{\ \text{def } I, \circ\ \} \\ & \forall(x,y :: \; x = y \Leftarrow \exists(z :: x\, f\, z \wedge z\, f{\cup}\, y)) \\ \equiv & \quad \{\ \text{def } \cup\ \} \\ & \forall(x,y :: \; x = y \Leftarrow \exists(z :: x\, f\, z \wedge y\, f\, z)) \\ \equiv & \quad \{\ \exists \text{ elimination }\ \} \\ & \forall(x,y,z :: \; x = y \;\Leftarrow\; x\, f\, z \wedge y\, f\, z) \end{array}$$

We see then that $I \sqsupseteq f \circ f{\cup}$ expresses that f is a partial function: for all x, there exists at most one y such that $y\ f\ x$. In keeping with [4], we use the term *imp* (abbreviating "implementation") for a spec f (recall, spec abbreviates "specification") satisfying $I \sqsupseteq f \circ f{\cup}$. Using the special term "imp" rather than simply "function" avoids confusion with the other notion of functionality introduced in this paper, that in the pers as types setting (for which we use the special term "difunctional".)

Definition 23: $imp.f \ \hat{=}\ I \sqsupseteq f \circ f^{\cup}$

If $f^{\cup}$ is a imp, we refer to f itself as a *co–imp*; just as imps correspond to functional relations, so co–imps correspond to injective relations. (As noted by van Gasteren in [5], the symmetry between functional and injective relations is lost in many texts, through restricting the notion of injectivity to functions.)

Definition 24: $co\text{–}imp.f \ \hat{=}\ imp.f^{\cup}$

The notion of functionality is not case in stone, but depends upon our notion of type. Working with monotypes, we have $imp.f \ \hat{=}\ I \sqsupseteq f \circ f^{\cup}$. We assert that with pers as types, the functional specs are precisely those satisfying $f \sqsupseteq f \circ f^{\cup} \circ f$. Such specs are known as *difunctionals* [6]. (Difunctional relations have also been called "regular" relations and "pseudo–invertible" relations [7].)

Definition 25: $difun.f \ \hat{=}\ f \sqsupseteq f \circ f^{\cup} \circ f$

We always use small letters $f, g, h, \ldots$ to denote difunctional specs. (This does not clash with the use of these letters to denote imps, since as we shall see, every imp is difunctional.) Since the containment $R \sqsubseteq R \circ R^{\cup} \circ R$ holds for all specs [1], we are free to replace the containment in the above definition by an equality:

Lemma 26: $difun.f \ \equiv\ f = f \circ f^{\cup} \circ f$

Our assertion that the functional specs are precisely the difunctionals is verified by the three results below. The first shows that every functionally typed spec is difunctional, the remaining two that every difunctional can be functionally typed.

Lemma 27: $f \in A \leftarrow B \ \Rightarrow\ difun.f$

Lemma 28: $difun.f \ \Rightarrow\ per.(f \circ f^{\cup}) \wedge per.(f^{\cup} \circ f)$

Lemma 29: $difun.f \ \Rightarrow\ f \in f \circ f^{\cup} \leftarrow f^{\cup} \circ f$

The last lemma above encodes that the pers $f \circ f^{\cup}$ and $f^{\cup} \circ f$ are respectively left and right domains for difunctional f. We conclude this section with the result that these pers are in fact the least domains for f under the "$\lhd$" ordering.

Lemma 30: $difun.f \ \Rightarrow\ (f \in A \sim B \ \equiv\ f \circ f^{\cup} \lhd A \wedge f^{\cup} \circ f \lhd B)$

6 More about difunctionals

In the last section we showed that with pers as types, the functional specs are precisely the difunctionals. In this section we document some properties of difunctionals. In particular, we give some conditions under which certain operators preserve difunctionality, and give three other ways to think about difunctionals.

Lemma 31: $per.A \Rightarrow difun.A$

Lemma 32: $imp.f \Rightarrow difun.f$

Lemma 33: $difun.f \equiv difun.f^{\cup}$

Lemma 33 is where the prefix "di" in difunctional comes from, telling us that every difunctional is not just functional, but in fact *bijective*. In conjunction with lemma 32, we see then that every co–imp is difunctional.

Difunctionals are closed under intersection:

Lemma 34: $difun.(f \sqcap g) \Leftarrow difun.f \wedge difun.g$

We might suspect difunctionals to be similarly preserved under "$\sqcup$", but this is not so. Disjointness provides however a simple condition to ensure preservation:

Lemma 35: $difun.(f \sqcup g) \Leftarrow difun.f \wedge difun.g \wedge disj.f.g$

In general, difunctionals are not closed under composition. For example,

$$f = \{(a,x),(a,y),(b,z)\}$$

$$g = \{(x,a),(y,b),(z,b)\}$$

are both difunctional (f is an imp, g is a co–imp), but their composition $f \circ g$ is not, as the reader may wish to verify. A simple "type check" however is all that is needed to ensure closure: the composition ($f \circ g$) of two difunctionals is itself difunctional provided that the least right domain of f subsumes the least left domain of g:

Lemma 36: $difun.(f \circ g) \Leftarrow difun.f \wedge difun.g \wedge f^{\cup} \circ f \sqsupseteq g \circ g^{\cup}$

Flipping the role of least right and left domains also works:

Lemma 37: $difun.(f \circ g) \Leftarrow difun.f \wedge difun.g \wedge g \circ g^{\cup} \sqsupseteq f^{\cup} \circ f$

6.1 Disjoint bundles

The full relation on a set $\mathcal{S}$ is given by $\mathcal{S} \times \mathcal{S}$. Relaxing the constraint that both sides of a full relation must be the same set gives what we call *bundles*: relations of the form $\mathcal{S} \times \mathcal{T}$, where $\mathcal{S}$ and $\mathcal{T}$ may differ. Just as pers can be written in terms of full relations, so difunctionals can be written in terms of bundles:

> **Lemma 38:** every difunctional can be written in a unique way as the union of disjoint bundles.

The bundles interpretation of difunctionals is particularly useful in understanding conditions under which operators such as composition preserve difunctionality.

6.2 Co–imp/imp factorisation

Every relation can be factorised in the form $f \circ g^{\cup}$, where f and g are imps. Flipping things around, it is a simple exercise to show that for imps f and g, the spec $f^{\cup} \circ g$ is always difunctional. In fact, we have the following result:

> **Lemma 39:** precisely the difunctional specs can be factorised as the composition of a co–imp and an imp.

This property of difunctionals has important applications in deriving programs that take the form of "representation changers". (See [8] for more details.)

6.3 Invertible specs

An *inverse* of a spec $R \in A \sim B$ is a spec $S \in B \sim A$ satisfying $R \circ S = A$ and $S \circ R = B$. Not all specs $R \in A \sim B$ are invertible, but those that are have a unique inverse, namely $R^{\cup}$. (See Lemma D22 in [4] for the proof.)

> **Lemma 40:** $S \in B \sim A$ is an inverse of $R \in A \sim B \;\Rightarrow\; S = R^{\cup}$

Which specs can be inverted ? Precisely the difunctionals:

> **Lemma 41:** $R \in A \sim B$ is invertible $\Rightarrow$ *difun.R*

> **Lemma 42:** *difun.R* $\Rightarrow$ $R \in R \circ R^{\cup} \sim R^{\cup} \circ R$ is invertible

(That the typing is valid in the last result follows from Lemma 30.)

7 Summary and future directions

Backhouse et al in [4] present a calculational theory of programming, with binary relations as programs and partial identity relations (monotypes) as types. We in this article work within the same framework, but adopt a more general notion of type: partial equivalence relations (pers). Working with pers allows us to handle types with laws. (This is explained in detail in [1].) For example, recalling that $\mathcal{S}^2$ abbreviates the full relation $\mathcal{S} \times \mathcal{S}$, imposing the law $a = b$ on the monotype $\{a\}^2 \cup \{b\}^2 \cup \{c\}^2$ gives the per $\{a,b\}^2 \cup \{c\}^2$. A quite different treatment of types with laws in the *F-algebra* style of type definition has recently been given by Fokkinga [9]; the relationship with our approach is clearly an interesting topic for study.

Working with monotypes, the functional specs (imps) are precisely those f satisfying $I \sqsupseteq f \circ f^{\cup}$. With pers, we found the functional specs to be precisely those f satisfying $f = f \circ f^{\cup} \circ f$, the so-called difunctionals. Moreover, we presented three alternative ways to look at difunctionals: as the union of disjoint bundles, co-imp/imp factorisable specs, and invertible specs. Pers are being used in many areas in computing science (e.g. modelling the λ-calculus and in analysing lazy functional programs.) It seems likely then that difunctionals, not a familiar concept to most computing scientists, have many other interesting applications.

Difunctionals generalise imps; another such generalisation is *causal relations* [10], throwing away the constraint that inputs must always appear on the right-side of a functional relation, and outputs on the left-side. Causal relations are important in the derivation of programs that can be implemented in hardware, being "implementable relations" in Jones and Sheeran's calculational approach to circuit design known as Ruby [11]. A simulator for causal Ruby programs has been produced [12]. We are experimenting with implementing difunctional relations, with a view to producing a more general simulator based upon causal relations as a generalisation of difunctionals rather than imps. Since pers are now adopted as types in Ruby [13, 8], such a simulator should accept Ruby programs earlier in the design process, and in some cases even the initial specification itself.

Acknowledgements

Thanks to the referees and to Erik Meijer for useful comments.

References

[1] Graham Hutton and Ed Voermans. *A calculational theory of pers as types.* Appears in [14]. [To appear as technical reports from Eindhoven and Glasgow, January '92.]

[2] Richard Bird. *Lectures on constructive functional programming.* Oxford University 1988. (PRG–69)

[3] Grant Malcolm. *Algebraic data types and program transformation.* Ph.D. thesis, Groningen University, 1990.

[4] Roland Backhouse, Ed Voermans and Jaap van der Woude. *A relational theory of datatypes.* Appears in [14].

[5] A.J.M. van Gasteren. *On the shape of mathematical arguments.* LNCS 445, Springer–Verlag, Berlin, 1990.

[6] J. Riguet. *Relations Binaires, Fermetures, Correspondances de Galois.* Bulletin de la Societé mathématique de France. Volume 76, 1948.

[7] A. Jaoua, A. Mili, N. Boudriga, and J.L. Durieux. *Regularity of relations: A measure of uniformity.* Theoretical Computer Science 79, 323–339, 1991.

[8] G. Jones and M. Sheeran. *Designing arithmetic circuits by calculation.* Glasgow University, 1991. [In preparation]

[9] Maarten Fokkinga. *Datatype laws without signatures.* Appears in [14].

[10] Graham Hutton. *Functional programming with relations.* Proc. Third Glasgow Workshop on functional programming (ed. Kehler Holst, Hutton and Peyton Jones), Ullapool 1990, Springer Workshops in Computing.

[11] Geraint Jones and Mary Sheeran. *Relations + higher–order functions = hardware descriptions.* Proc. IEEE Comp Euro 87: VLSI and Computers, Hamburg, May 1987.

[12] Graham Hutton. *A simple guide to the Ruby simulator.* Glasgow University, August 1991.

[13] Geraint Jones. *Designing circuits by calculation.* Oxford University, April 1990. (PRG–TR–10–90)

[14] Proc. EURICS Workshop on Calculational Theories of Program Structure, Ameland, The Netherlands, September 1991.

Getting your wires crossed

Geraint Jones*

Things should be as simple as possible 'and no simpler', so they say. This paper is about simplifying a construct in Ruby, to reduce the complexity of the algebra without sacrificing expressive power. Ruby, for which Mary Sheeran is largely responsible, is a language of relations and a collection of rules – equalities – for algebraic transformation of expressions in that language.

The presentation here is by way of being a natural history of the combining forms that build state machines. It shows that over time the operators have evolved as we have been able to simplify calculation by chosing to name combining forms which have simple properties, rather than naming those forms which correspond to the original intuition about the application area, and this apparently without making it significantly harder to relate the calculations to reality. Whether there are any general lessons which can be drawn from this history, I leave to the reader.

μ, Mealy, Moore and Mary

μFP is a language of functions [6], from which Ruby has been developed. The μ in its name is the operator which constructs a state machine from its transition function, something traditionally denoted by μ. This operator constructs an automaton $\mu[f,g]$ from two functions, f which delivers the output as a function of the present state and input, and g which delivers the next state also as a function of the present state and input.

This is the characterisation of a state machine known as a Mealy machine, as opposed to Moore machines, which describe the same machine by a different pair of functions. An implementation is likely, for detailed operational reasons like propagation delay, to be more like a Mealy machine than the apparently simpler corresponding Moore machine which calculates its output as a function of its state. So it was the Mealy machine that was chosen as a named combining form to be added to Backus' FP [1]. It is an odd coincidence that Mealy, Moore, and Mary might all be being spelled with a capital μ.

The μ operator of μFP satisfies the equation

$$\mu[f,g]\cdot\mu[h,j] \quad = \quad \mu[f\cdot[h\cdot[1,2\cdot 2],1\cdot 2],[g\cdot[h\cdot[1,2\cdot 2],1\cdot 2],j\cdot[1,2\cdot 2]]]$$

which is called $C\mu$ in reference [6]. Here the dot is (forward) composition of functions, the ones and twos are the FP notation for the projection functions which deliver the first and second components of a pair, and $[f,g]$ is the function that returns the pair of results of applying each of f and g to its argument.

*Address: Programming Research Group, Oxford University Computing Laboratory, 11 Keble Road, Oxford OX1 3QD, England; Email: *geraint.jones@comlab.oxford.ac.uk*.

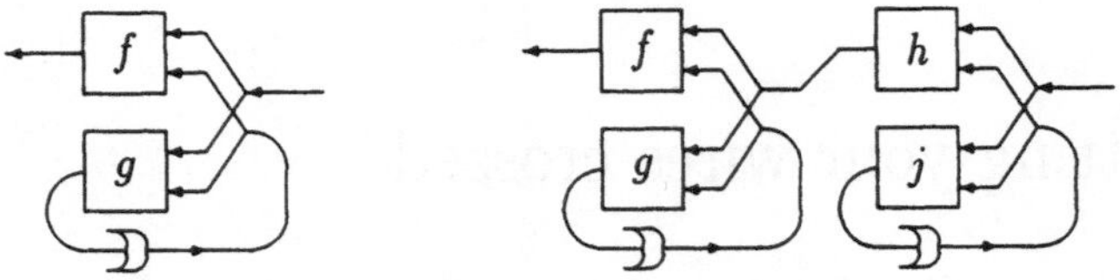

Figure 1: the μFP form $\mu[f,g]$, and the composition $\mu[f,g]\cdot\mu[h,j]$, each drawn with the conventions of [6], inputs on the right, outputs on the left, indexed from top to bottom

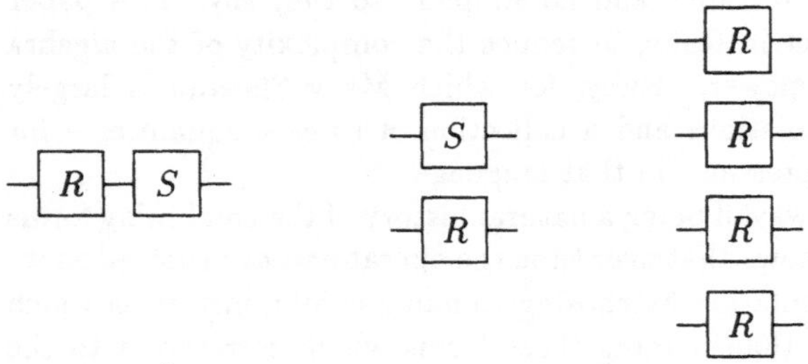

Figure 2: $R\,;S$ and $[R,S]$, and an instance of **map** R, drawn with the Ruby conventions: domain on the left, range on the right, indexed from bottom to top

The law Cμ expresses the composition of two state machines – that is a circuit in which the output of one machine is supplied as input to another, as illustrated in figure 1 – as a single state machine, albeit with a more complicated state and a more complicated output function and a much more complicated next-state function. The composite machine just has as its state the states of the two machines as a pair, although this is difficult to see from the form of Cμ.

This law has two possible applications: having composed two machines in this way, it might be possible to simplify the expressions $f\cdot[h\cdot[1,2\cdot 2],1\cdot 2]$ and $[g\cdot[h\cdot[1,2\cdot 2],1\cdot 2],j\cdot[1,2\cdot 2]]$ which describe its output function and its next-state function. More likely, the law would be used to factorise a large state-machine into two smaller ones: for distributed implementation, or for VLSI implementation, it pays to have the state as near as possible to the places where it is going to be used.

Unfortunately, in order to use the law to factorise some machine $\mu[F,G]$ it would be necessary first to be able to find f, g, h and j for which $F=f\cdot[h\cdot[1,2\cdot 2],1\cdot 2]$ and $G=[g\cdot[h\cdot[1,2\cdot 2],1\cdot 2],j\cdot[1,2\cdot 2]]$. On the face of it this is a daunting prospect, since there is no obvious approach.

Ruby

This section treats rapidly most of the Ruby notation used in this paper. If you are unfamiliar with the notation an introduction can be found in, for example, reference [3].

A circuit is represented by the relation between the signals at its terminals, rather than a function. This abstracts from the distinction between inputs and outputs. We think of binary relations with domain on the left and range on the right so that the relational composition, $R;S$, defined by $x\,(R\,;S)\,z \iff \exists y.\,x\,R\,y\,\&\,y\,S\,z$, reads naturally from left to right, as illustrated in figure 2. We tend to give to

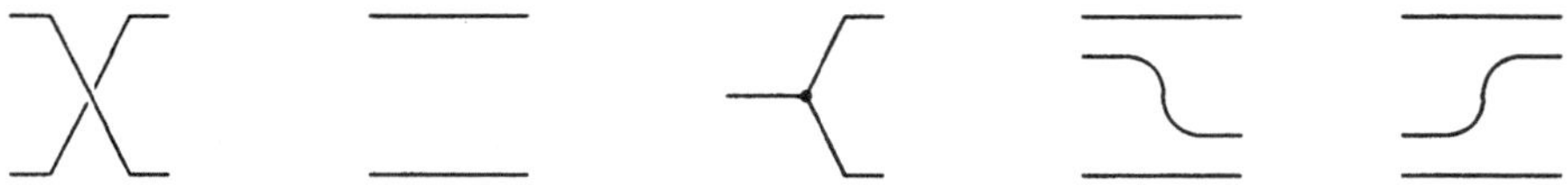

Figure 3: *swp*, 2, *fork*, *rsh*, and *lsh*, with grouping of signals represented by spacing

circuits names that suggest input in the domain and output in the range, but this is just a matter of convention and not part of the formalism.

One of the advantages of using relations is that we can easily treat the inverse (or more properly 'converse'), R^{-1}, of any relation, for which $x\, R^{-1}\, y \iff y\, R\, x$. Frequently this appears as a part of a conjugation, $R \setminus S = S^{-1} \,;\, R \,;\, S$, where the S is effectively a translation applied to all the signals from R.

The parallel composition of two circuits, $[R, S]$, relates a pair of signals in the domain to a pair of signals in the range if and only if the components are related by the corresponding component circuits, $\langle a, b\rangle\, [R, S]\, \langle x, y\rangle \iff a\, R\, x \;\&\; b\, S\, y$. In drawings, such as figure 2, the convention is that lists read from left to right if you stand in the range of the relation, facing into the domain. In the frequent case that one of the circuits is just an abstract wire – a wire or perhaps a bundle of wires, represented by the identity (or 'equality') relation, *id* – we abbreviate this to $\mathsf{fst}\, R = [R, id]$ or $\mathsf{snd}\, S = [id, S]$.

Parallel composition and sequential composition distribute over each other, meaning that $[A, B] \,;\, [C, D] = [A \,;\, C,\ B \,;\, D]$. Be careful that parallel composition in Ruby differs from the $[f, g]$ of μFP, which supplies one input to both f and g to produce a pair of outputs. That would correspond more closely to something like $fork \,;\, [R, S]$ where $x\, fork\, y \iff y = \langle x, x\rangle$.

Repeated composition we write as exponentiation, so that $R^1 = R$ and $R^{n+1} = R^n \,;\, R$. Similarly for negative powers, $R^{-n} = (R^{-1})^n = (R^n)^{-1}$. The repeated parallel composition of R is denoted by $\mathsf{map}\, R$, and relates two lists of signals if they are the same length and corresponding elements are related by R, that is $x\, (\mathsf{map}\, R)\, y \iff \#x = \#y \;\&\; \forall i.\, x_i\, R\, y_i$.

In this paper we need also a small number of primitive circuits, essentially wiring like *fork*, which we define here. The identity on pairs we write $2 = [id, id]$, and *swp* is the relation between pairs whose components are reversed, $\langle x, y\rangle\, swp\, \langle y, x\rangle$. Each of 2 and *swp* is its own inverse. The right- and left-shift relations on pairs are defined by $\langle x, \langle y, z\rangle\rangle\, rsh\, \langle\langle x, y\rangle, z\rangle$ and $\langle\langle x, y\rangle, z\rangle\, lsh\, \langle x, \langle y, z\rangle\rangle$. Clearly each is the other's inverse.

The wiring *zip* represents the interleaving of two buses of wires: it relates a pair of lists of signals to a list of pairs, provided the lists are of equal length and corresponding values are equal, that is $\langle x, y\rangle\, zip\, z \iff \#x = \#y = \#z \;\&\; \forall i.\, \langle x_i, y_i\rangle = z_i$.

Delay, statelessness, and state

As outlined so far, Ruby is a language in which only combinational circuits can be described. To deal with sequential circuits there is a slightly more sophisticated reading of the same formulae. A sequential circuit is a relation between two signals, and a signal is a doubly infinite sequence of samples. The samples can be thought of as the values of signals sampled on consecutive cycles of a logical clock. There need not be a physical clock, nor need the circuit be synchronous.

Simple combinational circuits like the wiring relations are promoted to time-sequences by acting pointwise: in the new reading, $x\ R\ y$ if and only if in the old reading, $x_t\ R\ y_t$ for all times t. Any circuit which is the promotion of some moment-by-moment relation like this is *stateless*.

The meaning of sequential composition, inverse, conjugate, and so on can be read immediately from the definition. However in the case of parallel composition, since all circuits are relations between a single signal in the domain and a single signal in the range, the $\langle a, b\rangle$ in the definition must be read as interleaving – *zip*-ping together – a and b into a sequence for which $\langle a, b\rangle_t$ is the pair of a_t and b_t for each time t. Similarly **map** R relates a single time-sequence consisting of the interleaved domain signals, a list of values at each time, to a similar sequence in the range.

The properties of the operators are preserved by this reading, for example that sequential and parallel composition distribute over each other, so the algebra of the language is unchanged by the change of semantics. Moreover any expression consisting only of combinational primitives and the operators introduced so far can be read by promoting all the primitives and applying the new readings of the operators. It will be stateless, and its meaning in this reading will be the stateless promotion of its combinational reading.

In order to deal with state, one more primitive is needed. A delay, $\mathcal{D}$, relates two signals which are shifted by one time unit, $x\ \mathcal{D}\ y \iff \forall t.\ x_t = y_{t+1}$. It might be a latch or register with its input in the domain and output in the range, supplying its output one time unit later in the range. Its converse, the anti-delay $\mathcal{D}^{-1}$, appears to be a circuit which predicts in the range what its domain signal is going to be one unit later. This need not be as unrealistic as it seems at first sight, because it may be a circuit taking its input in the range and giving output in the domain.

Delay and anti-delay are cancellable, that is $\mathcal{D}\ ;\ \mathcal{D}^{-1} = id = \mathcal{D}^{-1}\ ;\ \mathcal{D}$, because there is no 'first time' and so there is no initial undefined state of the latch. Note that $\mathcal{D}$ does not have any combinational reading: any expression with $\mathcal{D}$ in it must necessarily mean a relation between time-sequences. However equations in the Ruby operators remain true even when circuits with state, such as expressions containing $\mathcal{D}$, are substituted for the variables.

Although $\mathcal{D}$ does not appear as such in μFP, it is possible to define an isolated delay circuit by the μFP expression $\mu[2,1]$, but notice that it is not possible to construct a circuit which behaves like an anti-delay. Moreover (at least in the semantics given in reference [6], where there is a first instant and the output of the latch is initially undefined) there is no function which can be cancelled on *whichever* side of this delay it is composed.

The μFP operator in Ruby

The first thing to do, to make later comparison fairer, is to cast the original μ operator into Ruby. I claim that the operation on relations which corresponds to the μ operator in μFP is μ_{M}, defined by

$$i\ (\mu_{\mathrm{M}}\, R)\ o \iff \exists s, s'.\ \langle i, s\rangle\ R\ \langle o, s'\rangle\ \&\ s'\ \mathcal{D}\ s$$

and illustrated in figure 4. It takes a transition relation R and returns a machine

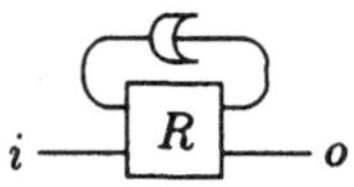

Figure 4: $\mu_M R$ drawn with the conventions of Ruby

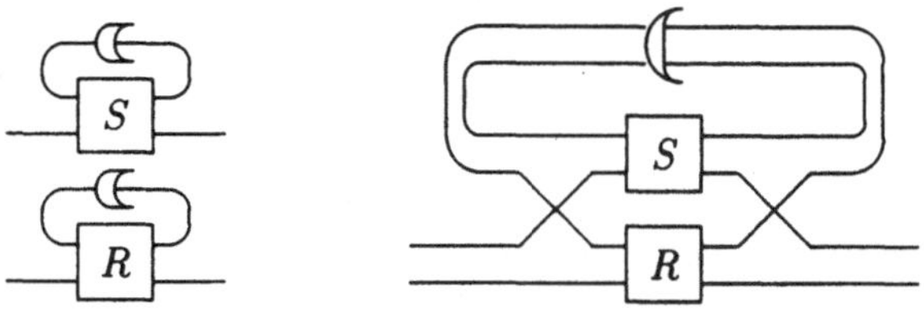

Figure 5: $[\mu_M R, \mu_M S]$ and $\mu_M([R,S] \setminus zip^{-1})$

$\mu_M R$. The transition relation relates a pair consisting of an input and a present state, to a pair consisting of an output and a next state. The definition says that the next state, s', is related to the present state, s, by a single delay $\mathcal{D}$; that is to say that the present state is the previous value of the next-state terminal of the relation.

This is in some ways a more natural description of a state machine, because the description in μFP tends to lead you to have as part of the transition-function the fork (on the right of the pictures in figure 1) which copies the input to each of the components of $[f,g]$. Parts of this wiring might not be needed in any particular machine.

A pair of these machines operating in parallel can always be rewritten as a single machine, using the fact that $\mathcal{D} ; 2 = [\mathcal{D}, \mathcal{D}]$

$$[\mu_M R, \mu_M S] \quad = \quad \mu_M([R,S] \setminus zip^{-1})$$

as illustrated in figure 5. This says that the parallel composition of two state machines is a state machine whose transition relation is the parallel composition of those of the constituent machines, but with the state and input/output suitably interleaved.

There seems to be nothing in reference [6] that corresponds to this law, because there is nothing in μFP which corresponds simply to Ruby's parallel composition – the $[R,S]$ on the right-hand side would be difficult to express. Parallel composition in Ruby generalises to **map**, and the rule about the parallel composition of μ_M machines generalises to

$$\mathsf{map}\, \mu_M R \quad = \quad \mu_M(\mathsf{map}\, R \setminus zip^{-1})$$

which might have been expressed in μFP, but seems never to have been, at least not in anything I have read so far, although a circuit like $\mathsf{map}\, \mu_M R$ is mentioned in passing in reference [7].

In fact the form used in reference [7], which was a first published attempt at choosing a reasonable suite of combining forms for Ruby, is

$$i\ (\mathsf{loop}\ R)\ o \quad \Longleftrightarrow \quad \exists s.\ \langle i, s\rangle\ R\ \langle o, s\rangle$$

which omits the delay from the feedback path. This makes no difference to the algebraic laws quoted so far, and Mary quotes as justification the symmetry of

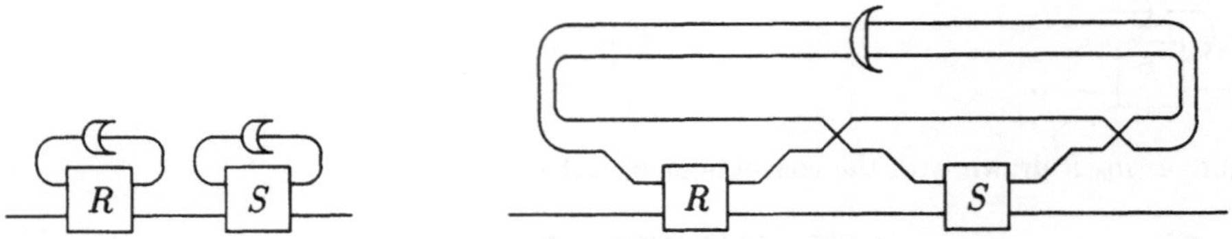

Figure 6: $\mu_{\mathrm{M}}\, R\,;\mu_{\mathrm{M}}\, S$ and $\mu_{\mathrm{M}}(rsh\,;\mathsf{fst}\,R\,;lsh\,;\mathsf{snd}\,swp\,;rsh\,;\mathsf{fst}\,S\,;lsh\,;\mathsf{snd}\,swp)$

$(\mathsf{loop}\,R)^{-1} = \mathsf{loop}(R^{-1})$, in contrast to $(\mu_{\mathrm{M}}\,R)^{-1} = \mu_{\mathrm{M}}(R^{-1}\,;\mathsf{snd}\,\mathcal{D}^{-2})$. I will return to the advisability of omitting the delay once I have sorted out the wiring.

Sequential (de)composition of state machines

As I said earlier, we are really interested in sequential decomposition: in taking large state machines and expressing them as compositions of machines with simpler transition relations. In search of techniques for this, consider first how to represent the composition of two state machines as a single machine. The equality about expressions in μ_{M} that corresponds to $\mathrm{C}\mu$ is

$$\mu_{\mathrm{M}}\,R\,;\mu_{\mathrm{M}}\,S \;=\; \mu_{\mathrm{M}}(rsh\,;\mathsf{fst}\,R\,;lsh\,;\mathsf{snd}\,swp\,;rsh\,;\mathsf{fst}\,S\,;lsh\,;\mathsf{snd}\,swp)$$

each side of which is illustrated in figure 6.

Already some progress has been made by arranging the plumbing as a collection of applications of fst and snd and instances of *lsh* and *swp*. Indeed this equation is so much simpler than the original that you might think that it does not capture the same thing. In a sense that is true: this equation is only about the merging of the two state machines into one. The original statement of $\mathrm{C}\mu$ in μFP has also interleaved the transition relations, that is it has gone on to simplify $rsh\,;\mathsf{fst}\,R\,;lsh\,;\mathsf{snd}\,swp\,;rsh\,;\mathsf{fst}\,S\,;lsh\,;\mathsf{snd}\,swp$, given the knowledge that in the case that corresponds most closely to the μFP the relations R and S are of the form $fork\,;[f,g]$ and $fork\,;[h,j]$.

Pursuing those assumptions is probably not worth doing in general, since in the cases which happen to arise in applications it may be much easier to simplify the particular $rsh\,;\mathsf{fst}\,R\,;lsh\,;\mathsf{snd}\,swp\,;rsh\,;\mathsf{fst}\,S\,;lsh\,;\mathsf{snd}\,swp$ than to deal with a more complex expression in separate relations determining the outputs and next states. There is clearly a pattern in this composite transition relation and the next thing to do is to study that pattern.

Beside and below

Ruby has been particularly successfully applied to describing and designing regular arrays connected in Cartesian grids. These are particularly attractive for the implementer, because they have simple connections, each of which is local. Yet they are sufficiently general to describe anything that might reasonably be built on a silicon surface.

To describe these grids, we use two new combining forms, $R \leftrightarrow S$, read 'R beside

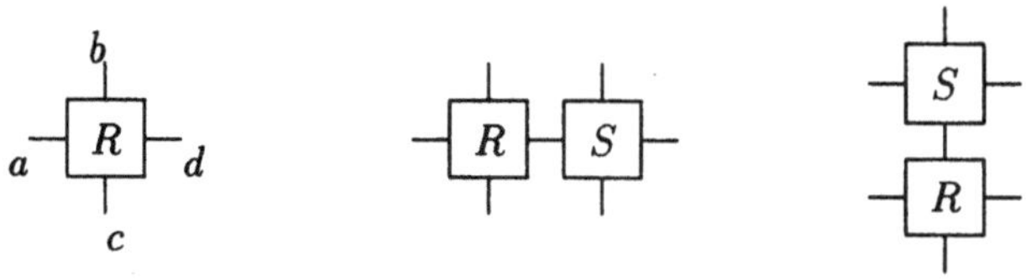

Figure 7: $\langle a, b\rangle\ R\ \langle c, d\rangle$ and layouts suggested by $R \leftrightarrow S$ and $R \updownarrow S$

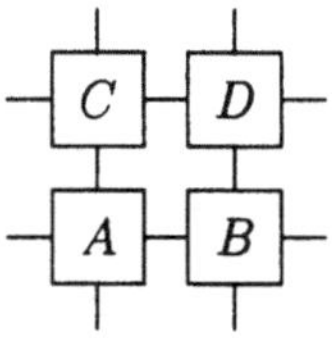

Figure 8: $(A \leftrightarrow B) \updownarrow (C \leftrightarrow D) = (A \updownarrow C) \leftrightarrow (B \updownarrow D)$

S', and $R \updownarrow S$, read 'R below S', defined by

$$\langle a, \langle b, c\rangle\rangle\ (R \leftrightarrow S)\ \langle\langle x, y\rangle, z\rangle \iff \exists n.\ \langle a, b\rangle\ R\ \langle x, n\rangle\ \&\ \langle n, c\rangle\ S\ \langle y, z\rangle$$
$$\langle\langle a, b\rangle, c\rangle\ (R \updownarrow S)\ \langle x, \langle y, z\rangle\rangle \iff \exists n.\ \langle a, n\rangle\ R\ \langle x, y\rangle\ \&\ \langle b, c\rangle\ S\ \langle n, z\rangle$$

and illustrated in figure 7, which uses the convention that wires on the left and top of the picture are in the domain of the relation and those on the bottom and the right are in the range. The ordering is the same as for all the other pictures: stand in the range, facing the domain, and read from left to right; and the division between left and top is that between elements of a pair, as is that between bottom and right. Consequently, inversion of a relation corresponds to reflecting it about the line from bottom-left to top-right which divides domain from range. (This is the Tees-Exe convention, after the geographical dividing line from the Tees estuary in the North East of England to the Exe estuary in the South West, which divides the moors and the mountains from the mud and the money.)

Beside and below need not be thought of as new primitives, for

$$R \leftrightarrow S = \mathit{rsh}\ ;\ \mathsf{fst}\ R\ ;\ \mathit{lsh}\ ;\ \mathsf{snd}\ S\ ;\ \mathit{rsh}$$
$$R \updownarrow S = \mathit{lsh}\ ;\ \mathsf{snd}\ S\ ;\ \mathit{rsh}\ ;\ \mathsf{fst}\ R\ ;\ \mathit{lsh}$$

However it is very useful to have names for these forms both because they occur often in practical circuits, and because they have a simple algebra: for example they distribute over each other in the sense that both of

$$(A \leftrightarrow B) \updownarrow (C \leftrightarrow D) = (A \updownarrow C) \leftrightarrow (B \updownarrow D)$$

describe the same relation, illustrated in figure 8. Beside and below are duals of each other in the sense that $(R \leftrightarrow S)^{-1} = (R^{-1}) \updownarrow (S^{-1})$ and $(R \updownarrow S)^{-1} = (R^{-1}) \leftrightarrow (S^{-1})$. Moreover, $\mathit{rsh} = 2 \leftrightarrow 2$ and $\mathit{lsh} = 2 \updownarrow 2 = \mathit{rsh}^{-1}$, where 2 is the identity on pairs, as illustrated in figure 9.

In the same way that parallel composition can be generalised to **map**, the beside and below operators generalise to row and column operators, defined by

$$\langle a, bs\rangle\ \mathsf{row}\ R\ \langle ys, z\rangle$$
$$\iff \#bs = \#ys\ \&$$
$$(\exists ps.\ a = ps_0\ \&\ \forall i.\ \langle ps_i, bs_i\rangle\ R\ \langle ys_i, ps_{i+1}\rangle\ \&\ ps_{\#bs} = z)$$

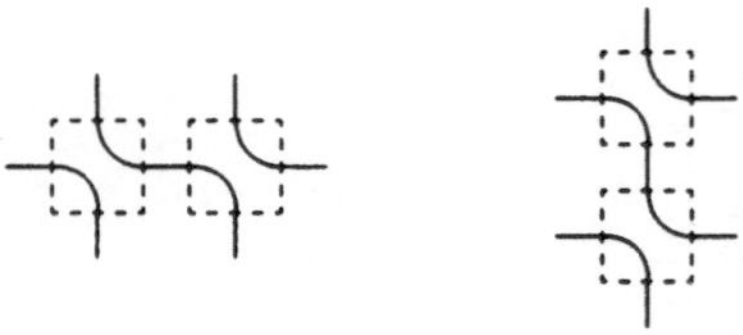

Figure 9: $rsh = 2 \leftrightarrow 2$ and $lsh = 2 \updownarrow 2$

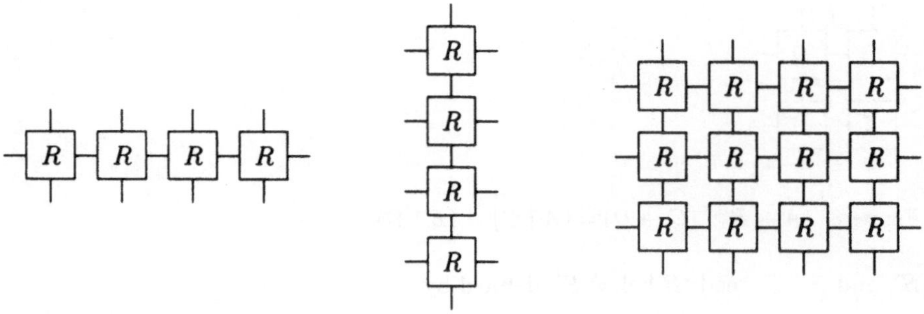

Figure 10: layouts for instances of $\mathsf{row}\, R$, $\mathsf{col}\, R$, and $\mathsf{row}\,\mathsf{col}\, R = \mathsf{col}\,\mathsf{row}\, R$

and

$$\begin{aligned} &\langle as, b\rangle\ \mathsf{col}\, R\ \langle y, zs\rangle \\ \iff\ & \#as = \#zs\ \& \\ & (\exists ps.\, b = ps_{\#as}\ \&\ \forall i.\, \langle as_i, ps_{i+1}\rangle\ R\ \langle ps_i, zs_i\rangle\ \&\ ps_0 = y) \end{aligned}$$

and row and col are also duals, meaning that $(\mathsf{row}\, R)^{-1} = \mathsf{col}(R^{-1})$ and $\mathsf{row}(R^{-1}) = (\mathsf{col}\, R)^{-1}$, so we might write col as $\overline{\mathsf{row}}$ and and row as $\overline{\mathsf{col}}$. Figure 10 shows the expected layouts for row and column. It is a consequence of the distribution of beside and below over each other that row and col commute, meaning that $\mathsf{row}\,\mathsf{col}\, R = \mathsf{col}\,\mathsf{row}\, R$. Unsurprisingly if we define $\mathsf{grid}\, R = \mathsf{row}\,\mathsf{col}\, R$, an instance of which also appears in figure 10, then grid is its own dual.

A good idea pinched from Wayne

Wayne Luk and I spent a considerable time, as part of an Alvey project, applying Ruby to the designs of regular arrays. As a result we fell into a way of thinking where rows and columns, besides and belows were almost simpler to deal with than sequential and parallel compositions. I do not know how he came to think of the idea, but it was at his suggestion that I adopted a slightly different state-machine operator in the lecture notes for my Ruby course [2].

This is one for which the composition of two state machines is a machine whose transition relation is made by putting the component translations together with the beside operator. Specifically,

$$i\,(\mu_{\mathrm{W}}\, R)\,o \iff \exists s, s'.\, \langle i, s\rangle\ R\ \langle s', o\rangle\ \&\ s'\,\mathcal{D}\, s$$

so $\mu_{\mathrm{W}}\, R = \mu_{\mathrm{M}}(R\,;swp)$ and $\mu_{\mathrm{M}}\, R = \mu_{\mathrm{W}}(R\,;swp)$. This is shown laid out following

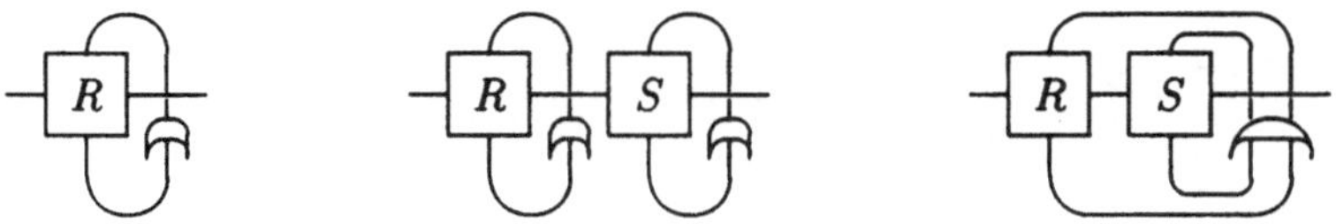

Figure 11: $\mu_W R$, the composition $\mu_W R ; \mu_W S$ and $\mu_W(R \leftrightarrow S)$

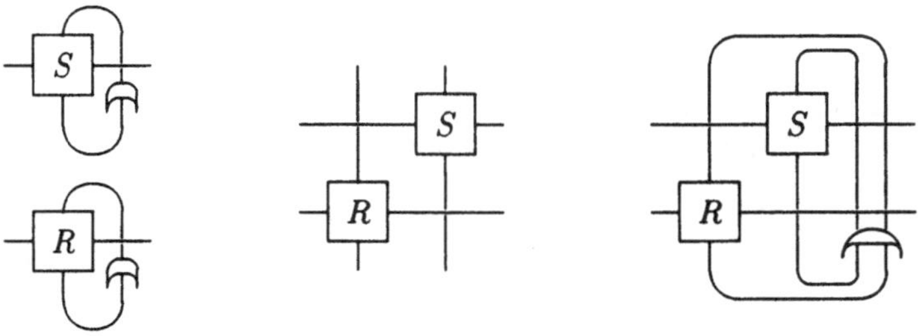

Figure 12: $[\mu_W R, \mu_W S]$, $[R, S] \setminus zip^{-1}$, and $\mu([R, S] \setminus zip^{-1})$

the Tees-Exe conventions in figure 11, along with a composition of machines which satisfies

$$\mu_W R ; \mu_W S \quad = \quad \mu_W(R \leftrightarrow S)$$

That, which is now the statement of Cμ, is so much simpler than the original form that I find it difficult to see why we did not think of it sooner! You can of course calculate one form of Cμ from the other, given the definitions and a bit of patience with the properties of the plumbing relations.

The law describing the parallel composition of two state machines, when cast in term of μ_W turns out to be formally identical to that for μ_M, that is

$$[\mu_W R, \mu_W S] \quad = \quad \mu_W([R, S] \setminus zip^{-1})$$

as is immediate from the definition, because $[swp, swp] ; zip^{-1} = zip^{-1} ; swp$. This law is illustrated in figure 12, and generalises to

$$\mathsf{map}\, \mu_W R \quad = \quad \mu_W((\mathsf{map}\, R) \setminus zip^{-1})$$

Retiming and slowing

One of the uses to which Ruby is put is called *retiming.* The highest clock frequency at which a synchronous clocked circuit can be operated, giving the highest throughput, is limited by the longest propagation delay from the output of a latch to the input of the next. In the course of optimising performance, latches are introduced and moved about to reduce the longest paths, but without changing the specified behaviour of the circuit.

A Ruby relation R for which $R ; \mathcal{D} = \mathcal{D} ; R$ is called *timeless.* Compositions of timeless relations are easy to retime, and this makes timeless relations particularly interesting. Suppose E is some expression in Ruby, that is an expression made up of Ruby operations and constants, and perhaps some variable names. Then on the assumption that all the variables in E are timeless, so also is E itself. That

Figure 13: $\mathsf{slow}(F\,;\mathcal{D}\,;G\,;\mathcal{D})$ and $(\mathsf{slow}\,F)\,;\mathcal{D}^2\,;(\mathsf{slow}\,G)\,;\mathcal{D}^2$

is because each of the Ruby operators preserves timelessness, and all the constant circuits we usually deal with are timeless (even $\mathcal{D}$ itself).

At first it may seem surprising, but both μ_M and μ_W also preserve timelessness. Even though there is state held in the feedback latches, it is still the case that if $\mathcal{D}\,;R = R\,;\mathcal{D}$ then necessarily $\mathcal{D}\,;\mu_M R = \mu_M R\,;\mathcal{D}$ and $\mathcal{D}\,;\mu_W R = \mu_W R\,;\mathcal{D}$. What this means is that the fed-back state is not anchored to a particular time: Ruby delays are not reset at any particular time, and any initial setting has to be by explicit reset signals. This means that we could add either of these operators to a suite of basic operators in Ruby without loosing the property that all operators preserve timelessness.

Another manipulation which is used in optimising performance is *slowing*. A slow version of a circuit can be obtained by taking some expression which describes the circuit, and substituting $\mathcal{D}^2$ (or some other multiple delay, with consequent changes) for every instance of $\mathcal{D}$ in that expression. The slow circuit is one that has to be clocked twice as often, or rather at twice the frequency, to get the same outputs for the same inputs. This might not seem in itself a good thing, but it allows the designer to introduce extra latches which can be moved around in the course of retiming.

Since all the delays appear in pairs, it takes two clock cycles for the signal at the input to each delay to appear at the output. On even-numbered clock cycles, the circuit will be performing the same calculation as an unslowed circuit. The state trapped between the two latches in a pair of delays is never involved in the even-cycle calculation, but after one clock cycle only this state is connected to the rest of the circuit, so the circuit is also performing the same calculation on odd-numbered clock cycles.

That is to say, a slow R behaves like two copies of R, alternately connected to their environment so that they operate on interleaved inputs to produce interleaved outputs. Figure 13 is meant to suggest this: the circuit on the left contains two copies of $F\,;\mathcal{D}\,;G\,;\mathcal{D}$, clocked on alternate cycles of the clock which switches the multiplexers between the two copies. Its behaviour is the same as that of $(\mathsf{slow}\,F)\,;\mathcal{D}^2\,;(\mathsf{slow}\,G)\,;\mathcal{D}^2$, and if F and G are stateless this is $F\,;\mathcal{D}^2\,;G\,;\mathcal{D}^2$.

This correspondence is interesting because it shows that we can define **slow** as an operator on relations, rather than on Ruby expressions. That is, we define **slow** as the interleaving operation, and if R and S are different expressions which denote the same relation, $R = S$, it is necessarily the case that $\mathsf{slow}\,R = \mathsf{slow}\,S$. Substituting $\mathcal{D}^2$ for $\mathcal{D}$ in *any* expression which describes a circuit will give the same slow circuit.

That is not obvious: a substitution which is not of equals for equals need not be a well-defined operation on the meaning of an expression! It works for **slow** in Ruby because apart from $\mathcal{D}$ the primitives are all stateless, which means that $R = \mathsf{slow}\,R$, and **slow** distributes over all the combining forms, for example $\mathsf{slow}(R\,;S) = \mathsf{slow}\,R\,;\mathsf{slow}\,S$, and $\mathsf{slow}[R, S] = [\mathsf{slow}\,R, \mathsf{slow}\,S]$.

Figure 14: two layouts for μR and two for $\bar{\mu} R$

However this property would be lost by adding either of the the state-machine operators to Ruby, because $\mathsf{slow}\, \mu_M R \neq \mu_M\, \mathsf{slow}\, R$, and $\mathsf{slow}\, \mu_W R \neq \mu_W\, \mathsf{slow}\, R$. If we define slow by the interleaving of relations, $\mathsf{slow}\, \mu_M R = \mu_M((\mathsf{slow}\, R)\,;\mathsf{snd}\,\mathcal{D})$ and likewise $\mathsf{slow}\, \mu_W R = \mu_W((\mathsf{slow}\, R);\mathsf{fst}\,\mathcal{D})$ so there is a substitution which corresponds to slowing, but it is more complicated because it has to deal specially with the μ operators as well as with $\mathcal{D}$.

A new μ and its dual

Clearly the problem with slowing state machines is that I have stubbornly retained the delay - hidden in the feedback path - which is the difference between slowing a machine and making a machine from a slowed transition relation. The difficulty that this causes can be overcome simply by omitting the delay, so I finally propose another μ operator defined by

$$i\,(\mu\, R)\, o \iff \exists s.\ \langle i, s\rangle\ R\ \langle s, o\rangle$$

illustrated in figure 14. It can be used to implement either of the earlier operations because $\mu_W R = \mu(R\,;\mathsf{fst}\,\mathcal{D})$ and so $\mu_M R = \mu(R\,; swp\,;\mathsf{fst}\,\mathcal{D})$. Moreover, it should be entirely unsurprising that $\mathsf{slow}\,\mu\, R = \mu\,\mathsf{slow}\, R$.

The dual of this operation is given by $\bar{\mu}\, R = (\mu(R^{-1}))^{-1}$, and satisfies

$$i\,(\bar{\mu}\, R)\, o \iff \exists s.\ \langle s, i\rangle\ R\ \langle o, s\rangle$$

so $\mu\, R = \bar{\mu}(R \setminus swp)$ and $\bar{\mu}\, R = \mu(R \setminus swp)$.

This is again a simplification over the earlier operators, whose duals introduced odd anti-delays. It would hardly have been worth noting that $\bar{\mu}_M R = \mu_M(R\,;\mathsf{snd}\,\mathcal{D}^{-2})$, nor that $\bar{\mu}_W R = \mu_W((R \setminus swp)\,;\mathsf{fst}\,\mathcal{D}^{-2})$, and while the excess anti-delays that appear on the right-hand sides can be moved about in the expression they cannot be eliminated. The loop operation is its own dual, $\overline{\mathsf{loop}}\, R = \mathsf{loop}\, R$, so there would be no way of re-expressing $\mathsf{loop}(R \setminus swp)$.

The delay-less μ operator has just as simple a form of $C\mu$ as before,

$$\mu\, R\,;\mu\, S \;=\; \mu(R \leftrightarrow S)$$

as illustrated in figure 15, and the same simple law for parallel composition,

$$[\mu\, R, \mu\, S] \;=\; \mu([R, S] \setminus zip^{-1})$$

as illustrated in figure 16. Moreover, the operation dual to this new constructor

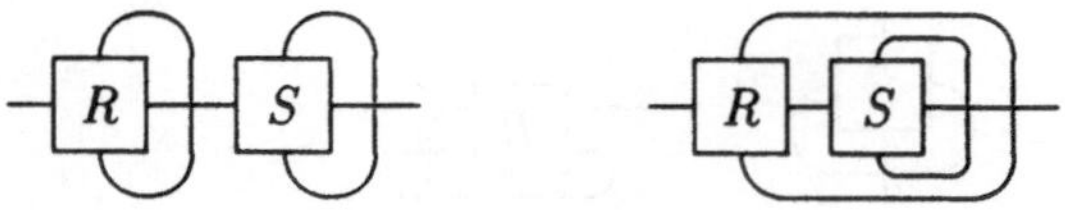

Figure 15: $\mu R ; \mu S$ and $\mu(R \leftrightarrow S)$

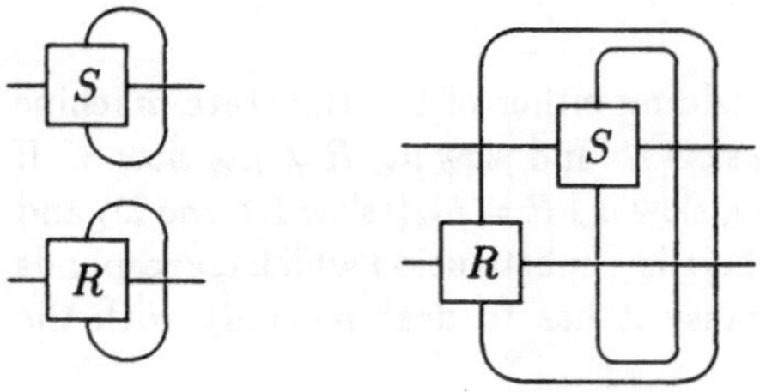

Figure 16: $[\mu R, \mu S]$ and $\mu([R,S] \setminus zip^{-1})$

has similarly simple laws, for

$$\begin{aligned}\bar\mu R ; \bar\mu S &= (\mu R^{-1})^{-1} ; (\mu S^{-1})^{-1} \\ &= (\mu S^{-1} ; \mu R^{-1})^{-1} \\ &= (\mu(S^{-1} \leftrightarrow R^{-1}))^{-1} \\ &= \bar\mu(S^{-1} \leftrightarrow R^{-1})^{-1} \\ &= \bar\mu(S \updownarrow R)\end{aligned}$$

and

$$\begin{aligned}[\bar\mu R, \bar\mu S] &= [(\mu R^{-1})^{-1}, (\mu S^{-1})^{-1}] \\ &= [\mu R^{-1}, \mu S^{-1}]^{-1} \\ &= (\mu([R^{-1}, S^{-1}] \setminus zip^{-1}))^{-1} \\ &= \bar\mu(([R^{-1}, S^{-1}] \setminus zip^{-1})^{-1}) \\ &= \bar\mu([R,S] \setminus zip^{-1})\end{aligned}$$

which gives μ and $\bar\mu$ the same standing in calculations.

Other laws which these new operators satisfy are also simplified. For example, the interface laws

$$\begin{aligned}A ; \mu R ; B &= \mu(\mathsf{fst}\, A ; R ; \mathsf{snd}\, B) \\ A ; \bar\mu R ; B &= \bar\mu(\mathsf{snd}\, A ; R ; \mathsf{fst}\, B)\end{aligned}$$

are broadly the same as for the earlier operators, but the laws capturing the idea of change of state

$$\begin{aligned}\mu(R ; \mathsf{fst}\, S) &= \mu(\mathsf{snd}\, S ; R) \\ \bar\mu(R ; \mathsf{snd}\, S) &= \bar\mu(\mathsf{fst}\, S ; R)\end{aligned}$$

are much simpler, because there are no side-conditions about the timelessness of the change of state, S. Indeed they would be true for any relation S, even relations which are not themselves expressible in Ruby.

Many people, when they first see a delay-free μ operator, are concerned about whether μR means anything in case the signal in the first component of the range depends immediately (that is, with no delay) on that in the second component of

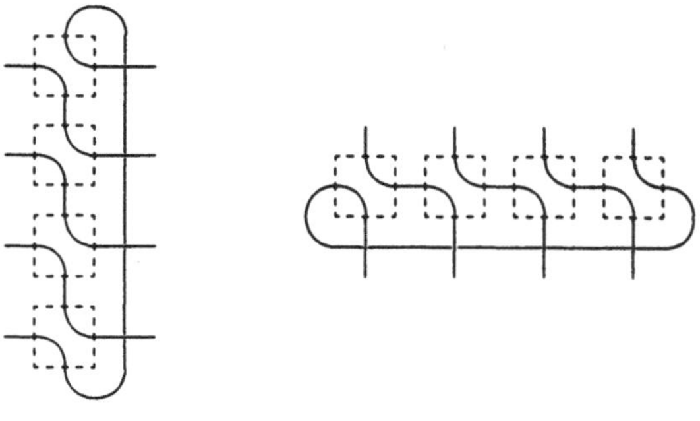

Figure 17: μ col 2 and its inverse, $\bar{\mu}$ row 2

the domain. The delay in the loop in the μFP primitive was there to ensure that any loop in the implementation of a μFP expression would contain a positive number of delays. There could therefore never be any loops in the causal dependency, and all signals in a circuit described in μFP are therefore necessarily defined.

This is not the case in Ruby, because it is not possible to guarantee that there are no loops in the causality graph: the delay in the feedback loop can be cancelled in, for example, $\mu_{\mathrm{M}}(R;\mathsf{snd}\,\mathcal{D}^{-1})$. Even if $\mathcal{D}$ and $\mathcal{D}^{-1}$, and even the taking of inverses, are omitted from the language, they can be constructed from μ_{M} and some plumbing, for $\mathcal{D} = \mu_{\mathrm{M}}\, swp$ and $\mathcal{D}^{-1} = \mu_{\mathrm{M}}(any \setminus fork)$, where $\langle a, b\rangle\, (any \setminus fork)\, \langle c, d\rangle \iff a = b \;\&\; c = d$.

However, this is to confuse the definedness of the signals with the definedness of the relations between them. Whatever the relation R, it yields a well-defined relation $\mu\, R$, and anything you can prove about $\mu\, R$ will be true whether or not the signal on the feedback path is defined by R. The causal relationship between inputs and outputs is one of the things from which Ruby chooses to abstract, and in consequence so is the definedness of signals whose definedness is not material to the observable behaviour of a circuit.

$\mathcal{D}$-light μ-using

It seems that I was not paying too much attention to Wayne's suggestion. While I adopted Wayne's wiring for μ_{W} in my course notes it was actually the delay-free μ that he used in reference [5] (where *it* also is called **loop**). In that paper he proves and uses properties of the delay-free operator, such as that $(\mu\, R)^n = \mu\, \mathsf{row}_n\, R$, where $\mathsf{row}_n\, R = \mathsf{snd}\, n\, ; \mathsf{row}\, R\, ; \mathsf{fst}\, n$ is a row with a size of exactly n. (This follows immediately from Cμ by an induction on n.)

However it turns out that all the uses of **loop** in the paper are instances of $\mu(R; \mathsf{fst}\,\mathcal{D})$ and so might as well have been uses of μ_{W}. Moreover, all the properties used are also properties of μ_{W} as well!

The thinking in the present paper came about from a need to express a particular $\mu(\mathsf{slow}\, R\, ; \mathsf{fst}\,\mathcal{D})$ in a form in which the **slow** was at the outside. This arose in the course of the formal development of a bit-serial circuit [4]. It happens that there is no S for which $\mu(\mathsf{slow}\, R\, ; \mathsf{fst}\,\mathcal{D}) = \mathsf{slow}\, S$, because the behaviour of the circuit is different on different phases of the clock. We need to do more work on such multi-phase circuits. Clarity of thought in the reasoning in that paper was only

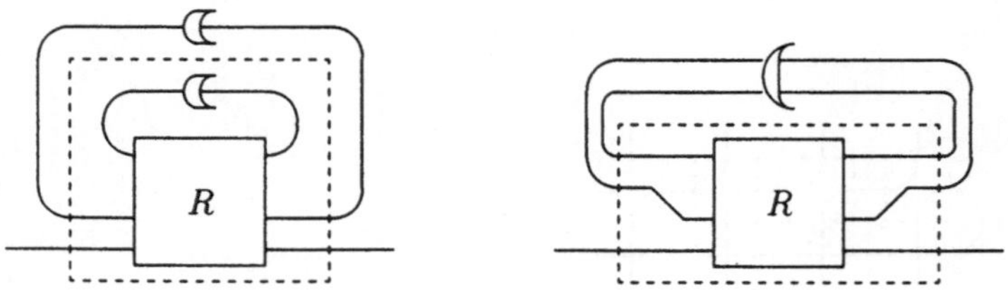

Figure 18: $\mu_{\mathrm{M}}\,\mu_{\mathrm{M}}\,R$ and $\mu_{\mathrm{M}}(R \setminus lsh)$

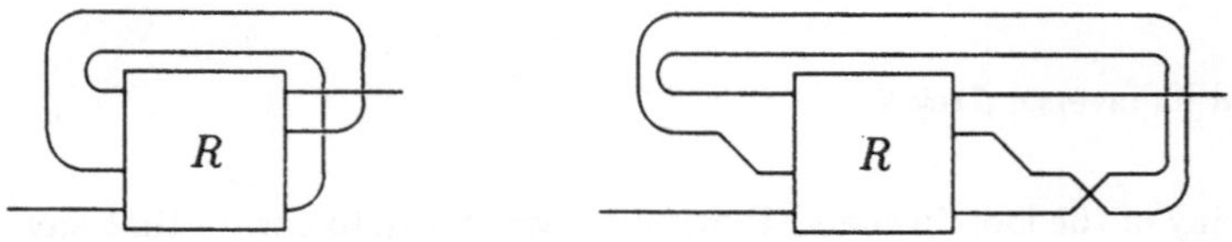

Figure 19: $\mu\,\mu\,R$ and $\mu(rsh\ ;\ R\ ;\ rsh\ ;\ \mathsf{fst}\ swp)$

possible by divorcing the feedback and the delay.

In the course of the reasoning about that bit-serial arithmetic circuit other instances of μ with no delays on the feedback path arose naturally in the calculations. Consider the circuit $\mathsf{col}\,2$, which relates a pair $\langle as, b\rangle$ to a pair $\langle y, zs\rangle$ if and only if $as +\!\!+ \langle b\rangle = \langle y\rangle +\!\!+ zs$. That is to say it is a left-shift operation, generalising $lsh = \mathsf{col}_2\,2$, and similarly $\mathsf{row}\,2$ is a right-shift operation on an arbitrarily wide tuple. In both cases a single signal is moved in at one end of the tuple, and a single one is carried out at the other end. The circuits $\mu\,\mathsf{col}\,2$ and $\bar{\mu}\,\mathsf{row}\,2$, illustrated in figure 17, similarly accomplish cyclic shifts. Of course, in the case of rows and columns of length two, $\mu\,\mathsf{col}_2\,2 = \bar{\mu}\,\mathsf{row}_2\,2 = swp$.

Things that are less simple

One of the μFP laws in reference [6] shows that a state machine whose transition function is itself a state machine can be simplified; in the μFP notation, that

$$\mu\,\mu[[f, g], h] \;=\; \mu([f, [g, h]] \cdot [[1, 1\cdot 2], 2\cdot 2])$$

Here the $[[1, 1\cdot 2], 2\cdot 2]$ is just the function corresponding to the rsh relation of Ruby, and $[f, [g, h]] = [1\cdot 1, [2\cdot 1, 2]] \cdot [[f, g], h]$ and $[1\cdot 1, [2\cdot 1, 2]]$ is the function that corresponds to lsh, so the nearest corresponding equation in the notation of this paper would be

$$\mu_{\mathrm{M}}\,\mu_{\mathrm{M}}\,R \;=\; \mu_{\mathrm{M}}(R \setminus lsh)$$

which is illustrated in figure 18. This form would be the same, whether or not there were a delay in the feedback loop. The corresponding equation for the new μ operator, illustrated in figure 19, is

$$\begin{aligned}\mu\,\mu\,R &= \mu(rsh\ ;\ R\ ;\ rsh\ ;\ \mathsf{fst}\ swp)\\ &= \mu(\mathsf{snd}\ swp\ ;\ rsh\ ;\ R\ ;\ rsh)\end{aligned}$$

which reveals the twist in the wires, and it would be similar for μ_W. I do not think I have ever had need to use this sort of law. However

$$\mu\,\bar{\mu}\,R \;=\; \bar{\mu}\,\mu(lsh\,;R\,;lsh)$$

and so, taking inverses throughout,

$$\bar{\mu}\,\mu\,R \;=\; \mu\,\bar{\mu}(rsh\,;R\,;rsh)$$

should those ever arise in practice.

Much ado about...

There is nothing extraordinary in anything I am reporting here: the sequential composition of μs was all in Mary's original Cμ in her thesis [6] almost ten years ago. In fact it is no easier to factorise a relation into $R \leftrightarrow S$ than into

$$rsh\,;\mathsf{fst}\;R\qquad;lsh\,;\mathsf{snd}\;swp\,;rsh\,;\mathsf{fst}\;S\qquad;lsh\,;\mathsf{snd}\;swp$$

because $R \leftrightarrow S$ is equal to

$$(rsh\,;\mathsf{fst}\,(R\,;swp)\,;lsh\,;\mathsf{snd}\;swp\,;rsh\,;\mathsf{fst}\,(S\,;swp)\,;lsh\,;\mathsf{snd}\;swp)\,;swp$$

and the three extra *swp*s are exactly the difference between μ_M and μ_W. On the other hand, I think I can justifiably claim that the simpler algebra of the present form of the Ruby μ has encouraged more creative exploration of circuits built from state machines than I could contemplate if faced with expressions like $f \cdot [h \cdot [1, 2 \cdot 2], 1 \cdot 2]$ and $[g \cdot [h \cdot [1, 2 \cdot 2], 1 \cdot 2], j \cdot [1, 2 \cdot 2]]$.

In this case it is not so much a matter of getting the names of things right as of getting to name the right things.

References

[1] Backus J. Can programming be liberated from the von Neumann style? a functional style and its algebra of programs. Commun ACM 1978;21:613–641

[2] Jones G. Designing circuits by calculation. Programming Research Group technical report PRG–TR–10–90. Oxford University Computing Laboratory, 1990

[3] Jones G, Sheeran M. Circuit design in Ruby. In: Staunstrup J (ed) Formal methods for VLSI design. North-Holland, 1990, pp 13–70

[4] Jones G, Sheeran M. Deriving bit-serial circuits in Ruby. In: Halaas A, Denyer P (eds) VLSI'91. (Proc IFIP TC10/WG10.5 Intl Conf, Edinburgh, Scotland, Aug 1991) North-Holland.

[5] Luk W, Brown G. A systolic LRU processor and its top-down development. Sci Comp Prog, 1990;15:217–233

[6] Sheeran M. μFP - an algebraic VLSI design language. Programming Research Group technical monograph PRG–39. Oxford University Computing Laboratory, 1984

[7] Sheeran M. Describing and reasoning about circuits using relations. In: McEvoy K, Tucker JV (eds) Theoretical foundations of VLSI design. (Proc Leeds workshop, 1986) Cambridge University Press, 1990, pp 263–298

Bernard of Chartres used to say that we are like dwarfs on the shoulders of giants, so that we can see more than they, and things at a greater distance, not by virtue of any sharpness of sight on our part, or any physical distinction, but because we are carried high and raised up by their giant size.

John of Salisbury, Metalogicon (1159)

If I have seen further it is by standing on the shoulders of giants.

Isaac Newton, in a letter to Robert Hooke

Implementing Projection-based Strictness Analysis

Ryszard Kubiak, John Hughes, John Launchbury
Department of Computing Science
University of Glasgow

Abstract

Projection-based backwards strictness analysis has been understood for some years. Surprisingly, even though the method is fairly simple and quite general, no reports of its implementation have appeared. This paper describes ideas underlying our prototype implementation of the analysis for a simple programming language. The implementation serves as a case study before applying the method in the Glasgow Haskell compiler.

1 Introduction

The method of projection-based backwards strictness analysis for first-order, lazy functional languages was first presented by Wadler and Hughes [8] in 1987. Since then it has been generalised by Hughes [4] and Hughes and Launchbury [3] to work for user-defined types and for polymorphism. Yet, to our knowledge, it has never been implemented even though the method is fairly simple and quite general. The time has come for projection-based strictness analysis to meet practice.

This paper describes a prototype implementation. Initially we expected that building the prototype would involve little more than a routine application of the theory developed over the last few years. We were wrong. Many difficulties arose which corresponded either to loose ends, or to issues that were not explored in previous papers. Specifically, these involved the combination of polymorphism and user-defined types. To overcome these problems, we had to spend considerable effort tying the theory down sufficiently for its implementation to become practicable. The prototype is based on a heavily cut down version of Haskell, as our ultimate aim is to incorporate a projection-based strictness analysis phase in the Glasgow Haskell compiler. In particular, we restrict ourselves to a first-order polymorphic language.

Another reason for expecting the implementation to be straightforward was that an implementation of projection-based program analysis already existed. In his thesis [7], Launchbury implemented a *binding-time analysis* using projections, which analysed programs written in a polymorphic, first-order language with user defined types. In particular, he demonstrated that projections (which are functions) can effectively be manipulated in a concrete implementation. Unfortunately, strictness analysis involves additional complications which meant that the extensions to the binding-time analyser were not trivial.

In this paper we begin with a brief review of the method of projection-based strictness analysis. Then we introduce our example language, with its model for types and its semantics. We provide an abstract semantics based on projections which defines a strictness analysis. Implementation issues follow. We provide a generic method of generating finite lattices of projections (called *contexts*) over user-defined data types, and show how to model certain operations by manipulating their concrete representations. Finally, after covering more details of the implementation and giving some examples, we discuss the difficulties we face in extending it to Haskell.

The contributions this paper makes may be summarised as follows.

- We provide an explicit closure semantics for our example language, and give a new presentation of the projection analysis.
- We provide a complete set of rules for constructing finite domains of projections over polymorphic ground types, and describe how operations on these may be performed by an implementation.
- We provide a short suite of examples of the analyser at work, showing how the analysis of polymorphism and data structures interacts.

2 Projection-based Strictness Analysis

Early strictness analysis methods could discover nothing informative about functions on lazy data-structures, and projection-based strictness analysis was developed in an attempt to solve this problem. Recall that, in domain theory, a projection is a function p such that $p \circ p = p$ and $p \sqsubseteq Ide\ (= \lambda x.x)$. The essential intuition is that a projection performs a certain amount of evaluation of a lazy data-structure. For example, the projection

$$\begin{array}{lcll} \mathit{Left} : \mathit{Nat} \times \mathit{Nat} \rightarrow \mathit{Nat} \times \mathit{Nat} & & & \\ \mathit{Left}\ (x, y) & = & (\bot, \bot) & \textbf{if } x = \bot \\ & = & (x, y) & \textbf{if } x \neq \bot \end{array}$$

may be thought of as evaluating the first component of a pair, while

$$\begin{array}{lcll} \mathit{Both} : \mathit{Nat} \times \mathit{Nat} \rightarrow \mathit{Nat} \times \mathit{Nat} & & & \\ \mathit{Both}\ (x, y) & = & (\bot, \bot) & \textbf{if } x = \bot \textbf{ or } y = \bot \\ & = & (x, y) & \textbf{otherwise} \end{array}$$

evaluates both. Now we can regard a function as *Both*-strict—performing as much evaluation as *Both*—if evaluating its argument with *Both* before the call does not change its result. For example, the function $+ : Nat \times Nat \rightarrow Nat$ evaluates both its arguments, and so $+ = + \circ Both$. More generally, there may be parts of a function's argument that are evaluated only if certain parts of its result are evaluated—a function may evaluate more or less of its argument depending on context. Take *swap* for example.

$$\begin{array}{l} \mathit{swap} : \mathit{Nat} \times \mathit{Nat} \rightarrow \mathit{Nat} \times \mathit{Nat} \\ \mathit{swap}\ (x, y) = (y, x) \end{array}$$

While *swap* is not *Both*-strict, but it is *Both*-strict in a *Both*-strict context since $Both \circ swap = Both \circ swap \circ Both$. Thus, if both components of *swap*'s result will be evaluated, then the components of its argument can be evaluated before the call without changing the meaning. We make the following definition:

Definition
Let f be a function and p and q be projections. We say f is p-strict in a q-strict context if $q \circ f = q \circ f \circ p$ (or equivalently, $q \circ f \sqsubseteq f \circ p$). □

Projections capture the notion of evaluating a component of a data-structure. To capture evaluation of a single value we must embed it in a "data-structure" with a single component, which we can think of as representing an unevaluated closure. Thus we think of a closure of type t as an element of $t_\perp$, and we "evaluate" it with the projection

$$\begin{array}{lcll} Str : t_\perp \rightarrow t_\perp & & & \\ Str\ \ \perp & = & \perp & \\ Str\ (\mathit{lift}\ x) & = & \perp & \textbf{if } x = \perp \\ & = & \mathit{lift}\ x & \textbf{if } x \neq \perp \end{array}$$

(writing the lifted elements in the form *lift* x). Now, any function $f : s \rightarrow t$ induces a function $f_\perp : s_\perp \rightarrow t_\perp$ which behaves like f on elements of s, but maps the new $\perp$ to $\perp$. It is easy to show that,

$$f \text{ is strict if and only if } Str \circ f_\perp \sqsubseteq f_\perp \circ Str$$

From f, together with a projection q representing the demand for the result of f, we want to find an p such that $q \circ f_\perp \sqsubseteq f_\perp \circ p$. We can always choose p to be *Ide*, but this is uninformative: *Ide* corresponds to performing no evaluation at all. We would like to find the smallest p such that the condition holds. In general this is equivalent to the halting problem, but [8] gives methods for finding quite small ps, for monomorphic functions. Later in this paper we give a revised version of these methods.

There are four fundamental projections over lifted types which capture various degrees of evaluation. We have already seen *Ide* (no evaluation), and *Str* (evaluate). In addition there is *Abs* defined by

$$\begin{array}{lcl} Abs : t_\perp \rightarrow t_\perp & & \\ Abs\ \ \perp & = & \perp \\ Abs\ (\mathit{lift}\ x) & = & \mathit{lift}\ \perp \end{array}$$

and the constant bottom function *Bot* $(= \lambda x.\perp)$. These are discussed in more detail later.

3 The Language

The language we use for the prototype implementation is a polymorphic, first-order lazy functional language with user-defined data types.

3.1 Syntax

Programs consist of type definitions, then function definitions, and finally an expression giving the meaning of the program. Each function definition and final expression must be given explicit type information. An example program is

```
List a = Nil + Cons a (List a)

append:: List a -> List a -> List a;
append xs ys = case xs
               in Nil -> ys
               || Cons u us -> Cons u (append us ys)
               end;

append (Cons Nil Nil) Nil:: List (List a)
```

In the abstract syntax which follows, we use {*pattern*} to signify zero or more repetitions.

```
Prog     → {TypeDef} {FnType FnDef} e::t
TypeDef  → T {a} = Sum
FnType   → f::{t ->}t
FnDef    → f {x} = e;
e        → x
         | c {e}
         | f {e}
         | case e in c_1 {x_1}-> e_1 ...c_n {x_n}-> e_n end
Sum      → c_1 {t_1}+ ... +c_n {t_n}
t        → T {t}
         | a
```

The grammar uses the following (possibly indexed) variables to denote the elements in various syntactic classes.

e	∈	*Expr*	[Value Expressions]
x	∈	*Var*	[Value Variables]
f	∈	*Fname*	[Function names]
c	∈	*Cname*	[Constructor names]
t	∈	*Texpr*	[Type Expressions]
a	∈	*Tvar*	[Type variables]
T	∈	*Tname*	[Type names]

Note that the language does not have a special syntax for products and tuples. The programmer may introduce a type of polymorphic pairs, say, and define selectors appropriately. For example,

```
type Pair a b = MkPair a b;

fst:: Pair a b -> a;
fst z = case z in MkPair x y -> x end;
```

The reason for this omission is to remove confusion between pairing in the language, and product in the semantics. The former is modelled by a lifted product.

3.2 Semantics

In order to use *Str* to discover simple strictness, the methods of [8] demand that instead of analysing a function $f : A \to B$, its lifted version $f_\perp : A_\perp \to B_\perp$ is used instead. At first this seems to be just a technical trick. However, lifting plays a role both in theory and in practice for modelling lazy evaluation.

Non-strict semantics requires that the evaluation of an argument to a function call should be postponed until it is certain the argument is needed. In practice, when evaluating a function call, the arguments are stored in the form of *closures*, i.e. graphs representing the expressions, and it is only evaluation of the function's body which causes evaluation of the closures. We model closures by lifted values.

3.2.1 Denotations of Types

We depart slightly from the standard model of types in lazy functional languages. Usually the right hand side of a type definition of the form

```
F a b = C1 R S + C2 T
```

is modelled by the domain

$$R \times S \ + \ T$$

where R, S and T model `R`, `S` and `T` respectively, the product is cartesian product, and the sum is separated sum. Instead, we model the type by

$$R_\perp \otimes S_\perp \ \oplus \ T_\perp$$

using smash sum and smash product. Because of the well-known isomorphisms $R + S \cong R_\perp \oplus S_\perp$ and $(R \times S)_\perp \cong R_\perp \otimes S_\perp$ this is isomorphic to the usual, but it is more convenient for us as it allows us to make explicit where closures reside. As an example, consider lists, defined as follows.

```
List a = Nil + Cons a (List a);
```

We model this type by the domain (actually functor),

$$List = \Lambda\alpha \ . \ \mu L \ . \ \mathbf{1}_\perp \ \oplus \ (\alpha_\perp \otimes L_\perp)$$

We write in^s_{Nil} and in^s_{Cons} for the injection functions into a named smash sum. Normally, we will drop the explicit $\Lambda\alpha$, and simply use successive Greek letters for successive polymorphic parameters (a sort of de Bruijn index).

3.2.2 Dynamic Semantics

The semantics are given in terms of two semantic functions,

$$\mathcal{PR} : \mathit{FunDefs} \rightarrow \mathit{FunEnv}$$
$$\mathcal{E} : \mathit{FunEnv} \rightarrow \mathit{Expr} \rightarrow \mathit{ValEnv} \rightarrow \mathit{Value}$$

where

$$\begin{array}{lcl} \nu \in \mathit{Value} & = & \bigcup_{\tau \in \mathrm{Type}} \tau \\ \rho \in \mathit{ValEnv} & = & \mathit{Var} \rightarrow \mathit{Value}_\perp \\ \phi \in \mathit{FunEnv} & = & \mathit{Fname} \rightarrow (\mathit{Value}_\perp \otimes \cdots \otimes \mathit{Value}_\perp \rightarrow \mathit{Value}) \end{array}$$

Given a program containing function definitions, the semantic function $\mathcal{PR}$ constructs a global environment of functions. $\mathcal{E}$ interprets expressions in a given function environment. $\mathcal{E}$ is defined as follows.

$$\mathcal{E}_\phi[\![\, \mathtt{x} \,]\!]_\rho \quad = \quad \mathit{drop}\ (\rho\ (\mathtt{x}))$$

$$\mathcal{E}_\phi[\![\, \mathtt{f}\ \mathtt{e}_1 \ldots \mathtt{e}_k \,]\!]_\rho \quad = \quad \phi\ (\mathtt{f})\ (\mathit{lift}\ \mathcal{E}_\phi[\![\, \mathtt{e}_1 \,]\!]_\rho \otimes \cdots \otimes \mathit{lift}\ \mathcal{E}_\phi[\![\, \mathtt{e}_k \,]\!]_\rho)$$

$$\mathcal{E}_\phi[\![\, \mathtt{c}\ \mathtt{e}_1 \ldots \mathtt{e}_k \,]\!]_\rho \quad = \quad \mathit{in}^s_{\mathtt{c}}\ (\mathit{lift}\ \mathcal{E}_\phi[\![\, \mathtt{e}_1 \,]\!]_\rho \otimes \cdots \otimes \mathit{lift}\ \mathcal{E}_\phi[\![\, \mathtt{e}_k \,]\!]_\rho)$$

$$\begin{array}{l} \mathcal{E}_\phi[\![\, \mathtt{case\ e\ in}\ \cdots \mathtt{c}_j\ \mathtt{x}_1 \ldots \mathtt{x}_k\ \mathtt{->}\ \mathtt{e}_j \cdots]\!]_\rho \\ \quad = \quad \mathit{case}\ \mathcal{E}_\phi[\![\, \mathtt{x} \,]\!]_\rho\ \mathit{in} \\ \qquad\qquad \begin{array}{lcl} \perp & \rightarrow & \perp \\ \vdots & & \\ \mathit{in}^s_{\mathtt{c}_j}\ (\nu_1 \otimes \cdots \otimes \nu_k) & \rightarrow & \mathcal{E}_\phi[\![\, \mathtt{e}_j \,]\!]_{\rho[\mathtt{x}_i \mapsto \nu_i]_i} \\ \vdots & & \end{array} \end{array}$$

Note our overloading of the symbol $\otimes$, here to operate on values. Any ambiguity about the use of such overloaded notation can be resolved by the context.

The novel aspect of the definition of $\mathcal{E}$ is the use of explicit closures. For example, when a variable is dereferenced, it's closure is collapsed (i.e. it is evaluated) using the function $\mathit{drop} : t_\perp \rightarrow t$ which maps $\perp$ to $\perp$, and $\mathit{lift}\ x$ to x. Conversely, when a function is called, a tuple of closures is constructed strictly containing its arguments, and so on. This is an accurate simulation of what actually happens within the machine: if for any reason the tuple of closures for the arguments cannot be created (e.g. the lack of memory) the function returns $\perp$. While the definition of $\mathcal{E}$ looks unusual, it may be obtained from the usual semantics via the isomorphisms of Section 3.2.1.

The function environment is constructed as the least fixed point of the function definitions, as follows (where $\underline{\lambda}$ produces a strict function),

$$\begin{array}{l} \mathcal{PR}[\![\cdots,\ \mathtt{f}\ \mathtt{x}_1\ ..\ \mathtt{x}_k\ \mathtt{=}\ \mathtt{e},\ \cdots]\!] \\ \quad = \mathit{fix}\ (\lambda\phi.\{\cdots, f \mapsto \underline{\lambda}(\nu_1 \otimes \cdots \otimes \nu_k).\mathcal{E}_\phi[\![\, \mathtt{e} \,]\!]_{[\mathtt{x}_i \mapsto \nu_i]}, \cdots\}) \end{array}$$

3.3 Non-uniform Types

The syntax of types allowed by most lazy functional languages (including the language used in this paper) allows for *non-uniformly* recursive types. A type is *uniformly-recursive* if it may be defined by equations of the form $\mu X.F(X)$, where F is a functor from domains to domains (i.e. $F(X)$ is a type-valued expression depending on X).

The following are two examples of non-uniform types.

```
type Moo a b = Msimple + Mcompl (Moo b a);
type Foo t = Fsimple + Fcompl (Foo (Foo t));
```

To model such types requires abstraction over functors, rather than just over types. Furthermore, while fairly trivial programs containing non-uniform types can be successfully type-checked using the widespread Hindley-Milner type system, the obvious versions of **map** and **fold** for such types cannot.

If we allowed them, non-uniform types would also cause problems for us later on when we define lattices of contexts over each type. For these reasons we rule out non-uniform types. This may be done with a syntactic check.

It is worth mentioning that the restriction does not exclude definitions such as

```
type Goo a = Gsimple + Gcompl (List (Goo a))
```

in which `Goo a` is the instantiation parameter for `List`.

4 Abstract Semantics

In this section we define an abstract semantics for our language to perform backward strictness analysis. It takes the form of a projection transformer.

Wadler and Hughes introduced two operations for combining projections: $\sqcup$ and &. The first is usual least upper bound (i.e. pointwise). The second is defined as follows.

$$\begin{array}{rcll} (p\&q)\ x & = & \bot & \textbf{if } p\ x = \bot \textbf{ or } q\ x = \bot \\ & = & (p \sqcup q)\ x & \textbf{otherwise} \end{array}$$

This operation is used in the analysis to capture conjunction of demand. In our presentation, we extend these operations to denote corresponding pointwise operations on abstract environments. In such an environment

$$env \in AbsEnv = Var \rightarrow Proj$$

names are associated with projections over lifted types. We use $[\,]$ to denote the initial environment in which every identifier is mapped to *Bot*. By $[(\mathbf{x}, p)]$ we mean the initial environment extended by binding the variable $\mathbf{x}$ to the projection p, and by $\rho \setminus \{\mathbf{x}_1, \ldots, \mathbf{x}_k\}$ we denote the environment differing from ρ in that the variables $\{\mathbf{x}_1, \ldots, \mathbf{x}_k\}$ are mapped to *Bot*.

A forwards projection analysis such as appears in Launchbury's thesis [7] is defined by abstract functions which mimic the concrete semantic functions.

$$\mathcal{PR}^{\#} : FunDefs \rightarrow ForwardAbsFunEnv$$
$$\mathcal{E}^{\#} : ForwardAbsFunEnv \rightarrow Expr \rightarrow (AbsValEnv \rightarrow AbsValue)$$

In the case of backwards strictness analysis the direction of the final arrow is reversed.

$$\mathcal{PR}^{\#} : \mathit{FunDefs} \rightarrow \mathit{AbsFunEnv}$$
$$\mathcal{E}^{\#} : \mathit{AbsFunEnv} \rightarrow \mathit{Expr} \rightarrow (\mathit{AbsValue} \rightarrow \mathit{AbsValEnv})$$

where,

$$\begin{array}{lcl} p \in \mathit{AbsValue} & = & \text{some domain of projections} \\ \rho^{\#} \in \mathit{AbsValEnv} & = & \mathit{Var} \rightarrow \mathit{AbsValue} \\ \phi^{\#} \in \mathit{AbsFunEnv} & = & \mathit{Fname} \rightarrow (\mathit{AbsValue} \rightarrow \mathit{AbsValEnv}) \end{array}$$

The *projection transformer* $\mathcal{E}^{\#}$, takes an expression $\mathbf{e}$ and a projection p (which expresses the demand on the value of $\mathbf{e}$), and builds an environment $\rho = \mathcal{E}^{\#}_{\phi^{\#}}[\![\mathbf{e}]\!]p$ in which all free variables $\mathbf{x}_i$ of $\mathbf{e}$ are assigned projections. The environment ρ is constructed so that the following *safety* condition is satisfied for all projections p of appropriate type:

$$\begin{array}{l} p \;\circ\; \underline{\lambda}(\nu_1 \otimes \cdots \otimes \nu_k).\mathit{lift}\ \mathcal{E}_{\phi}[\![\mathbf{e}]\!]_{[\mathbf{x}_i \mapsto \nu_i]} \\ \qquad \sqsubseteq \underline{\lambda}(\nu_1 \otimes \cdots \otimes \nu_k).\mathit{lift}\ \mathcal{E}_{\phi}[\![\mathbf{e}]\!]_{[\mathbf{x}_i \mapsto \nu_i]} \;\circ\; (\rho(\mathbf{x}_1) \otimes \cdots \otimes \rho(\mathbf{x}_k)) \end{array}$$

The environment $\rho(\mathbf{x}_i)$ is the demand on parameter $\mathbf{x}_i$ given a demand p on the value of $\mathbf{e}$, so this condition is just a multi-argument generalisation of the condition given in Section 2. The best possible environment is one in which variables are associated with the least projections for which the safety condition is still guaranteed.

To capture strictness properties we will re-express the projection *Str* using a strict form of the lifting operation, written $(-)_{\oplus}$. On domains, $t_{\perp} = t_{\oplus}$, but on functions,

$$\begin{array}{lcll} f_{\oplus}\ \perp & = & \perp & \\ f_{\oplus}\ (\mathit{lift}\ x) & = & \perp & \textbf{if } f\ x = \perp \\ & = & \mathit{lift}\ (f\ x) & \textbf{otherwise} \end{array}$$

Strict lifting is functorial except that it doesn't preserve the identity. In fact, $\mathit{Ide}_{\oplus} = \mathit{Str}$. Writing $f_{\oplus}$ provides a more convenient and compact notation for $(\mathit{Str} \circ f_{\perp})$, as occurs in earlier papers.

Our first use of strict lifting is in the definition of the projection transformer $\mathcal{E}^{\#}$. The first equation realises the guard operation from [8].

$$\mathcal{E}^{\#}_{\phi^{\#}}[\![\mathbf{e}]\!](p_{\perp}) \;=\; \mathcal{E}^{\#}_{\phi^{\#}}[\![\mathbf{e}]\!](p_{\oplus}) \;\sqcup\; \lambda x.\mathit{Abs}$$

Recall that all demands are projections over lifted domains. Such projections may always be expressed in the form either $p_{\perp}$ or $p_{\oplus}$. The intuition behind a demand of the form $p_{\perp}$ is, "this value may or may not be required, but if it is then p's worth will be needed." Conversely, a demand of the form $p_{\oplus}$ means, "this value *will* be required, and what's more, p's worth of it will be needed." With this intuition, the equation above may be read as follows, "to compute the demand propagated from a lazy demand, first compute it as if the demand was strict, and then make all the resulting demands lazy." Note that *Abs* is the weakest lazy demand, as $\mathit{Abs} = \mathit{Bot}_{\perp}$.

The rest of the equations apply to projections expressible as $p_{\oplus}$

$$\mathcal{E}^{\#}_{\phi\#}[\![\mathtt{x}]\!]p \;=\; [(\mathtt{x}, p)]$$

$$\begin{aligned}&\mathcal{E}^{\#}_{\phi\#}[\![\mathtt{f}\ \mathtt{e}_1 \ldots \mathtt{e}_k]\!]p_{\oplus}\\ &\quad= \mathcal{E}^{\#}_{\phi\#}[\![\mathtt{e}_1]\!]p_1 \;\&\cdots\&\; \mathcal{E}^{\#}_{\phi\#}[\![\mathtt{e}_k]\!]p_k\\ &\quad\quad \textbf{where } (p_1 \otimes \cdots \otimes p_k) = (\phi^{\#}\ f)\ p\end{aligned}$$

$$\begin{aligned}&\mathcal{E}^{\#}_{\phi\#}[\![\mathtt{c}\ \mathtt{e}_1 \ldots \mathtt{e}_k]\!](\cdots \oplus (p_1 \otimes \cdots \otimes p_k) \oplus \cdots)_{\oplus}\\ &\quad= \mathcal{E}^{\#}_{\phi\#}[\![\mathtt{e}_1]\!]p_1 \;\&\cdots\&\; \mathcal{E}^{\#}_{\phi\#}[\![\mathtt{e}_k]\!]p_k\end{aligned}$$

$$\begin{aligned}&\mathcal{E}^{\#}_{\phi\#}[\![\mathtt{case}\ \mathtt{e}\ \mathtt{in}\ \cdots \mathtt{c}_i\ \mathtt{x}_1 \ldots\ \mathtt{x}_k\texttt{->}\mathtt{e}_i \cdots\ \mathtt{end}]\!]p_{\oplus}\\ &\quad= \textstyle\bigsqcup_i \left(\mathcal{E}^{\#}_{\phi\#}[\![\mathtt{e}]\!](\delta_i)_{\oplus} \;\&\; \rho_i \setminus \{\mathtt{x}_1, \ldots, \mathtt{x}_k\}\right)\\ &\quad\quad \textbf{where}\\ &\quad\quad\ \ \rho_i = \mathcal{E}^{\#}_{\phi\#}[\![\mathtt{e}_i]\!]p_{\oplus}\\ &\quad\quad\ \ \delta_i = \mathit{Bot} \oplus \cdots \oplus (\rho_i\ \mathtt{x}_1 \otimes \cdots \otimes \rho_i\ \mathtt{x}_k) \oplus \cdots \oplus \mathit{Bot}\end{aligned}$$

In these rules we assume that the structure of the contexts corresponding to their underlying types. For example, in the rule for constructor applications the projection is a sum of products of projections; the particular summand given is assumed to be the one associated with the constructor c. Similarly, the *Bots* appearing in the rule for case expressions should be understood as the bottom projections over the target types of the remaining constructors, different from c.

It is worth noticing that our transformer is slightly more efficient than the one given originally [8]. Like Davis and Wadler [2], we collect the result of the analysis in an environment of projections, so allowing the contexts for all the arguments to be found by a single pass through the function's body.

Because of the first equation for $\mathcal{E}^{\#}$ we only need to construct the function environment for strict demands. Again it is constructed as the least fixed point of the function definitions.

$$\begin{aligned}&\mathcal{PR}^{\#}[\![\cdots,\ \mathtt{f}\ \mathtt{x}_1\ ..\ \mathtt{x}_k\ \texttt{=}\ \mathtt{e},\ \cdots]\!]\\ &\quad= \mathit{fix}\ (\lambda\phi^{\#}.\{\cdots, f \mapsto \lambda p\ .\ \mathcal{E}^{\#}_{\phi\#}[\![\mathtt{e}]\!]\ (p_{\oplus}), \cdots\})\end{aligned}$$

5 Manipulating Projections

Projections are functions, yet our analyser needs to perform a variety of operations on them, including comparing for equality. To achieve this we work with a concrete representation of the projections, syntactically modelling the semantic constructions and operations. This is reflected in the following development where we use the semantic notation to represent a syntactic construction.

5.1 Contexts for strictness analysis

Following the approach of Launchbury [6] and Hughes and Launchbury [3] we define for each type a finite collection of projections called *contexts*. The following rules define the family of all contexts by induction on the structure of the denotations of types.

$$\mathbf{1}\ \mathbf{cxt}\ \mathbf{1} \qquad \alpha\ \mathbf{cxt}\ \alpha$$

$$\frac{p\ \mathbf{cxt}\ T}{p_\perp\ \mathbf{cxt}\ T_\perp} \qquad \frac{p\ \mathbf{cxt}\ T}{p_{\oplus}\ \mathbf{cxt}\ T_\perp}$$

$$\frac{p_1\ \mathbf{cxt}\ T_1\ \ldots\ p_n\ \mathbf{cxt}\ T_n}{p_1 \oplus \ldots \oplus p_n\ \mathbf{cxt}\ T_1 \oplus \ldots \oplus T_n}$$

$$\frac{p_1\ \mathbf{cxt}\ T_1\ \ldots\ p_n\ \mathbf{cxt}\ T_n}{p_1 \otimes \ldots \otimes p_n\ \mathbf{cxt}\ T_1 \otimes \ldots \otimes T_n}$$

$$\frac{P(p)\ \mathbf{cxt}\ T(t) \qquad [p\ \mathbf{cxt}\ t]}{\mu p.P(p)\ \mathbf{cxt}\ \mu t.T(t)}$$

$$\frac{p\ \mathbf{cxt}\ F \quad q_1\ \mathbf{cxt}\ T_1\ \ldots\ q_n\ \mathbf{cxt}\ T_n}{p\ q_1 \ldots q_n\ \ \mathbf{cxt}\ \ F\ T_1 \ldots T_n}$$

As an example of contexts we present the familiar head-strict and tail-strict projections [8] over the the list type $\mu L\ .\ \mathbf{1}_\perp\ \oplus\ \alpha_\perp \otimes L_\perp$.

$$H = \mu l\ .\ \mathbf{1}_\perp\ \oplus\ \alpha_{\oplus} \otimes l_\perp$$
$$T = \mu l\ .\ \mathbf{1}_\perp\ \oplus\ \alpha_\perp \otimes l_{\oplus}$$

Strictly speaking, the polymorphic projections are represented by (H *Ide*) and (T *Ide*), but we will often be sloppy and understand that uninstantiated parameters α, β etc. are actually instantiated to *Ide*.

5.2 Modelling Operations

The analysis is defined in terms of operations on projections. In order to implement the analysis we need to model these semantic operations on contexts. To help us do this, we need to explore some of the properties of the operations.

First, the least upper bound operation $\sqcup$. If p, q are projections then $p \sqcup q$ defined point-wise is also a projection. Furthermore, the following equalities hold.

$$
\begin{array}{lcl}
p \sqcup p & = & p \\
p \sqcup q & = & q \sqcup p \\
(p \sqcup q) \sqcup r & = & p \sqcup (q \sqcup r) \\
p \sqcup Bot & = & p \\
p \sqcup Ide & = & Ide \\
p_\perp & = & Abs \sqcup p_{\oplus} \\
(p \oplus q) \sqcup (r \oplus s) & = & (p \sqcup r) \oplus (q \sqcup s) \\
(p \otimes q) \sqcup (r \otimes s) & = & (p \sqcup r) \otimes (q \sqcup s) \\
p_\perp \sqcup q_\perp & = & (p \sqcup q)_\perp \\
(p_{\oplus}) \sqcup q_\perp & = & (p \sqcup q)_\perp \\
(p_{\oplus}) \sqcup (q_{\oplus}) & = & (p \sqcup q)_{\oplus} \\
\mu p.P(p) \sqcup \mu q.Q(q) & = & \mu p.(P \sqcup Q)(p)
\end{array}
$$

All these but the last can be easily checked from appropriate definitions. The last rule requires induction over the context structure of P and Q. The equalities in the distributivity rules guarantee that if p and q are contexts, then $p \sqcup q$ is a context too.

Unfortunately, although contexts are closed under $\sqcup$ they are not closed under &, and so we may need to introduce extra approximation. The following properties of & may be derived straight from its definition.

$$\begin{array}{lcl}
p \,\&\, p & = & p \\
p \,\&\, q & = & q \,\&\, p \\
(p \,\&\, q) \,\&\, r & = & p \,\&\, (q \,\&\, r) \\
(p \sqcup q) \,\&\, r & = & (p \,\&\, r) \sqcup (q \,\&\, r) \\
p \,\&\, Bot & = & Bot \\
p_{\perp} \,\&\, Abs & = & p_{\perp} \\
Str \,\&\, Ide & = & Str \\
p_{\oplus} \,\&\, q_{\oplus} & = & (p \,\&\, q)_{\oplus} \\
p_{\oplus} \,\&\, q_{\perp} & = & (p \,\sqcup\, (p \,\&\, q))_{\oplus} \\
p_{\perp} \,\&\, q_{\perp} & = & (p \sqcup q)_{\perp} \\
(p \oplus q) \,\&\, (r \oplus s) & = & (p \,\&\, r) \oplus (q \,\&\, s) \\
(p \otimes q) \,\&\, (r \otimes s) & = & (p \,\&\, r) \otimes (q \,\&\, s)
\end{array}$$

While the & operation distributes nicely over products and sums it is not the case with the fixed-points. This means $\mu p.P(p) \& \mu q.Q(q)$ is not necessarily equal to $\mu p.(P \& Q)(p)$. The familiar projections H and T over lists provide us with an example of this, that is, $H \& T \neq \mu l \,.\, \mathbf{1}_{\perp} \,\oplus\, Ide_{\oplus} \otimes l_{\oplus}$.

To see this, consider applying each to the list $u = 1 : \perp : [\,]$. We see that $T\;\; u = 1 : \perp : [\,]$ and $H\;\; u = 1 : \perp$. As neither returns $\perp$,

$$(H \& T)\;\; u = (H\;\; u) \sqcup (T\;\; u) = 1 : \perp : [\,]$$

However, $(\mu l \,.\, \mathbf{1}_{\perp} \,\oplus\, Ide_{\oplus} \otimes l_{\oplus})\;\; u = \perp$ and so it is not equal to $H \& T$.

This apparently peculiar behaviour of H and T comes from the fact that T is strict over its recursive calls while H is not. The actual projection $H \& T$ treats the head of its argument differently from the tail, and so is not a context. Because we want to disallow such projections in order to retain finite domains, we need a way to find the least context approximating $H \& T$ from above. We may start from unfolding H and T in $H \& T$.

$$\begin{array}{lcl}
H \& T & = & (\mathbf{1}_{\perp} \,\oplus\, Ide_{\oplus} \otimes H_{\perp}) \,\&\, (\mathbf{1}_{\perp} \,\oplus\, Ide_{\perp} \otimes T_{\oplus}) \\
 & = & \mathbf{1}_{\perp} \,\oplus\, Ide_{\oplus} \otimes (T \,\sqcup\, H \& T)_{\oplus}
\end{array}$$

This shows that the desired approximation to $H \& T$ cannot be less than $T \,\sqcup\, H \& T$. We may continue with unfolding the latter

$$\begin{array}{l}
T \sqcup H \& T \\
\quad = \;\; (\mathbf{1}_{\perp} \oplus Ide_{\perp} \otimes (T_{\oplus})) \,\sqcup (\mathbf{1}_{\perp} \oplus Ide_{\oplus} \otimes (T \sqcup H \& T)_{\oplus}) \\
\quad = \;\; \mathbf{1}_{\perp} \oplus Ide_{\perp} \otimes (T \sqcup H \& T)_{\oplus}
\end{array}$$

We obtain a recursive equation with respect to $T \sqcup H \& T$ to which the minimal solution is the context $\mu l \,.\, \mathbf{1}_{\perp} \,\oplus\, Ide_{\oplus} \otimes l_{\oplus}$. This is actually T which is therefore the least context above $H \& T$.

Let us find out what can be the best approximation to $\mu p.P(p)\&\mu q.Q(q)$ in general. To ease the notation we will write $\mu p.P(p)$ as μP, and likewise for $\mu q.Q(q)$.

A closer look at the properties of &, especially those dealing with lifted projections, allow us to conclude that whenever μP & μQ is unfolded we will obtain one of the following combinations: μP & μQ, $\mu P \sqcup \mu P\&\mu Q$, $\mu Q \sqcup \mu P\&\mu Q$ or $\mu P \sqcup \mu Q$. Which of these appear depends on which of the recursive calls inside μP and μQ are lifted with strict-lifting, and which with usual lazy lifting. There are four possible cases for the conjunction of the unfolded context:

- it depends only on μP & μQ; in this case $\mu P \& \mu Q = \mu(P\&Q)$, the latter being a context (by induction), and we do not need to approximate;
- the conjunction contains $\mu P \sqcup \mu Q$; this is equal to the context $\mu(P \sqcup Q)$ and we cannot do better than taking this as the approximation;
- both $\mu P \sqcup \mu P\&\mu Q$ and $\mu Q \sqcup \mu P\&\mu Q$ appear in the result; a further unfolding of any of these will show the dependence on $\mu P \sqcup \mu Q$ and we again must take $\mu(P \sqcup Q)$ as the approximation; and
- only one of $\mu P \sqcup \mu P\&\mu Q$ or $\mu Q \sqcup \mu P\&\mu Q$ occurs (possibly together with μP & μQ); a further unfolding will show that $\mu P \sqcup \mu P\&\mu Q$ or, respectively, $\mu Q \sqcup \mu P\&\mu Q$ is the best approximation.

The last case corresponds to our previous example $H\&T$ for which T is the best approximation.

Our implementation does not unfold μP & μQ when it evaluates its value. Instead, all the pairs of corresponding recursive calls inside μP and μQ are analysed. For each pair of calls only the information whether the call is lifted strictly or lazily is recorded. Assuming an ordering on pairs as in the picture

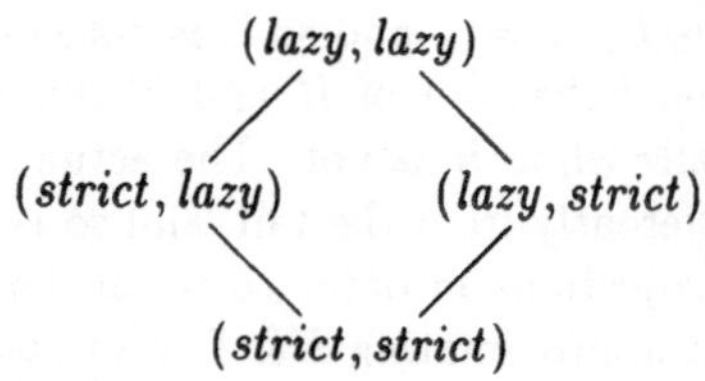

the implementation evaluates the least upper bound of all pairs and on this basis one of the four discussed cases applies. This approach requires a single traversal through the structure of μP and μQ in order to find the best approximation to $\mu P\&\mu Q$.

6 Implementation

6.1 Finding Fixed Points

A program containing recursive function definitions gives rise to recursive abstract equations, which have to be solved at compile time. Of the variety of methods for finding such solutions (fixed points) we use minimal function graphs [5]. Our implementation follows that of Launchbury [7].

The minimal function graph contains abstract function results (tuples of contexts representing the demand for the arguments to the function) for selected abstract arguments (contexts representing the demand for the function's result) for the functions in the program. The process of evaluating the fixed-point starts by constructing a graph containing the arguments we are interested in, along with an initial approximation for the function's result. The following iterative process is applied in order to improve these approximations.

At each iteration all argument-value pairs recorded in the current function graph are reevaluated according to the projection transformer. This is done by applying the transformer to the function body and the argument. When a function application is encountered within the body, two cases are possible depending on whether we can find the function value for an argument in the current graph. If we can, the value of the application is taken from the graph. If we cannot, we compute the best approximation derivable from the current graph, and add the new point to the graph.

At each iterative step we construct a fresh graph containing improved approximations to the values previously recorded, together with argument-value pairs for newly met arguments. With this new graph the iterative process continues until successive graphs are equal, that is until the fixed-point solution for the whole program is reached. As an optimisation to this process, we split the graph into mutually dependent units, and only iterate those parts that might have changed.

Minimal function graphs appear to be crucial for obtaining strictness analysis results in a practically acceptable time, given that the number of possible contexts over arbitrary data types can be quite large. The gain comes from the fact that we rarely require the whole fixed-point, but only its value for a few specified arguments.

6.2 Concrete Representation of Projections

The following is the LML [1] definition of the type that represents projections in the implementation

```
type proj = PStr proj
          + PLift proj
          + PBot
          + PProd (List proj)
          + PMu name (List proj)
          + PRec name
          + PSum (List proj)
```

The term `PLift p` corresponds to $p_\perp$ and `PStr p` represents $Str \circ p_\perp$. Data of the form `PProd [`$p_1, \ldots, p_k$`]`, `PSum [`$p_1, \ldots, p_k$`]` stand for strict products $p_1 \otimes \ldots \otimes p_k$ and sums $p_1 \oplus \ldots \oplus p_k$, respectively.

The structures `PBot` and `PProd []` represent the monomorphic bottom and identity projections over the two-point domain $\mathbf{1}_\perp$, as well as the polymorphic projections *Bot* and *Ide*, respectively. This overloading does not confuse us in practice because when needed we can deduce from a surrounding context what is the underlying domain for a projection.

A data of the form `PMu f [p1,...,pk]` represents a context over a recursive type. As we admit mutual recursion on types the representation allows for mutually recursive contexts `p1,...,pk` over domains mutually recursive with `f`. Of course, among these contexts there should be a context over `f`. The `PRec g` form can only be met inside a recursive projection and the name g selects one of the surrounding mutually recursive projections.

On the `proj` type a library of basic operations is defined such as generating the bottom or the identity contexts for a given type, calculation of the $\sqcup$ and &, factorisation of an instance of a polymorphic projection into its polymorphic and instance parts. The abstract function graphs stores the argument-value pairs for abstract functions also as data of the type `proj`.

6.3 Sample Results

Below we present results obtained by the strictness analyser. In the projections which follow, we write the constructor names in explicitly to aid understanding.

6.3.1 Lists

We begin with some standard list-based examples.

```
type List alpha = Nil + Cons alpha (List alpha);

append ::  List alpha -> List alpha -> List alpha;
append  xs zs   = case xs in
                      Nil -> zs
                  || Cons y ys  -> Cons y (append ys zs)
                  end;

reverse :: List alpha -> List alpha;
reverse rs = case rs in
                 Nil -> Nil
             || Cons y ys -> append (reverse ys) (Cons y Nil)
             end;
```

First *append*. Consider the demand $(\mu l\ .\ Nil : \mathbf{1}_\perp \ \oplus\ Cons : \alpha_{\oplus} \otimes l_\perp)_{\oplus}$ for *append*'s result. This is a strict demand (hence the final strict lifting) which is recursively strict in each list element (hence the strict lifting on the α), but lazy in the list tails (the non-strict lifting of l). This is what we previously wrote as $H_{\oplus}$. From this result context, the demand on *append*'s arguments is computed as,

$$(\mu l\ .\ Nil : \mathbf{1}_\perp \ \oplus\ Cons : \alpha_{\oplus} \otimes l_\perp)_{\oplus} \ \otimes\ (\mu l\ .\ Nil : \mathbf{1}_\perp \ \oplus\ Cons : \alpha_{\oplus} \otimes l_\perp)_\perp$$

In summary, a strict, head-strict demand $H_{\oplus}$ for *append*'s result is translated to a strict and head-strict demand for the first argument, and a lazy, head-strict demand for the second, i.e. $H_{\oplus} \otimes H_\perp$.

Alternatively, given a demand $(\mu l \,.\, Nil : \mathbf{1}_\bot \;\oplus\; Cons : \alpha_\bot \otimes l_{\obar})_{\obar}$ (that is, strict and tail-strict, $T_{\obar}$) for the result of *append*, the analyser deduced a demand of

$$(\mu l \,.\, Nil : \mathbf{1}_\bot \;\oplus\; Cons : \alpha_\bot \otimes l_{\obar})_{\obar} \otimes (\mu l \,.\, Nil : \mathbf{1}_\bot \;\oplus\; Cons : \alpha_\bot \otimes l_{\obar})_{\obar}$$

for its arguments, i.e. both arguments strict and tail strict, $T_{\obar} \otimes T_{\obar}$.

The analyser obtained the following facts about *reverse*. If its result is demanded in a strict and head-strict context

$$(\mu l \,.\, Nil : \mathbf{1}_\bot \;\oplus\; Cons : \alpha_{\obar} \otimes l_\bot)_{\obar}$$

then its argument is in a strict and tail-strict context

$$(\mu l \,.\, Nil : \mathbf{1}_\bot \;\oplus\; Cons : \alpha_\bot \otimes l_{\obar})_{\obar}$$

Likewise, if the result is demanded strictly and tail-strictly, then so is its argument. Combining these facts, we see that *reverse* is strict and tail strict, in both $H_{\obar}$ and $T_{\obar}$ contexts.

6.3.2 Trees

For the next examples we introduce a polymorphic tree type. As with lists, the contexts over trees are generated automatically, having a structure which corresponds to the structure of the type definition.

```
type Tree alpha = Leaf alpha + Node (Tree alpha) (Tree alpha);

flat :: Tree alpha -> List alpha;
flat t = case t in
             Leaf x   -> Cons x Nil
          || Node l r -> append (flat l) (flat r)
          end;
```

Whereas particular contexts over lists like H and T have standard names, allowing the results of the analysis to be written compactly, contexts over trees do not. However, as with the list contexts, it is very easy to read the strictness from the contexts.

The function *flat* collapses a tree down to a list. If that result list is demanded by a strict, and head-strict context, $H_{\obar}$, that is,

$$(\mu l \,.\, Nil : \mathbf{1}_\bot \;\oplus\; Cons : \alpha_{\obar} \otimes l_\bot)_{\obar}$$

then the analyser deduces a demand on the tree argument of,

$$(\mu t \,.\, Leaf : \alpha_{\obar} \;\oplus\; Node : t_{\obar} \otimes t_\bot)_{\obar}$$

That is, a strict, *Leaf*-strict, left-strict context. When a tree is built in such a context its left spine may be constructed strictly, all the way down to the leaf. The rest of the tree is left unevaluated. If any other part of the tree is required, again its left spine is evaluated all the way to the leaf, and so on.

Alternatively, if the result of *flat* is demanded in a strict, and tail-strict context, $T_{\oplus}$, that is,

$$(\mu l\ .\ Nil : \mathbf{1}_{\perp}\ \oplus\ Cons : \alpha_{\perp} \otimes l_{\oplus})_{\oplus}$$

then the demand on *flat*'s argument is,

$$(\mu t\ .\ Leaf : \alpha_{\perp}\ \oplus\ Node : t_{\oplus} \otimes t_{\oplus})_{\oplus}$$

which is a strict and left-and-right-strict context. The structure of the tree will be evaluated, but none of the leaves.

6.3.3 Instances of Polymorphic Functions

All the examples so far have been of polymorphic functions on their own. The final series of examples are of instances of polymorphic functions. We define a type of Peano numerals together with addition, and use these to define a function which sums the leaves of a tree.

```
type Nat = Zero + Succ Nat;

add :: Nat -> Nat -> Nat;
add a b = case a in Zero -> b || Succ c -> Succ (add c b) end;

sum :: Tree Nat -> Nat;
sum t = case t in
           Leaf t    -> t
        || Node l r -> add (sum l) (sum r)
        end;
```

Because the numerals are non-atomic, *add* has some interesting strictness. A result context of

$$(\mu n\ .\ Zero : \mathbf{1}_{\perp}\ \oplus\ Succ : n_{\oplus})_{\oplus}$$

produces an argument context of

$$(\mu n\ .\ Zero : \mathbf{1}_{\perp}\ \oplus\ Succ : n_{\oplus})_{\oplus}\ \oslash\ (\mu n\ .\ Zero : \mathbf{1}_{\perp}\ \oplus\ Succ : n_{\oplus})_{\oplus}$$

Conversely, a result context of

$$(\mu n\ .\ Zero : \mathbf{1}_{\perp}\ \oplus\ Succ : n_{\perp})_{\oplus}$$

generates the argument context

$$(\mu n\ .\ Zero : \mathbf{1}_{\perp}\ \oplus\ Succ : n_{\perp})_{\oplus}\ \oslash\ (\mu n\ .\ Zero : \mathbf{1}_{\perp}\ \oplus\ Succ : n_{\perp})_{\perp}$$

In other words, if the complete result of *add* is demanded then both is arguments are demanded completely. Conversely, if the result of *add* is only demanded strictly, then its first argument is demanded strictly, but it's second lazily.

Now let us examine *sum*. If *sum*'s result is demanded hyper-strictly then the analyser deduces that its argument is also demanded hyper-strictly. That is, a result context,

$$(\mu n\ .\ Zero : \mathbf{1}_{\perp}\ \oplus\ Succ : n_{\text{Ⓓ}})_{\text{Ⓓ}}$$

is converted to the argument context,

$$((\mu t\ .\ Leaf : \alpha_{\text{Ⓓ}}\ \oplus\ Node : t_{\text{Ⓓ}} \otimes t_{\text{Ⓓ}})\ (\mu n\ .\ Zero : \mathbf{1}_{\perp}\ \oplus\ Succ : n_{\text{Ⓓ}}))_{\text{Ⓓ}}$$

Notice the explicit application of one context to another. As we mentioned earlier, all the polymorphic contexts like *H* and *T* should actually have been applied to *Ide*, but this would have cluttered up the examples unnecessarily.

As a final example, suppose the demand for *sum*'s result is merely strict. Then the demand for *sum*'s tree argument is strict, leaf-strict and left-strict. That is, the analyser converts the result context

$$(\mu n\ .\ Zero : \mathbf{1}_{\perp}\ \oplus\ Succ : n_{\perp})_{\text{Ⓓ}}$$

to the argument context

$$((\mu t\ .\ Leaf : \alpha_{\text{Ⓓ}}\ \oplus\ Node : t_{\text{Ⓓ}} \otimes t_{\perp})\ (\mu n\ .\ Zero : \mathbf{1}_{\perp}\ \oplus\ Succ : n_{\perp}))_{\text{Ⓓ}}$$

7 Extending the Prototype to Haskell

As mentioned previously, our language is pretty close to the Haskell Core language as used in the Glasgow compiler as an intermediate language after desugaring and type-checking the input program. However, the Core language is richer the one here as it covers various phenomena present in Haskell programs.

First of all, Haskell is higher-order. As our method works only for first order languages we are unable to do more than discover simple strictness when we encounter a higher-order function. That is, we produce poor but safe results for higher-order functions. A similar solution applies to non-uniformly recursive types. The only contexts we use over such types are $Ide_{\text{Ⓓ}}$, $Bot_{\text{Ⓓ}}$, $Bot_{\perp}$, $Ide_{\perp}$.

Another difference between the Core language and ours is that the former admits local definitions in the form of `let` and `letrec` expressions. This means that in the minimal function graphs we should not only keep the values for the functions defined at the entire level but also the values of functions defined by `let` and `letrec`s.

Similarly, Haskell allows partial function applications. This, and the presence of `let`s, `letrec`s and lambda expressions forces us to change the resulting type of the projection transformer. The transformer has to distinguish between the free and bound variables. So, when applied to an expression and a context the transformer returns a pair consisting of a tuple of safe contexts for the bound variables and a projection environment for the free variables. Such pairs will also be recorded in the minimal function graph. Only for the globally defined functions can we be sure the free-variables part of the result is empty.

The most serious problem comes from modules. If the strictness analyser is to return results, strictness properties have to be passed from one module to another. Currently, it is far from clear how to do this.

The only problem that type classes (the major innovation of Haskell) introduce is that many previously first order functions become higher-order when the dictionary is passed as an extra parameter. Again, this is a topic for further work.

8 Acknowledgements

Our thanks to Simon Peyton Jones whose many comments were very useful in improving the paper. This work was funded by ESPRIT basic research action 3124 *Semantique*.

Bibliography

[1] L. Augustsson. *A Compiler for Lazy ML.* Proceedings of Lisp and Functional Programming Conference, Austin, Texas, 1984.

[2] K. Davis and P. Wadler, *Strictness Analysis in 4D*, Third Annual Glasgow Workshop on Functional Programming, Ullapool, *Workshops in Computing*, S-V, 1990.

[3] R.J.M. Hughes and J. Launchbury, *Projections for Polymorphic Strictness Analysis*, To appear in *Mathematical Structures in Computer Science*, C.U.P.

[4] R.J.M. Hughes, *Projections for Polymorphic Strictness Analysis*, In *Category Theory in Computer Science*, Manchester, 1989.

[5] N.D. Jones and A. Mycroft, *Data Flow Analysis of Applicative Programs Using Minimal Function Graphs*, Proc. of the Thirteenth ACM Symposium on Principles of Programmng Languages, St. Petersburg, Florida, pp. 296-306, 1986

[6] J. Launchbury, *Projections for Specialisation*, in Bjørner, Ershov and Jones (eds), *Partial Evaluation and Mixed Computation.* Proceedings IFIP TC2 Workshop, Denmark, Oct 1987. North-Holland, 1988.

[7] J. Launchbury, *Projection Factorisations in Partial Evaluation*, Ph.D. thesis, Glasgow University. *Distinguished Dissertations in Computer Science*, Vol 1, CUP, 1991.

[8] P. Wadler and R.J.M. Hughes, *Projections for Strictness Analysis*, In *Functional Programming and Computer Architecture*, Portland, USA, LNCS 274, 1987

Vuillemin's Exact Real Arithmetic

David R Lester
Department of Computer Science
Manchester University
Manchester M13 9PL

1 Introduction

If we are content with using only rational numbers, accurate computer arithmetic is easy to implement. Unfortunately, as was discovered early in the history of mathematics, there are numbers, such as $\sqrt{2}$, which are *irrational*. The discovery of computable functions by Turing [15] and Church [4] led to work on computable numbers [13, 2]. This work used a radix representation along with intervals. This is fine from the point of correctness, but as the implementation is *memoryless*, it could be quite inefficient[1].

This paper was written in an attempt to understand and interpret the work of Jean Vuillemin [16], in which he describes a representation of computable real numbers using continued fractions. In this paper we will hopefully see the benefits of using a lazy functional language to implement algorithms that are intrinsically lazy. We also explore some of the algorithms in more detail than [16], paying particular care to ensure that lazyness is preserved.

The advantage with using continued fractions as a representation of numbers is that if, for example, we calculate π to a high degree of accuracy at some stage, this accuracy is then available everywhere else that π is used without further calculation being necessary.

Because we will be using the terms frequently, and because the concepts may not be familiar, the introduction continues by informally introducing three key concepts used in this paper. They are *Real Numbers*, *Computable Real Numbers*, and *Continued Fractions*. Readers already familiar with this material should feel free to skip the remainder of the introduction.

In Section 2 computable continued fractions are discussed. We show how to produce rational approximations to continued fractions in Section 3. A gentle introduction to Gosper's algorithm is provided in Section 4; the main algorithm is given in Section 5. The continued fraction representation of the exponential and logarithm functions is given in Section 6. These representations make it necessary to be able to convert continued fractions of rationals and reals into the standard form of **E**-fractions.

---

[1] Boehm and Cartwright claim otherwise in [3].

1.1 What are Real Numbers?

The best way to think of the various stages in the development of number theory is that of a closure operation. If you start with the integer one, and the operation of + you can generate all of the positive natural numbers $\mathcal{N}^+$. Augmenting the set of operations with − it is possible to generate all of the integers, $\mathcal{Z}$. We may therefore make the statement: the closure of operations + and − with the number one is $\mathcal{Z}$, the integers. Multiplication adds no new numbers, but when we consider the division operation we must include fractions. These constitute the rational numbers, which we represent by the symbol $\mathcal{Q}$. We can restate this as: the closure of the operations of +, −, ×, and / on the number one is $\mathcal{Q} \cup \{\perp, \infty\}$. (We use $\perp$ to represent the number 0/0 and ∞ to represent $n/0$, whenever $n \neq 0$).

If we think in terms of a pencil and paper implementation for the moment, then provided that we have a sufficiently large piece of paper we can perform operations on rational numbers to any desired degree of accuracy. In the context of the implementation of rational number arithmetic, this can be paraphrased as: provided that the memory does not overflow we can perform operations on rational numbers to any desired degree of accuracy.

But of course – as the Greek Mathematicians discovered[2] – this is not the whole story. There exist numbers (such as $\sqrt{2}$) that cannot be represented by any finite fraction. Such numbers are said to be *irrational*. There are a many beautiful generalisations that arise from this, but for the moment we simply observe that numbers such as square roots arise from finding the roots of quadratic polynomials. The rational and irrational numbers that are generated as roots to polynomial equations are called *algebraic numbers*.

At this stage you may wonder where this process stops; *i.e.* how many operations must we use to generate all of the real numbers? The answer is that the process doesn't stop and no finite set of operations will generate all of the real numbers.[3] The solution is to restrict attention to a subset of $\mathcal{R}$ which I shall call $\mathcal{A}$; which has only a limited set of operations. The set $\mathcal{A}$ will constitute a useful set of computable real numbers for engineering applications.

$$
\begin{aligned}
1 &\in \mathcal{A}\\
\mathcal{A}+\mathcal{A} &\subset \mathcal{A}\\
-\mathcal{A} &\subset \mathcal{A}\\
\mathcal{A}/\mathcal{A}_{\neq 0} &\subset \mathcal{A}\\
e^{\mathcal{A}} &\subset \mathcal{A}\\
\log \mathcal{A}_{>0} &\subset \mathcal{A}
\end{aligned}
$$

Notice that by removing the restrictions on the argument for the logarithm function we would obtain a subset of the complex numbers, $\mathcal{C}$, which would include trigonometric functions. This should provide a sufficient range of basic arithmetic operations for most engineering applications. The next subsection high-lights the major problem involved in producing an arithmetic package for real numbers.

---

[2] The theory of irrationals in [5] is attributed to Theætus.

[3] This is a direct consequence of Cantor's Diagonalization Argument. It is normally stated as: The real numbers are not effectively ennumerable.

1.2 What are Computable Real Numbers?

Informally, a number is said to be computable if we can write a program which will print its value to some specified degree of accuracy. Following Pour-El and Richards [12], we may formalise this definition.

Definition 1.1 A real number x is *computable* if there exists a computable sequence $\{r_k\}$ of rationals which converges effectively to x.

Definition 1.2 A sequence $\{r_k\}$ of rational numbers is *computable* if there exist three recursive functions a, b, and s from $\mathcal{N}$ to $\mathcal{N}$ such that $b(k) \neq 0$ for all k and

$$r_k = (-1)^{s(k)} \frac{a(k)}{b(k)} \text{ for all } k.$$

Definition 1.3 A sequence $\{r_k\}$ of rational numbers *converges effectively* to a real number x if there exists a recursive function $e : \mathcal{N} \to \mathcal{N}$ such that for all N:

$$k \geq e(N) \text{ implies } |r_k - x| \leq 2^{-N}.$$

A cardinality argument suffices to show that non-computable numbers exist: the set of programs is countable, the set of real numbers is not. It seems reasonable that in dealing with numbers for computers, we should restrict our attention to just the subset of real numbers that is computable. In fact for the engineering applications that we have in mind this set may be further restricted to the closure of the arithmetic operations on the singleton set: $\{1\}$ – as outlined above.

Life is seldom simple. It is an unfortunate fact of life that it is not even possible to tell whether a computable real number is 0. Let us suppose that we are given a monotonically decreasing sequence of rationals that converges to 0. One such sequence is 1, 0.1, 0.01, 0.001, ...; proving the convergence establishes that this sequence represents the computable real number 0. Similarly we might wish to consider the monotonically increasing sequence: −1, −0.1, −0.01, −0.001, ...; again this is another representation of the real number 0. In general, for each integer n, we will refer to a monotonically increasing sequence of rationals as n^- and to a monotonically decreasing sequence as n^+; these numbers will be called Zeno Integers[4], and are useful in developing informal arguments about the computability of real number operations. Generalising this there are also Zeno Rationals – numbers such as 2.5^+ and 2.5^-.

There are more operations that not computable; some of these are listed in Theorem 1.4, which is a combination of results from Turing [15] and Rice [13]. Proofs of these results may be found in [16].

Theorem 1.4 (Turing, Rice) *There is no algorithm, which for an arbitrary computable real number $r \in \mathcal{R}$, can compute:*

1. *whether the number r is zero;*

[4] This seems ironic as it was Zeno of Elea's attack on the foundations of Greek Mathematics that led indirectly to the discovery of the irrationals, and hence has caused us to go to all this trouble in implementing arithmetic [14].

2. whether $r > r'$ for any fixed $r' \in \mathcal{R}$;

3. whether the number is rational;

4. the first digit of the decimal expansion of r;

5. the first term of the regular continued fraction expansion of r (which is $\lfloor r \rfloor$);

6. the value $f(r) \in \mathcal{R}$ of any function f which is not continuous at r.

This is all very disturbing. However, facing facts is infinitely preferable to facing defeat, so we must cast around for ways to avoid the Turing/Rice Theorems.

The first "fix" is reasonably obvious: we must give up any idea that exact comparisons are available. They are replaced by what I shall refer to as ε-comparisons. Two numbers r and r' are said to be $=_\varepsilon$ if $|r - r'| < \varepsilon$. Similar properties hold for the other comparison operations. This is not so very different to the properties of comparison operations available in floating point packages.

The second "fix" is implied by the fourth observation in Theorem 1.4, where we notice that we can't even find the first digit of a computable number. To see this consider the Zeno Integer $1^- = 0.\dot{9}$. The first digit of each rational approximation is 0, but of course the first digit of the number 1 is 1. The solution: use a redundant representation of the computable numbers. This is implicit in the decimal representation of numbers: as we have seen $0.\dot{9}$ and 1 are both representations of the same number.

We now move on to consider continued fractions.

1.3 What are Continued Fractions?

In this section we will see how to represent numbers by continued fractions. Continued fractions are an attractive representation of real numbers because: we are able to take advantage of what functional programmers would call *laziness*, and there exist algorithms to perform the arithmetic operations we require.

Definition 1.5 A finite continued fraction representation of the number r is a sequence of numbers $[x_0, x_1, \ldots x_n]$, satisfying:

$$r = x_0 + \cfrac{1}{x_1 + \cfrac{1}{\ddots + \frac{1}{x_n}}}$$

There is no reason why we should only consider finite continued fractions, so infinite fractions are also permitted.

For the time being, in this paper, we will make the numbers in the sequence $x_0 \ldots x_n$ be integers[5]. A finite continued fraction with integer terms can be used as a compact method to represent a rational number. It is possible to calculate the values of the integers $x_0, x_1, \ldots x_n$ from r in the following way. Let $r = r_0$; we compute

$$r_0 = x_0 + \frac{1}{r_1}, \; r_1 = x_1 + \frac{1}{r_2}, \; \ldots, \; r_n = x_n$$

[5] It is to be understood that these integers may be arbitrarily large.

where at each step we choose an integer x_n that is *close* to r_n. Let us give x_n the value $x_n = f(r_n)$. There are a number of choices for the function f. Obvious candidates are the rounding operations.

$$\begin{array}{llcll} \textbf{floor} & \lfloor r \rfloor & = & z \text{ such that} & 0 \le r - z < 1; \\ \textbf{round} & \lfloor r \rceil & = & z \text{ such that} & -\frac{1}{2} < r - z \le \frac{1}{2}; \\ \textbf{ceiling} & \lceil r \rceil & = & z \text{ such that} & -1 < r - z \le 0. \end{array}$$

The choice of **floor** leads to **N**-fractions, which are characterised by the following theorem.

Theorem 1.6 (Hurwitz) *Let* $r = [z_0, z_1, \ldots, z_n, \ldots]$ *be the* **N***-fraction expansion of some finite number. Then*

1. *All terms after the first are positive.*

2. *If the fraction is finite, then its last term is greater than* 1.

Another choice is that of **round**, leading to **Z**-fractions, which are characterised by the following theorem.

Theorem 1.7 (Hurwitz) *Let* $r = [z_0, z_1, \ldots, z_n, \ldots]$ *be the* **Z***-fraction expansion of some finite number. Then*

1. *All terms after the first have absolute value greater than or equal to* 2.

2. *Whenever* $|z_{n+1}| = 2$, *the subsequent term has the same sign.*

3. *If the fraction is finite, then its last term is different from* -2.

Proofs of Theorems 1.6 and 1.7 are given by Vuillemin [16]. Using these definitions it is possible to construct continued fractions for irrational numbers. We can do so, for both the **N**-fraction and **Z**-fraction forms. We begin with the **N**-fraction forms for $\sqrt{2}$, $\sqrt{3}$, $\phi = \frac{1+\sqrt{5}}{2}$, and e.

$$\begin{array}{lcl} \sqrt{2} & = & [1, 2, \ldots, 2, \ldots] \\ \sqrt{3} & = & [1, 1, 2, \ldots, 1, 2, \ldots] \\ \phi & = & [1, 1, \ldots] \\ e & = & [2, 1, 2, 1, \ldots, 1, 2n+2, 1, \ldots] \end{array}$$

As an alternative, we can give the **Z**-fractions for the same numbers.

$$\begin{array}{lcl} \sqrt{2} & = & [1, 2, \ldots, 2, \ldots] \\ \sqrt{3} & = & [2, -4, 4, \ldots, -4, 4, \ldots] \\ \phi & = & [2, -3, 3, \ldots, -3, 3, \ldots] \\ e & = & [3, -4, 2, 5, -2, -7, \ldots, 2, 4n+5, -2, -4n-7, \ldots] \end{array}$$

The interested reader can use the definitions given earlier, in conjunction with a series expansion for each irrational number, to prove that these continued fractions are correct. There are a number of useful properties that **N**-fractions and **Z**-fractions have, which are outlined in Lagrange's Theorem.

Theorem 1.8 (Lagrange) *Let $r = [z_0, z_1, \ldots, z_n, \ldots]$ be the* **N**-*fraction or* **Z**-*fraction expansion of some finite number. Then*

1. *The continued fraction has only one term if and only if $r \in \mathcal{Z}$ is integer.*

2. *The continued fraction is finite if and only if the number $r \in \mathcal{Q}$ is rational.*

3. *The continued fraction is eventually periodic if and only if $r \in \sqrt{\mathcal{Q}_{>0}}$ is the irrational square root of a positive rational.*

4. *The continued fraction approximants $r_n = [z_0, z_1, \ldots, z_n]$ converge to r with speed: $|r - r_n| < \phi^{-n}$, where $\phi = 1.618\ldots$ is the golden ratio.*

Again proofs are available in [16], to which interested readers are referred. At this stage you may feel that continued fractions are all very well, and an interesting representation of real numbers, but what use are they? In the next section we combine the material already covered, to consider computable continued fractions and operations upon them.

2 Computable Continued Fractions

Although continued fractions are a good representation because they can be used lazily, there remains a problem with selecting either **N**-fractions or **Z**-fractions as representations of real numbers: neither **floor** nor **round** are computable operations. This means that for some numbers it is not possible for a computer to construct the continued fraction, even though it exists. What is needed is a computable analogue to **floor** or **round**; the operation required is that of finding the Euclidean Part.

2.1 A Digression upon Euclidean Division

In order to find the Euclidean Part, $z = r \div 1$, of a real number, r, we define a measure, Δ, for the *distance* between two arbitrary real numbers. One simple measure would be to simply take $|x - y|$, but this causes problems when one of x or y is infinite. A better measure, in the sense that it is finite for all x and y is given in [16].

Definition 2.1 The measure, Δ, is defined:

$$\Delta(x, y) = \frac{2|x - y|}{\sqrt{(1 + x^2)(1 + y^2)}}$$

This defines a finite distance between any two numbers: in particular $0 \leq \Delta(x, y) \leq 2$. It therefore permits us to discuss convergence at ∞ in a natural fashion.

Definition 2.2 Let $r \in \mathcal{R}$ be an arbitrary computable real. The *Euclidean Part* $z = r \div 1$ of r is an integer $z \in \mathcal{Z}$, computed in finite time, such that $\Delta(r, z) < 1$.

The simple way to calculate $r \div 1$ is to take rational approximations, r_n, to r until the error in the approximation is small enough. In other words, if the value of r is known to lie in the closed interval $[i_n, s_n]$ (because of the value of r_n), then the error is small enough when $\Delta(i_n, s_n) < 1$. Later it will be necessary to consider how we implement the algorithm for various representations of real numbers. Before that, we consider the use to which we will put the operation of finding the Euclidean Part.

2.2 Euclidean Continued Fractions

It is now possible to specify how *Euclidean Continued Fractions* (henceforth **E**-fractions) may be constructed for an arbitrary computable real number, r. Let $r_0 = r$; then:

$$r_0 = z_0 + \frac{1}{r_1},\ r_1 = z_1 + \frac{1}{r_2},\ \ldots,\ r_n = z_n + \frac{1}{r_{n+1}},\ \ldots$$

where at each step $z_i = r_i \div 1$. In the same way that **N**-fractions and **Z**-fractions were characterised, **E**-fractions may be characterised.

Theorem 2.3 *Let $r = [z_0, z_1, \ldots, z_n, \ldots]$ be some* **E**-*continued fraction expansion of r. Then r is in the open interval:*

$$\left(\frac{-4z_0 + (z_0^2+1)\sqrt{3}}{z_0^2-3}, \frac{-4z_0 - (z_0^2+1)\sqrt{3}}{z_0^2-3}\right)$$

The open interval (x, y) is interpreted as the set of points $(-\infty, y) \cup (x, \infty)$ whenever $x > y$.

Proof of 2.3

Obtain bounds on the value of r by solving the quadratic polynomial $\Delta(r, z_0) = 1$. Remember: for z_0 to be eligible, it must satisfy $\Delta(r, z_0) < 1$.

□

Notice that this result contradicts that given by Vuillemin in [16, Theorem 6(ii)] for the case where $z_0 = 1$. Vuillemin gives the interval $(1/2, -1/2)$, we obtain $(2-\sqrt{3}, 2+\sqrt{3})$. This means that, for Vuillemin the value of $1 \div 1$ is any non-zero integer, whereas my algorithm permits $1 \div 1$ to have only the values 1, 2 and 3. The important point to note about **E**-fractions is that although we have weakened the conditions upon the terms in the continued fraction so that there is redundancy, the conditions are still strong enough to ensure effective convergence of the rational approximations.

In the next section we consider ways of obtaining rational approximations to continued fractions.

3 Printing and Comparing Continued Fractions

In this section we see how to print continued fractions as decimal numbers and how we can arrange the ε comparison operations. What is needed for both operations is a way of determining a sequence of rational approximations, with the aim of using the first one that is *sufficiently accurate.* In this context we will say that the rational approximant r_n is sufficiently accurate whenever $|r - r_n| < \varepsilon$. To do this efficiently we will be making use of some of the properties of Euler's Q-polynomials.

3.1 A Digression upon Euler's Q-polynomials

Given a convergent continued fraction $r = [z_0, z_1, \ldots, z_n, \ldots]$, we define the approximant r_n to be the continued fraction $[z_0, z_1, \ldots, z_n]$. Obviously the approximants $\{r_i\}$ are rationals whose limit is r. We need a way to compute these rationals. One obvious way is as follows.

$$r_n = z_0 + \cfrac{1}{z_1 + \cfrac{1}{\ddots + \frac{1}{z_n}}}$$

There are a number of difficulties with this approach. First the number of terms has to be given, when what is normally needed is a rational that is to within a certain accuracy of r. Secondly it is not incremental, by which I mean that knowing the values of r_i for $i < n$, does not make it any easier to compute r_n.

Euler's Q-polynomials provide a means to overcome the second problem, which in turn solves the first. Euler gives the following expansion for the continued fraction $r_n = [z_0, z_1, \ldots, z_n]$.

$$r_n = [z_0, z_1, \ldots, z_n] = z_0 + \frac{1}{q_0 q_1} + \frac{-1}{q_1 q_2} + \cdots + \frac{(-1)^{n-1}}{q_{n-1} q_n}$$

where

$$\begin{aligned} q_0 &= 1 \\ q_1 &= z_1 \\ q_{n+2} &= z_{n+2} q_{n+1} + q_n \end{aligned}$$

In other words there is a recurrence relation for the term q_{n+2} involving the previous values q_{n+1} and q_n. Every functional programmer will know what to do in this situation!

3.2 Error of Rational Approximants

The question we now address is: when have we calculated a rational approximant to the desired accuracy? We observe that $|r - r_n|$ is given by the error term:

$$\frac{1}{q_n([z_{n+1}, \ldots] q_n + q_{n-1})}.$$

From this, and Theorems 1.6, 1.7, and 2.3, we can obtain limits on this term, for each sort of continued fraction.

Theorem 3.1 *In the case of* **N**-*fractions the error term is less than:*

$$\frac{1}{q_n(q_n + q_{n-1})}.$$

This follows because each Q-polynomial term q_i is positive and $q_{i+1} > q_i$. Furthermore, the number $[z_{n+1}, \ldots]$, being a **N**-fraction is an element of $(1, \infty)$.

Theorem 3.2 *In the case of* **Z**-*fractions the error term is less than:*

$$\frac{1}{q_{n-1}^2}.$$

This follows because each Q-polynomial term satisfies $|q_{i+1}| > |q_i|$. Furthermore, the number $[z_{n+1}, \ldots]$, being a **Z**-fraction is an element of $[2, -2)$.

Theorem 3.3 *In the case of* **E**-*fractions the error term is less than:*

$$\frac{1}{|q_n(xq_n + q_{n-1})|}$$

with x in the range:

$$\left(\left|\frac{4z_{n+1} + (z_{n+1}^2 + 1)\sqrt{3}}{z_{n+1}^2 - 3}\right|, \left|\frac{4z_{n+1} - (z_{n+1}^2 + 1)\sqrt{3}}{z_{n+1}^2 - 3}\right|\right),$$

provided that the term $xq_n + q_{n-1}$ doesn't change sign in this range.

The theorem for **E**-fractions is more complicated, because we have no ***a priori*** bound for the continued fraction $[z_{n+1}, \ldots]$. The result follows because we ***can*** assign a bound once the first term, z_{n+1}, is known.

We now consider ways to implement arithmetic on continued fractions.

4 The Algebraic Algorithm

Having seen various sorts of continued fractions, and how to turn them into rational approximations, we move on to consider the implementation of ordinary arithmetic operations on them. The simplest is the algebraic algorithm **aa**, which we investigate in this section.

The algebraic algorithm satisfies the following condition:

$$\mathbf{aa}\begin{pmatrix} N & n \\ D & d \end{pmatrix} r = \frac{Nr + n}{Dr + d}$$

That is: **aa** is a function that takes a state (consisting of four integers) and a real number (represented by a continued fraction) and returns the real number $(Nr + n)/(Dr + d)$ (again represented as a continued fraction).

The main use of the **aa** is to perform operations on real numbers, such as adding a rational to a real or multiplying a rational by a real. Adding the rational n/d is achieved by using the following initial configuration:

$$\frac{n}{d} + r = \mathbf{aa}\begin{pmatrix} d & n \\ 0 & d \end{pmatrix} r,$$

and multiplication by n/d is given by:

$$\frac{n}{d} \times r = \mathbf{aa} \begin{pmatrix} n & 0 \\ 0 & d \end{pmatrix} r.$$

We observe that the following properties arise with the continued fraction representation of the number r and the result. Firstly if the continued fraction is finite, then at some stage we will need to consider the case where r is infinite; we define the algebraic algorithm in this case in the following manner[6]:

$$\mathbf{aa} \begin{pmatrix} N & n \\ D & d \end{pmatrix} \infty = \frac{N}{D}.$$

Let us now suppose that the number we are applying the function **aa** to is of the form $x_0 + \frac{1}{r}$. Then it is easy to verify the following identity:

$$\mathbf{aa} \begin{pmatrix} N & n \\ D & d \end{pmatrix} (x_0 + \frac{1}{r}) = \mathbf{aa} \begin{pmatrix} Nx_0 + n & N \\ Dx_0 + d & D \end{pmatrix} r.$$

Another identity that holds for the function **aa** is that for any y_0:

$$\mathbf{aa} \begin{pmatrix} N & n \\ D & d \end{pmatrix} r = y_0 + \frac{1}{\mathbf{aa} \begin{pmatrix} D & d \\ N - Dy_0 & n - dy_0 \end{pmatrix} r}.$$

These two identities define the *consumption* and *emission* of terms in the continued fraction representations of the initial real number r or the resultant real number. The critical question is therefore: which of these operations should we choose to perform, given a choice? The answer is straightforward if we wish to be as lazy as possible: we emit a term provided it is sufficiently close to the value we require for an **E**-fraction, otherwise we consume a term from the input.

Let's be a bit more explicit: to evaluate the following state

$$r = \mathbf{aa} \begin{pmatrix} N & n \\ D & d \end{pmatrix} (x + \frac{1}{x'}),$$

the Algebraic Algorithm goes through the following steps.

1. After checking that the input continued fraction hasn't terminated, we use the first term x to determine the bounds for $x + 1/x'$, using the *criterion* that $\Delta(x, x + 1/x') < 1$.

2. From this we can determine the bounds on the value of r.

3. If the bounds $(i,\ s)$ on r are such that $\Delta(i,\ s) < 1$, then any integer between i and s can be the Euclidean Part of r, then we output the Euclidean Part. Alternatively, we absorb the term x.

The main use to which we will put the Algebraic Algorithm is as a base case for the more useful Quadratic Algorithm, which we now consider.

---

[6] The fraction N/D will need to be converted to a continued fraction – but this is easy.

5 Quadratic Algorithm

The problem at the moment is that we are limited to rational operations on any particular real number we care to consider. What we would really like to do is to add and multiply two real numbers represented as continued fractions.

This is what Gosper's Quadratic Algorithm does. His original papers [8, 9] are unfortunately a little difficult to obtain but a précis is available in [11]. This paper has as an added bonus, an implementation of continued fractions in SASL. The Quadratic Algorithm calculates the following function (which, as we shall see, can be used to implement the basic arithmetic operations):

$$\mathbf{qa}\begin{pmatrix} N & N' & n & n' \\ D & D' & d & d' \end{pmatrix} x\, y = \frac{(Nx+N')y+(nx+n')}{(Dx+D')y+(dx+d')}.$$

Notice that this time the state consists of eight integers and that the function **qa** takes two real numbers (represented as continued fractions) returning another real number.

We first observe that the following base cases can be given:

$$\mathbf{qa}\begin{pmatrix} N & N' & n & n' \\ D & D' & d & d' \end{pmatrix} \infty\, y = \mathbf{aa}\begin{pmatrix} N & n \\ D & d \end{pmatrix} y,$$

and

$$\mathbf{qa}\begin{pmatrix} N & N' & n & n' \\ D & D' & d & d' \end{pmatrix} x\, \infty = \mathbf{aa}\begin{pmatrix} N & N' \\ D & D' \end{pmatrix} x.$$

As we would expect, we can derive similar identities to those deduced for the algebraic algorithm. Firstly, absorbing a term from each continued fraction[7], we observe that the following holds:

$$\mathbf{qa}\begin{pmatrix} N & N' & n & n' \\ D & D' & d & d' \end{pmatrix} (x_0+\frac{1}{x})\,(y_0+\frac{1}{y}) =$$

$$\mathbf{qa}\begin{pmatrix} Nx_0y_0+N'y_0+nx_0+n' & Ny_0+n & Nx_0+N' & N \\ Dx_0y_0+D'y_0+dx_0+d' & Dy_0+d & Dx_0+D' & D \end{pmatrix} x\, y.$$

Emitting a term, y_0, remains essentially as described for the Algebraic Algorithm:

$$\mathbf{qa}\begin{pmatrix} N & N' & n & n' \\ D & D' & d & d' \end{pmatrix} x\, y =$$

$$z_0 + \cfrac{1}{\mathbf{qa}\begin{pmatrix} D & D' & d & d' \\ N-Dz_0 & N'-D'z_0 & n-dz_0 & n'-d'z_0 \end{pmatrix} x\, y}.$$

To use the Quadratic Algorithm to add two numbers x and y we observe that

$$x+y=\mathbf{qa}\begin{pmatrix} 0 & 1 & 1 & 0 \\ 0 & 0 & 0 & 1 \end{pmatrix} x\, y$$

Similar initial states may be computed for the other arithmetic operations. We next consider the problem of transcendental functions.

---

[7] To be as lazy as possible, we should follow Gosper[9] and only absorb a term one of the continued fractions at a time. The idea is to select the one which will cause the most rapid convergence.

6 Transcendental Functions

If we are not able to compute logarithms, exponentials, and trigonometric functions then our real number implementation is severely limited. Fortunately these functions can be represented as continued fractions, as has long been known.[8]

Wall [17] gives a continued fraction expansion for exp(r) which, when transformed, may be given as:

$$\exp(r) = [1, \frac{1}{r}, 2, \frac{3}{r}, -2, \frac{5}{r}, 2, \frac{7}{r}, -2, \ldots].$$

In the same work we also find a definition for log(r) which is equivalent to

$$\log(r) = [0, \frac{1}{r-1}, \frac{2}{1}, \frac{3}{r-1}, \frac{2}{2}, \frac{5}{r-1}, \frac{2}{3}, \ldots].$$

As we can see, we must be prepared to deal with continued fractions having non-integer terms. So we now consider the problem of turning a Euclidean continued fraction with real valued terms into a Euclidean continued fraction with integer terms. We must be careful to ensure that the operations we use are computable.

A consequence of the desire to deal with transcendental functions of arbitrary real numbers is that traditional continued fraction expansions will generate a continued fraction with real-valued coefficients. For example, using Gauss' continued fraction to calculate $e^{\sqrt{2}}$ will give:

$$[1, \frac{1}{\sqrt{2}}, 2, \frac{3}{\sqrt{2}}, -2, \ldots]$$

We therefore desire a function which will convert this continued fraction into a Euclidean continued fraction, *in a lazy fashion.*

The solution is to adapt the Algebraic Algorithm of Section 4 so that the state is a 4-tuple of E-fractions. Calculating the bounds of the output is straightforward, and we have computed an output value when the distance between the two bounds is less 1, using the Δ metric. This comparison will have to be performed by using ε-comparison and setting the limit as $1 - \varepsilon$.

7 Conclusion

To an extent the paper's title of Exact Real Arithmetic is misleading. The system only computes the answer to some arithmetic expression to whatever accuracy you specify. It may run out of memory (in which case the program will inform you of this fact); it may fail to compute any answer whatsoever (in which case you will wait for ever to observe the output of the program). It does have major advantages over traditional floating point numbers. Firstly, you may be sure that any answer it provides is accurate. Secondly, there is no need to re-code an algorithm when more accuracy is required.

---

[8] The British Library kindly provided a copy of Gauss' work [7]; this includes his work on the hypergeometric series [6], which, unfortunately, is in Latin.

8 Acknowledgements

Jean Vuillemin's work [16] is clearly the major source for the implementation work that I have undertaken. I have used the arbitrary precision integer package produced by Richard Bird and Phil Wadler [1]. Thanks are also due to Quentin Miller for providing the implementation of Orwell [10]. I would also like to thank Geoffrey Burn, Simon Peyton Jones, John Robson, Peter Sestoft, and Geraint Jones who have all contributed comments upon preliminary versions of this paper. Of course, all errors and indiscretions remain my own work.

References

1. R.S. Bird and P.L. Wadler. *An Introduction to Functional Programming.* Prentice-Hall Series in Computer Science. Prentice-Hall International (UK) Ltd., Hemel Hempstead, Hertfordshire, England, 1988.

2. E. Bishop and D. Bridges. *Constructive Analysis.* Springer Verlag, 1985.

3. H. Boehm and R. Cartwright. Exact real arithmetic: Formulating real numbers as functions. In D.A. Turner, editor, *Research Topics in Functional Programming*, University of Texas at Austin Year of Programming, pages 43–64. Addison-Wesley, 1990.

4. A. Church. *The Calculi of Lambda-Conversion.* Princeton University Press, Princeton, N.J., 1941.

5. Euclid. Elements.

6. C.F. Gauss. Disquisitiones generales circa serium infinitam $1 + \frac{\alpha\beta}{1.\gamma}x+$ etc. pars prior. In *Werke*, volume 3, pages 123–162. Königlichen Gesellschaft der Wissenschaften, Göttingen, 1812.

7. C.F. Gauss. *Werke*, volume 3. Königlichen Gesellschaft der Wissenschaften, Göttingen, 1876.

8. R.W. Gosper. Continued fraction arithmetic. HAKMEM 101b, MIT, 1980.

9. R.W. Gosper. Continued fraction arithmetic. Unpublished Draft Paper, 1981.

10. Q. Miller and P. Wadler. *An Introduction to Orwell 6.00.* Programming Reasearch Group, 8–11 Keble Road, Oxford, UK, January 1990.

11. S.L. Peyton Jones. Arbitrary precision arithmetic using continued fractions. Internal Note 1530, Deptartment of Computer Science, University College London, January 1984.

12. M.B. Pour-El and J.I. Richards. *Computability in Analysis and Physics.* Perspectives in Mathematical Logic. Springer-Verlag, Heidelberg, 1989.

13. H.G. Rice. Recursive real numbers. *Proceedings of the American Mathematical Society*, 5(5):784–791, 1954.

14. D.J. Struik. *A Concise History of Mathematics.* Dover Publications, Mineola, New York, 1948.

15. A.M. Turing. On computable numbers, with an application to the Entscheidungsproblem. *Proceedings of the London Mathematical Society,* 42(3):230–265, 1936.

16. J. Vuillemin. Arithmétic réelle exacte par les fractions continues. Technical Report 760, Instituit National de Recherche en Informatique et en Automatique, Domaine de Voluceau, Roquencourt, BP105, 78153 Le Chesnay Cedex, France, November 1987.

17. H.S. Wall. *Analytic Theory of Continued Fractions.* Van Nostrand, Inc., 250 Fourth Avenue, New York 3, 1948.

A Semantics for Relational Programming

David Murphy,
Department of Computing Science,
University of Glasgow,
Glasgow G12 8QQ, Scotland.

Abstract

This paper presents an elementary model of relational programming as a generalisation of functional programming. We present well-known models of features of functional programming and show one way that they generalise to the relational case. This is achieved by giving a uniform construction of a category of types and relations from a category of types and functions.

Our construction of a relational from a functional calculus is used to discuss data-types and polymorphism in relational languages, and to show how they can be modeled by extensions of functional techniques. We also discuss the class of *causal* relations that can be implemented particularly efficiently and characterise them.

1. Introduction

The paucity of the type structure, and of the semantics for relational programming is remarkable in comparison with the functional case. In this paper these deficiencies are partly addressed; we present a simple but uniform categorical model for relational programming. This model has the advantage of generalising extant models of functional programming languages, so that some results and constructions carry over. Our intention is not to provide a 'state of the art' approach, but rather to try to understand the computer science content of an elementary construction. Thus, the level of the category theory we use is deliberately simple; familiarity with material around the level of Part I of Lambek and Scott [18], is assumed. To a certain extent, then, this paper is a collection of well-known sources, but one that may offer some intuition for how they might fit together.

The structure of the rest of the paper is as follows. In the remainder of this section we introduce relational programming, motivate our concerns, and discuss a naïve semantic approach. This being found wanting, the next section introduces a more satisfactory formalism: we show how to extend well-known models of functional programming to models of relational calculi. In particular, we present standard notions of data-type and of polymorphism and show how they can be extended. Finally, we take a class of relations, the *causal relations*, that are particularly useful for the programmer, and characterise them in the model.

1.1. Why relational programming is interesting

Relations have been used for various purposes in computer science: to model non-determinism, as in [4] and [27]; to specify behavioural properties of programs, as in [11]; and to model hardware, as in [21]. Various dataflow and logic programming languages are also relational in nature. This interest in the uses of relations has not been matched by a large theoretical effort; we cite merely the early interest in the axiomatics of the calculus of relations shown by Tarski in [28], and the later categorical study based on this by Freyd and Scedrov [10].

The plethora of uses for relations indicates that there is a place for a relational programming languages. Here we study ones that are extensions of *functional programming*. A good example of the sort of language we shall describe is *Ruby*, introduced in [25] and explained more carefully in [22]. This relational calculus concentrates on the structural feature of programs; it has Hindley–Milner polymorphism, and makes frequent use of polymorphic relations. It is of proven usefulness in the design of (parallel) algorithms and hardware; see, for instance, [17]. We assume familiarity with such a calculus.

Ruby is a 'design–by–calculation' language; one starts with a "clearly correct" relational specification and refines it into an implementation. Refinement proceeds via algebraic laws concerning the combinators, initiality of datatypes and so on; these are used to transform the specification. Within this paradigm,—which is similar to that of the *Bird/Meertens formalism* [2],—it is particularly important for the semantics to give these laws more or less for free. Moreover, many useful laws deal with polymorphic combinators, so a proper treatment of Hindley–Milner polymorphism is essential. These features of Ruby will dictate the pattern of study we make of the relational calculus. (An alternative, axiomatic treatment with a similar Bird/Meertens-oriented style is given by Backhouse et al. in [3].)

The reader should be warned that we will not deal with many topics fully; full second–order polymorphism, for instance, is omitted, as is a thorough treatment of the general semantics of datatypes in terms of the algebras of (strong) endofunctors. Footnotes are sometimes used to refer to more comprehensive accounts.

1.2. Naïve models

It is well–known that a very simple model of functional programming can be given in the category $\mathfrak{Set}$, so the question 'why can't we give a similarly–naïve account of relational programming in the category of sets and relations $\mathfrak{Rel}$?' suggests itself. The answer is that $\mathfrak{Rel}$ does not have very nice properties as a category to give a semantics to a programming language. We can summarise the undesirable properties of $\mathfrak{Rel}$ thus:

- It is self-dual.
- It is not cartesian-closed.
- It is not even complete or cocomplete.

These properties mean that it is hard to define a rich type structure in $\mathfrak{Rel}$, and to deal with fixed points. Thus $\mathfrak{Rel}$ is not much help, as it does not automatically admit the type structure we want to use. So, instead of using categories like $\mathfrak{Rel}$ directly, we will study them as structures derived from better behaved categories. Our approach will be to select a category $\mathfrak{C}$ that is a model of functional programming and derive properties of the associated relational language. Such properties often give laws are useful for transforming relational programs.

2. Categories of Relations

In this section we investigate a general approach to the description of relational constructions in programming languages. We shall start with the notion of a language of types and total functions modeled, as usual [1], as a category, $\mathfrak{C}$. From this category we will construct a category of types and relations, $\mathfrak{C}^r$, which inherits some of the structure of $\mathfrak{C}$, giving a model of relational programming. Much of the work presented here is due to de Moor [9]; the reader is referred there for a more extensive analysis. That work, in turn, draws on the early study of Barr [5].

2.1. Constructing $\mathfrak{C}^r$

Given a category $\mathfrak{C}$, a *span* of two objects a and b in $\mathfrak{C}$ is an object m and a pair of arrows $g : m \to a$ and $h : m \to b$. A *span morphism* between two spans (m, g, h) and (m', g', h'), is an arrow $\alpha : m \to m'$ such that $g = g' \cdot \alpha$ and $h = h' \cdot \alpha$.

If there is a span morphism from (m, g, h) to (m', g', h') we say $(m, g, h) \lesssim (m', g', h')$. Two spans (m, g, h) and (m', g', h') are said to be *equivalent* if there are span morphisms so that $(m, g, h) \lesssim (m', g', h')$ and $(m', g', h') \lesssim (m, g, h)$; i.e. figure 1 commutes.

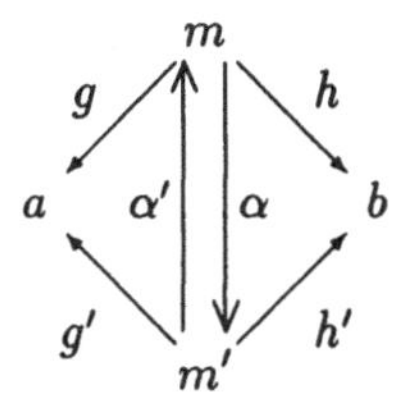

FIGURE 1. A diagram evincing the equivalence of the spans (m, f, g) and (m', f', g').

We will think of a relation as a class of equivalent spans, and write $[g, h]$ for the relation between the types a and b witnessed by the span (m, g, h).

Notice that in $\mathfrak{Set}$ a class of equivalent spans $[g, h]$ determines a relation $R \triangleq \{(g\ w, h\ w) \mid w \in m\}$ in the obvious way. Here it makes sense to think of w as witnessing the relatedness of objects in a and objects in b. Taking classes of equivalent spans indicates that we do not care what is the witness of this relatedness. We call a the *domain* of $[g, h]$ and b the *range* of the relation; obviously this designation gives no input/output information.

Composition of relations can be defined using weak pullbacks; given spans $(m, g, h : m \to b)$ and $(n, j : n \to b, k)$ we can define the relations $R \triangleq [g, h]$ and $S \triangleq [j, k]$. Then, the *sequential composition* $R\ ;\ S$ is defined to be the relation $[g \cdot j', k \cdot h']$ where $j' : b' \to m$ and $h' : b' \to n$ form a weak pullback of h and j; see figure 2. (A weak pullback is a pullback where the mediating arrow need not be unique. Mac lane discusses weak limits in general. Note that all weak pullbacks of a given pair of arrows with common target give rise to equivalent spans.)

We now have our construction of a category of relations; given a category $\mathfrak{C}$ with weak pullbacks, we can define the category $\mathfrak{C}^r$ which has the same objects as $\mathfrak{C}$ and classes of equivalent spans as arrows, composition being given by taking weak pullbacks. Thus $\_^r$ should be a functor from the category of all small categories with weak pullbacks to the category of all small categories, $\_^r : \mathrm{WP}\mathfrak{Cat} \to \mathfrak{Cat}$.

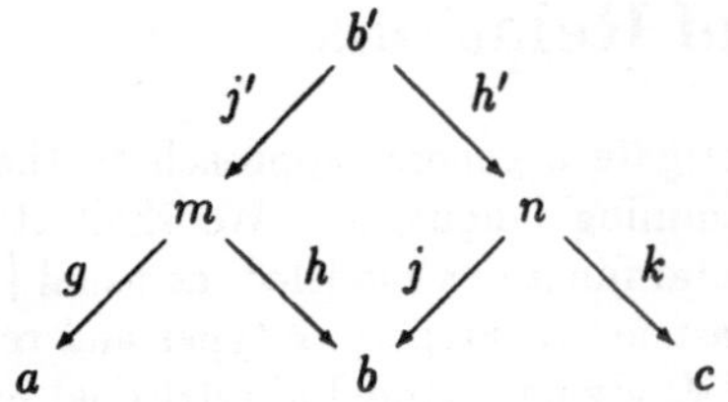

FIGURE 2. The Composition of Relations as a Weak Pullback.

Notation: we write $R \triangleq [g, h]$ to name the relation witnessed by the class of equivalent spans $[g, h]$ as R. If $g : m \to a$ and $h : m \to b$ then we say that $R \triangleq [g, h]$ *has type* $a \sim b$ and write $R : a \sim b$. Clearly if $R : a \sim b$ and $S : b \sim c$ then $R \,;\, S$ is defined and has type $a \sim c$.

2.2. Functors and Natural Transformations in $\mathfrak{C}^{\mathrm{r}}$

Relational *converse* is modeled by a contravariant endofunctor $\_^{\leftharpoondown} : \mathfrak{C}^{\mathrm{r}} \to \mathfrak{C}^{\mathrm{r}}$ which just takes $[g, h]$ to $[h, g]$ and leaves objects unaffected. We extend this notation, writing $R^{\leftharpoondown}$ for the converse of a relation R. Obviously if $R : a \sim b$ then $R^{\leftharpoondown} : b \sim a$.

All functions are relations: to interpret a function $f : a \to b$ in $\mathfrak{C}$ as a relation, make one leg of the span the identity. This gives a functor $G : \mathfrak{C} \to \mathfrak{C}^{\mathrm{r}}$ known as the *functioning* or *graph functor*:

$$G\,a \triangleq a$$
$$G\,f \triangleq [\mathrm{id}_a, f]$$

The functor G provides us with an embedding $\mathfrak{C} \hookrightarrow \mathfrak{C}^{\mathrm{r}}$; it is this on which the semantics of relational languages are based, since it allows us to carry some properties from $\mathfrak{C}$ into $\mathfrak{C}^{\mathrm{r}}$.[1]

Suppose $\mathfrak{A}$ and $\mathfrak{B}$ are categories with weak-pullbacks, and that $F : \mathfrak{A} \to \mathfrak{B}$ preserves these, so that compositions are preserved. What should it mean for a functor to extend F to the relational structure ? It seems reasonable to suppose that any *extension* of F, $F^{\mathrm{r}} : \mathfrak{A}^{\mathrm{r}} \to \mathfrak{B}^{\mathrm{r}}$ say, should preserve converses, and should view functions as relations in the same way. So, we say F^{r} extends F if it is a functor and

$$F^{\mathrm{r}} \cdot G^{\leftharpoondown} = (G \cdot F)^{\leftharpoondown}$$
$$F^{\mathrm{r}} \cdot G = G \cdot F$$

Theorem 1 (de Moor). *The construction* $\_^{r}$ *is 'reasonable.' Specifically:*

(i) $\mathfrak{Set}^{r} \equiv \mathfrak{Rel}$.

(ii) *Suppose* $\mathfrak{A}$ *and* $\mathfrak{B}$ *have weak pullbacks and* $F : \mathfrak{A} \to \mathfrak{B}$ *preserves them. Then the following defines a unique functor* F^{r} *that extends* F*:*

$$F^{r} a \triangleq a$$
$$F^{r}[g, h] \triangleq [F\,g, F\,h]$$

---

[1] Notice that if $\mathfrak{C}$ is a topos with choice, then our category of relations can be characterised monadically,—a style advocated by Moggi, [20]: it is the Kleisli category of the powerset monad, so in this case the graph functor has a right adjoint.

Thus there is a way to extend a category of total functions to a category of relations in such a structure–preserving way, and our desire that $\_^{\mathrm{r}}$ be functorial is satisfied.[2]

It should be clear that given a natural transformation $\eta : F \dot{\rightarrow} H$ we would like there to be a natural transformation $G \cdot \eta : F^{\mathrm{r}} \rightarrow H^{\mathrm{r}}$. Clearly this is only reasonable if F^{r} and H^{r} are functors, so we assume F and H preserve weak pullbacks. Then:

Theorem 2 (Barr, de Moor). *Given $\eta : F \dot{\rightarrow} H$, $G \cdot \eta$ is a natural transformation when its converse $(G \cdot \eta)^{\leftarrow}$ is. In particular, η^{r} is a well–defined natural transformation with components ${\eta_a}^{\mathrm{r}} : F^{\mathrm{r}}(a) \rightarrow G^{\mathrm{r}}(a)$ if η_a is always an isomorphism. (Recall that the composition of a functor G with a natural transformation η is itself a natural transformation with components $(G \cdot \eta)_a = G(\eta_a)$.)*

2.3. The Ordered Structure of $\mathfrak{C}^{\mathrm{r}}$

The category $\mathfrak{C}^{\mathrm{r}}$ is *order–enriched*; there is an order on hom–sets given by $\lesssim$. In $\mathfrak{Set}$, this order is just the familiar relational inclusion:

$$R \lesssim S \iff x\,R\,y \implies x\,S\,y$$

This 2–categorical structure is studied in [12] and [15]; we do not treat it further here.

2.4. Choice

Our construction of a category of relations is by no means the standard definition; the more usual one is:

A standard relation between a and b is a subobject of the product $a \times b$. (This is reasonable if we remember that we can type R as $R : a \sim b$ iff $R \subseteq a \times b$.) We can think of this as a span (m, g, h) where $g \times h : m \rightarrow a \times b$ is monic. Two such (m, g, h) and (m', g', h') give the same relation when they code the same subobject, i.e. when $m \equiv m'$, so a standard relation is an equivalence class of spans under isomorphism rather than under equivalence of spans. We will write $\mathfrak{C}^{\mathrm{s}}$ for the standard category of relations derived from $\mathfrak{C}$.[3]

Much of the relevant literature taking this approach is cited in the excellent introduction of Spenser [26]. The purpose of this subsection is to compare our construction to the standard one:

---

[2] The reader may wonder if it is possible to do without the (mild) restriction of preserving weak pullbacks. It is possible, but one obtains for F^{r} a structure weaker than that of a functor. These 'upfunctors' and their associated weak and lax transformations, adjunctions etc. are mentioned by de Moor [9], and discussed extensively by Jay [15].

[3] It would be disingenuous to pretend that this is the full story; all that is really needed for relations to make sense in a category is that it should be *regular*. Thus we might expect that a standard way of constructing a relational calculus would be to take the free regular category over a model of the functional case. This construction has been elucidated in some cases by Carboni in as-yet-unpublished work. Another approach we also deliberately skim over is the Karoubi construction used extensively by Freyd, whose [10] is a fairly readily-available reference. There is some reason to believe, given this multiplicity of constructions, that it will be some time before the whole story on using categories to generalise functional to relational programming is known; this confusion offers a shred of justification for the naïve position taken here.

Theorem 3. *For $\mathfrak{C}$ a topos, the standard construction of relations on $\mathfrak{C}$ is equivalent to ours (i.e. there is an equivalence of categories $\mathfrak{C}^r \cong \mathfrak{C}^s$) only if all epis split in $\mathfrak{C}$.*

Proof. Consider an arrow of $\mathfrak{C}^r$, i.e. a span (m, f, g). We can form the product arrow $\langle f, g\rangle : m \to a \times b$. Since $\mathfrak{C}$ is a topos, we can perform an epi/mono factorisation on this arrow to get a composite $\langle f, g\rangle = \langle f', g'\rangle \cdot e$ where $e : m \to m', \langle f', g'\rangle : m' \to a \times b$. Our aim is to show that if the span (m', f', g') is equivalent to (m, f, g) then there is an arrow e' which splits the epi e (i.e. $e \cdot e' = \mathrm{id}_{m'}$). But for (m', f', g') to be equivalent to (m, f, g) there must be arrows $\alpha : m \to m', \alpha' : m' \to m$ such that the diagram in figure 1 commutes. However, epi/mono factorisations are unique up to isomorphism, and so we can take $\alpha = e$. Next, consider α'; diagram chasing gives us $e \cdot \alpha' = \mathrm{id}_{m'}$ so this is the required e'. □

This result is rather damaging to the construction; it means we can only really make sense of our relations if the underlying category $\mathfrak{C}$ has choice.

3. Datatypes

In this section we will study the datatypes available in categories of relations. We will assume as fixed some base cartesian closed category $\mathfrak{C}$, and show how datatypes given over $\mathfrak{C}$ can be extended to datatypes given over $\mathfrak{C}^r$. Notation and material are taken freely from the functional case as discussed in Verwer's [29]. We will write π_a or $\pi_a^{a \times b}$ for the projection $a \times b \to a$, and b^a as usual for the exponential. Given $f : a \to b$, we will write $\ulcorner f \urcorner$ for the 'name' of f, $\ulcorner f \urcorner = \text{curry}\ (f \cdot \pi_a^{1 \times a})$; further information, for those unfamiliar with CCCs, is given in [18].

3.1. Transformation and Internal Languages

We want to be able to derive algebraic laws that enable us to transform relational programs. The other subsections of this section will provide the laws; this section is devoted to mentioning relevant work on internal languages which capture these transformations.

It is well known that cartesian closed categories 'model' the first order typed λ-calculus. The sense in which they do so is this; there is a functor L from the category of CCCs to the category of typed λ-calculi, and a functor C the other way: these functors define an equivalence of categories [18], with the functor L giving the *internal language* of a CCC. Thus, there is a model of the transformational semantics of $\mathfrak{C}$; $L(\mathfrak{C})$. Moreover, as we will outline, we can sometimes reason about $\mathfrak{C}$'s datatypes in it.

The question of internalising the laws of $\mathfrak{C}^r$ that do not derive via G from those of $\mathfrak{C}$ is much more involved. Moggi has done some work on a related problem, the internal language of the *partial λ-calculus*, [19], but there has been, to my knowledge, essentially no work on this area yet. This is not a crucial lack as it turns out that $L(\mathfrak{C})$ suffices for nearly all the manipulations of, for instance, [17].

3.2. Data types as F-algebras

We have been thinking of the underlying category $\mathfrak{C}$ as a category of types and functions. It is often convenient to define data types in $\mathfrak{C}$ by means of *F-algebras*. In this subsection we discuss this kind of construction and show to what extent it carries over to categories of relations. A *type functor* F is a endofunctor $F : \mathfrak{C} \to \mathfrak{C}$ with certain properties. It is defined by giving

- A binary components functor $\ominus : \mathfrak{C} \times \mathfrak{C} \to \mathfrak{C}$.
- A constructors isomorphism $\gamma_a : F(a) \ominus a \to F(a)$ for each object a.

One of the advantages of defining datatypes with functors is to emphasise the operation such constructions on terms; to construct lists, we must give not just a list type $\mathsf{lst}\ a$ for each type a (thus defining F on objects) but also an arrow $\mathsf{map}\ f : \mathsf{lst}\ a \to \mathsf{lst}\ b$ for each arrow $f : a \to b$.

The object $F(a)$ is defined as the least fixed point of $(\_ \ominus a)$. The existence of this fixed point follows standardly if $\mathfrak{C}$ has finite colimits and $(\_ \ominus a)$ is ω-cocontinuous.

Moreover, $(F(a), \gamma_a)$ is a free initial algebra. This means that for every object b and arrow $f : b \ominus a \to b$ there is a unique *homomorphism*, i.e. an arrow $\langle f \rangle : F(a) \to b$ satisfying

$$\langle f \rangle \cdot \gamma_a = f \cdot (\langle f \rangle \ominus \mathrm{id}_a)$$

These homomorphism properties often give rise to useful laws; cf. [2].

Defining datatypes this way is loosely known as the Hagino style; a good introduction is [31]. (We have only given one half of the technique; dually there are terminal F-coalgebras.) The advantage of this style is that it emphasises the importance of the constructors, which have good properties:

Theorem 4. *As our notation hints, the constructors γ_a are components of a natural isomorphism $\gamma : \Lambda x \,.\, F(x) \ominus x \dot{\to} F(x)$.*

This is worth proving, since it brings out the functoriality, and gives us a familiar construction, the map of functional programming [6].

Proof. Given an arrow $g : a \to b$, define the F-map of g as $F(g) = \langle \gamma_b \cdot (\mathrm{id}_{F(b)} \ominus g) \rangle$.

$$\begin{aligned} F(g) \cdot \gamma_a &= \gamma_b \cdot (\mathrm{id}_{F(b)} \ominus g) \cdot (F(g) \ominus \mathrm{id}_a) \\ &= \gamma_b \cdot (F(g) \ominus g) \end{aligned}$$

Example. Cons-lists[4] of type a can be specified by giving the component functor $x \ominus a = \mathbf{1} + (a \times x)$ and the two constructors $\mathsf{nil}_a : \mathbf{1} \to \mathsf{lst}\ a$, $\mathsf{cons}_a : \mathsf{lst}\ a \times a \to \mathsf{lst}\ a$. (Here $\mathbf{1}$ is the terminal object.) The reader might find it helpful at this point to verify that the $\mathsf{lst}-\mathsf{map}$ of a function $f : a \to b$ is just the usual $\mathsf{map}\ f$.

Notice that the usual (pattern matching) decomposition of lists follows from the invertability of γ_a; the converse $\gamma_a^{-1} = \langle \gamma_a \ominus \mathrm{id}_a \rangle : F(a) \to F(a) \ominus a$ breaks $F(a)$ up into its components.

The results of the last section now enable us to lift type functors over $\mathfrak{C}$ to functors over $\mathfrak{C}^{\mathrm{r}}$, constructors isomorphisms to isomorphisms and so on. (Note, however, that in general if F is a type functor over $\mathfrak{C}$ it will not be a type functor over $\mathfrak{C}^{\mathrm{r}}$ even if it preserves weak pullbacks and ω-colimits.)

It would be nice to be able to reason about datatypes in the internal language $L(\mathfrak{C})$. That is possible if the type functor is *strong*. This means intuitively that it is representable in $\mathfrak{C}$:

---

[4] We will define what Jay (after Cockett) [8], [16] calls 'right list objects.' These cons-lists are isomorphic to snoc lists (left list objects) in a CCC, the proof being accomplished by showing that a cons $as = \mathsf{reverse}\ (a\ \mathsf{snoc}\ (\mathsf{reverse}\ as))$.

An endofunctor $F : \mathfrak{C} \to \mathfrak{C}$ is strong if it has a *functorial strength*, i.e., for objects $a, b \in \mathfrak{C}$, there is a natural transformation

$$\tau_{a,b} : (b^a) \to (F(b)^{F(a)})$$

such that for every $f : a \to b$,

$$\tau_{a,b} \cdot \ulcorner f \urcorner = \ulcorner F(f) \urcorner$$

The details need not detain us here,—see [29],—suffice it to say that in a cocomplete category $\mathfrak{C}$ we need merely prove that the components functor $\ominus$ is strong in order to have the homomorphism and constructor equations available in the internal language.[5]

4. Polymorphism

Our problem is to model Hindley–Milner style polymorphism in a relational language. The model used will be a simplification of Seely's model for the full second order λ-calculus due to Hilken. Seely's version is presented in [24]. We follow the excellent explanation of [1]:

4.1. Ideas of Polymorphism

We start off with the idea of a *kind*; this is a collection of types. We write Ω for the kind of all types; notice this is not a type. Next, we form a category of kinds (objects) and type expressions (arrows), $\mathfrak{T}$. Base types are arrows such as $\mathsf{Int} : \mathbf{1} \to \Omega$, and we have the usual arrows like lst: $\Omega \to \Omega$ and function types $\_ \longrightarrow \_ : \Omega \times \Omega \to \Omega$. We will assume this category $\mathfrak{T}$ has products, so we can model types with more than one free type variable. (Thus all we will assume about $\mathfrak{T}$ is that it has a $\mathbf{1}$, a distinguished object Ω and is cartesian closed; other objects are just junk. It may be helpful to think of $\mathfrak{T}$ as just a λ-calculus, but one at the type level, with polymorphic terms as first class citizens.)

Notice first that indeterminate arrows $\Omega \to \Omega$ act like type variables. A polymorphic type is one with a universally quantified type variable, so expressions like $\Lambda T : \Omega \,.\, t$ are of interest. Clearly, then, to model 2nd-order Λ-abstraction we need a map from type variables into types

$$\forall : (\Omega \to \Omega) \to \Omega$$

However, we are just interested in the Hindley–Milner fragment of the calculus where all quantification appears at the outside, so we can take the sort of polymorphic types to be something different;

$$\forall : (\Omega \to \Omega) \to \mho$$

[5] Again, we have shied away at this point from adding a further level of technicality that could clarify matters. What we really want for dealing with datatypes is that *all* endofunctors have initial algebras and final coalgebras and that these coincide. A category where this happens is called (by Freyd) *algebraically compact*. Such categories arise naturally via the standard construction of relations over a CCC and via the Karoubi construction, although no details have yet been published to my knowledge. This insight have be of long-term interest.

Let σ be a type variable; then $\forall(\sigma)$ intuitively represents the collection of polymorphic terms t such that, given a type $T : \Omega$ we can apply it to t so that $t\,T : \sigma(T)$. We will write $t\,T$ as t_T for obvious reasons.

The other side of type abstraction is type application; we need a projection to instantiate a polymorphic term $\forall(\sigma)$ at a type. Thus, there should be an operation $\mathrm{proj} : (\Omega \to \Omega) \times \Omega \to (\mho \to \Omega)$ where

$$\mathrm{proj}\,\sigma\,T \qquad \text{is an function} \qquad \forall(\sigma) \to \sigma(T)$$

This means that we can think of $\forall(\sigma)$ as a sort of product over types.[6]

Now, there should be an isomorphism between the polymorphic terms in $\forall(\sigma)$ and the collection of all families $\{t_T : \sigma(T) \mid T \in \Omega\}$ indexed over all types. We will call this isomorphism ϕ: it relates

$$\{t_T : \sigma(T) \mid T \in \Omega\} \qquad \text{to} \qquad \Lambda T : \Omega \,.\, t : \forall(\sigma)$$

We now have enough machinery to express the proper relationship between polymorphic types and the collection on their instantiations:

(i) If we define a polymorphic function from a collection of functions $\{t_T \mid T \in \Omega\}$, and then consider the instance relative to a specific type S, this is just the original instance t_S;

$$\mathrm{proj}\,\sigma\,S\,(\phi\{t_T \mid T \in \Omega\}) \;=\; t_S : \sigma(S)$$

(ii) If, given a polymorphic function $t : \forall(\sigma)$, we consider the collection of all its instances, then rebuild the function using those instances, we get the original

$$\phi\,\{\mathrm{proj}\,\sigma\,T\,(t) \mid T \in \Omega\} \;=\; t : \forall(\sigma)$$

So, in order to show that we have a well-behaved model of polymorphism, we need to point out $\forall$ and proj behaving thus.

4.2. A Model of Polymorphism

Our first step is to associate with each object of $\mathfrak{T}$ a category, so we have an indexed category $\rho : \mathfrak{T}^{\mathrm{op}} \to \mathbf{Cat}$. The idea is that $\rho(x)$ will be the category of types and terms polymorphic over x. Thus $\rho(x)$, often called the *fibre* over x, will model a λ-calculus and thus should be cartesian-closed, and we will want the functor $\rho(y) \to \rho(x)$ in $\mathbf{Cat}$ induced by $x \xrightarrow{f} y$ in $\mathfrak{T}$ to preserve the cartesian structure. (This functor is often written f^*.) A suitable indexed category, therefore, will be at least of the form $\rho : \mathfrak{T}^{\mathrm{op}} \to \mathrm{CC}\mathbf{Cat}$, where $\mathrm{CC}\mathbf{Cat}$ is the category of all small cartesian-closed categories with functors that preserve the structure 'on the nose.'

Consider a type $T : x \to \Omega$. An instance of a polymorphic term $t : \forall(\sigma)$ at T is clearly an object t_T in the fibre over x, $\rho(x)$. We will represent $\forall(\sigma)$ as an object t in $\rho(\Omega)$; this works because given T we can form $T^* : \rho(\Omega) \to \rho(x)$ and apply it to t to get an object $T^*(t)$ in $\rho(x)$, modelling proj.

We need to know that polymorphic types are 'just' the collection of all their instances, so we require an natural isomorphism

$$\psi : \mathrm{Hom}_{\mathfrak{T}}(\_, \Omega) \dot{\to} \mathrm{obj}\;\rho(\_)$$

[6] It cannot be a real categorical product as there are too many types. However, the insight that polymorphic terms should behave somewhat like the product of their instances leads to the most productive idea of internal categorical models of polymorphism, nicely introduced by Phoa [23].

This means in particular that objects in the fibre over Ω only come about from terms with a free type variable $\sigma : \Omega \to \Omega$, as required. Notice that, by Yoneda's lemma, $\psi_x : \mathrm{Hom}(x, \Omega) \to \rho(x)$ is determined by the image of the identity and so the object of $\rho(\Omega)$, $\psi_\Omega(\mathrm{id}_\Omega)$ acts like a polymorphic type variable.

The formalisation of these results is due to Seely [24]:

Theorem 5. *There are indexed categories $\rho : \mathfrak{T}^{op} \to CC\mathfrak{Cat}$ having an isomorphism*

$$\phi_t : \{t_T : \sigma(T) \mid T \in \Omega\} \to \Lambda T : \Omega \,.\, t : \forall(\sigma)$$

So that

$$proj\,\sigma\; S\; (\phi\{t_T \mid T \in \Omega\}) \equiv t_S$$
$$\phi\; \{proj\,\sigma\; T\; (t) \mid T \in \Omega\} \equiv t$$

4.3. (Some) Polymorphic Relations Categorically

Now notice that if the T^*s preserve weak pullbacks, and the $\rho(x)$s have them, we can build the categories $\rho(x)^r$ with $(T^*)^r$ induced by T^*. Since the fibres are CCCs and the substitution functors preserve this structure, our assumptions hold, and we have a model of a polymorphic calculus of relations.

Notice that each fibre $\rho(x)^r$ is well-behaved, being just the relation calculus derived from a given functional calculus $\rho(x)$ polymorphic over x. However, collectively the polymorphic relations are not well-behaved since there are nonextensional elements i.e. polymorphic relations R and S which are equal at all types but are not the same object of $\rho(\Omega)$.

5. Causal Relations

While programming in a relational framework has much to offer over the functional style in terms of expressiveness, computing with relations is less efficient, and sometime harder to reason about. In this section, we describe a class of relations which offers a novel blend of the functional and relational styles. This class of *causal* relations inherits much of the expressive power of pure relations, but naturally extends the functional style without excessive loss of efficiency; in particular, interpreters of tolerable efficiency exist for the causal relations; much good work has been done here by Hutton [13], [14].

As an example of the usefulness of causal relations, we mention the correlator derivation of [25]. Here a functional description of a hardware component is transformed into one using causal relations. The new specification is susceptible to more efficient implementation; the causal relations allow us to express the inherent bidirectionality of the design without resorting to the full complexity of the relational calculus: the final design can still be driven functionally, and the presence of a causal representative captures this.

5.1. Causality

A relation is causal if we may identify an 'input' part of the relation, which uniquely determines the remaining 'output' part:

Definition 6. *Suppose $\mathfrak{C}$ has finite products. Consider a relation $R \triangleq [g,h]$ in $\mathfrak{C}^r$. R is causal if there is an arrow $f : i \to o$ of $\mathfrak{C}$ with $(id_i, f) \in [g,h]$. (That is, there is an isomorphism $\iota : i \times o \to a \times b$ and projections $\pi_i : a \times b \to i, \pi_o : a \times b \to o$ such that $(\pi_a \cdot \iota \cdot (id_i, f), \pi_b \cdot \iota \cdot (id_i, f)) \in [g,h]$.)*

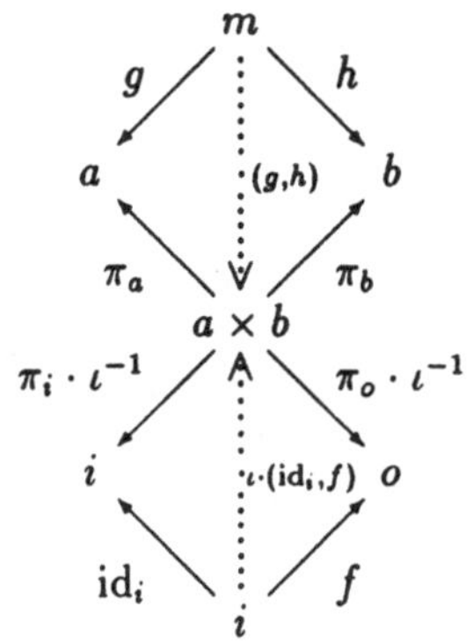

FIGURE 3. The notion of causal representative

The diagram is shown in figure 3. Here the arrows $\pi_i \cdot \iota^{-1} \cdot (g,h)$ and $\pi_o \cdot \iota^{-1} \cdot (g,h)$ respectively pick out the input/output parts of the relation, such that the first uniquely determines the second, as witnessed by the arrow f. Thus f can be thought of as a *causal representative* of $[g,h]$. (Notice that composing a relation $R = [g,h] : a \sim b$ with a function $k : b \to c$ gives us a relation $[g, k \cdot h] : a \sim c$.) The fact that there may be many possible choice of f just means that there are many functional interpretations — many ways to 'drive' the relation.

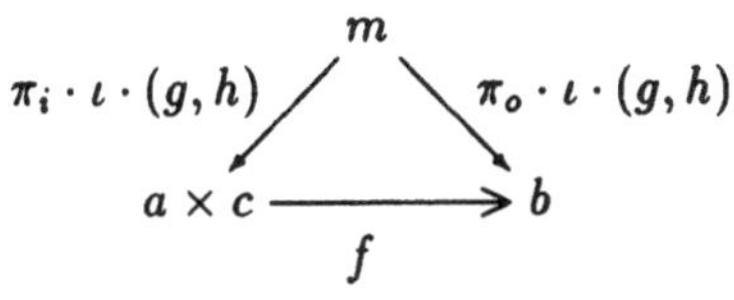

FIGURE 4. Picking a way to drive a causal relation.

Example. Suppose $R \triangleq [g,h]$ is a relation of type $a \sim b \times c$. If we know that R is really a function $f : a \times c \to b$ in disguise, how does this fit with our definition of causality? Take $i = a \times c$, $o = b$ and ι as the natural isomorphism $a \times (b \times c) \to (a \times c) \times b$ and we quickly see that the diagram in figure 4 commutes.

5.2. Causal Representatives

The causal representatives are well-behaved: given $R : a \sim b$ and $S : c \sim d$, pick causal representatives $f : i \to m$ and $g : m \to o$ respectively. Trivially, $g \cdot f$ is a causal representative of a relation, but that relation is not necessarily $R \; ; \; S$. Moreover, if f is a causal representative of R, and f has an converse, then f^{-1} is a causal representative of R and of $R^{\leftarrow}$. Thus we have a primitive closure under the idea of being a causal relation. Finally if f is a causal representative of R and g is a causal representative of S, then $f \times g$ is a causal representative of $R \otimes S$, where $\otimes$ is the weak product/coproduct of $\mathfrak{C}^r$. It is also the case that the causal representatives are just the images of $\mathfrak{C}$ in the graphing functor:

Theorem 7. *A relation R is in the wide subcategory $G(\mathfrak{C})$ of $\mathfrak{C}^r$ iff it is causal.*

Proof. Suppose that R has a causal representative f. Then clearly f is an arrow of $\mathfrak{C}$. Moreover, if $f : i \rightarrow o$ is an arrow of $\mathfrak{C}$, then $[\mathrm{id}_i, f]$ is an arrow of $\mathfrak{C}^r$ and obviously in $G(\mathfrak{C})$. □

Notice that the business of picking a causal representative tells us how we are planning to 'drive' R,– what the input and output will be. The set of all causal representatives of a relation captures all the deterministic ways it can be used; a design, then, should specify both components (relations) and how they are used (causal representatives); that way, since the causal representatives have good closure properties, it can effectively be simulated. (Specifying causal representatives is equivalent to giving what Hutton [13] calls relations and their 'directions'.)

Notice that the causal polymorphic representatives are well-behaved in the sense that they are just the collection of their instances:

Theorem 8.

$$Hom_{\mathfrak{T}}(\_, \Omega) \equiv G(\rho(\_))$$

Proof. Obvious since G is an embedding. □

6. Concluding Remarks

Some standard constructions that give models of various features of functional programming have been presented. These were extended to models of the same features in associated relational languages.

Work on semantics is often useful because it gives insight into programming. The semantics of Ruby certainly emphasises the importance of polymorphic combinators, and the functoriality of data–type constructors. These features provide a large range of laws with which to transform Ruby programs. Using these features often leads to algorithms with a regular structure, which can usually be implemented efficiently.

Further work

Our treatment of polymorphism is inadequate for three reasons. Firstly, as we have pointed out, it does not contain all the polymorphic relations that might be of interest; it is rather hard to see how to deal with this. Secondly, it only describes the Hindley-Milner fragment of the calculus; there should be no difficulty in extending it to the full PL–categorical description in the style of Seely; that is beyond the scope of this paper, though. Finally, we have seen that the indexed categorical model we present is not the end of the story, as it contains some 'nonparametric' polymorphic relations; the solution is to apply the extensional collapse of [7] or to try to internalise our constructions [23]. This should give us insight into a relational version of Wadler's 'Theorems for Free' [30].

A fuller treatment of our model would include a reasonable discussion of polymorphic isomorphisms (the 'plumbing' relations) and their coherence properties. The monadic datatypes introduced by Moggi and popularised by Wadler might also be of interest.

Acknowledgments

My thanks are due to Mary Sheeran, for encouraging this work, and to Geraint Jones, Clare Martin and especially Oege de Moor for aiding my understanding while on visits to Oxford. I have greatly benefited from conversations with Barney Hilken, Barry Jay and Phil Wadler. Graham Hutton made several careful contributions to this work at various stages; my special thanks go to him. This work was supported by IED project 1759; funding is gratefully acknowledged.

The final draft of this paper was completed while the author was at the GMD Schloss Birlinghoven. Without considerable effort from the systems support staff there, the final version would have been prepared much more quickly and easily.

Bibliography

1. A. Asperti and G. Longo, *Applied category theory: an introduction to categories, types and structures for the working computer scientist*, M.I.T. Press, 1991, To appear.
2. R. Backhouse, *An exploration of the Bird–Meertens formalism*, Technical Report CS 8810, Department of Computing Science, Groningen University, 1988.
3. R. Backhouse, P. de Bruin, E. Voermans, and J. van der Woude, *A relational theory of datatypes*, Proceedings of the Workshop on Constructive Algorithmics, Ameland, The Netherlands, 1990.
4. J. de Bakker, *Semantics and termination of nondeterministic recursive programs*, in Automata, Languages and Programming (S. Michaelson and R. Milner, Eds.), (1976), Edinburgh University Press.
5. M. Barr, *Relational algebra*, in the Reports of the Midwest Category Seminar IV, (1970), Springer-Verlag LNM 137.
6. R. Bird and P. Wadler, *Introduction to functional programming*, Prentice Hall, 1988.
7. V. Breazu-Tannen and T. Coquand, *Extensional models for polymorphism*, Theoretical Computer Science, Volume 59 (1988), Pp. 85–144.
8. J. Cockett, *List-arithmetic distributive categories: locoi*, Journal of Pure and Applied Algebra, Volume 66 (1990), Pp. 1-29.
9. O. de Moor, *Categories, relations and dynamic programming*, Technical Report PRG–TR–18–90, Programming Research Group, Oxford University, 1990.
10. P. Freyd and A. Scedrov, *Categories, allegories*, North Holland, 1990.
11. C. Hoare and J. He, *The weakest prespecification*, Technical Report PRG-44, Programming Research Group, Oxford University, 1985.
12. C. Hoare, J. He, and C. Martin, *Pre-adjunctions in order enriched categories*, Manuscript, Programming Research Group, Oxford University, 1990.
13. G. Hutton, *A simple guide to the Ruby simulator*, Department of Computing Science, University of Glasgow.
14. G. Hutton, *Functional programming with relations*, in Functional Programming (G. Hutton, C. Holst, and S. Peyton-Jones, Eds.), (1990), Springer-Verlag Workshops in Computer Science.
15. C. Jay, *Extending properties to categories of partial maps*, Technical Report ECS–LFCS–90–107, Laboratory for Foundations of Computer Science, 1990.

16. C. Jay, *Tail recursion from universal invariants*, in Category Theory and Computer Science, (1991), Springer-Verlag LNCS 530.
17. G. Jones and M. Sheeran, *The study of butterflies*, Technical Report PRG-TR-14-90, Oxford University Computing Laboratory, 1990, to appear, proceedings of the IVth Banff Higher Order workshop.
18. J. Lambek and P. Scott, *Introduction to higher order categorical logic*, CUP, 1986.
19. E. Moggi, *Categories of partial morphism and the partial λ calculus*, in Category Theory and Computer Science (D. Pitt et al., Ed.), (1985), Springer-Verlag LNCS 240.
20. E. Moggi, *Computational λ-calculus and monads*, in Proceedings of Logic in Computer Science, (1989).
21. D. Murphy, *Formal Design of Regular Architectures*, in Algorithms and Parallel VLSI Architectures II (P. Quinton et al., Eds.), (1991), North Holland.
22. D. Murphy, *Type refinement in ruby*, in Functional Programming (G. Hutton, C. Holst, and S. Peyton-Jones, Eds.), (1990), Springer-Verlag Workshops in Computer Science.
23. W. Phoa, *Two results on set-theoretic polymorphism*, in Category Theory and Computer Science, (1991), Springer-Verlag LNCS 530.
24. R. Seely, *Categorical semantics for higher order polymorphic lambda calculus*, Journal of Symbolic Logic, Volume 52 (1987), Number 4, Pp. 969-989.
25. M. Sheeran, *Describing and reasoning about circuits using relations*, in Proceedings of the workshop on theoretical aspects of VLSI design (J. Tucker et al., Ed.), (1990), CUP.
26. D. Spenser, *A survey of categorical computation: Fixed points, partiality, combinators ... control?*, Bulletin of the EATCS, Volume 43 (1991), Pp. 285-312.
27. E. Stark, *Compositional relational semantics for indeterminate dataflow networks*, in Category Theory and Computer Science (D. Pitt et al., Ed.), (1989), Springer-Verlag LNCS 398.
28. A. Tarski, *On the calculus of relations*, Journal of Symbolic Logic, Volume 6 (1941), Pp. 73-89.
29. N. Verwer, *Categorical semantics as a basis for program transformation*, Technical Report RUU-CS-90-38, Department of Computer Science, Utrecht University, 1990.
30. P. Wadler, *Theorems for free!*, in Functional Programming and Computer Architecture, (1989), Springer-Verlag LNCS.
31. G. Wraith, *A critique of Hagino's thesis*, Manuscript, Department of Mathematics, University of Sussex, 1988.

From Primitive Recursive Functions to Silicon through Relations

Lars Rossen*

December 23, 1991

Abstract

We introduce a new semantics for Ruby, to facilitate reasoning about temporal abstractions. In this frame we show how to encode primitive recursion. This gives us a transformation system form function to relations, and this can be used as a first transformation towards silicon.

1 Introduction

During the past decade there have been numerous attempts at silicon compilation. The intent is to produce a compiler that works in much the same way as traditional compilers, they just produce silicon instead of low level code. The problem that faces us when producing such compilers is that not only do we have a desire to produce correct silicon, we also want to produce compact and efficient silicon. This is complicated by the fact that many optimising algorithms for 2 dimensional layout are NP-hard.

The relational language Ruby [5, 4, 6] is a formal language that addresses some of these layout problems. However there are other problems with the language; one is that it is difficult to express temporal abstraction. We therefore propose a different semantics for the language to facilitate this abstraction mechanism. This semantics views the Ruby relations as relations over possible traces of values instead of relations over functions from time instances to data values. It is important to note that this is a move away from the lockstep synchrony traditionally used in Ruby.

Having introduced temporal abstraction we can present an algorithm for transforming a recursive function into a Ruby description using this abstraction mechanism to hide the recursion. This description can then be used either directly to produce layout or it can be manipulated via traditional Ruby methods to gain more efficient and compact layout.

---

* Technical University of Denmark, 2800 Lyngby, Denmark; *lr@id.dth.dk*

In the next section we introduce the new semantics for the Ruby language, and we also introduce some of the Ruby forms that we need to transform and reason about recursive functions. In section 3 we introduce the definition of primitive recursion. Primitive recursion serves as the formal basis for the transformation algorithm we introduce in chapter 4. It is not our intent to present a full featured transformation system; we just want to illustrate how specifications that are naturally expressed with recursion can be expressed in Ruby. At the end of this paper we take a naive recursive specification of a multiplier and transform it into a Ruby description.

2 The Relational Language

Our aim is to make a transformation from functions into relations using abstraction over time. To facilitate this approach we define a variant of the relational language Ruby that is suitable for reasoning with temporal abstractions.

In this variant the Ruby relations are relations over possible traces. Traces can be described with a set of trace operators. () denote a empty trace, this is the situation where nothing happens on the channel. The trace (a, b, c) denote the situation where we have observed the c value followed by the b and a value on the channel. Note that the leftmost element in a trace is the most recent value. Note further that we only describe finite streams.

We use : to concatenate a value to a trace, and we use ˆ to append one trace to an other:

$$\begin{aligned}\text{Concatenation:}\quad & a{:}(a_1, a_2, \ldots) = (a, a_1, a_2, \ldots)\\ \text{Trace appending:}\quad & (a_1, \ldots, a_n)\hat{\ }(b_1, \ldots) = (a_1, \ldots, a_n, b_1, \ldots)\end{aligned}$$

Following the traditional Ruby approach all relations are binary and more complex relations are defined by grouping traces in tuples. We use the symbol $\langle\rangle$ for trace tuple construction. An example of a tuple of traces is $\langle(), \langle(a_1, a_2), (b), (c)\rangle\rangle$, the tuple contain an empty trace and a tuple with three traces as elements.

2.1 The Ruby Base

When using streams to describe wire values the basic definitions of the Ruby combinators are slightly different:

$$()\text{spread}(r)() \triangleq \textbf{true} \tag{1}$$

$$a_h{:}a_t \ \text{spread}(\mathbf{r})\ b_h{:}b_t \triangleq a_h\ \mathbf{r}\ b_h \ \wedge\ a_t\ \text{spread}(\mathbf{r})\ b_t \tag{2}$$

$$()\mathcal{D}_{st}(st) \triangleq \textbf{true} \tag{3}$$

$$a_h{:}a_t\ \mathcal{D}_{st}\ b_h{:}b_t \triangleq a_h = b_h \ \wedge\ a_t\ \mathcal{D}_{st}\ b_t \tag{4}$$

$$a\ F;G\ b \triangleq \exists c \cdot a\ F\ c \ \wedge\ c\ G\ b \tag{5}$$

$$\langle a_1, a_2\rangle[F, G]\langle b_1, b_2\rangle \triangleq a_1 F\, b_1 \ \wedge\ a_2 G\, b_2 \tag{6}$$

The definition above (and the following) should be read as the *smallest* relation satisfying the definition. Note that the delay element now has a starting value. This gives rise to certain problems concerning retiming, but we will not investigate it further here. Ruby delay with initial value was introduced in [3].

In [7] most of the Ruby language was defined as an extension to the above 4 primitives. The same extension is still valid with this new model for the primitives and in the following we will use many of the operators and relations from this extension. Some of the simple wire primitives are:

$$
\begin{aligned}
\langle\rangle \ \mathsf{NIL} \ \langle\rangle &\triangleq \mathbf{true}\\
a \ \mathsf{ID} \ a &\triangleq \mathbf{true}\\
\langle a,b\rangle \ \pi_1 \ a &\triangleq \mathbf{true}\\
\langle a,b\rangle \ \pi_2 \ b &\triangleq \mathbf{true}\\
a \ \mathsf{Dub} \ \langle a,a\rangle &\triangleq \mathbf{true}\\
\langle a,b\rangle \ \mathsf{Cross} \ \langle b,a\rangle &\triangleq \mathbf{true}\\
\langle a,b\rangle \ \mathsf{apr} \ a\hat{}\langle b\rangle &\triangleq \mathbf{true}\\
\langle\langle a,b\rangle,c\rangle \ \mathsf{reorg} \ \langle a,\langle b,c\rangle\rangle &\triangleq \mathbf{true}
\end{aligned}
$$

As we will be dealing with numbers we need some primitive number functions.

$$
\begin{aligned}
\mathbf{0} &= \mathsf{spread}(\lambda ab \cdot a = b = 0)\\
\mathsf{S} &= \mathsf{spread}(\lambda ab \cdot b = a + 1)
\end{aligned}
$$

The parallel and serial primitives and the identity can be used to construct new combining forms:

$$
\begin{aligned}
\mathsf{Fst}(F) &\triangleq [F, \mathsf{ID}]\\
\mathsf{Snd}(F) &\triangleq [\mathsf{ID}, F]\\
B \setminus A &\triangleq A^{-1};B;A
\end{aligned}
$$

We can also work with 4 sided circuits, in that case we require that the domain and range of the relation are pairs. Some of the forms we will be using are:

$$
\begin{aligned}
\langle a,\langle b,c\rangle\rangle \ F \leftrightarrow G \ \langle\langle e,f\rangle,g\rangle &\triangleq \exists h \cdot \ \langle a,b\rangle F\langle e,h\rangle \ \wedge \ \langle h,c\rangle G\langle f,g\rangle\\
F \updownarrow G &\triangleq (G^{-1} \leftrightarrow F^{-1})^{-1}\\
A \rightarrow F &\triangleq \mathsf{Fst}(A);F\\
A \downarrow F &\triangleq \mathsf{Snd}(A);F\\
F \leftarrow A &\triangleq F;\mathsf{Snd}(A)\\
F \uparrow A &\triangleq F;\mathsf{Fst}(A)
\end{aligned}
$$

A graphical interpretation of these forms can be seen in figure 1. All these forms are used in gluing circuits together. $\mathsf{row}_n^i(F_i)$ is used to make a row of n F_i's, the leftmost beeing F_1 and the rightmost beeing F_n. loop_4 is used to make a loop around a 4 sided circuit.

$$\begin{aligned}\langle a,b\rangle\ \mathsf{loop}_4 F\ \langle c,d\rangle &\triangleq \exists e\cdot\ \langle\langle a,e\rangle,b\rangle F\langle c,\langle d,e\rangle\rangle\\ \mathsf{row}_0(F) &\triangleq [\mathsf{ID},\mathsf{NIL}];\mathsf{Cross}\\ \mathsf{row}_{n+1}^i(F_i) &\triangleq (\mathsf{row}_n^i(F_i)\leftrightarrow F_{n+1})\setminus \mathsf{apr}\end{aligned}$$

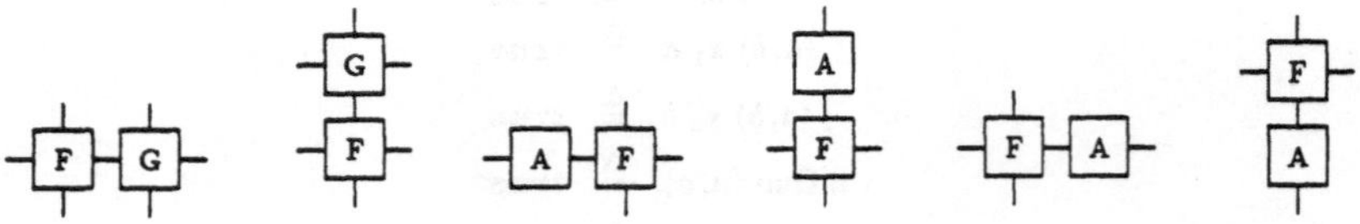

Figure 1: Graphical interpretations of $F\leftrightarrow G$, $F\updownarrow G$, $A\rightarrow F$, $A\downarrow F$, $F\leftarrow A$ and $F\uparrow A$

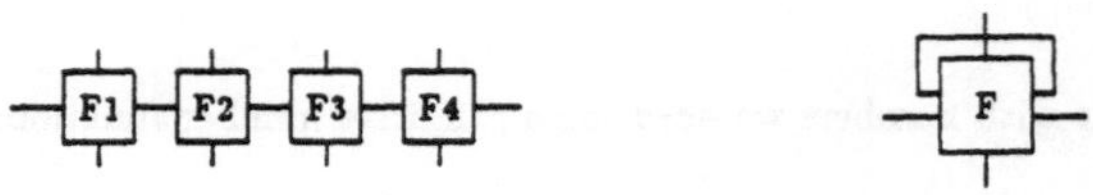

Figure 2: Graphical interpretations of $\mathsf{row}_4^i(F_i)$ and $\mathsf{loop}_4(F)$

2.2 Trace Related Relations

In the Ruby literature different primitives have been invented for reasoning with a differentiated time basis (**bundle** in [9] and **pair** in [5]). When using traces a multiplexor seems to be a natural choice. The multiplexor should not be confused with the traditional Ruby multiplexor that discards values that are not selected. The Multiplexor consumes a value from the selected trace and leaves the other untouched:

$$\langle\langle\langle\rangle,\langle\rangle\rangle,\langle\rangle\rangle\mathbf{M}\langle\langle\rangle,\langle\rangle\rangle \triangleq \mathbf{true} \tag{7}$$

$$\langle\langle a_h\!:\!a_t,b\rangle,0\!:\!ns\rangle\mathbf{M}\,\langle a_h\!:\!c,0\!:\!ns\rangle \triangleq \langle\langle a_t,b\rangle,ns\rangle\mathbf{M}\,\langle c,ns\rangle \tag{8}$$

$$\langle\langle a,b_h\!:\!b_t\rangle,n{+}1\!:\!ns\rangle\mathbf{M}\,\langle b_h\!:\!c,n{+}1\!:\!ns\rangle \triangleq \langle\langle a,b_t\rangle,ns\rangle\mathbf{M}\,\langle c,ns\rangle \tag{9}$$

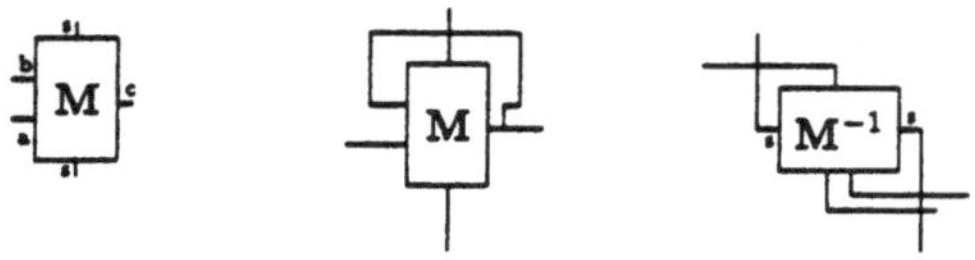

Figure 3: The multiplexor and the two latch circuits

Where the multiplexor is used to combine two traces, the **tap** is used to split a trace in two, the one being a copy, the other a subset. This can be define in terms of the multiplexor.

$$\mathbf{tap} \;\triangleq\; \mathsf{Dub};\mathsf{Snd}(\pi_1{}^{-1};\mathbf{M};\pi_2;\pi_2) \tag{10}$$

Examples of traces **M** and **tap** relates:

$$\begin{array}{rcl}
\langle\langle(1,3,4),(2,5)\rangle,(0,1,0,0,1)\rangle & \mathbf{M} & \langle(0,1,0,0,1),(1,2,3,4,5)\rangle \\
\langle\langle(3,1,3,4),(2)\rangle,(0,0,1,0,0)\rangle & \mathbf{M} & \langle(0,0,1,0,0),(3,1,2,3,4)\rangle \\
(1,12,12,3,4,12) & \mathbf{tap} & \langle(1,12,3,4,12),(1,12,4)\rangle \\
(1,12,12,3,4,12) & \mathbf{tap} & \langle(1,12,3,4,12),(1,4)\rangle
\end{array}$$

The **M** and **tap** give rise to a new set of derived relations. We need a couple to investigate primitive recursion. A useful circuit element is the latch. The latch exists in two different forms. One makes copies of the input stream and can be described as a simple multiplexor loop:

$$\mathbf{L}_1 \;\triangleq\; \mathsf{loop}_4(\mathbf{M} \leftarrow \mathbf{tap}) \tag{11}$$

The other latch is close to being the opposite; it takes a stream of values and only passes through selected elements. This can be described as a different multiplexor loop:

$$\mathbf{L}_2 \;\triangleq\; (\mathbf{M}^{-1} \setminus \mathsf{Cross}) \leftarrow \pi_2 \tag{12}$$

Here are examples of traces they accept:

$$\begin{array}{rcl}
\langle(1,3,4),(0,1,1,0,0,1)\rangle & \mathbf{L}_1 & \langle(0,1,1,0,0,1),(1,1,1,3,4,4)\rangle \\
\langle(1,12,12,3,4,12),(0,1,1,0,0,1)\rangle & \mathbf{L}_2 & \langle(0,1,1,0,0,1),(1,3,4)\rangle
\end{array}$$

A sequence element produces a sequence of numbers for each consumed number. $\lhd$**seq** produce the sequence $0 \ldots n$ for each n, $\rhd$**seq** produce the sequence $n \ldots 0$.

$$\begin{array}{rcl}
()\lhd\mathbf{seq}() & = & \mathbf{true} \\
n_h{:}n_t \lhd\mathbf{seq}(0,\ldots,n_h)\hat{\ }c & = & n_t \lhd\mathbf{seq}\, c \\
()\rhd\mathbf{seq}() & = & \mathbf{true} \\
n_h{:}n_t \rhd\mathbf{seq}(n_h,\ldots,0)\hat{\ }c & = & n_t \rhd\mathbf{seq}\, c
\end{array}$$

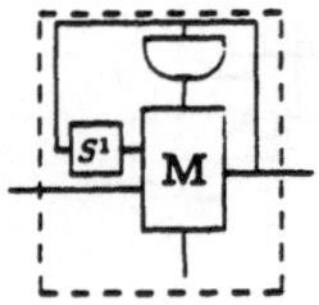

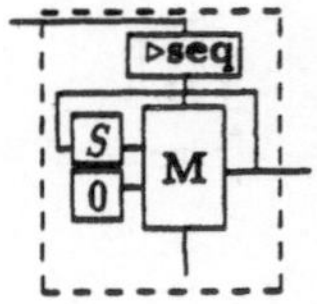

Figure 4: Down– and Up–sequence circuits

This can be defined in terms of M, tap and $\mathcal{D}$:

$$\triangleright\text{seq} \triangleq \text{loop}_2(\text{Snd}(\text{Dub};[\text{S}^{-1}, \mathcal{D}_0]);\text{reorg};\text{M} \leftarrow \text{tap};\pi_2) \quad (13)$$

$$\triangleleft\text{seq} \triangleq \triangleright\text{seq};{\pi_2}^{-1};\text{loop}_4([0, \text{S}] \rightarrow \text{M} \leftarrow \text{tap});\pi_2 \quad (14)$$

3 Primitive Recursion

Our starting point is the definition of primitive recursive functions ($\mathcal{PRF}$). According to [1] (and with a slight change in notation) numerical $\mathcal{PRF}$'s are the functions that can be constructed from the following rules:

1. $0 \in \mathcal{PRF}$
2. $\lambda x \cdot x{+}1 \in \mathcal{PRF}$
3. $(\lambda n_1, \ldots, n_k \cdot n_i) \in \mathcal{PRF}$ if $k \geq 1$ and $1 \leq i \leq k$
4. $(\lambda n_1, \ldots, n_k \cdot h(g_1(n_1, \ldots, n_k), \ldots, g_m(n_1, \ldots, n_k))) \in \mathcal{PRF}$ if $h, g_1, \ldots, g_m \in \mathcal{PRF}$
5. $f \in \mathcal{PRF}$ if $h, g \in \mathcal{PRF}$ and
   $f(m_1, \ldots, m_k, 0) = g(m_1, \ldots, m_k)$
   $f(m_1, \ldots, m_k, n+1) = h(f(m_1, \ldots, m_k, n), m_1, \ldots, m_k, n)$

For instance by allowing the range of functions to be pairs of numbers and by taking additions as a primitive we can define the Fibonacci function as:

$$\begin{aligned} fib(n) &= \text{fst}(f(n)) \\ f(0) &= \text{Pair}(1,1) \\ f(n+1) &= h(f(n), n) \\ h(\text{Pair}(a,b), n) &= \text{Pair}(b, a+b) \end{aligned}$$

For an explanation of how pairs can be encoded using primitive recursion see [2].

4 From Functions to Relations

We define a transformation (meta-)function $\mathcal{T}$ that takes a $\mathcal{PRF}$ and translates it into a Ruby relation. For the translation to be correct we want the resulting Ruby relation to be a relation between two traces such that at any instance of the trace the transformed $\mathcal{PRF}$ must be satisfied, this correspond to the spread() definition:

$$\forall ab \cdot \; a\mathcal{T}[f]b \;\Leftrightarrow\; a\,\mathsf{spread}(\lambda ab \cdot b = f(a))\,b$$

Transformation of an expression into Ruby proceeds as an recursive process on the length of the expression. The possible transformation steps follow the definition of primitive recursion.

- Base case.

  We assume that we have primitive combinational circuits corresponding to the relations **0** and **S**. If we have other primitive circuits (f) we can consider them base cases as well:

$$\mathcal{T}[0] = \mathbf{0} \tag{15}$$
$$\mathcal{T}[\lambda x \cdot x + 1] = \mathsf{S} \tag{16}$$
$$\mathcal{T}[f] = \mathsf{spread}(\lambda ab \cdot b = f(a)) \tag{17}$$

- Functional application:

$$f = h(g_1(n_1, \ldots, n_k), \ldots))$$
$$\mathcal{T}[f] = \pi_2{}^{-1};(\mathsf{row}_n^i(\pi_2;\mathsf{Dub};\mathsf{fst}\;\mathcal{T}[g_i]);\pi_2;\mathcal{T}[h] \tag{18}$$

- Recursive definitions are transformed into a circuit with a loop to enable recursion:

$$f(m_1, \ldots, m_k, 0) = g(m_1, \ldots, m_k)$$
$$f(m_1, \ldots, m_k, n+1) = h(f(m_1, \ldots, m_k, n), m_1, \ldots, m_k, n)$$

  have the transformation:

$$\mathcal{T}[f] = (\mathsf{Dub};[\,\triangleright\mathbf{seq};\mathsf{Dub};\mathsf{Snd}(\mathsf{Dub}),\ \triangleleft\mathbf{seq};\mathbf{Neg}])\downarrow ((\mathsf{Dub} \rightarrow (\mathsf{Cross} \updownarrow \mathbf{L}_1)) \leftrightarrow \mathsf{loop}_4(\mathsf{reorg} \rightarrow (\mathsf{reorg};[\mathcal{T}[g], \mathcal{T}[h]]);\pi_2{}^{-1} \leftrightarrow \mathbf{M} \leftarrow \mathbf{tap}) \leftrightarrow \mathbf{L}_2;\pi_2) \tag{19}$$

Figure 5 illustrates the two last transformations. The proof of correctness of this transformation is done inductively on the length of the transformed function f.

As we can see, the functional application has a rather complicated transformation. Fortunately most of the functional applications we use can be reduced to a simpler form. For example:

$$\mathcal{T}[\lambda x \cdot h(g_1(x))] = \mathcal{T}[g_1];\mathcal{T}[h] \tag{20}$$
$$\mathcal{T}[\lambda x \cdot h(g_1(x), g_2(x))] = \mathsf{Dub};[\mathcal{T}[g_1], \mathcal{T}[g_2]];\mathcal{T}[h] \tag{21}$$
$$\mathcal{T}[\lambda xy \cdot h(g_1(x), g_2(y))] = [\mathcal{T}[g_1], \mathcal{T}[g_2]];\mathcal{T}[h] \tag{22}$$

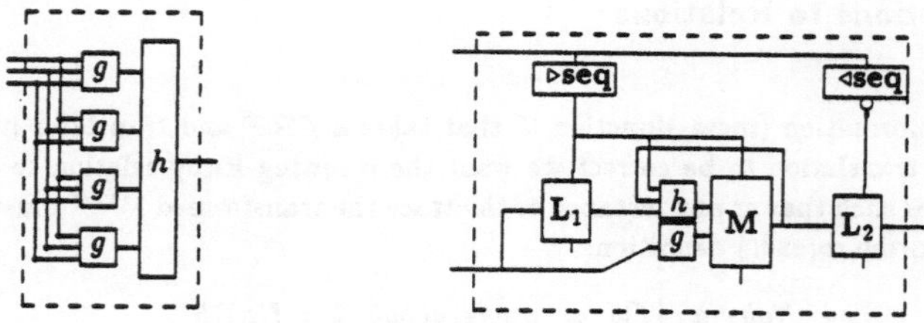

Figure 5: Ruby implementation of application and recursion

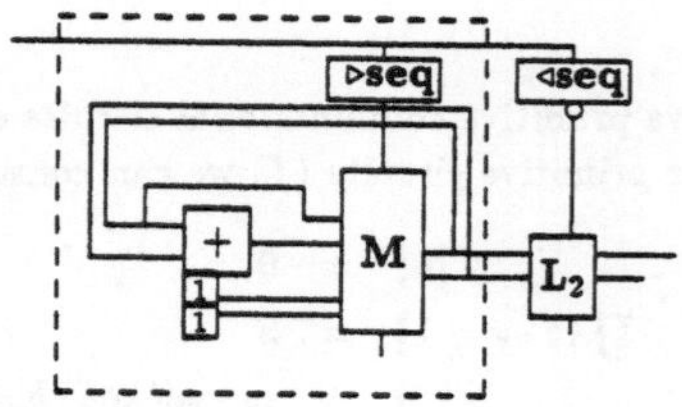

Figure 6: The implementation of the Fibonacci function

A proof of rule 20 is (rule 21 and 22 has similar proofs):

$$
\begin{aligned}
& \mathcal{T}[\lambda x \cdot h(g_1(x))] \\
= \; & \{\text{use rule 18}\} \\
& \pi_1{}^{-1};(\mathsf{row}_1^i(\pi_1;\mathsf{Dub};\mathsf{Fst}(\mathcal{T}[g_i])));\pi_1;\mathcal{T}[h] \\
= \; & \{\text{row def}\} \\
& \pi_1{}^{-1};(\pi_1;\mathsf{Dub};\mathsf{Fst}(\mathcal{T}[g_1]));\pi_1;\mathcal{T}[h] \\
= \; & \{\text{Removal of extra wires}\} \\
& \mathcal{T}[g_1];\mathcal{T}[h]
\end{aligned}
$$

We can reduce the definition for transforming recursion in the same way, if we have a simpler form of recursion. For example:

$$
\begin{aligned}
f(0) &= g \\
f(n+1) &= h(f(n))
\end{aligned}
$$

has the transformation:

$$
\mathcal{T}[f] \;=\; (\mathsf{Dub};[\,\triangleright\mathsf{seq},\ \triangleleft\mathsf{seq};\mathsf{Neg}]);(\mathsf{loop}_4([g,h] \rightarrow \mathbf{M} \leftarrow \mathbf{tap}) \leftrightarrow \mathbf{L}_2) \setminus \pi_2
$$

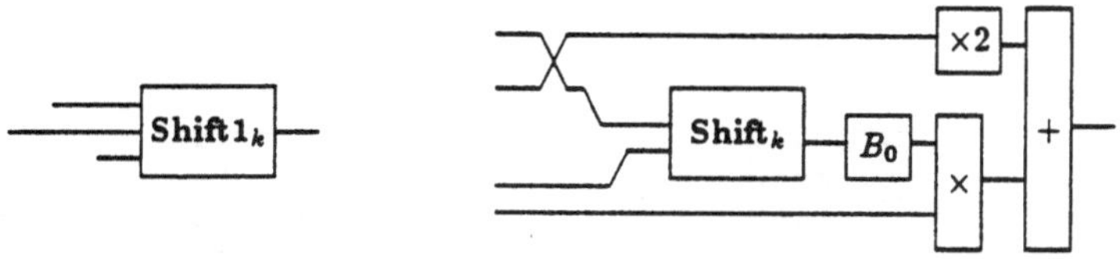

Figure 7: Drawings of the step function (h) and **Shift** circuits for the **BitMult**.

Let us return to the Fibonacci function. We define it in terms of an auxiliary function that returns a pair:

$$\begin{aligned} fib(n) &= \mathsf{fst}(f(n)) \\ f(0) &= g \text{ where } g = \{1,1\} \\ f(n+1) &= h(f(n)) \text{ where } h(\{a,b\}) = \{b, a+b\} \end{aligned}$$

If we use $\mathcal{T}$ to transform *fib* into Ruby we get:

$$\begin{aligned} \mathcal{T}[g] = G &= \mathsf{spread}(\lambda ab \cdot b = \{1,1\}) \\ \mathcal{T}[h] = H &= \mathsf{Dub};[\pi_2, +] \\ \mathcal{T}[f] = F &= (\mathsf{Dub};[\,\triangleright\mathbf{seq},\ \triangleleft\mathbf{seq};\mathbf{Neg}]);((\mathsf{loop}_4([G,H] \rightarrow \mathbf{M} \leftarrow \mathbf{tap}) \leftrightarrow \mathbf{L}_2) \setminus \pi_2);\pi_2 \end{aligned}$$

A drawing of this can be seen in figure 6.

5 An Example

To illustrate some aspects of optimising Ruby calculation we investigate a sequential multiplier. The sequential multiplier has the following definition:

$$\begin{aligned} \mathbf{BitMult}(x,y,0) &= 0 \\ \mathbf{BitMult}(x,y,n+1) &= 2 \times \mathbf{BitMult}(x,y,n) + \mathbf{Bit0}(\mathbf{Shift}_k(y,n)) \times x \end{aligned}$$

Here **Bit0** returns the parity bit of a number, and $\mathbf{Shift}_k$ returns a k bit number shifted n bits to the left (k assumed to be a constant of the circuit). We assume that we have a primitive circuit that can perform a select of the least significant bit (**Bit0**) and a circuit that can perform a shift left one bit ($\mathbf{Shift1}_k$). $\mathbf{Shift}_k$ then becomes:

$$\begin{aligned} \mathbf{Shift}_k(y,0) &= y \\ \mathbf{Shift}_k(y,n+1) &= \mathbf{Shift1}_k(\mathbf{Shift}_k(y,n)) \end{aligned}$$

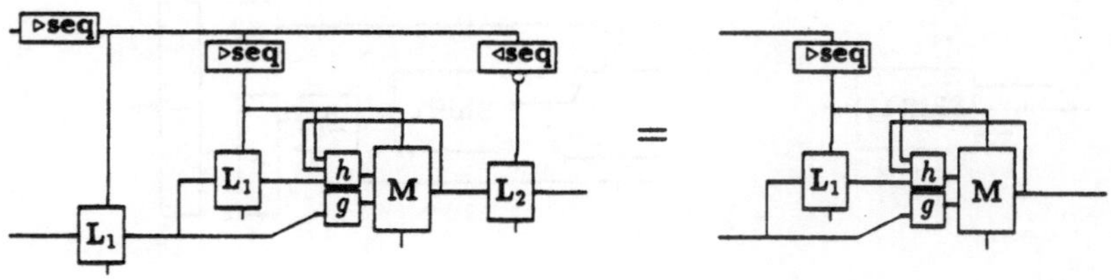

Figure 8: A complex reduction rule

Following the scheme from the previous section we get the following Ruby expressions for $\mathbf{Shift}_k$ and **BitMult**:

$$
\begin{aligned}
\mathbf{S}_g &= \mathsf{ID} \\
\mathbf{S}_h &= \pi_1;\pi_2;\mathbf{Shift1}_k \\
\mathcal{T}[\mathbf{Shift}_k] &= (\mathsf{Dub};[\,\triangleright\mathbf{seq};\mathsf{Dub};\mathsf{Snd}(\mathsf{Dub}),\ \triangleleft\mathbf{seq};\mathbf{Neg}])\downarrow \\
&\quad ((\mathsf{Dub} \rightarrow (\mathsf{Cross} \updownarrow \mathbf{L}_1)) \leftrightarrow \mathsf{loop}_4(\mathbf{reorg} \rightarrow (\mathbf{reorg};[\mathbf{S}_g,\mathbf{S}_h]);\pi_2{}^{-1} \leftrightarrow \mathbf{M} \leftarrow \mathbf{tap}) \\
&\quad \leftrightarrow \mathbf{L}_2;\pi_2) \\
\mathbf{B}_g &= \mathbf{Zero} \\
\mathbf{B}_h &= \mathsf{Snd}(\mathsf{Cross});\mathbf{reorg}^{-1};[\mathbf{reorg};\mathsf{Snd}(\mathbf{Shift}_k;\mathbf{Bit0});\times, 2\times];+ \\
\mathcal{T}[\mathbf{BitMult}] &= (\mathsf{Dub};[\,\triangleright\mathbf{seq};\mathsf{Dub};\mathsf{Snd}(\mathsf{Dub}),\ \triangleleft\mathbf{seq};\mathbf{Neg}])\downarrow \\
&\quad ((\mathsf{Dub} \rightarrow (\mathsf{Cross} \updownarrow \mathbf{L}_1)) \leftrightarrow \mathsf{loop}_4(\mathbf{reorg} \rightarrow (\mathbf{reorg};[\mathbf{B}_g,\mathbf{B}_h]);\pi_2{}^{-1} \leftrightarrow \mathbf{M} \leftarrow \mathbf{tap}) \\
&\quad \leftrightarrow \mathbf{L}_2;\pi_2)
\end{aligned}
$$

A drawing of S_h and B_h can be seen in figure 7. A thing to note when optimising this circuit is the way $\mathbf{Shift}_k$ is driven. First it produces y shifted 0 times, then 1, then 2 ... up to n. It is possible to let the circuit operate in a more natural way by avoiding producing the n–bit shift from the initial value. Instead we produce an n–bit shift as a single shift of the previous value. This can be captured in a rather complex ruby transformation (can be seen in figure 8):

$$
\begin{aligned}
&\mathsf{Snd}(\triangleright\mathbf{seq};\mathsf{Dub});\mathbf{L}_1;(\mathsf{Dub};[\,\triangleright\mathbf{seq};\mathsf{Dub};\mathsf{Snd}(\mathsf{Dub}),\ \triangleleft\mathbf{seq};\mathbf{Neg}])\downarrow \\
&\quad ((\mathsf{Dub} \rightarrow (\mathsf{Cross} \updownarrow \mathbf{L}_1)) \leftrightarrow \mathsf{loop}_4(\mathbf{reorg} \rightarrow (\mathbf{reorg};[g,g]);\pi_2{}^{-1} \leftrightarrow \mathbf{M} \leftarrow \mathbf{tap}) \leftrightarrow \mathbf{L}_2;\pi_2) \\
&= \triangleright\mathbf{seq};\mathsf{Dub};\mathsf{Snd}(\mathsf{Dub})\downarrow \\
&\quad (\mathsf{Dub} \rightarrow (\mathsf{Cross} \updownarrow \mathbf{L}_1)) \leftrightarrow \mathsf{loop}_4(\mathbf{reorg} \rightarrow (\mathbf{reorg};[g,g]);\pi_2{}^{-1} \leftrightarrow \mathbf{M} \leftarrow \mathbf{tap})
\end{aligned}
$$

Using this transformation produces the Ruby circuit presented in figure 9. This circuit correspond to a traditional implementation of a multiplier, where the two multiplexors (and the corresponding loops) implement the two multiplication registers.

6 Conclusion

We have presented a method for transforming (primitive) recursive function into a Ruby description. To facilitate reasoning with recursive functions a trace based semantics for Ruby forms was

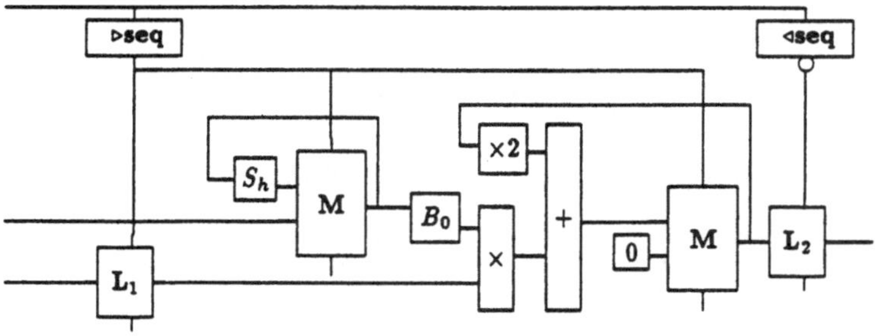

Figure 9: The optimised sequential multiplier

developed. This view led us to introduce a new Ruby primitive M, a multiplexor. With the aid of this multiplexor we could express the temporal conditions surrounding recursive functions and their implementation as hardware loops.

The general idea here is to have every recursive function as a simple loop surrounded with a temporal abstraction mechanism. This mechanism hides the actual loop (and use of time). We investigated how it was possible to manipulate this abstraction in the traditional Ruby way by calculating with equivalences.

6.1 Future work

A lot of work lies ahead of us in investigating this extension of the Ruby method. If would be natural to investigate how this variant of Ruby can be used together with the theory of asynchronous circuits. This is partly being investigated in [8].

We also intend to investigate other temporal abstractions and theorems for calculating with these abstractions.

7 Acknowledgement

I am grateful to Robin Sharp for the many inspiring discussions that preceded this paper. I also wish to thank Jørgen Steensgaard-Madsen for providing me with good references to primitive recursion theory. Finally I would like to thank the Danish Technical Research Council for the economic sponsorship I have received through the research program RapID.

BIBLIOGRAPHY

[1] Peter B. Andrews. *An introduction to mathematical logic and type theory.* Academic Press, Inc., 1986.

[2] Martin Davis. *Computability and Unsolvability.* Dover Publications, Inc. New York, 1982.

[3] Graham Hutton. Functional programming with relations. In Simon L. Peyton Jones et al., editors, *Functional Programming, Glasgow 1990.* Springer-Verlag Workshop in Computing, 1991.

[4] G. Jones and M. Sheeran. Relations and refinement in circuit design. In Morgan, editor, *Proc. BCS FACS Workshop on Refinement.* Springer-Verlag Workshop in Computing, 1990.

[5] Geraint Jones and Mary Sheeran. Circuit design in ruby. In J. Staunstrup, editor, *Formal Methods for VLSI Design.* Elsevier, 1990.

[6] Lars Rossen. Proving (facts about) ruby. In G. Birtwistle, editor, *The IVh Higher Order Workshop.* To appear in Springer Verlag, 1990.

[7] Lars Rossen. Ruby algebra. In G. Jones and M. Sheeran, editors, *Designing Correct Circuits, Oxford 1990.* Springer-Verlag Workshop in Computing, 1991.

[8] Lars Rossen and Robin I. Sharp. Sequence semantic of ruby. To appear at DCC 1992, Lyngby, 1991.

[9] Mary Sheeran. Retiming and slowdown in ruby. In G. Milner, editor, *The Fusion of Hardware Design and Verification.* North Holland, 1986.

Functional Compilation from the Standard ML Core Language to Lambda Calculus

Nick Rothwell

December 17, 1991

1 Introduction

This paper describes a compiler from the Standard ML core language to a simple intermediate code based on the lambda calculus. It forms an optional part of the SML Kit, an "open" interpreter written in SML which implements the complete SML language faithfully according to the Definition[4], and with an internal modular structure reflecting the structure of the Definition. The interface presented by the compiler to the rest of the Kit is identical to that presented by the Kit's "pure" interpreter. The lambda compiler is not intended to be an example of how to generate highly efficient code for SML; instead, it serves to illustrate in a clear, modular fashion some of the techniques which are needed to compile core SML into a simple intermediate language. It also shows that a code generating "subsystem" can be added to a pure interpreter so that no details of the compiler or the code generation (or even whether there *is* a compiler) are visible to the rest of the system.

It should be stated that some of the main ideas in the compiler (such as the adoption of an intermediate lambda language with unique variables, and the use of higher-order functions to compile declarations) were first seen in Standard ML of New Jersey [2], and the reader is referred to [1] for a more extensive coverage of SML code generation, together with some of the techniques employed in the Kit. Suffice to say that the Kit's compiler section is a lot simpler in overall structure and function, but operates in a similar way to the back-end and runtime system of SML/NJ.

2 Structural Overview

The SML Kit's evaluation stage revolves around the concept of *dynamic basis* presented in the Definition. The evaluator takes a dynamic basis representing the current top-level environment, and a top-level declaration, and attempts to evaluate it. The evaluation is either successful, yielding the dynamic basis corresponding to the declaration, or else it fails due to an exception propagating to the top level. The `EVALTOPDEC` signature is given in figure 1[1].

---

[1] The code examples have been beautified slightly: "*" (for type tuples) is written "×", "->" (for the function type) is "→", and type variables are written "α", "β" and so on (or "$\alpha_=$", "$\beta_=$" if they have the equality attribute).

The interpreter and the compiler each form a subsystem which conforms to this interface. The underlying implementation of the dynamic basis is different in each case, although both implementations provide the operations of the dynamic semantics (`E_in_B`, `E_of_B`, `B_plus_B`). The rest of the SML Kit accesses the evaluation modules through the interfaces provided by the signatures `EVALTOPDEC` and `DYNAMIC_BASIS` (figure 2), and has no knowledge of any of their internals.

The compiler contains a number of modules associated with analysing, compiling and executing declarations. These are brought together in a single linkage module which evaluates top-level declarations. This top-level module of the compiler translates (core-level) declarations to lambda code which is fed through a simple optimiser and then executed. If successful, the execution results in a new set of dynamic bindings to add to the top-level environment. As far as the rest of the Kit is concerned, the interface is just an evaluator for declarations; the compiler is totally hidden.

3 Variables and Environments

Where the dynamic semantics retains the notion of a *variable* in the source language, and builds environments as mappings from these variables, we introduce a new type of identifier, the *lvar*, which is known only to the compiler and lambda interpreter. Lvars are represented numerically and are generated uniquely during compilation. Therefore, even though the same variable can be bound in several places in the source text, with different meanings, an lvar is bound exactly once. This property simplifies much of the compiler since a lot of environment analysis is no longer necessary; many operations on the intermediate code can be performed with respect to an lvar without worrying about the same lvar being rebound in a nested scope[2].

Corresponding to the various environments of the dynamic semantics, the compiler has two sorts, whose interfaces are shown in figures 3 and 4. The *dynamic environment*, or DEnv, maps lvars to runtime objects. The *compiler environment*, or CEnv, maps SML variables to lvars (with a special mechanism for making available the pervasive functions, such as the arithmetic operators). CEnvs are used during compilation to deal with SML identifiers occurring in the source text being compiled; DEnvs are used during execution to deal with the evaluation of lvars.

When a declaration is compiled, each variable bound by the declaration is associated with a new, unique, lvar. This mapping of SML variables to lvars constitutes the CEnv for the declaration. The code is then executed to yield a set of objects, one for each variable. These objects are bound to the lvars to form the DEnv for this declaration. Finally, the CEnv and DEnv are incorporated into the top-level environment. In subsequent declarations, the compiler will translate occurrences of the newly-bound SML variables into their corresponding lvars via the CEnv; during execution, the lvars will be mapped to their runtime values by the DEnv.

Recall from section 2 that the compiler must match the signature `EVALTOPDEC` in order to link with the rest of the system. This it does by implementing the type `DynamicBasis` as a pair (`CEnv` × `DEnv`). This allows SML identifiers to be mapped to

[2] and some cannot; beta-reduction of functions, for example, requires variable renaming.

```
signature EVALTOPDEC =
  sig
    type DynamicBasis
    type topdec

    datatype result = SUCCESS of DynamicBasis
                    | FAILURE of string

    val eval: DynamicBasis × topdec → result
  end
```

Figure 1: The signature EVALTOPDEC

```
signature DYNAMIC_BASIS =
  sig
    type DynamicBasis
    type Env                    (* (StrEnv × VarEnv × ExConEnv) *)

    val E_in_B: Env → DynamicBasis
    val E_of_B: DynamicBasis → Env
    val B_plus_B: DynamicBasis × DynamicBasis → DynamicBasis
    val emptyDynamicBasis: DynamicBasis
    val initialDynamicBasis: DynamicBasis
  end
```

Figure 2: The signature DYNAMIC_BASIS

runtime objects by looking them up in the CEnv and then looking up the resulting lvars in the DEnv.

4 Runtime Data Objects and Representations

The Definition has a large selection of dynamic, or "runtime", data objects, including constructors, records, exception packets, and various kinds of environment. These semantic objects are defined abstractly at a fairly high-level, and some (records and environments) are defined using other high-level constructs (finite maps). The compiler has a small number of simple data objects and a single notion of environment, in which the semantic objects are implemented. This scheme requires the compiler to make choices of representation; some of the choices require information from the typechecker.

The compiler's OBJECTS signature is shown in figure 5. This is essentially an interface to a (hidden) datatype, but there are advantages to making the interface

```
signature DYNAMIC_ENV =
  sig
    type DEnv
    type lvar
    type object

    val emptyDEnv: DEnv
    val declare: (lvar × object × DEnv) → DEnv
    val plus: DEnv × DEnv → DEnv
    val REC: DEnv → DEnv        (* Semantics V4, p48 *)
    val lookup: DEnv → lvar → object
  end
```

Figure 3: The signature DYNAMIC_ENV

functional—in particular, closures are built in a clean way. The types **lvar** and **DEnv**, as described above, are needed for building closures, as is the type **LambdaExp** of lambda expressions (section 5).

The simplest runtime objects correspond to the *special values* of the Definition: integers, reals and strings. In addition, there is a *void* object used in the representation of **unit** and of nullary exception and data constructors (section 6). **vector** and **select** allow vectors (non-assignable arrays) of objects to be built and decomposed. **Ref** and **deRef** build and decompose references. **equal** provides equality on objects; it respects the identity of references, and is undefined on closures.

The representation of closures corresponds very closely to that in the Definition, but has an extra component. **bodyEnv** and **recEnv** correspond to the elements E and VE in the closures of the semantics. In place of the *match*, we have an lvar and a lambda expression. Where the Definition applies the match to an argument, we instead evaluate the lambda code in an environment which binds the lvar to the argument. The dynamic environment signature (figure 3) provides the *Rec* operation described in the Definition.

5 The Lambda Language

We now describe the lambda language generated by the compiler. The signature specifying the lambda language datatype is shown in figure 6. The language is at a level usually associated with compiler intermediate codes, but the Kit interprets it directly rather than compiling it down into lower-level code. The lambda language is essentially lambda calculus with one or two simple extensions. It contains constants of the base types associated with SML's special values, and also *switches* (simple case expressions) over them. There are operations on vectors, and an exception mechanism. We consider the lambda language to be *untyped*, in that there is no provision for defining or expressing types in the language. The integers, strings and reals of the lambda language can be considered to have SML types **int**, **string** and **real** respectively, but there is no notion of type abstraction, datatype and so on.

```
signature COMPILER_ENV =
  sig
    type CEnv
    type var                          (* Unqualified variables *)
    type longvar                      (* Qualified vars (for lookup) *)
    type excon                        (* Unqualified exception constructors *)
    type longexcon                    (* Qualified excons (for lookup) *)
    type lvar                         (* Unique lambda identifiers *)

    val emptyCEnv: CEnv
    val initialCEnv: CEnv

    val declareVar: (var × lvar × CEnv) → CEnv
    val declareExcon: (excon × lvar × CEnv) → CEnv

    val plus: CEnv × CEnv → CEnv

    datatype result = LVAR of lvar
                    | PRIM

    val lookupLongvar: CEnv → longvar → result

    val lookupLongexcon: CEnv → longexcon → lvar

    val lvarsOfCEnv: CEnv → lvar list
  end
```

Figure 4: The signature COMPILER_ENV

```
signature OBJECTS =
  sig
    type lvar
    type LambdaExp                (* For building closures.   *)
    type DEnv                     (* lvar→object environment.  *)
    type object

    val void: object

    val integer: int → object
    val deInteger: object → int

    val real: real → object
    val deReal: object → real

    val string: string → object
    val deString: object → string

    val closure: {arg: lvar, body: LambdaExp, bodyEnv: DEnv} → object
                                  (* The recEnv part is created empty.  *)

    val deClosure:
      object → {arg: lvar, body: LambdaExp, bodyEnv: DEnv, recEnv: DEnv}

    val vector: object list → object
    val select: int × object → object

    val Ref: object → object
    val deRef: object → object

    val equal: object × object → bool
  end
```

Figure 5: The signature OBJECTS

The variables of the language are the lvars introduced in section 3. Lvars are bound in function (**FN**) expressions and recursive declarations (**FIX**) and referenced by **VAR** leaf nodes. The Definition's *special constants* map to lambda-expressions of the sort **INTEGER**, **STRING** or **REAL**, which have corresponding sorts of object (section 4). Similarly, there is a **VOID** lambda constructor which yields a `void` object. (The name **VOID** is used rather than **UNIT** since there are many circumstances in which a **VOID** lambda term might be used, and the word **UNIT** might misleadingly suggest some relation to SML's `unit` data object.)

Function (`fn`) expressions in SML are compiled into **FN** expressions in the lambda language. These only take a single lvar as argument, so a fair amount of work is involved in transforming SML function expressions containing matches into lambda functions; most of the work is done by a match compiler (to be described in a forthcoming technical report).

Mutually recursive function definitions compile into **FIX** expressions which bind a set of lvars in parallel. The right hand sides of the bindings are expected to be function (**FN**) expressions. The **APP** constructor represents application of one lambda-expression to another in the obvious way. **PRIM_APP** is used for pervasive functions (the *basic values* of the Definition) in a manner not described in this paper.

Corresponding to the many data objects of the Definition (records, data constructors, exception constructors, references), the lambda language has two data manipulating constructors. **VECTOR** takes a list of lambda expressions and returns a fixed-length list of objects from which elements can be extracted using the **SELECT** constructor. **REF** is a constructor for creating a reference to an object using a new address, as in the Definition.

The lambda language has conditional expressions over the three basic types (integers, strings, reals); comparison of reals is assumed to make sense because it is required by the Definition. There are three "branch" operations (**SWITCH_I**, **SWITCH_S** and **SWITCH_R**), one for each corresponding object type, although the switches have identical structure (and in fact the switch datatype is polymorphic). Finally, the lambda language provides for exception raising and handling. **RAISE**(e) raises the exception packet denoted by e (and whose format is described in section 6). **HANDLE**(e_1, e_2) evaluates e_1; if an exception is propagated, e_2 is evaluated to yield a **FN** expression, and the result of the **HANDLE** expression is e_2 applied to the exception packet. Any exception resulting from this application is propagated outward.

6 The Declaration Compiler

6.1 Conventions and Representations

The declaration compiler is central to the Kit's compiler subsystem, since the interface presented to the rest of the Kit is of an interpreter which executes declarations.

The declaration compiler has two purposes:

- to translate declarations in the SML core language into expressions in the lambda language;
- to generate a compiler environment (CEnv) for the variables bound in each declaration.

```
signature LAMBDA_EXP =
  sig
    type lvar
    type (α₌, β) map

    datatype α option = NONE | SOME of α

    datatype LambdaExp =
        VAR of lvar                (* Lambda variables *)
      | INTEGER of int             (* Constants... *)
      | STRING of string
      | REAL of real
      | FN of lvar × LambdaExp (* Function-terms *)
      | FIX of lvar list × LambdaExp list × LambdaExp
                                   (* Mutually recursive fns *)
      | APP of LambdaExp × LambdaExp (* Function application *)
      | PRIM_APP of int × LambdaExp (* Primitive function application *)
      | VECTOR of LambdaExp list (* Records/tuples *)
      | SELECT of int × LambdaExp (* Con/record indexing *)
      | SWITCH_I of int Switch (* Switch on integers *)
      | SWITCH_S of string Switch (* Switch on strings *)
      | SWITCH_R of real Switch (* Switch on reals *)
      | RAISE of LambdaExp         (* Raise exception *)
      | HANDLE of LambdaExp × LambdaExp (* Exception handling *)
      | REF of LambdaExp           (* ref(expr) *)
      | VOID                       (* nil, () etc *)

    and α Switch = SWITCH of {arg: LambdaExp,
                              selections: (α, LambdaExp) map,
                              wildcard: LambdaExp option
                              (* Wildcard mandatory for *)
                              (* REAL or STRING switches *)
                             }

      (* Some convenient lambda-building utilities: *)
    val pair: LambdaExp × LambdaExp → LambdaExp
    val first: LambdaExp → LambdaExp
    val second: LambdaExp → LambdaExp
    val Let: ((lvar × LambdaExp) × LambdaExp) → LambdaExp
  end
```

Figure 6: The signature LAMBDA_EXP

However, since (SML) declarations yield environments and (lambda) expressions yield values, there is no obvious translation from declarations to lambda expressions. The following, rather elegant, convention is due to Andrew Appel [2].

The compiler is a function **compileDec** with type

```
CEnv → dec → (CEnv × (LambdaExp → LambdaExp))
```

Every SML declaration is treated as if it had a *scope*. For top-level declarations, the scope does not actually exist, although each such declaration *dec* is treated as if it occurred as part of an expression of the form

let *dec* **in** *scope* **end**

The result of compiling a declaration is a CEnv for the declaration, plus a function which, when applied to a compiled *scope* for the declaration, returns a lambda expression corresponding to the declaration compiled locally for that scope. (The knot is tied in the top-level interface, as described in section 7.)

There are two reasons for this particular convention. The first is abstraction—an alternative approach would have been to have the compiler translate declarations directly into lambda expressions with some convention for the scope of the declaration (such as a vector of lvars corresponding to the identifiers ordered lexically), but it is more elegant to choose the convention elsewhere, separately from the compiler itself. The second reason for the higher-order nature of **compileDec** is that it makes sequential and local declarations easy to deal with: the functions resulting from compilation of the sub-phrases can just be composed together (as shown in subsection 6.2).

This convention carries down into the internals of the compiler. Functions which compile expression-like phrases (expressions, atomic expressions and so on) return a **LambdaExp**. Functions which compile declaration-like phrases (declarations, value bindings, and so on) return a function of type **LambdaExp → LambdaExp**.

The compiler has a simple set of runtime data structures, onto which it must map the runtime data structures (the dynamic semantic objects) of the Definition. Records become vectors whose elements are ordered lexically according to label. Constructed datatypes become pairs of integer tag and value. Exception values and packets are represented as pairs of data value and a reference denoting the exception name. Value-carrying data and exception constructors compile into closures.

Atomic expressions are compiled as follows. Special constants (integers, reals and strings) have direct counterparts in the lambda language, and are trivially compiled into these without reference to the CEnv. Identifiers are more complicated, since by this stage they have been resolved by the elaborator into one of three classes: variable, data constructor or exception constructor. Variables (other than the pervasives) are looked up in the CEnv yielding lvars. Nullary data constructors compile into pairs whose first element is **VOID** and second is an integer tag denoting the constructor. Unary (value-carrying) constructors compile into closures which perform the pairing operation.

Exception constructors are treated similarly to data constructors, but the Definition requires than exceptions be generated dynamically during execution. If an exception declaration serves to introduce a new exception (as opposed to a new identifier binding for an existing exception), then each execution of that declaration creates a new, distinct, exception. (By contrast, datatype declarations compile to no code.) Exceptions may be nullary or they may carry values, in the same way as constructors. And, exceptions may be pattern-matched, in which case they must be matched sequentially according to their dynamic identity, rather than by identifier or their occurrence in the source text. By contrast, data constructors are not generative, and may not be directly renamed; hence, constructors in patterns may be distinguished merely by their source identifiers.

To implement exceptions faithfully, each declaration of a new exception binds an lvar to a new *string reference*, regardless of whether the exception carries a value. The string holds the exception's textual name for the purposes of printing. This representation is most convenient for pattern matching, since exception matching then becomes a matter of determining identity of references. When an exception identifier is encountered in an expression, it must be converted into a form consistent with a value of type `exn` or $\alpha \rightarrow$ `exn`. For nullary exceptions, the lambda code pairs the string reference with `VOID`. For unary exceptions, the code builds a closure.

SML expressions are compiled in the context of a CEnv, yielding a lambda expression. Function application is simple to compile, because the type of the functional part is not discriminated at application time; instead, the compiler ensures that it will always be a closure. Function (`fn`) expressions are dealt with by the match compiler. `raise` expressions are compiled into `RAISE` lambda terms and `handle` expressions are compiled into `HANDLE` lambda terms, which are implemented in the lambda interpreter with exceptions. In the case of `HANDLE`, the lambda term contains a function `FN` sub-term built by the match compiler.

6.2 Compiling Declarations

We shall dismiss the simple cases first. Type declarations play almost no part in SML's dynamic semantics, and so the compiler can ignore their effect[3]. Therefore, `compileDec` compiles each `type` and `datatype` declaration into an empty CEnv together with the identity function. Empty declarations and infix declarations[4] are treated similarly. For phrases of the form

abstype *datbind* **with** *dec* **end**

the *datbind* is discarded. `local` and sequential declarations are similar to each other; they differ only in the CEnv produced as a result. In both cases, the first declaration is compiled yielding a CEnv ce_1 and result function f_1. The second declaration is compiled in an environment augmented with ce_1, yielding ce_2 and f_2. The resulting CEnv is $ce_1 + ce_2$ (for sequential declarations) or ce_2 (for `local` declarations); in each case, the result function (of type `LambdaExp` $\rightarrow$ `LambdaExp`) is $f_1 o f_2$.

Recursive function declarations are straightforward; SML disallows any other kind of object to be declared recursively, and even places syntactic restrictions on the

---

[3] We say *almost* no part because there is an obscure situation, highlighted in the SML Commentary [3], which requires **datatype** declarations to have an effect at evaluation time. However, this situation occurs in connection with the modules system which the Kit currently does not implement.

[4] Infix declarations find their way into the abstract syntax, although they are omitted from the semantic rules of the Definition.

functions (recursive declarations may not, for instance, bind variables to expressions which just happen to have functional type).

Within a `rec` declaration (of which `fun` is just a syntactic derived form), there may only be function bindings and further, nested, occurrences of `rec` (which serve no purpose). The entire topmost `rec` declaration is flattened out to yield a set of mutually recursive function bindings, which are then translated into a `FIX` declaration in the lambda language. The recursive declaration is compiled in two passes. The first pass assembles the function identifiers to be bound and creates new lvars for them. The second pass compiles the declaration's right hand sides (which must all be lambda expressions) in the outer CEnv plus the CEnv for the function identifiers. The resulting lvars and compiled functions are then assembled into a `FIX`.

Finally we consider plain value bindings. These are actually the most complicated, because value bindings may contain patterns and must therefore use the match compiler.

An expression of the form

`let` *pat* `=` *exp* `in` *scope* `end`

is regarded as the equivalent

`(fn` *pat* `=>` *scope*`)` *exp*

which can be dealt with by the match compiler without any complicated code specific to value bindings.

7 Execution

Recall that `compileDec` has type

`CEnv → dec → (CEnv × (LambdaExp → LambdaExp))`

which allows the compiler to deal with declarations rather than expressions. At the top-level of the compiler, each core declaration is passed to `compileDec`, to return a CEnv for the declaration plus a function f of type `LambdaExp → LambdaExp`. From the CEnv is built a `VECTOR` lambda expression containing all the lvars in some canonical order, and f is applied to this. The result is a lambda expression for the top-level declaration over a scope containing a tuple of the variables bound by the declaration. This lambda expression is then executed, to return (if successful) a vector of object values, one for each variable. The vector is then decomposed to form a DEnv for the declaration. Finally, the top-level basis is augmented with the CEnv and the DEnv.

The interface to the lambda interpreter is shown in figure 7, and is fairly self-explanatory. In practice, the implementation is fairly simple as well. Lambda expressions are passed to a function

`run: DEnv → LambdaExp → object`

```
signature RUN_LAMBDA =
  sig
    type DEnv
    type LambdaExp
    type object

    exception UNCAUGHT of string

    val run: DEnv → LambdaExp → object
  end
```

Figure 7: The signature RUN_LAMBDA

which executes them in a DEnv representing the current top-level environment. Free lvars in the lambda expression are retrieved directly from the DEnv. Constants evaluate directly to the corresponding objects. Function (FN) expressions evaluate to closures encapsulating the current environment. The treatment of FIX is similar to the treatment of `val rec` in the Definition, using an unfolding operation on the closures to provide recursion. (This scheme is described more fully in the SML Definition and the SML Commentary.)

Application (APP) of one lambda expression to another results in the function and argument being evaluated, and then the body of the function being executed in the closure environment of the function extended by an lvar binding for the argument. VECTOR and SELECT produce calls to `Objects.vector` and `Objects.select`.

Exception handling is done in a meta-circular manner; the lambda interpreter contains a single exception called PACKET. When a lambda expression raises an exception, the interpreter raises PACKET with the exception packet. Expressions of the form HANDLE(e_1, e_2) cause e_1 to be interpreted in a context which handles PACKET, in which case e_2 (which must be a FN lambda term) is applied to the packet's value. If PACKET propagates to the top level it is transformed into an exception called UNCAUGHT which carries a string denoting the printed value of the packet, so that it can be reported.

The implementation of SML references and assignment (i.e. the constructor `ref` and the function `:=`) is currently incomplete, and so we defer a discussion of references to a future paper.

8 Conclusions

We have attempted to show that it is possible to build an SML to intermediate lambda language compiler which is modular and which uses simple data structures. Our thesis is that modularity and abstraction are initially more important than raw efficiency—a well-structured compiler can be made more efficient by optimising the modules and refining the interfaces between them, but an efficient compiler can rarely be improved in modularity and structure.

The lambda language is small and simple, with nice properties (such as the unique identity of lvars) and yet it is a full functional language in its own right. Currently, many projects depend on making alterations and enhancements to the SML source text or treating it in some special way; we hope that the lambda language can be used in this way instead, thus avoiding the complexity and ambiguities of the SML language itself.

Bibliography

1. Andrew W. Appel. *Compiling with Continuations.* Cambridge University Press, 1992. To appear.

2. Andrew W. Appel and David B. MacQueen. A Standard ML compiler. In *Functional Programming Languages and Computer Architecture*, pages 301–324. Springer-Verlag, 1987.

3. Robin Milner and Mads Tofte. *Commentary on Standard ML.* MIT Press, 1991.

4. Robin Milner, Mads Tofte, and Robert Harper. *The Definition of Standard ML.* MIT Press, 1990.

TIP in Haskell
— another exercise in functional programming

Colin Runciman
University of York*

1 Introduction

Several years ago, Peyton Jones [3] tested some of the claims made for functional programming by re-implementing a well-known parser generator (YACC) in a lazy functional language (SASL) and comparing the result with the original imperative implementation. His conclusions were positive so far as the expressive power of functional programming was concerned — laziness and higher-order functions both proved valuable — but he bemoaned SASL's lack of type-checking, abstract data types and modules, and also the difficulties of correcting errors and optimising performance in the presence of lazy evaluation.

This paper describes another experiment in the same spirit, but with a new programming language (Haskell) and a new application (TIP). Between the development of SASL (circa. 1975) and the development of Haskell (circa. 1990) there were several developments in functional programming systems, and we expect to see the benefits. Working on a fresh application presents fresh problems, and also retains the element of rethinking a procedural program in a functional language, not just translating between functional languages.

Haskell is a language recently designed by an international team, with the intention that it should become a common lazy functional language providing "faster communication of new ideas, a stable foundation for real applications development, and a vehicle through which others would be encouraged to use functional languages" [2]. Like several other functional languages, it has a polymorphic type system, abstract data types and modules. More distinctively, Haskell includes *type classes* for the systematic expression of ad hoc polymorphism, *array types* whose values are aggregated collections of indexed values, and an I/O scheme requiring every program to be a function whose result is a list of *requests* and whose argument is a list of *responses.*

TIP [8] is a software package for use in interactive terminal-based programs; it is an important part of a commercially successful tool-kit for the rapid construction of UNIX applications. TIP enables the application programmer to work with a

---

* Author's address: Department of Computer Science, University of York, Heslington, York YO1 5DD, United Kingdom. Electronic mail: **colin@uk.ac.york.minster**

virtual terminal, abstracting away from the low level protocols and detailed screen-update strategies that are involved in communication with an *actual terminal*. There were two particular reasons for choosing TIP as a functional programming exercise:

1. it is an *abstraction of interactive I/O*, posing questions about program structure and modularity;

2. it requires the expression of a *complex and changing state with an indefinitely long lifetime*, posing questions about data abstraction and space-efficiency.

These are the questions we shall concentrate on. In the course of examining them, the I/O system and array types of Haskell will be discussed. Apparent opportunities to make use of the type class mechanism will also be discussed.

2 The Original TIP

The original TIP is implemented in C. We shall therefore refer to it as C-TIP to distinguish it from H-TIP, the Haskell version. An application program uses C-TIP by calling appropriate routines[1] from a large number available. Most routines are used to make changes to a *virtual screen* without any immediate effect on the *actual screen* of the computer terminal. But calling the special routine `trefresh()` causes TIP to transmit an efficient update sequence to the actual screen so that its contents become those of the virtual screen. There is also a *virtual keyboard* in which multi-character input sequences, as transmitted by some keys of the *actual keyboard*, are mapped to numeric constants with mnemonic names.

For the application developer, the "Level 1" C-TIP interface can be summarised as in Figure 1. Note the predominance of `void` as result type; the significant outcome of calling one of these `void`-typed routines is not the result it returns, but the state-change it accomplishes within the C-TIP package. The collection of routines may appear modest, but some of them are quite sophisticated: boxes, for example, including lines as degenerate cases, may intersect yet be drawn or erased independently. According to the manual Level 1 is "sufficient for TIP to be used effectively on any terminal but with no more than one visual attribute [single colour, single font etc.]". H-TIP is therefore restricted to Level 1, not to avoid particular problems that other levels pose[2], but to limit the scale of the programming exercise.

3 The Application Interface of H-TIP

Our first concern in the development of H-TIP must be to formulate the application interface. What is an appropriate functional equivalent of the C-TIP routines?

---

[1] The term *function*, though conventionally applied to C routines, is misleading when they are called almost entirely for their side effects.

[2] A *complete* re-implementation of TIP in Haskell would present a few difficulties; some of these are mentioned at the end of the paper.

`void tbell()`	*ring bell on next refresh*
`void tbox(xl,yl,xh,yh)`	*draw box given opposite corner co-ords.*
`void tnobox(xl,yl,xh,yh)`	*erase box ditto*
`void ttitle(xl,yl,xh,yh,s)`	*draw box with given title*
`void tclear()`	*clear the virtual screen*
`void tmove(x,y)`	*absolute move of virtual cursor*
`void trelmove(x,y)`	*relative move ditto*
`void tprintf(x,y,w,f,...)`	*print values given place, width and format*
`void tputc(c)`	*print given character*
`void tputs(s)`	*print given string*
`int tread()`	*read key from virtual keyboard*
`void trefresh()`	*send update to actual terminal screen*
`void tstart()`	*set initial conditions: must be first call*
`void tstop()`	*reset and release resources: must be final call*
`int txmax()`	*max column number on screen*
`int txpos()`	*current column of virtual cursor*
`int tymax()`	*max row number on screen*
`int typos()`	*current row of virtual cursor*

Figure 1: Level 1 C-TIP Interface.

3.1 Packages as Collections of "Stately" Functions?

Perhaps the routines should become what Fairbairn and Wray call *stately functions* [13]: the manipulation of state implicit in a procedural interface can be made explicit in a functional interface by the addition of state-valued arguments and by returning states as (components of) result values. Some C-TIP routines carry out I/O operations as a side-effect: H-TIP input streams can be incorporated into the state, and result structures can be further extended to allow for output. For example, the types of `tstart`, `tputc` and `trefresh` under this scheme might be:

```
tstart   :: String -> TipState
tputc    :: TipState -> Char -> TipState
trefresh :: TipState -> (TipState, String)
```

where the `String` argument of `tstart` represents the keyboard input stream, and the `String` component in the result of `trefresh` is the appropriate update sequence that should be transmitted to the terminal.

Although this approach of making state transitions and I/O traffic explicit in the function signatures is workable, it has two unfortunate consequences:

1. the application program is obliged to "carry around" the TIP state, to ensure that it is duly supplied as argument whenever a TIP function is used and to extract its new value from the result returned;

2. the application program is further obliged to conduct input and output associated with the actual terminal, acting as a low-level messenger conveying lists of characters to and from TIP.

These obligations are surely unwelcome news for the application programmer, who hoped using TIP was going to make life simpler! True, the necessary programming can be facilitated by suitable *combining forms* for stately I/O functions [9], or by adopting a *monadic* style of programming [10]. But the fact remains that by including functions with extended signatures in the interface, essential tasks that are properly the responsibility of the TIP package are instead put upon the application. This is both insecure and inconvenient.

3.2 Packages as Higher Order Functions

A quite different approach is to represent the entire package as a single function: this takes an *abstract program* as its argument and yields a *concrete program* as its result. In Haskell the type of a (concrete) program is

```
main :: [Response] -> [Request]
```

so an H-TIP application might be expressed as an abstract program of type

```
application :: [TipResponse] -> [TipRequest]
```

where the types `TipRequest` and `TipResponse` are suitably defined to represent the calls and results of C-TIP routines. This means that a TIP package represented as a higher order function should have type

```
tip :: ([TipResponse] -> [TipRequest]) -> [Response] -> [Request]
```

so that a complete concrete program can be expressed simply by applying `tip` to the abstract `application`.

```
main = tip application
```

Comparing this scheme with the one we considered before:

1. the manipulation of TIP state and all the associated low-level I/O is safely and conveniently encapsulated in the `tip` function where it belongs;

2. application programmers are on familiar ground, writing programs in which I/O is expressed using a request & response model — whatever auxiliary functions and programming techniques they usually use for I/O are likely to remain applicable.

So this is the scheme we shall adopt.

3.3 Abstract Requests and Responses

Working from the C-TIP routine headers of Figure 1, it is a straightforward exercise to write most of the corresponding definitions of `TipRequest` and `TipResponse` shown in Figure 2. The introduction of the type `YX` for screen co-ordinates is perhaps the most immediately apparent change, but other less obvious changes are more significant. The new relationship of function and argument between TIP and the application means, first, that there is no need for requests `Tstart` or `Tstop`: `tip` simply wraps the evaluation of its argument in an appropriate context. Secondly,

```
data TipRequest =                data TipResponse =
    Tbell                            Tkey Char
  | Tbox YX YX                     | Tres Response
  | Tnobox YX YX                   | Tvoid
  | Ttitle String YX YX            | Tyx YX
  | Tclear
  | Tmove YX
  | Trelmove YX
  | Tprintf YX Int String [String]
  | Tputc Char
  | Tputs String
  | Tread
  | Trefresh                     type YX = (Int,Int)
  | Treq Request
  | Tmax
  | Tpos
```

Figure 2: Level 1 H-TIP Interface.

```
+-----+       +-----+        +-----+     +-----+
|     |       |     |        |     |     |     |
|     +--+ ==> |     |        |  +--+ ==> |
|     |  | (a) |     |        |  |  | (b) |
+-----+--+     +-----+        +--+--+     +--
```

Figure 3: The shared edge restriction in C-TIP.

```
class (Eq a) => Booly a where       class Baggy a where
   add :: a -> a -> a                  ins :: a -> [a] -> [a]
   sub :: a -> a -> a                  del :: a -> [a] -> [a]
   nul :: a                            set :: [a] -> a

         instance (Booly a) => Baggy a where ...
```

Figure 4: Polymorphic bags — a special case.

since `tip` controls *all* I/O on behalf of the application (the function producing actual requests and consuming actual responses is the result of `tip`) it is necessary to provide some way of passing across the interface any I/O requests and responses that are *not* to do with the terminal (eg. those to do with file-handling). This is the reason for including `Treq` in the definition of `TipRequest`, and `Tres` in the definition of `TipResponse`.

Abstraction and Polymorphism

The `printf()` routines in C are classic examples of *ad hoc polymorphism*, something which Haskell classes are designed to express. Moreover, there is in Haskell a standard class `Text` of printable types. It is therefore surprising that one cannot define in H-TIP a `Tprintf` request with anything like the flexibility of C-TIP's `tprintf()` routine.

Suppose, for now, that we are willing to do without the interpretation of format control characters, using the `%` character in format strings as a simple place-holder. Then we might hope to make the following definition.

```
| Tprintf YX Int String [(Text a) => a]
```

But this is illegal: a context such as `(Text a)` cannot be embedded in a type; we cannot have "a list of values, each of some textual type", the best we can hope for is "a list of values, each of the *same* textual type". Reluctantly accepting this restriction, we revise the definition.

```
| (Text a) => Tprintf YX Int String [a] .
```

But this too is illegal: types of constructor functions cannot have contexts in their own right. A context *could* be placed on the type of `TipRequest` as in

```
data (Text a) => TipRequest a =
   ...
   | Tprintf YX Int String [a]
   ...
```

but this defines a whole family of different request types; we want just one.

In fact, we are forced to give up the idea of polymorphic `Tprintf` requests altogether, making the values just strings (say).

```
| Tprintf YX Int String [String]
```

An application must itself apply `show`, or some other function, to values of `Text` types in order to form suitable `Tprintf` arguments. This requirement can be eased by providing a function to do the job.

```
tprintf :: (Text a) => YX -> Int -> String -> [a] -> TipRequest
tprintf yx w f xs = Tprintf yx w f (map show xs)
```

It seems strange that `tprintf` can exhibit polymorphism of a kind forbidden to `Tprintf` — though even `tprintf` restricts each value list to be of uniform type. A slight loss of polymorphism and one exceptional case in the application programmers' interface may not seem too bad, but being unable put the `show` application inside

H-TIP, where each `TipRequest` is processed, could become a more serious problem. What if a full implementation is required that *does interpret* codes in the formatting string? Must the *application* be responsible for applying functions (supplied by H-TIP) to decompose the string, and to interpret its contents? What if the format also depends on information maintained within H-TIP? The lack of polymorphism in message passing interfaces, despite what type clases provide, is a significant limitation.

4 State and State-Transition

In order to service application requests, H-TIP has to maintain information about the state of the virtual terminal and the state of communication with the actual terminal. The overall definition of state in H-TIP is

```
data TipState = TS String [Response] Display YX YX Bool
```

where the `String` is a suffix of what the program receives along the `stdin` channel (from the actual keyboard), the `[Response]` is a suffix of the concrete response stream, the `Display` records the current contents of actual and virtual screens, the two `YX` co-ordinates are those of the actual and virtual cursors, and the humble `Bool` indicates whether the alarm is set to ring when the screen is updated.

Transitions corresponding to each `TipRequest` are coded in the defining clauses of a function `trans`.

```
trans :: TipState -> TipRequest ->
         (TipState, ([Request], TipResponse))
```

This stately signature is strongly reminiscent of the rejected scheme for the application interface — but we are now *within* the TIP package. The `tip` function itself can be defined along the following lines.

```
tip application rps =
    rqs where trqs = application trps
              (rqss,trps) = mapstate trans (stinit rps) trqs
              rqs = concat rqss
```

The function `mapstate trans` implements a state machine, which is applied to an initial state `stinit rps` and a list of TIP requests `trqs` forming the input stream for the machine. A dual output stream `(rqss,trps)` comprises actual I/O requests `rqss` (bundled into lists since there may be zero or many concrete I/O requests as a result of each abstract one) and the TIP responses `trps`.

4.1 Structure and Manipulation of Displays

In C-TIP, display information is represented by an array of line descriptors together with minimum and maximum line numbers for changes since the last refresh. Similarly, line descriptors are arrays of character cell descriptors with bounds on column numbers where changes have been made.

```
typedef struct { cell *col; subscr lmin, lmax; } line;

typedef struct { line *row; subscr smin, smax; } screen;
```

(These declarations have been slightly simplified: the real `line` and `screen` structures also contain wide-scale fonts, and the real `screen` structure contains things like cursor and alarm state too.)

Self-supporting Delta Structures

The close similarity of the `screen` and `line` structures suggests that, even if there is some variation in the operations performed on them, the two data structures should ideally be instances of the same polymorphic type. This type might be defined by

```
data DeltArray a = DA (Array Int a) (Maybe (Int,Int))
```

where the introduction of a `Maybe` type [6]

```
data Maybe a = Just a | Nothing
```

is preferred to the C-TIP representation of "no changes" which assigns special values to the bounds [4]. Now the `Display` and `Line` types can be defined as follows.

```
type Display = DeltArray Line
type Line    = DeltArray Cell
```

In order to define operations conveniently over the entire nested `DeltArray` structure, without breaking the data type abstraction, the module implementing `DeltArray` types is *self-supporting*: the polymorphic functions it defines meet their own requirements for functions over the parametric component type. A simple example by way of illustration is a function

```
daiap :: Int -> (a->a) -> DeltArray a -> DeltArray a
```

which yields an array with a pending change recorded for some index position, given a *change function* over the component type: the result of a partial application of `daiap` to two arguments is itself a possible change function. The benefits of this can be seen in the concise expression of update operations: for instance, given indices `x,y::Int` and function

```
f :: a -> Cell -> Cell
```

it is easy to formulate a corresponding `Display`-level function.

```
daiap y . daiap x . f :: a -> Display -> Display
```

A more complex example is a polymorphic function `daupd` which extracts a *delta value* representing all pending changes in a `DeltArray` and also computes a new `DeltArray` with these changes made and none pending. To do this it requires as its first argument a *delta function* for the component type — and a couple of other functions to convert between the two levels of delta values.

```
daupd :: (a->b->(a,b)) -> (Int->c->a) -> (a->c) ->
         c -> DeltArray b -> (c, DeltArray b)
```

The point to note is that any result of a partial application of daupd to three arguments is itself a possible delta function.

The discipline of self-support involves identifying the signatures of required functions, and ensuring that they are provided. This sounds like the role of type classes; but classes as currently defined in Haskell cannot express it, partly because they are restricted to a single type parameter[3]. Although we can *begin* an instance declaration of the form

```
instance (Delta a) => Delta (DeltArray a) where ...
```

we cannot complete it — or even define the Delta class adequately in the first place — because the relevant functions involve other parametric types. Even with multiple type parameters, we could only formulate specific classes such as Delta; there is no way to formulate the general class of self-supporting types.

Arrays and Indexed Trees

In the definition of the DeltArray type above, the underlying structure was shown as a Haskell Array. Since arrays are used in C-TIP, and arrays are regarded as an important provision of Haskell, the choice may seem obvious. However H-TIP actually uses balanced indexed trees because[4] an explicitly defined data structure gives the option to share substructures, in ways not possible using arrays, and to exercise closer control over the timing of display evaluation (see section 4.2). So the definition of the DeltArray type becomes

```
data DeltArray a = DA (IndexTree a) (Maybe (Int,Int))
```

where the IndexTree type can be defined as follows.

```
data IndexTree a = Leaf a | Fork Int (IndexTree a) (IndexTree a)
```

The Int value held in a Fork construction is the maximum index for which the associated element is in the left IndexTree branch. Construction of an IndexTree from other values is by applying the function

```
itgen :: Int -> a -> IndexTree a
```

where itgen n x yields a tree with n leaves, all sharing the value x.

Why is the index type specified as Int? Shouldn't it rather be any type of class Ix as for arrays? No, it is not sensible to put Ix type indices in an IndexTree, since there is no efficient way to obtain Ix mid-points: in the context Ix a we have a function

```
index :: (a,a) -> a -> Int
```

---

[3] Recent contributions posted to the haskell mailing list have proposed generalisations; in particular, a posting from Mark Jones at Oxford described his *Gofer* implementation of Haskell which supports multi-parameter classes.

[4] Also, the prototype Haskell compiler used for H-TIP implements arrays as lists, incurring access and update costs linear in the size of the array.

but no inverse. Precisely because of the `index` functions, it would be straightforward to provide polymorphic indexing in a higher level data type. But in H-TIP, `Int` indices are fine.

Why bother to keep indices in the tree anyway? Wouldn't omitting the indices significantly reduce storage space occupied by trees? (Not only would each `Fork` construction be smaller, but also there would be more opportunity for structure sharing — eg. substructure representing blank parts of a screen.) This is a space/time trade-off. Storing indices speeds access by avoiding the need to refer to index bounds and also avoids a series of repeated mid-point calculations.

On Cells, Bits and Bags

Now consider individual character cells in the display. A `cell` in C-TIP is a `struct` with four fields: character values and fonts for each of the virtual and actual screens.

```
typedef struct { char vc,ac; font vf,af; } cell;
```

In Level 1 TIP it suffices to think of a `font` as having just two possible values: one indicates that the associated `char` is an ordinary character code, and the other that it is an eight bit byte code for a section in the edge of a box or boxes. C-TIP encodes edges in such a way that overlapping boxes, including boxes with some edges in common, can be created and deleted independently provided that any two boxes with a shared edge have centres on opposite sides of it. Figure 3 shows the effect of a `nobox()` call when an edge is shared by boxes centred (a) on opposite sides, and (b) on the same side. Something like the shared edge restriction is inevitable if the edge cells have a fixed size representation, because an application can request an arbitrarily deep overlay of boxes. Ideally TIP would maintain *bags* (or *multisets*) of edge segments to represent these cells. C-TIP uses a `char`-sized approximation because having a display state of fixed size simplifies memory management — a single allocation suffices, performed by `tstart()` — and enables the application programmer to predict accurately how much space C-TIP will need.

In H-TIP the similar but separate nature of the virtual and actual parts of the cell is expressed by defining a `Cell` to be a `HemiCell` pair.

```
type Cell = (HemiCell, HemiCell)
```

Viewing the font information as the *tag* for the union of character codes and edge codes, suggests that the `HemiCell` type should be defined as follows.

```
type HemiCell = Plain Char | Fancy Bits
```

But this would perpetuate the shared edge restriction. In Haskell, dynamic memory management is (a) *inevitable* and (b) *free* (at least so far as programming is concerned), so why not do the job properly with bags? There isn't a `Bits` type with the desired characteristics anyway! So we redefine

```
type HemiCell = Plain Char | Fancy (Bag Char)
```

to support unrestricted sharing of edges. The implementation of bags must include a cheap operation to extract the associated set, because the function to derive appropriate printed characters from edge cells has to be efficient. One solution is to represent multisets as a sequence of non-empty sets $s_1 \supseteq s_2 \supseteq \ldots \supseteq s_n$ in a list: the associated set is empty if the list is empty; otherwise the associated set is that at the head of the list.

Of course, we should like the bag implementation to be polymorphic and to be instantiated automatically given a suitable set type. But the class system cannot express the general case, *again* because of the restriction to a single parametric type. A putative instance declaration beginning

```
instance (SetEl s e) => BagSetEl [s] s e where ...
```

is not even syntactically well-formed. If we try hard, we can express a special case where sets and elements are identified in a single Boolean system (this is true in the H-TIP setting — for example, the character `'+'` can be used to represent the set {`'-'`, `'|'`}) and the list of ordered sets is the only implementation of bags admitted. Figure 4 outlines the relevant declarations. The return does not seem great for the effort involved.

4.2 The Pragmatics of State Transition

Although the previous section described the `TipState` type in some detail, the *size* of its values was hardly mentioned. Excluding the residues of lazily evaluated input streams the `Display` component is dominant. On a largish physical display, such as an A3 workstation, there may be several thousand character cells. A *fully evaluated* `Display` value contains double this number of `HemiCell` structures in the worst case, and these are only the leaves of the `DeltArray` and `IndexTree` structures with their many numeric indices and bounds.

Laziness and Space Leaks

In the initial `Display`, however, a single blank `Cell` structure is shared across the entire `YX` space. Moreover, under the normal regime of lazy evaluation, a `Display` value is *most unlikely* to be fully evaluated. Branches of `IndexTrees` corresponding to parts of the screen not in use will be held as closures — unevaluated expressions. This sounds like good news. In practice, however, it is disastrous because the closures involved become ever more complex and enormous. Our intuition about state transition may suggest that previous states are "left behind", and that the memory they occupied can be recovered. But under lazy evaluation, components of the current state may be held as closures including references to the previous state; this in turn may have component closures referring to the *previous* previous state, and so on. In short, the entire state-history of the program may steadily accumulate in memory. Indeed, in experiments with a "naturally lazy" version of H-TIP, using a benchmark test involving many `Tbox` and `Tnobox` requests over large screen areas, garbage collection was found to take 95% of the time[5] and the rapidly expanding heap soon exhausted the available memory space of several megabytes.

The observation of this kind of *space-leak* in a lazy functional program is not new [7], and it has been made before in the context of long-running interactive

[5] The semispace garbage collector repeatedly made copies of the large closures.

programs [12]. In each application there are particular pitfalls to avoid — an example in H-TIP is inadvertently releasing a `TipState` to the application as part of a closure in a `TipResponse` — but the nature of the underlying problem is much the same.

Normalisation and Closure Space

Even if the *problem* has been discussed before, not much has been said about *solutions.* A special primitive, such as a hyperstrict identity function, is sometimes used to force evaluation. Even without such a primitive, a programmer can resort to tricks such as testing a structure for equality with itself! But such techniques are too indiscriminate to deal with values where some components, such as input streams, must remain unevaluated. Also, since a forcing function necessarily traverses every part of its result, it is a very expensive solution when the argument is a large structure most parts of which are already evaluated. Some languages permit constructor definitions to be annotated to show *strictness* in selected arguments. Bird and Wadler [1] assume a polymorphic primitive `strict` that can be applied to *any* function: evaluation of `strict f x` reduces `x` to head normal form before applying `f` to it.

The solution adopted for the TIP program exploits the class mechanism to obtain both polymorphism and selective control of evaluation. We introduce a class `Norm` of types over which a predicate `normal` is defined.

```
class Norm a where normal :: a -> Bool
```

The intention is that `normal` functions are so-defined that the result of an application `normal x` is always `True`, but computing this truth guarantees that `x` is evaluated to at least a specified minimal extent. One way to declare a data type to be a `Norm` instance is simply to define `normal` to yield `True` for each possible outermost construction. The `IndexTree` type is a suitable example.

```
instance Norm (IndexTree a) where
  normal (Leaf _) = True
  normal (Fork _ _ _) = True
```

To avoid keeping an `IndexTree` with branches that are only (history-retaining?) closures any function building an `IndexTree` should not use the lazy `Fork` constructor but rather a *normalising constructor* `fork`.

```
fork :: Int -> IndexTree a -> IndexTree a -> IndexTree a
fork m lt rt | normal lt && normal rt = Fork m lt rt
```

If the `IndexTree` has a `Norm` component type, a normalising `leaf` constructor can be defined similarly.

```
leaf :: Norm a => a -> IndexTree a
leaf x | normal x = Leaf x
```

From this example it should be clear how `Norm` can be used to define data structures with selectively strict constructors, say. But we have more than that. The definitive constructors are lazy, and remain available. And the strictness of `leaf` is not fixed, for there are as many `leaf` functions as there are `Norm` types; some may not evaluate their argument at all, others may evaluate it fully, and still others may determine whether to evaluate one component of their argument by examining another.

In H-TIP, `normal` functions are applied *only* in `normal` definitions and in guards (where their role of forcing evaluation is akin to that of argument patterns). Use of `normal` in guards is further restricted to definitions of normalising constructors, apart from a single use in the main state-transition function. Consequently, normalisation is easily separated from other mechanisms in the program. The `HemiCell` structures with their edge multisets are left lazy, but in all other respects each successive `Display` is fully evaluated as a result of state normalisation after each transition. The benchmark test mentioned earlier was repeated for a normalising version of the program. The heap grew rapidly to about 100K bytes but then remained at about that size, sometimes shrinking, sometimes expanding.

5 Conclusions & Future Work

Many software packages written in a procedural language are similar in form to TIP — a collection of procedures operating on a shared state internal to the package, some also performing I/O. For example, there are database packages, graphics packages, equation-solving packages and so on. The use of an abstract response-request type in functional versions of such packages is an attractive alternative to the extended signature approach. Extended signatures may be more flexible if an application makes use of more than one package. However, by making the concrete request type a parameter of each abstract request type, it is possible to compose layers of several different response-request packages for use by a single application. For example, if `database` is a function representing a package, an abstract application program of type

```
application :: [DbResponse (TipResponse Response)] ->
               [DbRequest  (TipRequest  Request )]
```

can be made concrete by the following definition.

```
main = tip (database application)
```

Polymorphic data types with functional constructors are well established in functional languages: in H-TIP they once again proved pleasant to work with. The polymorphic type system caught most errors in programming with data structures; the one exception was an invariant violation involving `IndexTree` indices — this was easy to track down because it had such bizarre effects on the actual display! In due time, there will be more sophisticated implementations of Haskell arrays. A future compiler might compile an array-based version of H-TIP to code performing safe destructive updates: since there is just one abstract terminal and the interactive application is serial, it should be possible to make the use of display arrays *single threaded* or even *linear* [11].

It is disappointing to realise that despite the complex machinery of the present Haskell class system, there are constraints which curtail its use in practice. During the development of H-TIP, the restriction of classes to a single type parameter cropped up several times, and the limited scope for ad hoc polymorphism in data type constructions prevented the definition of an interface as flexible as the original.

On the other hand, classes did provide a handy way to control space problems caused by lazy evaluation. Such problems are likely to arise in a wide range of applications, and it is important to devise programming techniques to solve them in a systematic, efficient and general way that does not intrude on a natural lazy style. The `Norm` class worked well for TIP, but surely more refined schemes are awaiting discovery.

We still do not have the tools to determine whether a functional program has a space leak of some particular class and, if so, which are the offending structures. A stable heap of 100K bytes is certainly better than a fast-growing one of several megabytes, but is the 100K byte figure what we should expect, and if so by what calculation? Even basic information from compilers about the size of individual constructions could be useful in this respect; ideally implementations would support *heap profiling* [5].

Finally, some of the functionality of the original TIP package could not be implemented in standard Haskell. For example, in C-TIP an optimisation inhibits `refresh()` operations when the application user has "typed ahead", interrupts can be generated from the keyboard and handled appropriately, and limits can be set to the time between key-strokes. There is as yet no consensus about the best way to program this kind of behaviour in a functional language.

Acknowledgements

Thanks to Dave Wakeling and Iain Checkland for comments and suggestions. H-TIP was implemented using a prototype Haskell compiler developed at Glasgow as part of the GRASP project; particular thanks to Kevin Hammond for speedy response to reported problems. The work described in this paper was supported by SERC (Science and Engineering Research Council) as part of the FLARE (Functional Languages Applied to Real Exemplars) project.

References

1. R. Bird and P. Wadler. *Introduction to Functional Programming*. Prentice-Hall, 1988.

2. P. Hudak and P. Wadler (editors). Report on the programming language Haskell, a non-strict purely functional language (Version 1.0). Technical report, University of Glasgow, Department of Computing Science, April 1990.

3. S.L. Peyton Jones. YACC in SASL — an exercise in functional programming. *Software — Practice and Experience*, 15(8):807–820, August 1985.

4. C. Runciman. What about the *natural* numbers? *Computer Languages*, 14(3):181–191, 1989.

5. C. Runciman and D. Wakeling. Problems and proposals for time and space profiling of functional programs. In *Proceedings of 3rd Glasgow Workshop on Functional Programming*, pages 237–245. Springer-Verlag, 1990.

6. M. Spivey. A functional theory of exceptions. *Science of Computer Programming*, 14(1):25–42, June 1990.

7. W. Stoye. *The Implementation of Functional Languages Using Custom Hardware.* PhD thesis, University of Cambridge Computer Laboratory, December 1985. Technical Report No. 81.

8. H.W. Thimbleby. The design of a terminal independent package. *Software — Practice and Experience*, 17(5):351–367, May 1987.

9. S.J. Thompson. Interactive functional programs. Technical Report 48, Computing Laboratory, University of Kent at Canterbury, 1987.

10. P.L. Wadler. Comprehending monads. In *Proceedings of ACM Conference on LISP and Functional Programming*, pages 61–78, June 1990.

11. D. Wakeling and C. Runciman. Linearity and laziness. In *Proceedings of 5th ACM Conference on Functional Programming Languages and Computer Architecture*, pages 215–240. Springer-Verlag, August 1991. LNCS 523.

12. S.C. Wray. *Implementation and Programming Techniques for Functional Languages.* PhD thesis, University of Cambridge Computer Laboratory, January 1986. Technical Report No. 92.

13. S.C. Wray and J. Fairbairn. Non-strict languages — programming and implementation. *The Computer Journal*, 32(2):142–151, April 1989.

Experiments in Haskell - A Network Simulation Algorithm

Paul Sanders
Systems Research Division
British Telecom Laboratories
Martlesham Heath, Ipswich. IP5 7RE

Abstract

This paper summarises some of the results of a study into the use of Haskell for a network simulation application. These results are compared with a Pascal implementation of the same program to give an indicator of how well Haskell performs against conventional languages for this task.

1. INTRODUCTION

The area of network simulation is an important one for telecommunications companies. It is essential to be able to predict the effect of any change of protocol, routing strategy, call rate etc. on a network before any changes are implemented. There are, therefore, many network simulation models and programs to implement them.

A key feature of network simulation programs is the use of complex data structures and highly recursive algorithms. They are, consequently, difficult and time-consuming to write and maintain. Furthermore, as different strategies are devised, new simulation programs must be developed or old ones extended to cope with the changes.

This suggests that functional programming languages (fpls) will prove advantageous since it is believed that:

- complex data structures and their manipulation are generally easier to express in fpls than in imperative languages;
- functional language programs are easier to understand and maintain than their equivalent imperative language programs;
- recursive algorithms are very easily expressed in an fpl.

All these factors suggest that considerable savings and improved quality will be achieved if fpls were to be used for network simulation.

The FLARE [1] project aims to evaluate the use of functional languages on large applications and this paper gives the results of BT's first input to the project. A small network simulation model was implemented in the lazy functional programming language Haskell [2], and this was compared with an existing Pascal implementation of the same program. Each implementation was carried out by a programmer experienced in the relevant language.

Section 2 gives an overview of the results of the study. Section 3 presents some concluding remarks.

2 SOME RESULTS FROM THE STUDY

The results can be split into two categories - quantitative and qualitative.

2.1 Quantitative Results

The most important metrics for the study were lines of code, development time and bugs found. The first two results are summarised in the following table:.

	Pascal Version	Haskell version
Lines of code	1840	1050
Development time	22 days	12 days

Note that these figures are approximations but are close enough to illustrate the differences. Also, both programmers were proficient in the language they were using.

The Haskell program is almost half the length of the Pascal one. This fraction is higher than expected; earlier studies, such as [3], indicated that the Haskell program would probably be a third of the length or less. An examination of the program revealed the major cause. As stated earlier, there are many data types in the program with a large number of components. Since they are defined as abstract datatypes, constructor and destructor functions are defined for each component, and this has added roughly 200 lines to the program. The relative verbosity of Haskell (to the languages surveyed in [3]) accounts for some of the other 'extra' lines.

The Haskell program development time was close to half that of the Pascal program and was in accordance with that expected from the earlier study. This is a good result for

Haskell since it indicates that despite its initial complexity it retains the development benefits that other functional languages offer.

Only seven bugs were found during the development of the Haskell program. This is due to a combination of:

- not needing to handle data storage and manipulation explicitly
- strong typing

The former is one of functional programming's biggest assets. Debugging pointer references in any language is a difficult process; eliminating it is bound to simplify a programming task. Type checking was found to identify almost all the bugs in the program. Bug-fixing was mostly an exercise in type-debugging which is, in general, easier than finding logical errors.

2.2 Qualitative Results

The most striking difference in the two programs lies in the better clarity of the Haskell code. This can be mostly attributed to the fact that datatype manipulation is much easier and much clearer than in Pascal. For example, it is not easily apparent what the following Pascal fragment achieves:

```
PROCEDURE appenda (VAR aptr:altlistptr ; a : numb) ;
VAR ptr: linklistptr;
BEGIN
IF aptr = NIL THEN BEGIN
    new (aptr); aptr^.alt := a; aptr^.tail := NIL END
ELSE BEGIN
    ptr := aptr;
    WHILE ptr^.tail <> NIL DO ptr := ptr^.tail;
    new (ptr^.tail); ptr^.tail^.alt := a; ptr^.tail^.tail := NIL
END END;
```

The Haskell equivalent is much easier to understand:

```
appenda :: [a] -> a -> [a]
appenda [] i = [i]
appenda (a:as) i = a : (appenda as i)
```

and has a more general type. Note that if a "list append" function was needed for another element type in the Pascal program then the Pascal fragment would need to be duplicated.

A further improvement to readability derives from the lack of global variables in the Haskell program. There are a large number of these in the Pascal version of the simulator and it is often difficult to work out when and how something is being updated. The lack of destructive update also aids understandability in the Haskell program - it is always clear when something is being 'updated' and, more importantly, the changes that are being made are easily apparent from the program code.

Another benefit gained from using Haskell was in the ease with which the algorithm was expressed. The mathematical description of the algorithm was easily expressed in the declarative programming style and the algorithm naturally decomposed into modules and some higher-order functions. We are of the opinion that this made debugging and extending the program easier than it was for the Pascal program but, not being the authors of that program, we cannot say for certain.

The main problems encountered during the program's development lay in the following two areas:

- the inability to deal elegantly with global variables
- the development system

The simulation program keeps a lot of data which must be available to many routines but much of this data is write-once. In the Pascal program there are 23 global variables with various subsets of these being used in each procedure. In the Haskell program this figure can be reduced to 15 global "variables" but this is still a large amount of data to have to pass to every function. The solution adopted was to partition the data into volatile and non-volatile segments so that updates would not involve duplicating the non-volatile data. This cut down a large part of the storage requirements of the program and made the code clearer to read but it did not fully solve the problem. Changing just one element of a large, say, ten element datatype makes the code look quite cumbersome. A record structure like that found in Standard ML provides an elegant way of handling this and would be a useful addition to Haskell in a future revision.

The final problems with the development lay with the compiler being used. This was found to be slow, cryptic in its error messages and contained many bugs. The compiler used was a prototype and so some problems were to be expected, nonetheless, the problems encountered hindered the development of the application and went some way to souring the favourable impression obtained from using Haskell for the coding. It is doubtful whether any non-enthusiast of functional languages would be encouraged to take up Haskell using the currently available compilers: a robust compiler is urgently needed.

3 CONCLUSIONS

This paper has given an overview of the findings of an experiment in the use of Haskell for a network simulation application. The benefits and drawbacks of using Haskell were identified when compared with using Pascal for the implementation of the same program.

The results of the study show that Haskell, and similar functional languages, are well suited to this kind of application and that their use leads to clearer and more concise code. The high level of abstraction in Haskell leads to less code and smaller development times. For this study a significant improvement in both areas was achieved. If these benefits could be realised in a true commercial environment then the cost of software development could be significantly decreased.

In comparison with other functional languages the study has shown that Haskell suffers no lack of quality for its increased richness. Its main drawback (at the time of this study) is the lack of a robust, reliable compiler. This situation will improve in the very near future as the many prototype compilers that are available mature.

4 REFERENCES

[1] British Telecom Research Laboratories, University of Glasgow, University of Kent, University College Swansea, University of Swansea. *Functional Languages Applied to Realistic Exemplars - a detailed proposal for research submitted to Information Engineering Advanced Technology Programme*. September 1990

[2] Hudak P, Wadler P (Eds). "Report on the programming language Haskell, Version 1.0". Technical Report, Yale University and Glasgow University, April 1990

[3] Sanders P: An Evaluation of Functional Programming for the Commercial Environment. In: B De Neumann D Simpson G Slater (Eds).Mathematical Structures for Software Engineering. Clarendon Press, Oxford, 1991, pp 275-291

Operational Theories of Improvement in Functional Languages

(Extended Abstract)

David Sands*
Imperial College†

Abstract

In this paper we address the technical foundations essential to the aim of providing a semantic basis for the formal treatment of relative efficiency in functional languages. For a general class of "functional" computation systems, we define a family of improvement preorderings which express, in a variety of ways, when one expression is more efficient than another. The main results of this paper build on Howe's study of equality in lazy computation systems, and are concerned with the question of when a given improvement relation is subject to the usual forms of (in)equational reasoning (so that, for example, we can improve an expression by improving any sub-expression). For a general class of computation systems we establish conditions on the operators of the language which guarantee that an improvement relation is a precongruence. In addition, for a particular higher-order nonstrict functional language, we show that any improvement relation which satisfies a simple monotonicity condition with respect to the rules of the operational semantics has the desired congruence property.

1 Introduction

The mathematical tractability of functional programs gives us the ability to show that operations on programs preserve meaning, and has lead to much interest in formal methods for program construction. However, although an underlying aim of these activities is to derive efficient programs from inefficient specifications, formal techniques for reasoning about efficiency (and how operations on programs affect it) have received little attention.

This work focuses on the problems of providing semantic notions efficiency improvement for functional languages; possible applications include the the construction of program logics for reasoning about the relative efficiency of program

* This work was partially funded by ESPRIT BRA 3124, *Semantique*.

† Department of Computing, 180 Queens Gate, London SW7 2BZ email: ds@uk.ac.ic.doc

fragments, the construction or validation of efficiency-improving transformations, and the development of calculi for reasoning about the execution-related properties of programs.

In this paper we describe a class of improvement relations definable over a variety of functional languages, and address the technical foundations essential to the aim of providing a semantic basis for the formal treatment of efficiency.

Informally, the notions of improvement that we have in mind are binary relations, R, between programs such that pRq if q is at least as good as p, both *observationally* (can match any observable evaluation) and *intensionally* (is operationally "better"). We study this concept in the context of lazy programming languages, where we associate the term "lazy" with an evaluation process which terminates as soon as the outermost *constructor* of the result is known—practically all higher-order functional languages have a lazy component, in the form of a lambda-abstraction (or partial application), where "λ" plays the role of a lazy constructor.

With the above applications in mind, what we want is a notion of improvement that satisfies the following: it should be a preordering (*i.e.* p is improved by p, and, if p is improved by q, and q is improved by r, then p is improved by r) and it should be substitutive, *i.e.* we can reason about improvement by substitution of "improvement for improvement" (*c.f.* "substitution of equals for equals", a.k.a. equational reasoning). These requirements are summarised by saying that improvement should be a *precongruence.*

One way of defining such relations would be to make these conditions true by construction. However, in order to verify improvement "laws", such a definition is rather unhelpful. A more useful form would be a definition for which reasoning about improvement reduces to reasoning about some basic evaluation relation. However, the basic evaluation relation for a lazy language is too "shallow", in itself, to capture the behaviour of a term in any context; as a generalisation of "applicative bisimulation" [1] we define the desired improvement relation, *improvement simulation*, by analogy with strong (bi)simulation in process algebra [8]. The remaining problem is to verify, for a given language and a particular notion of improvement, that improvement simulation is a precongruence. This problem is the primary focus of this paper.

In the first part of this paper we define an improvement simulation relation for a broad class of "lazy" languages. The main technical result of this section is that an improvement simulation is a precongruence exactly when a certain *improvement extensionality* condition holds for each of the operators of the language. This result is based on, and generalises, the main result of Howe's study of equality in lazy computation systems [5]; as in [5], the significance of the condition is that in practice it seems relatively simple to check.

In the second part of the paper we study a particular lazy computation system, a variant of the lazy lambda calculus with constants. Using the result of the previous section we show that any improvement simulation induced by a particular computational property is guaranteed to be a precongruence whenever the property satisfies a simple monotonicity requirement with respect to the rules of the operational semantics. The significance of this characterisation is that many computational properties can be given by simple inductive definitions, for which the required monotonicity condition is easily checked. We illustrate these ideas with some examples, and note that the the result is applicable to a variety of languages defined by structural operational semantics, and in particular those defined by the *structured computation system* format of [6].

In conclusion we consider related works, and possible further developments.

2 Improvement in Lazy Computation Systems

2.1 Lazy Computation Systems

A lazy computation system [5][1] is a particular syntactic form well-suited to specifying the syntax of strict and non-strict functional languages (although nondeterminism can also be handled in this framework), together with an evaluation relation. We begin with the language. A lazy computation language is reminiscent of the syntax of terms in combinatory reduction systems [7] and Martin-Löf's type theory, although unlike these, application is not a predefined construct (*c.f.* Aczel's syntax, [7], remark 1.5).

DEFINITION 2.1 *A* lazy computation language *L is specified by a triple $(\mathbf{O}, \mathbf{K}, \alpha)$, where $\mathbf{O}$ is a set of* operators *of the language, $\mathbf{K}$ is a subset of $\mathbf{O}$, the* canonical operators, *and α is a function $(\mathbf{O} \to \{(k_1, \ldots k_n) | n, k_i \geq 0\})$ specifying the* arity *of each operator.* □

The arity of an operator is given as a list whose length corresponds to the to the number of *operands*, and whose respective elements correspond to the number of bound variables that will be "attached" to that operand.

DEFINITION 2.2 *Fix an infinite set V of variables x, y, x_1, x_2 etc. The terms, $T(L)$, ranged over by a, b, a_1, a_2 etc. are formed as follows:*

- $V \subseteq T(L)$
- *if $F \in \mathbf{O}$, $\alpha(F) = (k_1, \ldots, k_n)$ and $a_1, \ldots, a_n \in T(L)$, then*

$$F((\bar{x}_1).a_1, \ldots, (\bar{x}_n).a_n) \in T(L)$$

where each $\bar{x}_i$ is a list of k_i variables.

□

For example, in an ML-like language, a list case-expression of the form:

```
case E of nil  => A
     (cons x y) => B
```

could be expressed in a lazy computation language, using an operator *case* of arity $(0, 0, 2)$, as a term of the form $case(E, A, (x, y).B)$, where, as in the sequel, we abbreviate operands of the form $().e$ as simply e. Some other notational conventions used are summarised below.

---

[1] We adopt the slightly generalised notion as suggested in [6].

NOTATION

Variables A list of zero or more variables $x_1, \dots x_n$ will often be denoted $\bar{x}$, and similarly for a list of operands. Variable-binding structure in $T(L)$ is given by specifying that in an operand of the form $(\bar{x}).b$, the free occurrences of variables $\bar{x}$ in b are bound. The closed terms, written $T(L)^\circ$, are the defined to be the terms with no free variables.

Substitution We use the notation $a\{b_1, \dots, b_n/x_1, \dots, x_n\}$ to mean term a with free occurrences of $x_1, \dots, x_n$ simultaneously replaced by the terms $b_1, \dots, b_n$. A formal definition of substitution is omitted. Let $\equiv$ denote syntactic equality on terms, which will be taken to include pairs of terms which are the same up to renaming of bound variables (alpha-conversion).

Relations If R is a binary relation on $T(L)^\circ$ then we extend R to $T(L)$ by: $a\ R\ b$ if and only if $a\sigma\ R\ b\sigma$ for all closing substitutions σ. If we have a relation S on T(L), extend S to operands by:

$$(x_1 \dots x_n).b\ S\ (x'_1 \dots x'_n).b' \iff b\{z_1, \dots, z_n/x_1, \dots, x_n\}\ S\ b'\{z_1, \dots, z_n/x'_1, \dots, x'_n\}$$

where $z_1, \dots, z_n$ are not free in b, b'. We will use variables e,e_1,e_2 *etc.* to range over operands. For commonly-indexed lists of operands $\bar{e}$, $\bar{e}'$ we will write $\bar{e}\ R\ \bar{e}'$ to mean $\forall i.\ e_i\ R\ e'_i$. Finally, let ';' denote relation composition, so $a\ R;S\ c$ if and only if there exists a b such that $a\ R\ b$ and $b\ S\ c$. □

Evaluation

A lazy computation system is essentially an evaluation relation which relates closed terms (of a particular lazy computation language) to their "values". The values are the *canonical terms*, which are defined to be any closed term of the form $C(\bar{e})$ where $C \in \mathbf{K}$. The evaluation relation is expressed as a family of relations over which we have a well-founded ordering which encapsulates notion of (induction on) the "size" of a computation.

DEFINITION **2.3** *A lazy computation system is a pair* $(L, \{\stackrel{w}{\longrightarrow}\}_{w \in W})$ *where* L *is a lazy computation language,* $\{\stackrel{w}{\longrightarrow}\}$ *is a family of binary relations indexed by a well-founded ordering* $<_W$*, between closed terms and canonical terms.* □

EXAMPLE **2.4** The lazy lambda calculus [1, 11] shares the syntax of the pure untyped lambda calculus, but has an operational semantics given by an evaluation relation $M \Downarrow N$ ("M converges to principal weak head normal form N") defined inductively over closed lambda terms as follows:

$$\bullet\ \ \lambda x.M \Downarrow \lambda x.M \qquad \bullet\ \ \frac{M \Downarrow \lambda x.P \quad P\{N/x\} \Downarrow Q}{MN \Downarrow Q}$$

We can recast this as a lazy computation system as follows: writing $\lambda x.M$ as $\lambda((x).M)$, and MN as $@(M,N)$, define $\mathbf{O} = \{\lambda, @\}$, $\mathbf{K} = \{\lambda\}$ with $\alpha(\lambda) = (1)$ and $\alpha(@) = (0,0)$. Now take the set W to be the set of proofs built with the above rules, with the well-founded ordering being the "subproof" relation. Then define $M \stackrel{w}{\longrightarrow} N$ whenever w is a proof of $M \Downarrow N$. □

In the remainder of the paper it will be convenient to define the following abbreviations on evaluation judgements:

- $a \longrightarrow b \iff \exists w.\ a \stackrel{w}{\longrightarrow} b$,
- $a{\downarrow}^{w} \iff \exists b, w.\ a \stackrel{w}{\longrightarrow} b$,
- $a{\uparrow} \iff \neg(a{\downarrow}^{w})$.

2.2 Improvement Simulation

In our consideration of lazy computation systems, the choice of set W will be of particular importance, since it will not only be used to formalise a general notion of induction on the "size" of a computation (via the well-founded ordering, $<_W$), but also to capture information pertaining to the *computational* properties of evaluation. In what follows we will consider additional structure on the set W provided by a *computation preorder*, $\succeq$. Intuitively, $w \succeq w'$ means that some computational property associated with w is improved by the computation property associated with w'. So, for example, W might be the set of possible computation traces (*e.g.* sequences of abstract machine states), then we could define $w' <_W w$ if w' is a strict sub-trace of w, and $w \succeq w'$ if w' contains fewer evaluations of arithmetic operators.

Roughly speaking, the basic notion of "improvement" between closed terms is the largest relation that satisfies the following:

> *if A is "improved by" B, then whenever A can be evaluated to some canonical term, then B can be evaluated in an "improved fashion" ($\succeq$) to a term with a matching outermost canonical operator, and "improved" operands.*

We formalise this notion of improvement with the following definitions:

DEFINITION **2.5** *For any given improvement preorder, $\succeq$, define the monotone function $\langle\!|\text{-}|\!\rangle_{\succeq} \in T(L)^\circ \times T(L)^\circ \to T(L)^\circ \times T(L)^\circ$ as follows. For any binary relation R on closed terms, let $\langle\!|R|\!\rangle_{\succeq}$ be the least relation on closed terms such that $a_1 \langle\!|R|\!\rangle_{\succeq} a_2$ if*

> *whenever $a_1 \stackrel{w_1}{\longrightarrow} C(\bar{e}_1)$ then there exist w_2, $C(\bar{e}_2)$ such that $a_2 \stackrel{w_2}{\longrightarrow} C(\bar{e}_2)$, with $\bar{e}_1\ R\ \bar{e}_2$ and $w_1 \succeq w_2$*

□

DEFINITION **2.6**
A relation R is an improvement simulation *(with respect to $\succeq$) if $R \subseteq \langle\!|R|\!\rangle_{\succeq}$* □

DEFINITION **2.7** *Let $\trianglelefteq_{\succeq}$ denote the largest improvement simulation.* □

Since $\langle\!|\text{-}|\!\rangle_{\succeq}$ is a monotone function on the powerset lattice of all binary relations on $T(L)^\circ$ then by the Knaster-Tarski fixed point theorem it has a greatest fixed point (given by $\bigcup\{R | R \subseteq \langle\!|R|\!\rangle_{\succeq}\}$, *i.e.* the union of all improvement simulations), so the above definition is well defined with $\trianglelefteq_{\succeq}$ equal to this greatest fixed point. We will refer to this relation as *the* improvement simulation. The importance of this maximal fixed point definition is that it comes with a useful proof technique, sometimes referred to in the context of process algebra as "Park Induction" (in reference to [12]), or in a more general setting as "co-induction" ([9]):

To show that $R \subseteq \trianglelefteq_{\succeq}$, for some binary relation R on $T(L)^\circ$, it is sufficient to show that R is an improvement simulation.

...

So, in order to show that two closed terms are related by $\trianglelefteq_{\succeq}$ it is sufficient to exhibit any improvement simulation which relates them.

In what follows we will routinely omit the $\succeq$-subscripts, unless we are specifically considering different computation preorderings over the same lazy computation system.

PROPOSITION **2.8** *If R and S are binary relations on $T(L)^\circ$ then $\langle\!| R |\!\rangle; \langle\!| S |\!\rangle \subseteq \langle\!| R; S |\!\rangle$.*

PROOF Suppose $a\ \langle\!| R |\!\rangle; \langle\!| S |\!\rangle\ c$. If $a\!\uparrow$ then for all binary relations P on $T(L)^\circ$, and all $d \in T(L)^\circ$, $a\ \langle\!| P |\!\rangle\ d$, so in particular $a\ \langle\!| R; S |\!\rangle\ c$. Otherwise, if $a \xrightarrow{w_1} C(\bar{e}_1)$ then $\exists b \in T(L)^\circ.\ b \xrightarrow{w_2} C(\bar{e}_2)$, with $w_1 \succeq w_2$ and $\bar{e}_1 R \bar{e}_2$, and such that $c \xrightarrow{w_3} C(\bar{e}_3)$ with $w_2 \succeq w_3$ and $\bar{e}_2 S \bar{e}_3$. Transitivity of $\succeq$ gives $w_1 \succeq w_3$, so $a\ \langle\!| R; S |\!\rangle\ c$ as required. □

It follows from this result that if R and S are improvement simulations then so is $R; S$.

PROPOSITION **2.9** *$\trianglelefteq$ is a preorder.*

PROOF It is easily established that syntactic equivalence ($\equiv$) on closed terms is an improvement simulation[2], and hence that $\trianglelefteq$ is reflexive. Transitivity follows from the fact that since $\trianglelefteq$ is a improvement simulation, so is $\trianglelefteq; \trianglelefteq$. □

2.3 Improvement Extensionality

We want to establish conditions which guarantee that $\trianglelefteq$ is a precongruence, *i.e.* that $F(\bar{e}) \trianglelefteq F(\bar{e}')$ whenever $\bar{e} \trianglelefteq \bar{e}'$. A simple inductive argument on any term a establishes that this is equivalent to the requirement that $\trianglelefteq$ be closed under substitution, *i.e.* $a\{\bar{e}/\bar{x}\} \trianglelefteq a\{\bar{e}'/\bar{x}\}$ whenever $\bar{e} \trianglelefteq \bar{e}'$.

For a particular language, one method for giving a direct proof that the (bi)simulation is substitutive is to form an intermediate relation which is substitutive by construction, and to show that this is equal to the (bi)simulation relation in question.

The improvement-extensionality condition which we develop is expressed in terms of conditions on just such an intermediate relation. Here we adopt the intermediate relation given in [5], albeit defined relative to a different maximal simulation relation:

DEFINITION **2.10 (Howe)** *Define $a \trianglelefteq^\star b$ inductively on the syntax of a:*

$$\begin{array}{rll} x \trianglelefteq^\star b & \textit{if} & x \trianglelefteq b \\ F(\bar{e}) \trianglelefteq^\star b & \textit{if} & \exists F(\bar{e}').\ \bar{e} \trianglelefteq^\star \bar{e}' \textit{ and } F(\bar{e}') \trianglelefteq b \end{array}$$

□

[2] We assume that the evaluation relation respects syntactic equivalence.

The definition of $\unlhd^\star$ is best understood in terms of the properties that it satisfies, *viz.*,

PROPOSITION 2.11 *$\unlhd^\star$ is the smallest binary relation on $T(L)$ such that:*

(i) $\unlhd \subseteq \unlhd^\star$, *i.e.*, $a \unlhd b \Rightarrow a \unlhd^\star b$

(ii) $F(\bar{e}) \unlhd^\star F(\bar{e}')$ *if* $\bar{e} \unlhd^\star \bar{e}'$

(iii) $\unlhd^\star; \unlhd = \unlhd^\star$, *i.e.*, $a \unlhd^\star b$ *and* $b \unlhd c$ *imply* $a \unlhd^\star c$

PROOF Properties (i)–(iii) follow easily from the definition 2.10, together with the fact that $\unlhd$ is reflexive. Binary relations on $T(L)$ which satisfy (ii) and (iii) form a sub-lattice of the powerset lattice of all binary relations on $T(L)$, so a smallest relation satisfying (i)–(iii) exists (and is given by the intersection of all relations above $\unlhd$ in this sub-lattice). It is straightforward to show that $\unlhd^\star$ is minimal, and hence the smallest of such relations. □

One particularly useful consequence of the definition of $\unlhd^\star$ is the following:

PROPOSITION 2.12 (Howe) *If $a \unlhd^\star a'$ and $b \unlhd^\star b'$ then $b\{a/x\} \unlhd^\star b'\{a'/x\}$.*

PROOF (By induction on b) □

To prove that $\unlhd$ is a precongruence it is necessary and sufficient to prove that $F(\bar{e}) \unlhd F(\bar{e}')$ if $\bar{e} \unlhd \bar{e}'$, since this amounts to proving that $\unlhd = \unlhd^\star$. Therefore to show that $\unlhd$ is substitutive it is necessary and sufficient to show that $\unlhd^\star \subseteq \unlhd$. Since $\unlhd$ is the maximal fixed point of $⦃\cdot⦄$, it is sufficient to prove that $\unlhd^\star$ is an improvement simulation, *i.e.* that $\unlhd^\star \subseteq ⦃\unlhd^\star⦄$.

Following [5] we give a characterisation of when $\unlhd^\star$ is a precongruence, in terms of a condition on the operators of the language (analogous to Howe's extensionality condition).

DEFINITION 2.13 *An operator F is* improvement extensional *if for any closed terms $F(\bar{e}_1)$, $F(\bar{e}_2)$, whenever*

(i) $\bar{e}_1 \unlhd^\star \bar{e}_2$,

(ii) $F(\bar{e}_1){\downarrow}^{w_1}$, *and*

(iii) $\forall a_1, a_2 \in T(L)^\circ$, *if* $a_1{\downarrow}^{w}$ *with* $w <_W w_1$, *then* $a_1 \unlhd^\star a_2 \Rightarrow a_1 ⦃\unlhd^\star⦄ a_2$

then $F(\bar{e}_1) ⦃\unlhd^\star⦄ F(\bar{e}_2)$. □

Now if we say that a lazy computation system is improvement extensional whenever all of its operators are, we have the following result:

THEOREM 2.14 *A lazy computation system is improvement extensional if and only if $\unlhd$ is a precongruence.*

PROOF

($\Leftarrow$) If $\unlhd$ is a precongruence then from proposition 2.11 it is easily shown that $\unlhd = \unlhd^\star$. Improvement-extensionality then follows from the definition of $\unlhd$.

($\Rightarrow$) It is sufficient to show that $\unlhd^\star \subseteq \langle\!\![\unlhd^\star]\!\!\rangle$, *i.e.* that

$$\forall F(\bar{e}), b \in T(L)^\circ,\ F(\bar{e}) \unlhd^\star b \Rightarrow F(\bar{e})\ \langle\!\![\unlhd^\star]\!\!\rangle\ b.$$

In the case where $F(\bar{e})\uparrow$ then $F(\bar{e})\ \langle\!\![\unlhd^\star]\!\!\rangle\ b$ immediately follows. Otherwise, suppose $F(\bar{e})\downarrow^{w_1}$, then we prove by induction on w_1 that $F(\bar{e})\ \langle\!\![\unlhd^\star]\!\!\rangle\ b$. By the definition of $\unlhd^\star$ we have a term $F(\bar{e}')$ such that $\bar{e} \unlhd^\star \bar{e}'$ (and hence that $F(\bar{e}) \unlhd^\star F(\bar{e}')$), and $F(\bar{e}') \unlhd b$. By proposition 2.12 we can assume that $F(\bar{e}')$ is closed. The induction hypothesis coincides with condition (iii) in the definition of improvement extensionality, so we conclude that $F(\bar{e})\ \langle\!\![\unlhd^\star]\!\!\rangle\ F(\bar{e}')$. Then we have that $F(\bar{e})\ \langle\!\![\unlhd^\star]\!\!\rangle ; \unlhd\ b$. Now since

$$\begin{array}{rcll} \langle\!\![\unlhd^\star]\!\!\rangle ; \unlhd & = & \langle\!\![\unlhd^\star]\!\!\rangle ; \langle\!\![\unlhd]\!\!\rangle & \\ & \subseteq & \langle\!\![\unlhd^\star ; \unlhd]\!\!\rangle & \text{(Prop. 2.8)} \\ & = & \langle\!\![\unlhd^\star]\!\!\rangle & \text{(Prop. 2.11)} \end{array}$$

we conclude that $F(\bar{e})\ \langle\!\![\unlhd^\star]\!\!\rangle\ b$ as required.

□

3 Monotone Improvement in the Lazy Lambda Calculus

Unlike the standard notions of operational approximation and equivalence, it is likely that we may wish to consider a variety of improvement relations over a fixed lazy computation system. In particular we are interested in various notions of improvement over variants of the lazy lambda calculus, which include constants and lazy constructors, as a prototypical non-strict functional language.

For such languages we have found that the improvement extensionality condition holds, and is straightforward to check, for a number of simple notions of improvement. However it is somewhat tedious to re-establish improvement extensionality for each minor variant of the computation ordering[3]. In this section we give a structured operational semantics for a lazy lambda calculus (which defines a lazy computation system), and define a simple monotonicity condition on computation preorderings. Using the results of the previous section it is possible to show that any improvement simulation induced by a monotone computation order is guaranteed to be a precongruence.

Although we present this result in the context of a specific computation system, we believe that it is widely applicable; as evidence, we note that it applies to the class of *structured computation systems* defined by Howe [6].

To illustrate the usefulness of this characterisation, we give some examples of monotone computation orders.

---

[3] Notwithstanding certain simple closure conditions for precongruent improvement simulations, *i.e.* that if $\unlhd_I$ and $\unlhd_J$ are precongruences, then so are the improvement simulations $\unlhd_{I^{-1}}$ and $\unlhd_{I\cap J}$

3.1 A Lazy Lambda Calculus with Constants

We take the lazy computation language defined in example 2.4, and add a lazy list-constructor, **cons** (a canonical operator of arity $(0,0)$), together with a list case expression built with a noncanonical operator, **case** (of arity $(0,0,2)$). We add some constants, $c \in$ Const, (*i.e.* canonical operators of arity $()$) including the empty list, **nil**, and some strict primitive functions, $p \in$ Prim, over these constants. For convenience we write $\lambda((x).a)$ as $\lambda x.a$, application as $a\, b$, constants $c()$ as simply c, and operands of the form $().b$ as just b.

A lazy computation system for this language is then specified by first giving an operational semantics: figure 1 defines rule schemas which allow us to conclude evaluation judgements of the form $a \Downarrow b$ ("closed term a converges to principal weak head normal form b"). We will treat rules c and p are shorthand for a set of rules,

$$\frac{}{\lambda x.b \Downarrow \lambda x.b}\,\lambda \qquad \frac{}{\mathsf{cons}(e_1,e_2) \Downarrow \mathsf{cons}(e_1,e_2)}\,\mathsf{cons} \qquad \frac{}{c \Downarrow c}\,c$$

$$\frac{e_1 \Downarrow \lambda x.b \quad b\{e_2/x\} \Downarrow a}{e_1\ e_2 \Downarrow a}\,@$$

$$\frac{e_1 \Downarrow \mathsf{nil} \quad e_2 \Downarrow a}{\mathsf{case}(e_1,e_2,(x,y).e_3) \Downarrow a}\,\mathsf{case1} \qquad \frac{e_1 \Downarrow \mathsf{cons}(e_h,e_t) \quad e_3\{e_h,e_t/x,y\} \Downarrow a}{\mathsf{case}(e_1,e_2,(x,y).e_3) \Downarrow a}\,\mathsf{case2}$$

$$\frac{e_1 \Downarrow c_1 \cdots e_n \Downarrow c_n \quad ([\![p]\!](c_1,\ldots,c_n) = a)}{p(e_1,\ldots,e_n) \Downarrow a}\,p$$

Figure 1: Operational Semantics

one for each $c \in$ Const and $p \in$ Prim; informally we assume that each primitive function p of n arguments is given meaning by some partial map $[\![p]\!]$, from a tuple of n constants to a constant. Now we define the lazy computation system as in example 2.4: let W be the set of closed proofs (derivations) in the above system, *i.e.* proofs of judgements of the form $a \Downarrow b$, where a and b are closed terms. Define the family $\{\xrightarrow{\Delta}\}_{\Delta \in W}$ as $a \xrightarrow{\Delta} b$ whenever Δ is a proof of the judgement $a \Downarrow b$. The well-founded ordering $<_W$ is taken to be the immediate-subproof relation.

3.2 Monotone Computation Preorders

Definition 3.1 *A computation preorder* $\succeq$ *is* rule-monotone *if for all judgements* S, S', *and all* $\Delta_1,\ldots,\Delta_n$, $\Delta'_1,\ldots,\Delta'_n \in W$, *if*

$$\Phi = \frac{\Delta_1,\ldots,\Delta_n}{S}\,\mathbf{r} \quad \Phi' = \frac{\Delta'_1,\ldots,\Delta'_n}{S'}\,\mathbf{r}$$

are proofs (by rule $\mathbf{r}$*), and if for each* i, $\Delta_i \succeq \Delta'_i$, *then* $\Phi \succeq \Phi'$. □

Theorem 3.2 *If* $\succeq$ *is rule-monotone, then* $\trianglelefteq_{\succeq}$ *is a precongruence.*

PROOF Assume that $\succeq$ is rule-monotone, then by theorem 2.14 it is necessary and sufficient to show that each operator is improvement extensional. Details not included for lack of space, but fairly straightforward: the case for @ requires prop. 2.12, and the lack of restrictions on the exact set primitive functions relies on the fact that they are partial maps between constants, not arbitrary terms. □

It turns out that this result generalises to a large class of lazy computation systems, namely those definable by the so-called *structured computation systems* of [6]. A structured computation system is a lazy computation system defined by SOS-style rules which obey certain simple syntactic restrictions (basically, a requirement that meta-variables in the antecedents of a rule do not form cyclic dependencies, and that the expression schemes should be sufficiently "simple"). Howe shows that any structured computation system is extensional. Analogously, a simple adaptation of this proof yields the result that a structured computation system is improvement-extensional with respect to any monotone computation preorder. The details of this result will be reported elsewhere.

Deriving Computation Orders from Property Maps

In an abstract setting, the actual choice computation preorder, $\succeq$, is somewhat arbitrary. However, in choosing W to be the entire derivation tree of an evaluation judgement, and by identifying computational properties with properties of the proof tree, we can obtain definitions of various computation preorders which are, to some extent[4], correct with respect to the operational semantics.

For example, suppose the constants of the above language include the integers, and we have integer multiplication as a primitive function; then one notion of improvement, could be based on the number of multiplications performed, *viz.* the number of instances of the rule p for which $p \equiv \textsf{multiply}$ in respective proofs.

Following this approach, it is convenient to define various computation orders by providing a map from proofs to a set of "computational properties". The set of computational properties will represent some aspect of resource-use, and therefore will have some natural ordering. We require that this should be a preorder, although in practice, for a sufficiently abstract notion of property we would expect a partial order.

If we call a function from W to any preorder $(P, \sqsubseteq)$ a *property map*, then any property map $f \in (W \to (P, \sqsubseteq))$ induces an improvement preordering on W, $\succeq_f$ by:

$$\Delta_1 \succeq_f \Delta_2 \iff f(\Delta_1) \sqsupseteq f(\Delta_2).$$

By a small abuse of notation, will denote the corresponding improvement simulation by $\trianglelefteq_f$. A natural way of defining a property map is by induction on proofs, by cases according to the last rule applied. For such definitions, the rule-monotonicity property is usually straightforward to check.

[4] In general, this assumes that we can identify the *computation process* and the *proof tree*. For some languages (unlike this one and most other functional languages we have considered) the proof-construction process (*i.e.* interpretation) may involve backtracking, in which case this computational information would not be present in the final proof.

3.3 Examples

In the remainder of this section we give some examples of rule-monotone improvement orderings, defined in terms of various property maps.

(i) The property map, $W \to \{*\}$ gives (trivially) a rule-monotone improvement ordering, and the corresponding notion of improvement simulation is essentially just the usual "applicative simulation" [1].

(ii) Define the property map **@time** $\in (W \to (\mathbf{N}, \leq))$, as

$$\mathbf{@time}(\Delta) = \textit{the number of instances of the } \mathbf{@}\textit{-rule in } \Delta.$$

This gives an improvement simulation simple measure of sequential time complexity.

(iii) The property map **callset** $\in (W \to (\mathcal{P}(\text{Prim}), \subseteq))$ gives the set of primitive functions called in a given proof (ordered by subset inclusion).

(iv) Define the property map **depth** $\in (W \to (\mathbf{N}, \leq))$ inductively as follows:

$$\mathbf{depth}\left(\frac{\Delta_1, \ldots, \Delta_n}{S}\,\mathbf{r}\right) = \begin{cases} 1 + \text{Max}(\mathbf{depth}(\Delta_1), \ldots, \mathbf{depth}(\Delta_n)) & \text{if } \mathbf{r} \in \text{Prim} \\ 1 + \mathbf{depth}(\Delta_1) + \cdots + \mathbf{depth}(\Delta_n) & \text{otherwise.} \end{cases}$$

A proof that $\succeq_{\mathbf{depth}}$ is rule-monotone is left as an exercise for the interested reader. The depth property gives an improvement simulation, $\trianglelefteq_{\mathbf{depth}}$, which describes improvement of parallelism for a simple parallel implementation of the semantics in which the arguments to primitive functions are evaluated in parallel, and computation is sequential otherwise. A theory of improvement for this relation may contain laws such as

$$\begin{aligned} &\mathsf{case}(x, p(x_1, \ldots x_n), (y_1, y_2).p(x_1, \ldots, x_k, e, x_{k+2}, \ldots, x_n)) \\ &\quad \trianglelefteq_{\mathbf{depth}} \; p(x_1, \ldots, x_k, \mathsf{case}(x, x_{k+1}, (y_1, y_2).e), x_{k+2}, \ldots, x_n) \end{aligned}$$

which can be verified by the Park induction principal, *i.e.* by constructing a relation which contains every ground instance, and by showing that this relation is an improvement simulation (definition 2.6)

4 Conclusions

4.1 Related Work

The class improvement preorders developed here generalises *cost equivalence* and *program refinement* developed in the author's previous work [13, 15] (the above cost equivalence can be generated as the derived the equivalence relations $\trianglelefteq \cap \trianglerighteq$). The motivation for the development of cost equivalence was to provide substitutive equivalences with respect to a simple calculus for time analysis—for the relationship to other work on time analysis of programs in lazy languages see [13, 15]. From the development of cost equivalence a program refinement relation arose naturally. This is a simple instance of the improvement simulation in a language which can easily be shown to be improvement extensional.

In [16] a class preorderings called *comparison relations* are considered for a side-effect free lisp derivative. The class of comparison relations is sufficiently general to express relations analogous to the kinds of improvement relation considered here, and indeed it is suggested that certain comparison relations could be developed to provide soundness and improvement proofs for program transformation laws. Only the maximal comparison relations (essentially, the standard operational approximation and equivalence relations) are considered in detail, and the results are specific to a particular language and model of computation.

As mentioned previously, section 2 is inspired by, and is a generalisation[5] of [5], although by contrast the motivation in Howe's case is in connection with the study of open-endedness and type-free reasoning in type theories. Astesiano *et al* [3] consider a highly parameterised definition of bisimulation which also could have been adapted for our purpose, although as far as we know there is no general study of congruence for such relations.

The form of simulation we introduce is related to Thomsen's extended bisimulation in CCS induced by a preorder on *actions* [17], particularly if we consider a notion of improvement bisimulation as $\trianglelefteq_I \cap \trianglerighteq_{I^{-1}}$. More recently, Arun-Kumar and Hennessy [2] have considered a specific efficiency preorder for CCS processes based on the number of internal (silent) actions performed by a process, and expressed as a refinement of weak bisimulation. They prove that it is preserved by all CCS contexts except summation, and develop a proof system for finite processes.

Moggi's categorical semantics of computation [10] is intended to be suitable for capturing broader descriptions of computation than just input-output behaviour. Gurr [4] has studied extensions of denotational semantics to take account of resource-use, and has shown how Moggi's approach can be used to model a notion computation for which program equivalence also captures equivalence of resource-requirements (and hence corresponds with the kind of cost equivalences generated by $(\!|\_|\!)$). Gurr extends Moggi's λ_c-calculus (a formal system for reasoning about equivalence) with sequents for reasoning about about the resource properties *directly* (although the ability to do this depends on certain "representability" issues, not least of all that the resource itself should correspond to a type in the metalanguage). This is analogous to the approach in [13, 15] where cost-equivalence (a "resource" equivalence) is used in conjunction with a set of *time rules* which are used to reason about the cost property directly. An important difference is that in our approach these concepts are derived from (and hence correct with respect to) the operational model, so we may argue, at least, that an operational approach provides a more appropriate starting point for a semantic study of efficiency—although the deeper connections between these approaches deserves some further study. In addition, Gurr gives an account of a semantic formalisation of non-exact complexity, which although outside the scope of our study, begins naturally by introducing a partial ordering on resources.

4.2 Further Work

The main limitation of this work is in it's treatment of nonstrict functional languages. In the example of the lazy lambda calculus the operational semantics

---

[5] If we take $\succeq$ to be the whole of $W \times W$ then the improvement extensionality condition can be shown to correspond exactly to the extensionality condition of [5].

describes a *call-by-name* evaluation mechanism, when most actual implementations of lazy evaluation use *call-by-need.* In the case of standard notions of operational equivalence and approximation this is not a problem, but in the case of improvement simulations, this becomes a major shortcoming, since we cannot safely derive appropriate improvement orderings from the model as we did in section 3, since the model nolonger reflects many operational properties accurately. It remains to be investigated whether lazy computation systems with "correct" notions of improvement can be derived from appropriate call-by-need operational semantics.

As an alternative patch consider the following: suppose we take a call-by-name notion of improvement simulation (which is a precongruence), and by some indirect means identify some subset of improvement simulation which is valid in a call-by-need model. (What we have in mind is the use of some notion of (sub)linearity or single-threadedness to identify when call-by-need and call-by-name are essentially the same.) Then we conjecture, for many simple notions of improvement (such as the examples in the previous section) that we can safely (w.r.t. call-by-need improvement) close-up this subset under substitution into any context, not just the linear ones. It is likely that notions such as strictness may, as in [14], have an important role to play in such an approach.

Acknowledgements Thanks to numerous members of the *Semantique* project for constructive feedback on the material presented here, and to the referees for their helpful comments on an earlier draft.

Bibliography

1. S. Abramsky. The lazy lambda calculus. In D. Turner, editor, *Research Topics in Functional Programming.* Addison Wesley, 1990.

2. S. Arun-Kumar and M. Hennessy. An efficiency preorder for processes. In *TACS.* LNCS 526, 1991.

3. E. Astesiano, A. Giovini, and G. Reggio. Generalized bisimulation in relational specifications. In *STACS.* LNCS 294, 1988.

4. D. Gurr. *Semantic Frameworks for Complexity.* PhD thesis, Department of Computer Science, Edinburgh, 1991. (Available as reports CST-72-91 and ECS-LFCS-91-130).

5. D. J. Howe. Equality in lazy computation systems. In *Fourth annual symposium on Logic In Computer Science.* IEEE, 1989.

6. D. J. Howe. On computational open-endedness in Martin-Löf's type theory. In *Sixth annual symposium on Logic In Computer Science*, 1991.

7. J.W. Klop. *Combinatory Reduction Systems*, volume 127 of *Mathematical Centre Tracts.* Mathematischen Centrum, 413 Kruislaan, Amsterdam, 1980.

8. R. Milner. Calculi for synchrony and asynchrony. *Theoretical Computer Science*, 25:267–310, 1983.

9. R. Milner and M. Tofte. Co-induction in relational semantics. *Theoretical Computer Science*, 1990. *(to appear).*

10. E. Moggi. Computational lambda-calculus and monads. In *Fourth annual symposium on Logic in Computer Science*, 1989.

11. C.-H. Luke Ong. *The Lazy Lambda Calculus: An Investigation into the Foundations of Functional Programming.* PhD thesis, Imperial College, University of London, 1988.

12. D. Park. Concurrency and automata on infinite sequences. In *5th GI conference on Theoretical Computer Science.* LNCS 104, Springer Verlag, 1980.

13. D. Sands. *Calculi for Time Analysis of Functional Programs.* PhD thesis, Imperial College, September 1990.

14. D. Sands. Complexity analysis for a lazy higher-order language. In *Proceedings of the Third European Symposium on Programming*, number 432 in LNCS. Springer-Verlag, May 1990.

15. D. Sands. Time analysis, cost equivalence and program refinement. In *Proceedings of the Eleventh Conference on Foundations of Software Technology and Theoretical Computer Science.* Springer, December 1991.

16. C. L. Talcott. *The Essence of Rum, A Theory of the intensional and extensional aspects of Lisp-type computation.* PhD thesis, Stanford University, August 1985.

17. B. Thomsen. An extended bisimulation induced by a prorder on actions. Master's thesis, Aalborg University, Institute of Electronic Systems, 1987.

Combining Single-Space and Two-Space Compacting Garbage Collectors*

Patrick M Sansom†
University of Glasgow

December, 1991

Abstract

The garbage collector presented in this paper makes use of two well known compaction garbage collection algorithms with very different performance characteristics: Cheney's two-space copying collector and Jonker's single-space sliding compaction collector. We propose a scheme which allows either collector to be used. The run-time memory requirements of the program being executed are used to determine the most appropriate collector. This enables us to achieve a fast collector for heap requirements less than half of the heap memory but allows the heap utilization to increase beyond this threshold. Using these ideas we develop a particularly attractive extension to Appel's generational collector.

1 Introduction

Many programming environments have a heap storage management system with automatic garbage collection. In these systems storage that is no longer referenced from outside the heap is automatically reused. It is now widely accepted that, for good performance, it is essential to allocate storage from a contiguous block of memory, rather than a free list [1]. It is also highly convenient when allocating variable-sized objects. To be able to do this the garbage collector is required to compact objects into one block, so the remaining memory is left in a contiguous block ready for allocation.

The main contribution of this paper is to present a collection scheme which brings together two very different collectors: Cheney's two-space copying collector [3] and Jonkers' single-space compacting collector [4], in a way that utilises the desirable characteristics of both collectors. This idea is then combined with Appel's generational collector to produce a particularly attractive garbage collection scheme.

---

* An earlier and more detailed version of this paper, entitled "Dual-Mode Garbage Collection", may be found in [8].

† Author's address: Department of Computing Science, The University, Glasgow, G12 8QQ, UK. E-mail: sansom@dcs.glasgow.ac.uk

1.1 Background

Over recent years Cheney's two-space copying garbage collection scheme has provided the basis for most compacting garbage collectors. Numerous attempts have been made to improve on his basic algorithm. Generational schemes which make use of the short expected lifetimes of recently created objects have improved performance greatly [2,5].

Cheney's scheme and most of these extensions suffer a serious drawback. The heap space utilised by objects in the heap is limited to half of the memory allocated to the heap. Schemes which do use generational collections to increase heap utilization impose additional costs (see section 5). This problem may be overcome in virtual memory systems where large virtual address spaces and virtual allocation can be used to expand the heap memory as required — at the cost of additional paging.

Though virtual memory is common on single processor systems, we are interested in developing garbage collection schemes for processing elements of parallel systems. Current technology does not provide these systems with virtual memory and shows little sign of doing so in the near future. As they are required to maintain a local heap the shortcomings of the copying garbage collector working within a fixed physical address space need to be addressed.

Jonkers has presented a single-space compacting collector which utilises the entire memory allocated to the heap. Though it solves the memory utilization problem, it suffers from a collection time proportional to the size of the heap, regardless of the current heap requirements.

We set out to design a compacting collection scheme which makes use of both Cheney's and Jonkers' collection schemes. The aim being to provide a fast collector for heap requirements less than half of the available memory while allowing the heap to grow beyond this without breaking the collector.

1.2 Outline

Section 2 briefly describes the two collection schemes. Section 3 provides an analysis of the performance of the two collectors. In section 4 we present our scheme which combines the two collectors. Section 5 describes how the dual-mode ideas can be incorporated into other schemes. In particular we describe an extension to Appel's generational collector which incorporates this approach. Some initial performance results are presented in section 6.

Finally, in section 7, we outline the ongoing work being undertaken to evaluate these ideas.

2 The Basic Collectors

This section outlines Cheney's two-space and Jonkers' single-space compacting collection schemes. Rather than describing the intricate details we highlight the significant characteristics of the two collection schemes. This sets the scene for the analysis presented in section 3.

2.1 Two-Space Copying

Cheney's two-space copying garbage collection scheme [3] divides the heap into two semi-spaces, called *from-space* and *to-space*. New cells are allocated in from-space. When from-space is full execution stops and the garbage collector is called. During a collection all live objects are copied from from-space to to-space leaving any free memory within the semi-space at the end of to-space. Semi-spaces are then *flipped* and execution resumed. In the next collection cycle copying objects in the opposite direction.

Cheney's algorithm is very attractive because:

- A complete garbage collection only requires one pass through the live objects. Each live object is copied once and all live references are examined once. A collection requires a fixed number of instructions for each object and a fixed number for each reference. This gives the algorithm a time complexity proportional to the size of the live memory.
- It requires no collector stack or other auxiliary data structures.
- The only requirement on the heap object structure is that objects that have been evacuated are large enough to hold a forward pointer, indicating the new address of the object in to-space, and that this can be recognised as such.

The major shortcoming of this algorithm is the restriction of the heap size to half of the available memory. As the live memory requirements of a program approach the size of a semi-space the performance of the garbage collector deteriorates because the amount of free space recovered during each collection falls. Programs which require more memory than the size of a semi-space cannot run.

2.2 Single-Space Compaction

Jonkers' single-space compacting collector is of the Mark-and-Sweep variety. It proceeds in two phases. In the first phase the collector marks all live objects. In the second, the collector sequentially scans the entire memory compacting the live objects towards one end of the heap. The compaction process used actually requires two scans.

Marking the heap is achieved using Deutsch-Schorr-Waite's pointer reversal algorithm [9]. This threads the stack through the objects, avoiding the need for an auxiliary stack. In addition to marking each live object we need to be able to record, for each object, the point within the object that is currently being marked.

The basic idea of Jonkers' algorithm [4] is to scan through the entire heap threading the live locations that reference an object to the object itself. This results in the locations that reference an object being made accessible from the object itself via a linear list. When this object is scanned the locations that have been threaded to the object are restored with the object's new heap location. After all the references have been threaded and subsequently restored with the new address the objects are "slid" to their new locations. The details of this are quite complex and are omitted here for brevity.

The main advantage of this collector is that it allows the entire memory allocated to the heap to be utilised by heap objects. On the negative side the time performance of this garbage collection scheme is significantly worse than the two-space copying scheme.

1. The requirement to scan the entire heap memory — not just the live memory — gives a garbage collection a time complexity of the order of the entire heap size! It should be noted that the actual work required for the garbage memory is very small. For each garbage object all we require is to recognise it as such and move on to scanning the next object in the heap.

2. The amount of processing required for each live object and reference is significantly larger than that required by the two-space scheme.

In addition there are also a couple of significant requirements placed on the objects within the heap. We have to be able to:

- Record our position within an object during pointer reversal marking.

- Thread locations that reference an object to the object. We require a pointer size field that can be distinguished from a heap location so the end of the threaded list can be identified. If the heap objects do not have such a field it is possible to add an extra field to all the objects (with a considerable space overhead). This field could also be used to encode our position during pointer reversal.[1]

- Recognise the beginning of the next object when scanning the heap.

Though this algorithm appears to be a lost cause the analysis in the following sections shows that it does still have a useful role to play.

3 Analysis of Performance

We now compare the performance characteristics of the two garbage collection schemes described above. First some definitions:

- Let $_1$ and $_2$ be subscripts used for the single-space (one-space) and two-space garbage collection schemes respectively.

- Let t_x be the time taken to perform a garbage collection of scheme x and m_x be the memory reclaimed by a collection of scheme x.

- Let M be the total heap memory available and R the amount of live memory currently required by the program running. Define $r = R/M$ to be the residency of the program running — the proportion of memory currently required.

[1] Our particular implementation for the STG-machine avoids adding any additional words to the heap objects.

- Finally, we define the efficiency of a garbage collection scheme to be the number of words reclaimed in a unit time.

$$e_x = \frac{m_x}{t_x}$$

We note that $1/e_x$ gives the time required to reclaim a word. If we assume that the residency does not change quickly, the number of words reclaimed will be approximately equal to the number of words allocated. This gives us a measure of the garbage collection overhead associated with the allocation of a word. Clearly we wish to minimise this value, or equivalently, maximise the efficiency.

From the discussion in sections 2.1 and 2.2 we derive the following performance equations:

$$\begin{aligned} t_2 &= aR & (1) \\ t_1 &= cR + b(M - R) & (2) \end{aligned}$$

We observe that we would expect $c > a$ as the overhead in the single-space collector is greater.

$$\begin{aligned} m_2 &= M/2 - R & (3) \\ m_1 &= M - R & (4) \end{aligned}$$

$$e_2 = \frac{M/2 - R}{aR} = \frac{M}{2aR} - \frac{1}{a} = \frac{1}{2ar} - \frac{1}{a} \qquad (5)$$

$$e_1 = \frac{M - R}{cR + b(M - R)} = \frac{1 - r}{cr + b(1 - r)} \approx \frac{1 - r}{cr} = \frac{1}{cr} - \frac{1}{c} \qquad (6)$$

The approximation in equation 6 is justified only for residencies of a reasonable size when the cr term dominates the $b(1 - r)$ term. We note also, that we would expect b to be very small as the code for garbage objects simply moves the scan along to the next object in the heap.

Looking at the efficiency graphs (figure 1) we observe that up to a particular program residency r^* the two-space collector is more efficient but beyond this the single-space collector performs better. We propose to consider running the single-space collector only for these large residencies justifying the approximation made in equation 6.

Determining r^*

Observing that r^* is the residency when $e_2 = e_1$, we have:

$$\begin{aligned} \frac{1}{cr^*} - \frac{1}{c} &= \frac{1}{2ar^*} - \frac{1}{a} \\ \frac{c - a}{ca} &= \frac{c - 2a}{2car^*} \\ r^* &= \frac{c - 2a}{2(c - a)}, r^* \neq 0 \end{aligned}$$

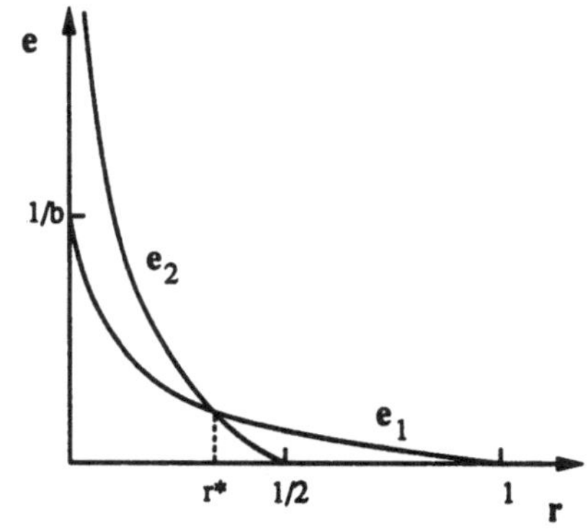

Figure 1: Efficiency of the two garbage collectors

Defining k to be the residency coefficient ratio of the two garbage collection schemes ($k = c/a$) we get:

$$r^* = \frac{ka - 2a}{2(ka - a)} = \frac{k-2}{2(k-1)} = \frac{k/2 - 1}{k - 1} \tag{7}$$

From this we see that a value of $k = 4$ would give $r^* = 1/3$.

The actual value of k needs to be determined experimentally for particular implementations of the garbage collection schemes. A reasonable approximation can be obtained quite easily by measuring the average time for each garbage collection on a residency of sufficient size to justify the approximation in equation 6, say 1/3, and taking the ratio $k \approx t_{1,r=1/3}/t_{2,r=1/3}$.

Initial results from the implementation outlined in section 6 indicate a value of $k \approx 3.5$ giving $r^* \approx 30\%$.

4 Combining The Collectors

The above performance comparison shows that neither collector is "best" over all possible program residencies. It would be beneficial to be able to determine which collector to use based on the current residency of the program being run. We propose to do exactly this. While the residency is less than r^* the two-space collector will be used but for residencies greater than r^* the single-space collector will be used (see figure 2).

We calculate the residency immediately following a garbage collection:

$$r = \frac{Hnext - Hlow}{HTop - HBot} \tag{8}$$

This is used as an estimate to determine which garbage collection scheme to use on the following collection. If the residency changes significantly between collections this estimate may result in the least appropriate garbage collection scheme being used when the garbage collection is required. We note that it will only be used

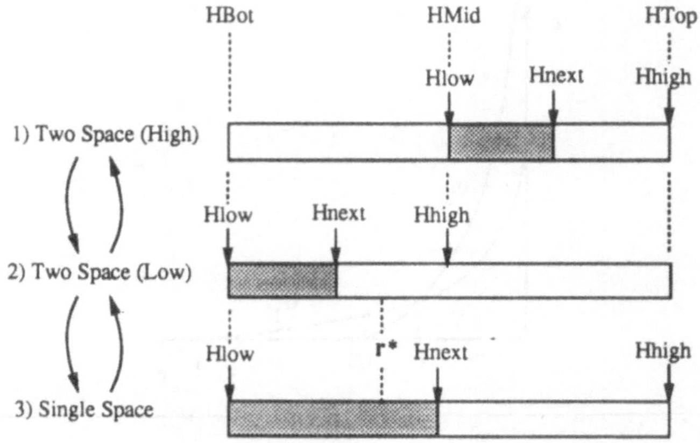

(1) and (2) are both states after a two-space collection is completed. We move between them each time we flip the semi-spaces. After flipping from (1) to (2) we can test the residency and decide to change our collection scheme to a single-space collector (3). We change back to a two-mode (2) collector after any single-space collection determines the residency to be less than r^*. Note that after performing a two-space collection which results in a flip from (2) to (1) it is not easy to switch to a single-space collector. The simplest solution is to wait until we have performed the next two-space collection which will flip back to (2).

Figure 2: Switching between collectors

for one collection (or possible two in the case of the two-space collector (figure 2)) before the new residency is determined and the more appropriate scheme used.

The work required to change the current collection scheme is minimal. To change from 2 to 3 (in figure 2) all we have to do is modify `Hhigh` and change the `Mode` to single-space. To change back we reset `Hhigh` to `HMid` and change the `Mode` back to two space. The `Mode` is used to determine which collector to invoke when garbage collection is required.

As switching collection schemes is cheap and the collector's performance are similar near the decision point, r^*, we are not concerned with occasionally choosing the least appropriate collector. We can avoid an oscillating situation by using two residency thresholds: one for changing from a two space to single-space collector; and a lower threshold for changing back.

4.1 Characteristics of the Dual-Mode Collector

The basic achievement of the Dual-Mode collector is to allow the residency to grow beyond half of the heap memory. It has the performance of the two-space collector for residencies below r^* and of the single space collector for residencies above r^*. This does not come free:

1. We require code to perform both collection schemes. The extra memory required by the collection code reduces the memory available for the heap.

2. The objects in our heap have to comply with the requirements and restrictions placed on them by both garbage collection schemes. In particular, we have to be able to:

   - Leave a forward pointer in from-space when copying,
   - Record our position within an object during pointer reversal marking and
   - Link all references to a particular object during compaction.

Where the dual-mode scheme performs well is when the residency is not constant. There are two main sources of variation in the residency. One is the basic residency required by the particular task a program is performing. The residency required by different tasks within a program may vary. The other source is more obscure and much harder to determine. It arises as a result of the build up and destruction of intermediate data structures during execution. The variations here can be quite large — the work on space leaks highlights this problem.

Consider a program which has a residency that remains low most of the time, but at one point during execution the residency grows significantly, before settling down again. A standard two-space collector would require a memory size of at least twice the peak heap requirements, to cope with this. Our collector only requires a memory size equal to the peak heap requirements. When the residency is low the two-space collector will be used. It is only during the sudden peak that we have to change to use the single-space scheme until the residency settles down again. We achieve a much more efficient use of the memory resources available.

We note that virtual memory systems can avoid this problem to some extent as more virtual memory can be requested as required. The problem with this is that this additional memory may impose a significant paging cost. It may be more efficient in virtual memory machines to use a slightly less efficient single-space collector instead of incurring the additional paging cost.

5 Dual-Mode Ideas and Generational Collectors

Having introduced the idea of dual-mode garbage collection we pause to consider its application to the more sophisticated generational garbage collection schemes. We first observe that it is possible to use the dual-mode ideas wherever a two-space collector is used. This allows us to remove the requirements to maintain a to-space of a particular size. We can fall back to the single-space collector when the copying collector does not have a to-space large enough at its disposal. The merits of doing this will depend on the particular scheme under consideration.

Some generational schemes, such as that proposed by Lieberman and Hewitt [5], do allow heap utilization to increase beyond half by using a copying collector to collect smaller units of heap at a time (generations). This only requires a piece of memory the size of a single generation to be reserved for use as to-space. These schemes have other costs associated with them. All these schemes keep track of the hopefully infrequent pointers from older to newer generations. In addition they require a scheme to identify new-to-old pointers into the generation being collected.

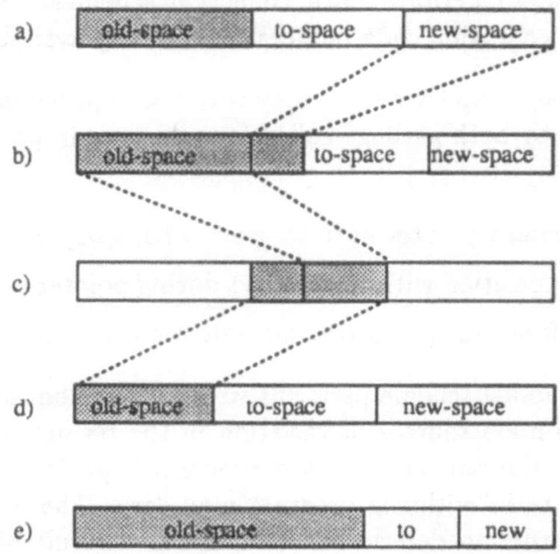

The basic heap organization of Appel's collector is depicted in (a). New objects are allocated in *new-space*. When this fills a minor collection is performed. This collects new-space moving it into *to-space* using a coping scheme. *Old-space* is then extended to include the objects just collected, compare (b). The free heap is split again and allocation can continue in new-space. At some point after a minor collection a major collection is performed. This copies the, as yet, un-collected parts of old-space, see (c), and then moves all of old-space back to the lower end of the heap, compare (d). (e) shows a situation that is not possible in Appel's collector but using dual-mode ideas can be coped with by using the single-space collector to collect old-space.

Figure 3: Appel's Generational Collector

This problem is approached in different ways. Lieberman and Hewitt require all younger generations to be scavenged to identify such pointers. To collect the entire heap therefore requires time proportional to the *square* of the live memory. Other schemes have proposed complex bookkeeping to keep track of all references into a generation — complicating the collector greatly.

Appel has described a particularly simple two generation garbage collection scheme based on a copying collector [2]. We spend the rest of this section discussing how the dual-mode ideas can be applied to his scheme. The result is a very attractive collection scheme.

Appel's scheme divides the heap into just two generations, *old* and *new*. The old generation is placed in the lower end of the heap memory. The remaining memory is split into two semi-spaces. The higher space is allocated to the new generation and the lower is used when collecting the new generation, during a *minor* collection, as to-space. This is depicted in figure 3. Whenever the new generation is collected all the objects are promoted onto the end of the old region and the old region extended. Because young records have a high mortality rate the new region contains few live objects. As a result, copying these onto the end of the old region is relatively fast. When the old region grows to half of the heap space a *major* collection is performed.

This collects the entire old generation by copying it into the other half of the heap memory and using a move operation to move the old generation back to the lower end of the heap.

Appel developed his scheme for a virtual memory system where the heap space could be extended as required. A major shortcoming of Appel's scheme, when considered for a system without virtual memory, is that it can only function while the residency remains below half the memory allocated to the heap. This arises because the old generation must be copied during a major collection. We observe that a single-space collection scheme could be used to collect the old generation. This would actually have the same effect as the combined copy and move that Appel uses during a major collection.

Our dual-mode ideas are particularly suited to Appel's collector. Most garbage collection is spent doing minor collections. These always use the two-space copying scheme, which is relatively fast — especially if there is a high proportion of garbage. Occasionally a major collection is required which we perform using the single-space collector. This allows the old generation to be extended beyond half the heap without breaking the collector.

The performance of Appel's collector is dependent on the mortality rate of the objects in the new generation. By only using two generations the size of new space is maximised to increase the time between collections. This increases the likelihood of a young object becoming garbage before the next minor collection. As the old generation grows, the size of the new generation decreases, reducing the performance of the minor collections as a larger proportion of the objects will be live. Our extension allows the residency to grow beyond half of the heap memory, but has to accept the decrease in the performance associated with this. These performance trade-offs still need to be carefully examined.

6 Initial Performance Results

We have implemented the two-space, single-space and dual-mode collection schemes for the STG machine with the intention of incorporating them into the new Haskell compiler being developed at Glasgow [6]. The implementation avoids interpreting the structure and current state of closures by attaching specific code to heap objects. This code *knows* the structure and current state of the object and performs the appropriate actions without having to test any flag or arity fields. It should be noted that our implementation of the single-space compacting collector requires no additional storage to be associated with each heap object. As a result heap-objects have the same structure regardless of the collector being used. Space prevents us describing these ideas here. The interested reader is referred to [8].

Our garbage collection code has been written in C as the compiler uses C as an intermediate assembler. Unfortunately the compiler is not yet in a state to run real applications so our initial results have been obtained using a test bed which constructs a heap and then invokes the garbage collector to collect it.

During each run it builds a heap of the required size and structure with an appropriate proportion of garbage dispersed through it. It then invokes the garbage collector, noting the time it takes to collect the heap. This is performed a number of times and the averaged recorded.

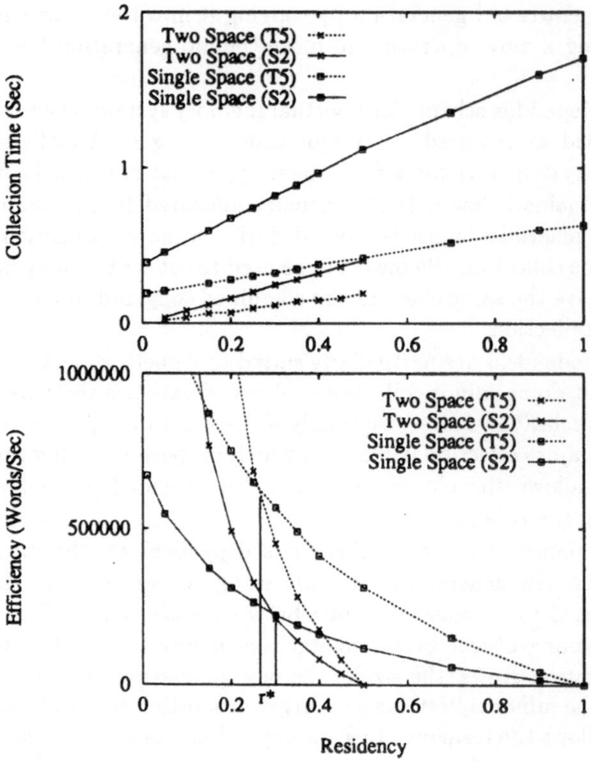

Figure 4: Comparison of Garbage Collection Schemes (Sun 3/60, Heap=1Mb)

The graphs in figure 4 show the time and efficiency of the two-space and single-space collectors averaged over five runs. The different heap structures shown are: a five-way branching tree (T5), where each object contains five pointers except for the leaves which contain five non-pointers words; and a shared list structure (S2), where each object contains two pointers and has two references to it.

The results were consistent with our predictions from section 3. Though the various heap structures investigated gave significantly different performance figures, arising from different heap object sizes and degrees of sharing, they all had the same shaped curves and similar threshold residencies. Depending on the structure the approximation for the value of k was between 3 and 3.5 giving a resulting threshold residency, r^*, of between 25% and 30%. This can be observed in figure 4.

A noticeable drawback of the scheme is the significantly larger time required by the single-space collector to perform a collection. This increases any pause experienced by the user, though the frequency is reduced.

The most striking feature about these results is the huge improvement in two-space collector performance for small residencies. Any program which has a large basic residency will suffer, regardless of whether a two-space or single-space scheme is used, because this heap is repeatedly collected without releasing any garbage. It is in this situation where we hope that Appel's collector will perform well as it avoids repeatedly collecting this part of the heap.

7 Ongoing Work

Though these ideas look promising they have yet to be fully explored. Considerable practical work aimed at evaluating the ideas is still required. In particular we want to:

- Examine and compare the performance of the two-space, single-space, and dual-mode collection schemes when used as collectors for real Haskell applications.
- Implement the dual-mode version of Appel's collector and evaluate its performance.
- Examine the performance trade-offs of increasing the heap size in a virtual memory vs. using a collector that utilises the entire heap.

Acknowledgments

Thanks to my supervisor, Simon Peyton Jones, for many useful discussions and comments. This work was supported by a scholarship from the Commonwealth Scholarship Commission.

Bibliography

1. AW Appel, "Garbage collection can be faster than stack allocation," *Info Proc Lett* 25 (1987), 275–279.
2. AW Appel, "Simple generational garbage collection and fast allocation," *Software — Practice and Experience* 19 (Feb 1989), 171–183.
3. CJ Cheney, "A nonrecursive list compacting algorithm," *CACM* 13 (Nov 1970), 677–678.
4. HBM Jonkers, "A fast garbage compaction algorithm," *Info Proc Lett* 9 (July 1979), 26–30.
5. H Lieberman & C Hewitt, "A real-time garbage collector based on the lifetimes of objects," *CACM* 26 (June 1983), 419–429.
6. SL Peyton Jones, "The spineless tagless G-machine: a second attempt," Dept of Computer Science, University of Glasgow, 1991.
7. M Rudalics, "Multiprocessor list memory management," RISC-LINZ Series no 88-87.0, Reasearch Inst for Symbolic Computation, Johannes Kepler University, Dec 1988.
8. PM Sansom, "Dual-mode garbage collection," in *Proc Third International Workshop on Implementation of Functional Languages on Parallel Architectures*, CSTR 91-07, Dept of Electronics and Computing Science, University of Southampton, June 1991.
9. H Schorr & WM Waite, "An effecient machine-independent procedure for garbage collection in various list structures.," *CACM* 10 (Aug 1967), 501–506.

External Function Calls in a Functional Language

Manfred Schmidt-Schauß[†]

Abstract

In order to perform IO's in the pure, nonstrict functional language NATURAL EXPERT LANGUAGE (NEL) via subroutine calls, we have extended functional programming by nondeterministic functions. These functions are hyperstrict and their input and output must be data. This makes it possible to write functional programs that run under (multi-user) TP-monitors, furthermore it makes programming cleaner and easier. Integration into commercial mainframe DP-environments is improved since such programs behave like usual commercial dialog programs. Some source-level transformations and optimisations can no longer be used such as: unfolding, common subexpression elimination and fully lazy lambda-lifting.

Acknowledgements. I thank Nigel Hutchison, Ute Neuhaus and David Earlam for their comments on a draft of this paper. Special thanks to Will Partain, whose comments contributed to the final version.

Introduction

Interaction of a pure functional program with its environment via function calls like "get" or "put" is usually considered as not referentially transparent, since the same function called with the same arguments gives different answers for different calls. Consider for example the function ASK_INT of type TEXT → INTEGER. An evaluation of this function will send a pop-up window to a terminal displaying the text and asking for an integer value, returning as result the value typed by the user. This function applied to "`type some number`" may have as result any valid integer. In the normal framework of pure nonstrict functional languages this is not considered as referentially transparent, since the two expressions

(ASK_INT "?") + (ASK_INT "?")

and

2 * (ASK_INT "?")

may have different values, and thus equational reasoning does not apply.

In commercial functional languages, simple, clean and understandable interfaces to devices such as terminals, databases, other languages, TP-monitors and to the operating system have a high priority. A commercial functional language with ugly or incomprehensible interfaces will not be accepted and hence will be a loss-making business. Looking for example at the papers [5] and [3] the conclusion would be that it is impossible to combine pure functional programming languages with programming

† Software AG, Uhlandstr 12, 6100 Darmstadt, Germany

IO's by local calls as in third and fourth generation languages. In this paper we will discuss an alternative approach.

Before going on, let us try to clarify the notion of referential transparency. In [8] there is a discussion of this and some related notions. They define referential transparency as the property of a language that the value of every expression depends only on the values of subexpressions, not on their syntactic form. We will call this notion *weak referential transparency*. A language permits *unfolding*, if it is safe to syntactically replace variables by their defining expression. Then *referential transparency* is the conjunction of weak referential transparency and unfoldability.

With regard to these definitions, the above mentioned papers criticise the loss of unfoldability. Without unfolding, the expression 2 * (ASK_INT "?") cannot be transformed into (ASK_INT "?") + (ASK_INT "?"). But this is not a surprise, since [8] gives a strong hint that unfoldability and nondeterminism cannot coexist.

I will try to isolate three different kinds of behaviours or events of external functions that may collide with the usual understanding of pure functional programming.

Event type 1: The same external function call may result in different answers in a different run of the program.

Event type 2: The same external function call may have different results if called twice in the same run of the program.

Event type 3: One external function call may influence another such external function call via the external environment. (for example, updating a database may influence a subsequent request).

Event type 3 violates purity, since this is a way to reintroduce global variables misusing the environment. Thus the conclusion is that this must be avoided at any cost.

Event type 1 may be acceptable even for a hard-core functional programmer, as long as event type 2 and event type 3 are not possible, by the following argument: We can assume that the meaning of all the nondeterministic functions is chosen at the start of the program. An implementation method would be memoization.

Event type 2 is the one we permit. This provides an acceptance problem for the functional programming community, since it is taken for granted that this type of event marks the boundary between pure functional programming and misusing pure functional programming in a procedural style. NATURAL EXPERT permits this event in a restricted form. In this paper we will provide arguments that it is not off the limits of pure nonstrict functional programming.

The approach where the functional program is considered as a big function that accepts an input stream and outputs a stream of answers is attractive, since referential transparency is not compromised. In Haskell [2] streams are used, and dialog functions map a list of responses to a list of requests. This works (in a UNIX environment), however, if a dialog-oriented functional program uses this paradigm for performing IO's, the programming style is rather counterintuitive. The input stream (output stream) must be passed around and the construction of the output stream must be made with care, since otherwise the question-answering sequence may become unsynchronised. A dialog-oriented functional program that runs under a TP-monitor cannot even use this view of an input-stream, since the TP-monitor does not provide such an input-stream. TP-monitor programs work on the basis of send and receive.

My motivation to propose a different method is our work on the commercial product NATURAL EXPERT LANGUAGE (NEL) (see [4],[7]), a pure nonstrict functional programming language with strong polymorphic type-checking. The underlying abstract machine is a graph reducer [6] of the G-machine-type. There are so-called gateway functions that can be viewed as externally defined functions. Their task is to communicate via a fourth generation language with the environment, such as databases, printers, and terminals. Based on our experience with a dozen or so systems that are in production, we can state that calling these gateway functions from within a functional program works very nicely and exhibits the expected behaviour.

The paper has three sections, first we give some examples of our usage of external calls, in the second we present some coniderations on semantics, and in the third we describe some experiences and applications.

1. Usage of Gateways in Natural Expert Language

Basically, we use gateways for three purposes: communication with a user, communication with databases, and for importing functionality (like text-processing or trigonometric functions). Since the last one requires no discussion, we will discuss only the first two in this section.

Calling external subprograms or routines via a so-called gateway is roughly done as follows: Before the control is passed to the external program, all its input is evaluated in a hyperstrict fashion. The input to a gateway can only be data. This data is then transferred from the heap into a (nested) record-structure. Note that the storage that is used by the gateway subprogram is not under control of NATURAL EXPERT. If the subprogram has finished, it has to transfer its data back to the heap. These transfer-routines are automatically generated and compiled at compile time of the corresponding gateway function. In our environment it is not possible to pass closures to the external subprograms and then request more evaluation from the subprogram, if some values are needed. The reason is that this evaluation may in turn demand a gateway call, but then the flow of control will be destroyed, since the fourth generation environment does neither support coroutines nor a recursive invocation of NATURAL EXPERT (with the same environment).

1.1 Usage of Gateways to Communicate with the User.

Suppose we have a dialog system for giving advice for car insurances. Then a step in the dialog would be that the user selects a district. This is done by presenting a table of districts on the terminal where the user may select one by marking a check-box. Looking at the functional program, this is done via a general purpose function SELECT_FROM_LIST of type (TEXT, LIST(α,TEXT)) $\rightarrow$ α . The input is a header text, and a list of pairs consisting of the objects and their text representation. This function is (in NEL-syntax) programmed as follows:

```
SELECT_FROM_LIST ($HT, $INLIST) :=
  FST( PICKED($SEL,$INLIST) )
  WHERE $SEL IS GATE_SELECT_FROM_LIST ($HT,$LIST),
                $LIST IS MAPPED(SCND,$INLIST)
```

The function GATE_SELECT_FROM_LIST has type (TEXT, LIST(TEXT)) $\rightarrow$ INTEGER, FST returns the first element of a pair, and SCND the second element of a pair. (The identifiers starting with $ are local variables, the other identifiers are globally defined). The function GATE_SELECT_FROM_LIST is hyperstrict, that is, it evaluates its arguments to head normalform, i.e. it evaluates its arguments in full depth. The handling of the map, such as paging and help and others, is all in the called 4th generation program.

The function does the following. The input parameter $INLIST is a list of pairs consisting of the object and the corresponding text; $LIST is an extraction of only the texts. This avoids the evaluation of all the object-expressions. The gateway GATE_SELECT_FROM_LIST returns an integer that is the position of the selected item in the list. We can assume that the corresponding program guarantees that the integer is a valid position in the list. Thus, we can view the gateway GATE_SELECT_FROM_LIST as a nondeterministic function that returns an integer value, but it cannot be predicted which one.

The rule above is also able to provide menus. The text then points to an action to be performed and the action is performed after the selection. The separation of texts and objects ensures that the right action is performed after the selection. Our experience with a menu-driven map-editor that is written in NEL shows that it is not sufficient to rely on data-dependency. The programmer has to take into account the extent to which the action-expressions are to be evaluated. The serialisation operator *⇒ may help in such situations to enforce the right extent of evaluation. The implementation of *⇒ is as follows: To evaluate _(exp1 *⇒ exp2)_, first evalute _exp1_ to weak head normal form, ignore the result, then evaluate _exp2_.
The following (simplified) example is a demonstration of using serialisation to solve that problem.

Assume MODIFY_PAIR: (INT,INT) →(INT,INT) is a function that permits a user to modify a pair of integers. The dialogue should be as follows: First a menu is displayed with three choices: i) MODIFY_THE_FIRST, ii) MODIFY_THE_SECOND, iii) NUMBERS ARE OK, the user selects one and then a window opens for changing the appropriate number or returning the pair.
The first try is:

```
MODIFY_PAIR($I1,$I2) :=
    SELECT_FROM_LIST ("SELECT AN ACTION",
     <("modify first arg", MODIFY_PAIR(ASK_INT (LEGIBLE $I1),$I2)),
      ("modify second arg", MODIFY_PAIR($I1, ASK_INT (LEGIBLE $I2)) ,
      ("Return ", ($I1,$I2)) > )
```

(LEGIBLE returns a string representation for an integer argument.)

Unfortunately, this function does not behave the right way: It asks again and again whether to modify the first or the second number until "Return" is selected and then asks again and again to modify the integers according to the selections made before. A possible remedy is to insert serialisation at the beginning of MODIFY_PAIR:

```
MODIFY_PAIR($I1,$I2) := $I1 *⇒ $I2 *⇒
        SELECT_FROM_LIST ("SELECT AN ...
```

Now the function has the desired behaviour.

The following example deals with some special problems concerning lambda-lifting. It demonstrates that fully lazy lambda-lifting provides some problems in the presence of nondeterministic functions.

```
GUESS_INT $MSG := ($GET_EQ_INT 120)
    WHERE $GET_EQ_INT $I :=
            ((IF $A NE $I  THEN $GET_EQ_INT $I  ELSE $A)
                WHERE $A IS ASK_INT $MSG)
```

The call of (GUESS_INT "Guess the right number") is intended to behave as follows:

It should display a message on the terminal "Guess the right number" and then wait for an integer input. If the number is not 120, the question is asked again. If it is 120, then the returned value is 120. The problem here is how lambda-lifting is implemented. Suppose, we use maximal free expressions, then the lambda-lifted version of $GET_EQ_INT may look as follows:

```
    ($GET_EQ_INT_LL (120, ASK_INT $MSG ))
     WHERE $GET_EQ_INT_LL ($I,$A_I_MSG) :=
                ((IF $A_I_MSG NE $I
                  THEN $GET_EQ_INT_LL ( $I,$A_I_MSG)
                  ELSE $A_I_MSG)
```

But now the program doesn´t work as intended: If the answer is 120, then the returned value is 120. If the user doesn´t hit the first time, which is very likely, the function loops. Thus our implemented version of lambda-lifting does not use the maximal-free-expression optimisation. Currently, only variables are lifted, thus our lifted version is as follows:

```
 $GET_EQ_INT_LL ($I,$MSG) :=
           ((IF $A NE $I THEN $GET_EQ_INT_LL ( $I,$MSG)  ELSE $A)
                    WHERE $A IS ASK_INT $MSG)
```

This works as intended, starting a dialog, asking again and again until the user types the right number. We could improve upon this by permitting lambda-lifting using something like "maximal free deterministic expressions"

1.2 Gateways accessing databases

In NATURAL EXPERT, reading and updating databases via a gateway-call is possible, since a programmer can write arbitrary code in such a subroutine, but we consider this as dirty programming. To do this via gateways as nondeterministic functions means that we could never reason about the behaviour of such calls. For example, we could not even prove that the same query to the same database will result in the same answer. In our view the correct method is to carry around something like a pointer to the database and view the gateway call as deterministic. For example, DB_GET(query, DB) may return an answer to a query. The answer is always the same, as long as the query is the same, where equality of the database (database-pointer) means that the whole databases denote exactly the same. DB_UPDATE (parms, DB) results in DB', which is (a pointer to) the updated DB. It may be remarked that a database DB must be passed as parameter to the program, and cannot be obtained from the environment during the run, since the results of gateway calls cannot be coupled to the value of some external entity. This is from a certain point of view similar to Trinder´s approach [9], however, in the method given here, existing databases can be accessed.

A problem with such accesses to databases is that the unrestricted use of the method above would require an existing database system that can support several hypothetical database states, since there may be several references to the DB-argument. Conceptually, that means that the DB-system can maintain several copies of the whole database. Almost all commercial database systems have only a linear history, thus to access these databases using this method, there must be some restrictions to ensure that all requests are submitted using the newest version. A similar problem arises in using arrays in a functional language, however, it is not problematic to copy an array. Presumably, it is possible to ensure a correct behaviour by an appropriate check during compile-time. Several methods have been proposed so far: update-analysis, path-analysis or linear types (see e.g. [1], [10], [11]).

A real database access gives either the desired answer or a response-code. This may collide with the assumption that these database accesses being deterministic, since besides deterministic response codes like "duplicate record" or "invalid request", there are nondeterministic ones, like "record in use", "disk full", "IO-error", or "database not available". Thus there are two possibilities: to terminate the run of the functional program with error, or to consider also partially nondeterministic gateways.

2. Some Remarks on Semantics

A discussion of the problem of adding nondeterminism to functional languages is given in [3]. They study the addition of an explicit set data type to the language with the intended meaning that the sets denote different outcomes. This approach is very close to a nondeterministic one, but they refuse to provide a choice operator.

The semantics of a functional language that permits nondeterminism is a problematic issue, since it is no longer possible to interpret a programmed function in a simple way as a function in some domain.

Let's suppose there exists a nondeterministic semantics similar to the set-method of [3]. Every first-order function would then be interpreted as a relation: it relates all possible inputs to the possible outputs. For example, the ASK_INT function mentioned above is then interpreted as a relation in the cross-product of all strings with all integers. Since there are no restrictions, it is the full cross-product. The intended meaning of other nondeterministic gateways is similar: Every input can produce every output. Deterministic functions are interpreted as functions. Note that if there are no nondeterministic gateway functions, then there should be no difference to the usual formalism, i.e., the relations are functions. We can even say what a partially nondeterministic database-access means: It is interpreted as a relation, whose restriction to the return-code "OK" is a function.

In general we assume that gateways terminate, if the hyperstrict evaluation of the input terminates. This is adequate, since reasoning about nontermination should not take into account that the user never types something.

As an example let's look at the functions *F1 $X := 2*(ASK_INT $X)* and *F2 $X := (ASK_INT $X) + (ASK_INT $X)* . The first one can be interpreted as a relation that relates all texts to all even integers, the second one as a relation that relates all texts to all integers. With respect to this interpretation, there would be no difference between the second function and *F3 $X := (ASK_INT $X)* .

An issue related to the meaning is "What can be proved about a program?". For this we can ignore several side-effects of a program that do not influence its behaviour or its value, such as printing something, or displaying on a terminal, as long as there is no feedback. With nondeterministic functions, it should remain possible to reason about termination, correctness of database-updates, about static program properties, like strictness of functions in some arguments, and evaluation order of expression.

3. Practical Experiences with the System.

Currently, about 10 licences for NATURAL EXPERT have been sold, and there are about 30 installations. Up to now, a dozen applications are in production. The most complex one is a spanish natural language interface to the databases of Telefonica de España [12]. This system contains two subsystems written in NEL and is used as a query interface. It is intended as a tool for a class of users without any knowledge about the database structure, the names of the fields, where the data is, how to write programs to acces it, etc. So, this class of users can´t use a query language like SQL. The system accesses more than 60 files and saves a lot of money.

One of the other applications in production is a loan evaluation system used in a spanish bank. This system first uses a statistical, package to evaluate the loan requests. This leaves 40% as doubtful. The cases are then fed into an NEL-system that successfully resolves half of them.

Integrated in the NEL-editor is the so-called type-compiler which is a module written in NEL. This module runs every time a new type is encountered, and uses gateways to update a database and report errors. This module has superseded a previous system written in a fourth generation language. Tho old one was not entirely reliable and also not maintainable, whereas the new one has proven to be very reliable and easy to maintain. The next release of NEL will contain more than 6 internal NEL-applications. All these systems employ gateways for communication with the end-user and with data-bases.

The success of these applications relies on the emphasis of NATURAL EXPERT LANGUAGE on integration and smooth interfaces to the commercial data processing environments. This includes the nondeterministic gateways as well as the corresponding programming style.

Conclusion

The addition of nondeterministic (hyperstrict, data->data) gateways in a commercial functional language permits programming dialogs as is usual in a TP-monitor environment, where dialog-IO´s are made in block-mode rather than as a stream The calls to get an input from the user can be programmed without an argument that stands for the environment. This is adequate, since a user in general behaves almost as a random variable.

Pure functional programming can be combined with deterministic and nondeterministic external function calls as in the procedural style. Dialog calls like ASK_INT "?" are interpreted as nondeterministic function calls, database accesses can be seen as a call of a deterministic external function. Whether our framework retains referential transparency or not, depends on its defintion in the presence of nondeterministic functions. Anyway, reasoning about programs should provide no problems, however, as far as I see, a corresponding theory has not yet been worked out. I encourage functional programming theoreticians to do further investigations into a combination of functional programming and nondeterminism.

The hyperstrictness of gateway calls can not only be seen as violating laziness, but seems attractive for using a graph reducer on a parallel machine, since it is like an annotation for performing parallel evaluation.

References

[1] A. Bloss, Update analysis and the efficient implementation of functional aggregates. In FPCA'89, pp.26-38,ACM Press, 1989

[2] P. Hudak, S.P.Jones, P, Wadler et. al, Report on the programming language Haskell: A nonstrict, purely functional language

[3] R.J.M. Hughes and J.O'Donell , Expressing and Reasoning about nondeterministic functional programs, Proc. of Functional Programming, Glasgow, 1989

[4] N. Hutchison, U. Neuhaus, M. Schmidt-Schauß, NATURAL EXPERT: A commercial functional programming environment, submitted to J. Functionl Programming

[5] L.McLoughlin and E.S.Hayes, Imperative Effects from a Pure Functional Language, Proc. of Functional Programming, Glasgow, 1989

[6] S. Peyton Jones, The Implementation of functional programming languages, Prentice Hall, (1987)

[7] Software AG, NATURAL EXPERT, Reference Manual, Version 1.1.3, (1990)

[8] Søndergaard, H., and Sestoft, P., Referential transparency, definiteness and unfoldability, Acta informatica 27, 505-517 (1990)

[9] P.Trinder, Referentially transparent database languages, Proc. of Functional Programming, Glasgow, 1989

[10] P. Wadler, Linear types can change the world!, In IFIP working conference on Programming concepts and methods, North Holland, 1990

[11] D.Wakeling, C. Runciman, Linearity and Laziness, Proc FPCA 1991, LNCS 523, pp. 215-240, (1991)

[12] Telefonica and Software Ag España, "Satelite: Exploiting Natural Language", Journal of the Asociacion Española para la Inteligencia Artificial, March 1991

A note on abstraction in Ruby

Mary Sheeran*

Abstract

This note points out that the abstraction relations that we use when designing representation changers in Ruby are exactly the difunctional relations. A simple characterisation of when the composition of two abstractions is an abstraction is also presented.

Introduction

A lot of hardware design is about data abstraction: representing complex datatypes in ways that can be implemented directly on silicon. Recent work in Ruby has concentrated on the development of a systematic way of designing circuits that change the representation of data. To do this, one needs to be precise about exactly what is an abstraction relation.

This note points out that the Ruby abstraction relations are exactly the difunctional relations that have been studied, quite independently, by those who work on relational methods of modelling types. The purpose of the note is to highlight this coming together of two apparently independent lines of research.

Proofs in this paper are presented in the 'Eindhoven style' proposed by Dijkstra, Feijen, van Gasteren and others. The style may appear verbose, but in practice it is a good way of doing proofs.

Ruby

In Ruby, we model circuits (or programs) as binary relations, and the ways of structuring circuits as functions from relations to relations. Two such structuring functions are relational composition and relational inverse. They are defined as follows:

$$
\begin{aligned}
a\,(R\,;S)\,c &\Leftrightarrow \exists b.\, a\,R\,b \wedge b\,S\,c \\
a\,R^{-1}\,b &\Leftrightarrow b\,R\,a
\end{aligned}
$$

and have the expected mathematical properties. For example,

$$
\begin{aligned}
R\,;(S\,;T) &= (R\,;S)\,;T \\
(R^{-1})^{-1} &= R \\
(R\,;S)^{-1} &= S^{-1}\,;R^{-1}
\end{aligned}
$$

*Address: Computing Science Dept., Glasgow University, Glasgow G12 8QQ, Scotland; Email: *ms@dcs.gla.ac.uk*.

Relational union is defined in the standard way and has the usual properties:

$$\begin{array}{rcl} a\,(R \cup S)\,b & \Leftrightarrow & a\,R\,b \vee a\,S\,b \\ (R \cup S)^{-1} & = & R^{-1} \cup S^{-1} \\ Q\,;(R \cup S) & = & (Q\,;R) \cup (Q\,;S) \\ (R \cup S)\,;T & = & (R\,;T) \cup (S\,;T) \\ R\,;R^{-1}\,;R \cup R & = & R\,;R^{-1}\,;R \end{array}$$

The last of these equalities is presented (and proved) in a different form by Hutton and Voermans [2], where it is called the triple rule. It is also used extensively in the paper by Hutton and Voermans in this volume. I use it once (and call it the triple rule) in the last proof in this paper.

For the purposes of this note (and as a notational experiment), I introduce an abbreviation for the form $A^{-1}\,;A$.

$$A\!> \;=\; A^{-1}\,;A$$

Read $A\!>$ as 'A right'. Some properties of 'right' are

$$\begin{array}{rcl} (A\!>)^{-1} & = & A\!> \\ (A\,;B)\!> & = & B^{-1}\,;A\!>\,;B \end{array}$$

The dual operator is defined by

$$<\!A \;=\; A\,;A^{-1}$$

and satisfies

$$\begin{array}{rcl} <\!A & = & (A^{-1})\!> \\ (<\!A)^{-1} & = & <\!A \\ <\!(A\,;B) & = & A\,;<\!B\,;A^{-1} \end{array}$$

A useful operator and its properties

In calculations, equations of the form $A\,;B = A$ arise very often. We think of them as assertions about the range of A and we introduce the abbreviation $A \vdash B$ for $A\,;B = A$. The dual of $\vdash$, which we write as $\dashv$, is also useful

$$A \dashv B \Leftrightarrow A\,;B = B$$

The two operators are dual because

$$A \dashv B \Leftrightarrow B^{-1} \vdash A^{-1}$$

Two useful properties of $\vdash$ are

$$\begin{array}{rcl} B \vdash C & \Rightarrow & A\,;B \vdash C \\ B \vdash C\,;D & \Rightarrow & B\,;C \vdash D\,;C \end{array}$$

These two rules will be referred to as 'composition on the left of $\vdash$' and 'left shift' in calculations. The assertion $B \vdash C\,;D$ means $B \vdash (C\,;D)$ and not the nonsensical $(B \vdash C)\,;D$.

No link with logic is implied in the use of the turnstile symbol. It would be interesting to know if there is in fact any link.

Types in Ruby

Data types in Ruby are partial equivalence relations (pers). This method of modelling Ruby types was introduced by Jones in reference [4] we have used it to structure Ruby calculations since then (see references [5] and [6] for instance). It is convenient to model data types as relations because then they can be 'pushed about' in calculations using our existing transformation rules. Originally, we used identity relations to model types, but this proved to be too restrictive. Partial equivalence relations give us more flexibility.

Voermans has independently proposed that pers should play the rôle of types in the relational calculus being developed by Backhouse and his research group (see reference [2] and also the paper by Hutton and Voermans in this volume).

A partial equivalence relation is a relation R that satisfies $R = R^{-1} = R \,;\, R$ or, equivalently, $R \vdash R^{-1}$. We say that R has type $A \sim B$ if A and B are pers and $A \,;\, R \,;\, B = R$. A is then a domain type of R and B is a range type. (A relation may have many different types.) For types A and B, the assertion $R : A \sim B$ is equivalent to $A \dashv R \wedge R \vdash B$; it is making two unlinked statements about the domain and range of R and does not capture the ways in which changing A might change B.

Difunctional relations

A relation R is difunctional if $R \vdash R{>}$, that is if $R \,;\, R^{-1} \,;\, R = R$. The paper by Hutton and Voermans in this volume shows that when one has partial equivalence relations as types, the difunctional relations play the rôle of functions. The reader is referred to that paper for further discussion of the theoretical aspects of having partial equivalence relations as types. Difunctional relations have also been called *regular* relations [3].

Abstraction and representation

In earlier work by Jones and Sheeran (reference [5]), a relation with range type A is defined to be an abstraction onto the type A if $a{>} = A$. (Lower case letters are used to denote abstractions.) If a relation is an abstraction, it is also difunctional, since it follows from $a \vdash A$ and $a{>} = A$ that $a \vdash a{>}$.

Furthermore, the abstractions are *exactly* the difunctionals. If a is difunctional, it follows that $a{>}$ must be a type and a an abstraction onto that type.

$$\begin{aligned} a \vdash a{>} \;&\Rightarrow \{\text{ composing } a^{-1} \text{ on the left of } \vdash \} \\ &\quad a^{-1} \,;\, a \vdash a{>} \\ &\Leftrightarrow \{\text{ definition of } a{>}\text{, and } a{>} = (a{>})^{-1} \} \\ &\quad a{>} \vdash (a{>})^{-1} \end{aligned}$$

That last judgement says that $a{>}$ is a partial equivalence relation, and so a type. It is a range type of a since $a \vdash a{>}$. Similarly, if a is difunctional, ${<}a$ is a type and is a domain type of a, since

$$\begin{aligned}
a \vdash a{>} \quad &\Leftrightarrow \{\text{definition of } a{>}\}\\
&\quad a \vdash a^{-1} ; a\\
&\Rightarrow \{\text{left shift by } a^{-1}\}\\
&\quad a ; a^{-1} \vdash a ; a^{-1}\\
&\Leftrightarrow \{\text{definition of } {<}a\}\\
&\quad {<}a \vdash {<}a\\
&\Leftrightarrow \{{<}a = ({<}a)^{-1}\}\\
&\quad {<}a \vdash ({<}a)^{-1}
\end{aligned}$$

and

$$\begin{aligned}
a \vdash a{>} \quad &\Leftrightarrow \quad a ; a^{-1} ; a = a\\
&\Leftrightarrow \quad {<}a \dashv a
\end{aligned}$$

Thus, if a is difunctional then it has type ${<}a \sim a{>}$. We say that a is an abstraction onto the type $a{>}$. Earlier, we showed that if a relation is an abstraction then it is difunctional. It follows that our abstraction relations are exactly the difunctionals.

The inverse of a difunctional relation is also difunctional.

$$\begin{aligned}
a \vdash a{>} \quad &\Leftrightarrow \quad a ; a^{-1} ; a = a\\
&\Leftrightarrow \quad a^{-1} ; a ; a^{-1} = a^{-1}\\
&\Leftrightarrow \quad a^{-1} \vdash (a^{-1}){>}
\end{aligned}$$

This means that the inverse of an abstraction is also an abstraction, which is a little surprising. Reference [5] states wrongly that the inverse of an abstraction is not necessarily an abstraction.

However, the composition of two abstractions is not necessarily an abstraction. Again, reference [5] is wrong on this point, as it states that composition preserves abstraction. Here is a simple condition on types that characterises two abstractions whose composition is an abstraction.

Assume that a and b are abstractions. The composition $a ; b$ is an abstraction if and only if the composition of the two types $a{>}$ and ${<}b$ is its own square, that is

$$a ; b \vdash (a ; b){>} \quad \Leftrightarrow \quad a{>} ; {<}b \vdash a{>} ; {<}b$$

The equivalence is proved by proving the implication in each direction.

$$\begin{aligned}
&a ; b \vdash (a ; b){>}\\
&\qquad \Leftrightarrow \{(a ; b){>} = b^{-1} ; a{>} ; b\}\\
&\qquad\quad a ; b \vdash b^{-1} ; a{>} ; b\\
&\qquad \Rightarrow \{\text{composing } a^{-1} \text{ on the left of } \vdash\}\\
&\qquad\quad a^{-1} ; a ; b \vdash b^{-1} ; a{>} ; b\\
&\qquad \Rightarrow \{\text{left shift by } b^{-1}\}\\
&\qquad\quad a^{-1} ; a ; b ; b^{-1} \vdash a{>} ; b ; b^{-1}\\
&\qquad \Leftrightarrow \{\text{definitions of } a{>} \text{ and } {<}b\}\\
&\qquad\quad a{>} ; {<}b \vdash a{>} ; {<}b
\end{aligned}$$

Note that the above proof did not rely on the fact that a and b are abstractions. That fact is used in the proof of the reverse implication, which is

$$\begin{aligned}
& a{>}\,;{<}b \vdash a{>}\,;{<}b \\
& \qquad \Leftrightarrow \{\text{definition of } \vdash\} \\
& \qquad\qquad a{>}\,;{<}b\,;a{>}\,;{<}b = a{>}\,;{<}b \\
& \qquad \Rightarrow \{\text{composing } a \text{ on left, and } b \text{ on right}\} \\
& \qquad\qquad a\,;a{>}\,;{<}b\,;a{>}\,;{<}b\,;b = a\,;a{>}\,;{<}b\,;b \\
& \qquad \Leftrightarrow \{a \text{ and } b \text{ are abstractions}\} \\
& \qquad\qquad a\,;{<}b\,;a{>}\,;b = a\,;b \\
& \qquad \Leftrightarrow \{\text{definitions of } \vdash \text{ and } {<}b\} \\
& \qquad\qquad a\,;b \vdash b^{-1}\,;a{>}\,;b \\
& \qquad \Leftrightarrow \{(a\,;b){>} = b^{-1}\,;a{>}\,;b\} \\
& \qquad\qquad a\,;b \vdash (a\,;b){>}
\end{aligned}$$

A corollary of this result is that if a and b are abstractions and the composition of the corresponding types $a{>}\,;{<}b$ is itself a type, then $a\,;b$ is an abstraction. This follows from the fact that if R is a type then $R \vdash R$.

Interestingly, the condition

$$a{>}\,;{<}b = {<}b\,;a{>}$$

also guarantees that $a\,;b$ is an abstraction, since

$$\begin{aligned}
& a{>}\,;{<}b = {<}b\,;a{>} \\
& \qquad \Rightarrow \{\text{composing } a{>} \text{ on left, and } {<}b \text{ on right}\} \\
& \qquad\qquad a{>}\,;a{>}\,;{<}b\,;{<}b = a{>}\,;{<}b\,;a{>}\,;{<}b \\
& \qquad \Leftrightarrow \{a{>} \text{ and } {<}b \text{ are types}\} \\
& \qquad\qquad a{>}\,;{<}b = a{>}\,;{<}b\,;a{>}\,;{<}b \\
& \qquad \Leftrightarrow \{\text{definition of } \vdash\} \\
& \qquad\qquad a{>}\,;{<}b \vdash a{>}\,;{<}b
\end{aligned}$$

In general, the composition of two types is itself a type if it is its own inverse.

It is also the case that if the relational *union* of the two types $a{>}$ and ${<}b$ is its own square (and so a type) then $a\,;b$ is an abstraction. To prove this, we must show that for a and b abstractions,

$$a{>} \cup {<}b \vdash a{>} \cup {<}b \Rightarrow a{>}\,;{<}b \vdash a{>}\,;{<}b$$

The proof is

$$\begin{aligned}
& a{>} \cup {<}b \vdash a{>} \cup {<}b \\
& \qquad \Leftrightarrow \{\text{definition of } \vdash\} \\
& \qquad\qquad a{>} \cup {<}b = (a{>} \cup {<}b)\,;(a{>} \cup {<}b) \\
& \qquad \Leftrightarrow \{\text{composition distributes over union, and } a{>} \text{ and } {<}b \text{ are types}\} \\
& \qquad\qquad a{>} \cup {<}b = a{>} \cup a{>}\,;{<}b \cup {<}b\,;a{>} \cup {<}b \\
& \qquad \Rightarrow \{\text{composing } a{>} \text{ on left, and } {<}b \text{ on right}\} \\
& \qquad\qquad a{>}\,;{<}b = a{>}\,;{<}b \cup a{>}\,;{<}b\,;a{>}\,;{<}b
\end{aligned}$$

$$\Leftrightarrow \{\, a{>} \text{ and } {<}b \text{ are types} \,\}$$

$$a{>} \,;\, {<}b \;=\; a{>} \,;\, {<}b \cup a{>} \,;\, {<}b \,;\, (a{>} \,;\, {<}b)^{-1} \,;\, a{>} \,;\, {<}b$$

$$\Leftrightarrow \{\, \text{triple rule} \,\}$$

$$a{>} \,;\, {<}b \;=\; a{>} \,;\, {<}b \,;\, (a{>} \,;\, {<}b)^{-1} \,;\, a{>} \,;\, {<}b$$

$$\Leftrightarrow \{\, a{>} \text{ and } {<}b \text{ are types} \,\}$$

$$a{>} \,;\, {<}b \;=\; a{>} \,;\, {<}b \,;\, a{>} \,;\, {<}b$$

$$\Leftrightarrow \{\, \text{definition of } \vdash \,\}$$

$$a{>} \,;\, {<}b \vdash a{>} \,;\, {<}b$$

In their paper in this volume, Hutton and Voermans present conditions under which the composition of two difunctionals is difunctional that are also corollaries of the stronger result proved here.

How do these results influence calculation?

These results about abstractions are interesting because many circuits behave as abstractions. Circuits that change data from one representation into another are very common; for example, arithmetic and digital signal processing circuits fall into this class. Representation changers can be specified as the composition of one abstraction with the inverse of another. That is, a representation changer is of the form $a \,;\, b^{-1}$ where a and b are abstractions.

For example, if bin_n is the abstraction that relates an n–bit binary number to the natural number that it represents, and csv_n relates an n–place carry–save number to the natural number that it represents, then the conversion from carry–save to binary would be specified as $csv_n \,;\, bin_{n+1}^{-1}$. This specification manipulates natural numbers internally and so cannot be implemented directly in silicon. It must be refined into a network of hardware primitives, each of which manipulates only bits. Reference [5] studies ways of refining representation changers specified in this style into circuits. A more recent paper builds on that work and makes it more systematic [7].

The results about inverting and composing abstractions presented above indicate that a representation changer is just a particular form of abstraction, in which two concrete types are related through an abstract type. In the real circuit examples that we have studied so far, the conditions under which the composition of two abstractions is itself an abstraction are met, so that all of the representation changers are also abstractions. This means that we should be studying ways of refining abstractions into networks of smaller abstractions. Such a refinement is useful if it reduces the complexity of the types manipulated internally by the network. Ultimately, the types on internal arcs should be so simple that they can be implemented using just wires. The preliminary results about composing abstractions presented above should form a useful basis for a more top–down approach to the refinement of abstractions.

Acknowledgements

When I gave my talk at the Portree workshop, Phil Wadler asked me if the abstraction relations that I was discussing were the same as the difunctional relations presented by Graham Hutton. I said that the abstraction relations were certainly difunctional but that I didn't think that the reverse implication held. This note is by way of a correction to my answer! Thanks to Phil for asking the question. Thanks to John Hughes, Graham Hutton, Geraint Jones, David Murphy and John O'Donnell for comments and suggestions.

References

[1] Graham Hutton and Ed Voermans, *Making functionality more general*, in this volume.

[2] Graham Hutton and Ed Voermans, *A calculational theory of pers as types*, Technical report, University of Glasgow, November 1991.

[3] A. Jaoua, A. Mili, N. Boudriga and J. L. Durieux, *Regularity of relations: A measure of uniformity*, Theoretical Computer Science 79, 1991. pp. 323–339.

[4] Geraint Jones, *Designing circuits by calculation, MSc Course Notes*, Programming Research Group technical report PRG–TR–10–90, April 1990.

[5] Geraint Jones and Mary Sheeran, *Relations and refinement in circuit design*, in [8]. pp. 133–152.

[6] Geraint Jones and Mary Sheeran, *Circuit design in Ruby*, in [9]. pp. 13–70.

[7] Geraint Jones and Mary Sheeran, *Designing arithmetic circuits by refinement in Ruby*, in preparation.

[8] Carroll Morgan and Jim Woodcock (eds.), *Proc. BCS FACS 3rd Refinement Workshop, Jan. 1990*, Springer Workshops in Computing, Springer Verlag, London, 1991.

[9] Jørgen Staunstrup (ed.), *Formal methods for VLSI design*, North-Holland, 1990.

Requirements for a Functional Programming Environment

Ben A. Sijtsma
Koninklijke/Shell - Laboratorium, Amsterdam
(Shell Research B.V.)
P.O. Box 3003, 1003 AA Amsterdam, The Netherlands
e-mail: sijtsma1@ksla.nl

Abstract

In this paper we discuss the requirements we would like a functional programming environment to fulfill. These requirements are divided into two groups: one for prototyping and one for regular program development. The requirements are primarily based upon three case studies we have performed. Some of the requirements are not new, but their importance was once more stressed in our studies. The overall conclusion is that a functional programming environment is should offer at least the same level of support as a conventional one offers, including the ability to interface with existing packages and systems, such as a library of numerical routines and an user-interface management system.

1 Introduction

In this paper we discuss the requirements we would like a functional programming environment to meet. The requirements depend on the usage of functional languages: if these languages are used for prototyping in the sense described below certain requirements are to be met, but if they are used for program development at the Laboratory, then additional requirements exist. Prior to explaining what we mean by regular program development, we will discuss the use of a functional language for prototyping.

There are many models for software development (see [5] for a review). Almost all models include the parts *Requirements*, *Specification*, *Design*, and *Coding*. In *Requirements* the customer states, or should state, the behaviour of the system to be built. The requirements are generally not sufficiently detailed or rigorous for the *Design* and *Coding* phases. The customer cannot be blamed for the lack of detail and rigour, because he generally does not, and perhaps even cannot, know the necessary level of detail. It is here where the specifier comes in. In cooperation with the customer he augments and transforms the requirements into the specification of the intended system. In this cooperation the customer has to decide on many issues, the relevancy and consequences of which he might be unable to judge or to comprehend. Furthermore, it is likely that the customer is asked to decide only on those issues which are raised by the specifier. It might very well be that he, with the best of intentions, decides on his own on other issues which in his opinion are straightforward or of little importance. As a consequence the specification might not fully reflect the intended system.

Moreover, there are other complications. To avoid misinterpretation of the specification in the *Design* and *Coding* phases the specifier could use a formal language to write the specification in. It is our experience that executing these phases is facilitated by the existence of a formal specification. However, the customer generally is unfamiliar with these formal languages and hence might be unable to read the formal specification.

The last complicating factor we will mention is the following. It has been asserted that

> ... *it is really impossible for a client, even working with a software engineer, to specify completely, precisely, and correctly the exact requirements of a modern software product before trying some versions of the product [3].*

This is in line with the observation that the customer can change his perception of the system to be built dramatically after being confronted by an implementation of the product [1]. So even if the specification reflects the intended system there is no guarantee that the system, after being built, will be a success.

To overcome the above mentioned problems many workers in the field advocate the use of prototypes, see e.g. [3, 4, 6, 7, 8, 11]. We are in favour of writing formal specifications and using prototypes. The first stages of our software development cycle can be depicted as follows.

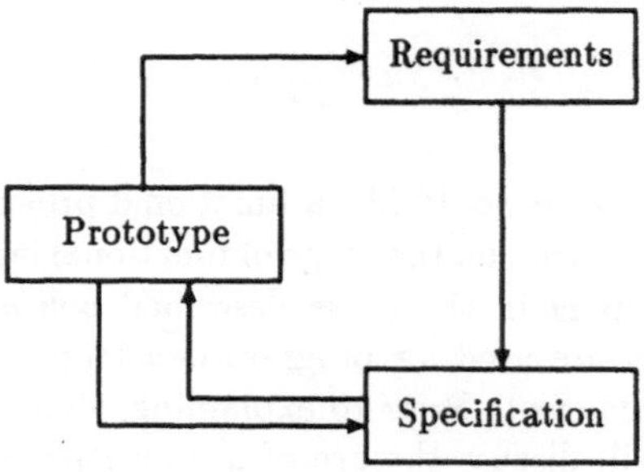

The prototype in every iteration serves three purposes:

- Since writing formal specifications is difficult the prototype serves as a feedback to the specifier that the formal specification indeed describes what he intended to specify. This accounts for the *Specification-Prototype-Specification* loop.

- The prototype is a means of communication between the developer and the customer. In the prototype (part of) the formal specification is visualised, i.e. the customer can see how the developer has interpreted his requirements. Prototyping circumvents the problem that the customer might be unable to read the formal specification.

- The prototype can be regarded as a (incomplete) version of the system. Hence it offers the customer the opportunity to work with the prototype and helps him to define more accurately the system he actually wants.

The previous two points account for the *Specification-Prototype-Requirements-Specification* loop. In our software development methodology prototypes are used to arrive at a good formal specification. In the literature there is a whole classification of software development methods using prototypes (see [4, 5, 11]). Our approach can be characterised as *specification prototyping.*

We now briefly discuss regular program development at the Laboratory. This will provide the background needed to understand the additional requirements. The Shell Laboratory in Amsterdam is a highly technical environment and is quite different from a software production environment such as a software house. At the Laboratory software is not an end in itself: software is mainly written to *explore* a problem and/or possible solution. Hence the lifetime of a program is generally very short. Moreover, the requirements are not always known in advance. In the Laboratory a researcher does not follow standard software development method: he writes a program and revises it numerous times until he is satisfied with the result. The resulting software is frequently not the main result, but the knowledge encapsulated in it is. Neither written-down requirements nor formal specifications enter the picture. This is of course in strong contrast with the prototype program development cycle described above.

Our observations are primarily based upon three cases. In two cases we constructed a formal specification from a set of requirements using the prototype approach. In the other case we used a functional language to explore a problem and its solution. We used Miranda[1][15] and LML[2] for writing functional programs.

The structure of this paper is as follows. In Section 2 we discuss the requirements to be met by a functional programming environment for prototyping. Similarly, Section 3 contains some requirements for regular program development. Some final remarks can be found in Section 4.

2 Prototyping

All our three cases had no numerical aspects, like integrating differential equations or solving a set of linear equations, but were rather of a combinatoric nature. In our environment modelling of physical phenomena is important. Such models frequently use a mixture of algebraic and differential equations. The NAG [12] library is used within our Laboratory to solve such equations. Although we are aware that in principle numerical algorithms can be written in a functional language, even very elegantly (see [10]), it is an expert's job to provide a set of robust, efficient and accurate numerical routines. The availability of such a library for functional languages is a prerequisite for prototyping such applications using functional languages.

We have found that the ideal prototyping language is domain-dependent. Some examples might clarify this point. Two of our case studies used mathematical

---

1 *Miranda* is a trademark of Research Software Ltd.

relations quite a lot. Relations can be regarded as a set of ordered pairs, but there exist specific notations for relations. For example:

- R^+ denotes the transitive closure of a relation R,
- $a\ R\ b$ denotes the boolean value whether the pair $(a, b) \in R$,
- $R_0 \circ R_1$ denotes the composition of two relations, and
- $a\ R$ denotes the set $\{b \mid a\ R\ b\}$.

For our case studies we have developed some modules providing functionality that could be regarded as "basic" to the domain of the applications. This enabled us to construct prototypes very rapidly.

We would like the prototype language to allow definition of notation such that standard notations of a domain can be closely mimicked. Although it might be argued that "it's just syntax," we argue that it is an important point for our prototype program development cycle. A notation in the functional language that mimics the notation used in the specification allows for a rapid construction of the prototype. Furthermore, this could prevent errors arising in the translation from specification to prototype and hence it is more likely that errors in the prototype are errors in the specification and not of the translation.

This also raises the question whether the prototype language and the specification language could be the same. From our experience we are inclined to conclude that there is an essential difference between these two languages. The need to be able to demonstrate the prototype entails constraints that do not have their counterpart in the specification. Furthermore, in the prototype certain implementation choices can be made that need not be adequate for an implementation in another language. To give an example, consider a problem that has to deal with identifiers. For a prototype it can be sufficient to store identifiers in a linear list. If the prototype is also the specification, this would preclude the use of more efficient data structures, such as a hash table.

The restriction to an executable specification language can make specifications unnecessarily complex. In one of our cases a set S was defined by

$$S = \{g(a) \mid a \in A \wedge (\exists f \in B \rightarrow C : Q(f) : P(f, a))\},$$

where A, B, and C are known sets, P and Q are predicates, and g is a function. An executable specification of the set S above could very easily obscure such a definition, making it intractable to change.

The purpose of writing prototypes is to demonstrate their functionality to future users and to elicit good requirements. Hence the prototype should be able to solve reasonably sized problems in a reasonable span of time. This is a rather vague statement: what do we mean by "reasonable." The size of the problems should be such that the future user understands the functionality of the prototype and its limitations. It is our experience that the user is not satisfied by running the prototype on some toy examples. Problems of a realistic size are required.

The best way to elicit requirements is to let the future user play with the prototype. This implies that response times should not be very long, since then the feedback process is bound to fail. In two of our cases some prototypes took hours to solve even small problems and we had to do some extensive reprogramming (in a functional language) to obtain a prototype that was fit to be demonstrated. So fast execution is still required. More on this point is to be found in the following section.

3 Regular programming

Functional languages can only be used for regular programming at the Laboratory if additional requirements are fulfilled. The most important ones are discussed below.

In our cases we have only prototyped the technical core of a program. We did not attempt to prototype any graphical user interface. Such interfaces form an important part of many applications and are frequently subject to change. A program developed at the Laboratory can be considered as a vehicle of knowledge transfer, because it embodies a piece of technology and makes this technology available to users of the program. A good user interface can significantly

- lower the initial hesitation a new user has to overcome, and
- improve the usage of the program.

Hence the user interface can well determine the success of an application and is therefore an essential factor in knowledge transfer via programs.

Good user-interface management systems (UIMS) are available that allow prototyping and development of user interfaces. Generally, user interfaces developed with a UIMS communicate with the rest of the application by means of "call-back routines." These call-back routines are often expected to be written in C (the majority), C++, or Fortran. If functional languages are to be used within our environment, linkage between such a language and UIMS is required.

Another requirement concerns databases. Applications increasingly use databases: they retrieve model parameters and other input data and/or store certain results in databases. In may areas data is more persistent than the functions to be performed on that data. So, we expect that in the near future a database will be the heart of many applications that will access, modify and extend it. A familiar, but perhaps unexpected, example is contained in Unix. The database is the file system and a great number of programs exist, e.g. `cat`, `mv`, `rm`, `vi`, `ls`, `grep`, `touch` and many others, that change or inspect the file system. The implications regarding our requirements will be clear. For prototyping it generally suffices to use a mock-up of a database. For example, a file is used as a database or the run-time memory contains a data structure that acts as the whole database. For other applications, however, the existence of an interface to a (relational) database is necessary.

For prototyping the speed of execution need not necessarily be high, but for ordinary applications an implementation in a functional language should have a speed comparable to that of a more conventional implementation, e.g. in C or Fortran. It is insufficient to state that faster hardware will lower execution speeds significantly: this is undoubtedly true, but the size of the problems we want to solve still increases more rapidly than the MIPS and FLOPS of machines.

It is still an open question whether the use of dedicated hardware for the evaluation of functional languages is a viable option. If, with dedicated hardware, the execution speed of functional languages becomes comparable to that of C or Fortran, then the additional investment costs should be offset by the profits accruing from more cost-effective development and maintenance. There are indications that program development in functional languages can be more effective, but, to our knowledge, there is no evidence as yet regarding the reduction of the costs of maintenance. Such evidence is needed since the costs of maintenance for imperative programming are generally at least three times as high as those of development (see [9]).

4 Concluding Remarks

In the previous two sections we have given some elements we would like to find in a functional programming environment. In short they are:

- a library of numerical algorithms that can be linked with a functional language,
- extension of notation to be able to closely mimic standard notation,
- a high speed of execution,
- linkage with standard user-interface management systems, and
- linkage with (relational) database systems.

Of course tools that are available for software development in conventional languages are also required. For instance, an interactive debugger and/or interpreter are needed. In addition, the functional equivalent of tools such as the Unix "yacc" and "lex," which have already been implemented in a functional language (see [13]), should be made available. A similar remark holds for pretty-printers and cross referencers.

All these requirements can be summarised in the statement that a functional programming environment should offer at least the same level of support as a conventional one. This does not imply that we expect to see the same suite of tools (e.g. `cc`, `dbx`, `lint`, `lex`, and `yacc`) for functional languages. In the near future we expect that programs are developed using different tools and languages: the user interface will be developed by a UIMS, data presentation is done by using a graphical toolbox, commercially available numerical routines will be used for solving differential and algebraic equations, etc. Functional languages will only be used in industry if they can interface with such tools and other languages.

Some of the above requirements may be hard to fulfill. To give an example: consider an application using windowing facilities. Such an application is controlled by the window manager. The user behind his screen, using keyboard and mouse, generates "events" that are handled by the window manager. These events are translated in calls to the "call-back routines." After execution of the call-back routine control is returned to the window manager. Such a model of interaction is clearly based upon the availability of a state and routines manipulating it. It, therefore, remains to be seen whether it is possible to let functional languages and currently available UIMS communicate with each other. An attempt can be found in [14].

An aspect that is not a requirement, but is important for industrial acceptance of functional languages, is the following. Starting to use a new language is only viable if it can be trusted that the new language has sufficient support for a long span of time, i.e. at least ten to 15 years. With *sufficient* support we mean, for example, that the new language will become available on future architectures and "answer-line service" can be obtained. Furthermore, the tools that are used in functional program development should be fully supported. So also in this case functional languages should have the same level of support as exists for more conventional languages.

Acknowledgement We would like to thank the referees for making valuable remarks on a draft version of this paper.

Bibliography

1. Alter SA. *Decision support systems - current practice and continuing challenges.* Addison-Wesley, Reading, MA.

2. Augustsson L. *A compiler for lazy ML.* Proceedings of the ACM Symposium on Lisp and Functional Programming, Austin, 1984, pp. 218-227.

3. Brooks FP. *No Silver Bullet - Essence and Accidents of Software Engineering.* Computer, April 1987, pp. 10–19.

4. Budde R., Kuhlenkamp K., Mathiassen L., Züllighoven, H. (Eds) *Approaches to Prototyping.* Springer-Verlag, Berlin, 1984.

5. Graham DR. *Incremental development: review of nonmonolithic life-cycle development models.* Information and Software Technology, Vol. 31, No. 1, 1989, pp. 7–20.

6. Harker S. *The use of prototyping and simulation in the development of large scale applications.* The Computer Journal, Vol. 31, No. 5, 1988, pp. 420–425.

7. Henderson P. *Functional programming, formal specification, and rapid prototyping.* IEEE Transactions on Software Engineering, Vol. SE-12, No. 12, 1986, pp. 241–250.

8. Henderson P., Minkowitz C. *The* me too *method of software design.* ICL Technical Journal, Vol. 5, No. 1, 1986, pp.64–95.

9. Horowitz E., Munson JB. *An expansive view of reusable software.* IEEE Transactions on Software Engineering, Vol. SE-10, No. 5, September, 1984.

10. Hughes R. *Why functional programming matters.* The Computer Journal, Vol. 32, No. 2, 1989.

11. Ince D. *Rapid software engineering.* Second IEE/BCS Conference on Software Engineering 88.

12. The Numerical Algorithms Group Limited. *NAG, Fortran Library, Mark 13.*, 1988, ISBN 1-85206-046-8.

13. Peyton Jones S. *YACC in SASL – an exercise in functional programming.* Software, Practice & Experience, 1985.

14. Singh S. *Using XView/X11 from Miranda.* Proceedings of the Glasgow Functional Programming Workshop 1991, Portree, Scotland.

15. Turner DA. *Miranda: a non-strict functional language with polymorphic types.* In: Functional Programming Languages and Computer Architecture (LNCS 201), Jouannaud, JP. (Ed). Springer-Verlag, Berlin, 1985.

Debugging by Dataflow — Summary

Duncan C. Sinclair*
University of Glasgow

Monday 30th December 1991

Abstract

In this paper we discuss why debugging in the lazy functional paradigm should be different from the control-flow style adopted by imperative language debuggers. We look at some of the bugs that are peculiar to functional programming, and how they might be resolved in a proposed debugging system based around *dataflow* technology.

1 Introduction

Lazy functional languages are growing in popularity, but tend to lack useful programming tools which are expected in a serious development system. One obvious deficiency is the lack of good debugging tools for these languages. Debuggers for functional languages tend to be ad-hoc in design, and based upon the debugging style used for imperative programs.

These debuggers tend to have extensions to the debugging metaphor to accommodate the functional style, but we feel that we could produce a better debugger by starting from scratch, using new techniques where appropriate, and adopting parts of existing technology when it is found to be relevant.

2 Functional Programs get Bugs Too

Everybody suffers from programming bugs, no matter whether the language is imperative or functional. Some argue that fewer bugs occur in the functional style, due to greater expressiveness, statelessness or for some other reason. This is not the point: functional language programs get bugs too.

But what's wrong with the imperative languages' debuggers? Functional programs are totally different from imperative programs in the way they behave at run-time. Imperative programs follow a simple execution order, this means that a debugger can easily present the user with the evaluation flow of the program,

* Mail to: Department of Computing Science, University of Glasgow, Glasgow, G12 8QQ, UK. E-mail: `sinclair@dcs.glasgow.ac.uk`

which would be recognised as the ordering of the commands as they appear in the program listing.

In lazy languages, evaluation does not take on an easily recognised ordering, but is decided implicitly by data dependencies. This suggests that the average programmer would quickly get lost within a debugging session presented according to evaluation order. In Section 4 we argue this point further.

Hall et al [1] define a number of levels where debugging may take place. We shall categorise them into three:

Specification Errors in the specification, and the understanding of it.

Semantic Errors in the implementation of the program.

Pragmatic Errors due to language implementation techniques.

We shall concentrate on the semantic and machine levels, while conceding that specificational debugging has its place. We look at an example of a pragmatic bug, taken from [2, chap. 23], where there are further examples, and discussion.

Example — Space Leaks

> Space leaks occur when lazy semantics cause large parts of evaluated or unevaluated graph to be help in store, when they should be either disposed of, or evaluated.

Here we have an example:

```
f = drop 1000
drop n xs = xs                , if n = 0
          = drop (n-1) (tl xs)
... f ... f ...
```

What happens here, is that on the first evaluation of `f`, it will stay in memory fully evaluated, to be used again. Unfortunately, the machine representation of f is going to be very large, as it will be a 1000 deep recursive loop which has been unwound. This ensures that we will never need to do this recursion for each use of the function `f`, but it consumes too much memory in the process.

3 A Dataflow Debugger

We propose taking a *dataflow* approach to debugging. That is, we shall use dataflow as the unit of evaluation, rather than the typical function call debugger step.

Dataflow concerns the relationship between producers of data, and the respective consumers of that data. This can be expressed as a graph, where the nodes are consumers/producers, and the arcs show the dataflow between them. This graph is very different to the graph found in the graph reduction paradigm for functional language execution.

It is in fact common to program true dataflow architecture machines in functional languages. In these languages, the functions become nodes, and the data dependencies determine the arcs. We will now reverse this, so that dataflow will be a metaphor for the execution of functional programs running on conventional machines. A debugger can then follow the dataflow through a program, rather than following its evaluation order. We believe that functional programmers have a fair idea of the dataflow within their own programs, and because lazy evaluation does not alter this, it makes a workable basis for a debugging strategy.

3.1 Dataflow to the User

In this section we look at some of the details that make up dataflow debugging. This starts at the lowest level of dataflow with nodes and arcs, moving up to address more user-centred issues.

Low Level Dataflow

Dataflow is about *nodes* and *arcs*, which together form a dataflow graph. The nodes conceptually store and process data, which flows between them via the arcs.

In the dataflow paradigm for debugging of functional languages, a simple node is created and stands for each application of a function to a full set of arguments. This is analogous to the function being entered in normal graph reduction.

Arguments, and subsequently, the result of the function form the arcs of dataflow between the nodes. In the lazy environment we are working in, the dataflow can only be identified as it occurs, as a result of forced evaluation.

The user may wish to inspect values passing along an arc, and perhaps watch data structures being built up by the function feeding the arc.

High Level Dataflow

For recursive functions, and functions defined using higher order functions, there could be vast numbers of nodes created. Realistically, the user cannot cope with this. So, we allow clustering of nodes, either automatically, in the case of simple recursive functions, or, in more complicated cases, under user control.

These nodes will act in exactly the same way as a simple node, with any dataflow to or from other nodes going through the cluster node. Cluster nodes could be broken apart to see the internal structure, if required.

User-centred Dataflow Debugging

Still, all these nodes and arcs will be too much. In a similar way to the selective break-pointing and tracing offered by traditional debuggers, the dataflow debugger must be able to limit the amount of information kept and presented to the user.

We shall use two new techniques, which I call *focussing* and *filtering.*

Focussing is analogous to the selective break-pointing. In focussing, we limit the number of nodes to those the user specifically asks for. This choice is ideally made before execution, in order to specialise the data collection done by the debugger.

The user would make this choice by nominating function names. Then as the program is run, "highlights" of the dataflow graph would be shown to the user, with arcs of dataflow mapping out where data is travelling to or from focussed nodes.

In order to see active values within a node (i.e. within an active instance of a function), the debugger would allow the user to inspect inside a node to determine the values of named local variables. This basic feature is analogous to single-stepping within a break-pointed (focussed) function.

Unfortunately, we are now strictly limited to the data we can see, and our focussed nodes, if they are in any way complex will have a mess of dataflow arcs hanging off them attached to other nodes. We need a way of controlling the data we see, as well as the nodes.

There is one other useful feature from imperative debugging we would find useful. It is often the case that we wish to watch a particular variable during the life of the program, and be alerted when it changes.

An analogous feature in a functional debugger would be the ability to watch values of a particular type, or created by a particular function, and follow them as they flow through the dataflow graph.

For this we introduce filtering. This will allow us to specify data-streams and particular types of data that we are interested in. This solves both problems we found above. Not only can we limit the untidy dataflow around focussed nodes, we will also be able to ask for dataflow occurring away from the centre of attention.

This will allow us to trace back data to its origins, and watch what happens to in on the way to focussed nodes. Also, this could be used to watch data structures being build within the dataflow arc between two nodes. The process of the creation of a structure is sometimes more relevant in debugging than its internal values.

4 How to Get Lost

Why Dataflow is better than Evaluation Order

Imagine being shown two implementations of fib, one written in a standard lazy functional language, the other in an imperative one.

Now try to describe the evaluation order, and dataflow of each program. For the imperative program, evaluation order will be obvious and dataflow obscure, while the reverse will be true of the functional program.

This is due to the difference of the imperative language having an explicit state, where the functional language does not, and the functional language having explicit data dependencies, while the imperative language hides them within its state.

Within the imperative paradigm, we have the the state to hold on to. Running through the state-modifying commands, we understand what is happening, but the data dependencies become confused as they are not expressed explicitly, but implicitly in the state modifications. The important thing is that imperative programmers understand the "state" of their "state", and don't need the data dependencies, and so would not be worried.

For the functional paradigm, things are different, there isn't a state to carry us through the program execution, or to be looked after — but we do know what parts of the program depend on other parts. We can see the dependencies, without needing to know the eventual order of evaluation, which may have been dictated by far-off parts of the program.

Even if we worked out the evaluation order from the lazy semantics, some optimisations, such as those based upon sharing and strictness analysis, which are important to the efficient execution of the program can change this by altering when and how often values are computed.

This is also an argument against debuggers based on simple interpretation of the program, rather than integrated into the normal execution of the program. These debuggers would not present the same pragmatics of execution at run-time, and so would obscure some of the bugs linked with sharing and evaluation order.

5 Future Problems

This paper reports work in progress. A prototype has been completed, and a full implementation is under construction. In this short section, we shall look at some of the issues not yet addressed.

The exact visual representation and user interaction has yet to be worked out. More pragmatic still, focussing and filtering takes place at a higher level of dataflow than what is really happening within the executing program — I need to be able to specify, perhaps informally, how the high level dataflow relates to the raw dataflow.

What about higher-order values? For functions which are built up during the execution of the program, with code coming from various other functions, this will need to be presented without confusing the user. Somehow the debugger will have to encase these functions into their own nodes, and avoid having them strung out along a row of nodes. If further information is required inside the function, it could be split apart to show the separate functions which make it up, in the same way as that envisaged for recursive functions.

Which brings us on to recursive functions. How does the debugger tell the difference between a recursive and a non-recursive invocation in order to package up recursive functions into cluster nodes? It would perhaps need to use some analysis of the program to do this.

Often the user will wish to see the result of as-yet unevaluated computation. It is our wish that evaluation order should proceed in the natural order it would take without the debugger intervening. Anything else could affect the termination properties of the program, and might also result in incorrect sequencing required for interactive programs. Therefore we plan to allow forced evaluation of values, as long as no updates occur. This would mean that any computation would be lost, and values would be computed a second time when the value is required by the program.

Acknowledgements

Thanks to my supervisor John O'Donnell for helping me understand my own ideas. This work was supported by the Science and Engineering Research Council.

Bibliography

1. Cordelia Hall, Kevin Hammond & John O'Donnell, "An Algorithmic and Semantic Approach to Debugging in Haskell," in *Functional Programming, Glasgow 1990*, Workshops in Computing, Springer-Verlag, Aug 1990, 44–53.
2. Simon L. Peyton Jones, *The implementation of functional programming languages*, Prentice Hall, 1987.

Using XView/X11 from Miranda

Satnam Singh
Dept. Electronics and Electrical Engineering
The University of Glasgow, G12 8QQ

Abstract

Lazy functional programs typically have very primitive user interfaces. Poor interfaces with the outside world make it difficult to access machine resources like colour displays and mice. This paper presents a technique for using X11 and an associated toolkit XView [1] from the lazy functional language Miranda. [1] This has been done by building an interpreter for a subset of X11/XView.

1 Introduction

Lazy functional programming has been shown to have many benefits as a paradigm for elegantly representing many kinds of computation. Quick prototyping, ease of formal reasoning and powerful function and data abstraction mechanisms are just a few of the advantages enjoyed by functional programmers. However, functional programs usually have a poor interface to the external world.

The typical method of performing input/output in an imperative language is by using a library of functions which cause side effects. This is undesirable in a functional language because we want programs to have the property of referential transparency. This means that we can always replace the occurrence of a function call by its appropriately elaborated defining body. Thus, when we say $fx = 1 + gx$ in Miranda, we really mean that f is always the same as $1 + gx$. This property is most useful when transforming functional programs and when trying to prove their correctness.

Access to external graphics facilities are usually accomplished by linking to a library. This assumes that the correct external procedure definitions are available for the language you want to use and that you are going to compile your language into a standard machine code format that can be linked with such libraries. Many functional languages are interpreted e.g. Miranda. For these languages it is simply impossible to directly link into alien machine code libraries.

One popular method for accessing operating systems facilities is to make functional programs operate over streams of requests. The output of the functional program is a list of request to the operating system. The input is a list of responses from the operating system.

This paper describes such a system. The lazy functional language used is Miranda and the graphics system is X11. Enough details are given to allow the reader to build his or her own interface to a graphics system. However, some knowledge about X11 and UNIX system calls is assumed.

[1]Miranda is a trademark of Research Software Ltd.

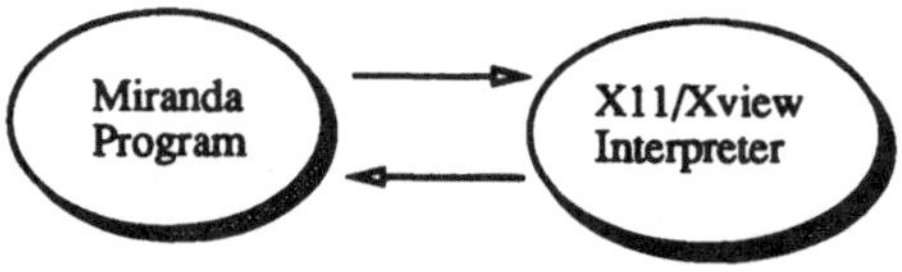

Figure 1: Cross coupled communication

2 Writing Miranda X11 Clients

The usual way of accessing X11 services is via procedure calls to the Xlib library or other libraries built on top of Xlib. This is not an option available to us because we cannot call C procedures from Miranda.

It would be very useful to be able to access the facilities of X and its toolkits from functional languages without sacrificing referential transparency. Even access to Xlib or the protocol level would allow specialised libraries tailored for functional languages to be built.

What is required is a controlled way of effectively making C function calls and passing information between Miranda and C programs. Our solution involves building an intermediate layer that translates Miranda X11 requests into C procedure calls to the X11 system. It also obtains information about events and other X11 information which is translated from C structures into a form that Miranda can digest.

An interface to the XView toolkit and some of the basic X11 drawing, networking and resource database management routines has been implemented. The interface allows Miranda clients to be written, but in principle makes XView/X11 available to any language that is capable of unbuffered text input/output. In an earlier version of the system, an interface was also provided for Lazy ML.

To write a Miranda X11 client, a library of XView definitions has been provided. This describes the most common XView objects and some X11 objects and provides some useful operations over them. It also provides support for colour and gives names to over 400 different colours.

A Miranda program that wants to perform file operations has to use the **sysmessge** type which contains constructors that correspond to system services. When one of these constructors is written to the output stream, a corresponding system function is executed.

The same technique has been used to provide access to external X11/XView services. However, whereas the execution of the system functions associated with the **sysmessage** constructors is done implicitly by the Miranda system, we have to connect the output of our program to another program which process the request and then executes the relevant X11/XView calls. Our Miranda program also has to receive input like window handles from this external program. Thus, the output of the Miranda program is the input of this external X11/XView interface program and this program's output is the Miranda program's input. This calls for cross-coupled communication between these two concurrent programs. This back-to-back arrangement is shown in figure 1.

3 An interface for X11/XView

A program that interprets the output of the Miranda program and then executes the corresponding X11/XView calls has been implemented. The program is called *xvi* (XView Interpreter) and is written in C, lex and yacc. It works under the UNIX operating system and relies on UNIX pipes for communication between subprocesses. It parses the input for commands that create windows and subwindows with buttons, panels etc. For each object created, it sends out a message giving a handle (or reference) to that object. Once all windows and subwindows have been created, the client then gives up control and waits to be notified of events. An event corresponds to a mouse click or button press. When this happens the *xvi* program notifies the client about which object caused the event and then waits to parse further commands. The client decodes the event information, decides upon an action which will involve sending further requests to the interpreter and then gives up control again. This process continues for each event until the application quits. The *xvi* program contains a parser which is started and stopped for each event.

The normal way of being notified of some action like a button press is to associate a *callback* function with each user interface object of interest. In XView, the callback corresponds to the address of a user supplied C procedure that is passed event information as parameters. Obviously, we can not generate C callback functions from Miranda. In an older version of this system that worked with the SunView windowing system, the interpreter contained a finite number of callback functions that each returned unique status information to the client. This was a very restrictive method but allowed the writer of the client to choose which objects had callbacks. In the *xvi* system there is a default callback function which simply notifies the client about the general class of event that has occurred. The client can choose to ignore this information or interrogate the interpreter further about the details of the event.

The *xvi* program returns handles to XView objects, rather than the pointers. It maintains a table of XView objects and uses the handle to index this table. When the first window is created a handle of value 1 is returned. The interpreter is designed to work with a range of languages. Some languages may not be able to deal with 32bit unsigned integers which would have to be used to represent pointers to XView objects. By using an intermediate table and giving out the index as a handle means that the client language needs only to deal with small integers. The table is very large. The computer is more likely to run out of swap space before the table is filled.

It is possible to run the *xvi* program by itself and type in commands using the keyboard and interactively created windows and drawings. The program can be given a command line argument which is the name of a program to take input from and send output to. To use a Miranda client, this would be a here script which evokes the Miranda interpreter to evaluate a given function. However, any program that generates the correct input syntax and parses the output properly can be run. To evaluate the function `run` in the file `miratool.m` we first have to make an executable UNIX file with the following contents:

```
#!/usr/local/bin/mira -exp
run $+
%include "miratool"
```

Thus runs the Miranda interpreter causing it to evaluate the function `run`. This function takes the value of its argument from the standard input, as specified by **$+**. The input is of a textual forms which is parsed at runtime. The include file specifies where to look for the definition of **run**.

This executable UNIX file now behaves like a command and can be used as an argument to *xvi*. To run the clients so that it connects to the X server we simply type:

```
ss@avon> xvi miratool
```

The *xvi* program can take any of the usual X and XView command line arguments. For example, it would be easy to make the window appear on the display of another machine.

The *xvi* program creates two pipes and then rewires them so that the communication between them is cross coupled. The named program is executed as a subprocess with its input/output associated with one pipe. The other pipe is associated with the input/output of the interpreter's parser.

Creating such pipes is a bit of a black art, so we explain here how in detail how it was done. The following code fragments are in C. We first declare a variable to hold the process id `pid` and declare two pipes. Here, `ParentPipe[0]` is opened for reading and `ParentPipe[1]` for writing. Similarly for `ChildPipe`.

```
int pid ;
int ParentPipe[2] ;
int ChildPipe[2] ;
```

We create the pipes by calling the system function `pipe`. In the actual implementation we take the precaution of checking that the pipe was indeed created. Here we just ignore the returned status value. See the UNIX manual page on `pipe` for more information.

```
(void) pipe(ParentPipe) ;
(void) pipe(ChildPipe) ;
```

Having created the pipes, we close the existing standard input/output and fork off a subprocess using the `fork` system call.

```
close(0);
close(1);
pid = fork() ;
```

The parent process now connects its input to `ChildPipe`'s input and its output to `ParentPipe`'s output. This is done by copying file descriptors using the `dup2` function. We check to see that the duplication was successful and signal an error message if something has gone wrong. Once the standard input and output are set up, the pipe descriptors are no longer needed and are deallocated using `close`. The parent process has a non-zero process id.

```
if (pid != 0) /* Let's do the parent re-wiring */
{ dup2 (ChildPipe[0], 0) ;
  dup2 (ParentPipe[1], 1) ;
  close(ParentPipe[0]) ;
```

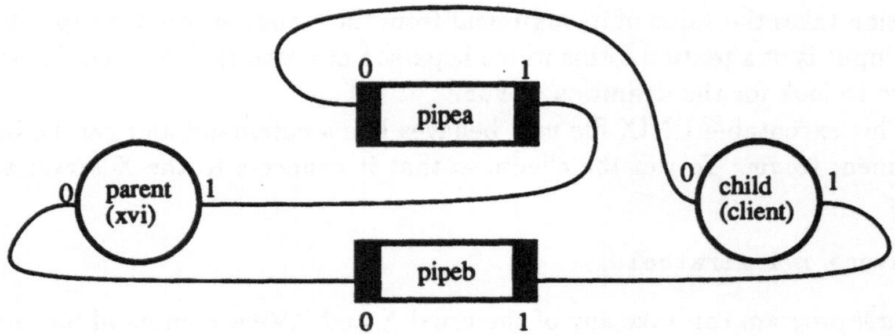

Figure 2: Pipe organisation for cross-coupled communication

```
    close(ParentPipe[1]) ;
    close(ChildPipe[0]) ;
    close(ChildPipe[1]) ;
} /* otherwise do child re-wiring... */
```

The child process performs similar actions. It's input is connected to **ParentPipe**'s input and it's output is connected to **ChildPipe**'s output.

This causes the input/output streams of the child and parent processes to be cross-coupled as shown in figure 2. Inputs (0) are shown on the left and outputs (1) are shown on the right. Following the lines it can be established that the the output of the parent is connect to the input of the child, and that the output of the child is connected to the input of the parent.

The parent process is the interpreter and the child process is executes the program given as the first argument by using the **execlp** system function. For a reason unknown to the author, it is not possible to have the interpreter as the child process. This prevents XView TTY subwindows from operating. The original version had the interpreter as the child process: it took many hours to work out the TTY subwindow was broken. Sun say that a program can have at most one TTY subwindow.

4 Miranda Interface to X11/XView

Miranda clients are written using a library module called **xview.m** which contains definitions of X11/XView objects. This module also contains many other useful definitions e.g. names given to over 400 different RGB colour triples. The output of a Miranda client is a list of requests to *xvi*. The list is of type **[xview]** where **xview** is defined as an algebraic type. Part of the definition of **xview** is given below.

```
> xview ::= Get_event
> | Get_event_bit window
> | Return
> | Frame_set_rect (num, num, num, num)
> | Frame_get_rect
> | Xv_create  num xv_type [attr]
> | Xv_init
> | Xv_main_loop window
> | Xv_set num [attr]
```

```
> | Window_fit window
> | Window_fit_width window
> | Window_fit_height window
> | Xv_get window attr
> | Textsw_save window (num, num)
> | Textsw_reset window (num, num)
```

The Miranda program receives as input replies from the interpreter. These replies are encoded in Miranda as:

```
> xview_reply ::= WinRef num | Notify num | PanRef num | Text [char] |
>       Event [num] | Bool bool | PanelEvent num | String [char]
```

The interpreter simply prints textual values like **WinRef 3**. The Miranda program takes a list of these values can automatically parses them to yield expressions of type **xviewreply**.

A description of the entire interface is beyond the scope of this paper. The library has been written to resemble to C interface as closely as possible. Before it can be used, one really has to be familiar with the XView and X11 programming. As a way of an example we present a simple Miranda client to give an idea of how the system is used.

5 An Example: Miratool

Miratool is a graphical front end to the Miranda System. It is styled after other programs like Tapetool and DbxTool which provide graphical interfaces to existing programs. Miratool is written itself in Miranda! Figure 3 shows a screen snapshot of the program in action.

The program allows the user to enter the filename of a Miranda script and it's directory on two separate text input lines. It is useful to separate the directory specification from the root file specification because often one wants to compile and edit several files in the same directory. Another way of selecting a file is to drag its icon onto the editing window. This will also change the text entries. This provides a much superior form of user interaction compared to simply getting the user to type in the name of a file that might not exist. Here, the user directly manipulates the object of interest by pointing at it and then dragging it over the Miratool application.

The load button will cause the script specified in the text entries to be loaded. The compile button causes the compilation of the specified script. This is done by inserting a string into the terminal emulation window which is running the Miranda interpreter. The last button causes a popup window to appear giving a simple message about the program. This window can be dismissed at any time and does not prevent other actions taking place.

The first row of buttons set the edit mode. This is useful when you want to browse through Miranda files but not allow any accidental edits. The choices on these buttons are mutually exclusive. The depressed (shaded) button signifies the current selection. The last row of buttons allows the user to control various aspects of the Miranda interpreter. Each represents an option which can be on or off. The choices on these buttons are not mutually exclusive: more than one can be depressed.

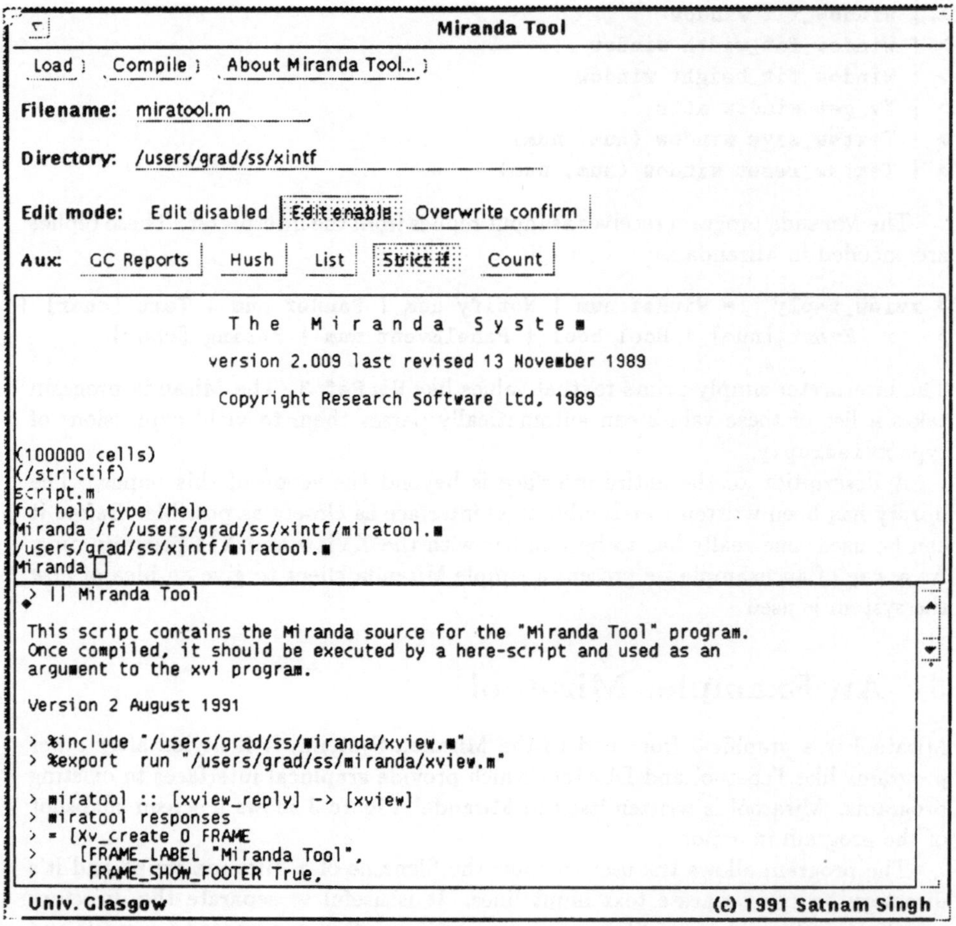

Figure 3: Miratool screen snapshot

The Miranda interpreter is running in a terminal emulation subwindow. The user can type into this window as if it were a terminal. the application also "types into" this window. The bottom subwindow is a text editing window. This is a fully featured text editor which can be completely controlled by the application. The snapshot shows the source code for Miratool itself in the text editing window.

Some of the source code for Miratool is given below The first few lines of the program import the interface library and create a base frame inside which subwindows are fitted. The type of the program is specified as being a function that takes a list of *xvi* responses and returns a list of *xvi* requests. The first "parameter" to the Xvcreate call is the ID of the enclosing window, or 0 if this is a base frame. The second argument states that a frame is being created and the third argument is a list of attributes to be associated with the frame. The list can be empty. There are a large number of possible attributes that modify the appearance and behaviour of objects. In this example the title of the window is set to "Miranda Tool", two footers are labelled and the window is set to be 45 rows in height.

```
> %include "/users/grad/ss/miranda/xview.m"
> %export  run "/users/grad/ss/miranda/xview.m"

> miratool :: [xview_reply] -> [xview]
> miratool responses
> = [Xv_create 0 FRAME
>     [FRAME_LABEL "Miranda Tool",
>      FRAME_SHOW_FOOTER True,
>      FRAME_RIGHT_FOOTER "(c) 1991 Satnam Singh",
>      FRAME_LEFT_FOOTER "Univ. Glasgow",
>      WIN_ROWS 45],
```

After this message has been sent to the interpreter (as a line of text) the objects described above are created and the interpreter returns a line giving a handle to the base frame. For the first object created, the response will be WinRef 1. Later on in the script, the value of the first response is associated with a Miranda variable:

```
>   where
>   WinRef base       = responses!0
>   WinRef main_panel = responses!1
```

In subsequent definitions, base is the handle to the base frame window.

The program then creates the panel items. The author has written some utility functions for creating panel items like buttons, text entries and choice button selections. The trailing numeric arguments specify positions in the panel, with (0, 0) pair specifying the default position to be used.

```
>     Xv_create base PANEL []] ++
>     panel_button main_panel "Load" 0 0 ++
>     panel_button main_panel "Compile" 0 0 ++
>     panel_button main_panel "About Miranda Tool..." 0 0 ++
>     panel_text main_panel "Filename: " "script.m" 0 1 15 ++
>     panel_text main_panel "Directory: " (getenv "PWD") 0 2 35 ++
```

```
>    panel_choice main_panel "Edit mode: "
> ["Edit disabled", "Edit enable", "Overwrite confirm"] 0 3 ++
>    panel_toggle main_panel "Aux: "
> ["GC Reports","Hush", "List", "Strict if", "Count"] 0 4 ++
>     [Xv_set edit_mode_entry [PANEL_NUM_VALUE 1],
>    Xv_set choice_entry [PANEL_NUM_VALUE 8],
>    Window_fit_height main_panel,
```

This code can be written more efficiently by eliminating , but we prefer using the concatenations as we feel this style results in clearer programs.

The utility functions are easily defined. The function panelbutton is shown below. The Xvcreate call creates a button inside the specified panel. The buttons label is set through the attribute PANEL_LABEL_STRING. If a non-zero position pair is given for x and y then the position of the button inside the panel is also explicitly set. Otherwise the panel package places the button automatically.

```
> panel_button pan label x y
>   = [Xv_create pan PANEL_BUTTON ([PANEL_LABEL_STRING label] ++ pos)]
>      where
>       pos = [XV_X (Xv_col pan x), XV_Y (Xv_row pan y)],
>                                                      if (x~=0) & (y~=0)
>           = [], otherwise
```

After all the subwindows and their components have been created the client tells the interpreter to enter its main loop by sending Xvmainloop.

```
>    Xv_main_loop base
>   ] ++ (do_events (drop 14 responses))
```

The client now waits for some event to to take place which will be signalled by the interpreter. Some of the Miratool code for dealing with its events is shown below.

```
>   do_events (r:rs)
>     = do_load rs ++ (do_events (drop 2 rs)),
>                                           if r = PanelEvent load_but
>     = do_compile rs ++ (do_events (drop 2 rs)),
>                                           if r = PanelEvent compile_but
>     = do_popup rs ++ (do_events rs), if r = PanelEvent about_but
>     = [Return] ++ do_events rs, otherwise

>   do_load rs
>     = [Xv_get filename_entry (PANEL_VALUE ""),
>        Xv_get directory_entry (PANEL_VALUE ""),
>        Xv_set textwin [TEXTSW_FILE (directory++"/"++filename)],
>                                                               Return]
>       where
>          String filename = rs!0
>          String directory = rs!
```

If the Load button is pressed then the function doload is called. This gets the value of the text entry fields, forms the full filename and then causes the specified file to be loaded. Once all this has been done, it returns control to the interpreter by sending the special request return. This stops the parser and puts the interpreter back into a state where it is looking for more events. While the event handling code is being interpreted, the button goes grey. For C clients the period buttons go grey for is very small. Miranda clients however are much slower so the button can go grey for seconds rather than milliseconds.

6 The Interpreter

The interpreter is written in yacc which is used to specify the syntax of the requests produced by the Miranda client. This syntax is standard textual representation of the algebraic data type used to describe requests. The yacc grammar simply specifies each of the constructors of this algebraic type and a corresponding action. This action is usually a call to the X11 or XView system to either set or get some information.

An extract from the yacc file is shown below. The start symbol for the grammar is interp. This describes a list of requests given by interp1.

```
interp : | interp1 interp ;

interp1 : Xv_init_TOK
  { xv_init () ; }

| Xv_main_loop_TOK window
  { xv_main_loop ($2) ; }

| Xv_create_TOK window window_kind
  { do_xv_create ($2, $3) ; } attr_list
```

The last rule matches against any request that creates windows like frames or canvases. When this rule is matched, the corresponding C routine given in brackets is called. The last term deals with the parsing of attribute lists.

As another example, consider a request that needs a value returned from the system. The following rule will return the string contained in a text panel item.

```
| PANEL_GET_TEXT_VALUE_TOK window
  { (void) printf ("Text \"%s\"\n", panel_get_value($2)) ; }
```

The output is read by the Miranda client which understands it to be a literal of the reply type of the Text constructor (the message read being in quotes). Notice that we do not need to write any input/output routines for the request and reply types: Miranda will do the work for us automatically.

7 Problems with the interpreter

Although the interpreter provides a much needed route for Miranda programs to have good interfaces and interactive graphics, there are still many problems with the system at present. The system implements much of the XView toolkit, but not all. However, this is simply due to lack of time, and in principle almost all of the XView toolkit could be coded. Also, only a very small part of the Xlib toolkit has been coded. Just enough is implemented to produce lines, rectangles, circles, colours, fonts, line styles, database resources and a few other features.

Clients written in Miranda runs slowly because Miranda runs slowly. Also, there is a communication overhead between the Miranda client and the interpreter. All communication is through UNIX serial pipes and the requests all passed in a textual form. Greater efficiency could be gained by encoding the requests into some numerical forms. However, the current method takes advantage of Miranda's ability to show and read automatically any expression (except functions) so that virtually no output or input code has to be written. The actual function that forms the output of the Miranda tool script is run and is defined simply as:

```
> run  = lay . map show . miratool
```

It is not possible to associate a callback function with just selected objects, as is the convention in C programs that use the XView toolkit. We settle for each object having a callback that notifies the client of every event. The client can then chose to ignore this information or take some appropriate action.

The technique used to read responses (by using a long where clause) is rather inelegant. Forgetting to cater for a response will cause the program to crash with little idea about where things went wrong. It would be nicer to use a continuation passing style, but this has not been done for the Miranda version. The interpreter does have a debugging flag, which when set will write all information to the standard error output reporting the progress of the program. In practise this has proved to be most useful for catching synchronization errors between the Miranda client and the interpreter.

8 Future Work

The current interface corresponds as closely as possible to the C program interface to XView. This makes it easier for someone who knows already how to write XView applications to write and convert to Miranda his or her XView applications. It also means that existing documentation on XView is still relevant. However, this interface is not the most natural for use in a function language. It would an interesting idea to design a more appropriate high level interface and then code it on top of the existing system. The author has coded Henderson's functional geometry primitives in this system and produced the Escher fish picture with them.

There are user interface design tools which allow XView interfaces to be created interactively. The user selects windows, buttons, sliders etc. and places them using the mouse. The system then generates a C or C++ skeleton which the user can then flesh out with callback routines for events of interest. These tools allow interfaces to be prototyped very quickly. It should be possible to write a utility to hook the skeleton code produced by such programs into the interpreter. This would mean that the Miranda client would no longer have to build the XView objects: it would only have to process the events. Such a system would be much more accessible to most Miranda programmers since it would not require a great deal of knowledge of the XView system.

Another improvement would be for the interpreter to be built into the Miranda system and a special type like **sysmessge** to be provided that causes some external action when objects of that type are evaluated. This would improve performance by eliminating the need to communicate through pipes and perform textual conversion. However, this work would have.to be carried out by the implementors of Miranda.

9 Summary

An interpreter for a useful subset of XView and X11 toolkits has been written. Copies of the system described are available from the author. This allows Miranda programs to take advantage of some of the facilities of these toolkits. In particular, it allows Miranda programs to employ high quality direct manipulation user interfaces. This is done without sacraficing referential transparency or modifying the source code of the Miranda system. In principle, it is possible to use this interpreter from any language, although it is tailored for Miranda. As an example, a graphical front end for the Miranda interpreter has been produced using this system.

References

[1] XView Programming Manual. Sun Microsystems Inc. 1990.

Author Index

Published in 1990

AI and Cognitive Science '89, Dublin City University, Eire, 14–15 September 1989
A. F. Smeaton and G. McDermott (Eds.)

Specification and Verification of Concurrent Systems, University of Stirling, Scotland, 6–8 July 1988
C. Rattray (Ed.)

Semantics for Concurrency, Proceedings of the International BCS-FACS Workshop, Sponsored by Logic for IT (S.E.R.C.), University of Leicester, UK, 23–25 July 1990
M. Z. Kwiatkowska, M. W. Shields and R. M. Thomas (Eds.)

Functional Programming, Glasgow 1989, Proceedings of the 1989 Glasgow Workshop, Fraserburgh, Scotland, 21–23 August 1989
K. Davis and J. Hughes (Eds.)

Persistent Object Systems, Proceedings of the Third International Workshop, Newcastle, Australia, 10–13 January 1989
J. Rosenberg and D. Koch (Eds.)

Z User Workshop, Oxford, 1989, Proceedings of the Fourth Annual Z User Meeting, Oxford, 15 December 1989
J. E. Nicholls (Ed.)

Formal Methods for Trustworthy Computer Systems (FM89), Halifax, Canada, 23–27 July 1989
Dan Craigen (Editor) and Karen Summerskill (Assistant Editor)

Security and Persistence, Proceedings of the International Workshop on Computer Architecture to Support Security and Persistence of Information, Bremen, West Germany, 8–11 May 1990
John Rosenberg and J. Leslie Keedy (Eds.)